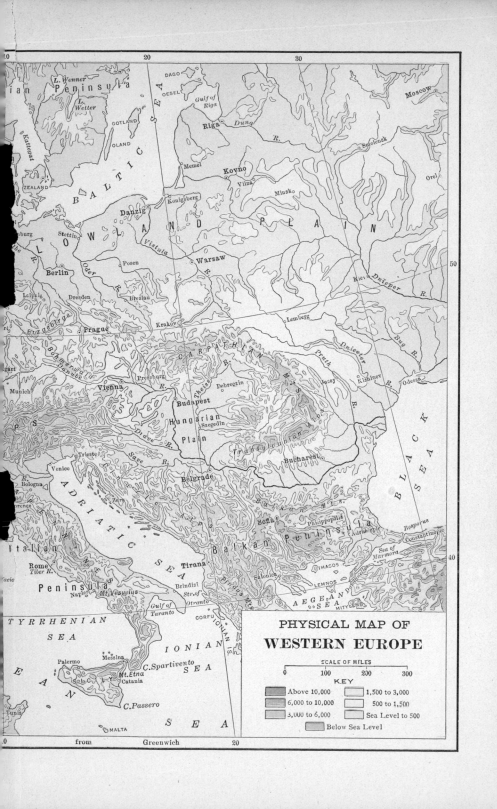

PHYSICAL MAP OF
WESTERN EUROPE

SCALE OF MILES

0   100   200   300

KEY

Above 10,000   1,500 to 3,000

6,000 to 10,000   500 to 1,500

3,000 to 6,000   Sea Level to 500

Below Sea Level

A HISTORY OF EUROPE

FROM THE REFORMATION TO OUR OWN DAY

BY

FERDINAND SCHEVILL

PROFESSOR OF MODERN HISTORY IN
THE UNIVERSITY OF CHICAGO

*WITH GENEALOGICAL TABLES
AND TWENTY-FOUR MAPS*

GEORGE G. HARRAP & CO., LTD.

LONDON   CALCUTTA   SYDNEY

PRINTED IN THE UNITED STATES OF AMERICA

CONTENTS

CONTENTS

SECTION IV

REVOLUTION AND DEMOCRACY FROM 1789 TO OUR OWN DAY

MAPS

A HISTORY OF EUROPE

A HISTORY OF EUROPE

CHAPTER I

CONCERNING HISTORY IN GENERAL AND THIS HISTORY IN PARTICULAR

An indispensable preliminary measure for every present-day historian is to explain to his readers what he means by history. For it can not have escaped even superficial observation that history has become a very elastic word with wholly indeterminate History a boundaries. It is hardly an exaggeration to say that there very elastic are today as many definitions of history as there are word historians and that in fact every historian writes his own kind of history.

This extension of the bounds of history is a development of relatively recent date. The English historian, Edward Freeman, who lived in the second half of the nineteenth century, was still able to proclaim narrowly and dogmatically that History "history is past politics." Not content with a cool, ob- traditionally jective statement, he rode into the lists against all adver- concerned saries and fought hotly for his definition on the double with politics ground that it alone accorded with the honorable tradition of his craft and that its surrender would bring loss and confusion in its train. And indeed the facts were so indisputably on his side that no one dreamed of denying that the European predecessors of Freeman as far back as the revivers of historical studies in the Renaissance had accepted history as substantially concerned with politics. More impressive still, the ancient historians from Herodotus to Tacitus, whom the modern writers regarded as half-gods and whom they continued humbly to imitate, had proceeded on precisely the same theory. It was unchallengeable that an ancient tradition gave its sanction to a purely political interpretation of history and that in view of the numerous brilliant disciples of the historical muse through the ages every departure from the customary ritual of her worship might be decried as impertinent and blasphemous.

1

And yet neither Freeman nor the long line of historical writers stretching in a shadowy column behind him as far back as Herodotus, father and fountain-head of history, could stop the movement that The modern broke down the old barriers. Like all strong revolutionary movement forces it had been quietly and secretly at work some breaks generations before men became aware of its existence. through the barriers of Undeniably it was tied up with the whole modern com- the Old plex, above all, it resulted from the observational and History scientific influences that had given birth to the new physics and astronomy, the new critical philosophies, and the new naturalistic phase of art and literature. Beginning more partic- ularly with the eighteenth century, man's various activities in society, not only his political institutions but also his courts of justice and legal practices, his life on the farm and in the city, his relation to his group and the relation of social groups to one another, together with a score of other matters shedding a novel and amazing light on the great issue of his destiny, had begun to receive a some- what timid attention. By the middle of the nineteenth century this new material, all of it strikingly illustrative of humanity's prolonged and many-sided struggle to make itself at home on earth, had reached immense proportions and could no longer be ignored by scholars who, calling themselves historians, instinctively felt that nothing apper- taining to the creature man might remain foreign to their sympathy. To be sure, the vigor inhering in the accepted practice of history was such that a conservative group continued to insist that only political data were relevant to the historian's business and that it was for economists, sociologists, and other new-fangled specialists but not for the honorable craft of the historians to utilize the new material. But with each new decade the membership of the con- servative school fell off until we come to the memorable fight made by Freeman. In spite of its having the appearance of a vigorous offensive, it was, regarded in the perspective of nineteenth century development, no more than a last-ditch rally fought under that most irrational and pathetic of slogans: "The old guard dies but does not surrender."

With the dawn of the twentieth century the New History had triumphed all along the line. And the immediate result was undeni- ably that confusion which the routed pundits had so confidently fore- told. Amidst a rush of more or less sincere avowals that history transcended politics every historical writer adopted a practice dictated by his individual attitude toward the world of today. While the state very generally continued to hold the main attention, one historian showed a disposition to take cognizance of data furnished by the geographer, another gave preference to economic material, and a third inclined to lend an ear to the voices emanating from literature and the arts. Although in the sudden levelling of the old restrictions every influence bearing on man and every one of man's activities had become theoretically relevant to a record professing to be a history, in practice each writer spread himself over as much territory as he was able to occupy and concocted under the name of history a very personal product. Of this regrettable confusion the only conceivable cure would be an agreement as to the true and exact ingredients of the New History, the relative importance of each element to all the others, and the method and principles of their interpretation. But before such an agreement could even be initiated, the labors of the numerous auxiliary workers such as geographers, ethnologists, economists, and sociologists, would have to be coördinated and made conveniently accessible; and following this achievement, by the putting out of new hypotheses constantly checked and corrected in the light of the facts, the formula would have to be worked out which would enable the New History competently to meet the obligation of a synthesis in conformity with the requirements of modern thought.

The twentieth century sees the dawn of the New History

So comprehensive a program signified the coöperative enterprise of many hands which might not culminate in a new and satisfactory world picture short of the labor of several generations. If an impatient historian here and there, refusing to wait longer, should rush to produce the synthesis demanded by the new outlook, he might by his shortcomings prove that his effort was premature, but he could hardly fail, provided he subjected his procedure to an honest self-criticism, to do useful pioneer work. It is in this light that we may regard certain recent experiments, notably the *Outline of History* by H. G. Wells. Although its sins both of omission and commission are considerable, it has rendered a hardly-to-be-exaggerated service in focussing the attention of historians and public alike on the desirability of a unified conception of the world which accords with the criteria of science and the fullness of modern knowledge. Discounting its weaknesses, we may, on the strength of its positive achievement, be reasonably sure

Premature historical syntheses. The case of H. G. Wells

that the path which it blazes will be followed until a history more adequately expressive of our present information and outlook will see the light. One advance will lead to another as step follows step until the staircase is completed which brings us to our goal.

Conceding that the New History is still in a fluid state, we may confidently assert that it will concern itself more and more vigorously with the total problem of man's earthly labors. The present writer is inclined to think that it will take the form of a his-tory of civilization, but not as if there were just one unified history of civilization involving all men from the beginning of time regardless of climate, continent, and color. More conformable to the facts, it would seem to him, would be a whole series of histories of civilization constructed with reference to a contentious, plural world where peoples have repeatedly risen and disappeared after having produced a civilization so individual that we can not but regard it as unique. Thus the Chinese people built up through centuries a civilization which stands unmistakably on its own feet. So did the people of India. What good purpose is served by studying these two distinct creations other than for their own sakes and as highly individual expressions of a search for an adjustment to the specific conditions encountered on earth by Chinamen and Hindus? In the same way there is or has been a Persian, an Arab, a Greco-Roman and many another civilization besides. Admitting the claim on our attention of all these civilizations, we may none the less assert that preëminently interesting to us alive today in Europe or the United States of America is the European or Occidental civilization of which we are a passionate, struggling, and inseparable element.

The New History will be a history of civilization

But enough of the New History and of its eventual crystallization in a history or in a series of histories of civilization! Undoubtedly the time for producing such works has arrived, but since they will still for a long time to come bear an experimental character, a book which, like the present, is avowedly a book for beginners is ill-suited for this pioneer service. For a text-book is not a fit platform for those theoretical discussions among the adepts which, as already indicated, must be brought to a certain degree of conclusion before the New History can take shape. Instead of inviting controversy and taking an advanced and problematical position a text-book can by its nature aim at nothing other than the assembling of a fund

This book a text-book concerned with European civilization

of more or less securely established results. It is frankly and overwhelmingly pragmatic in the persuasion that prior to every effort at interpretation of the facts are the facts themselves. For these reasons this work is not a History of European Civilization; but it is and desires to be looked upon as a portal to such a history. For what is its proceeding, with what is it steadily concerned? It directs the attention throughout on all of western Europe and on the European man, the *homo Europaeus*, in his several variations; it recognizes that there was a steady, developmental movement involving many stages from the primitive homogeneity of sixth century barbarism to the astonishing richness and heterogeneity of the twentieth century; it deals with the social classes and political forms of the emerging and evolving states; it takes account of new economic as well as new intellectual enterprises and registers the changing expression of literature and the arts. Because it does all these things it is substantially a history of European civilization; but as it is not constructed on the basis of a preceding theoretical discussion concerned with determining the relation of the constituent elements of civilization to one another it prefers, in view of this incompleteness, to call itself modestly a history and, more particularly, a History of Europe from the Reformation to Our Own Day.

An additional reason why the title History of European Civilization has been avoided for this book may be found in the above-indicated chronological limits. By the view already expounded European or Occidental civilization is a separate and unique historical entity. That does not of course mean that it has not absorbed important features of other, particularly the earlier Mediterranean civilizations. In the same way a people, which has made its appearance on the stage of history as a distinct and separate folk, does not necessarily lose its identity because it happens to incorporate in itself in the course of time a certain percentage of other racial stocks. In the interest of organic unity a History of European Civilization should therefore, ideally considered, begin with the beginning, that is, it should open with that earliest phase of its being which by an unhappy accident has been misnamed the Middle Age. Let us take note that every civilization necessarily has many phases because it is the product of a long evolutionary process. Adopting a biological analogy, we may think of the main phases of any civilization cycle as childhood, youth, young manhood and so on to the closing phase

This book a History of Modern Europe treated in four sections

of senility and death. But as it is only recently that civilization has been envisaged as a process, it has happened that labels, highly inappropriate from a modern evolutionary viewpoint, have got themselves attached to some of the stages of the European movement. The label Middle Age for the first or childhood phase is a case in point. The word Renaissance, customarily employed to designate the second phase, is hardly more relevant. However, these terms have become so thoroughly embedded in our consciousness that it would be foolish to attempt to dislodge them. They are therefore accepted in this book but the periods and experiences which they cover are only cursorily treated in an introductory section, numbered Section I. It is the phases following the Middle Age and the Renaissance, the phases collectively called the Modern Period, to which this work directs its effort. These modern phases are handled in three sections with chronological limits more or less clearly marked. They bear the following section numbers and titles; Section II, The Reformation and the Religious Wars from 1500 to 1648; Section III, The Absolute Monarchy from 1648 to 1789; Section IV, Revolution and Democracy from 1789 to Our Own Day. These, too, are commonly accepted periods and labels, and, like the designations Middle Age and Renaissance, are no longer wholly satisfactory. But as they indicate a succession of outstanding events and at least do not quarrel with the fundamental evolutionary concept, they may be permitted to stand. To the alert and inquiring student the text itself will suggest the possibility of divisions and designations different from the above and based on a more severely developmental analysis of the Modern Age.

If the writer may venture to offer a last counsel to the young student about to accept the guidance of this book, it is to put himself in a frame of mind hospitable to the idea that bigger than Europe is the concept European civilization, and that, a living **The proper** influence enfolding him and all of us alive today, it must **attitude** **with which** needs include the whole series of its earlier phases back **to approach** to its first beginning in the feudal age. Our remote, **this history** medieval ancestor was of course a backward barbarian checked and repressed by a hundred shackles made up largely of such tenuous things as his fears, his superstitions, and his tribal customs. However, because he was naturally active and enterprising he refused to sit with folded hands and passively face the hostile forces which surrounded him. He ventured forth, albeit timidly; he experimented until he broke one or another of his many bonds and gained a larger radius of action. Often, it is true, he straightway wove himself again a new shackle. None the less in the main he achieved from age to age a fuller liberty of movement and a more secure command of his environment. As soon as he had come upon a suitable legal device or had shaped a promising political institution, the probability was that he would tinker with his invention, constantly refitting it to meet his changing circumstances. Pursuing this restless course, the European man gradually developed innumerable activities and crowned his labors with immense creations in every field of mental and material endeavor. These in their successive unfolding are what we may call the evidences of European civilization and the true subject-matter of European history. Better were it not to have been born than not to feel the grandeur of these labors of our forebears and not to respond with heightened pulse-beat to the persistent heroism of their struggle with nature and with fate.

SECTION I

PRELIMINARY SURVEY

CHAPTER II

THE FIRST OR MEDIEVAL PHASE OF EUROPEAN CIVILIZATION

A history of Europe beginning with the Reformation labors under the disadvantage of an arbitrary starting-point. Plunging the reader without warning into a broad and agitated stream of human circumstance, it owes him at the least a few explanations which may enable him to discover where he is. If, holding fast to our announced purpose, we decline to ascend the human stream to its remote sources and content ourselves with a survey of that stretch which directly leads up to the Reformation, we shall find it advisable and even necessary to recede as far as the great bend in the stream marked by the fall of the Roman Empire and the incursion into Roman territory of the German and Slav tribes. Here undoubtedly is a towering mile-stone; here without question European, as distinct from Ancient or Mediterranean history, takes its start. From the fall of the Roman Empire to the Reformation is a stretch of a thousand years, during which enormous upheavals completely changed the face of western Europe and endowed it with a new civilization.

A review of the previous period necessary to the understanding of the Reformation

Of these thousand years an account, however brief, is indispensable if the reader would understand the situation confronting him in the Reformation. While it is not uncommon to consider the whole succession of ten centuries from 500 A.D. to 1500 A.D. as a single period, called the Middle Age, it is on the whole more advisable to break the ten centuries into two unequal parts and, while attributing the designation, Middle Age, to the eight centuries from 500 A.D. to 1300 A.D., to set off the period from 1300 to the Reformation as the Rebirth or the Renaissance. It hardly matters much if the Renaissance is regarded as an independent period or as a last, vanishing phase of the Middle

Middle Age and Renaissance chronologically determined

8

Age or even as the dawn of a new, the Modern Period. What alone really ever counts so far as chronological divisions of history are concerned is whether they serve a useful purpose; and that such is the case in regard to Middle Age and Renaissance admits of no dispute. Indeed the more we occupy ourselves with these two periods, the more we become aware that each is charged with its own distinctive characteristics. The outstanding differences between them, which will be developed fully later on, may be briefly anticipated here with the statement that the medieval epoch had a unique spiritual unity due to the unchallenged domination of religion and the Church, while the Renaissance cultivated a profusion of new activities and ideas sure in the long run to disperse the religious atmosphere which the Middle Age had cherished. In the slow manner characteristic of human movements and not without sharp setbacks the age ushered in about 1300 endowed man with a new attitude toward life. For this reason the Renaissance is, as the word signifies, a new birth or at least a new phase of west-European mankind.

In this chapter we shall undertake to define very briefly the Middle Age, while in the one that follows we shall deal in somewhat greater fullness with the characteristics of the Renaissance. The two chapters together may be thought of as a gateway leading to the period of our real concern, the Modern Age.

Among the decisive features which in a sweeping backward view stand out in the medieval landscape, none is more striking than the emergence with definite national characteristics of the great peoples of Europe, the Italians, the French, the Spaniards, the English, and the Germans. Not only do they emerge in the course of the Middle Age, but they emerge identified with certain geographic areas which have ever since been uninterruptedly their homes. Within these respective areas each was obliged to struggle with very much the same variety of political, social, economic, and religious problems. Undoubtedly it is these problems that give the measure of the Middle Age and communicate its *The Middle Age gave birth to the great peoples of Europe and to a special set of social and religious problems* peculiar temper. We shall best succeed in capturing that temper if we concentrate our attention on the three outstanding factors of medieval society, on feudalism, the towns, and the Church. These three features, above all the Church, give a particular character to the first phase of what we must regard as a new movement in civilization.

A. FEUDALISM

If we agree that the Middle Age began at the close of the fifth century with the frightful chaos produced by the simultaneous decline of the Roman Empire and the invasion of the German tribes, and if **Feudalism** we then reflect that in the course of the next seven or **a complex** eight centuries Europe raised itself to a relatively stable **of rude in-** order representing the early stages of a new and colorful **stitutions** civilization, we shall be cured of the unwarranted ten-**representing an effort** dency of superficial thinkers to regard this extraordinary **to rise above** period with contempt. It was of course raw and youthful **barbarism** — a circumstance which can not be sufficiently stressed and as a result of which the political, social, and economic problems of medieval Europe bear invariably a markedly primitive stamp. In their essence these problems are all comprehended under the term feudalism. But what is feudalism? Feudalism may perhaps best be thought of as the sum of the economic, social, and political institutions representing the first effort of a young and aspiring society to rise above an unmitigated barbarism. Under feudalism European society, in spite of bewildering local variations, presents itself to view in rarely simple terms. Essentially there are but two classes: the rulers who own the soil and the ruled who till it. Land is the only form of wealth and land determines the structure of society. The rulers are of course armed and have the pride of an hereditary caste of warriors, while the ruled, disarmed, are attached to the soil as an hereditary caste of peasant-serfs. Governments of the modern type, maintaining a well regulated administration over a large area, do not exist. Substantially each petty lord, though theoretically subject to an over-lord and ultimately to the king, is master in his own possessions with the result that for all practical purposes Europe is made up of thousands of loosely associated little lordships. The social-economic unit of this backward society is the type of farmstead called the manor. The manor is worked coöperatively by the peasants who dwell together in the village and are governed either in person or by deputy by their military lord and master residing in the outskirts of the village in the manor-house or castle.

Carefully weighing these various data, we may think of the early Middle Age as effecting, owing to the influx of victorious German and Slav tribes of a nomad and semi-nomad type, the reagrarianization of the Roman Empire. The notable Roman city culture, already in decline before the coming of the barbarians, broke down and suffered a complete eclipse. The agrarian settlement proceeded on the whole according to a simple formula: a select warrior class took over the ownership of the soil permitting the bulk of the population to work it in return for rent paid, in the absence of money, in personal services and natural products. The warriors ruled society as a privileged noble class, while the peasants, at the mercy of their masters, were depressed to the legal status of serfs, not very much above that of chattels. Feudalism is the comprehensive word which describes this complex situation, that is, feudalism sets forth the political, social, and economic conditions produced by the triumph throughout western Europe of a primitive agrarianism.

The Middle Age caused by the failure of urban civilization and a return to agrarianism

B. THE RISE OF THE TOWNS

During the first five centuries of the Middle Age this rude organization of society characterizes all western Europe until, around 1000 A.D., a new element made its appearance which not only complicated the structure but produced a mental ferment destined to undermine the spiritual foundations on which the Middle Age rested. I refer to the coming of the towns. Originating in a rebirth of trade and industry, the towns represented an agglomeration of men resolved to engage in new, non-agricultural activities, to multiply the conveniences of living, and to defend themselves against a baronage established on the soil and instinctively hostile to traders only too eager to free themselves from the political control of a tyrannical warrior caste.

Around 1000 A. D. urbanization again sets in

The springing up of towns all over the face of Europe completely changed the picture. Before long the lords in their scattered castles found themselves face to face with burgher groups which exceeded them in wealth, culture, and ultimately in military power. Not that, confronted with this phenomenon, the feudal warriors promptly disappeared from the scene or even noticeably reduced their pretentions; but relatively they lost ground, both socially and politically, in the face of the steady advance of the town-dwellers, themselves armed behind tall, battlemented walls and acquiring by their courageous enterprise increasing material resources and an ever expanding mental outlook.

Rapid material, political, and cultural advance of the towns

With the multiplication of towns and of the special activities by which town-folk lived medieval society in the twelfth and thirteenth centuries reached its climax. There are many people of our own day, especially philosophers and artists, who uphold the opinion that that climax represents such a balance and harmony of the forces of life and art as has been but rarely achieved in history. But impressive as the spiritual flowering of the Middle Age no doubt was, it is not the concern of this book. Confining our attention to the weighty phenomenon of the rising town, we shall be content to note what the town signified for European development in two directions, politically and culturally.

The addition of the urban element brings medieval civilization to its climax

On finding itself opposed by the existing feudal political order and obliged to fight for its life, the town boldly developed a political principle of its own, the principle of self-government. Wherever a town sprang up, there also, sooner or later, will be found a movement aiming at independence and self-help. By means of charters wrung from their lords, the towns gained their earliest liberties, which with the aid of additional grants they strove to enlarge whenever the occasion served. Some towns, notably those of Italy and Germany, succeeded finally in becoming free republics, detached or all but detached from the feudal state in the midst of which they had sprung up, while in countries like England and France the ever waxing urban centers consciously and unconsciously helped to build up the power of the king, because under the king the peace of the land so necessary to trade was more likely to be secured than under a turbulent nobility to whom war was hardly more than an intensification of their favorite sport, the hunt. Unmistakably the towns figure as the main historical agents in the gradual process of replacing the loose feudal régime with the royal centralized state. Although, exactly like the landlords with whom they locked horns, the vigorous townsmen, while engaged in their struggle for existence, thought only of themselves and of their selfish interests, they builded better than they knew for the simple reason that they represented economic forces which were bound in the end to effect a complete political reorganization of society. This reorganization, as we shall see, took the form of the centralized monarchy, which famous institution must therefore in last analysis be charged to the account of the towns.

Politically the towns promote self-government and ultimately the absolute monarchy

Culturally the town initiated a change no whit less significant. By living together within the narrow confines of the town wall, great numbers of men were brought into close contact, quarreled with one another over conflicting interests or worked out common plans, and extraordinarily stimulated their wits through the constant necessity of action in the face of new situations. Some townsmen, in the capacity of enterprising merchants, gained wealth and experience by seeking business and adventure in neighboring towns or distant countries, while others, engaged in weaving cloth, tanning leather, or forging weapons, effectively increased their mastery of life by the skillful practice of their respective crafts. Living experimentally and rewarded for their hardihood with constantly increasing possessions, these men tended to abandon the ruts of custom not only in matters affecting their material and political welfare but in mental and spiritual matters as well. How could it have been otherwise? When men acquire the habit of freely using their minds in the immediate concern of earning a living, will they not be moved to apply them also to the higher interests represented by philosophy and religion? Let us concede that philosophy and religion everywhere and always represent an attempt to give theoretical expression to the experiences accumulated by man on his earthly pilgrimage. This being so, it follows that if a primitive agricultural society, such as that which preceded the rise of the towns, develops a religion and philosophy which adequately expresses its intentions, a commercial and mobile society, like that produced by the urban movement, is sure to wax critical of its inheritance and to set about the formulation of ideas and theories of its own.

Culturally the towns prepare the ground for a new religious and philosophic outlook on life

However, before we can advantageously look into the new culture which the towns promoted, we must acquire some conception of the older culture by which the towns at their birth were surrounded and against which they reacted. The culture of the Middle Age is embedded in its religion and philosophy and can be crowded into a single word — Christianity. To secure Christianity's unchallenged domination there had grown up since Roman times a splendid and authoritative agency in the Christian Catholic Church. While the Christian *religion*, consisting of a body of firmly held beliefs, must be looked upon as the spiritual essence of the Middle Age, the *Church* may be conceived as an institution for the

The Middle Age an attempt to realize a Christian society through a dominant Church

inculcation and triumphant assertion of the spiritual values of Christianity. This institution is the keystone of the medieval arch, absolutely indispensable to an understanding of medieval Europe.

C. THE CHURCH

The origin of Christianity is to be found in a new and deeply emotional attitude on the part of the people of the Greco-Roman world toward the great questions of life and death. Wearied and disappointed by the sad actualities of life on earth, men in ever increasing numbers turned for comfort to a hoped-for life beyond the grave. Finally, under the inspiration of Jesus of Nazareth, hailed as savior and the Christ, and under the direction of a group of devoted disciples, a body of beliefs took shape which taught that this world was a vale of tears and which promised compensation for the many human ills by final rest in union with the one and only God, our heavenly Father. The new faith, called Christianity, had a remarkable success in gaining converts, who, scattered over the extensive Mediterranean area and confronted with a hostile pagan majority, felt before long the need of a close association. The result was the Christian Church, which, though periodically persecuted by the dominant pagans, had, by the beginning of the fourth century, grown strong enough to convince a new ruler, the famous Emperor Constantine the Great, of the advisability of granting it the protection of the law (Edict of Milan, 313 A.D.). And now, become fairly irresistible, the vigorous new institution undertook to crowd out and destroy all rival beliefs and religious organizations, until in the course of a few generations following its recognition it had become enthroned in exclusive majesty throughout the Roman world.

Rise of Christianity and the Church

When the northern barbarians, the Slavs and Germans, overwhelmed the Roman Empire, the Church, surviving the Empire, undertook to draw them into its fold, and by heroic missionary labors extending over many centuries succeeded in its purpose beyond its most extravagant dreams. As a result the European world, which gradually emerged from the medieval chaos was Christian, theoretically one in faith and Church. Actually, however, owing to ecclesiastical disputes which can not be examined here and which proved incapable of settlement, Europe witnessed the establishment of two Christian Churches, one of the east and the

Christianization of the barbarians and the establishment of two Christian Churches

other of the west. The eastern Church, organized under the patriarch of Constantinople, is usually referred to as the Greek Orthodox Church, while the western Church, called Catholic, centered about the pope of Rome and employed the Latin language as the medium of its thought and ritual. As the civilization with which we are concerned in this book grew up in the area dominated by the Latin Church, it is this Church with which the present sketch is exclusively concerned.

The central purpose of the Church was to serve as the means of saving men and women from the eternal damnation to which they were doomed by reason of the sin of their first parents, Adam and Eve. Through the vicarious sacrifice of Jesus Christ, the only begotten son of God, the primal curse had been lifted and the sole salvation first made a possibility. With the utilization of means of the new opportunity the Church, according to universal belief, had been entrusted by Christ himself, who was considered to have expressly named the apostle Peter as his successor in the government of the communion of his followers. ("Thou art Peter and upon this rock I will build my church." St. Matthew XVI, 18.) Not without resistance a considerable number of organizations, also claiming Christian inspiration, were gradually suppressed as unauthorized and heretical and all Christians brought under that Church which called itself Catholic, proclaimed Peter as its second founder, and set up its capital in the city of Rome. As the fundamental belief of all good Christians was that Jesus Christ, the son of God, had offered himself as a sacrifice upon the Cross in order to appease the wrath of God, the Father, with the seed of Adam, it was easy and natural to accept the Church, of which Christ was proclaimed the founder, as the sole and divinely appointed means for bringing salvation to each needy individual sinner. One of the Christian Fathers compactly stated this position when he said: "Outside the Church there is no salvation." It was this awe-inspiring power enabling the Church to open and shut the gates of heaven and hell which in large measure explains the tremendous hold it had on the minds of men.

In view of this towering eminence it behooved the Church to keep its members ever mindful of their sinful state by fairly enfolding them with its solicitude and love. To this end it evolved a number of important measures: it drew up a creed containing the essentials of the Christian faith; it developed a body of uplifting prayers suitable for all the varied circumstances of life; and it established

The Church the sole means of salvation

a noble succession of rites and services of which the most solemn
and impressive was the mass. Above all, however, it provided as the
necessary and effective means of that salvation which was the main
concern of every man, woman, and child the Seven
Sacraments. These, constituting what has been called
the sacramental system, contain so much of the teaching
and practice of the Church that an acquaintance with
them illuminates not only the overshadowing importance
of the institution throughout the medieval centuries but also the
utter dependence of the individual on its divine authority. By
means of the sacramental system the Church attended its subjects
all the days of their life, from the cradle to the grave.

The kernel of the Church the sacramental system

In dealing with the Seven Sacraments we may begin with *ordination*. Ordination was reserved for the clergy and was administered
by a bishop by the laying on of hands. It conferred upon the candidate for priesthood the sacerdotal character with the
authority and power to administer the other sacraments
except confirmation, also reserved to bishops. Ordination drew a
sharp dividing line through the Christian body since it marked off
the priesthood, specially called to the service of God, from the mass
of common men. By the *sacrament of baptism* the new-born infant
was received into the membership of the Church. The holy water
on its brow signified that its share in the guilt of Adam's fall was
washed away and that it had become a Christian and the child of
God. When the boy and girl reached the age of about twelve years,
they received, after due instruction in the creed and customs of
the Church, *confirmation* from the bishop, who rubbed holy oil and
balsam on their forehead. The significance of this act was to make
them strong to resist temptation in the approaching battle of life.
However, if a Christian yielded to temptation and sinned, he could
receive pardon by the *sacrament of penance*. This consisted of four
parts: (1) he must feel contrition or regret for the sin committed;
(2) he must confess orally to a priest; (3) he must receive absolution
from a priest; and (4) he must render satisfaction by performing
the particular penance, e.g. a pilgrimage or almsgiving, which the
priest might see fit to impose. At the hour of death the priest stood
by the bedside and by anointing the dying man with holy oil strengthened his soul for the eternal journey. This rite was called the
sacrament of extreme unction. The *sacrament of marriage* bound man
and wife in lawful Christian wedlock, held to be indissoluble by hu-

The Seven Sacraments

man power. Only the Church which made the marriage could annul it, and even the Church could only do so in case a holy ordinance had been overlooked when the marriage was celebrated. Finally, there was the *sacrament of the Holy Eucharist*. This developed from the Lord's Supper as described in the gospels and involved the consecration of bread and wine by the priest, its miraculous transformation into the body and blood of Christ, and its proffer in this consecrated form to the Father in renewal of Christ's original sacrifice upon the Cross. The change of substance effected at the altar is called in theological language transsubstantiation and is the central mystery of Catholicism. It was the sacrament of the Lord's Supper which, dignified with an elaborate chanted ritual and made impressive with candles, incense, and gorgeous vestments, finally evolved into the magnificent service called the mass.

Conceding that the spiritual guidance of mankind concentrated in the sacramental system was the chief function of the clergy, we must not overlook other duties of a more mundane sort which devolved on it. When we recall that to the clergy fell exclusively the government of the Church and that the Church on its material side consisted of innumerable houses of worship, clerical residences, manorial estates, and property of every conceivable kind, we are bound to admit that its worldly activities were neither few nor slight. To meet the various clerical obligations, spiritual as well as administrative, an elaborate organization had been worked out which extended from the parish priest at the foot of the ladder to the pope at the top. The *parish* was the territorial unit of administration, a convenient number of parishes being bound together into a *diocese*, at the head of which stood the *bishop*. A variable number of dioceses constituted a *province*, over which one of the bishops enjoyed authority under the title *archbishop*. The succession priest, bishop, archbishop, culminated in the pope, the unchallenged head of the Church, residing in his capital, in ancient and venerable Rome. Rome, as the hub of a vast administrative wheel, harbored an almost endless variety of officials, some attached to the papal chancellery, others to the law-courts, and still others to the treasury. The most distinguished group of these central officials was the *college of cardinals*. Appointed by the pope, the cardinals were associated with him in governing the Church, and upon them on the death of the ruling pope devolved the grave responsibility of electing his successor.

[marginal note: Government and administration of the Church]

At the side of the above-mentioned officials, whose shoulders bore the main burden of Church government, there had, in response to the ascetic spirit of the age, grown up another group of churchmen,
The monas- whom we must accept as a very characteristic feature of
tic orders a medieval Christianity. I refer to the monks and nuns. The
character-
istic expres- monks and nuns were organized in a great variety of ord-
sion of ers, founded by men and women animated by an un-
medieval quenchable religious fervor. Some of the more popular
piety monastic orders spread rapidly over the face of Europe, reached a large membership, and achieved through the free offerings of the faithful an enviable position expressed in terms of lands and houses. The oldest and most famous of the orders was that of the Benedictines founded by a dedicated spirit, St. Benedict, as early as the sixth century (529 A.D.), while the Cistercians, Carthusians, and others, who sprang into being at a later time, hardly, if at all, lagged behind the Benedictines in riches, popularity, and power.

In the thirteenth century the two famous orders, the Franciscans and the Dominicans, came into being, fashioned in the heat of a great religious revival and pledged to ideals somewhat different from
The begging those of their predecessors. The older orders — all or-
friars ganized more or less on the Benedictine model — empha-
sized the life of studious contemplation of divine things in seclusion from the world and its temptations. The Franciscans and Domini-
cans, on the other hand, sought out the crowded centers to dispense among the poor and heavy-laden the offices of Christian charity. Dedicated to poverty, chastity, and obedience, their three obligatory vows, and seeking their living, at least at first, from door to door, they were distinguished from the older monks under the name of begging brothers or friars (from Latin *frater*, i.e., brother).

The heads of monasteries were called abbots or priors. They and their flocks were usually subject to the jurisdiction of the bishop in whose diocese they resided, but occasionally individual abbots and,
Jurisdic- in the case of the begging friars, the orders themselves
tional had sought and obtained from the pope the right to be
disputes
between the responsible only to him. Naturally the pope profited by
pope and this arrangement, for he acquired an army of immediate
the bishops adherents scattered throughout Christendom. But the pope's gain was the bishop's loss. As a result of this rivalry between the local and the central authority in the Church many a diocese became the scene of a bitter, though generally subterranean,

conflict between the bishop and his following of priests on the one hand and the abbot or prior supported by the monks and friars on the other.

The officials of the Church from pope to priest and including the monastic orders constituted a sharply defined class or caste of medieval society called the clergy. The respect felt for the clergy is indicated by the circumstance that everywhere in feudal Europe they took the highest rank and were called the first estate. The remainder of the inhabitants of a feudal state constituted the laity, which fell into two classes, an upper class embracing the nobility and called the second estate, and a lower class composed of the common people or third estate. Neither in practice nor theory did the laity have anything to do with the government of the Church, which was reserved exclusively to the first estate, the clergy.

The clergy the highest medieval class or first estate

In the light of this brief review of the authority and government of the Church, we are thoroughly prepared to agree that its place in medieval society was very different from what it is at present. In fact, the Church was a state, so much greater than the various feudal states, at the side of which it played its part, that it completely overshadowed them. In consequence of this preëminence the Church had achieved what is known as immunity, that is, it had won from the civil authorities exemption from taxation as well as the right for the clergy to be amenable only to the law-courts of the Church. In consequence a member of the clergy, on being charged with an offense, was haled before an ecclesiastical tribunal and judged by ecclesiastical judges in accordance with the ecclesiastical law. This, commonly called canon law in distinction from the civil law of the secular courts, was composed of acts of Church councils and decisions of the popes, and so great was its importance in a world dominated by the clergy that it was pursued as a professional study at the universities. Moreover, in certain important matters, such as marriage and divorce and the proving of wills, the ecclesiastical courts possessed authority also over the laity. From these dispositions it follows that throughout western Europe the individual clergyman by being answerable in all respects to ecclesiastical authority was the unquestioned subject of the Church, while the individual layman owed obedience to two states, the Church and the civil state of his residence, each of which exercised authority over him in certain specified matters.

The Church functions as an independent state

Another important function of the Church by virtue of which it
met the definition of a state was that it levied taxes. Since the
Church owned immense manorial properties, for which it claimed
immunity and paid no contribution to the civil powers,
The Church
levies the   it enjoyed a considerable income. This income, of the
tithe and   nature of rent, constituted its basic revenue. However,
controls   it was not large enough to meet the great expenses of its
education
far-flung organization. In consequence the Church had, in
every country in which it was established, gained the right to levy
a tax, called tithe, amounting in theory to one-tenth of the annual
produce of the soil, although in practice it usually came to a good deal
less. If we add that since the Church undertook to direct the steps of
erring mankind, it very naturally assumed control of the education of
its followers and conducted such schools as existed, we join another
detail to the picture painting the influences by which the Church
counted in the affairs and overwhelmed the imagination of the faithful. But let no one dream for a moment that law-courts, taxes, and
education represented unlawful usurpations. In the confusion of the
early Middle Age, when the young states of Europe were only just
taking shape and were as weak as new-born babes, all the functions
which the Church cared to assume fell to its lot without a struggle
because it was the strongest and, in some extreme cases, the only
institution of any kind that in the general dissolution of society
continued to operate.

However, in measure as the civil states gained strength, and they
tended to do so, as we have seen, with the rise of the towns, the
extraordinary power of the Church would be felt to be excessive
The Church and a conflict was inevitable. In fact, the conflict started
claims   even before the towns had become an acknowledged power,
equality   the whole Middle Age resounding, as is well known, with
and, later,
superiority this struggle. But undeniable as is the sharp medieval
over the   contest between Church and state, we should not fail to
state   note that it ran counter to the accepted theory of the age.
For the theory affirmed that Church and state were equally of God,
who had created them for the service of his creatures, entrusting to
one the rule of the souls of men and to the other the rule of their
bodies. At the head of the two complementary institutions God had
placed the pope and the emperor, endowing them respectively with
the spiritual and material authority over mankind. But as, in point
of fact, pope and emperor, instead of working in harmony, were

involved in a struggle as constant as it was vehement, certain aggressive popes, like Gregory VII, Innocent III, and Boniface VIII, had been moved to brush the older equalitarian theory aside in favor of the view of the dependence of the emperor and all civil governors whatever on the pope, conceived as the only true spokesman and representative of God. Thus the later papal theory, formulated at the time of the greatest power of the Church, came to be that since civil as well as ecclesiastical authority had been divinely committed to the pope, the emperor and, of course, the other civil rulers as well held their thrones subject to the pope's pleasure. That the Renaissance with its powerful secular tendencies would challenge this extreme position and vindicate the independence of the civil sovereign goes without saying.

Since the clergy were the most exalted and richest class in Europe — the first estate — they paid the usual price of power by more than ordinary exposure to temptation. All through the Middle Age serious charges of corruption were preferred against them. Clerical Occasionally popes and prelates inaugurated a reform, but abuses in spite of these praiseworthy efforts the abuses persisted or cropped up again. Human nature is weak and frail even under surplice and cowl. The chief abuse was perhaps simony, which is the buying and selling of Church offices. The Church officially recognized simony as a sin, but many clergymen and even popes were none the less guilty of it. So long as abbacies and bishoprics produced huge revenues, it is easy to see how ambitious men should crave their possession even at the price of bribery. Another charge against the upper clergy was that they lived in a state of pride and worldliness quite out of keeping with humble followers of Christ and the apostles. Many rode to hunt and even to war and lived in splendid palaces amid an unbroken round of festivals. The lower clergy were accused of squeezing excessive fees out of their parishioners for marriage, burial, and other necessary services, and there is irrefutable evidence that many ecclesiastics of all ranks were guilty of gross carnal vices. This latter charge was more particularly levelled at the monks and friars, tending to become ever more shrill and vehement as we approach the Reformation.

The shortcomings of the clergy were scourged by ardent and upright priests all through the Middle Age, sometimes even by incumbents of the highest ecclesiastical positions. It did not derogate from the Church to make public recognition of the fact that some of its ministers were unworthy. The personal conduct of clerics was conceded to be a field of permissible criticism. But it was different with criticism which gnawed at the organization and doctrine of the Church, because these represented God's own handiwork stamped with a holy and unalterable character. Such critics were blasphemers and against them the Church was armed with formidable weapons. She branded them as heretics and launched her excommunication against them, excluding them from her fellowship and the association of the living. There she left them, for an ancient scruple forbade her to shed blood; but at this juncture, her partner and more often her subordinate rather than partner, the state, stepped in to seize the heretic as a public enemy and put him to death, usually by fire.

Criticism of doctrine and organization defined as heresy

In spite of this rigorous repression heresy and heretics were not uncommon in the Middle Age. Even in that period of Church omnipotence an occasional hardy spirit was moved to assert his individual convictions. Of these isolated heretics, who were perpetually cropping up at odd corners of Europe, there is here no need to speak, although they hold a not unhonored place in the intellectual history of the age. But in addition there were concerted heretical movements affecting a wide area and really jeopardizing the existence of the Church. Of these collective heresies, that of the Albigensians, belonging to the beginning of the thirteenth century, spread over much of southern France. The Albigensians went the length of attacking the sacramental system, and when excommunication proved ineffective, Pope Innocent III, in 1208, preached a crusade against the offenders and crowned his victory, won only after a furious struggle, by setting up a special tribunal called the Inquisition. This was charged with inquiring into the opinions of the suspects and with punishing every slightest departure from orthodoxy. Having drowned the Albigensian heresy literally in blood, the Inquisition persisted as a convenient tool of ecclesiastical repression and was destined to acquire an unenviable reputation for cruelty and bigotry, especially in Spain. However, in spite of the severity with which the Albigensian rebellion was punished, other movements of protest raised their heads from time to time. In the fourteenth century John Wyclif inaugurated a heretical agitation in England which taught that the individual needed no mediator between himself and God and which it took

The Middle Age witnesses the rise of numerous individual and collective heresies

several decades to stamp out; and, shortly after, John Hus began a similar movement of criticism against priestly domination in Bohemia. Although Hus, in 1415, paid for his audacity by being burned at the stake, the heresy which he started continued to agitate his country for several generations after his disappearance.

By such movements of concerted revolt and by many other signs as well it was in the course of the later Middle Age becoming clear not only that the Church no longer enjoyed its old unquestioned authority but that new ideas and forces were coming New ideas to the fore sure to alter the whole medieval inheri- and forces tance and outlook. What these agencies were and what presage a particular conditions were bringing them to the front must new age now engage our attention. Let us turn to examine the new or second phase of western civilization, commonly called the Renaissance.

REFERENCES

In this as in all subsequent lists of additional reading, general works are given first. In them the reader will usually find more ample bibliographies than are appropriate to an introductory work like this.

D. C. MUNRO, *Middle Ages*, ch. 14
E. EMERTON, *Introduction to the Middle Ages*, ch. 15; *Medieval Europe*, chs. 7–10, 16; *Beginnings of Modern Europe*, chs. 3, 7
H. W. C. DAVIS, *Medieval Europe*, chs. 4, 6, 9
L. THORNDIKE, *Medieval Europe*, chs. 15, 17–19, 30
D. C. MUNRO and G. C. SELLERY, *Medieval Civilization*, pp. 159–211, 240–47
G. KRUEGER, *The Papacy*, chs. 7–9
E. CHEYNEY, *Industrial and Social History of England*, chs. 3, 4
C. DAY, *History of Commerce*, chs. 5–14
E. M. HULME, *Renaissance and Reformation*, chs. 1, 2
A. L. CROSS, *History of England and Greater Britain*, ch. 13
J. N. FIGGIS, *From Gerson to Grotius*, ch. 2
Cambridge Medieval History, vol. II
A. LUCHAIRE, *Social France in the Age of Philip Augustus*, chs. 8–12
H. ADAMS, *Mont-Saint-Michel and Chartres*
A. JESSOP, *Coming of the Friars*
E. B. WORKMAN, *Evolution of the Monastic Ideal*
H. O. TAYLOR, *The Medieval Mind*
C. SEIGNOBOS (Dow), *Feudal Régime*

CHAPTER III

THE SECOND OR RENAISSANCE PHASE OF EUROPEAN CIVILIZATION

We have agreed that it does not matter much whether we regard the Renaissance as a last phase of the dying Middle Age or as an independent epoch ushering in the Modern Period. Beyond all question it is an era of transition, during which the peculiar social and political features of the Middle Age and, above all, the ideas in which these features had their roots, were undermined and new ideas saw the light which tended to embody themselves in novel forms and institutions.

The Renaissance an era of transition

It has been pointed out that the towns were the natural centers of the forces of transition because their peculiar activities were bound, in the long run, to prove disruptive of everything the medieval heart held dear. However, the towns developed slowly through long centuries and their inherent hostility to the medieval system did not at once appear, although the baronial class, threatened in its political domination, may be said to have scented the enemy instinctively and with very little delay. Following the natural tendency of youthful organisms, whose future is not yet assured, the towns were in their first phase driven to seek a compromise with the ruling powers, a sort of working arrangement. In this they succeeded to such a degree that they fitted themselves into the prevailing feudal system with sufficient grace and ease to produce a rather unusual balance of the forces and classes constituting society. The evidence of this accommodation is furnished by the fact that it was only after the coming of the towns, in the course of the thirteenth century, that the Middle Age came to a climax.

The towns in their first phase absorbed into the medieval political system

However, if the thirteenth century marks the flowering and culmination of the Middle Age, with the fourteenth century, owing to the continuous growth of the towns and the progressive social disequilibrium which that expansion entailed, the decay of the medieval world became open and palpable. The manifold changes soon

24

registered in every field of human thought and action give In their
the measure of the new stage of civilization and constitute second
the subject matter of every study concerned with the phase the towns dis-
Renaissance. In an effort to get as close as possible to rupt the
this great movement let us consider it under eight aspects. medieval
system

A. THE DEVELOPMENT OF COMMERCE AND INDUSTRY

The earliest medieval trade had necessarily been determined by
the political-economic conditions prevailing under feudalism. We
must think of the long centuries of the Germanic settlement as
substantially without security, without roads, without The towns
conveniences of living of even the humblest sort. Society arise in
satisfied at best an irreducible minimum of human wants response to
and was simpler, ruder, and more impecunious than we new human
can easily imagine. Therefore, when about 1000 A.D. trade needs and
began to revive, it crept slowly and cautiously along what are distrib-
in a socially chaotic world stood out as the safest routes uted
of travel. These were the shore-lines of the Mediter- according to
ranean, the North, and the Baltic seas, as well as the courses of the convenience and security
leading navigable rivers, such as the Po, the Seine, the Rhone, the
Danube, the Rhine, and the Thames. Along these sea and river
routes the first thriving towns came to life, though with the spread
of the movement the interior, in its turn, became gradually dotted
with settlements planted at bridges or crossroads or nestling under
the protecting shadow of some castle or monastery.

We have already seen that no sooner was a town formed than it
aspired to self-government and gained, in spite of the opposition of
the neighboring feudal lords, a measure of freedom which it was at
pains constantly to increase. The greatest success in this Preëm-
endeavor was achieved by the towns of Italy, first, be- inence of
cause the feudal opposition was weakest there, and second, the Italian
because, owing to the geographical factors involved, the towns
Italian towns enjoyed much greater opportunities for wealth and
power than those of any other country. And exactly because the
Italian towns assumed the unquestioned leadership of the town movement, the Renaissance, considered as a cultural process, is primarily
a creation of Italy, from which, as a center, it radiated over the rest
of Europe.

To clinch the argument of Italian preëminence let us consider

the location of the Italian towns with regard to the medieval world.
In the days of the Roman Empire Italy had, as is well known, been
a country of immense and busy towns, which, though fallen into
sad decay during the seizure of power by the Germanic
tribes, had but to pick up the threads of their past to
put themselves once more on the road to recovery. Their
ancient greatness had been largely due to the fact that
Italy lay in the center of the Mediterranean basin, from
gray antiquity the most populous and civilized area of the
world. At the time of the town revival, around 1000 A.D.,
this situation had changed, if at all, to the further advantage of the ancient peninsula. To its west and north lay the crude
and backward but aspiring societies of Spain, France, England, and
Germany, while to the east there loomed, first, the Byzantine empire,
still, though in patent decline, a highly civilized state, and second,
the Arab dominion, a once powerful organism, now threatened with
internal disruption and, since the eleventh century, exposed besides
to the attack of wild Turkish tribes from the central plateau of Asia.
As the Arabs had taken over much of the culture of the Greeks, they
dwelt on as high a plane of civilization as their Byzantine neighbors,
and, like them, were industrious and skillful artisans as well as busy
traders who spun the threads of an ambitious commerce all the way
to the remote regions of India and China. Within the compass of
both the Byzantine and the Arab empires conveniences and luxuries
were to be found of which backward and impoverished Europe had
lost the very knowledge. The eastern nobility wore garments of
silk and brocade, their ladies bedecked themselves with ropes of
pearls and many-colored jewels, while the houses of the enterprising
Moslem merchants of Syria and Egypt and the Christian churches
and palaces of Constantinople were hung with glowing tapestries
and enriched with ornaments of gold and ivory expressive of a
cultivated society and a refined taste. Although, as the crusades
amply proved, the east loomed vaguely as a region of fabulous riches
to the whole backward body of western Christendom, it appealed
particularly to the Italians. For not only did the peninsula lie in the
close outskirts of Arab and Byzantine power, but its southern tip together with the island of Sicily had served for generations as an Arab-
Byzantine battle-ground, thus bringing to the Italians an immediate
knowledge of eastern politics as well as an acquaintance with eastern
arts and wares. To the Italian folk the east was the Levant, Land

Significance of the Mediterranean position of Italy, particularly of its proximity to the Levant

of the Rising Sun, and they turned to it with longing and admiration in their eyes.

Under these circumstances the Italian merchants became the natural middlemen between east and west. In the great coastal cities, such as Amalfi, Pisa, Genoa, and Venice, enterprising individuals formed companies of merchant adventurers who sailed their galleys to Alexandria, Jaffa, Acre, and Constantinople to fetch back the silks, the jewels, the gold chains, the carved ivory, and, above all, the dyes, spices, and slaves obtainable in the markets of the Levant. That slaves were for a long time one of the most profitable commodities handled by the medieval traders throws a penetrating light on the primitive and predatory character of the age. The other eastern wares, however, were without exception luxuries of small bulk, and could, on being landed on the Italian wharves, be loaded on horseback to be carried to the Italian inland and thence over the Alpine passes to France and Germany. Later on, when the galleys became larger and the skill of the sailors greater, the oriental goods could be transported by an unbroken water-route past the straits of Gibraltar to the cities of the English channel and the North sea. In the long run, the shrewd Italians took advantage of every available land and sea path and, as their caravans radiated over Europe, they would stop at one settlement after another, displaying their eastern wares and causing the rude natives to gape with wonder over the marvels spread before their eyes. Desires before undreamed of were excited in their breasts, desires to satisfy which they were obliged to offer in exchange their crude gold and silver coins and such raw products, native to the north, as linen, wool, leather, and furs. These, carried back to Italy and refined by Italian industrial skill, would then make up the cargo with which the galleys returned to the Levant to complete the circle of exchange.

The Italians become the middlemen between east and west

This system, once inaugurated, stimulated an increasing intensity of intercourse, and while transforming the economic life, altered gradually even the superficial physical aspect of Europe by the throwing of bridges over streams and the reconstruction of the neglected Roman roads as well as the tracing of new highways. At the same time a tentative code of international law came into being by means of treaties conceding to merchants protection of life and goods at the hands of the authorities of the city or country in which they

Social, legal, and technical advances made by commerce

chanced to sojourn. Of course we must guard against exaggerating the advance made, since it is undeniable that feudal lawlessness was a long-lived and many-headed hydra. But the fact of progress remains, as appears also from the circumstance that the traders, profiting by their experience, uninterruptedly improved the technical devices of their profession. Learning to coöperate, they formed partnerships based on written contract; they set up banks as aids and stimulants of commerce; they invented bills of exchange to facilitate the transfer of credits between places geographically separated; and they did what they could to replace the debased and unreliable medieval coinage with a sound and stable currency.

A further important effect of an expanding trade was that it powerfully stimulated the industrial arts. If the west felt an irresistible longing for the precious eastern luxuries, it would imperatively have to give to the east equivalent goods of its own, and these, owing to the difficulties and expense of transportation, could not, to any large extent, be raw products. Soon, therefore, the original merchant organizations or merchant gilds, as they were called, were everywhere supplemented by the manufacturing associations or craft gilds of the woolen and linen weavers, the armorers, the leather-workers, the furriers and the rest, whose mounting success steadily increased the population of the medieval town as well as its general productivity and wealth. In this way every town came to be economically dominated by the gilds, which in their two fundamental types of merchant and craft gilds monopolized its entire business. Let us not fail to note, however, that the gild was more than an economic unit, for it served religious, social, and even political ends as well. Indeed some gilds, wholly non-economic, satisfied purely social and religious purposes, somewhat in the fashion of our modern fraternal orders. None the less the powerful gilds were doubtless the economic ones and their power was great enough to enable them or a combination of the wealthiest units among them to take over in most cases the town government. Gild membership implied individual political power collectively exercised. Thus the gilds fostered a justified pride, of which the most conspicuous outward sign were the meeting-places or gild halls. These together with the municipal center or town hall constituted the most expressive physical feature of each rising community, furnishing by their size, harmony of parts, and beauty of detail an accurate measure of its importance. In short, who would

Marginal note: Trade fosters industry and both adopt the gild organization

know well the town of this period must occupy himself with its organic cell, the gild.

A final word on the leading town areas during the Renaissance. They become intelligible on the basis of the general conditions of exchange just sketched. In Italy the northern half of the peninsula, because of the proximity of the Alpine passes behind which Enumeralay the markets capable of absorbing eastern wares, far tion of the outstripped the south in the development of town life; great town and in northern Italy two towns gradually took the lead areas in Italy, over all the others. They were Venice and Florence. France, and By building up a prosperous colonial empire in the eastern Flanders Mediterranean Venice largely succeeded in driving all the rival Italian cities from this scene of opportunity and of becoming the chief distributor of spices and other eastern articles through the western world, while Florence, by carrying the manufacture of textiles, both of wool and silk, to an unexampled proficiency, achieved both the industrial and the banking primacy of Europe. In southern France the valley of the Rhone became an important city area, which, however, gradually yielded ground to the Marne-Seine system of cities in the French north, among which Paris gained an early preëminence. The town movement was still young when the Rhine cities all the way from Strassburg to Cologne came to the front, their increasing commerce being favored by one of the most fruitful valleys of Europe as well as by a fairly easy connection *via* the Alpine passes with the Italian cities. In their favorable situation lay also the explanation of the rise of the Flemish towns, which served as the sea-ports of the rich Rhine hinterland. A further advantage accrued to this group from the proximity of England, one of the main sources in the Middle Age of the supply of that invaluable staple, wool. On the basis of this importation the Flemish cities, such as Ghent, Ypres, and Bruges, developed a textile industry which presents an interesting northern counterpart to that of Florence. The English cities across the channel from Flanders developed no equivalent industry and long remained industrially inferior, but being favorably located for commerce, several of them, and more particularly London on the broad-backed Thames, became flourishing emporiums.

A last town area to consider embraced the German settlements along the coast of the North and Baltic seas. In addition to exploiting the profitable herring fisheries of their waters, they acted as middlemen conducting the native products of Russia, such as leather, wax, and furs, and of Scandinavia, such as iron and tar, into the stream of world trade. Lübeck, Hamburg, and Bremen stood forth as leaders in this area. For the purpose of completely overawing the opposition of the neighboring feudal lords they had united several score of seaboard and inland cities with themselves in a mighty federation called the Hanse. During the fifteenth century, when the Hanse was at its height, it dominated politically and economically the basin of the North and particularly of the Baltic sea all the way from Novgorod in Russia to London and Bruges. At Bruges in Flanders the two greatest streams of European commerce, coming respectively from the Mediterranean and the Baltic, coalesced, making Bruges the leading world emporium until supplanted in the sixteenth century by Antwerp.

The German towns united in the Hanseatic League or Hanse

B. THE REVIVAL OF LEARNING

With the townsmen engaging in ever expanding trade and industry, journeying into far countries to make acquaintance with strange climes and peoples, struggling to dominate the chaotic social and political conditions of the feudal era, and courageously trying their hand at self-government, the world in which they lived began to assume a new form, making it indispensable for them to bring their inherited ideas into conformity with the reality about them.

A new experience gives rise to new ideas

We have already seen that medieval Europe lived its life in the great shadow cast by religion and the Church. And this shadow is by no means a figure of speech, for the substance of the religious teaching of the age was that the body of man, as well as the earth of which it was a part, was under the curse of Adam and invited the scorn of the true Christian. The only thing of value was the soul, which, having come from God, would be restless here below until it had been reunited with the Father. Houses, lands, feasts, and finery, as empty possessions, as things seen, counted less than the dust of the fields against the unseen treasures of the spirit. If this is an extreme, ascetic statement of the Church's teaching, it may yet be said to communicate the essential attitude toward the problem of living which the Church drove home to the faithful. Man was in tune with the divine will if he resolutely rejected this

The medieval Church upholds as its highest aim the contemplation of divine things

world for the better world to come. His best hope of salvation was to be other-worldly.

At a relatively early time the townsmen, engaging in activities which conferred pleasure in themselves as well as highly welcome material benefits, began to entertain doubts touching the invariable applicability to them and their affairs of the purely idealist doctrine of the Church. They were glad to be alive, they frankly enjoyed the sensuous and colored garment of the earth, and they delighted in the improved material position resulting from their increased resources. Since the Church was an elastic institution, extremely responsive to the society which it served, an immediate clash was avoided, although we can not fail to see that the development of town mentality took from the outset a direction abhorrent to fundamental ecclesiastical principle.

The earth-bound activities of the townsmen in contradiction with the main ecclesiastical trend

It was not so much the indulgent Church as one of its dependent institutions which gradually brought this secret inner conflict to the consciousness of the intellectual leaders of the cities. In the eleventh and twelfth centuries the Church had greatly enlarged its educational system by multiplying the monastery and cathedral schools and endowing them with a curriculum which inculcated the so-called Seven Liberal Arts — grammar, rhetoric, logic, arithmetic, geometry, astronomy, and music — but which in reality turned largely about Latin, the one wholly indispensable feature of an education aiming to fit a young cleric for his future work. In the twelfth century this system had flowered in a promising and ambitious institution, the university. Before long universities dotted the leading countries of Europe, but both in the renown of its teachers and in the number of its students the university of Paris outshone all the others.

The medieval school and university system

The university movement signified a meager but genuine intellectual revival based on such scraps of Greek and, more particularly, of Aristotelian philosophy as had survived the long neglect of the last phase of the ancient and the first phase of the new European civilization. Admittedly slight, the Aristotelian remains none the less furnished evidence touching one of the notable achievements of the Greek mind. The basic feature of Aristotelianism was a system of logic which had been elaborated by the famous Athenian as a means for testing truth. This logic had by a stroke of chance

The medieval intellectual movement aims at the reconciliation of faith and reason been preserved; and enraptured by its rediscovery and by the excitements inherent in the dialectic game, the university professors undertook the task of bringing the Christian doctrines, owing their origin to faith alone, into harmony with the Aristotelian norms of reason. This labor, enthusiastically embarked on, produced a philosophy which from its university champions, the *doctores scholastici* or schoolmen, has been called scholasticism. The acknowledged prince of the scholastics was St. Thomas Aquinas (d. 1274) who, coming at the end of a cumulative movement, solved in his famous *Summa* the philosophic problem of his age to the general satisfaction. The achievement of Aquinas consisted in adjusting the conflicting demands of faith and reason in so subtle and delicate a way that each came into its own without infringing on the rights of the other. With that success scholasticism had reached its goal and spent its energy; but, instead of dying, it unhappily lingered on, as movements ensconced in powerful institutions will, until, eternally chewing its ancient cud, it invited the irritated attention of the alert and mobile townsmen. What struck them was that the education served up in the schools and universities by the dull and dessicated schoolmen was wholly out of touch with the needs and problems of an urban group. They wanted, although they were perhaps only dimly aware of the fact, intellectual sanctions for their novel, mundane ways of living; and when they could not get them from the university professors, they took them from the only other authority available, the ancients.

There followed the intellectual revolt called the Revival of Learning; and it is notable that it took place, at least to a large extent, outside and even against the universities. It is in fact a town, not a university movement, and the best proof thereof is that it had its start in the great towns of Italy, more particularly in Florence. Its forerunners begin to put in an appearance as early as the thirteenth century, as may be illustrated by the case of St. Francis of Assisi (1182–1226). An extraordinarily pure and simple soul, he gave his life whole-heartedly to Christ and founded one of the great orders of begging friars, the Brothers Minor or Franciscans. In these respects he moved within the frame of the ascetic concepts of the Middle Age; but because he sent his friars not into monastic solitude but out into the world to serve their suffering fellow-men, and further, because he rejoiced with the simple pleasure of a child

The new feeling for life and nature illustrated by St. Francis of Assisi

or poet in the countless fair forms of nature, calling the beasts his brothers and the birds his sisters, he is on the way toward an affirmation of existence that is essentially modern.

One hundred years after St. Francis we come across the first open champion of a revival of classical studies, Francesco Petrarca or Petrarch (1304–1374). Of Florentine ancestry Petrarch, owing to the banishment of his father from the Arno city The first as the result of a political defeat, was born in upper great champion of the Tuscany at Arezzo and brought up beyond the Alps at new learnAvignon on the Rhone, whither the papal court had ing is recently transferred its seat. Having returned to Italy to Petrarch pursue the study of law in the renowned legal university of Bologna, the young Petrarch ended by rejecting a profession which was repugnant to his nature and courageously resolved to live his life precariously as a wandering scholar. To later ages he was chiefly known as a poet who poured out his troubled love for Laura in scores of musical sonnets. By adopting the vernacular for these expressions of a mercurial emotion he became one of the founders of Italian literature. However, among the men of his own time, Petrarch, the poet, counted less, much less, than Petrarch, the intellectual giant. For them the notable thing about him was that he inaugurated a conscious rebellion against the hide-bound university professors and that he proposed to replace their educational pabulum, which he considered as no better than thrashed straw, with the nourishment still abundantly stored in the literature of the classical period. What made that literature, produced more than a thousand years before, appeal as still vital to the fourteenth century was an important but simple circumstance. It was the self-expression of an active people engaged in wrestling with the very human problems born of contact with this earth. Naturally enough its frank but refined worldliness made a strong appeal to the new Italian urban class involved in essentially the same struggle.

The spirit of Petrarch's championship of classical literature should be clearly understood. Although the Greek language had been forgotten in the European west and its inestimable trea- Petrarch sures had become inaccessible, let no one dream that the champions great Latin authors had similarly sunk from view during the humanistic content the Middle Age. Not only had the Latin language been of classical made, as we already know, the corner-stone of the medie- literature val school curriculum, but the Latin authors, more particularly Virgil, were freely utilized as a convenient text for mastering a strange and difficult tongue. But these Latin studies, prescribed by the dogmatic system of the Seven Liberal Arts under the names of grammar and rhetoric, were at best hardly more than dry philological exercises. Wholly taken up with its peculiar theological preoccupations, the Middle Age made no effort to penetrate to the spirit of the classical authors, who with their glad acceptance of this earth dwelt in a realm incomprehensible and even hateful to ascetically minded men. Petrarch, therefore, did not so much recover the ancient books as he unsealed his mind to their vital contents, and, arising in his place, preached that content to all the seekers of life in his day. According to his reform program, the curriculum of the schools was still to be based exactly as before on Latin; only henceforth the young men were to receive the living message of the text in order to be guided by its light. Not Latin for the sake of a dead language and the dusty theological disputes conducted in it, but Latin as an avenue to a genial outlook on life became Petrarch's watchword. As this prized geniality of spirit was admirably expressed by the word *humanitas*, the Revival of Learning has often been indentified with humanism and Petrarch has been called the first humanist. In the same effort to emphasize his resolute departure from the austere ideals of a medievalism still widely prevalent in his age, he has, not without a certain exaggeration, been acclaimed the first modern man.

On the purely practical side Petrarch set himself as his main object the task of improving the manuscripts of Virgil, Horace, Livy, Cicero, and the other Latin poets, historians, and philosophers, whose texts, owing to the carelessness of many genera-

Petrarch inaugurates a new era in classical scholarship

tions of scribes, had become exceedingly corrupt. In addition he aimed to establish libraries, by which the precious manuscripts could be made more accessible to the studious, and to discover valuable lost works among the dusty shelves of forgotten monasteries. In support of these labors he collected an enthusiastic following of scholars who devoted a vast energy to the recovery, correction, and popularization of the classical remains.

Although Petrarch did not know Greek, he fully recognized its importance. Within a generation after his death a number of native scholars from the Greek east had been drawn to Italy as teachers, and in the first half of the fifteenth century these scattered forerunners were followed by a voluntary influx due to the gradual conquest of the Byzantine Empire by the Ottoman Turks. When, in 1453, Constantinople, the Greek capital, itself fell before the Asiatic onslaught, still greater numbers of scholars turned their footsteps toward Italy, taking with them as their most precious pos- *The conquest of Greek and the recovery of the classical viewpoint* session whatever manuscripts they managed to save from the wreck of their world. In this way the treasure-house of Greek literature, immeasurably richer than that of Rome, was made accessible to the western student, and a scholarly group of humanists, hopefully reaping the rich fields of classical philology, history, and philosophy, might be encountered in every great center of Italy. While some of these men were no better than bat-eyed pedants, who gave their days to such trifles as the enclitic particle or the aorist tense, others again steeped themselves so thoroughly in the issues of life which dominated Athens and Rome that they impress us in some of their manifestations as belated Greeks and Romans, more comfortably at home in a dead and buried age than in their own.

By the middle of the fifteenth century the vision of a new intellectual culture, based on antiquity, had seduced the whole educated world of Italy. Not only leading laymen associated with government or trade, but numerous churchmen, especially men *The new learning seduces the great churchmen and penetrates all classes* of the highest rank, shared in the general enthusiasm. In many instances when the great Church dignitaries did not themselves become scholars, they assumed the role of patrons and dilettanti and tolerantly discussed Stoicism, Platonism, and the other philosophic speculations of the Greeks as if they had been interesting early phases of Christianity. Thus by subtle and imperceptible stages the otherworldliness of the Middle Age made way for the avowed worldliness of the Renaissance, and a glad affirmation of this life, the precious gift of which we have an immediate consciousness, came to expression in all classes of society.

Of the peculiarly joyous temper of the period and of its happy expression in the arts we shall presently learn more; but one sinister concomitant of the mental liberation belongs here and must not escape our attention. It will cause no surprise to learn that *The spread of pagan sentiments* the continued occupation of the humanists with the pagan world threatened in the long run to estrange them from Christianity. To be sure this had not been the case with Petrarch, for the reason that he was still too close to the Middle Age to lose his sincere awe of the faith of his fathers. But after a hundred years of Cicero and Seneca, of Plato and Plotinus, this faith no longer loomed so large as formerly and as a result the mass of the humanists became infected with religious scepticism. And yet, if they broke inwardly with their inheritance, if they became more or less pagan in their outlook on life, they made no clamorous and inconvenient stir about it. The Church, governed by prelates themselves steeped in the new learning and cut adrift from the traditional moorings, practised an extreme toleration and carefully avoided bringing the humanists into open opposition with itself.

Judged from a purely religious standpoint the resulting situation in Italy was hollow and, in the long run, dangerous. For granting that under the popes of the fifteenth century, who, frankly attached **Danger for** to the pleasures and splendors of this world, may be **the Church** classified as a distinct group of Renaissance popes, the **in the pa-** Church appeared as a house magnificent, costly, and out- **ganization** **of the Ital-** wardly no less impressive than of yore, it was never the **ian prelates** less permissible to suspect that that house no longer sheltered the Christ in whose divine name it claimed the respect and obedience of the Christian world. And though the Italians, absorbed by their pagan enthusiasms, might not be shocked by this contradictory situation, it was not improbable that some other people, not yet paganized by the new learning, would rise to protest against what struck it as an intolerable scandal in the Christian family.

C. LITERATURE AND THE FINE ARTS

Since, during the Renaissance, men developed a new attitude toward the problems of living, literature and the Fine Arts, which serve as an outlet for whatever stirs the human heart, promptly **The Renais-** came to the front. Let us first briefly consider the move- **sance** ment of literature. In Italy and in every other country **stimulates** **the** as well writers arose who, moved in the depth of their **vernacular** souls by the freshening stream of life, felt that they had **literatures** something of value to communicate; and although some writers continued to use Latin, so long the authoritative medium of the learned classes of the world, others, especially poets, became convinced that their emotions could be adequately expressed only in the familiar mother-tongue. In this way the European vernaculars, the French, Italian, Spanish, English, and German languages acquired an incontestable literary standing, while at the same time the literatures in these languages, although they had begun to flourish in the Middle Age in connection with the epic poetry cultivated by the nobility, came into continuous being. Considered in their Renaissance phase, which alone concerns us here, these native literatures still possess a somewhat tentative character. They have come to stay but are not yet quite sure of the fact. Thus Italian literature, after introducing itself to the world, as to the sound of silver trumpets, with the three immortal Florentines, Dante, Petrarch, and Boccaccio, all of the fourteenth century, in the fifteenth century again dropped into comparative insignificance. In the same century which gave Italy its great Florentine constellation England gave birth to Chaucer (1340–1400), who produced the delightful *Canterbury Tales* but, like the Italian triumvirate, left no successor. Contemporary France was graced by Froissart (1337–1410), one of the most picturesque prose chroniclers of all time, and, shortly after, heard the natural, moving voice of the poet Villon (1431–1484), child of the city and its slums. Great names all these, but names whose distinctly sporadic performances leave the impression that the literary movement in the European vernaculars was not yet full-fledged.

Everything considered, the temper of the Renaissance in the period before the Reformation expressed itself much less fully in literature than in the Fine Arts. And in this field Italy so decisively led the other countries that we may be pardoned if, owing to lack of space, we confine ourselves to the artistic movement among the Italians. The several Fine Arts serve the function of expressing within the limits of their respective means and under the stimulus of the creative imagination the longings and ideals of a particular society. In other words, while architecture, sculpture, and painting always have specific tasks which they must satisfy each in its own material of stone, wood, or color, they will be found expressive and beautiful in a particular case in exact measure as they give convincing form to the aspirations of their time or of all times. No sooner had the townsmen, as early as the eleventh century, set themselves the task of building that new thing, a town, than they perforce called architecture into being; and architecture in its turn quite naturally wakened to life sculpture and painting. But as all this early activity had taken place while the Church still enjoyed an unquestioned authority, the Fine Arts in their purely medieval phase were steeped in the Christian

The Fine Arts in the Middle Age created the Gothic style

spirit. By historians of art the medieval phase of the Fine Arts is universally called Gothic, a name rather ill-chosen (for what had the Goths to do with medieval art?), but fully serving a purpose if we agree that it means no more than that medieval churches, statues, and paintings were conceived in a particular spirit and sound an identical religious note. Gothic, in short, is a purely conventional name for the self-expression, the *style* of the Christian Middle Age.

When, with the coming of the Renaissance, the town began to break away from the moorings of the Church, when it devoted itself to worldly ends and in this pursuit reëstablished the broken con-nection with antiquity, the Gothic style was gradually abandoned and a new manner of expression developed appropriate to the new age. Of course, this style too was, no more than Gothic, fixed and unchanged through successive generations; and connoisseurs distinguish at least three phases, early Renaissance, middle Renaissance, and late Renaissance, covering together the period from about 1400 to 1550 and even 1600. Concerned here with but the merest sketch, we shall be satisfied first, to characterize the Renaissance art as a whole, and second, to point to a few of the great artists who distinguished themselves in the respective fields of architecture, sculpture, and painting.

The Renais-sance style rules from 1400 to 1600

If we agree that Gothic feeling continued to rule the practice of the Italian artists till toward the year 1400, we are prepared to understand the conditions that helped mold the new style. Shortly after 1400 the artists, having had their attention called by the humanists to Greece and Rome, turned with the same fervor to the artistic monuments of the past as the scholars had already shown for its literature. With a sudden fiery enthusiasm for the new they coupled a wholly unde-served contempt for the forms which had enjoyed authority for so long a time. Gothic became positively taboo as they threw them-selves with the passion of proselytes on the Corinthian columns, the decorative motifs, and the marble statuary of antiquity. Innumer-able architectural and sculptural remains in a more or less complete state of preservation were still to be found in all the cities of Italy. If we consider more particularly the architects, in whose eyes the long neglected ruins suddenly again became beautiful, the practical issue for them came to be how the essential forms of the ancient monuments might be successfully adapted to the existing needs of society. The Renaissance town did not, like ancient Rome, call

The Renais-sance style defined by its elements

for amphitheaters, baths, and temples. It would normally require cathedrals, town halls, and gild houses, in so far as the need for these had not already been met in the Gothic period; and with the increasing wealth of the community and of its individual members a somewhat novel demand would make itself felt for parish churches, private chapels, and, above all, for palaces and villas. Add that the artists, more particularly the sculptors and painters, refusing to maintain the obligatory medieval attitude toward nature as the realm of Satan, knocked at her door with the request to be admitted to her kindly confidences, and we have the situation out of which the new style was born. Defining that style by its elements, we may therefore summarily say first, that it represented a revival of classical forms; second, that it was inspired with the freshness of nature; and, third that, while by no means wholly emancipated from religion and the Church, it served the interest and outlook of energetic groups which had risen to influence through the opportunities of trade and industry.

Turning first to architecture, we greet in Brunellesco (1377–1446) the harbinger of the Renaissance spirit. His great work, by which he illustrated the classical principle of spaciousness coupled with simplicity, is the dome with which he crowned the cathe- Architecture— dral of his native town of Florence. Such a church as ture— San Lorenzo, also in Florence, announces his decision to Brunellesco and turn from the massive piers which featured Gothic church Michael construction to the lighter and more graceful columnar Angelo row of the Roman builders. These suggestions of Brunellesco, taken over and elaborated by several generations of innovators, studded the Italian towns with that profusion of handsome edifices in the Renaissance style which still arouses the admiration of the visitor. The culminating structure, both historically and stylistically, is perhaps St. Peter's at Rome. Many of the greatest architects of the peninsula were at one time or another entrusted with its construction which continued throughout the sixteenth century; but the most famous name connected with the enterprise is that of the Florentine, Michael Angelo (1475–1564). In the far-seen dome, in which Michael Angelo outdid the lofty cupola of his fellow-citizen, Brunellesco, we hail one of the monumental achievements of all time.

In many ways, however, the private structures of the period were more interesting and more varied than the religious edifices. It was an age when military despots and merchant princes came to the front, desirous to commemorate themselves and their families with an enduring monument.   In Florence successful bankers, like the

The profusion of private palaces and country villas

Medici, the Strozzi, and the Pitti, erected heavy piles of masonry whose frowning, fortress-like, and medieval character, was only slightly modified by the urbanity of the new feeling, while in Venice, the sea city, where an unthreatened security reigned and the idea of a fortress as a family home had become a complete anachronism, the merchant residences rose in open, graceful, superimposed arcades, whose many-colored marbles softly mirrored themselves in the slow-moving canals.   But if Venice and Florence stand out in the front of the Italian cities, Rome, Padua, Bologna, Siena, and a score of others did not lag far behind.   They too were architecturally transformed; and since each town boasted a distinct town personality, its structures of this period sound a very individual note in the richly modulated Italian architectural chorus.

In the Florentine Donatello (1383–1466), the contemporary and friend of Brunellesco, we encounter the artist who inaugurated the Renaissance movement in sculpture.   While an occasional, religiously

Sculpture — Donatello and Michael Angelo

conceived figure, like that of his well-known St. George, would show that he still cherished the memories of the Middle Age, his work, considered as a whole, is, though not untouched with the spirit of antiquity, the frank expression of a whole-hearted realism.   As his numerous charming portrayals of childhood eloquently confess, Donatello was essentially a follower of nature.   His contemporary, Ghiberti (1378–1455), is the author of the two celebrated bronze gates of the Florentine baptistery.   They set forth in many scenes in high relief certain significant events, selected in one case from the life of Christ, in the other from the Old Testament.   How be just to Luca della Robbia, Desiderio da Settignano, and a score of others?   Enough that this Florentine school of sculpture culminated in Michael Angelo (1475–1564), who, by preference a wielder of the chisel, by no means confined himself to one art but practised also architecture, painting, and poetry.   He is one of the myriad-minded men, the universal geniuses, who are a distinguished and distinguishing feature of the age.   Abandoning the simple-hearted naturalism of Donatello which contented itself naïvely with the immediate aspect of the visible universe, he searched with persistence and austerity for the reality behind appearances, and in his Moses (in Rome) and in his figures for the Medicean tombs in Florence created an almost terrifying world of supermen, confronted with whom every living generation since has felt itself reduced to a race of pigmies.

Significant as were the achievements of architecture and sculpture, it was, however, the art of painting which the Renaissance chiefly utilized to voice its hopes and fears. That was perhaps because paint is a more fluid and expressive medium than stone or marble and because the restless spirit of the age felt itself more completely at home in the sensitive and fugitive effects of line and color. So much did painting become the chosen Italian art that every town of any importance developed its own painters, who constituted a local group or school with a style peculiarly their own. The inexhaustible richness and variety of Italian painting is due to these schools, to which to do justice here is entirely out of the question. Let us content ourselves with glancing at the schools of the two greatest centers, Florence and Venice.

Painting the outstanding art of the Renaissance

The Florentine school of painting was founded by Giotto (1266–1337) in a period still dominated by Gothic emotions. Though Giotto is rightly considered one of the greatest artists of all times, his work, steeped in medieval feeling, ceased to appeal to the generation that took delight in Brunellesco and Donatello and achieved the Renaissance civilization. Early in the fifteenth century, therefore, the art of painting was invaded by the same spirit which had already moved architecture and sculpture to fresh expression. The first painter to sound the new note was Masaccio (1401–1428?), a sturdy, convincing realist, as his frescos in the Brancacci chapel, still extant, amply prove. Paolo Uccello, Fra Filippo Lippi, Botticelli, and many others caught the realist note from him, delicately varying it according to their individual temper. In Botticelli the world still recognizes a personal utterance so rare, so puzzling that its mystic implications have never quite been plumbed.

Florentine painting from Masaccio to Botticelli

The Florentine school came to its final fruition in Michael Angelo (1475–1564) and Leonardo da Vinci (1452–1519). Of Michael Angelo it may be said that, though he became a painter against his will at the imperious bidding of a pope, he achieved in his scenes of the creation, depicted on the ceiling of the Sistine chapel at Rome, a masterpiece which has quickened the pulse of every generation of men since his time. Leonardo, like Michael Angelo, was a universal genius, who, in addition to painting, practised sculpture, Michael interested himself in scientific experiment, and was an Angelo and engineer and inventor. However, just as Michael Angelo Leonardo was by preference a sculptor, Leonardo was first of all da Vinci and preëminently a painter. Unfortunately some of his greatest works, like the Last Supper at Milan and the portrait of a lady, called Mona Lisa, at Paris, have been almost ruined by the tooth of time, owing, it would seem, to his over-hasty adoption of certain technical innovations.

At this juncture a word about the technical processes connected with painting may not prove amiss. At the time of Giotto and for several generations afterwards the Florentines commonly and preferably used what is known as the fresco method. By Fresco and this, a convenient style of large-scale wall-painting, the oil painting artist applies his color to the wet plaster, permitting plaster and paint to fuse into an indistinguishable mass in the process of drying. Largely because of its discouraging lack of permanence, fresco work was gradually abandoned for painting on specially prepared boards or canvas in substantial colors which owe their peculiar body to the circumstance of their being carried in a solution of oil. This extraordinarily solid technic, commonly called painting in oil, gradually gained the upper hand and was employed also by Leonardo; only, given as he was to scientific experimentation, he tried other media, besides oil, with the disastrous result above mentioned.

One of the last artists to use the fresco technic with outstanding success was Raphael (1483–1520), whose great allegorical presentations of theology, philosophy, and poetry in the private chambers Raphael of of the pope's palace of the Vatican, as well as whose Urbino numerous altar-pieces and portraits in oil, place him on the summit of the Renaissance movement. A certain grace achieved by Raphael, a sensuous harmony, too facile, it may be, but rarely winning, have made him the most beloved artist of all time. A native of the mountain town, Urbino, he is, let us not fail to note, a product not of the Florentine, but of the Umbrian school. To accord him a merited place in our brief record may serve to confirm us in the view that the great centers of Florence and Venice by no means enjoyed a monopoly of artistic genius.

Not only was the city of Venice remarkably secure in its day and its government unusually stable, but set in a silver sea under a blue and radiant sky, it was and has remained one of the fairest and most stirring sights on earth. Inevitably these happy social and physical conditions were reflected in the school of paint- Venetian ing, which, springing from the fresh vigor of the Renais- painting — sance, revelled in a liveliness and charm of color never Titian before or afterwards achieved. Since it is futile simply to call off the roster of illustrious Venetian names, let us rest content with the artists who stand on the summit of accomplishment. They are Giorgione, Titian, Tintoretto, and Paul Veronese; but Titian (1477–1576) tops them all as the embodiment of peculiarly Venetian purposes. Whether he produced portraits — and he produced many, since all the prominent people of his time desired to be limned by him — or whether he painted altar-pieces for the gorgeous churches lining the canals, his work no longer bears a trace of medieval provincialism or piety. Let us for a moment transport ourselves into the presence of that gorgeous panel in the Venetian Academy called the Presentation of the Virgin. Instead of any act or gesture specifically Christian, we have a magnificent procession of gentlefolk moving with a dignity and arrayed with a sumptuousness which suggest not the Holy Family but the merchant princes under whose patronage Titian and his school developed their refined, aristocratic, and frankly worldly art.

D. NATURAL SCIENCE AND INVENTION

That the Middle Age neglected the natural sciences was no more than might be expected of a period which looked askance at this earth as a vale of tears and taught that the happiest hour of life was the hour on which one left it. The common people held Medieval that nature was inhabited by sprites, elves, and devils, science whom it was the part of wisdom to propitiate, and even limited to astrology the upper classes were very generally dominated by similar and superstitions. Under these circumstances anything like alchemy a sane or systematic study of man's physical environment was out of the question and the closest medieval approach to scientific inquiry, as we understand the term, is represented by the quack sciences of astrology and alchemy. Astrology, which did indeed include some slight observation of the heavens, owed its amazing popularity to the specious belief that the individual human destiny is determined by the stars, while alchemy, which undoubtedly encour-

aged a small measure of laboratory experimentation, was practised
in the illusive hope of fabulous riches to be achieved by converting
the baser metals into gold. Conceding that astrology and alchemy
served as forerunners of the genuine sciences of astronomy and
chemistry, owing to the absurd hypotheses on which they were
based, as well as because of the total absence of a critical method,
we can not agree that they contributed greatly to a truly helpful
and exact knowledge of man and his world.

With the advent of the Renaissance the negative attitude toward
the earth popularized by medieval Christianity gradually made way
for a happy affirmation, which imperceptibly led to a closer observation of natural forms and processes. The intellectual
stimulus supplied by humanism contributed to the same
end, for with the uncovering of classical literature there
was uncovered also the remarkable science of the Greeks,
more particularly in the fields of physics, astronomy,
medicine, and mathematics. The result was that at some universities, notably at Padua, by slow, indeed, very slow degrees a new
scientific spirit began to prevail. Not till the beginning of the
sixteenth century, however, did it celebrate any considerable triumphs, and these, moreover, were long limited to medicine. It was
a notable advance when such studies as anatomy and physiology
were put on a frankly experimental basis by the dissection of dead
bodies. The greatest Paduan name is that of a native Fleming,
Dr. Vesalius. In 1543 he published his anatomical treatise, *Fabrica
Corporis Humani*, wherein he took the bold position that it was
necessary to challenge every past authority, even the awe-inspiring
Greeks, and to be guided exclusively by an examination of the facts.
The facts — that was the sign in which science was destined to win
its imposing modern victories.

But since, after all, it was only toward the year 1500 that medicine
took a distinctly original turn, we are justified in putting at the head
of the studies that first yielded novel results the related sciences of
geography and astronomy. In fact, investigation will
make perfectly clear that the medieval scientific petrifac-
tion was first shaken by the introduction of new geographical knowledge. This originated in the simplest possible
way as a by-product of the journeys undertaken by merchants over
land and sea in search of markets. As soon as the Mediterranean
area had become fairly familiar, men took to travel, very often as

Margin notes: Slow improvement of observational methods: medicine

The solid advances of geography

much in the spirit of adventure as from the lust of gain. As early as the second half of the thirteenth century the celebrated Venetian, Marco Polo, penetrated overland all the way to China and left a record of his hazards which still inflames the imagination of the reader. Before long the scattered new information was incorporated in maps, made by cartographers who addressed themselves quite as much to man's mounting passion for knowledge as to the practical needs of traders and sea-captains. Then, in the fifteenth century, through the developments of humanism, the geography and astronomy of the ancient Greeks was made accessible. The last of the great Alexandrian astronomers was Ptolemy, who had lived in the second century after Christ and who had taught not only that the earth was round but also had calculated its circumference at an astonishingly close approximation to the true figure. Eager to pick up every crumb from the Greek table, the humanists were not slow to give up the common medieval view that the earth was flat in favor of the more authoritative Ptolemaic teaching. By the fifteenth century, therefore, the geography of the world had taken on a changed aspect: to abundant new data touching Europe, Africa, and Asia was added the advantage of fuller maps and charts and of the Ptolemaic hypothesis with its thought-provoking implications. If, in connection with these facts, we now consider the alluring profits of the oriental trade, we shall easily understand how men fell victim to that strange fever compounded of romance, love of knowledge, and low greed, which we call the voyages of discovery and which did not exhaust itself till man had entered into complete possession of the earth.

Of the voyages of discovery more will be said later on. At this juncture it behooves us to point out that the new geography led with unescapable logic to the new astronomy, connected with the famous name of Copernicus (1473–1543). This native of the city of Thorn on the Vistula river passed ten formative years of his life in Italy, where he absorbed in eager draughts the new ideas so generally diffused through the peninsula. The new astronomy — Copernicus Impressed by the Ptolemaic astronomy, which placed a round, stationary earth at the center of the universe with all the other celestial bodies revolving around it, he was none the less led to question some of its dicta and formulated, after years of study, his own hypothesis. This upheld the view that the earth with the other planets revolved around the sun, and that, in addition to this motion, it spun every twenty-four hours around its axis.

Owing to the general currency of the Ptolemaic or geocentric theory, a currency made practically obligatory because of its endorsement by the Church, Copernicus hesitated so long to announce his heliocentric views that it was not till the year of his death that his epoch-making astronomical treatise issued from the press (1543). Not greatly noticed at first, its teachings filtered very slowly into the European consciousness. However, in measure as the new hypothesis captured the thinking minds, not only did it revolutionize the whole picture of the universe, but it helped decisively to put the natural sciences on a solid foundation by spreading the conviction that the modern, as distinct from the medieval, knowledge would have to begin with the challenge of tradition and pass on thence to new data accumulated through fresh, individual observation.

General stimulus to science of the Copernican astronomy

Because the Middle Age was conspicuously indifferent to natural science it must not be thought to have been wholly without distinction in the field of invention. While, as our own age would abundantly prove, invention is greatly stimulated by scientific discovery, it is not entirely dependent on it, since some of the most important inventions ever made by man have resulted from nothing more than from his inborn ingenuity. Even in the relatively slothful Middle Age men, on being confronted in the field of their immediate interests with perplexing problems, brought or tried to bring them to a satisfactory solution. Thus, since the liturgical service of the Church stimulated a love of music, the singers invented a system of notation, which, with additions imposed by later phases of development, is the system we still use. Again, the sailors of the Mediterranean, finding it difficult to steer their course as soon as they lost sight of land, either invented the mariners' compass or, what comes to much the same thing, took it over from the Arabs, who in their turn had borrowed it from the Chinese. As for the medieval painters, they first solved their particular difficulty, as we have seen, with the fresco method and, when that proved unsatisfactory, turned to oil and canvas.

The Middle Age not undistinguished by invention

When, with the quickening of intercourse in the Renaissance, problems of a technical kind rapidly multiplied, inventions, representing more or less complete solutions of the new problems, multiplied also. Two in particular had such far-reaching consequences that we must single them out for attention. In the course of the second half of the fourteenth century gun-powder came into use and gradually, very gradually, revolutionized the European methods of warfare, since gun-powder led to the invention of artillery and muskets, at first of exceedingly rude construction but destined relentlessly to supplant the earlier weapons. In the wake of these technical improvements, certain social and political changes were not slow to announce themselves. A little reflection will show that the ascendancy of the feudal baron was to a considerable extent dependent on his exclusive possession of an expensive equipment of horse, lance, and armor. Since the new weapons, even though they long remained almost ludicrously clumsy, were far more effective, when it came to the business of killing, than pike and sword, they tipped the balance in favor of the military rivals of the baronage, the low-born mercenaries, who, equipped at the king's expense and employing a tactics appropriate to the new instruments, were able, on the one hand, to break the attack of the noble cavalry and, on the other, to batter a breach into the hitherto impregnable walls of the feudal castle. The strong monarchy, of which we shall presently hear more, made its advent with the fifteenth century; it owed its replacement of the feudal system substantially to the rise of the towns, but there is no room to doubt that the feudal decline was greatly accelerated by the military revolution signified by gun-powder and the new weapons.

Gun-powder destroys the military advantage enjoyed by the nobility

A still more significant invention, doubtless one of the most far-reaching in the annals of the human race, was printing. So long as books were written laboriously by hand, they were necessarily few in number and expensive, a prerogative of kings and princes, lay and ecclesiastical. With the rise of the towns the problem of a simpler and cheaper method of communicating ideas became pressing, and was met, as is usually the case, not with a single invention but with a whole interlocking series of them. The situation becomes reasonably clear if we remember that in the Middle Age the scribes wrote chiefly on parchment, prepared from the skins of animals, preferably of sheep. To supersede the costly handwritten parchment a long succession of steps would be necessary, of which the invention of *paper* and *movable type* were the most important. Toward the middle of the fifteenth century an excellent linen paper, made of the fiber of flax, had come into use as a substitute for parchment; and shortly after, in 1454, the first book printed from movable type dropped from the press. Char-

Printing involves a series of inventions

acteristically for an age still predominantly ecclesiastical the first creation of the new labor-saving device was a version of the Bible. That Bible, one would be inclined to say after weighing all the facts, was more than the work of its immediate printer: it was the composite achievement of a great number of men, each of whom, nameless though he has remained, contributed an invaluable fraction to the final product. However, as they apparently all resided in the flourishing cities dotting the course of the Rhine, printing may not improperly be represented as the collective offering to mankind of the Rhenish towns. The crowning invention, that of the movable type, is usually ascribed to John Gutenberg of the city of Mainz.

Within a few decades printing had spread from the Rhine to all the countries of Europe. Books, once a rarity, were multiplied as though by magic, and, sold for a small price, carried the old and the new knowledge far afield. Not only was learning, the proud and barricaded learning of the schools, henceforth made more generally accessible, but an enormously potent engine for the promotion of his program was put into the hands of every innovator and reformer. Though it would be a mistake to think of the broad masses of men as now taking to reading and lifting themselves without more ado to a new level of understanding, it is certain that the middle classes, the true carriers of the Renaissance, still further clinched the triumph which was already theirs. Printing, even more than gun-powder, heralded their advent to power; and it is clear evidence of their rise that before many decades had passed, the books printed in Latin, the vehicle of a limited group of scholars, were greatly outnumbered by those published in the various European vernaculars. Plainly whoever wished to be widely read had to be content to circulate his ideas in the language of the street and home. But if the new invention helped the common tongues to win their final victory over Latin, it also tended to replace the many dialectic variations in each European country with a fixed language norm accepted as authoritative for literary purposes. In other words, the Italian, French, Spanish, German, and English languages substantially received their modern dress in the sixteenth century through the wide diffusion of printed books.

The immeasurable revolution wrought by printing

E. INDIVIDUALISM

It is difficult for a modern man to realize to what an extent the Middle Age was a period of classes and class discipline. Whether you were a knight, a merchant, a craftsman, or a peasant, you lived out your life in the spirit of class loyalty and in strict submission to the firmly established customs of your group. In case you were injured in your rights you appealed for justice to the court which functioned for your social level. That means that there were baronial, ecclesiastical, town, and peasant (manorial) courts, to which the individual was amenable according to his status. Above the various civil courts, it is true, was the court of the king, but it did not always function because the king was frequently without power. Each class had its own dress, its own art, its own literature, even its own amusements and table manners. In sum, so tyrannical was the class code that the individual was bound and dominated in every concern of life by a vast multitude of meticulous prescriptions. *The rigorous class system of the Middle Age*

In the Renaissance, through the operation of the forces which we have been studying, the stout barriers of custom began to give way and men were prompted to modify their group allegiance in favor of the new and persuasive ideal of individual freedom. The great merchant of Venice or Florence chafed at the numerous restrictions imposed by his fellows of the gild of merchants regarding buying and selling, and nursed the smouldering conviction that if he were given a free hand, he would much more rapidly mount the golden ladder of success. With such ideas simmering in his head *The individualist creed produces a galaxy of brilliant personalities* he favored an economic policy of untrammeled enterprise, just as his contemporary, the humanist, enamoured of classical literature and advocating a new educational program, desired to cut loose from the intellectual and moral restrictions of the Church and university. Whenever you draw close enough to a Renaissance situation to see what is really happening, you discover that the men who figure as leaders in the field under examination are liberating themselves from the fetters of the past and aiming at fuller self-expression. Philosophically stated the Renaissance is therefore an age of emerging individualism, the essence of which is freedom. Freedom — what a seductive battle-cry! It has rung sonorously through all the succeeding centuries and continues in our day to make itself heard with all its old persuasiveness. To the attempt to achieve the greatest possible measure of free self-expression is to be mainly attributed the amazing galaxy of fifteenth and sixteenth century personalities, more brilliant perhaps and more sharply defined than those of any other epoch of history.

If individualism with its demand that every man seek his own fullest development came to the front at this time to remain a characteristic spiritual ingredient of the whole Modern Age, it carried Individual- with it certain ethical consequences which must not be ism with its overlooked. By its policy of minute and vigorous control ideal of the medieval class régime taught men to find their hap- freedom piness in service to the group, in humble self-suppression. fosters an The Renaissance, on the contrary, with its individualist appropriate creed tended to ignore and sacrifice the group in favor of ethics its most energetic and highly endowed members and to set up a criterion by virtue of which the gifted and successful ones, regardless of the methods they employed, were accorded universal honor. Two types of conduct, or, to speak philosophically, two systems of ethics were thus brought into confrontation with each other; and if the pagan-individualist type irresistibly surged to the surface in the Renaissance, the older medieval, or, as we may term it, Christian-socialist type was by no means entirely driven from the scene. In fact it is plain to see that both have existed side by side, often enough in open discord, to the present generation. What further complicates the situation is the circumstance that the modern man, as the historical heir of two ethical codes, most often tries to combine them both in his single person. The result is in most cases like the meeting of fire and water. Certainly it will not do to make out that men and women in our day adopt and tenaciously cling to either one or the other ethical system, seeing that in practice they pay a disconcertingly sincere homage to both.

Making all allowances for a situation varying from place to place and class to class, we are still forced to admit that the Renaissance The main ushered in a new moral code. Its main elements are a elements of powerful individualist assertiveness, the proclamation of individual- freedom from inherited trammels, and an ethical and, by ism implication, an aesthetic practice in harmony with the new libertarian attitude toward the problem of living.

F. THE VOYAGES OF DISCOVERY AND EUROPEAN COLONIZATION

If the constant interaction of the Renaissance forces, here artificially separated for purposes of analysis, has already been emphasized, it is borne in on us with renewed persuasiveness in taking up the voyages of discovery. Can the voyages of discovery be logically separated from the commercial expansion of the towns already treated? Certainly not, since following directly in the wake of that expansion they are preëminently a commercial movement. Are they intimately tied up with the Revival of Learning? Most decidedly, since it was the new scholarship that revived the Ptolemaic geography and popularized the idea that the earth was round. Without doubt too the discoveries owe much to the new passion for self-expression and adventure which during the Renaissance burned like fire in the hearts of men. *The voyages of discovery not an isolated event*

It would be entirely proper to introduce this division of our Renaissance summary with the cautious voyages which, during and after the crusades, first familiarized the Italian merchants with the Mediterranean, since it was these early, modest enterprises which gave birth to the passion for the sea. However, as commonly understood, the voyages of discovery concern themselves with the open ocean and begin very definitely with Portugal. A fundamental feature in this little country's commercial position was that it did not participate in the benefits of the spice trade monopolized by the Italians. Moreover, geographically Portugal lay opposite Africa, to which continent it gave an enforced attention since northwestern Africa was inhabited by hostile Mohammedan Moors, whose favorite out-door amusement was to prey upon Portuguese trade. *The voyages of discovery inaugurated by Portugal*

In the first half of the fifteenth century a prince of the Portuguese royal house, known to fame as Prince Henry the Navigator, championed the idea, more or less in the air by reason of the enlarged geographic vision connected with humanism, of sailing around Africa to the Indies, the fabulous region whence the precious spices came. A deep Christian religious feeling added its peculiar stimulus to his purpose by filling him with the hope of pleasing God by the conversion of the African infidels. Moved to fit out expeditions, he received his reward before long by the discovery of the Azores and Cape Verde Islands. When he died *The Portuguese discoveries* in 1460, his bold mariners in their tiny ships had traced the coast of Africa almost to the equator. However, in spite of anxious prayers the land stubbornly refused to take the desired angle to the northeast which would show that the continent had been rounded. At last, in 1486, Diaz achieved this brilliant success and penetrated a few leagues beyond the Cape of Good Hope; and twelve years later, in 1498, Vasco da Gama crowned a century of heroic effort by sailing across the Indian ocean to Calicut in Hindustan. Since from now on the Portuguese could acquire the spices, silks, and other luxuries of the orient directly in the countries of their origin, the European trade in these commodities was put on a new foundation. The Italian cities, with Venice at their head, unable to compete with Portugal, suffered a mortal blow. Although the Adriatic metropolis might not immediately realize the fact, its heyday was over and its decline had set in.

The startling discoveries inaugurated by Prince Henry aroused the emulation of all the hardy spirits throughout the maritime world. Since the Portuguese had dedicated themselves to the task of reaching the Indies by rounding Africa, why should not the attempt be made to beat them to their goal by sailing west over the Atlantic? If the Ptolemaic theory, which had become the common property of scholars, was correct, it was impossible to miss the Indies by that route. A certain bold skipper, Christopher Columbus (1446–1506), a native of the Italian city of Genoa, pondered the idea until he became firmly convinced of its feasibility. Much derided by cautious stay-at-homes and long unable to find the necessary financial sponsors, he at last secured the support of a woman of vision, Queen Isabella of Castile. Supplied by her with three small caravels, on August 3, 1492, he set out from Palos, a port of western Spain. Over two months later, on October 12, when all his companions had already despaired of success, he touched land in the small island group of the Bahamas; and before turning his prow back to Europe he discovered also the large neighboring islands of Cuba and Haiti.

Christopher Columbus sails west for the Indies

Owing to his undercalculation of the earth's circumference, Columbus believed that he was on the fringe of the desired spice lands, the fabled Indies, and the name Indians, which he gave to the western aborigines, has clung to them to this day. On his return to Spain he was heartily acclaimed by court and people. Queen Isabella raised him to the rank of admiral, conferred a patent of

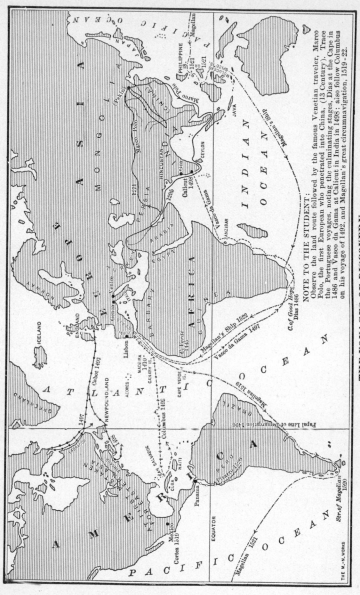

NOTE TO THE STUDENT:
Observe the land route followed by the famous Venetian traveler, Marco Polo, the first European who penetrated into China, (13 Century). Trace the Portuguese voyages, noting the culminating stages, Dias at the Cape in 1486 and Vasco da Gama at Calicut in India in 1498; also follow Columbus on his voyage of 1492, and Magellan's great circumnavigation, 1519–22.

THE VOYAGES OF DISCOVERY

nobility on him, and invested him with the viceroyalty of the new lands. In three subsequent voyages he learned nothing which led him to correct the impression that he had reached the outskirts of Asia and the Indian spice lands. A choleric man by nature with a host of enemies, he experienced many strange vicissitudes, of which perhaps the strangest is that he was, on the occasion of one of his later visits to the lands he had discovered, arrested and sent back to Spain, a prisoner in irons. On his death in 1506, near Valladolid, he was rapidly forgotten, and by a tragic mishap the world, which he had, so to speak, called out of the void,[1] was named, not after him, but after a relatively unimportant traveler and geographer, the Florentine, Amerigo Vespucci.

Columbus's mistake about his discovery

In consequence of these startling successes discovery became a passion, especially among the Portuguese and Spaniards. Though the seas were wide and perilous, every adventurer's soul felt a personal summons to strike out into the unknown regions whence fame and riches beckoned. Voyage soon trod upon the heel of voyage, each new enterprise contributing its mite to the completion of the world's geography. In 1497 John Cabot, a Venetian citizen in the employ of Henry VII of England, reached Cape Breton Island, off the coast of North America; and in 1499 Pinzon, who had accompanied Columbus on his first voyage, skirted the shore of Brazil. Thus the great continental mass behind the curtain of islands discovered by Columbus slowly hove in view and it became clear that this was neither India nor China. A fitting climax of this multiplied endeavor was reached when Magellan, a Portuguese in the Spanish service, attempted in 1519 to reach Asia by a passage to the south of the American continental barrier. Having successfully rounded Cape Horn, he was the first European to furrow the Pacific, and in 1522, after a journey of three years, his ship, fittingly named Victory, reached its European starting-point. Magellan himself did not live to see the end, for he was killed upon the Philippine Islands; but the honor of the first circumnavigation of the globe is undeniably his.

Discovery becomes a passion

As the discoveries had their origin in man's commercial instincts,

---

[1] It may be noticed in passing that the Northmen, proceeding from Iceland, had discovered America in the tenth century and called it Vinland. But as their discovery was not followed up, it had no results for civilization and does not detract in the least from the well-earned fame of Columbus.

they were utilized at once for purposes of trade. But that was not all. Energized by their successful labors, the Portuguese and Spaniards undertook also to Christianize the new regions and to settle them with colonists from the home-lands. In other words they adopted a policy of thorough-going Europeanization. However, it became apparent before long that this ambitious program would be successful only in the savage and sparsely inhabited continents of North and South America. In the thickly settled regions of Asia, especially in India and China, where the natives boasted a civilization, which, if different, was by every objective standard equal to that of Europe, both Christianization and colonization encountered insurmountable obstacles. In consequence we note a difference: Asia remained, as it began, a field purely of commercial exploitation; the Americas, on the other hand, were gradually planted with settlers and Europeanized.

Different treatment of Asia and the Americas

In this work of colonial appropriation Portugal and Spain, as first upon the ground, had an advantage over the other European states. For a moment they even dreamed of excluding all third parties and sharing the immense booty between themselves. Appealing to the pope to serve as arbiter, after much haggling they agreed (1496) on a division of the New World based on the meridian which lay three hundred and seventy leagues west of the Cape Verde Islands. All the new lands to the east of this meridian were to belong to Portugal, all to the west to Spain. But this arrangement, so immensely profitable for the partitioning powers, could not be maintained. In the long run, even as between Portugal and Spain, each power was likely to hold only what it could actually lay its hands on; and both together would find it impossible to shut out determined rivals. Sooner or later England, France, and, very likely, other countries would join in the scramble for the new possessions, and, in view of the resources at their disposal, were almost certain to effect a lodgment.

Attempt of Portugal and Spain to monopolize the new lands

The fierce colonial rivalry among the European powers is one of the most important interests of the Modern Period and will play no small part in this history. For the present, however, we shall merely associate the various European powers with the main regions to which in the first instance they directed their colonial enterprise. The Portuguese planted trading posts along the coast of Africa and the southern shore of Asia, and by means of an unbroken chain of fortified establishments long dominated the trade of the Indian Ocean. They also settled Brazil, which lay to the east of the meridian agreed upon with Spain, with sufficient numbers of their own people to make it gradually Portuguese in speech and manners. The Spaniards located their chief colonial centers at the following points: (1) The West Indies, whither Columbus himself had first directed the stream of immigration; (2) Mexico, which was won for the Spaniards by the intrepid conqueror Cortez; (3) Peru, which was acquired by the equally undaunted Pizarro; (4) the Philippine Islands, secured by Magellan. With the West Indies, Mexico, and Peru as outlying bases of action, Spain surrounded and soon occupied the whole region of Central and South America (except Brazil), while by means of the Philippine Islands she acquired an important foothold in Asiatic waters. *The main colonial objectives of Portugal and Spain*

The northern countries of Europe entered late, and with only gradually increasing vigor, into the struggle for the new continents. The little which Henry VII of England did to secure a share for his nation in the great extension of the world is of importance only by reason of consequences which he did not foresee. In 1497 he fitted out John Cabot, a Venetian, who, as already noted, reached the coast of North America. After Henry's time English enterprise slumbered, to be directed on its revival toward the discovery of still another passage, a passage by the waters of the northwest, to that goal of all desires, the spice lands of Asia. By this route it was hoped to repeat the feat of the Portuguese and Spaniards, who had reached Asia by following respectively a southeasterly and a southwesterly course. Although, owing to the far projection of North America into the Arctic sea, the English plan was doomed to failure, it had the effect of at least keeping alive the English interest in the North American coast. Not till the early seventeenth century, however, did the English fully realize their opportunities and set about the systematic colonization of the Atlantic seaboard. *England slowly turns to the American coast*

The French proved even more lax than the English in colonial enterprise and it was not till the reign of Henry IV (1589–1610) that they seriously undertook to carve out a conquest for themselves. They then hastened to undo, as far as possible, the consequences of their neglect by settlements in Canada, and, later, in Louisiana, that is, in the great basins of the St. Lawrence and Mississippi rivers. *France secures a lodgment in Canada and Louisiana*

Colonial success was in every instance assured by the support of a strong home government. By mastering that fact we have the expla-

Germany and Italy do not participate in the colonial movement nation why Germany, where the feudal lords had reduced the central sovereign to impotence, had no part in the voyages of discovery and in this matter of colonial increase came off with empty hands. In the case of Italy, too, it was its unhappy political atomization which accounts for its failure to share in the Asiatic and American spoils. These vast potential benefits were reserved for the united and the strong.

G. THE RISE OF CAPITALISM

A feature of the Renaissance which we can not afford to overlook is that it matured a new form of economic organization in which we recognize the germ of modern capitalism. In considering the

Medieval economy is town economy and its unit is the gild growth of the town we noted that the expanding economic life centered around the gild. The gild was an admirable institution in its way and for its time. It supplied the town market, of which it was conceded a monopoly, but it also assumed proportionate obligations in that it guaranteed the town residents a sound article at a fair price. Although competition was not entirely eliminated among the members of the same gild, it failed to raise its head effectively against the prevailing equalitarian ideal of a living on a decent burgher level secured to the whole membership. A further purpose of the gild economy was to eliminate the middle man, the mere trader, by requiring whoever produced an article to display and sell it in his shop.

However, fashioned for local ends, the gild became ineffective the moment the question of a lively export trade arose. This called for foresight and initiative, that is, for the promoter and enterpriser

Foreign trade appropriated by the merchant-adventurer who was free to arrive at independent decisions and who was not hampered by the minute regulations concerning buying and selling which governed the gilds. As soon therefore as a foreign trade of considerable dimensions developed such, for instance, as the Italian trade with the Levant during and after the crusades, it eluded the control of the gild and was appropriated as his playground by the merchant endowed with a particular genius for business. Though the risks involved in these distant enterprises were enormous, the profits, correspondingly large, produced riches undreamed of by the stay-at-home craftsman and shopkeeper and presently gave rise, first in the towns of Italy and later, throughout the west, to a relatively small body of merchant princes and capitalists who towered head and shoulders over the rest of the community.

While wealth might be and usually was individually owned, in accordance with the requirements of the age it was amassed by means of the coöperative or company venture. Consider the case of an intelligent Venetian who saw the chance of profit by importing a cargo of spices from Alexandria. He could not from his own resources supply the ships, the wages of a large number of seamen, and the articles of the out-bound voyage which were to be sold on the Egyptian market. He would have to find partners who would share in the prospective profits in proportion to their contribution to the enterprise. Formed in the first instance for a single voyage, the association, if successful, might take on a permanent form. Because of the greater trust existing among blood relations it is noticeable that most early partnerships possessed a family character. Moreover, as the merchant companies were alert to utilize every opportunity, they engaged not only in trade but also in financial operations, without which, owing to the bewildering coinage situation, no trade in goods was possible. All early trading companies without exception did also the business of banks; and those of Florence, which with creditable intelligence developed to the highest degree the possibilities of the banking field, acquired for their city a financial preponderance like that of London or New York in our day. That already by the fifteenth century money had become king, more particularly of course in Italy, is illustrated by the company of the Medici. Substantially a family bank, which had accumulated its huge capital under the leadership of several generations of eminent merchants, it engaged in the manner typical of early capitalism in trading and exchange operations in every part of the known world. By the second half of the fifteenth century the Medici operated a subsidiary bank in every important center of Europe. At the same time the family insinuated itself into the government of Florence with the result that the head of the institution gradually emerged as the ruler of the city.

A similar, if more tardy, development in the regions north of the Alps, particularly in Flanders, prepared the way for the subjection of the whole economic life of Europe to the power of money; for, while capitalism originated with the export trade, it was not long before it influenced the whole medieval gild economy. The ex-porter with connections in all markets and commanding ample resources could buy the raw products, such as wool or leather, much more cheaply than the local gild, and by giving out limited quantities from his store and further, by contracting for the total annual output of the individual master, could bring the gilds more or less under his control. As early as the fourteenth century the flourishing cloth manufacture of Florence was already so completely in the power of a handful of great pro-moters who merely bought up the cloth for export without them-selves producing a single yard that the gild system no longer squared with its original principle. In the altered circumstances the masters of the wool gild leave the impression of having been reduced to a body of small shop-foremen while the journeymen and apprentices look for all the world like a proletariat of modern wage-earners.

Capitalism undermines the gild economy

The same movement may be noted somewhat later in Flanders and, somewhat later still, in England. It indicates an economic evolution which would end by crowding the socialistic gilds entirely from the scene and by establishing a competitive, capitalist order of society. Nor does it admit the least doubt that this was a fated development since it falls in perfectly with all the forces abroad in the Renaissance, with the enlargement of the world and of its opportunities, with the individualist philosophy inviting every man to make the most of his powers, and with the replacement of the town as the economico-political unit of society with the nation ruled by the "strong," the modern king. Monarchs like Louis XI of France and Henry VII of England or, in the following century, like King Francis I and Emperor Charles V, leaned heavily on the monied men, the bankers and capitalists, and never ceased to favor them as against the little men, the shopkeepers, who fought desperately to maintain the familiar but steadily slipping system of the gilds.

The rise of a capitalist society

H. THE STRONG MONARCHY

It remains to discuss the characteristic political movement belong-ing to the Renaissance. That already in the Middle Age the town had flung a challenge to the feudal baron we are aware; also that the town had become steadily more powerful, even though the feudal class had remained a factor, and a powerful factor, in the situation. Under the constitutional conceptions which ruled the Middle Age the monarch was himself a baron, though a baron-in-chief, to whom was conceded an honorary and strictly limited headship over his fellow-barons. He was *primus inter pares* (first among equals). On account of his feudal origin and prejudices he frequently failed to understand that the town movement offered itself as a convenient means for strengthening his position as against the nobility. In the long run the fact could hardly escape him, while, regardless of his far or shortsightedness, the cities would be only too eager to give him their support against an overweening baronage whose lawless control of the countryside interfered with their freedom of trade. Throughout Europe it comes to this: the towns and the monarch were natural political allies.

The political alliance between towns and monarch

Owing to special circumstances belonging to medieval history, Germany and Italy constituted the Holy Roman Empire and had the same monarch, the Holy Roman emperor. Confronted in Germany with the great landed nobility and in Italy with the pope supported by the towns, the emperor was in the course of the twelfth and thirteenth centuries so completely worsted that in both countries, but more particularly in Italy, he was reduced to impotence. In Italy the towns and other local agencies became substantially independent, while in Germany the largest of the barons acquired a power tantamount to sovereignty. In the period of the Renaissance this medieval decision against the emperor became irrevocable. In Italy he practically disappeared from the scene; in Germany, though he made a belated effort to strengthen his hand by favoring the towns, he remained so feeble that he conveys the impression of being hardly more than tolerated by the great dukes and archbishops, the real masters of the land.

Decline of the monarch's power in Italy and Germany

In Spain, France, and England, on the other hand, the feudal monarchy in this same Renaissance period traveled the opposite road and steadily waxed in strength. In these countries for reasons that belong to medieval history the king was not exposed to the combination of circumstances which sapped the vigor of the Holy Roman emperor. Owing to this immunity he was enabled to profit to the full from the rise of that strong urban element which was opposed to the barons and actively engaged in multiplying the wealth of the

country. When the king needed money, as he constantly did since
the jealous nobles systematically kept him poor, he found that the
easiest way to get it was to apply to the men with the moneybags,
The   his doughty burghers. But as these naturally asked for
monarchs   a return favor, they received it, on the one hand, by
of Spain,   enlarged municipal charters and, on the other, in the form
France, and
England   of a constitutional concession: they were admitted to the
lean on the feudal assembly of the realm. The feudal assembly or
towns   parliament was originally composed of clergy and nobles
and constituted the national council of the king. When to clergy and
nobles, who in feudal law were regarded respectively as the first and
second estates, the representatives of the towns were added, these,
having gained a foothold within the feudal frame, acquired the character and designation of a third estate. It was essentially in the
Renaissance period that this advance in political status was secured
by the towns of all three feudal states under discussion.

To the bonds of a financial and constitutional order created
between the townsmen and their king a powerful emotional element
was presently added in the rise of nationalism. As one of the decisive
Nationalist influences in the history of modern Europe nationalism
sentiment   can not be too closely scanned by the student. Although
comes to   not entirely lacking in the medieval period, it became
the aid of   clearly manifest as a political factor only in the Renais-
the king   sance, from which time it has grown steadily until, like
a slowly developing motif in an orchestral piece, it mounted to a
thundering climax in the nineteenth century. Nationalism is a
sentiment based on community of language and customs and is
historically associated with the new social order inaugurated by the
towns. Latent and unimportant in the period of unchallenged feudalism, it made its appearance in the Renaissance, most often under
circumstances involving an attack by a foreign foe on the collective
interests and ideas of the urban class. Thus Spanish nationalism
developed as a reaction against the Mohammedan Moors, who had
taken possession of the land in the eighth century; and it strengthened and consolidated itself in the long struggle with the alien
invader. Similarly French nationalism, as the name of Joan of Arc
eloquently attests, was the child of the English invasion and the
Hundred Years' War. Again, the English largely achieved their
own powerful group consciousness in the same struggle. We must
guard against exaggerating the new national fervor of the western

peoples, since so long as the baronial class held aloof from the common people, considering itself a special breed infinitely superior to the vulgar herd, a harmonious sentiment, binding all classes, was out of the question. However, it can not be denied that the towns, which in the first phase of their existence had been animated by nothing more than a very local type of patriotism, became the champions of the more inclusive sentiment and, in measure as they prospered, spread among the people of the same speech a more generous love of country. But as the head of the country was the king, as, in fact, he was the visible embodiment of the nation, it followed that every increase of patriotic sentiment redounded to his benefit.

Thus a powerful combination of circumstances connected with the towns and their new civilization came to the aid of the king in his struggle with the nobles. But to the nobles, as outstanding rivals of the royal power, must be added the clergy, who in the *Growth of* medieval period had acquired a body of rights and im- *the royal* munities amounting in their sum to substantial independ- *power* ence of the state. When we further recall that at the *implied also a struggle* height of the Middle Age the pope, as chief representative *with the* of the clergy throughout Europe, had gone the length of *Church* declaring that kings held their states by his grace as papal benefices, we shall have to admit that the medieval monarch faced a difficult situation. It was indisputable that if ever he was to become the effective head of a united people, the vast clerical pretensions and privileges would as imperatively have to be reduced as those of the nobility. In fact the only conceivable way by which a united nation could be created was by the subjection by all classes alike to a common law embodied in the king. Wherever therefore the national unification movement was inaugurated, a struggle with the Church followed as logically and inexorably as with the nobles.

It must now be clear that the cue for an active sovereign of the age of the Renaissance was to enlarge in every way the monarchy centered about his person. This states substantially the royal program pursued alike in Spain, France, and England; and though *Measures* its execution exhibits considerable variation in each coun- *by which* try, there is noticeable a broad identity of result. With- *the king* out necessarily disturbing the numerous judicial tribunals *increased* inherited from the feudal régime, the king confirmed his *his power* position as court of final appeal and head of the national system of justice; he multiplied the officials who looked after the royal interests in the provinces, thereby building up a royal administration; he increased his income by subsidies from the towns, which he was concerned to render fixed and regular; and with his enlarged means he laid the foundation of a permanent armed force dependent on no one but himself. All these measures partook in reality of a more tentative character than is indicated by the above over-definite statements. Often enough, as, for instance, in England during the War of the Roses, it seemed as if the monarchy, instead of winning its cause, was on the point of being engulfed in disaster; but, beneath the surface, the tendencies here sketched continued to operate and ended by producing that novel political phenomenon, the strong monarchy.

As a result of this political evolution Spain, France, and England, on the eve of the Reformation, present themselves to view with a new unity and vigor; and though they will long continue to be engaged in the process of extricating themselves from feudal bonds, it may be said of them around 1500 that they have become fairly provided with a modern centralized organization, enabling them to exercise a power undreamed of in their earlier history.

Spain, France, and England become strong monarchies

The eight heads under which we have attempted to familiarize ourselves with the Renaissance are so many paths by which the European man ventured into new fields. If we hold fast to the idea that he was carrying forward a movement of civilization the foundations of which had been laid in the Middle Age, his many activities during the new period become amazingly unified. For, viewed in this organic manner, the Renaissance signified in substance a breaking away from childhood with its innumerable bondages. Surely it is not merely fanciful to see in the man of the Middle Age essentially a child, a timid stay-at-home clinging to his familiar hearth and disinclined to look beyond the narrow limits of his home and parish. Besides, the Church, which led him like a mother by the hand, bade him not to make too much of this life of troubles but to feast his eyes on the vision of the life to come. There was in consequence something repressed and passive about the Middle Age. By the hundreds and the thousands men sought the seclusion of a monastic cell, voluntarily renouncing life before its natural close. Yet within other thousands and tens of thousands a spark gleamed and a sap stirred which would not be extinguished or denied. And when in due time the child became a youth, west-

Summary

ITALY
IN THE
RENAISSANCE

SCALE OF MILES

0   50   100   150   200

THE MATTHEWS-NORTHRUP WORKS, BUFFALO, N.Y.

European civilization entered upon a new and higher stage. Here lies the significance of the Renaissance, here is the reason why the eight aspects under which we have examined the movement exhibit with the often wanton breaking of bonds the courageous testing of new opportunities. The Renaissance triumphantly affirmed that the special characteristic of European civilization was to be experimentation and love of danger in a degree beyond that of any other civilization of which there is record; it declared that for better or worse European civilization was not to be held under the authoritative direction of the Church in a fixed and predetermined mold, but that by combining curiosity with enterprise it was to impose on the European man the obligation of an unceasing self-renewal.

REFERENCES

E. EMERTON, *Beginnings of Modern Europe*, chs. 5, 8–10
E. M. HULME, *Renaissance and Reformation*, chs. 3–9
E. SICHEL, *Renaissance*
Cambridge Modern History, vol. I, chs. 1, 2, 5, 6, 8, 15, 16
J. BURCKHARDT, *Renaissance in Italy*, pp. 129–53, 203–29, 309–27
J. H. ROBINSON AND H. W. ROLFE, *Petrarch The First Modern Scholar and Man of Letters*
J. A. SYMONDS, *Short History of the Renaissance*, chs. 1, 7–11
C. R. BEAZLEY, *Prince Henry the Navigator*, Introduction
M. I. NEWBIGIN, *The Mediterranean Lands, a Study in Human Geography*
C. L. BECKER, *Beginnings of the American People*, ch. 1
J. E. SANDYS, *History of Classical Scholarship*, II, pp. 1–123
J. N. FIGGIS, *From Gerson to Grotius*, ch. 3
R. L. POOLE, *Illustrations of the History of Medieval Thought*
C. DAY, *History of Commerce*, pp. 70–139
E. CHEYNEY, *Industrial and Social History of England*
S. REINACH, *Apollo*, chs. 15–18
R. MUTHER, *History of Painting*
E. FAURE, *History of Renaissance Art*
B. BERENSON, *The Florentine Painters of the Renaissance; The Venetian Painters of the Renaissance, The Central Italian Painters of the Renaissance*
R. STEINER, *Mystics of the Renaissance*, pp. 52–182, 246–68
W. C. ABBOTT, *Expansion of Europe*, I, chs. 3, 6, 9, 10
E. CHAPMAN, *History of Spain*, chs. 22–26
R. B. MERRIMAN, *Rise of the Spanish Empire*, II, chs. 16–18

THE REFORMATION AND THE RELIGIOUS WARS FROM 1500 TO 1648

CHAPTER IV

THE EUROPEAN STATES ON THE EVE OF THE REFORMATION

The emergence among the peoples of western Europe of the strong monarchy, of which we have just heard, is in striking contrast with the increased disintegration among the peoples of central Europe. **Desirability** This contradictory phenomenon suggests the necessity of **of a detailed** a detailed survey of the whole European political situa- **survey of** tion at the beginning of the sixteenth century. And as **Europe** at that time Italy was in most essential respects the center of the western world it is proper to begin our survey with the Mediterranean peninsula.

ITALY

The central fact of Italian political history during the Middle Age is that the Holy Roman emperor lost his hold on the peninsula. He suffered defeat, in part because he represented feudalism and **Italy breaks** thwarted the growth of city life, but in still larger part **away from** because, as a German, he represented the idea of foreign **the Empire** domination. In consequence the towns, representative of a young and sturdy nationalism, joined forces with the pope, violently opposed to the emperor as the leading check on his political ambitions, and the combination proved too much for the imperial strength. With the death in 1250 of Frederick II of the house of Hohenstaufen the sun of the Empire may be said to have set in Italy. Nor did the occasional reappearance of an emperor in the fourteenth and even in the fifteenth century alter the situation: Italy had thrown off the imperial yoke.

The casting off of the imperial yoke is part of the great outburst of energy which led to the Renaissance. Scores of towns of northern and north-central Italy, chiefly in Lombardy and Tuscany, became free republics, and having no more to fear from the emperor, engaged in violent conflict with one another; in the mountain areas of the Alps and Apennines occasional feudal lords, more *The Italian* or less formidable, continued to maintain themselves; the *chaos and* central area, with Rome as capital, was claimed by the *the* pope as his temporal dominion; and finally, the spacious *emergence of five* south, including the island of Sicily, constituted the king- *dominant* dom of Naples (officially called the kingdom of Sicily). *states* The most novel and promising features in the complicated situation were the northern and north-central towns, which had gained political liberty and overflowed with bubbling vigor; but unfortunately, like the Greek cities of antiquity, neither could they keep the peace with one another nor preserve the necessary inner harmony among the citizens. As a result a double movement was soon manifest among them: the large towns swallowed up their small neighbors, and all towns, large and small, becoming a prey to domestic faction, tended to fall under the rule of some bold adventurer eager to assume despotic control. Before many decades had passed the city of Milan embraced all Lombardy, while Venice and Florence, equally aspiring and ambitious, achieved a position of corresponding eminence in the provinces respectively of Venetia and Tuscany. Around 1450 therefore the towns of Milan, Venice, and Florence exercised such power that only the state of the Church, dominated by the pope, and the kingdom of Naples could be compared with them. These five outstanding states ruled the politics of Italy and while there were still some feudal lords, such as the dukes of Savoy and Ferrara, who represented survivals of an older order, they brought little effective power to bear on the situation. Let us take a closer view of the five leading states.

Milan. Even before Milan acquired the control of Lombardy by subjecting the neighbor-cities to her rule, her local government had suffered the typical transformation from free republic to despotism. It was the penalty the citizens paid for being *The ruling* unable to bring their local feuds to an amicable settlement. *houses of* The first tyrant was of the native house of Visconti, which *Visconti* by its bold and unscrupulous conduct succeeded in making *and Sforza* its power permanent. In sign thereof the Visconti despot presently took the title duke and converted the Milanese republic into a duchy. In 1447 the last Visconti died without male heirs. Thereupon the city reasserted its freedom, but lacking the energy to carry out its purpose, it was in 1450 obliged to accept a new despot, a military adventurer by the name of Francesco Sforza. Like the Visconti before him Sforza fastened his power on the state. The second ducal line set up a brilliant court at Milan and with the Milanese revenues at its disposal entered with zest into the political rivalries of the peninsula.

Venice. From early medieval times it was clear that the city of Venice was destined to play a large role not only in Italy but also in Europe. A sea-city, planted among the islands of the Adriatic

Venice founds a maritime empire
lagoons, she was secure from attack by land, while her position at the very center of the contemporary world imposed upon her, as it were by decree of nature, the part of intermediary in the commerce between east and west. Alert to the opportunity, not only did her merchants succeed in gradually monopolizing the trade of the Levant, but in order to make their position impregnable they built up a colonial empire, which at its height included the Dalmatian coast as well as the islands of Corfu, Crete, and Cyprus together with a large number of smaller islands constituting an unbroken chain of posts stretching all the way across the waters of the eastern Mediterranean. When the poet Wordsworth, reviewing her medieval greatness, began an apostrophe to her with the words: "Once did she hold the gorgeous east in fee," he uttered no more than the bare truth.

But their colonial empire did not suffice the ambitious traders of the Queen of the Adriatic. Desiring to secure the passes of the Alps, necessary for their trade with Germany, they began an expansion

Venice becomes an Italian land power
movement on the continent; and at the very time when neighboring Milan was consolidating her rule in Lombardy the Venetians set up the banner of their patron saint, St. Mark, throughout the northeastern province of the peninsula, the province of Venetia. Already deeply involved in the engrossing politics of the eastern Mediterranean, the city of the lagoons was by this acquisition plunged also into the territorial problems of Italy.

Venetian domestic government presents a very different face from that exhibited by the average Italian town. The main reason is that the enterprising merchants who had been particularly instrumental in building up the wealth and the greatness of the city were firmly resolved that the political control should never pass from their hands. In this purpose they were aided by the circumstance that, preëminently commercial, Venice never developed a powerful industrial proletariat. In consequence of the weakness of the common people the merchants succeeded not only in gradually eliminating the democratic features originally embodied in the Venetian constitution, but also in establishing themselves as a full-fledged hereditary oligarchy. It was in 1297 that they carried the decisive measure which declared *The Venetian government a merchant oligarchy* that the government inhered in perpetuity in the citizens who at that date were members of the Grand Council and in their descendants. Naturally the limited number of families thus exalted above their fellow-citizens thenceforth designated themselves as noble and, in proof of their unusual intelligence and moderation, maintained themselves in unchallenged control for many centuries. Although an hereditary Grand Council thus became the sovereign body over Venice, the actual administration was placed in the hands of various commissions elected by the Grand Council. The system culminated in the duke or doge, who was chosen for the term of his life but bound to a strictly constitutional and severely limited exercise of power. In view of her prosperity, political stability, and, last but not least, her brilliant contribution to the culture of the Renaissance, Venice may be regarded as probably the most successful merchant oligarchy in European annals.

Florence. The only Italian city which matched and possibly exceeded Venice in wealth and culture was Florence. In political stability, on the other hand, the Tuscan town was decidedly inferior. The explanation lies in the circumstance that Florence, though by no means eschewing over-sea trade, developed primarily as an industrial and banking center and became densely populated with workingmen engaged, above all, in the manufacture of woolen cloth. At a relatively *The republic supplanted by the house of Medici* early time the gilds, twenty-one in number, around which the economic life of the town revolved, took over the government of the city. However, in point of fact the few large and powerful merchant gilds of bankers and wholesalers successfully kept the lesser or craft gilds in the background, while the common workers, forbidden to organize gilds of their own, brooded over their wrongs in sullen discontent. In spite of these inner rifts and because of a really genuine passion for political liberty, Florence retained a republican form of government longer than any city of Italy. In the long run, however, the class divisions, fanned by ambitious individuals for their own ends, proved disastrous to her. Early in the fifteenth century a local family of merchants and bankers of the name of Medici succeeded in organizing a political machine, which, while preserving the established forms, took over the government by underground manipulations. The Medici system was much like that of the average American city "boss," except that the Medici succeeded in making their control hereditary. As a result a Medici of the third generation, Lorenzo by name, ventured to set up his power in the open and both at home and abroad was honored as the head of the government. This Lorenzo (d. 1492), called the Magnificent, was an intelligent and gifted statesman, besides being a poet and a liberal patron of poets, philosophers, and artists; but even he so far continued to respect the republican tradition as to refrain from taking a title such as prince or duke.

The State of the Church. How the pope, spiritual head of western or Latin Christendom, slowly built up a temporal dominion around the city of Rome is an impressive chapter of medieval Uncertain history. For us it will suffice to note that the gradual control by failure of the imperial power in Italy clinched the papal the popes of claim to a territory, which extended from the mouth of their the Tiber in a northeasterly direction all the way across temporal the peninsula to the Adriatic sea. Considerable in extent, dominion the papal lands were for the most part a difficult mountain area of small hill-towns bent on independence, and of feudal lords securely ensconced in inaccessible castles. Even when, at the height of his power, the pope issued commands to all the monarchs of Europe, his control of his immediate dominion was very precarious; and when, at the beginning of the fourteenth century, he abandoned Rome for Avignon, entering on what is known as the Babylonian Captivity (1305–1377), his rule over the State of the Church broke down completely. On its return to Rome, in the last quarter of the fourteenth century, the papacy resolutely took up the plan of at last reducing its territory to submission but met with such resistance on the part of the hill-towns and the castle-lords that more than a hundred years passed before the battle was won.

The long drawn out political struggle between the popes and their recalcitrant lieges so fully occupied the papal strength that this purely local conflict constitutes perhaps the main element in the fifteenth century story of the papacy. Nor need the frank papal bid for temporal and worldly power surprise us. The Renaissance had dawned over Italy and the Renaissance signified in essence a brisk turning toward earth and earthly things. On the side of politics it prompted state-building, that is, a more effective organization of government; and with all the world intent upon this matter, how could the popes, themselves temporal sovereigns since the early Middle Age, remain untouched by so universal a development? In sum, the Renaissance *Policy and character of the Renaissance popes* made the popes political-minded in the specifically Italian sense indicated by the movement toward despotism. But the Renaissance influence did not stop there. Steeped in the atmosphere of their time and country, the pontiffs took up humanism, became admirers of pagan philosophy, and gloried in the patronage of literature and the arts. Certainly from Nicholas V (d. 1455) to Leo X (d. 1521) we encounter a succession of popes who reflect so much of the color of their time that we may think of them as constituting a distinct Renaissance group. Considered as a body they are decidedly worldly individuals, enjoying life on the same terms as any Renaissance despot; their chief political concern is to consolidate their Italian state; and liberating themselves from medieval austerity to the point of losing all sense of the spiritual obligations of their office, they multiply the financial burdens of Christendom in order to acquire abundant means wherewith to maintain a splendid court, to build palaces and churches, and to exercise a munificent patronage of scholars and artists.

Although, owing to their close intimacy with humanists and painters, the Renaissance popes often appear in an agreeable personal light, it is also true that some of them, mastered by their passion for fame and their dream of power, fell into extraordinary excesses. In fact, morally, some popes are indistinguishable from the worst tyrants that forced their way to the front in the city republics. Take, for example, *Alexander VI and Caesar Borgia* Alexander VI (1492–1503) of the house of Borgia. Without crediting all the monstrous scandal which circulated concerning him in his own time, it is yet undeniable that he indulged himself in every sensual pleasure forbidden to his sacred office and that at the same time he abused his ecclesiastical power by employing it to advance the fortunes of his many illegitimate children. The most famous of these was his son, Caesar Borgia, who, uniquely vicious and unscrupulous, was nevertheless a man of remarkable courage and attainments. Caesar entertained the astounding dream of acquiring the State of the Church as his personal possession. Supported by the criminal connivance of his father, he might have succeeded but for Alexander's premature death, caused in all probability by his mistakenly swallowing the poison which he had planned to administer to one of his guests.

Like and yet very unlike Alexander were his successors, Julius II (1503–1513) and Leo X (1513–1521), the latter a son of the Florentine usurper, Lorenzo the Magnificent (Medici). Of Julius it may be said Julius II that he holds the honor of having at last completed the and Leo X reduction of the State of the Church to papal obedience, while both he and Leo are memorable as lavish builders and patrons. Julius II, a dynamic character who brooked no opposition, laid the foundations of the famous church of St. Peter at Rome and, attaching Michael Angelo and Raphael to his person, assigned them the respective commissions of the Sistine chapel and the Vatican frescos in which they attained their greatest heights. Leo X, who lacks the large proportions of the forceful Julius, presents himself to view as a cultured, easy-going sybarite. He is sufficiently characterized by his cheery invitation to his intimates, on the occasion of his election, to join him in "enjoying the papacy." Such an attitude and the worldly spirit it implies, acceptable though it may have proved in an ordinary secular ruler, ran violently counter to the ancient traditions of the Christian Church. Besides — a by no means unimportant prudential consideration — it necessitated a huge outlay of money. No wonder that in certain countries of Europe a protest began to make itself heard inspired, on the one hand, by an immediate moral revulsion against the pagan splendors of Rome and, on the other, by indignation against the increasing taxes of all kinds laid upon the faithful in order to defray the papal program. Here is the seed of what in the very reign of the spendthrift Leo became a religious rebellion of world import.

The Kingdom of Naples. The southernmost of the Italian states was structurally so different from the others that, except geographically, it hardly seemed to belong to the peninsula. It was a A feudal feudal state governed by a king set over a body of unsurvival ruly barons and, besides Naples, the capital, hardly developed any city of note. In consequence the town movement, which inwardly and outwardly transformed the Italian north, left the southern kingdom essentially unaffected, permitting it to retain its medieval social and political organization right through the Renaissance. In fact the Renaissance hardly made itself felt even in the field of art and letters.

But if the kingdom constituted a conservative, relatively unchanging society, its size gave it such power that it counted heavily in the world of Italian politics. On the failure, in the twelfth century, of its original Norman dynasty the crown had passed to the German house of Hohenstaufen, which, because of its overshadowing power in Italy, the popes pursued with a deadly hatred. As the Norman kings had acknowledged the pope as their suzerain, the Holy Father always had a convenient pretext at hand for interfering in the affairs of Naples. Finally, to rid himself once and for all of the *The succession of foreign dynasties: Norman, German, French, and Spanish* Hohenstaufen incubus, he offered the crown to the duke of Anjou, brother of the French king. The ensuing struggle, one of the most tragic in the history of the thirteenth century, ended (1268) with the victory of the duke of Anjou, who took the title Charles I. But the new Angevin dynasty encountered grave difficulties in its turn. Before long (1282) Sicily revolted and, appealing for help to the king of Aragon, committed itself to his hands; and when, in 1435, the last direct descendant of Charles I died, the Aragonese ruler of Sicily crossed the straits of Messina and took possession of Naples too. However, as certain French relatives of the last Angevin sovereign did not fail to put forth a claim to Naples based on ties of blood, there followed a tedious conflict between the houses of Anjou and Aragon which did not however alter the fact of Aragonese possession. In 1481 the last Anjou pretender died, leaving all his claims to the crown of France. For over a decade the claim was permitted to slumber, but in 1494 the youthful French king, Charles VIII, bethought himself of his shadowy Neapolitan rights and made them the basis of an invasion of Italy. That invasion, as we shall see later on, changed the face of the peninsula and, to a not inconsiderable measure, of Europe.

GERMANY OR THE HOLY ROMAN EMPIRE

What determined the history of Germany in the Middle Age more than any other one thing was that through the coronation of the Frank king, Charles the Great, as emperor on Christmas day, 800 A.D., it became involved in the attempt to unite Europe by reviving the Roman Empire. The restored Empire, because of its close association with the Christian Church, became known as the Holy Roman Empire; and without doubt the Holy Roman Empire did for some centuries occupy a preëminent position, although it never effected the union of all Europe but only of its middle area comprising chiefly Germany and Italy. When, in the thirteenth century, in the days following the defeat of the house of Hohenstaufen, Italy repudiated the imperial connection, the Holy Roman Empire became substantially restricted to Germany. Thenceforth the Holy Roman Empire and Germany became interchangeable terms.

The Holy Roman Empire reduced to Germany

The emperor had originally been a powerful sovereign of the feudal type. But his defeat in Italy reacted disastrously on his position in Germany. On finding him engaged to his full strength in Italy his leading German vassals, the great dukes, counts, and bishops, had raised their head against him, had forced him to make heavy political concessions whenever he asked for military help, and by slow degrees had reduced him to a puppet. By the middle of the fourteenth century the triumph of the great feudataries was so complete that they resolved to incorporate it in a constitutional enactment which from its official seal (*bulla*) has received the name of the Golden Bull (1356). The situation created by the Golden Bull is illuminating, especially in the matter of the emperor's dependence on the great lords. Elected in the past by the whole baronage, he was now made the nominee of a select body of the seven greatest princes of the realm. Of this number three, the archbishops of Mainz, Trier (Treves), and Cologne, were ecclesiastical princes, while four, the king of Bohemia, the duke of Saxony, the margrave of Brandenburg, and the count palatine of the Rhine, were lay lords. On the demise of an emperor these seven, who assumed the title electors (*Kurfuersten*), met and elected a new emperor. Thereupon the successful candidate was qualified to take the title German king and to exercise the authority still inhering in the Roman emperor, though, in theory at least, he was not supposed to be clothed with the full Roman rights until he had completed the process of his elevation to the purple by crossing the Alps to Italy to be crowned in Rome at the hands of the pope.

Decline of the emperor's power

Another feature connected with the Golden Bull was that the traditional legislative and administrative dependence of the emperor on the feudal assembly, called the *Reichstag* or diet, was confirmed and strengthened. The diet was composed of two houses, the upper of the seven electors and the lower of the lesser barons, lay and ecclesiastical; but as, in the period after the Golden Bull, those cities, which, having won self-government, were known as the free imperial cities (*Freie Reichsstaedte*), were con- stituted as an additional house, the German diet in its final form was composed of three houses. Under German constitutional practice the emperor was incapable of taking any action without the consent of all three houses; and as two of the houses were made up of feudal magnates ⸢bent on playing the master in their respective territories, it was clear that the emperor was likely to be kept in close bondage. He was in point of fact left without army, navy, administration, or taxes and became no better than a graven image draped for merely decorative purposes in the mantle of royalty. While the form of a united Germany was maintained, to all practical intents the rights of sovereignty had been taken over by the members of the three houses called the estates of the realm. Thus Germany was broken up, or at least entered on a phase preliminary to being broken up, into several hundred little sovereignties.

The German diet

Toward the end of the fifteenth century, as a result of the breath of nationalism which stirred every country of Europe in connection with the Renaissance, an attempt was made to revive the central power of the emperor. The nationalist sentiment was strong enough to create a party of constitutional reform within the diet. Putting itself behind the young and attractive Emperor Maximilian, who had mounted the throne in 1493, it excited high hopes, which, owing to the persistent separatist tendencies, came in the long run to nothing. True, a few measures were adopted somewhat strengthening the decrepit German organization. The old feudal right of private warfare was abolished by the proclamation of internal peace (*ewiger Landfrieden*); a national tribunal (*Reichskammergericht*) was established as a court of last resort; and a first move was made toward a national administration by dividing the country into ten districts to serve as a skeleton for military and financial action. But as the emperor was endowed neither with an army nor taxes nor officials of any kind, Germany remained, as before, impotent, unrespected, and disorganized to the point of chaos.

The German nationalist movement fails to unify the German government

The Emperor Maximilian (1493–1519) belonged to the house of Hapsburg established in the old east mark of Germany, called

Austria. Possessing a mobile mind and hospitably disposed to the new influences of the Renaissance, he was none the less so greatly under the sway of the colorful medieval dreams of chivalry that his contemporaries were well inspired to hail him as "the last knight." Driven by contradictory emotions, he steered an uncertain and quixotic course and by a long string of failures proved himself one of the poorest politicians that ever lived. However, his father, the Emperor Frederick, had evolved a matrimonial program which, extended by the son, succeeded in the course of two generations in raising the house of Hapsburg to a leading position in Europe. In 1477 Maximilian himself was joined in wedlock to Mary of Burgundy, heiress of the Netherlands, one of the busiest and wealthiest city areas of Europe. Then, in 1496, the son of this union, Philip, married another and even greater heiress, Joan, daughter of Ferdinand and Isabella of Spain. The oldest-born of this match, Charles by name, represented the junction of three great reigning houses and in due course entered upon possession of Austria, the Netherlands, and Spain. In the eyes of the aging Maximilian his grandson Charles must have been more than a compensation for his many political disappointments, since the young man was the visible proof and symbol of the greatness of the house of Hapsburg, for which Maximilian and his father before him had labored and intrigued during a long life.

Emperor Maximilian prepares the greatness of the house of Hapsburg by his marriage alliances

In 1519 "the last knight" ended an inglorious career. When thereupon the electors raised Charles, who took the title Charles V, to the imperial dignity, it may have seemed to superficial observers as if the dimmed glories of the Holy Roman Empire had been brilliantly renewed. But if Charles's reign, which was destined to be filled with the uproar of the Reformation, amply proved that he was a powerful monarch, it also proved that he was strong not by reason of any power conferred on him by Germany and the imperial office, but solely because he commanded the immense resources represented by the lands of which he was master by right of inheritance. Preëminent among these was Spain.

Emperor Charles V

SPAIN

While the Spanish people were still in an early formative stage, they suffered a crushing experience by being conquered by the Mohammedan Moors from across the straits in Africa. The event occurred in the eighth century and the victory of the followers of Allah and his Prophet was so complete that only in the shelter of the northern mountains did scattered Christian groups manage to maintain themselves in freedom. Before long, however, they took courage, advanced against the enemies of both their country and their faith, and slowly pushed them southward toward the sea. On the liberated territory a number of Christian states were formed which, though hampered by jealousy, usually tended to act together against the hated infidel. In the course of time, either through matrimonial alliances or by conquest, the Christian states, possessing alike a feudal and military character, amalgamated with the result that by the second half of the fifteenth century two of them, Castile and Aragon, dominated the situation. It was now only necessary for Isabella, heiress of Castile, to marry Ferdinand, heir of Aragon, for the country's lost unity to be in the main restored. Complete peninsular unity, however, had been made very difficult and perhaps unattainable by the emergence along the western coast of the state of Portugal, whose people gradually developed a national consciousness of their own. As Portugal comprised less than one fifth of the trans-Pyrenean area, the peninsula was not hindered from becoming preponderantly Spanish.

Christian versus Mohammedan Spain

The states of Castile and Aragon owed their greatness to the fact that by accepting as their mission the expulsion of the Moors from the peninsula they served as rallying points of the national and religious sentiment of the Spaniards. Therefore no sooner had Ferdinand and Isabella become a royal pair than they turned their combined arms against Granada, the last foothold maintained in the peninsula by the Moors. In the year 1492 they completed the difficult work of conquest. It was a triumph such as only a few sovereigns have ever tasted, for it meant the final disappearance of a power which had exercised a hateful, alien rule for almost eight centuries.

The conquest of Granada

But if the state of the Moors had vanished, the Moors themselves had not. In certain sections, chiefly along the southern coast, they constituted a leading urban element, while agriculture too, in which they had distinguished themselves by the introduction of an efficient system of irrigation, gave a livelihood to many thousands of their faith and blood. In religious and racial respects the Spanish situation was still further complicated by the presence in most towns of flourishing communities of Jews. In an effort to propitiate these two alien groups they had originally been treated with liberality.

The rising tide of Christian intolerance They had even been endowed with charters guaranteeing their rights. But when the last Moorish fortress was about to fall, a wild Christian and national fanaticism flared up which demanded nothing less than the forcible conversion of both Jews and Moors to the ruling faith or, in lieu thereof, their death or expulsion. Clergy, nobility, and common people shared this lamentable intolerance, which, quite as much political as it was religious, reached the height of its expression in an institution with as sorry a fame as any in history, the Inquisition.

The Inquisition took the form of a central governing committee, with branches in all the provinces of Spain charged to ferret out heretics and infidels with the idea either of bringing about their

The Spanish Inquisition conversion or else of visiting an exemplary punishment upon them. Avowedly a Christian institution, its main purpose was, after all, political rather than religious in that it aimed to consolidate the state. To this end it was subjected to the crown and the pope's control entirely eliminated. The head of the dread machine was called the Grand Inquisitor and under the first incumbent, Thomas de Torquemada, who held the office from 1483 to 1498, some two thousand persons suffered death by fire and some tens of thousands were sentenced to prison terms and money fines. Rather than submit to a debasing tyranny innumerable families of self-respecting and well-to-do Jews and Moors fled to foreign countries. Let us admit that Protestant writers have frequently exaggerated the horrors of the Spanish Inquisition. With ample deductions made on the score of partisanship, enough remains to revolt every sensitive spirit. And a consideration of another sort falls heavily into the scales — the injury which Spain did herself by her policy of uncompromising violence. For, aside from the manifest economic loss and the still more serious intellectual setback resulting from the suppression of what were, mentally, probably the most alert groups of the community, the settled religious intolerance developed a national pride and exclusiveness which petrified the Spanish mind and hindered it from making as large a contribution to European civilization as, in view of its many notable endowments, might have been justly expected.

Queen Isabella, a resolute, gracious, and deeply religious woman,

THE UNIFICATION
OF FRANCE

Fiefs resumed by the crown
in the time of Louis XI and
Charles VIII.

0   50   100   150   200
SCALE OF MILES

THE UNIFICATION
OF SPAIN

0   50   100   150   200
SCALE OF MILES

who died in 1504, was survived twelve years by her husband Ferdinand, a remarkably capable but harsh and unscrupulous ruler. Owing to the death of their only son, the crown was destined to pass to their daughter Joan, who in 1496 had been married to Philip of Hapsburg, son of Emperor Maximilian. But as Philip died in 1506 and Joan was adjudged insane and therefore incapable of government, the successor of the famous unifiers of Spain was the oldest issue of the Hapsburg marriage, Charles. When on the death of Ferdinand in 1516, Charles assumed the crown, he was but sixteen years old.

The succession passes from Ferdinand and Isabella to their grandson, Charles

To understand Charles's role in Spanish history we must thoroughly grasp the constitutional position to which he fell heir. In medieval times the monarchy, both in Castile and Aragon, had exhibited the usual feudal character and the sovereign had ruled with the advice of a baronial assembly, called *cortes*. As early as the thirteenth century the commoners had risen to consideration by gaining admission to the cortes for representatives of the fast growing cities. Unfortunately the democratic promise contained in this broadening of the parliamentary system was not realized, for the eternal struggle with an alien conqueror violently inflamed the national sentiment which naturally rallied around its visible symbol, the king. In consequence the king was able to extend his administrative and judicial system, to maintain a fighting force, and to insinuate his tax-gatherers into the towns, although the constitutional custom was not abrogated that the taxes had to be authorized by the cortes. The movement toward centralization was subtle and imperceptible but necessarily led to the exaltation of the king whose person served as the focus of constantly multiplying administrative threads. In short, though both in Castile and Aragon the cortes continued to function with all their traditional rights apparently intact, there fell across them in an ominous way the constantly lengthening shadow of the king.

Growing power of the king

During the reign of Ferdinand and Isabella there took place so memorable a territorial expansion that it may not be overlooked. If it was Isabella, who, by putting her faith in Columbus, acquired a title to the new world beyond the Atlantic, it was her Aragonese husband who pushed Spanish influence in the opposite direction, that is, eastward along the Mediterranean. Not that he was the originator of this policy, for long before his time his ancestors had spread their power from the Balearic islands to Sardinia and Sicily, while an illegitimate branch of the royal line had seated itself on the throne of Naples. In this situation was indicated a possible control of Italy and the Mediterranean basin which Ferdinand of Aragon, one of the most grasping and enterprising sovereigns of his day, was sure not to lose from sight. In consequence when Charles VIII of France tried to seize Naples for himself (1494), he inevitably encountered lively opposition from his royal cousin of Spain. We shall presently look into the Franco-Spanish conflict which ensued; but in connection with this summary of Spanish territorial growth we may anticipate the outcome by noting that Ferdinand more than held his own against his French rival. In 1504 he acquired the kingdom of Naples and somewhat later (1512) the southern or Spanish section of the small mountain-kingdom of the Pyrenees known as Navarre.

The growth of Spanish territorial power during the reign of Ferdinand and Isabella

FRANCE

So successful was the French monarchy in initiating a process of consolidation at the expense of the feudal barons that, as early as the thirteenth century, it stood out as the most efficient governmental machine in Europe. But owing to a series of disasters, of which the greatest was the Hundred Years' War with England, the advantages won were in the fourteenth and fifteenth centuries again largely sacrificed. In the end the long English occupation reacted in favor of the French king by creating such a passion of nationalism as the country had never known. Its unforgettable exponent was the heroic maid of Orleans, Joan of Arc, under whose inspired leadership the French people successfully inaugurated the task of driving the English back across the channel. For Joan as well as for all others dedicated to the idea of liberation the natural leader was the king; and though the king, Charles VII (1422–1461), was a man of very ordinary character and capacity, he succeeded in greatly advancing his prestige and power by his consistent championship of the national cause. By 1453 the English had lost every foot of their French conquest except the port of Calais.

The French monarchy and the Hundred Years' War

Theoretically the French king was, even in the Middle Age, the source of all authority. In practice, however, his power was limited not only by the great nobles and the Church but also by the States General, which was the feudal assembly composed originally of clergy and nobles and strengthened since the beginning of the fourteenth century by the addition of representatives of the commoners or bourgeoisie. Since the States General bear an undeniable resemblance to the Spanish cortes, the German diet, and the English parliament, it becomes clear that all the European states boasted a somewhat similar political structure and developed along parallel lines. True, the States General appear as rather feeble compared with the English parliament; nevertheless, without their consent the king could not collect the *taille*, the tax on land or property values constituting his chief revenue. In 1439 the States General voluntarily divested themselves of their right of consent and from that moment their fate was sealed. Assured of a permanent income, the king increased the royal armed forces and was soon beyond the control of his subjects. From the earliest times ample revenues and a standing army have constituted the foundations of absolute monarchy. If the French people did not protest against the constitutional turn taken under Charles VII, it was owing mainly to the fact that no sacrifice seemed too great to purchase liberation from the English yoke; but hardly in less degree than to the English situation the monarchy owed its steady advance to the favor of the urban element which looked upon a strong king as the surest means for enforcing peace and order against the lawless feudal lords.

Increasing concentration of power in the hand of the king

It was under Charles's son and successor, Louis XI (1461–1483), that the menace of the great lords, which periodically threatened to overwhelm the monarchy, was so effectively met that the edifice of absolutism was still further fortified. Louis was a conspicuous example of the new order of ruler, just coming to the front, whose game was to spin a web as fine and elastic as a spider's and to gain his cause by diplomacy rather than by war. Faced by such powerful, semi-independent vassals as the dukes of Burgundy, Orleans, Anjou, and Brittany, he met their plots by a mixture of force and cunning and let no opportunity pass to add their fiefs to the royal domain. He was aided by the feudal custom of escheat, under which a fief reverted to the crown on the failure of male heirs. In this manner on the death (1477) without a son of Charles of Burgundy, Louis acquired Burgundy (the duchy) and Picardy, while by the death (1481) of the duke of

Territorial unification under Louis XI

Anjou, he laid his hand on the rich patrimony of Anjou, Maine, and Provence. When Louis's successor, Charles VIII (1483–1498) married Anne, the heiress of the duchy of Brittany, he acted in strict accord with his father's policy of absorbing the great semi-independent fiefs. The addition of Brittany to the crown practically completed the process of French territorial unification.

In measure as the power of the great nobles paled, the power of the king grew, chiefly by the multiplication of the instruments of government at his command. He distributed his administrative

Growth of the royal power secured by increase of the royal services agents more generally through the land and established beyond challenge the ascendancy of the royal courts of justice, particularly of the several courts of ultimate appeal, called *parlements*. As the States General had abdicated their power by the perpetual grant of the taille, they were rarely called together after the middle of the fifteenth century and gradually lost prestige. Nor did the Church escape the general trend. In 1438 in the Pragmatic Sanction of Bourges the independence of the Gallican (i.e. the French) Church had been strongly asserted as against the usurpations of the pope. But the enforced loosening of the papal hold only prepared the way for the encroachments of the king, who increasingly appointed bishops to office without regard either for the recent claims of the pope or for the more ancient rights of election by the cathedral chapters. The constitutional development indicated by the above measures is not limited to the reign of Charles VII or Louis XI but extends over the whole fifteenth and into the sixteenth century. As in Spain the constitutional movement, if slow, was sure and its meaning as clear as day: it signified the coming of one-man power, the system of absolutism.

ENGLAND

The medieval history of England is dominated by the conquest effected in 1066 by William of Normandy, who became King William I. By this event England acquired the benefit of a strong

Government vested in king and parliament monarchy and was spared some of the worst excesses of feudal lawlessness. Neither William nor his successors, however, dispensed with the assembly of barons, lay and ecclesiastical, known as the parliament. By taking advantage of certain difficulties in which some of William's successors became involved, the parliament gradually increased its powers, more particularly under John I, whom it obliged to sign (1215) the famous document, the Magna Charta, which signified an important limitation of the royal prerogative. Toward the end of the thirteenth century, in 1295, the parliament was expanded by the admission of representatives of the towns (boroughs); and thus strengthened, it organized in the course of time in two houses, the first made up of the great barons, lay and ecclesiastical, and the second of the representatives of the boroughs together with the representatives of the smaller holders of fiefs, called knights.

The parliament of two houses proved so effective an organization of the social classes interested in keeping an eye on the monarchy that the king might have been obliged to renounce all his special prerogatives, if a number of grave national upheavals had not interrupted the quiet tenor of domestic evolution. The most important of these was the Hundred Years' War with France, which by inflaming the national sentiment tended to redound to the benefit of the king, the country's natural head in a conflict with a foreign foe. But in spite of brilliant triumphs in the field, the Hundred Years' War ended disastrously (1453); the English lost all their gains across the channel except Calais; and, to make a bad matter worse, under the weak Henry VI (1422–1461) they became entangled in the civil struggle familiar under the name of the War of the Roses. When the War of the Roses ended with the victory of Henry Tudor at the battle of Bosworth (1485), England was an exhausted country ready to welcome a dictatorial ruler, provided he brought the peace she needed and passionately longed for. *Constitutional development interrupted by two great national upheavals*

The War of the Roses, ostensibly a struggle between two branches of the Plantagenet dynasty, the houses of York and Lancaster, was really waged between various factions of the feudal lords and was such an upflare of baronial lawlessness as England had never before known. The new sovereign, Henry VII (1485–1509) signified the advent of a new house, the house of Tudor, though he boasted through his mother the possession of Lancastrian blood. As he was wise enough to marry a princess of the house of York, he could urge the appeasement of the civil brawls on the ground of the convergence in him and his queen of the rival royal strains. Even with these precautions Henry was repeatedly disturbed by pretenders, who obtained a following among the people *The accession of Henry VII* by the false claim of Yorkist descent. All such crises he met with unusual subtlety and sagacity, with traits, in a word, that are rather a modern than a medieval specialty. Naturally such a keen penetration as his would not fail to see and grasp the opportunity afforded by the civil exhaustion for establishing a strong monarchy of the kind just then triumphantly emerging in France and Spain. Manifestly the rivals of the royal power were, on the one hand, the great nobles who had made the crown their plaything during the War of the Roses and, on the other, the parliament, which in an earlier period had established its right to a substantial share in the government.

In a lifetime of narrowly concentrated effort Henry put a curb on both of his opponents. By virtue of a law depriving the nobles of the right to keep under arms great bodies of retainers, he extinguished the centers of provincial resistance to the royal will; and to make assurance doubly sure he established an extraordinary court, the court of Star Chamber, which sat in London under his eye and visited dire punishment on the recalcitrant nobles as well as on all other malefactors whom the local courts were not strong enough to punish. In curbing the parliament he took a far less drastic course because the parliament was an integral feature of the English constitution and well entrenched in the affections of the nation. With shrewd self-restraint he even adopted a policy of ostensible coöperation with the rival institution. Since he owed his throne to the circumstance of his having been victor in a social broil, that is, to military force, he honored the representatives of the nation — and incidentally put the authority of the law behind his claim — by asking them to endorse his accession in a formal resolution. Furthermore he scrupulously observed the ancient custom by which the king could raise no taxes except with parliamentary consent. But, his supplies once obtained, he husbanded the returns like a miser in order not to be obliged to demonstrate more often than was necessary his dependence on a popular body. In the last thirteen years of his reign he took counsel with his parliament only twice and, partly out of gratitude for his reëstablishment of the domestic peace, it showed no disposition to hew out a path of its own. No doubt the legal claim of parliament to be associated with the king in governing England remained intact; but from failing to appear in London the legislature tended to fall into oblivion, leaving the king to occupy

Henry's policy toward nobles and parliament

the national stage alone. All facts carefully considered, it is incontrovertible that Henry Tudor renewed the prestige of the crown and created, certainly not a royal absolutism, but a strong monarchy looking in that direction.

The predecessors of Henry Tudor, while chiefly occupied with the conquest of France, had not failed to concern themselves with the annexation of the three smaller states nearer home, Wales, Ireland, and Scotland. Their progress, though often inter- *England* rupted, had been notable, for in the thirteenth century *encroaches* Wales had been brought definitely under the English *on her* crown, while even earlier, in the twelfth century, in the *neighbors,* reign of Henry II, Ireland had been invaded and reduced to *Ireland,* vassalage. Unfortunately for the native Irish they were *and* split into numerous warring tribes incapable of acting to- *Scotland* gether except on very rare occasions. Even under these untoward circumstances the Irish resistance was vigorous enough to make the English hold on the western island precarious, nay, at times wholly illusive. Henry VII, cautious by nature and fully occupied with the English domestic situation, contented himself with holding the coastal section around Dublin, called the English pale, and relegated the task of a genuine and sweeping conquest to his successors. As for Scotland, wars with it had been frequent throughout the Middle Age but the Scots and their king had thus far successfully escaped the English noose. Without doubt the Hundred Years' War, which had kept England occupied in France for several generations, had favored the independence of the northern neighbor. But with the Hundred Years' War at an end, it became probable that England would scan the situation beyond the Tweed somewhat more narrowly. The effect of such unsolicited interest would be to prompt the alarmed Scots to draw closer to France. In fact the probable partnership of Scotland and France was a circumstance with which Henry and all his Tudor successors would be obliged to reckon.

His delicate position between the French hammer and the Scottish anvil partly explains why Henry VII felt little inclination to renew the traditional struggle with the Capetian monarchy. But it is also true and wholly to his credit that he had no love *Henry's* of military adventure for its own sake. Of course he was *policy of* in a measure drawn into the intricate game of continental *peace* diplomacy; and it was natural enough that he should usually align himself against France. But as soon as serious conflict or embarrassing expense threatened he quietly withdrew. On the whole he held to the view that his safest policy was to maintain good and even intimate relations with Spain; and in 1501 he gave expression to this opinion in the fashion of the time by arranging a marriage between Arthur, prince of Wales, and Catherine, daughter of Ferdinand and Isabella. When Arthur died shortly after the ceremony, his widow was retained in England with a view to a later marriage to the king's second son, afterwards Henry VIII. In a commendable effort to detach Scotland by friendly means from her traditional ally across the channel Henry, in 1502, gave his daughter, Margaret, in wedlock to the Scottish king, James IV. In short the first Tudor was a man of peace. If he kept a sharp lookout toward France he was content in the main with such diplomatic measures for keeping his rival in check as amicable relations with Spain and Scotland.

. . . .

At the end of the fifteenth century there occurred an event which profoundly affected the relation toward each other of all the European states just passed in review. I refer to the invasion of Italy by Charles VIII of France in 1494. Although Charles pretended that he invaded Italy in the interest of his rightful claim to the kingdom of Naples, he was really prompted by an ungoverned ambition fortified by the circumstance that the French monarchy had become so strong that it overflowed like a brimming cup. The first result of the invasion was to show that Italy, home of the humanists and artists, was politically too feeble to offer an effective resistance to the new centralized type of monarchy. If her five most important states had stood together, there might have been a different tale to tell, but their incurable jealousies made a united front impossible. Charles marched the whole length of the peninsula without meeting a trace of serious opposition, drove the Aragonese incumbent from the throne of Naples, and crowned himself king. But there his triumph ended. King Ferdinand of Spain was not the man to let a rival pick a fruit which he regarded as his own and, allying himself with some of the Italian states, obliged the French king to beat a precipitate retreat. In 1495 Charles stood again on the soil of France with nothing but a few stirring memories to show for his lavish expenditure of blood and money.

However, the French king had proved that the trick could be

turned and that Italy was the predestined victim of a neighbor with a will to conquer. On dying in 1498, Charles left this conviction to his successor, Louis XII, and when, after a reign of seventeen years, Louis was succeeded by Francis I (1515–1546), the new king shaped his policy on the same ambitious assumption. It would be a tedious undertaking to follow in detail the Italian campaigns of these three rulers and mortally dull to trace the fluctuations of their shifty diplomacy. Let it suffice that France's rival, Spain, moved heaven and earth to hinder the consummation of the French designs and that in the battle of the two giants the pigmy states of Italy were at first pawns and ultimately victims.

Charles's Italian ambitions pursued by his successors, Louis XII and Francis I

Although France and Spain were on the whole well-matched, the scales tended from the first to incline in favor of the latter. As early as 1504 the issue over Naples was settled by its unconditional cession to King Ferdinand. In return Louis XII hoped to be left in possession of the duchy of Milan, on which he had fixed his eye as more desirable than Naples because nearer to France and which he had seized (1499) immediately on coming to the throne on the pretext, dearly beloved by the monarchs of his day, of an hereditary claim. But Ferdinand was not minded to leave Louis in possession of Milan either and in 1512, by means of a new combination of Italian princes and European powers, successfully ousted him. Thereupon Francis I, on the morrow of his accession to the throne, returned to the attack and once more gained a firm lodgment in the Lombard duchy (1515). Shortly after Ferdinand ended his days (1516), leaving the quarrel with France over Italy to his grandson and heir, Charles. How the poor Italian bone was worried by Francis and Charles all the days of their life we shall see in a later chapter.

The struggle in Italy turns around Naples and Milan

However, long before the struggle between France and Spain over Italy was brought to a settlement, it had become plain that the peninsula was a doomed land. Helpless before the might of the two western monarchies, the small Italian states wasted their resources in a frenzied and indecent scramble for mere self-preservation. Moreover, their abasement availed them not at all, for so long as Italy failed to present a united front to her aggressors she was, in the long run, certain to lose her independence. Worse, much worse from a cultural viewpoint, ground under the heel of brute force, she was sure

Political and cultural decline of Italy

to lose also the fine intellectual zest which had made the Renaissance such a brilliant and imaginative episode. In point of fact a general decline of Italian life set in, which, hardly noticed at first, became as legible as print toward the middle of the sixteenth century. It signified that the country's subjection to its foreign masters kept accurate pace with the extinction of those spiritual fires which had enabled Italy to produce a literary and artistic treasure still cherished by the world as one of its most precious possessions.

In this tragic decay the destiny meted out to the individual states deserves a passing word. As Naples and Milan were the main objectives of the Franco-Spanish conflict, these two states quickly lost Fate of the their independence, even though the question whether individual they would lose it to France or Spain long continued to states hang in the balance. The other three states, Venice, Florence, and the State of the Church, were not so much threatened in their immediate sovereignty as in a general diminution of importance due to the projection into peninsular affairs of two large-scale powers. In fact all three native states continued to assert a technical independence for many succeeding generations, Venice and the State of the Church under essentially the same form of government they had given themselves in the Renaissance. Only Florence passed through a number of stirring domestic changes which may be briefly noted here since the vicissitudes of the lively Arno city, mother of such a host of distinguished sons, have always enlisted a sympathetic attention.

The reader will remember that we have traced the political evolution of Florence to the Medicean domination under Lorenzo the Magnificent. On the heels of Lorenzo's death in 1492 came the The invasion of Italy by Charles VIII. Taking advantage restored of the general disturbance of the peninsula, the Floren-Florentine tines rose against Piero, the feeble heir of Lorenzo, drove republic him and all his family to flight, and again set up a republic. The new government lived for a time in the shadow of the famous Dominican friar and stern moralist, Girolamo Savonarola, and represented a curious reversion to the Middle Age. It was characteristic of Savonarola that while he hated the Medici as destroyers of the ancient liberties of Florence, he abominated them still more as the embodiment of the pagan spirit of the Renaissance. The strange attempt to throw Florence, beacon and inspiration of the new age, back into the twilight of the thirteenth century continued as long as the fanatical friar succeeded in dominating the common people. By 1498 his many enemies had sufficiently knocked his props from under him to compass his downfall and burn him at the stake on a trumped-up charge of heresy. Thereupon the political control slipped promptly into the hands of the business elements traditionally in command of the situation; but to no avail, since their valiant efforts to appease the bitter domestic divisions by a constitution on the Venetian model had only a temporary success. For the student of European thought the most memorable circumstance connected with the renewed Florentine republic in the days following the overthrow of Savonarola is that it employed as its secretary of state Niccolo Machiavelli, in whom we hail by virtue of his historical studies, particularly *The Prince*, one of the most penetrating political observers that ever lived. In *The Prince* Machiavelli shows not only that he had a remarkably keen appreciation of the movement toward tyranny and absolutism going on all over Europe in his day but also that he welcomed it as an escape from feudal and republican disorder.

The grievous lesson reserved for the renewed Florentine republic was that the days of a free Italy were over and that the small native states could not possibly escape the dilemma presented by the Franco-Spanish rivalry. Obliged to lean on one or the other of the two dominating powers, the republic threw in its lot with France with the result that when King Louis XII went down in defeat (1512), the government promptly collapsed. **The triumph of the Medici** With the help of Spain the Medici now returned to the city; and though they were once again driven out (1527) and the republic set up anew, the struggle for liberty was hopeless since under the altered circumstances it was directed not so much against the Medici as against the titan behind them, Spain. The renewed and final restoration of the Medici (1530) was the solemn evidence of Spanish invincibility. Convinced that it was useless to kick against the pricks, the Florentines now sullenly accepted the yoke of the Medici, who in their turn wore with fitting meekness the yoke of Spain. With the consent of their Spanish protector they converted their Florentine possession into the duchy (ultimately the grand duchy) of Tuscany. Thus at last was their ancient dream realized: they became hereditary lords of their native city, sacrificing to this petty ambition the liberty of their fellow-citizens as well as their own.

Beside these purely local consequences, certain other effects of the
prolonged Franco-Spanish duel over Italy began slowly to outline
themselves. They literally embrace all Europe and have helped

Passing of the medieval political ideal
shape its history to the present day. To gain the proper
approach to these general consequences let us recall that
the Middle Age cherished a noble ideal of European unity.
Championed in the first instance by St. Augustine in his
famous City of God, it envisaged in its developed form a
world-state of Christian humanity committed to a program of peace
under the double guidance of pope and emperor. But this program
of a Christian commonwealth failed in the course of the Middle Age
and was replaced by the actuality of separate and independent civil
states engaged in frank rivalry for the control of lands, commerce,
and other evidences of material wealth. The Renaissance with its
strong secular drift marks the definite emergence of these competing
civil entities; and the Franco-Spanish conflict over Italy presents
to view the first struggle among two leading powers in which there
is hardly traceable any longer the least vestige of medieval ideology.
The Franco-Spanish struggle is a naked power issue in which the
two combatants make use of war without scruple as a perfectly
legitimate weapon.

It is therefore plain that toward the end of the Renaissance Europe
had become endowed with a new political system which, since it
continues to this day, may be called the modern system, and which

Europe works out a system of coöperation based on treaties and a diplomatic and consular service
is distinguished by an unlimited competition among its
component parts logically culminating in the shock of
war. But even when war is reckoned a legitimate tool,
the *ultima ratio*, which each state reserves to itself as
its court of last appeal, it is undoubtedly a weapon of
destruction; and the Modern Period which, just beginning to dawn, was dedicated to commerce and industry and the multiplication of wealth, was sure to develop,
at least at intervals, a strong aversion for war's indiscriminate application. To conduct their enterprises the burgher classes, with whom the
control of society was coming to rest in constantly increasing measure,
required peace; and therefore as soon as the patriotic intoxication
which war released had evaporated, they welcomed the treaty of
peace which muffled the din of battle and at the same time cleared
once more the highways and opened the markets. Treaties of peace,
though chiefly of a political nature, usually contained also commercial

provisions or else were supplemented by express treaties of commerce. To be sure, each new war cancelled all treaties existing between the belligerent states, but on the termination of the conflict new treaties, which were the old treaties modified in accordance with the issue of the recent struggle, were promptly negotiated. To secure their precise execution there were gradually developed two special administrative services, the one diplomatic for political matters and the other consular for purely commercial affairs. Placed under the supervision of the department of state or foreign office, the two services taken together constituted the administrative machinery for maintaining and developing the relations among states according to the letter of the current agreements.

The sum of all the treaties negotiated among sovereign states for any end whatsoever may be conceived as making up the body of international law. Increasing in bulk with each new generation, international law has served to bind Europe into a single, *The constantly developing code of international law* more and more compactly organized commonwealth. Undeniably so long as each sovereign state, large or small, insisted that it was its inalienable right to bring every difference of opinion or of interest to the arbitrament of war, this delicate organization of the European states would be periodically exposed to anarchic disorganization; but for all that we should not overlook the substantial gain for political coöperation and economic interdependence that lay in basing all peace-time dealings among the jealously sovereign units of the European system on an expanding code of international law.

Although this emerging modern system comprised all states, great and small alike, only the powerful states, powerful in last analysis because of their military and naval strength, figure in the system as great powers. With them during the last four centuries has rested the control of Europe and, in measure *The great powers and the principle of balance* as Europe has expanded over-seas, the control of the rest of the world. But as each great power has been unceasingly engaged in the attempt to outstrip its rivals in defensive and offensive strength, there has developed the curious phenomenon called the balance of power. It comes into play when one great power, either by reason of its actual resources or by an alliance with other powers or by attaching to itself a group of lesser client states, achieves a position which points or seems to point to domination. Almost automatically the opponents draw together in order to redress the scales — a complicated diplomatic operation touching which enlightening evidence was supplied during the Franco-Spanish wars. Whenever in the struggle for the Italian prize France was in-the ascendancy there was an immediate rush on the part of the other powers of Europe to come to the aid of Spain; and whenever Spain was in the lead the rush was the other way.

To the reflective reader it must be reasonably clear that with a developing code of international law supplemented by the principle of balanced power, albeit precariously maintained, Europe should be conceived as a single commonwealth. Its political unity was however constantly challenged and at times completely nullified by the persistent and stubborn claim of each member-state to an unlimited sovereignty culminating in the right of war. Before a more harmonious commonwealth than this was possible the individual European citizen would have to learn to think in terms of Europe rather than in terms of the country of his particular allegiance. And that time was in the sixteenth century still far off; in fact it may be doubted if even yet, in this, the twentieth century, it has dawned for more than a handful of men, the hopeful and courageous vanguard of a new political order.

Europe a single but imperfect commonwealth

REFERENCES

C. H. HAYES, *Political and Social History of Modern Europe*, vol. I, pp. 74–86
E. M. HULME, *Renaissance and Reformation*, ch. 10
A. H. JOHNSON, *Europe in the Sixteenth Century*, chs. 1, 2
Cambridge Modern History, I, chs. 9–12, vol. II, chs. 2, 3
W. C. ABBOTT, *Expansion of Europe*, I, chs. 4, 5
R. LODGE, *Close of the Middle Ages*
P. VILLARI, *Life and Times of Savonarola; Life and Times of Machiavelli*
E. F. HENDERSON, *Short History of Germany*, I, chs. 7, 8, 9
R. W. S. WATSON, *Maximilian I*
C. E. CHAPMAN, *History of Spain*, chs. 18–22
R. B. MERRIMAN, *Rise of the Spanish Empire*, II, chs. 12–15
C. HEADLAM, *France*, chs. 13, 14
R. M. MACDONALD, *History of France*, II, ch. 19
A. L. CROSS, *History of England and Greater Britain*, chs. 17, 18

CHAPTER V

THE GERMAN REFORMATION TO THE PEACE OF AUGSBURG (1555)

The House of Hapsburg

Maximilian I (1493–1519)
     m. Mary, heiress of Burgundy

Philip the Handsome (*d.* 1506) *m.* Joan, heiress of Spain

Charles V (1519–56)   **Ferdinand I**(1556–64)

                                 m. Anne, heiress of
                                     Hungary and
                                     Bohemia

                    Maximilian II (1564–76)

We have seen that Germany, identical with the Holy Roman Empire (the Empire, for short), was a loose federation of several hundred semi-sovereign states, and that in the reign of the Emperor Maximilian (1493–1519) it experienced a national revival which, however, did not in any essential respect strengthen the feeble national government. The national revival was itself an effect of the general awakening that came to all sections of Europe alike with the Renaissance. Only *{The Renaissance a forerunner of the Reformation}* a somewhat detailed understanding of the particular stir which the Renaissance brought to Germany will prepare us to grasp the origin of the great sixteenth century movement called the Reformation.

As an instructive introduction to both Renaissance and Reformation let us examine the implications of the unshaken domination in Germany, and almost alone in Germany, of the Church. We are aware that the Middle Age was so thoroughly ruled by organized Christianity that the pope was able to proclaim the theory that, since all power came from God and he himself was God's earthly vicar, all government, civil as well as ecclesiastical, was of right

vested in his person. Of course, the doctrine of papal authority in
this, its extreme form, never enjoyed universal acceptance and
never hindered the European monarchs from asserting their independence in the civil field. None the less, in every
country of Europe, the Church secured a position which
placed it outside the national frame; and in view of the
fact that the pope succeeded in acquiring substantial control of each national Church, he rose in every instance to
a coördinate position with the monarch, exercising
sovereignty in the monarch's territory, chiefly by laying
taxes on ecclesiastical property and by controlling the higher ecclesiastical appointments.

*The medie-
val popes
exercise
powers
which prej-
udice the
rights of
civil rulers*

When, during the Renaissance, the strong monarchies developed
in France, Spain, and England, they undertook to challenge the
pope's power exercised within their boundaries. In each instance
they scored successes, which, if incomplete, showed that
the wind had veered and was now no longer filling the
pope's sails. Thus in France King Charles VII issued
(1438) a royal ordinance, known as the Pragmatic Sanction of Bourges, challenging the papal pretensions to control the French Church; and letting the deed follow the boast, Charles
VII as well as his successors by degrees took over the nomination of the
French bishops and abbots, in this way successfully usurping a power
to which the popes had never ceased to pretend. Again, in Spain,
under Ferdinand and Isabella, the crown took over (1482) the right
to nominate to bishoprics and forbade appeals from the Spanish
ecclesiastical courts to Rome; while in England by the celebrated
statutes of Provisors (1351) and of Praemunire (1353), a similar
anti-papal policy took shape, the former measure denying the pope's
claim to appoint to English benefices and the latter forbidding the
carrying of appeals outside the realm.

*Decline of
the pope's
power in
the strong
monarchies*

In Germany where, in distinction from the western monarchies,
the crown instead of growing stronger had, especially during the
long, disgraceful reign of Frederick III (1440–1493), become steadily
more feeble, the papal ascendancy over the German
Church had been confirmed (Concordat of Vienna, 1448).
In consequence the popes of the Renaissance exercised
a more arbitrary power in Germany than anywhere else in Christendom. They abused their appointive rights by taking money from
candidates to office — the sin of simony; they taxed the clergy

*Abuses of
papal power
in Germany*

(and that means ultimately the laity) by a frequent levy of tithes on the pretext of a crusade against the Turks which never materialized; and they unflinchingly exacted annates or first-fruits. The impost called annates involved the surrender of one-half of his revenues during the first year of office by each new episcopal incumbent. The German diets of the second half of the fifteenth century never ceased voicing their dissatisfaction with the innumerable papal abuses by loud complaints (*gravamina*) dispatched to Rome, which, quietly pigeon-holed on their arrival, proved no more effective than if they had been messages from Mars. In this connection we must not forget that this was the period of the Renaissance group of popes, who, indifferent to spiritual appeals, desired money and ever more money to satisfy their political ambitions and their sumptuous patronage of the arts. Since such men had but little conscience where their pockets were concerned, they agreed to every shifty measure for replenishing the treasury which their unscrupulous financial advisers might suggest. In an evil hour they agreed to a sale of indulgences in Germany on an unusually extensive scale.

Who would understand what is meant by an indulgence must be willing to have a look at the rather abstruse world of medieval theology and, more particularly, to scan the sacrament of penance.[1] The sacrament of penance dealt with acts of sin which **Indul-** God for his part forgave the sinner on contrition and **gences —** confession. Absolution by the priest was the evidence **the theory** of that forgiveness. However, there still remained the temporal penalty which the sinner must satisfy either in this world by acts classifiable as good works or in the next by enduring a purifying punishment in purgatory. It is here that the indulgence comes in. An indulgence is a remission of the temporal penalty by means of the Treasure of Grace, defined as the sum total of the merits of Jesus Christ and the great company of saints and martyrs. The Treasure of Grace came into existence because the ancient founders and confessors of the Christian faith offered much more satisfaction (that is, suffered much graver penalties) than their state of sin required. All such works in excess of what was needed to balance the account are called works of supererogation and comprise the Treasure of Grace. It is administered by the pope who may at his discretion apply it to the benefit of others lacking in good works. The document declaring the remission of the temporal penalty by

[1] See p. 10

a draft on the unexhausted and inexhaustible treasure of the Church is called an indulgence.

Granted that the indulgence, considered in the light of theory, is for us moderns somewhat intricate and difficult, we must agree that it so closely conforms to medieval concepts that it would have

The abuse of indulgences aroused no criticism, had it not in its practical application lent itself to abuse. In the Middle Age the popes issued indulgences with a certain restraint and conscientiously applied the returns to legitimate Christian ends such as a crusade. But with the coming of the Renaissance and its pressing financial necessities the sale of the papal certificates was converted into a device for raising taxes. They were consigned to licensed venders who penetrated into every nook and corner of Europe, except where they were excluded by a strong civil power. Because the pope exercised more influence in Germany than anywhere else, the hawkers disported themselves with particular freedom in German territory with the result that they fanned the already dangerous anti-papal sentiment.

In view of all these facts it is easy to understand the rising tide of national indignation directed against the pope. But unless we understand that this indignation, while possessed of a moral char-

The rising anti-papal tide acter, was also fed by political and economic considerations, we shall fail to grasp the nature of the hurricane released by Luther's challenge. By a remarkable coincidence all the forces of society were, at the beginning of the sixteenth century, focussing on the papal issue. While some groups, the simply and honestly pious of every social level, were offended with the pope because of his brilliant court and worldly policy, others, the growing mass of narrowly patriotic men, looked askance at him because he was a foreigner exercising more influence in their country than the emperor or the Reichstag. This latter group of passionate nationalists was recruited largely from the rising burghers; and the burghers possessed a further incentive to hostility in the vast sums of money said to be annually drained to Rome. To the town-dwellers of an age, the expanding energies of which called for capital, the steady stream of gold and silver pouring out of Germany across the Alps caused a veritable nightmare. In raising their voices to stop the exploitation they found sympathizers among all classes of the population including the clergy itself. It is useless trying to decide whether the economic or the moral motive predominated in the mounting

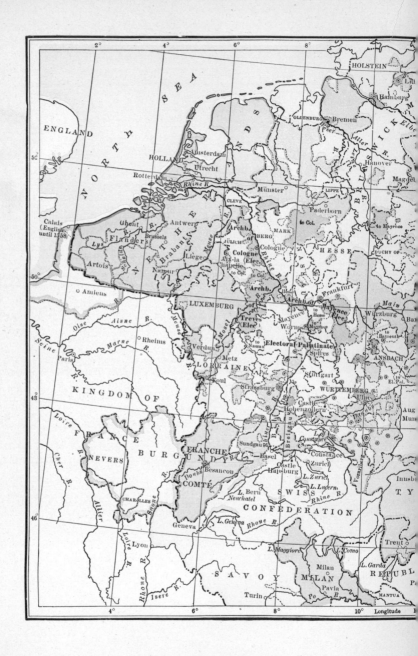

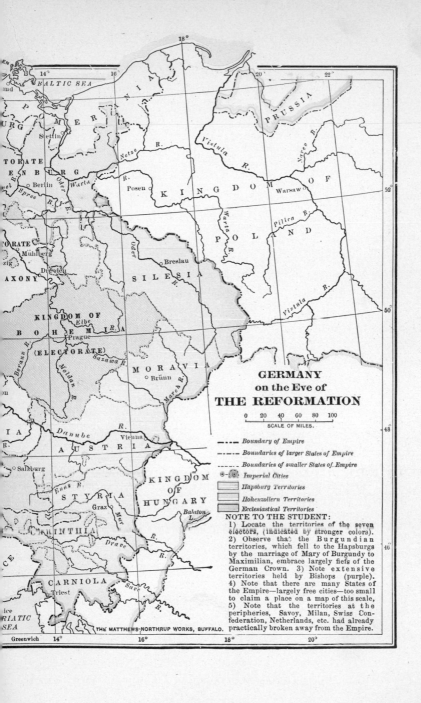

GERMANY
on the Eve of
THE REFORMATION

0   20   40   60   80   100
SCALE OF MILES.

- - - - - *Boundary of Empire*
- - - - - *Boundaries of larger States of Empire*
- - - - - *Boundaries of smaller States of Empire*
- *Imperial Cities*
Hapsburg Territories
Hohenzollern Territories
Ecclesiastical Territories

NOTE TO THE STUDENT:
1) Locate the territories of the seven electors, (indicated by stronger colors). 2) Observe that the Burgundian territories, which fell to the Hapsburgs by the marriage of Mary of Burgundy to Maximilian, embrace largely fiefs of the German Crown. 3) Note extensive territories held by Bishops (purple). 4) Note that there are many States of the Empire—largely free cities—too small to claim a place on a map of this scale, 5) Note that the territories at the peripheries, Savoy, Milan, Swiss Confederation, Netherlands, etc. had already practically broken away from the Empire.

THE MATTHEWS-NORTHRUP WORKS, BUFFALO.

anti-papal sentiment or whether both motives were not merely subsidiary aspects of the new nationalism. The situation in Germany was complex as human situations always are, and it will suffice if we agree that, given the papal abuses, the Renaissance spirit, which was a spirit of criticism, was bound to create a protest which would seek reënforcement from the moral, economic, and every other resource at man's service.

Turning from the politico-religious to the intellectual aspect of Germany, we are confronted with the phenomenon of humanism. Originating in Italy and taking the form of a passionate search among the ruins of antiquity for a new foundation of life and knowledge, it spread slowly to the other regions of Europe and, of course, also to Germany. But, as was only natural, the German humanists modified the movement in accordance with their temperament and outlook. So completely did the Italians identify themselves with the new learning that they were tempted to cut loose entirely from their medieval anchorage; some of them actually abandoned Christianity and avowed themselves to be pagans. The Germans felt no such inclination. Barbarian forest-dwellers in the days of the Caesars, they had had no share in ancient Rome, which was as remote and unreal to them as the fabric of a dream. On the other hand, the Christian faith, received by them in the early Middle Age, had entered their souls and, as an unexhausted force, stimulated their deepest affections. Hence they put their own interpretation on the new learning hailing from Italy and, while accepting its classical mission, preferably and enthusiastically directed its energies into a Christian channel. Turning first to the Fathers, they penetrated beyond them to the Bible, until this occupation with the origins of Christianity filled them with a sense of the amazing chasm between the simplicity of the apostolic age and the papal and ecclesiastical grandeur which was dangled before their eyes and which in the form of innumerable exactions pressed on their country like an incubus. Let it not for a moment be imagined that they were suddenly persuaded that the existing structure of the Church was an unnatural growth; in fact, because of their devotion to custom and tradition, they yielded the ecclesiastical institution a full and willing obedience. None the less the accumulation of fresh knowledge about so many phases of the Christian past gradually produced a viewpoint which was very different from the blind credulity of their forebears.

German humanism turns to the origins of Christianity

The German humanists were a relatively small body of men who served the usual provocative function of an intelligentsia. Since the universities, with certain notable exceptions, opened their doors to **Humanism** them, the ascendancy of the old barren scholasticism was **gets a foot-** gradually shaken. When men like Rudolph Agricola **hold in the** (d. 1485) and Conrad Celtis (d. 1508), who had gone to **universities** Italy to imbibe the new learning at its fountain-head, returned to their native land, they were received with enthusiasm by swarms of students who crowded to their lectures. Under these circumstances the familiar battle of conservatives and liberals was soon joined all along the line and early in the sixteenth century led to a memorable crisis. Its central figure was John Reuchlin in whom we encounter a typical expression of German humanism.

Like his predecessors, John Reuchlin (1455–1522) had made first-hand acquaintance with humanism by travel and study in Italy. An acknowledged master of both Latin and Greek, none the less by **John** a preference which he shared with most of his German **Reuchlin** countrymen he turned enthusiastically to the Fathers and **and the** from them to the Bible. But no sooner had he plunged **quarrel over** **Hebrew** into the Christian sources than he became persuaded of **studies** the necessity of knowing Hebrew. Not only had this language been neglected, but, owing to the hatred commonly felt in the Middle Age for the Jews, the outcast people who had crucified the Lord, it was under a general and severe taboo. In 1506 Reuchlin performed an important scholarly service for all Europe by publishing a Hebrew grammar and lexicon. It immediately aroused a storm of reprobation among the old-time schoolmen, whose main German stronghold was the university of Cologne. As this university was in the hands of the Dominican order of friars, identified since the thirteenth century with the scholastic system, the petrified faculty uttered a cry of alarm and in violent language put themselves on record against the lifting of the Hebrew ban. At their summons the stalwarts of the old régime gathered to their flag, while the friends of the new learning rallied around Reuchlin. It was a miniature war, in which the combatants denounced each other in fiery pamphlets and which culminated in a number of trials for heresy preferred by the exasperated Dominicans against the bold champion of Hebrew studies. Appeased only to flare up again, the combat dragged along for ten years and, though tiresome in detail, possessed the merit of bringing the issue, which was, in substance, the freedom of learning, to the attention of every educated group in Germany.

What regularly determines the victory in a conflict of this sort, a conflict of minds, is the swing of public opinion. And public opinion, veering slowly toward Reuchlin, was finally almost stampeded into his camp by the *Epistolae obscurorum virorum* (Letters of The Letters Obscure Men, 1515–1517). The work was the product of Obscure of a group of gay and emancipated spirits, champions of Men the new philosophy, and constitutes as telling a satire as the young and impertinent have ever aimed at their grave and stodgy elders. Taken at its face value, it was a collection of epistles written by students and admirers to one of the Cologne stand-patters; and the fun lay in having the bat-eyed correspondents, who blinked feebly at the new light, reveal by means of intimate communications, written without restraint and in an exaggerated version of the grotesque Latin current among the schoolmen, their secret viciousness and abysmal ignorance. True, much of the sport was in the nature of rude horse-play, but it did its work and fairly buried the old scholasticism under a tempest of inextinguishable laughter.

Although he stood with Reuchlin and smiled with characteristic malice at the broad humor of the Letters, Desiderius Erasmus (1467–1536) had no hand in their composition. In this remarkable scholar we meet the greatest figure of the humanistic circles of Erasmus his generation not only in Germany but throughout Europe. Though born on the lower Rhine, in Rotterdam, he lived in turn in every country of Europe and not only professed himself to be a cosmopolitan but, what is much more rare, actually succeeded in suppressing in himself every trace of nationalism. Like all humanists, north and south of the Alps alike, he employed the Latin language as his medium of expression; and as this tongue was still the foundation of every educational system, he was enabled to reach the cultivated classes throughout Christendom. In the main he was a scholar, rarely competent in both the classical and patristic fields and winning golden opinions by his editions of the ancients and the Fathers; but his fame as an intellectual leader was enhanced by his activity as a reformer, for, aroused by the evils of the day, he did not scruple at times to desert his study and make an open attack on the false idols of the market-place.

Erasmus's most famous contribution to scholarship was a New Testament in the original Greek accompanied by a Latin translation which ventured to expose the numerous errors of the version of the Bible stamped with the official approval of the Church and known as the Vulgate. The Vulgate dated back to the fifth century and His Chris- was regarded by pedantic theologians as sacrosanct. tian schol- While the New Testament of Erasmus illustrates the arship common effort of northern scholars to put Christian learning on a sound foundation, regardless of what tradition was upset and whose withers were wrung, it betrays the equally important attitude of this group toward the Scriptures as the true and supreme fountain of faith. "I long," he wrote in explanation of his occupying himself with the fundamental Christian documents, "that the peasant should sing the Scriptures to himself as he follows the plow, that the weaver should hum them to the tune of his shuttle, and that the traveler should beguile with them the weariness of his journey." This is the subtle evangelical note, sounded by him and Reuchlin and the whole body of the northern humanists steadily, if with no set and conscious purpose, against the prevailing ceremonious ecclesiasticism. Magnified by the succeeding generation to a vast cry, it became the trumpet blast before which the walls of Jericho went down.

We have already noted that though Erasmus was in the main a quiet scholar whose chief thought was personal tranquillity, he lived enough in the world to be moved to speak out against its evils. His sharp in- The Praise telligence put him, in the literary satire, in possession of a of Folly weapon which he wielded unsparingly and to the round applause of critics and reformers the world over. In his most famous production in this kind, the Praise of Folly (1509), he presents Folly as a woman adorned with cap and bells and engaged in boastingly recounting her innumerable earthly triumphs. Her merry discourse becomes a fierce lashing of the vile customs of monks, the ignorance of schoolmen, the venality of the clergy, the ambition of kings, and the gross superstition of the masses, in sum, a biting exposure of all the hoary evils of the age.

The Europe which cheered to the echo this attack on its social and political inheritance was already, even though it might not be conscious of the fact, in the throes of a mental revolution. To the humanists, champions of the new outlook, the name of Erasmus became a battle-cry; and when presently Martin Luther made his appearance and went a step farther by flinging his challenge directly at the Church, he counted, not unnaturally, on Erasmus's support.

He proved himself mistaken, not only in the single Erasmus but, to a considerable extent, in the whole older generation of humanists; for, though they regarded him at first not without favor, as soon as he definitely broke with pope and Church, they drew back in alarm. Why? Partly because they were timid scholars with a temperamental aversion for the heat and dust of the arena, but in still greater measure because, as they viewed the situation, they had preached not revolt but reform. In particular Erasmus, their honored chief, had cherished, futilely perhaps but earnestly, the dream that the increasing spread of knowledge would automatically reduce the evils of the world. His whole life-work was, on its moral side, an advocacy of reasonableness and toleration, and, instead of joining the ranks of violence and revolution, he resolutely turned his back on the Lutheran movement and sulked in his tent. Protestant writers, who, on this account, have often angrily berated Erasmus as a white-livered knave, fail to do justice to his fundamental conviction that the only reforms which are ever worth while come through gradual enlightenment; on the other hand, there is undeniably a modicum of truth in the pithy summary of the situation credited to a Catholic contemporary: Erasmus laid the egg; Luther hatched it. To bitter, partisan Catholics Erasmus was quite as great a criminal as Luther.

Erasmus does not accept the Lutheran revolt

Martin Luther was born November 10, 1483, in a village of Thuringia at the foot of the Harz Mountains. His ancestry for many generations back had been hard-working peasants, and much of peasant sturdiness and simplicity, with much of peasant obstinacy and superstition, remained characteristic of this son of the soil to the end of his days. By personal sacrifices his parents managed to send young Martin to school and later, to the university of Erfurt, where he prepared himself for the law; but in the year 1505, during a thunder-storm which overtook him on the highway and filled him with wild terror he made the vow to become a monk. It was a characteristically medieval act inspired by a sense of sin and the need of salvation. He joined the Augustinian order of friars at Erfurt and took his duties so seriously that a distinguished clerical career opened before him. In 1507 he was ordained a priest and, immersing himself in his theological studies, he was in 1512 promoted to the doctorate and, shortly after, called to the professorship of theology at the university of Wittenberg. This institution had been recently founded by the Elector Frederick of

Martin Luther

Saxony at the seat of his government. Luther immediately became a leading professor, largely because in the spirit of the new learning he based his instruction not on the medieval schoolmen but on the living Christian sources, the Fathers and the Bible.

But these externals of Luther's career do not touch the substance of the terrible inner problem which agitated him throughout his early manhood nor do they explain how it happened that he became a re-

Luther's inner agony and its solution former and altered the course of human history. To him, as to every true and sincere Christian, the supreme concern of life, before which everything else shrank to nothingness, was the question of salvation. The medieval Church had arrived at a solution which represented an amazingly delicate adjustment between faith and good works, that is, between simple surrender to God's love and the conscientious performance of the many holy acts enjoined by the sacraments. Neither one way nor the other sufficed by itself; you traveled each in turn according to the need of the hour and, so proceeding, met your reward in heaven. Luther tried the traditional Catholic combination, or, according to his Catholic critics, committed the error of trying works too exclusively; in any case he felt crushed by an agony of doubt touching his future fate until the certainty came to him like an illumination from on high that God accepted all who surrendered their stubborn will into His hands. By faith and faith alone did sinful man win his way to peace and forgiveness. In this the humble friar originated nothing new and never claimed he did; in fact he owed his trust in the way of faith to his discovery of it first, in the writings of St. Augustine, the great Latin father, and later, in the epistles of the impetuous Apostle Paul, in whom Luther detected a remarkable spiritual kinsman. Faith had therefore high and highest authority behind it, as the Church itself in no way denied. Only faith as the *sole* pillar of the edifice of salvation — that was not a position which a good Catholic, heir of an unbroken and authoritative tradition, could accept.

We must, if we would understand all that followed, hold to the view that bitter and tormenting doubts wrung Luther's soul for many years. By the time he became professor at Wittenberg he had begun to see the light, but his full position was not formulated till some time afterwards, in fact not till he had engaged in battle with the Church. It is highly characteristic that Luther found himself and grew to his full stature in the heat of conflict. Moreover, that the battle occurred at all, taking on something of the inevitableness of a natural event, was the result of his fiery personality, aided and abetted by his having achieved a personal religion, bringing him into so direct a relationship to God that the whole elaborate mediatory apparatus of the Church became a mere embarrassment. Luther was slow to see this sweeping consequence of his position, but he suspected it sufficiently to show signs of a growing impatience at any interference with the free flow of his spirit. *Implications of Luther's doctrine: faith and faith alone* Unescapably the time came when the Church, scenting an enemy, defended its ground. Thereupon his doubts, receiving wings from his wrath, brushed the clergy aside, only to find that behind the clergy rose the holy sacraments, with the administration of which the clergy was entrusted. We now begin to have an inkling of what it meant that so whole-hearted and uncompromising a character as Luther followed an individual line of development. He had, in opposition to the custom of his day, achieved a purely personal religion conferring the confident assurance of salvation through faith and faith alone; and with nothing but this conviction as his weapon he was gradually led to attack the majestic and historic edifice of the Church based on faith indeed but also on the equally significant foundation of clergy, sacraments, and works.

Luther was still far from seeing all the above implications of his position, he was still searching St. Augustine and St. Paul for their teaching about faith, when there occurred the event which flung him into the center of the world's interest and inaugurated the movement which Catholics call the Protestant revolt and Protestants the Reformation. *Luther challenges a vendor of indulgences* In 1517 a Dominican friar, Tetzel by name, appeared on the confines of Saxony to sell indulgences and Luther came forward to protest against the abuses with which they had become tainted. He showed his still conservative viewpoint in that he raised no objection against the ecclesiastical doctrines on which indulgences were based.

We have seen that indulgences were letters of pardon issued by the pope, and that, rightly or wrongly, the Germans had come to suspect that they were a financial device to minister to the scandalous luxury of the Roman court. Apparently Luther's protest against the indulgence hawked by Tetzel was mainly inspired by the report that among other exaggerations the Dominican did not scruple to lure purchasers by telling them that it was not only the penalty which was remitted but the sin itself. His protest took the form of ninety-five points or theses, which, in the scholastic manner still fashionable, he proposed to argue in learned debate before a university audience. **The reverberation of the ninety-five theses** Composed, according to usage, in Latin, they were affixed by him to the door of the castle church of Wittenberg on October 31, 1517. They produced a tremendous reverberation, were translated into German, and in a few weeks known throughout the land. Since they were, in the main, abstrusely theological, their popularity can be accounted for solely on the ground that they sounded an anti-papal note and therefore appealed to that anti-papal sentiment which, as we have seen, had procured a general lodgment in Germany.

That Luther was surprised by the tumult he had raised is certain, for he was still at the time a good son of the Church and not consciously opposed to the pope. His thoughts, born of keen spiritual **The critical period from 1517 to 1520** agony, had revolved solely about the question of salvation and had neither faced the many implications of his new convictions nor the purely historical issues involved in the evolution of the Church. But since the ninety-five theses loosed a torrent of discussion, he was swept off his feet, hurried into investigations he had hitherto neglected, and moved to broaden the basis of his criticism. The three years from 1517 to 1520 constitute an extraordinarily important interlude when there was still some hope that a compromise might be effected which would restrain the audacious friar from taking an irrevocable step. But Luther's fundamental impetuosity was as inimical to long drawn-out debate as to spineless formulas framed to skillfully evade the issue. Besides, the Catholics who broke into the discussion were as obstinate as he and, with flint striking flint, caused the sparks to fly in every direction. A debate, into which he was drawn at the university of Leipzig with a certain Dr. Eck (1519), proved particularly decisive for his revolutionary development, owing to the fact that during his preparations for the contest he arrived at the conclusion that the papacy was not evangelically instituted but the result of a gradual historic process. As for the pope, Leo X, his attitude toward the distant northern tempest was typical of the cultured Italian gentleman of the Renaissance: he mildly wondered why the faithful in Germany were showing such excitement over "a squabble of monks." Nevertheless, as head of the Church, he was sensitive to every attack upon its position and by characteristically cunning diplomacy tried to lure Luther to Rome, where he would have had him in his power. But the agents whom he dispatched to Germany were haughty and unskillful, and their attempts suffered shipwreck not only on Luther's unflinching stand but also on the resolution of his prince, the Elector Frederick of Saxony, to protect him to the utmost.

When, amid all these agitations, three years had passed, Luther had succeeded in clarifying his views and in a number of ringing pamphlets [2] boldly attacked the pope, the clergy, and the sacraments themselves. The bold step meant war, war to the The issue knife! Leo X did not misread the sign and, abandoning is war! futile negotiations, issued a bull declaring Luther a heretic and threatening him with the usual consequences unless he recanted. The friar met the challenge with a dramatic counter-blast. Amid a concourse of applauding Wittenbergers he consigned the papal judgment to the flames and to leave no doubt as to the revolutionary meaning of his act he threw in the books of Canon Law which recorded all the immunities and privileges accumulated by the Church in the Middle Age. The breach was complete. It remained to be seen for which side the German people would declare.

Germany had just passed through the throes of an imperial election. In January, 1519, the Emperor Maximilian had been gathered to his fathers, and after a particularly spirited contest, in which the kings of Spain, France, and England appeared The acces- as imperial candidates, the choice of the seven electors sion of fell on the king of Spain, who assumed the crown under Charles V the name of Emperor Charles V. But let no one imagine that Charles owed his election to his occupancy of the Spanish throne. It was due exclusively to his being the head of the house of Hapsburg and the most powerful prince of Germany. In the year 1520 he left Spain for the Low Countries to travel thence to Aachen, where he was crowned with the usual elaborate ceremony. Then he called a diet at the city of Worms on the Rhine. Many matters demanded his attention but all were overshadowed by the conflict which raged around Luther. The Wittenberg professor had just been condemned by the pope. It was incumbent on emperor and diet to declare their stand with reference to the papal sentence.

[2] These pamphlets, containing the gist of early Protestantism, are very important. They bore the titles: Address to the Christian Nobility of the German Nation; On the Babylonian Captivity of the Church; Concerning Christian Liberty. They have been made accessible in English by Wace and Buchheim under the title, Luther's Primary Works.

The sovereign who confronted his German subjects for the first time at Worms was a lad of but twenty-one years. He had passed his life in the Netherlands and in Spain, where he had been brought up **Charles** as a good Catholic who might acknowledge the existence **summons** of abuses in the Church, but who, in the main, gave it **Luther to** an unhesitating allegiance. Therefore he, personally, **Worms** was prepared to dispose of Luther without more ado. But there were certain considerations which could not be overlooked. So large a section of the German princes and people were secret or open supporters of Luther that to condemn him unheard might cause an armed insurrection. Accordingly, Charles agreed to have him summoned to Worms for a public hearing under a special pledge of safety. Luther's friends besought him not to walk into the lion's mouth, reminding him of the fate of Hus at Constance. "I would go even if there were as many devils there as tiles on the house-roofs," he answered. As the devil and his cohorts were to him not a figure of speech but a reality, it was a characteristically fearless reply. On April 17, 1521, he appeared before the diet.

The scene is one of those historical spectacles which dramatize a world conflict. The friar, whose audacity had given voice to the latent opposition of a people, was confronted with his supreme civil **Luther** judge, the emperor, who sat upon a throne encircled by **before the** a brilliant gathering of ambassadors, princes, and bishops. **diet** As he let his eye travel over the faces of the throng, he encountered all gradations of expression, ranging from deep devotion through indifference to fierce hatred. Would he recant the heresies he had uttered? Had he met this demand of the emperor, he might have won forgiveness and the fire he had lighted have been extinguished. But he insisted that he should be proved wrong by the words of Holy Writ. That was the crucial issue: for him the authority of the Bible had replaced the traditional authority of pope and Church. "Here I stand. I can not do otherwise. So help me God. Amen." If these were not his exact words, they concisely state that right of private judgment which he claimed and which was to become the common basis of every form of Protestantism. To cow this man was out of the question, especially as Worms was seething with his partisans. Permitted to depart in accordance with the imperial promise, he was seized on the highway by servants of his prince, the Elector Frederick, and carried secretly to the castle of Wartburg in the Thuringian forest. There let him lie concealed, was the thought of his protector, until the crisis be over and he might once more show himself without danger.

It did not take Charles long to come to a decision. He had nothing but abhorrence for a movement which threatened the spiritual authority of the Church and the unity of Christendom. Moreover, his attention at that moment was fixed not on Germany but on Italy, where the predominance won by his Spanish predecessors was again in question. In dealing with this sovereign we must never forget that he had interests *Luther condemned by imperial edict* in the most widely separated regions, in Spain, the Netherlands, Germany, Italy, and America. In Italy the king of France had recently renewed the Franco-Spanish struggle for ascendancy with the successful seizure of Milan (1515). From this vantage-point, from which he threatened the Spanish control of the peninsula, Charles was firmly resolved to oust him. Clearly in such an enterprise an alliance with the pope would prove helpful. But unless he gave support to the papal bull against Luther how could he hope for papal assistance against France? Accordingly, on May 26, 1521, Charles published the edict of Worms, which, not without a measure of deceit, he had wrung from the diet and which pronounced the ban of the empire against the heretic. In the hope that he had thus disposed of a dangerous religious crisis Charles turned his attention to other matters, more particularly to the French war and the reconquest of Milan.

But the Reformation had already acquired too great a momentum to be stopped by an imperial gesture. If Charles could have remained in Germany to see personally to the execution of his decree against Luther, or if the civil power in Germany had not substantially lain with the princes, who, from the nature of the case, were divided in their sympathies, the history of the Reformation might have been different. As it *The edict against Luther not executed* happened, Charles remained away from Germany for the next decade, and the princes and imperial cities, left to themselves, found agreement impossible in the face of the strong national support behind Luther. For to most of his countrymen he was since Worms a hero sent from heaven. Consequently the hostile decree remained a dead letter and the party of reform, encouraged by the vacillation of the central government, grew so strong that, by the time Charles saw fit to return to Germany, it could defy him as well as the pope.

It is important to understand what in the crucial decade of Charles's absence from Germany took place wherever the party of reform succeeded in gaining a foothold. To Lutheran enthusiasts

Religious changes effected by Lutheranism
it appeared imperative at a very early stage to proceed from opinion to action. The result was that some of the most familiar aspects of medieval Christianity began gradually to disappear. Monks and nuns renounced their vows, resumed their civil status, and in many cases married. Luther himself set an example by marrying (1525) Catherine von Bora, a former nun. Monastic and other ecclesiastical property was appropriated by the state and was devoted partly to the maintenance of the new religion, partly to the increase of the revenues of the prince. Further, the pope and hierarchy were set aside and their authority flouted, while in accordance with the evangelical tendency characteristic of the new doctrine many medieval practices such as indulgences, pilgrimages, worship of the Virgin and the saints were condemned as misleading works and abandoned. At the same time the religious service was materially altered. The impressive mass, conceived to be idolatrous, was more and more simplified until it had been stripped to the bare bones of a service composed of prayer, song, and sermon. Since the priesthood was no longer believed to be a privileged class, a necessary link between God and man, the communion in both bread and wine was conceded to the laity. Finally, Latin was driven from the service and replaced by German.

With an unparalleled ferment seizing on the whole country, visionaries and fanatics of every kind with a ready cure for the ailments of society rose to the surface and found willing converts. Not only

As the German kettle boils over Luther banks the fires
religious panaceas but political and social as well were shouted from every pulpit and platform. Such sweeping radicalism has manifested itself in connection with every great upheaval in history and has regularly proved the greatest enemy of the cause of moderate reform. As the alarmed Luther, confronted with these aberrations, deeply knew, it was moderate reform that he wanted, moderate *religious* reform; not the least hankering manifested itself in his mind in favor of the indiscriminate overthrow of the whole vast body of tradition. As he interpreted the grave crisis, to strive for the millenium here and now was to abandon the practical program of Christian reorganization and to invite certain shipwreck. Let us therefore admit that it was but natural that he should presently have put on the brakes and done

his best to defend himself against the imputation of being an anarchist by vigorously shaking off the extremists. In attempting to plumb his mind we should also remember that, overwhelmingly concerned with salvation, he refused to occupy himself for long with social and political problems and never acquired more than a meager understanding of them. His exclusively religious outlook made him desirous to carry through his movement by detaching it from every issue save his own and every leader save himself. It is possible that this sane if narrow decision saved the Reformation; but it is more than possible, it is highly probable, that Luther's extremely limited contacts with life helped sap the vigor of his movement by turning it too soon and too completely into the single channel of a reform of a moderate and exclusively religious character.

The first place at which the seething German kettle overflowed was at Wittenberg itself. Within a few months of Luther's condemnation at Worms this hearth of the reform movement threatened to pass over into the radical camp. Fanatics, calling themselves prophets, appeared in the town, inviting the people to rise in their might and break and burn the Catholic images and altars. Men of standing, including Carlstadt, one of Luther's colleagues on the Wittenberg faculty, did not scruple to join the disturbers. Luther lay concealed in the Wartburg, where he was turning his enforced leisure to account by the memorable task of translating the Bible into German; but the Wittenberg situation looked so serious that with his usual promptness he rushed into the arena and successfully rallied the people to his banner. The prophets fled, and though they continued their iconoclastic preachments elsewhere, Wittenberg, saved, became the citadel of the true, the moderate Lutheranism (1522). *[margin: Luther drives the prophets from Wittenberg]*

Simultaneously another revolution, involving a purely political and economic program, broke out among the petty knights of the Rhine region. This order of small landlords, theoretically directly under the emperor, had been ruined by the capitalistic development of the rising towns and was in consequence threatened with absorption by the more powerful princes. Resolved to utilize the general ferment to improve their status, they found an energetic leader in Franz von Sickingen and a literary champion with a really national outlook in Ulrich von Hutten. But, wretched medieval survivals with no footing in the modern world, the knights were, in spite of Hutten's enthusiasm, incapable of *[margin: Uprising of the Rhenish knights]* conceiving a program of national scope and fought only for their selfish ends. In a short war (1522–1523) they were crushed, not by the emperor but by the Rhenish princes, lay and ecclesiastical — an interesting and decisive indication of whither the German constitutional movement was tending.

Shortly after, a far greater disturbance than that of the knights shook the very foundations of society. Since the Lutheran ferment spread to every class it was clear that the humble tillers of the soil The rebel- would not be immune. Serfs, attached to the manors lion of the of the nobility and the Church, they had in recent dec- peasants ades frequently registered a protest against their hard lot by rising in insurrection. Not only had all their rebellions been cruelly suppressed, but their burdens had been multiplied by increased rents and services as well as through the seizure by the lords of the woods and pastures once owned by the villagers in common. With the expansion of trade characteristic of the Renaissance the old medieval simplicity was passing, and we need not think of the lords as necessarily harder of heart than their forebears if they tried to meet the higher cost of living by squeezing a larger return from their peasants. An economic adjustment attends every period of change, bringing an unusual pressure to bear on all classes alike. Such considerations do not alter the fact that the peasants dwelt in a deepening gloom, into which the wild hopes universally aroused by the Reformation fell like a ray of light. Not that the abused husbandmen responded particularly to the religious message of Luther, although it doubtlessly reached the hearts of many. Preëminently they were agitated by the conviction spread by innumerable visionaries of an era of social justice looming just beyond the horizon. In this mistaken hope they rose and armed themselves as best they could, first (1524) in the extreme south on the borders of Switzerland. Thence with surprising swiftness the revolt spread northward till all Germany between the lake of Constance and Thuringia was aflame. By the spring of 1525 armed hordes of peasants wandered over the land, killing the lords who ventured to resist them, burning castles and monasteries, and joyfully expecting the new age which was to rise phoenix-like from the ruins they had wrought.

Coolly considered, the great peasant insurrection was a midsummer madness and never had a chance of achieving success. The numerous bands of marauding rebels were uncoördinated; they were poorly armed; their leaders were insignificant men, all of them ignorant and deluded, some few vile and ready to betray the cause. They put forth several programs, some of which, like the famous Twelve Articles, demanded the restitution of the appropriated common lands, the abolition of excessive rents and services, and other perfectly reasonable items, while even the most extravagant were extravagant only for the sixteenth century and would sound like commonplaces on the lips of a present-day socialist. Having taken the road of force, the peasants were obliged to defeat the country's constituted authorities and at the same time persuade the alarmed urban classes that they possessed the constructive talent necessary to give the country a better organization. The test came when the outraged princes brought their forces into the field. The showing of the peasants was lamentable: unable to face the shock of arms, their phalanxes dissolved in a wild scramble for safety leaving the individuals to be butchered by the thousands by the ruthless conquerors. It has often been observed that no conflict unchains the beast in man more swiftly than the war of social classes. The hideous peasant war of 1525 is a case in point.

Ferocious suppression of the peasant revolt

Luther's attitude toward this great upheaval is illustrative of his determination to keep clear of extremes. While the peasant movement was still no more than the rumbling of a distant drum and before the era of violence had set in, he issued a pamphlet which was, in the main, a call to the lords to do justice to their offended serfs. But the battle once joined, a battle in which the peasants threatened the whole existing order of society, he sided with the princes without hesitation. If, in the light of his set purpose, such a decision was entirely comprehensible, it was unpardonable that in a second pamphlet on the peasant movement he should have given free rein to his hot temper and in language of unsurpassed coarseness have spurred on the princes, who certainly needed no spurring, to trample their adversaries in the dust. The tragic end of the peasant uprising stifled most of the visionary hopes entertained in connection with the Reformation. That in itself was perhaps no loss; but it was an irreparable injury to the general development of Germany that Luther, by tying his movement to the victorious chariot of the princes, broke with those popular forces which alone would have been able not only to renew Germany politically but also to assure the periodic freshening of the Reformation stream.

Luther against the peasants

While Germany was seething with these troubles, its absentee ruler, Charles V, was occupied with his many other interests and chiefly with the war with France. In fact, war with France was a leading feature of his reign and long prevented him from giving more than casual attention to the German problem. There were in Charles's time four wars between France and Spain, all concerned with the control of Italy. These wars occurred as follows: first war, 1521–1526; second war, 1526–1529; third war, 1536–1538; fourth war, 1542–1544. Toward the end of his life Charles conducted a fifth war against France which will be treated in due time and which differs from the others inasmuch as it was precipitated more particularly by the German situation.

The four wars of Charles V with Francis I

The first two wars were really a single war of almost a decade since they were broken by only a short and insincere peace. The military developments need not detain us. Suffice it that, in spite of all that King Francis I could do, the struggle went steadily in Charles's favor. In 1525, at Pavia, in northern Italy, a great battle was fought which proved a French disaster and led to the capture of the king. He was carried a prisoner to Madrid and there signed a peace (1526), by which he surrendered all his pretentions to Italy and, in addition, ceded the duchy of Burgundy, once held by Charles's Burgundian ancestors, to his Spanish rival. Released on the strength of a solemn oath that he would execute the peace, Francis none the less renewed the struggle as soon as he had crossed the Pyrenees and again touched the soil of France.

Defeat and capture of the French king at Pavia

The French king was encouraged to take this stand by the sudden friendliness of Pope Clement VII, Henry VIII of England, and other lesser potentates, chiefly of Italy. These rulers, alarmed by the completeness of Charles's victory, feared his universal ascendancy and swung instinctively to the weaker side to redress the balance. But the allies were neither energetic nor harmonious and failed to disturb Charles's grip upon the situation. Therefore the emperor was free to single out the vacillating pope for vengeance. In the spring of 1527 a combined army of Spaniards and Germans descended upon the Eternal City and took it by assault. The Spaniards were mercenaries, the Germans Lutherans, and between them the famished hordes, breaking all bonds of discipline, put the ancient

The pope turns against Charles and is punished with the sack of Rome

capital of Christendom to such a sack as no words can adequately describe. To superstitious Protestants the catastrophe took on the character of a divine punishment visited on the papacy for a long succession of misdeeds, while even faithful Catholics were inclined to regard the cruel pillage as a not unfitting conclusion to the selfish political game so passionately pursued by the whole group of Renaissance popes.

As for Clement VII, one of the least worthy sons of the Florentine house of Medici and as unspiritual a man as ever wore the triple crown of St. Peter, the chief thought that came to him as, from the castle of St. Angelo, he stared at the ruins wrought by The peace his policy, was that he was defeated and must come to of Cambray, terms with the all-powerful Charles. He opened negotia- 1529 tions, and although his allies continued the conflict yet a while, a general peace was at length arranged by the treaty of Cambray (1529). In return for a reconfirmation of the French retirement from Italy coupled with the payment of a money indemnity, Charles agreed to give up his claim to the duchy of Burgundy. Italy was his: that was the upshot of the ten years' struggle.

In the very year of the peace Charles visited the peninsula in order to set the Italian house in order and had the satisfaction of being fawned upon by the pope together with all the company of the petty princes as master of the land. With Naples Charles, and Milan definitely Spanish and secured by Spanish gar- master of risons, he straddled the peninsula like a colossus and over- Italy, is awed the pigmy powers at his feet. True, whenever emperor at France renewed the ambition which first drew her to Bologna Italy, the pope and his Italian compeers did not fail to rattle their chains in sign of mute sympathy, but it is clear that by 1529 fate had conclusively pronounced in favor of Spain. To put the final touch upon his victory, Charles, yielding to medieval precedent, had himself crowned emperor by the pope. The great pomp occurred at Bologna, in the month of February, 1530.

Encouraged by an unequaled triumph, Charles, after an absence of nine years, resolved once more to look into the affairs of Germany. For almost a decade the policy formulated by the condemnation of Luther at Worms had remained unfulfilled. In the The affairs emperor's absence the power in Germany indubitably of Germany rested with the princes, and if they chose to connive at 1521–1530 ecclesiastical changes there was no one to say them nay. In a diet held at Speier, in 1526, the paralysis of the central authority regarding religion was correctly expressed in a decree which permitted the estates to act in matters of faith as each could answer to God and to the emperor. It was a qualified recognition of the new Lutheran church. Three years later (1529) Charles had become reconciled with the pope, and with his fortunes mounting to the zenith, sent a peremptory command to a new diet, again convened at Speier, to revoke the concession of 1526. As the Catholic princes still commanded an overwhelming majority, the behest was complied with and Lutheranism outlawed. But the adherents of the new faith were no longer minded to yield, even at the risk of the emperor's displeasure. They drew up a document which declared with unusual fervor that their duty to God and conscience took precedence over their duty to their sovereign. On the strength of this ringing protest the reformers were for the first time welded into a party under the name, destined loosely to embrace all groups which successively fell away from the papacy, of Protestants.

Such was the decidedly taut situation which Charles confronted at a diet, called to meet him at the city of Augsburg (1530). Though his mind was even more completely made up than at Worms, he was, as then, persuaded that he would have to grant to the opposition the courtesy of a hearing. Asked to put their position in writing, the Protestants commissioned Melanchthon, a friend and fellow-worker of Luther's but a man of a more gentle and conciliatory disposition, to formulate the beliefs which represented the crystallization of opinion thus far attained by the secession from the Catholic Church. In a document which received the name of the Confession of Augsburg Melanchthon made a moderate and even conservative statement of the new tenets. So greatly did it appeal to his brothers in the faith that it became and has remained to this day the fundamental creed of the Lutheran church. True to his assumed role of judge, Charles listened to the Protestant defense and then, supported by the Catholic majority, firmly announced his decision. The innovators were given a respite of six months before action would be taken to bring them back by force into the Catholic fold. Would the movement collapse in the face of this threat? Thoroughly aroused, leading delegates of the Protestant estates called a meeting at the little town of Schmalkalden in Thuringia and organized a league for mutual protection (1531). It

Renewed condemnation of Lutheranism at the diet of Augsburg, 1530

meant the resolution to stand by the Protestant cause, if necessary by meeting force with force.

But just as a religious war seemed unavoidable, an event happened which adjourned it. In 1529 the Turks, who had established a vast Mohammedan power in the Near East on the ruins of the Byzantine Empire and other Christian states, had, in pushing west- *Civil war* ward up the Danube, reached the city of Vienna. Only *adjourned* the heroic defense made by the citizens themselves had saved the capital of Austria and eastern gate of Germany from capture. But, nothing daunted, Sultan Solyman resolved to renew the attack, and the rumor of a new and vaster Turkish expedition turned the concordant thoughts of emperor, princes, and people to the basin of the Danube. In need of Protestant support, Charles decided to adjourn action against the heretics and in a truce signed at Nürnberg (1532) agreed to refer the religious differences to a General Council of the Church. Such a Council had long appeared to him as the likeliest means of restoring the unity of Christendom, especially as the Protestants had frequently declared and now repeated that they were prepared to submit their case to this ultimate court of appeal.

Marching against the Turks with the forces of a united Germany behind him, Charles was enabled to make a display of power before which the Turks fell back without venturing a battle. On his return he found other interests of his wide dominions demanding *Charles's* his attention. Spain and his Italian provinces had long *many* suffered from the depredations of the Mohammedan pi- *political* rates established along the Barbary coast of Africa and *difficulties* encouraged by their powerful co-religionists at the other *keep him* end of the Mediterranean, the Turks. It was indispensable *crushing* to take up the problem of their punishment if Charles *Luther-* wished to keep the southern waterways open to Christian *anism* commerce. But once committed to an attack on the pestiferous corsairs of Tunis and Algiers, he was involved in enterprises requiring many years of labor and engulfing untold quantities of ships, men, and money. Besides, the slightest African mishap was sure to be taken advantage of by his enemies, Francis I and Sultan Solyman, either singly or in conjunction. To an occasional association, nay, even to a firm and lasting alliance with the infidel Turks, the French king had not the slightest objection, provided it would put a quietus on his hated rival of Spain. Thus, to the scandal of old-fashioned Christians a Franco-Turkish alliance, aimed at the emperor, was concluded and became operative in 1535. When in this year Charles returned from Tunis, where he had scored a great but temporary triumph over the confederated pirates, he encountered a diplomatic situation which developed into another French war (1536–38). No sooner had this been settled than he was obliged to launch another naval expedition against the Algerine corsairs, who, as usual, were strengthened by aid from Sultan Solyman. And, finally, from 1542 to 1544 he was obliged to fight a fourth war with Francis I. This war, concluded by the treaty of Crespy, served but to confirm that Spanish hold on Italy which a lifetime of effort on the part of Francis I had not succeeded in shaking.

This rapid summary of wars which shook the whole structure of Europe will once more make clear that Charles, owing to the vast extent of his dominions, had too many irons in the fire. He was an
Charles again faces the Lutheran issue intelligent and conscientious ruler, rarely restrained for so powerful a man. But though he had a temperamental preference for adjourning an important decision, to a program once adopted he held fast with the silent stubbornness of a tenacious nature. This trait will explain why, on his return to Germany in 1544, when, much as in 1530, he was for the moment disembarrassed of all his other difficulties, he took up the Lutheran schism, resolved by hook or by crook to put it at last out of the world. By the agreement of 1532 the threatening religious war had been avoided by referring the contentious issues to a General Council of the Church, still considered, as throughout the Middle Age, to be the highest ecclesiastical tribunal. Since 1532 Charles had been tireless in his effort to persuade the pope to convene such an assembly. The Holy Father, firmly opposed to a parliament only too likely to encroach on his prerogative, had employed every diplomatic device at his disposal to block the imperial request. The African campaigns, the French wars, even the Schmalkadic League were welcomed by the pope as checks on the too universal power of the emperor, but by 1545 Charles had triumphed over all obstacles and Pope Paul III, bowing his head, summoned a Council to meet in the Alpine city of Trent. It was too late. By 1545 the Protestants had passed beyond the stage of experimentation and were no longer willing to find their way back to mother Church on any terms. In the face of their refusal to recognize the Council, Charles, who had really never expected any other result, resolved to settle the issue on the battlefield.

Just before the outbreak of hostilities Luther died (February, 1546). Believing that God in His wisdom ordered the affairs of men and yet denying that He ordered them through the mediation of the pope, Luther had been brought to the belief that the Lord's highest earthly representatives were the various civil monarchs and that obedience to the particular ruler God had given him was every Christian's plain and undebatable duty. This doctrine of civil submission, as it has been called, made Luther a very uncertain supporter of the Schmalkaldic League formed to protect the new faith, if necessary by force of arms. However, with the aid of a little casuistry, his favorite political doctrine could be given an anti-imperial turn. By representing the true civil government in Germany to be vested not in the emperor but in the princes, it was possible for Luther to arrive at the position that under certain circumstances war against the emperor was justified. Inclined to quibble where the party interest was concerned, without a trace of talent for politics, and subordinating all life to the concepts of theology, the Wittenberg reformer has in these untheological times lost something of the glamour which he possessed for the earlier generations of Protestants. Nevertheless his simplicity and rude, vibrant sincerity still set him apart among the born leaders of men, lending him an authority which is heightened by his native gift for music and poetry. He was no mean performer on the lute, while the hymns which he contributed to the new church have a solemnity and strength unsurpassed among Protestant productions. We can now see that much about Luther was distinctly medieval, but, even so, his contribution to modern mentality is undeniable, for the appeal from pope and Church to the higher authority of the Bible was tantamount to the assertion, in matters of faith and conduct, of the right of private judgment. True, this right was not consistently asserted, but, once given to the winds, it could not again be recalled. Slowly gaining supporters, it served to fortify that individualism which was born in the Renaissance and which in the course of time led to the challenge not only of the universal Church but of every kind of traditional authority.

The first war of religion in Germany, usually called the Schmalkaldic war, broke out in the year of Luther's death (1546). The Protestant forces, commanded by the leading evangelical princes, John Frederick of Saxony and Philip of Hesse, acted without plan or energy. An additional difficulty resulted from an internal Prot-

[margin note: Final estimate of Luther]

estant division. While some princes weakly remained neutral,
Maurice of Saxony, a cousin of the Elector John Frederick, actually
turned traitor and, for the price of his relative's electorate, gave
The
Schmal-
kaldic war,
1546–47
military help to Charles. In consequence Charles was
able to outmanoeuver his opponents and to end the war
with one stroke at the battle of Mühlberg (April, 1547),
in which he crushed the Saxon army and took the elector
himself prisoner. At once all resistance broke down, leaving the
emperor master of the situation.

What now? Charles's plan was to reëstablish the unity of the
Church, but, though victorious, he was wise enough to see that he
would have to proceed with a certain moderation. He therefore had
German
rising and
defeat of
Charles
passed by the diet an ecclesiastical document, called the
Interim, which, while asserting every essential Catholic
position, contained a few concessions to the Protestant
viewpoint. This he imposed as law on all the Protestant
estates of Germany until the Council of Trent, which, under orders
from the pope, had adjourned its sessions, should reconvene and
render final, authoritative sentence. Imposed by force, the Interim
gave the false impression of an achieved reconciliation. Under the
surface, however, a sense of wrong filled the Lutherans and, slowly
mounting, became an irresistible force. Maurice of Saxony, made
elector in place of his deposed cousin, was as unscrupulously eager
to keep his booty as he had been to acquire it. A deft intriguer, he
secretly united the disgruntled Protestants around his person and did
not hesitate to spin his web as far as the court of France, where
Henry II now held sway. It redounded to the advantage of the
able plotter that Charles in the course of his reign had identified
himself more and more with his kingdom of Spain, becoming in
essence a Spanish national sovereign. While this made it impossible
for him to project himself sympathetically into the German situation,
it had the further drawback of alienating his German subjects and
inclining them more and more to look upon him as a foreign inter-
loper. Blinded by his Spanish outlook to the vigor of the national
resistance, he pursued a policy calculated to exalt his prerogative at
the expense of the estates and bound, in consequence, to arouse the
hostility of the Catholic as well as of the Lutheran princes. By the
year 1552 he stood practically alone in Germany with the princes
solidly arrayed against him. Taking the lead among them, the wily
Maurice delayed to drop the mask until he had received the full

assurance of French support. Then he pounced suddenly on Charles, obliging him to flee for his life southward over the Alps. Almost over night and without a battle the sweeping victory of 1547 had been turned into an equally sweeping defeat.

Reluctantly admitting his discomfiture, Charles empowered his brother Ferdinand to sign the preliminary Peace of Passau (1552), which permitted the reëstablishment of Protestantism on the pre-war basis. Then, with the German civil war composed, he turned with all his strength on France. Henry II, coöperating with the Protestant leaders, had invaded Germany from the west and seized the three bishoprics of Metz, Toul, and Verdun. Metz was a fortress on the Moselle and the key to western Germany. As, in Charles's view, this could never be left in French hands, he organized an expedition which tried to retake Metz but failed (January, 1553). France was not to be dislodged from the new vantage ground. The conquest affected in 1552 marks the beginning of an era of French encroachments on German territory destined to continue uninterruptedly for several centuries. *The Peace of Passau and the attempt to retake Metz*

His failure at Metz, taken in connection with the collapse of his German program, broke Charles's spirit. He retired from Germany, first to the Netherlands and thence to Spain, with the fixed, pessimistic resolve to throw off the burdens of office. Not till 1556 did he fully carry out his purpose; but from the time of his departure from Germany he left the conduct of German affairs entirely in the hands of his younger brother Ferdinand, who, more than two decades before, *Charles abandons the conduct of German affairs* had been designated by the electors as his successor in the imperial office. The first task confronting Ferdinand was to convert the preliminary arrangements of Passau into a definitive religious peace. At a diet held at Augsburg in 1555 this was accomplished in the famous document known as the Peace of Augsburg.

To the philosophically minded student perhaps the most memorable feature of the Peace of Augsburg is that it marks the abandonment of the unity of the Church, the central concept of medieval Christianity. By the side of the old Church the law henceforth recognized a heretical departure from Catholicism called Lutheranism and theologically defined by the Confession of Augsburg of 1530. To the student of German politics it may seem equally important that the legalization of the new faith *The Peace of Augsburg, 1555* signified a fresh victory of the territorial principle over the central power. It will be recalled that when Lutheranism first arose there was no question but that it belonged to the province of Charles to deal with it, in coöperation of course with the diet. But the princes had shielded the movement, and when Charles failed in his effort to suppress it, he thereby disastrously lowered the imperial prestige. The proof is furnished by the fact that the Peace of Augsburg declared that religion was primarily a territorial and not a national matter; and it confirmed this principle by giving to every estate the right to choose between the two legal religions and to impose its choice upon its subjects.

Clothed in the Latin formula, *cujus regio ejus religio* (religion pertains to the territorial government), this privilege of choice between two legal religions must not be confused with modern individual toleration with which it has nothing to do. The conceded **No** choice, narrow to begin with, pertained only to rulers **toleration** and not to their subjects, who, if they were Catholics, **in the** might be evicted from Protestant regions and vice versa. **modern** Indeed a fresh wave of intolerance may be said to have **sense** inundated Europe with the coming of the Reformation, since the theological fury of the Lutherans reacted on the Catholics and made them more rigidly doctrinal than they had been in the immediately preceding centuries. It would be difficult to prove that Lutheranism or any other form of Protestantism directly and intentionally promoted toleration in the modern sense; and yet it is clear that indirectly Protestantism helped considerably to bring about the triumph of this precious principle, since by emphasizing the right of private judgment it tended so greatly to multiply dissident faiths that in the end the idea of a uniformity enforced by penalties had to be given up as unrealizable. In 1555 individual toleration was still so far from the comprehension of men that not a voice was raised in its behalf.

With Lutheranism legalized it was easy to settle the question of former ecclesiastical property within the Lutheran territories. To all such property appropriated at the date of the treaty of Passau **Ambiguities** (1552) the Church was obliged to surrender title. But **of the peace** as nothing was said concerning property in Lutheran **of 1555** states which might be seized after 1552, there was the prospect of renewed wrangling wherever the Lutherans took over Catholic lands which for one reason or another had thus far been spared. A much more serious ambiguity marked the settlement of the issue of the prince-bishops. A prince-bishop was a bishop who was also a temporal ruler, and backward Germany was burdened with a goodly number of these feudal survivals. With regard to them the Lutherans contended that they were to have the usual right of choice between Catholicism and Lutheranism, while the most the Catholics would concede was the right of choice for their own persons. As, in the Catholic view, the bishoprics themselves were inalienably Catholic, the bishop who turned Protestant was at once to resign in order to permit a Catholic successor to be appointed in his place. This view was laid down in an article of the peace called the Ecclesiastical Reservation; and although the Protestants clamorously voiced their objection, it ended by being incorporated in the treaty. Since within a few years after the Peace of Augsburg had been signed a number of bishoprics, in spite of the Ecclesiastical Reservation, passed into Protestant hands, the Catholics nursed a serious and fairly justified grievance against their rivals. This and other difficulties finally led to the renewal of the religious struggle. Instead of being a peace, as it claimed to be, the Augsburg agreement settled nothing satisfactorily and was at best a truce.

Charles V saved himself the humiliation of putting his signature to the Peace of Augsburg by abdicating the crown, a step which, long meditated, he finally took in 1556. Two years later the man who had overshadowed Europe died, a modest recluse, in the cell of a Spanish monastery. *Sic transit gloria mundi*. Ever since Charles's accession to the empire his brother Ferdinand had exercised rule in the strictly Austrian lands; and as early as 1530 he had been named as Charles's successor to the empire. Thus Ferdinand became the founder of a second, a younger Hapsburg line, established in the German provinces of the house. The older line was continued by Charles's son, Philip, who was endowed with Spain (and her colonies), the Netherlands, and the Italian possessions. Henceforth until the extinction (1700) of Philip's progeny, we have to reckon with a Spanish and an Austrian branch of the house of Hapsburg.

Division of Charles's heritage

REFERENCES

C. H. HAYES, *Political and Social History of Modern Europe*, I, pp. 112–138
E. F. HENDERSON, *Short History of Germany*, I, chs. 10–15
Cambridge Modern History, I, chs. 16, 17, vol. II, chs. 4–8

W. Walker, *The Reformation*, chs. 3, 5

P. Smith, *Age of the Reformation*, chs. 1, 2; *Erasmus; Life and Times of Martin Luther*

T. M. Lindsay, *History of the Reformation*, I, pp. 189–258

E. M. Hulme, *Renaissance and Reformation*, chs. 12–14

E. Emerton, *Erasmus*

A. C. McGiffert, *Luther, the Man and his Work*

H. Boehmer, *Luther in the Light of Recent Research*

J. Koestlin, *Life of Martin Luther*

H. Grisar, *Luther and Lutheranism*

J. Janssen, *History of the German People* (a Catholic view), vol. III

E. Armstrong, *Charles V*

J. N. Figgis, *From Gerson to Grotius*, ch. 3

J. W. Richard, *Philip Melanchthon*

F. Schevill, *History of the Balkan Peninsula*, chs. 12–14

E. Troeltsch, *Protestantism and Progress*

J. S. Schapiro, *Social Reform and the Reformation*

H. C. Lea, *History of Auricular Confession and Indulgences*

CHAPTER VI

THE SPREAD OF THE REFORMATION AND THE COUNTER-REFORMATION OF THE CATHOLIC CHURCH

The movement of protest and revolt inaugurated by Luther spread rapidly through the northern, the Teutonic, area of Europe and even made threatening inroads on the Latin countries, Spain, Italy, and more particularly, France. This startling phenomenon may be accepted as proof that the cry for reform of the Church was more or less universal. However, no matter where the Protestant movement made its appearance, it regularly met with resistance, though of a varying intensity. In some countries, such as Italy and Spain, it was promptly and utterly suppressed. In others, such as France, it waxed strong enough to oblige the monarch to come to terms with it, while in still others it won the civil government to its side and completely replaced the old faith. We shall now follow the movement of reform on its journey through western Europe, prepared to take particular note of the new aspects it assumed due either to local conditions or to the influence of a strong personality, and ending our survey with a scrutiny of the effect on the Roman Church of the successful attack on its universal dominion.

The Reformation invades western Europe

Nowhere was the success of the Reformation more sweeping than in the Scandinavian north. Toward the end of the Middle Age the three Scandinavian powers, Denmark, Norway, and Sweden had become united under one king by virtue of the celebrated Union of Kalmar (1397). The concentration was more effective in name than in fact, since the king's residence in Copenhagen gave the government a Danish slant which aroused a frequent resistance in Norway and an almost uninterrupted opposition in Sweden. When, in the sixteenth century, King Christian II tried to reduce the recalcitrant Swedes by force of arms, he excited a revolution (1521) which, under the capable guidance of a Swedish nobleman known to fame as Gustavus Vasa, was crowned with complete success. In 1523 Gustavus Vasa was

Sweden breaks away from the Scandinavian union

invited by a meeting of the Swedish estates to assume the kingship in place of the deposed Christian II. He thus founded, together with the independence of his country, a royal house, the house of Vasa, destined to be identified with some of the most brilliant pages of Swedish history. Norway made no serious effort to follow the example set by its eastern neighbor. In fact, it fell even more completely than before under Danish rule, continuing in this state of subjection until the beginning of the nineteenth century.

Although the Swedish war for independence had nothing whatever to do with the Reformation, the disturbance which it caused throughout the Baltic area greatly favored the spread of Protestant opinions. Swedish and Danish students, returning from Wittenberg, preached the Lutheran innovations to the citizens of the larger towns and before long members of the two reigning houses and many leaders of the nobility as well fell under the influence of the new teachings. While it would be invidious to deny that conviction played a considerable part in these conversions, indubitably greed and ambition were by no means negligible factors. As in Germany, the sovereign who adopted Lutheranism stood to gain the immense Catholic properties, to which he would automatically fall heir in case Catholicism was proscribed. Since neither the newly fledged king of Sweden nor his Danish contemporary boasted other than meager and uncertain revenues, the temptation of each was necessarily great to strengthen his position by absorption of the landed wealth of the clergy. An element not to be overlooked was the envy and even hatred which the Church had excited throughout the impoverished north on the score of an excessive opulence and display. Consequently a policy of clerical spoliation was likely to meet with considerable popular approval, especially if the powerful nobility were won for the project by the shrewd proffer of a share in the booty.

The Scandinavian social-political situation favors Protestantism

These statements present no more than a very generalized picture of the politico-religious agitation astir in Scandinavia in the crucial decades during which Lutheranism gained an ineradicable foothold in Germany. It would hardly seem to have been so much a question in the Scandinavian countries of an irresistible popular movement as of revolutionary measures enthusiastically championed by a group of genuine religious converts and resolutely carried through by an interested ruling class. Admittedly the awakening national sentiment con-

The Scandinavian countries join the Lutheran camp

tributed to the relatively easy success of Protestantism, for, here as elsewhere, a native church divested of foreign influences made a mighty appeal to emotions deep-seated in every human breast. In sum, as early as 1527 Lutheranism had become effectively established as the state church of Sweden; and in the course of the succeeding decade Denmark with dependent Norway definitely broke with Rome by bringing its religious life into conformity with the Confession of Augsburg. Scandinavia — Sweden, Denmark, Norway — represents the one considerable conquest made by Lutheranism outside of Germany.

Turning next to Switzerland, we must, in order to grasp the crisis created by the Reformation, have at least a general knowledge of the political situation. The Alpine region familiar to us as Switzerland was in the Middle Age an integral part of Germany Origin of (the Holy Roman Empire). The sturdy peasants and Swiss independence herdsmen of the almost inaccessible inner valleys had always maintained a considerable measure of Germanic independence and naturally offered resistance when, in the course of the thirteenth century, the neighboring count of Hapsburg attempted to oppress them with dues and subject them to a typical feudal rule. In 1291 the men of the three cantons, Schwyz, Uri, and Unterwalden, surrounding the picturesque lake of Lucerne, formed a defensive alliance and with their solid peasant masses heroically and repeatedly beat off the onslaughts of the feudal hosts led against them by their enemy, the count of Hapsburg. In later generations their surprising victories crystallized in stirring legends, which, connected with such leaders as William Tell and Arnold Winkelried, still have the power to move the human heart. Victories and legends alike have served as a nursery of that liberty with which the fascinating story of Swiss independence begins and around which all its succeeding chapters are woven. For over two hundred years the house of Hapsburg clung to its dream of conquest, only to have it shattered on something stronger than dream, on the resolute will of the men of the mountains to be free. As late as the last decade of the fifteenth century Emperor Maximilian mobilized the whole imperial power in order to enforce the claim inherited by him in his capacity of count of Hapsburg; but this final effort too proved vain and in a new treaty signed at Basel in 1499, he was forced to acknowledge the freedom of the Swiss not only from the house of Hapsburg but to all intents also from the Holy Roman Empire.

The success of the three original cantons fired the enthusiasm of their neighbors and presently prompted the adjoining communities of peasants, as well as the two large towns of Zurich and Bern with The Swiss their dependent villages, to apply for admission to the form a loose league. There thus arose the Swiss Confederation, includ- federation ing before the last struggle with Emperor Maximilian as many as ten cantons and mounting to thirteen on the eve of the Reformation. However, the new and growing state never got beyond the phase of a loose association chiefly for defense against present and prospective enemies. The central agency of the Confederation was a diet composed of representatives from the thirteen cantons and strictly limited to the right of discussing peace and war owing to the fact that the strong passion of the local governments for independence would not permit them to divest themselves of their traditional powers. On this feeble framework the very successes of the Confederation put an almost impossible burden. In the course of their many victories the Swiss had conquered from the Hapsburgs and other feudal lords considerable territories, called common bailiwicks, which it fell to the lot of the Confederation to administer. But how could so weak a government maintain its rule in the common bailiwicks if ever there arose even a slight difference of opinion; and how could it possibly survive the buffeting of a fierce religious storm?

The test of the Swiss union came with the Reformation, first championed in Switzerland by a native son, Ulrich Zwingli by name, who always maintained that he had arrived at his religious opinions Ulrich independently of Luther. Zwingli was born on January 1, Zwingli 1484, in a village not far from the lake of Constance, and was therefore only a few weeks younger than the stormy petrel of Wittenberg. He came of an influential burgher family and received an excellent schooling which he crowned by attending the universities of Vienna and Basel. In both of these institutions humanism had come to the fore and Zwingli gave himself not only to the study of the classics but quite as enthusiastically, in accordance with good Erasmian precedent, to the mastery of the sources of the Christian faith. Ordained a priest in 1506, he was launched on his career by having the small parish of Glarus committed to his care. An even, balanced temper saved him from the religious crisis that troubled the youth of Luther and gave him a joyous confidence in the intellectual promises of humanism. At the same time, in his capacity

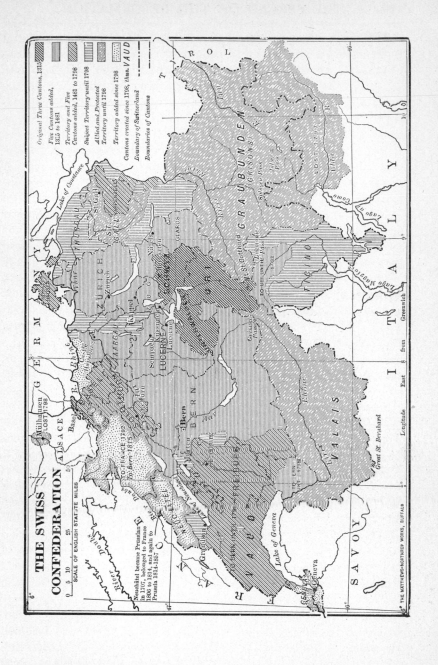

THE SWISS
CONFEDERATION

SCALE OF ENGLISH STATUTE MILES
0 5 10   25

Original Three Cantons, 1315
Five Cantons added, 1315 to 1481
Territory and Five Cantons added, 1481 to 1798
Subject Territory until 1798
Allied and Protected Territory until 1798
Cantons created since 1798, thus VAUD
Boundary of Switzerland
Boundaries of Cantons

Neuchâtel became Prussian in 1707, belonged to France 1806 to 1814, and again to Prussia 1814-1857.

THE MATTHEWS-NORTHRUP WORKS, BUFFALO

of free-born Swiss, he made acquaintance with the democratic system of government, becoming imbued with that virile patriotism which is the product of political responsibility.

Humanism and democracy, conceived as twin lode-stars, shaped Zwingli's labors and determined his fate. They explain why he began his public career not as a religious but as a social reformer intent on persuading his countrymen to break with that mercenary system of warfare by virtue of which they sold their bodies to the highest European bidder. He wanted his people to be too proud to fight for any but a national cause. So far as ecclesiastical abuses were concerned, he was, like Erasmus, content to drive them from the world by ridicule. Suddenly, around 1519, he swung his concentrated attention to religious reform, moved more perhaps than he could ever be brought to admit by the example of Luther. Once embarked on his new course, he took over practically all the doctrinal positions of his Saxon contemporary. However, when it came to the problem of ecclesiastical organization he followed a wholly independent line. We have seen that when in Germany the rule of the Church by pope and clergy was rejected, the control of the new, the Lutheran church was vested in the princes for the simple reason that they represented the existing civil power. As a result the Lutheran church became identified with and subservient to the secular lords, the princes. In Switzerland, where the civil power was exercised by magistrates elected by the people, a new and Reformed church would have to operate under the established authorities subject to the provision of as broad a measure of self-government for the individual religious communities as might prove workable. To this system Zwingli, the born republican, subscribed enthusiastically, thus favoring a form of church government much more responsive to popular currents than that of Germany. From his general position it also followed that Zwingli, far from feeling any aversion for politics as Luther did, regarded their practice not only as the plain duty of the citizen but as the necessary condition of a healthy and successful religious transformation.

Zwingli, humanist and democrat, adopts religious reform

As already said, Zwingli did not actively take up religious reform till 1519, in which year he was called to the city of Zurich, the most vigorous and thriving community of the whole Confederation, to take pastoral charge of the central church, the Great Minster. Luther had recently hurled his bolt against indulgences and Zwingli, taking the

Zwingli brings the Reformation to Zurich

same ground, was, exactly like the German friar, soon moved to broaden his criticism. In a surprisingly short time he had freed himself from the bonds of tradition and, breaking every connection with Rome, steered straight at independence. By 1525 his persuasive tongue had so completely swept the Zurich townsmen off their feet that he was enabled to set up his Reformed church with the consent and under the protection of the town council.

That, administratively, the Zwinglian church was to the Lutheran church just emerging in Germany as republicanism is to monarchy has already been remarked; let us note that, in point of doctrine, Zwingli, the two faiths, in spite of a general agreement, exhibited Luther, and slight, though by no means negligible, differences. The the Lord's most important variation unquestionably regarded the Supper Holy Eucharist or Lord's Supper. To the Catholic Church the Holy Eucharist had become the central mystery of Christianity and Luther, after first questioning the Catholic teaching, had in his conservative way ended by reverting to it. The orthodox position briefly was that the bread and wine of the service are changed into the actual body and blood of Christ by a miraculous process called transsubstantiation. True, Luther somewhat modified the traditional teaching, but his doctrine, usually called consubstantiation, hardly, except for professional theologians, differed by a hair's breadth from the Catholic position. To a certain rationalist tendency in Zwingli, a tendency which prompted him to test everything by the evidence of the senses, transsubstantiation and its little Lutheran brother, consubstantiation, were of a piece with every other medieval superstition, and he contemptuously tossed them on the scrap-heap together with fasts, pilgrimages, worship of the saints, and other so-called works. So sweeping an elimination of mystery from life and faith enraged Luther, who, miles removed from rationalism, had not even identified himself with Erasmian humanism, except where its positions happened to accord with the deep, religious demands of his nature.

It was natural that so long as Protestantism was weak and exposed to attack efforts should be made to draw the Lutheran and Zwinglian forces into an alliance. In 1529 when Charles V, having just brought The his war in Italy to a triumphant conclusion, was preparing Marburg to return to Germany to stamp out heresy by force, the conference outlook for the reformers became suddenly very black. In consequence Philip of Hesse, a Lutheran leader endowed with political understanding, urged the closing of the Protestant ranks, and as a preliminary measure brought Luther and Zwingli together in a conference at his city of Marburg in order to persuade them to iron out their doctrinal differences. Matters went smoothly enough until the Lord's Supper was broached. On this rock the meeting suffered shipwreck for the reason that Luther would not make the least concession to Zwingli's rationalism, and Zwingli, for his part, though ready to retain the Lord's Supper as a feature of his church service, refused to regard it other than as a purely symbolic act commemorative of an actual occurrence recorded in the gospels. Thus on the theological inflexibility of the two Protestant champions the plan of consolidating their movements came to naught. It was a piece of good luck that Charles, on coming to Germany, found himself diverted from his purpose by unforeseen circumstances, chiefly connected with the Turks, and that on this account he was obliged to adjourn his slaying of the serpent of heresy. But the disagreement between Luther and Zwingli, because the modern mind is inclined to regard it as mere hair-splitting, deserves an additional word of elucidation. The medieval development had identified the Church with sublime mysteries which, pouring an extraordinary glamour around life, had converted the individual existence, as has been aptly said, into a Christian epic. A humanism, inclining toward a cold, rationalist outlook, might eventually succeed in finding new and more acceptable formulas of living than those upheld by the Church, but it was highly improbable that mankind would suddenly and of one accord surrender a familiar and cherished body of traditions in exchange for an invitation to fare forth on an uncharted sea. Luther's position was evidence that great masses of men would long continue to value the emotional exaltations of faith above the chill satisfactions of reason.

From Zurich, its center, the Zwinglian movement spread into the adjoining Swiss areas, particularly into the towns which, here as elsewhere, proved to be the chief carriers of Protestantism. When Bern adopted his cause (1528), it looked to the sanguine Zwingli as if all Switzerland must ultimately fall like ripe fruit into his lap. But the five forest cantons, representing the original nucleus of Schwyz, Uri, and Unterwalden plus the two neighbors, Zug and Lucerne, clung to their ancient faith. In addition they were opposed to Zwingli's social reforms, which, by condemning the profitable mercenary service, threatened their well-being. Exactly as might be expected, it

Religious war followed by the Peace of Kappel, 1531

was over the subjected territory, the common bailiwicks, that the quarrel between the two groups finally came to a head. Dominating the federal diet, the five forest cantons planted their officials in the common bailiwicks and rigorously suppressed all Protestant teaching by the use of force. Against this Zwingli, hesitatingly backed by the Protestant cantons, protested with the result that civil war became inevitable. In the first clash in 1529, Zwingli by expeditious action won a bloodless victory and carried his point. In consequence each community of the common bailiwicks was conceded a free choice between the rival faiths. However, on the renewal of the struggle in 1531 the forces of Zurich were badly routed at Kappel (October 11) and the undaunted Zwingli himself slain. The defeated Zurichers had to sue for peace which, signed before the year was out at Kappel, cleared the atmosphere. The issue of the common lands was of course settled in the main in the Catholic interest, but the authority of each cantonal government to adopt the religion it preferred was freely recognized. The Kappel solution of the religious conflict closely resembles the one afterwards found by Germany and laid down in the Peace of Augsburg (1555) under the formula *cujus regio ejus religio*. That is to say, Switzerland, like Germany a weak federation, was obliged to leave the thorny religious issue to the local governments. Consequently each canton made its own choice between Catholicism and Protestantism, thereby giving to the religious map of Switzerland the same checkered appearance as marks Germany and characteristic of both of these countries to the present day. A constitutional effect of the religious factionalism was that the already feeble central government was for many generations to come reduced to complete impotence.

The Switzerland of the Reformation, though essentially a German state, had, by virtue of its westward expansion, already come to embrace a number of French districts. The territory of the Confederation stretched toward the lake of Geneva, at the western end of which lay, completely surrounded by the territories of the duke of Savoy, the city of Geneva. This French city, controlling the headwaters of the Rhone, was an important mart of trade and had a peculiar political régime which will be presently explained. By an amazing chain of circumstances Geneva, shaking off, early in the sixteenth century, its bondage to the duke of Savoy, established a free republic together with Protestantism, and immediately after became the home of an

The city of Geneva made famous by John Calvin

exile from France by the name of John Calvin. Not only did the alien Calvin become completely identified with Geneva, but breathing new life into the Reformation movement, he carried it much farther afield than Zwingli or even Luther had been able to do. Through Calvin the Reformation became militant and, effectively transcending national boundaries, developed an impetus which carried it to France, the Netherlands, Germany, Hungary, Great Britain, and ultimately across the Atlantic Ocean to America.

At the beginning of the sixteenth century Geneva had a form of government suggestive of the transition from medieval to modern conditions. Though the city, as an active community of merchants, had acquired a certain measure of self-government, it Geneva was still subject to its feudal lord, who was also bishop wins its of Geneva. As in the course of the preceding century, the independ-most powerful secular lord of the neighborhood, the duke ence of Savoy, had insinuated himself into the government as the lieutenant, in civil affairs, of the bishop, the town enjoyed the perilous luxury of a three-cornered rule. However, the unstable equilibrium might not have been destroyed, if the duke of Savoy, abetted by the bishop, had not formed the ambitious plan of bringing the town wholly into his power. This stirred the citizens' latent love of liberty and, rising in revolt, they attacked the conspirators with so much vigor that they drove them from the town. By 1536 Geneva had become a free republic recognizing no superior under heaven.

However, the victory of the Genevans would have been impossible without the help of the near-by Swiss cantons and particularly of the large and war-like canton of Bern. Since Bern was Protestant, it introduced Protestant preaching into Geneva and Geneva largely by its influence persuaded the citizens to adopt becomes the Reformation. They took this decisive step (1536) Protestant immediately after gaining their independence. No sooner had the double revolution been effected than Calvin appeared upon the scene.

John Calvin, a Frenchman by birth, saw the light of day at Noyon, in Picardy, on July 10, 1509. He received an excellent education in the classics, chiefly at the universities of Paris and Orleans. Originally intended for the Church, he switched at Orleans to jurisprudence, to which study, it may well be, he owed Calvin that clearness and precision which are the characteristics of his ripened thought. His steady and profound devotion to the great thinkers of antiquity may have helped to strengthen these out-standing mental traits.

Though a son of the sixteenth century might love the classics and give himself to the pursuit of law, he could not, more especially if he had the passion for righteousness which distinguished Calvin Calvin's from birth, avoid being drawn into the religious whirl-Institutes pool. While pursuing his studies Calvin came into touch with the circles in France which were nursing the seeds of the Refor-mation, and when the intolerant government of Francis I inaugu-rated an attack on heresy which brought many leading men to the stake, Calvin was obliged to seek safety in flight (1534). He settled in the Swiss city of Basel which some years before had adopted the Zwinglian reform, and here he published in 1536 his famous treatise *Christianae Religionis Institutio* (The Institutes of the Christian Religion). The Institutes, greatly enlarged in subsequent editions, constituted the most scientific and critical attempt that had yet been made to reconstruct the church of Christ on the basis of the evidence supplied by the New Testament. A positive achievement of profound scholarship, it was at the same time a daring exposure of the elaborate additions to the apostolic structure made by the medieval Church. No book had yet come from the Protestant camp combining so much historical information and method with such invincible logic. Some months after the publication of his great work Calvin paid a visit to his native France and on his return journey stopped for a night's rest at Geneva.

The Protestant faith, only recently adopted by Geneva, was still an exceedingly frail plant. The real difficulty was that the citizens, having turned Protestant largely on grounds of political expediency, Calvin had not felt the uplifting force of a great moral experience. settles in The leading preacher of Geneva, Farel by name, was Geneva aware of the evils of the situation and wrestled with them tirelessly. When the news was brought him that the famous young author of the Institutes had arrived in town, he called upon him at his inn and warmly solicited his aid in the great work of inner evan-gelization that still remained to be done. Calvin, enamored of the quiet life of the scholar, at first refused, but Farel plied him with such vigor that he at last agreed to make the sacrifice and plunge into the world of action.

The work on which Calvin now entered lasted, with the exception of a short setback and exile, till his death in 1564. By sheer force of will and ascendancy of genius he made himself the commanding figure within the city walls and with the consent of the citizens ruled their destinies like a dictator. His plan, one of the most audacious ever formed by man, was to realize in Geneva *Calvin* the original church of Christ outlined in the Institutes. Let *establishes* us be clear that it was this evangelical edifice which wholly *a theocratic* filled his mind. As for the political government to be *state* set up, its particular form did not matter much in Calvin's view, provided its magistrates were imbued with the sense of their Christian mission. He was therefore ready to take over the democratic régime already established at Geneva, provided it would accept the obligation to work in close association with and even subservience to his church to the end of producing as nearly perfect a Christian commonwealth as possible. Instead of separation of church and state, the much vaunted ideal of the present age more perfectly realized in the United States of America than anywhere on the older continent, he demanded the same intimacy and reciprocity between the two institutions for which the Middle Age had striven. According to him the state which governed temporal man and the church which ministered to his immortal spirit could not disjoin their labors if God's great purpose in regard to man was ever to be realized. This is a theocratic ideal substantially identical with that of the great medieval doctors, the reason for the agreement being that exactly like them Calvin held life to be worthless in itself and valuable only when lived under God with a constant view to salvation. Where Calvin and the scholastics differed — and the difference constitutes an unbridgeable chasm — was on the question of the means to a common end. While the medieval teachers exalted the Catholic Church as the divinely created instrument of salvation, the French reformer swept this vast intermediary structure aside with a single sweep of his arm and brought the individual face to face with God. The church in his view, the real but invisible church, was the body of believers throughout the world divided for practical purposes into separate units and guided by clergymen who preached and prayed, but who were completely impotent to promote by as much as a hair's breadth the salvation of the sinner.

Although Calvin's theocratic ideal possesses a decided interest, we are obliged to admit that it was his theories touching the meaning and application of Christianity which have chiefly impressed themselves on the world. His three major contributions belong to the respective fields, first, of church government, second, of morals, and third, of theology. We shall discuss them in turn and begin by noting that, regarding point one, he championed the Calvinism identifies itself with the democratic principle of government democratic principle. He did this because democracy seemed to be the system of the primitive church, in which every believer was equal to every other and all the believers together constituted a working, self-governing unit. By identifying itself with this principle Calvinism made a popular appeal which was absent from Lutheranism from the moment the Wittenberg reformer committed his movement to the control of the princes. Without the least doubt it was the democratic kernel of the Calvinistic system which was responsible for winning the hearts of the middle classes in so many European countries and which, by winning the middle classes, tied up the Genevan reform with those vigorous social and economic elements destined to be the carriers and exponents of the modern movement of progress. In short, a democratic church stirred the imaginations of all self-governing groups and greatly promoted democracy throughout the world.

A second memorable feature about Calvinism is the extraordinary emphasis which it put on conduct. According to the Genevan leader the conversion of the individual to the Reformed faith ought infallibly to mean a life lived on a plane of high endeavor in the consciousness of God's active and incessant grace. Hence the true Christian divorced himself from all weakness and frivolity and gained his daily bread and guided his relations with his fellow-men in the spirit of simple duty and dignified austerity. Without doubt Calvin is the first Puritan and his Genevan code of morals the source and model of all Puritanical codes whatever. But, cognizant of the frailty of the flesh and brought face to face with the backsliding and misdemeanors of his fellow-citizens, Calvin was unwilling to trust to pulpit exhortation to hold sinners to the narrow path. We must conceive him as a man of the grimmest resolution and, as such, a willing believer in the most drastic measures. He therefore created as an executive organ for his moral code a commission, called the consistory and made up of six ministers and twelve elders. The consistory was in substance an ecclesiastical or moral police and was empowered to arrest and bring to trial any man, woman, or child charged with failure to comply with the Genevan standard of conduct. The punishment imposed was carried

out by the civil authorities, which furnishes an excellent illustration
of how, in the Genevan system, state and church interlocked. The
records of the consistory, which still exist, show that children were
whipped for being disrespectful to their parents, men pilloried for
blasphemy, and money fines and imprisonment meted out for dancing, card-playing, the singing of profane songs, and non-attendance
at church. Of course, heresy and blasphemy were particularly
heinous offenses and in several instances led to the infliction of the
death penalty either by the sword or the lighted fagot. A community
subjected to a rigid standard of behavior by supervision and penalties
may become welded into an irresistible mass, but it will necessarily
learn to stifle that spontaneous human sympathy and to extinguish
those simple joys which under other systems have proved invaluable
elements of life. As in the case of every other code of ethics put
forth by man, the law of compensation provides that the credit and
debit accounts of puritanical Calvinism are in perfect balance.

The third feature of Calvinism destined to be historically important belongs to the province of theology and touches the Genevan
scholar's conception of God. He made the might and majesty of
the Creator so unapproachable and all-inclusive that it Calvin and
completely overshadowed the universe. No Christian predestina-
system has ever been set forth which reduced man to tion
such total insignificance, made him so entirely a helpless worm.
From this position it followed for Calvin, a reasoner who with characteristic firmness stood by every consequence of his logic, that
sinful man could not contribute an atom's weight to his own salvation either by the good works recommended by the Catholic Church
or by the faith extolled by Luther. God alone could save and His
saving was a pure act of mercy. But since God is eternal and omniscient He must know and has willed, even before birth, whether
a soul shall be saved or lost. Familiar under the name of election
by grace or predestination, this teaching has proved a rock on which
the waters of discussion have dashed themselves to spray for many
centuries down to the present hour. To men of a different temper
from the austere Calvin, to tender-minded men throughout the ages,
the doctrine that man is as utterly unimportant and God as rhada-
manthine and implacable as predestination implies has proved
extraordinarily repugnant. It was freely predicted, even in Calvin's
lifetime, that discouragement would seize upon the adherents of
this creed and that something akin to oriental fatalism would par-

alyze their wills. Rarely has a prophesy been more completely disproved by the facts, for history reveals that the Calvinistic form of Protestantism is associated with a remarkable display of human activity. What the belief in election by divine grace may have to do with an unexampled activism is a metaphysical problem beyond the scope of this book.

Calvin tried to bring the Lutheran and Zwinglian churches into union with his own. In this he scored a partial success, since in 1549 the Zwinglians signed with him the consensus of Zurich which **Relation of** established for Switzerland a single Reformed church. **Calvinism** The Lutherans, however, by refusing to budge from their **to Zwingli-** conception of the Eucharist secured the perpetuation of **anism and** **Lutheran-** the Protestant division. For the moment at least that **ism** misfortune hardly checked the astonishing vitality of Calvinism. From Geneva as a center and with the aid of an academy for the training of pastors, to which Calvin gave an unremitting attention, it radiated a missionary zeal unique among Protestants and excelled, among Catholics, only by the Jesuits.

The reform movement of which Luther, Zwingli, and Calvin were the protagonists could not possibly have achieved success, if it had not appealed to a conviction, which had been gathering strength **The papacy** for over a century, that the Church was corrupt in head **and the** and members. To all such criticism the popes not only **Reforma-** had turned a deaf ear but by a resourceful diplomacy **tion** had nullified every attempt to produce a reform by constitutional means. The failure of the General Councils of Constance (1414–1418) and Basel (1431–1449), assembled amidst the hopes of Christendom to inaugurate a new era, was due and due solely to the popes, jealously resolved to maintain their absolutism against the claims of a reforming parliament. Issuing with unshorn powers from the conciliar crisis, the Roman pontiffs plunged into the Renaissance and gave themselves whole-heartedly to worldly joys and schemes of temporal power. While many of the Renaissance popes by befriending humanism and patronizing the arts exhibited a spirit which elicits applause, it is also true that, practically without exception, they proved themselves morally so obtuse that the universal laxity of clerical manners and the scandalous financial corruption under their eyes failed to disturb their equanimity. Popes of this character would not be able to cope effectively with the northern revolt because they would be impenetrable to its moral fervor. They would continue to loiter in the pleasant gardens of the Renaissance and refuse to face the hard realities beyond the Alps. However, with the spread of the Protestant disaster certain more conscientious members of the papal court would feel alarm and raise their voice in favor of conciliating criticism by the abolition of some of the more flagrant scandals. In measure as this sentiment gained ground, it invaded even the college of cardinals and in the election of 1534 registered a first, if partial, success in the elevation to the curial chair of Paul III (1534–1549). Although this pope was undoubtedly a Renaissance product, still he showed a genuine concern for the evils of the Church and, intermittently at least, attacked the problem of the hour. For a few decades therefore the decision trembled in the balance until, with the election of Pope Paul IV (1555–1559), the papacy definitely and forever turned its back on the Renaissance and took up the urgent question of saving what was left of the universal Church. Under these circumstances began that famous movement of Church reform by Church action known as the Counter-Reformation.

Although the Counter-Reformation did not acquire its full momentum until the popes had put themselves at its head, let it be clearly understood that its energies had begun to accumulate long before the middle of the sixteenth century. Any attempt at a systematic presentation of these slowly gathering forces must start with the ecclesiastical reforms carried out in Spain under state direction and at the express instigation of Ferdinand and Isabella. These sovereigns entrusted the work to the learned and devoted Cardinal Ximenes, who in a lifetime of courageous service cleansed the Augean stables of the Spanish clergy. He renewed the spiritual life of the monastic orders; he brought the parochial clergy back to a sense of their obligations as guides and comforters of the people; and he established schools and seminaries which were made obligatory for all candidates for the priesthood and which put an end to the abysmal clerical ignorance so vigorously scourged by the humanists. It is true that the Spanish revival identified itself with scholasticism and was distinguished by a rigorous orthodoxy; it is no less true that it shaped for itself as its mightiest weapon the Inquisition and practised a fierce intolerance; but, in spite of these darker phases of the movement, Spain experienced a genuine renewal of religious life manifested by an energy which poured at last over the national boundaries and passed like an electric current through the paralyzed body of the universal Church.

One of the most conspicuous evidences of every religious renewal in the Middle Age had been the voluntary association of men and women in ascetic orders whole-heartedly devoted to some form of Christian service. Not only in Spain but in the other Catholic countries too, in measure as they caught the Spanish spirit, this medieval phenomenon was repeated with the result that organizations animated with the purest Catholic zeal came into spontaneous being and multiplied rapidly. Only the most important can be here enumerated. As early as the reign of Pope Clement VII a handful of ecclesiastics in his own capital of Rome founded the order of the Theatines (1524). Undeniably influenced by the Spanish example but certainly no less by the chilling blasts that blew from Wittenberg, they resolved that, above all, the parochial clergy must be aroused to a new sense of its duty. The Theatine order was planned, therefore, and rose to fame as an association of priests, who, turning away from idleness, ignorance, and self-indulgence, pledged themselves to the highest ecclesiastical ideals. Far more widely effective was a new order of friars, the Capuchins. Founded some two years after the Theatines as a reformed branch of the ancient Franciscans, the Capuchins practised simplicity and kindliness and, moving freely among the common people from whom they sprung and whose language they spoke, they became an important link in the chain of influences that kept the Italian masses loyal to the Church. However, as world forces, both of these rather local orders were completely overshadowed by the Jesuits. The Jesuits are unthinkable except as an expression of the narrowly concentrated Catholic fervor of Spain.

The Jesuits, or Society of Jesus, as the order is officially called, were founded by Ignatius Loyola. Loyola was a Spanish nobleman, who, as was natural in one of his birth, followed the profession of arms until during convalescence from a wound received at the siege of Pampeluna (1521), he chanced to read certain holy books dealing with the lives of Jesus and the saints. His high-strung and exalted nature was so fired with this reading that thenceforth he knew no other ambition than, in imitation of the early martyrs, to dedicate his life to the Church. His first efforts were wildly extravagant and ineffective. He eventually saw that he needed to put himself in possession

Margin notes: Evidences of Catholic revival: Theatines and Capuchins

Margin note: Loyola founds the order of the Jesuits, 1540

of a solid body of knowledge and at thirty-three years of age began the study of Latin, philosophy, and theology. While attending the university of Paris, he made the acquaintance of some kindred spirits who in 1534 solemnly bound themselves to him and to one another in the service of Christ and the Church. It is fascinating to linger on the strange coincidence that Loyola and his Protestant antipode, John Calvin, were students at Paris together and may have rubbed elbows on the same class-room bench. The group of seven companions (for that was the original number), welded into a unit by the inspired leadership of the Spanish nobleman, presently departed for Venice in the hope of crossing the sea to the Holy Land. When the outbreak of a new war with the Turks made the plan impossible, they contented themselves with taking the road to Rome to the end of gaining the papal blessing for their society. In 1540 Paul III officially authorized the order and at the same time approved its purpose and organization as sketched in Loyola's petition. In both these respects the Society of Jesus proved so different from the religious orders that preceded and followed it that it must be ranked as a highly original creation.

As recited in the charter of 1540, the objects of the Society were in the main three: (1) mission work in any part of the globe but more particularly in Protestant lands; (2) preaching and directing the conscience; and (3) educating the young. Since the Jesuit Society experienced an almost phenomenal growth, it was mission already by the time of the death of the founder (1556) work a factor to be reckoned with; and before it celebrated its fiftieth anniversary it boasted thousands of members together with some hundreds of colleges and houses distributed everywhere over Catholic Europe. And this enormous establishment remained with an indeed rare consistency dedicated to its original purposes, among which mission work held a conspicuous place. Not only did their Catholic enthusiasm carry these strange zealots to the ends of the earth, to India, China, and Japan, as well as among the Redmen of America, but it led them to display a particular energy in Protestant lands, where at the height of their power they scored many a triumph. Their practice was to single out for attention ruling families and officials in the highest walks of life and the conversion in the seventeenth century of the elector of that country, Saxony, which had been the cradle of the Reformation, and of the Scottish Stuarts on the British throne, shook the northern world with a sudden alarming sense of Jesuit missionary power.

If their missionary labors measure the courage and death-defying devotion of the Jesuits, their preaching and confessing illustrate their intellectual subtlety or, as their enemies phrased it, their trickery and dishonesty. So successfully did they exhort the faithful from the pulpits of their churches and so delicately did they direct their lives from the confessional that they were in eager demand in an age of religious doubts and convulsions. Practically without exception the Catholic sovereigns of Europe promoted Jesuits to the service of their private chapel, enabling them by this intimate intercourse to wield a wide though indefinable political influence. However, their most impressive service belonged without question to the field of education. Wisely aware that youth is the impressionable age, they gave their attention to the multiplication of schools and colleges and by virtue of their zeal and energy carried their instruction to a high degree of excellence. It was in part by championing better educational methods that Protestantism had won its victory, especially among the upper classes. To this Protestant movement the Jesuits opposed their own, carrying it through on a much more extensive and unified plan. The proof is furnished by the fact that by the seventeenth century the Jesuit colleges had acquired a very high reputation for efficiency in Italy, France, the Spanish Netherlands, and Catholic Germany, while in countries like Portugal and Spain they completely monopolized the educational field.

Jesuit preaching and education

Devotion, be it ever so sustained, can not by itself explain these remarkable achievements; they were due in no small part to an organization, which, although only gradually perfected, was implicit from the start in Loyola's conception. As was natural for an old soldier, he took the army as his model. Hence, establishing gradations of authority culminating in a commander-in-chief or general, he welded his machine together with the spirit of an iron military discipline. On being accepted as a novice a youth learned first and foremost complete subordination. As his best aid to this end he was made to live with and under the "Spiritual Exercises," a devotional book composed by Loyola and wonderfully adapted to the suppression of every trace of an individual will in the interest of the order. After a novitiate of two years' duration the youth became a scholastic. *Scholastics* took the course in arts and on graduation were permitted to qualify as teachers in their turn. Specially endowed scholastics were invited to study

The Jesuits organized as an army

theology and after a prolonged and successful application might hope to become priests and to be elevated to the rank of *spiritual coadjutors.* Individuals unsuited to serve either as teachers or priests were classified as *temporal coadjutors* and served the order to the best of their ability as laymen. They represented the lowest Jesuit rank, with the scholastics and spiritual coadjutors set above them in the order named.

Although these three classes embraced the bulk of the membership, they had no claim to the government of the Society. This was reserved to the "Professed of the Four Vows," a select body promoted from the spiritual coadjutors and composing the Society in the strict sense of the word. All Jesuits of whatever grade took the three vows sanctioned by monastic usage of chastity, poverty, and obedience, but the Professed *The inner governing group and the general* added a fourth vow (hence their name) of special and unalterable obedience to the pope. Even the Professed, however, were not so much a parliament as a general staff. They might advise the supreme general whom they elected to office for life, but they were absolutely at his will and pleasure, once he was installed in office. In the fourth vow resides the special significance of the order for the political history of the Counter-Reformation. The Jesuits conceived of themselves and, in fact, were the militia of the pope and first, defensively and finally, offensively waged perpetual war with heretics and infidels for the glory of the Church — *ad majorem gloriam ecclesiae.*

There remain for consideration three agencies with which the Church completed its armament in preparation for the war with its enemies. They are the Inquisition, the Council of Trent, and the Index.

We have seen that the Inquisition, conceived as a special board for the investigation and suppression of heresy, was intermittently employed throughout the Middle Age, sometimes locally by the bishops, sometimes more universally by the popes. One of the most famous instances of its papal use is in connec- *The Roman Inquisition* tion with the suppression of the Albigensian heresy at the beginning of the thirteenth century. In the following century the spread of humanism had discredited violence in matters of faith and had caused the discontinuation of the Inquisition until the Spanish government, faced by the special problem of the Jews and Moors, petitioned the popes for its resumption. In consequence, under Ferdinand and Isabella, the famous Spanish Inquisition was set up

in complete independence of Rome and operating as much and more
in the civil than in the ecclesiastical interest. Naturally when Pope
Paul III began to look about in order to strengthen the Catholic
defenses, he was much impressed with the work done in Spain and
in 1542, in compliment to the Spanish tribunal, issued a bull establishing a papal Inquisition which claimed universal authority. A
central board of cardinals sitting at Rome was empowered to hear
cases and pass sentence, acting at the same time as a court of appeal
from inquisitorial courts to be set up in the various European territories. As heresy, besides being a sin, was also accounted a crime,
the inquisitors were privileged, in consonance with the practice of
criminal courts throughout Europe at this time, to put the accused
to torture in order to extract a confession of guilt. This circumstance,
together with the fires which were presently lit at Rome, explains
why the Roman Inquisition soon spread a terror hardly inferior to
that connected with its Spanish exemplar.

Although it was the ambition of Paul III and his successors to
give the new institution a jurisdiction as wide as that of the Church
itself, they did not achieve their purpose. The Spanish government
politely notified Rome that in the future as in the past
it intended to do its own heresy-hunting and almost all
other Catholic states answered in the same vein. Not that
they were averse to persecution or, as we shall see, failed
to practise it, but they were averse to increasing the pope's
power by authorizing an infringement of the national jurisdiction.
In point of fact the new Roman Inquisition never exercised any
notable activity outside of Italy. Over Italy, however, it was completely effective and had no small part in stamping out not only the
new seeds of heresy but also many of the fair plants which had
grown up under the shelter of humanism. It is not enough to
explain the historic eclipse of Italy by pointing to the Spanish political conquest; it was caused even more by the fact that the
Italians, tiring of their splendid Renaissance audacity, succumbed
also spiritually to Spain.

The Roman Inquisition limited largely to Italy

It will be remembered that the Lutheran schism had no sooner
made its appearance than a General Council of the Church was
proposed as the natural and certain remedy. Emperor Charles V
was won over to the plan and from an early date importuned the
pope to call together the parliament of Christendom. But the pope
hesitated. The Councils of Constance and Basel, sitting in the first

half of the fifteenth century, had threatened his absolute control by championing a policy which would have lowered him to the rank of a mere constitutional sovereign.   It was only with the greatest difficulty that he had defeated these plans and preserved the power which he considered to be his by divine right as the successor of St. Peter.   However, stubborn as was the opposition of the popes of Luther's day to Charles's policy of a General Council, Charles was a very powerful man and could not be systematically flouted.   Sometimes he was almost omnipotent and on such occasions the pope had to make at least a show of acquiescence.   At last in 1542 Paul III issued the call for a Council to be held in the city of Trent on the southern slope of the Alps, but found occasion to adjourn it before a single session could be held.   In 1545 Pope Paul and in 1551 his successor went through the same comedy, except that the sessions were formally opened on these occasions and a limited amount of business transacted.   When finally, in 1552, the emperor was defeated by the German Protestants, he reached the conclusion that his conciliar remedy for the heretical poison was a failure and, resigning the imperial crown, retired to Spain to die in monastic seclusion.

Charles V advocates the calling of a General Council

Simultaneously with the disappearance of Charles from the scene the whole Catholic outlook dramatically changed.   The spirit of reaction triumphed, conciliation was rejected, and under Jesuit inspiration the whole Church drew its ranks closer together, committing its destinies into the hands of its traditional leader, the pope.   No longer fearful of a Council under these altered circumstances, Pope Pius IV (1559-1566) issued a new call which resulted in the famous and concluding session of Trent of 1562-1563.   With the trouble-breeding Protestant question eliminated from discussion, for this fighting body met to the battle-cry of "no surrender," the Council was able to perform a notable work. In response to the new moral fervor manifested by the clergy it began by correcting some outstanding abuses.   Thus it enforced episcopal residence, condemned pluralism (the practice of holding several benefices at once), and established seminaries to bring the clergy to a higher educational level.   Then it rolled up its sleeves to attack the real issues between itself and Protestantism, the issues of doctrine.   Without a shadow of equivocation the Council took its stand on tradition, reaffirming the labors of the scholastic doctors and restating in terms of medieval continuity every doctrinal posi-

The Council of Trent, 1562-1563

tion which Luther and his allies had attacked. Moreover, by laying a formal anathema on every contrary opinion, not only were the remaining bridges between the old and the new faith broken down but any plan to build bridges in the future was frustrated in advance. In short, "the Canons and Decrees of the Council of Trent," under which name the official acts were published, constitute a declaration of war; and from a purely military viewpoint they recommend themselves as a precise staking off of the ground which Catholicism was prepared to defend in the coming struggle. In that combat the Protestants were to learn that the lack of a common ground, due to their bitter doctrinal divergences, was a heavy handicap.

A result of the Council, surprising in view of the reluctance of the popes to call it together, was that the papacy emerged from the ordeal with added prestige, for, the Council settled, though not in The papal express words, the ancient constitutional issue as to absolutism whether the final authority in the Church rested with the pope or with the general assembly of Christendom. Though the papal absolutism had mounted steadily since the early Middle Age, it had always remained in dispute and was invariably challenged by the Councils whenever they met. Even in the Council of Trent there was a party of bishops who took their stand on the old platform of conciliar supremacy; but the papalists, ably assisted by the new champions of the pope, the Jesuits, won an undisputed victory. It was not the smallest service that Jesuit energy and discipline rendered its avowed lord and master. It would hardly be too much to say that the Council of Trent practically surrendered the historic conciliar claim and affirmed the absolutism of the pope in matters of government as well as of faith. Sufficient evidence of this assertion would seem to be supplied by the fact that the next ecumenical council did not meet till the nineteenth century (1870), when the final touch was added to the supremacy of the pope by the declaration of his infallibility.

Before adjourning the Council of Trent empowered the pope to draw up a list of forbidden books (*Index Librorum Prohibitorum*). Long before this act an occasional pope or a Catholic university had The Index taken cognizance of the flood of dangerous matter released by the new invention of printing and had attempted to bank it up by publishing the names of authors whom good Catholics should eschew. These haphazard efforts were now to be replaced by a careful attempt to put, as it were, in quarantine all writers and writings not strictly orthodox. The commission to which the work was entrusted brought out the papal Index of 1564, to which additions were afterwards made as occasion served. It was arranged in three categories, the first of which listed tainted individuals, so-called heresiarchs, who were condemned *in toto;* the second named individual dangerous works; and the third indicated forbidden passages within books otherwise sound. Wherever, as in Italy, the Index became effective, it must have contributed to the darkening of the intellectual skies. But many Catholic countries, doubtless to the advantage of the free play of ideas, refused to enforce it, and even a learned Jesuit was found, who, a white crow in a black flock, significantly hinted that the best way to discredit bad books was to write better ones.

In looking back over the movement in the Church which we have been describing, we would seem to be fully justified to speak of it as a Reformation inasmuch as it improved the manners and morals of the prelates, gave birth to new and highly disciplined orders, and raised the level of learning and devotion among the secular priests. But it is also clear that by breaking with the spirit of criticism and returning to the prison of medieval tradition the Counter-Reformation turned its back on humanism and the Renaissance. Of course, it might be argued that Protestantism had preceded Catholicism in declaring war on the Renaissance by reviving theological controversies and resting its case ultimately not on reason but on faith. In whatever ratio the responsibility for the phenomenon may be distributed, around the middle of the sixteenth century the promise of a liberated human spirit implied in the Renaissance was, temporarily at least, obscured by an era of religious strife between churches prepared to assert their respective theories of salvation not with the persuasions of the mind but with the drawn sword of the fanatic. By virtue of that blind and passionate struggle it might even come to pass that mankind would be permanently deflected from the advance indicated by the line of the Renaissance movement. But if something of the Renaissance freedom should be saved, enough to stimulate at some later time the courage of men to resume the great interrupted adventure of the fifteenth century, it would hardly be due to either Protestants or Catholics but rather to those rare individuals who, priests of the human spirit rather than of any church, were content to nurse the sacred flame outside the warring camps.

[marginal note: Reformation and Counter-Reformation extinguish the Renaissance]

REFERENCES

P. SMITH, *Age of the Reformation*, pp. 135–45, chs. 3–8
W. WALKER, *Reformation*; *John Calvin*
T. M. LINDSAY, *History of the Reformation*, II, Bk. 3, chs. 1–3, Bk. 5, ch. 2, Bk. 6
E. M. HULME, *Renaissance and Reformation*, chs. 15, 17, 18, 20–23
Cambridge Modern History, II, chs. 9, 11, 18, III, ch. 13
L. HAEUSSER, *Period of the Reformation*, chs. 10, 18–20, 31
A. PLUMMER, *Continental Reformation*, chs. 7–8
G. P. FISHER, *History of the Reformation*, chs. 5–9
G. KRUEGER, *The Papacy*, chs. 11, 12
C. E. CHAPMAN, *Spain*, pp. 213–17, ch. 27
M. JACKSON, *Huldreich Zwingli*
H. G. REYBURN, *John Calvin*
E. TROELTSCH, *Calvin*, Hibbert Journal, VIII, 102 ff.
T. C. HALL, *Was Calvin a Reformer or a Reactionary?* Hibbert Journal, VI, 171 ff.
H. D. FOSTER, *Calvin's Program for a Puritan State in Geneva*
A. C. McCABE, *Candid History of the Jesuits*
S. H. ROSE, *Loyola and the Jesuits*
F. THOMPSON, *Life of St. Ignatius*
T. J. CAMPBELL, *History of the Society of Jesus*
A. W. WARD, *The Counter-Reformation*
A. C. McGIFFERT, *Rise of Modern Religious Ideas*

THE POPES

Leo X (Medici), 1513–21
Hadrian VI, 1522–23
Clement VII (Medici), 1523–34
Paul III (Farnese), 1534–50
Julius III, 1550–55
Marcellus II, 1555
Paul IV (Caraffa), 1555–59
Pius IV, 1559–65
Pius V, 1566–72
Gregory VIII, 1572–85

CHAPTER VII

SPAIN UNDER EMPEROR CHARLES V AND HIS SON, PHILIP II; HER WORLD EMINENCE AND HER DECAY

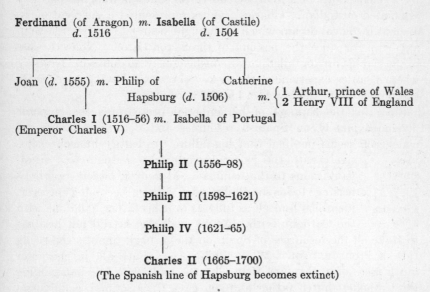

Ferdinand (of Aragon) *m.* Isabella (of Castile)
d. 1516   d. 1504

Joan (*d.* 1555) *m.* Philip of   Catherine
Hapsburg (*d.* 1506)   *m.* { 1 Arthur, prince of Wales
                                2 Henry VIII of England

Charles I (1516–56) *m.* Isabella of Portugal
(Emperor Charles V)

Philip II (1556–98)

Philip III (1598–1621)

Philip IV (1621–65)

Charles II (1665–1700)
(The Spanish line of Hapsburg becomes extinct)

When the grandson of Ferdinand and Isabella, Charles, who in 1516 mounted the throne of Spain, was, in 1519, elected to the Empire and became Emperor Charles V, the Spanish nation had cause to mourn rather than to rejoice at this increase of dignity; for, having duties henceforth in Germany, the monarch could no longer give an undivided attention to his Spanish task. In fact his interests which, besides Spain and Germany, embraced also the Netherlands and Italy, obliged him to abandon a narrowly national viewpoint and to broaden his policy till it assumed continental dimensions. Charles was by nature neither exceptionally energetic nor ambitious. Even as a young man he was taciturn, wary, and patient, but having once made up his mind to a particular course he was inclined to stick to it with singular tenacity. When a series of remarkable coincidences

Charles pursues an imperial rather than a Spanish policy

145

put him at an early age in possession of a large part of Europe, far
from having his head turned by the abundant favors of fortune, he
faced his responsibilities with, on the whole, extraordinary delibera-
tion and gradually elaborated a policy expressive of his position.
We have glanced at this policy in the chapter dealing with the
German Reformation and found that it involved a conception of
himself as arbiter (not master) of the states of Europe, held together
by a single faith of which the universal Church was the divinely
appointed custodian.   Charles's views represented a survival of an
ancient medieval dream which he brought nearer to realization than
any emperor since the passing of the Saxon Ottos.   None the less
in the end his dream failed, most conspicuously no doubt in Germany
where Charles experienced the heavy sorrow of having to concede
the protection of the law to a hateful heresy.

Since for the support of his imperial pretentions the emperor
depended largely on Spanish resources and Spanish soldiery the
conclusion seems justified that his failure to identify himself exclu-
Philip   sively with the particular interests of Spain was disad-
pursues a   vantageous to that country.   Moreover, he left a perilous
Catholic   heritage to his son Philip, who, without becoming emperor,
rather than
a Spanish   identified himself as fully as ever his father had done with
policy   the Catholic faith.   As we shall see, he did not hesitate
to stake all the resources of Spain on the struggle against the rising
tide of Protestantism.   While Philip was, above all, in character
much more of a Spaniard than Charles, and while by championing
the Catholic Church father and son gave their country a universal
significance it might otherwise have missed, the fact remains that
they put a burden on the Spanish people under which it in the end
calamitously broke down.

The reigns of the emperor and his son, covering almost the whole
of the sixteenth century, constitute an extraordinarily brilliant episode during which the history of Europe seems to revolve around
The   Spain.   With Philip's demise (1598) there is an eclipse
brilliance of so sudden as to bewilder the observer and so deep as to
the two   have remained substantially unbroken to our own day.
reigns
followed by We are forced to conclude that beneath the surface splen-
darkness   dor a slow dry-rot was at work which, when it at last
broke through the crust, produced disaster.   An examination of the
domestic situation, to which we shall now turn, will bear out this
deduction.   Beginning with the reign of Charles (1516–1556), we

shall examine the internal developments of Spain with a view to getting some light on the amazing Spanish collapse.

And first, the movement toward absolutism merits attention. We have seen [1] that Charles inherited a growing royal power which, exercised against the lawlessness of feudalism, had been the source of considerable social benefits. But, strong monarch that Charles was, in both of his kingdoms of Castile and Aragon he had to reckon with a parliament or cortes which controlled the purse and even insisted on being heard in legislative matters. In Castile, the real heart of Spain, there occurred early in Charles's reign a constitutional crisis. Angered by the sovereign's too arbitrary procedure, the cities of Castile, constituting the most active element represented in the cortes, revolted with the general plan of gaining more consideration for their wishes. As the movement was poorly coördinated, the royal forces were able to stamp out the fire (1522) so completely that Charles was left in a position to dictate the terms of peace. In consequence, some cities were, by way of punishment, deprived of their right of representation in the cortes, while all of them had to admit a royal appointee (*corregidor*) in their midst and to accept other serious curtailments of their municipal liberties. It was a body-blow aimed at popular government. Although the cortes of Castile was not deprived of its right to meet periodically and vote the taxes, henceforth that body was no better than a broken reed, lost heart, and became utterly subservient to the executive. In fact, following the rout of 1522, the once proud Castilian cortes degenerated to the level of a royal rubber stamp. As for the Aragonese cortes, it was made of sterner stuff than its Castilian counterpart and obliged Charles strictly to respect its financial and many other rights. Its turn to be humiliated did not come till the reign of Philip, who seized (1591) a convenient pretext to overrun Aragon with a Castilian army and to break, if not the Aragonese constitution, at least the will of the Aragonese people to use the cortes against the royal pleasure. Undoubtedly the line of movement in Spain throughout the sixteenth century is toward absolutism and away from constitutional practices; and in such a development of the purely arbitrary power of the crown we may detect a decline of public health ominous for the Spanish state.

Another cause of deterioration already noticeable under Charles

The growth of absolutism

[1] See p. 77.

but cumulatively effective under his successors carries us into the field of economics. The Spaniards were not a numerous people nor was their country naturally rich. Besides, owing perhaps to the The bad warm climate, they were characterized by a certain economic physical indolence. When the trans-Atlantic discoveries situation under Ferdinand and Isabella and the projection into world politics due to Charles lifted the Spanish people with dramatic suddenness into the first place in Europe, the necessity arose of increasing the country's productiveness if the rapidly rising expenses of the government were to be successfully met. The peninsula was a land of agriculture and sheep-raising with few and relatively unimportant manufactures. Instead of the economic activities being at once stimulated to more intensive life, they at first about held their own with the exception of sheep-raising, which has the drawback of involving a very destructive use of land; and after the middle of the century economic production visibly and definitely declined in practically every line. The reason is not far to seek. In large measure at least it may be ascribed to an unbelievably inept system of taxation. Since the clergy and the nobles, being privileged classes, were tax-exempt, the task of finding the national revenue fell almost exclusively upon the towns, the method adopted being to lay a burden of ten per cent on every commercial transaction. This senseless tax, called *alcabala*, had of course the effect of totally discouraging trade, that is, it shut off the air by which the urban classes lived. As for manufactures, which early in the sixteenth century were greatly stimulated by the rising demand for goods among the Spanish colonies across the seas, a complete ignorance of the laws of political economy led the government to burden the factories of silk and woolen textiles with so many regulations that the young enterprises were suffocated under a mountain of red tape. A stationary productiveness, on the one hand, and ominously growing government expenses, on the other, define a situation which simply obliged the monarch to become so extortionate as gradually to drain the wealth of the country. For a time, it is true, the steady economic enfeeblement remained hidden from view. The silver mines of Mexico and Peru poured a stream of bullion into the country which everybody fallaciously took for wealth and which did indeed enable the government to hire mercenaries and purchase military stores, that is, to engage in expenditures which were required by the exigencies of foreign policy, but which signified pure waste. In the long run the Spanish bullion regularly passed into the hands of commercial and industrial people, like the Dutch and English, who were able to supply the goods which the Spaniards wanted but which either through native indolence or stupid government interference they failed to create. In fact the paradox might be ventured that the American metal poured into the Spanish coffers was rather a curse than a blessing, since it had the evil moral effect of confirming this southern people in the fatal delusion that a nation can become rich without work.

From this analysis of the maladies of Spain the Inquisition must not be omitted. Established, as we have seen, under Ferdinand and Isabella, it retained its tragic effectiveness under Charles, who never wavered in his support of its main purpose. That The was to persecute the two alien groups, the Jews and the Inquisition Moors, until every trace of infidelity had disappeared from the land and the nationalist dream, " one people, one king, one faith," had been realized. We should not forget that the intolerance of the sovereign and the ruling classes was shared by the common people, who not only willingly bowed their necks to a secret and insufferable tyranny but who to testify to the hatred they felt for men of another blood and opinion crowded to the public executions, called *autos-de-fe* (acts of faith), at which the victims perished in rows by fire, as to a merry-making or a bull-fight. As the descendants of the Moors (usually called Moriscos) proved particularly difficult to uproot, there was in the eyes neither of Charles nor of his successors any reason for relaxing the royal vigilance against them. Occasionally the fanatic treatment to which these hunted groups were exposed caused them to break forth in a rebellion which in so far eased their fate as, instead of perishing singly by rack and fagot, they fell in multitudes by the avenging sword. When toward the end of Charles's reign the Lutheran opinions gained a foothold here and there, the Inquisition, rejoicing at the discovery of a new group of enemies, threw itself upon the Protestant heretics and stamped them out root and branch. Not in many pages could one exhaust the evils, moral, economic, and intellectual which flowed from the terrible system of oppression represented by the Inquisition. Suffice it to remark that a people which suffers the misfortune of having the free play of its spirit paralyzed by the terror emanating from a secret and invisible government can not long continue to carry the torch of civilization.

The last thirteen years of his rule Charles spent away from Spain closely occupied with German affairs. His failure to quell the Protestant movement broke his spirit and he resigned his crowns in 1556, Spain with Italy and the Netherlands to his son Philip, Germany to his brother Ferdinand. Philip II (1556–1598) found himself on his accession at the head of territories hardly less extensive than those which Charles had governed; and as he did not become emperor he had, from the Spanish point of view, the advantage over Charles of fixing his residence in Spain and of presenting himself to the world in dress, speech, and manners as a Spaniard. As such, his policy, although it was not so much dedicated to Spanish as to universal Catholic interests, aroused so little opposition that he came to be regarded by his people as a truly national king.

Philip an out-and-out Spaniard in feeling and carriage

Every historical personage has two aspects, depending on whether he is looked on with favor or disfavor. To his devoted Spaniards Philip II was a circumspect and estimable ruler, while for the other peoples of Europe, more particularly of the Protestant north, he was the darkest tyrant and the most persistent enemy of light the age produced. The modern historian can not adopt either of these partisan views. He sees in Philip a severe, formal, and narrow-minded man, who was animated by the Catholic fervor traditional among his people and his family, and who had acquired from the sad experiences of his father a perfect horror of religious diversity. Hence his guiding thought, while there was life in him, was to maintain the Catholic faith by repression of heresy through the Inquisition, where he had the power; by war, where war had become inevitable. Contemporary Protestants shuddered as they identified Philip with the horrors of the Inquisition. While from their angle their aversion was fully justified, it should not be forgotten, especially as it throws a penetrating light on this age of religious conflict, that there was not a feature of his reign of which he was more proud than of the Inquisition since, by means of it, he was doing God's will and securing the triumph of the divinely instituted Roman Catholic Church. However, apart from this one spark of religious enthusiasm, Philip's joyless nature was as foreign to elation as the head of a bank. He passed his days and his nights over state affairs. Every document had to go through his own hands. Historians who have examined his papers declare it incredible that so much matter should have been written by one man in

The character of Philip II

one lifetime. In fact, work was his failing, for work with him degenerated into a rage for minutiae and ended by enfeebling his grasp of essentials. Out of business hours this ogre of the Protestant mythology was a tender and devoted husband and father. Even his worthless son, Don Carlos, whose mysterious death in prison has been the cause of violent and frequent defamation of the royal name, he is now admitted to have treated with an exemplary forbearance.

This very ordinary man managed to loom like a titan on the stage of European politics for the simple reason that he stood forth as a party champion in a clash of world importance. At the very time that Philip succeeded to the throne of Spain the Counter- *Philip's* Reformation had at last organized its forces and was *world* prepared to take the offensive against Protestantism, *position due* which had thus far met with little or no systematic op- *to the iden-* position. Without doubt it accorded with Philip's fan- *tification of* atical devotion to the Church to put himself and his *himself* country at the service of this cause; but here again a *with the* judicious student will demur from the emotional Prot- *Counter-* estant view which presents him as the evil-minded and persistent *Reforma-* aggressor in the Catholic-Protestant conflict of the second half of *tion* the sixteenth century and will without difficulty agree that this struggle was inevitable and as much forced on Philip by the logic of events as determined by his own Catholic impulses. Nothing will lend better support to this argument than the narrative account of his reign, for it shows that he slipped into the role of Catholic champion gradually and under the unescapable pressure of circumstances.

On Philip's ascending the throne it looked as if the chief concern with him as with his father would be the purely political program of maintaining the Spanish hegemony in Europe by a close watch on France. Within a year of Philip's accession, the *The French-* French king, Henry II, showed that he nursed the same *Spanish war* ambitions as his ancestors, for, in conjunction with Pope *of 1557-59* Paul IV, he began (1557) a war, the chief object of which, *followed by* as on all previous occasions, was to wrest Italy from *the peace of* Spanish control. However, in this new struggle fortune *Cateau-* again decided in favor of the Spaniard. France gained some notable *Cambrésis* successes, above all, she captured Calais from the English, who had come into the struggle on the side of Spain; but after suffering two capital defeats in the channel area, one at St. Quentin (1557) and the other at Gravelines (1558), she agreed to come to terms. By the peace of Cateau-Cambrésis (1559), except that France was permitted to retain Calais, no territorial changes of note were carried out. Therefore the real import of the treaty may be said to have been once more to acknowledge the Spanish domination of Italy. As this admission ran counter to the trend of French ambition, we may be sure that Henry II, like all his predecessors as far back as Charles VIII, would have returned to the attack as soon as the occasion served, if the wheel of fortune had not now taken a novel turn. When the peace of Cateau-Cambrésis was signed, France was already simmering with heresy and rebellion and Philip, for his part, was morbidly aware that throughout his Netherland heritage, Protestant opinion had gained a powerful foothold. By these circumstances the two kings were diverted from their political rivalry and concentrated their attention on the domestic problem under their eye. Thus Cateau-Cambrésis marks an epoch. It rings down the curtain on the long struggle between France and Spain, a struggle chiefly over Italy which had begun more than half a century before, in 1494, with the famous expedition of Charles VIII; and it inaugurates an era of religious wars which cover the rest of Philip's reign.

The origin and development of the Protestant movements in France and in the Netherlands will be taken up in detail in later chapters. Here, where we are considering Spain, it will suffice to indicate the consequences which followed from Philip's mobilizing the Spanish resources against the Netherland heretics. Let us clearly understand that the Low Countries were not a part of Spain and that their association with that country was limited to the accidental circumstance that through a turn of luck (or ill luck) they owed allegiance to the same sovereign. There was therefore no reason why the Spanish state as such should concern itself with domestic happenings along the shores of the North sea; and as a matter of fact it did not do so. But Philip, as absolute ruler of Spain, could not be prevented from employing his Castilian soldiers and revenues to solve a problem that had arisen in another of his territories; and when in the course of the decade following Cateau-Cambrésis the Netherland situation culminated in an armed rising which Philip tried to stamp out with Spanish troops, the whole contemporary world became excited. In the eyes of the pope and his Catholic following Philip was doing nothing less than fighting

Heresy in the Netherlands develops into a general Catholic-Protestant struggle

their battle, while for Protestants, whether in Germany, France, or England, the Netherlanders were heroes defending a universal cause. Naturally both combatants took advantage of the wide appeal made by the struggle to summon all available help to their side. In this the rebels were, on the whole, more successful than the Spanish ruler, of whose excessive power even Catholics, nay, at times even the pope, continued to be fearful. Intermittently, it is true, but after all with much self-sacrificing fervor the Protestants of Germany and France and, most effectively of all, their co-religionists of England came to the aid of the hard-pressed sailors and merchants of the Netherlands. When we take up this struggle we shall see that it was, in large part at least, the help furnished the rebels by outsiders that balked every effort of Philip at their subjugation. Slowly and reluctantly Philip swung to the opinion that he would never master the situation on the lower Rhine until he had punished the leading supporter of his enemies. In what we may call the second phase of the conflict in the Netherlands he turned furiously on England.

The gist of Philip's plan was to gather an irresistible navy in the harbors of Spain, an irresistible army on the Flanders coast, and by a well-timed coöperative action to overwhelm the island-kingdom in order to make it harmless to succor continental Protestantism. In 1588 the great stroke was ready and was inaugurated by the dispatch of the magnificent fleet, called the Armada, against the English coast. In our English chapter we shall recount how the proud Armada proved a miserable fiasco for a great variety of reasons, among which the superior skill and audacity of the English seamen merit the first place. Philip bore his defeat with dignified resignation. He spoke unaffectedly of the deep grief it caused him "not to be able to render God this great service." And as soon as his exhausted means permitted he returned to the attack. But the English, made confident by success, not only parried every blow but even pushed the war to the Spanish coasts, capturing the treasure-ships which brought to Spain the plunder of America. Clearly the sending of the Armada was the climax of the general religious war and its failure defeated Philip's plans and settled a number of matters in a sense deeply distasteful to the champion of Catholicism. Not that during the ten years that were still his after his descent on England he weakly folded his hands in his lap. But for the historical reviewer it is clear that by 1588

Philip's life-work had come to naught; that both the Netherland rebels and the Protestant north in general were safe from overthrow; and that declining Spain was about to be superseded as ruler of the seas by the Netherlands and England.

It gives us the measure of Philip's difficulties and helps explain his failure in his war with Protestantism to recall to mind that he was heavily engaged at the same time on another, on the Mediter-

Philip's
Mediter-
ranean
difficulties

ranean front. Here he had to meet the naval power of the Turks and their corsair allies of the African coast. We are aware that this same combination troubled the Emperor Charles throughout his reign, and that, if he occasionally carried the war to Tunis and Algiers, both his ships and his shores continued to be exposed to the depredations of the pirates. With Philip's advent the situation changed, if at all, for the worse because of the concentrated attention he was obliged to give to the developments in northern Europe.

At length, in 1571, Pope Pius V persuaded Philip to join hands with Venice, still a considerable naval power commanding the remnants of a colonial empire in the eastern Mediterranean, in a resolute

The victory
of Lepanto

effort to set a term to the audacity of the Mohammedans. The pope himself made a contribution of money and ships and Philip, for once liberating himself from the administrative red tape which so often choked his activities, rapidly assembled a great fleet in the waters of Messina. The supreme command over the allied forces was entrusted to Don John, the handsome and chivalrous half-brother of the Spanish king and his exact counterpart in temper and demeanor. As soon as everything was ready Don John sailed his Armada eastward to find and fight the enemy wherever he might be. Sighting him in the gulf of Lepanto, off the western coast of Greece, the enthusiastic prince poured into his men his own unconquerable spirit. Dressed in white velvet trimmed with gold he had himself rowed between the lanes of galleys, crying exhortations to his men: "Christ is your leader. This is the battle of the Cross." In the combat that followed (October 7, 1571) the young commander's dash and courage contributed notably to the outcome, which was the greatest victory that had yet been won by any Christian force over the apparently invincible Turks. Of the two hundred galleys engaged on either side a squadron of only forty Turkish vessels managed to escape. The rest with all their men and armament were either sunk or captured. It was a by no means minor source of pleasure that 12,000 Christian rowers were freed from Moslem slavery.

Great was the exultation of the Christian powers and great and justified the satisfaction of the Spaniards who had made the main contribution to the brilliant victory. But its consequences fell far short of what was expected at the time. Torn violently Decline of apart through jealousy, the Christian allies by failing Ottoman to follow up their triumph permitted the Ottoman sultan power after to rebuild his fleet and resume the domination of his Lepanto home waters. After his one magnificent spurt Philip returned to his familiar bureaucratic jog-trot and starved his navy in so short-sighted a manner as to incapacitate it for further offensive fighting. In 1573 the disgusted Venetians signed a peace with the Turks on the best terms they could get, and though the war between Spain and the sultan dragged on, no further battle of any consequence took place. The Algerine corsairs continued to be a pest that weighed heavily on the commerce of Spain and Italy and perpetual vigilance toward them was an inalterable necessity of the situation; but the Turks, by renouncing an active policy in the western Mediterranean, ceased henceforth to lend encouragement to their African allies. The fact is, and it caused all Europe to heave a sigh of relief, that from approximately the date of the battle of Lepanto, the over-swollen Ottoman power entered definitely on a decline. That chronological succession does not however argue that the former event was the cause of the latter. Such an opinion would be hardly tenable in the light of the fact that the Turkish naval power recovered from the blow of Lepanto and forced Christian Venice to sign a peace (1573) which marked a further depression of its fortunes. Let us indeed agree that the Ottoman empire declined, but let us not make the mistake of ascribing that significant event to any but the actual causes. These, in the main, are undoubtedly to be found in the internal situation of the realm. About the time of Lepanto terrible domestic evils began to make themselves felt in administration and finance, spreading a corruption through Turkish public life that was like a consuming cancer. Simultaneously the sultanate, which, possessed of absolute power, could alone have cured these ills, fell into the hands of a succession of imbecile rulers, who, shut up in the imperial seraglio, thought only of their own pleasures and sat idly by while the ship of state drifted on the rocks. We shall in the future hear of an occasional recovery of the Ottoman state, but beginning with the last quarter of the sixteenth century, we may think of it as having effectively shot its bolt and as ceasing therewith to be the nightmare of Christian Europe.

Perhaps the most unqualified success associated with the reign of Philip was his winning of Portugal. The acquisition of this kingdom had, in the interest of peninsular unification, been an ancient object of the Spanish kings, but they had wisely refrained from the attempt to effect it by force of arms. Frequent marriages between members of the two reigning houses had fostered a dynastic intimacy, of which Philip took full advantage when, in 1580, the death of King Henry without direct heirs opened the question of the succession. While there were aspirants to the Portuguese crown with as good or a better claim than Philip, the Spanish ruler was close at hand with an irresistible army and by acting swiftly took possession of the throne before the opposition could gain momentum.

The acquisition of Portugal, 1580

Owing to the considerable trade and numerous colonies of Portugal its absorption greatly strengthened the Spanish position in the world; but it was not long before Philip discovered a fly in the ointment. Conscious of their separate nationality and intensely proud of their achievements during the Age of Discoveries, the Portuguese accepted the yoke of their greater neighbor unwillingly and never ceased to exhibit dangerous signs of restiveness. True, they organized no systematic rebellion against Philip II, but quietly nursing the precious memories of independence, they let the decline of Spain run its destined course. Some forty years after their first Spanish master's death they at length revolted and won back their freedom under a new royal house, the house of Braganza (1640). Thus ended in disaster what in Philip's lifetime was celebrated as the successful consolidation of the peninsula.

The union with Portugal ephemeral

On turning to the domestic situation under Philip we find there is little to add to the story of the country's ills under his predecessor except to say that they became steadily more deep-seated and incurable. In the face of the waxing absolutism the cortes of both Castile and Aragon, although they continued to be summoned from time to time to vote the taxes, paled to helpless, constitutional wraiths; the Inquisition completely dominated the social and intellectual life and fiercely made it its business to pounce upon and extinguish every spark of dissidence or originality as soon as it appeared; and the

Intensification of the domestic evils under Philip II

productiveness of both city and countryside declined until to a visitor from the busy north the Spanish people gave the impression of being a nation of idlers and beggars. Nor is this the end of the disheartening tale. In measure as misery spread the taxes mounted due to the high-flying foreign policy of the sovereign and his ceaseless embroilments with enemies in every part of Europe. Up to the very last year of his life Philip was engaged in sucking up as with a sponge the wealth of Spain with the result that when the ruler died who in the eyes of credulous Europeans was, owing to the bullion of America, as fabulously rich as Croesus, there was not enough money in the treasury to meet the most immediate wants of the royal household. The Inquisition, absolutism, insane administrative principles, and a spendthrift Catholic imperialism may be confidently named as the ills which engulfed Spain in her ruin.

The successor of Philip II, his son Philip III (1598–1621), was an utterly incapable man, the tool and puppet of his favorites. In 1609 he was forced to bend his pride so far as to sign a truce for twelve years with the Netherland rebels, thereby virtually acknowledging their independence. Thus did the seed sown by the emperor and his son begin to ripen under their successors. During the long reign of Philip IV (1621–1665) the shadows still further deepened, and in consequence of disasters suffered in the Thirty Years' War and its aftermath, the wretched country sank definitely to the second and third rank among European powers. How in the course of the Thirty Years' War France resumed the struggle for the supremacy in Europe interrupted by her religious difficulties and how, under the leadership of the great Cardinals Richelieu and Mazarin, she completely reversed the decision of Cateau-Cambrésis (1559) we shall see in due time. Let our last word on this swift review of Spanish glory and decay be that by the middle of the seventeenth century the decline of Spain was patent to the most superficial observer.

The rapid decline of Spain after Philip II

REFERENCES

C. H. HAYES, *Political and Social History*, I, pp. 87–107
P. SMITH, *Age of the Reformation*, ch. 9
T. M. LINDSAY, *History of the Reformation*, II, Bk. 6, chs. 2, 4
C. E. CHAPMAN, *History of Spain*, chs. 23–26
M. A. S. HUME, *Spain, its Greatness and Decay*, chs. 1–6
W. C. ABBOTT, *Expansion of Europe*, I, chs. 12–14

Cambridge Modern History, II, chs. 2, 3, III, chs. 15, 16, IV, chs. 22, 24
E. M. Hulme, *Renaissance and Reformation*, ch. 24
A. H. Johnson, *Europe in the Sixteenth Century*, chs. 3, 4, 5, 7
H. C. Lea, *Moriscoes in Spain*, chs. 3–11
R. B. Merriman, *Rise of the Spanish Empire*
C. Hare, *A Great Emperor*
E. Armstrong, *Emperor Charles V*

CHAPTER VIII

TUDOR ENGLAND: FROM THE ACCESSION OF HENRY VIII TO THE DEATH OF ELIZABETH

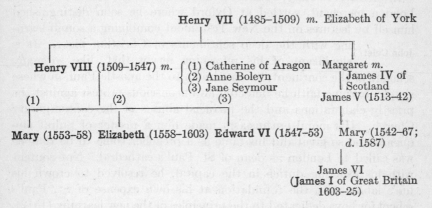

Henry VII (1485–1509) *m.* Elizabeth of York

Henry VIII (1509–1547) *m.* { (1) Catherine of Aragon
(2) Anne Boleyn
(3) Jane Seymour

Margaret *m.* James IV of Scotland

James V (1513–42)

(1)   (2)   (3)

Mary (1553–58)   Elizabeth (1558–1603)   Edward VI (1547–53)   Mary (1542–67; *d.* 1587)

James VI
(James I of Great Britain 1603–25)

It was during the pacification effected by the first Tudor monarch, Henry VII, a pacification in the course of which the civil rage loosed by the War of the Roses was gradually spent, that the Revival of Learning gained its first foothold in England. English travelers and scholars, returning from the continent and, more particularly, from Italy, communicated their humanistic enthusiasm to their countrymen until first, the university of Oxford and later, the sister institution at Cambridge became active centers for the promulgation of the new ideas. While the literature of the ancients was taken up with avidity, in accordance with the tendency generally exhibited among the peoples of northern Europe a preference was shown for the Christian learning which centered about the Bible and the Fathers. Throughout the Germanic area, let us recall, the Renaissance was as much and more a Christian than a classical movement, and England was no exception to the rule. On this account the great Dutch scholar, Erasmus of Rotterdam, was given an eager welcome when in 1499 he paid a visit to the circle of Oxford humanists. Erasmus was the spirit incarnate of northern scholarship and during the six visits he paid his English friends between the years 1499 and 1517 he gave and received a stimulus which had the happiest consequences for the

The Revival of Learning comes late to England

159

cause of letters. Innumerable as were the famous Dutchman's English contacts, his best friends as well as the leaders of the English movement were Colet and More. A review of their intellectual interests will serve as the best possible introduction to the prevailing mood of English humanism.

After travel in Italy, John Colet (1466–1519), the son of a wealthy London merchant, settled at Oxford where he soon distinguished himself by lectures on the New Testament combining a sound learn-

John Colet ing with the deep sentiments of Christian piety. It is significant of his reforming fervor that, like so many scholars of the continent, he was drawn to the apostle Paul, in whose simple, burning faith he detected an unconscious protest against the priestly elaborations and the financial abuses of the contemporary Church. His moral enthusiasm made him a master of pulpit eloquence and so great did his fame as a preacher come to be that he was called to London as dean of St. Paul's cathedral. Not content with his exacting duties in the capital, he resolved to crown his life's labors with the foundation at his own expense of St. Paul's school for boys dedicated to the principles of the new learning (1512). Here Latin and Greek, taught in a fresh way, crowded out the barren studies of the schoolmen, while Christianity was taught not in the form of a round of mechanical ceremonies but as a spiritual message pointing the true way to salvation.

A similar moral passion informed the thought and life of Sir Thomas More (1478–1535), friend and intimate of both Colet and Erasmus. Brought up in the humanistic circle of Oxford, he

Sir Thomas became a barrister, and adopting a public career, was at
More   an early age elected to the house of Commons. His distinguished qualities did not escape King Henry VIII, who drew him into his service, and advancing him from post to post, raised him in 1529, on the disgrace of Cardinal Wolsey, to the office of Lord Chancellor, the highest dignity in the realm under the sovereign. His public service and tragic end belong to the political history of the times which we shall presently take up.

At this juncture we are concerned with More's place in the English Renaissance and may agree that, though he promoted the cause of learning at every turn, his fame rests chiefly on a single volume, the

More's   well known Utopia. Written in Latin and published in
Utopia   1516, the Utopia is composed of two parts to meet a clear-cut double purpose. While Part One is a sweeping criticism, social,

political, and religious of the England of his day, Part Two unfolds the picture of an ideal commonwealth, Utopia, the kingdom of Nowhere, in which the wrongs and abuses of contemporary society are remedied and men live together in those conditions of labor and peace enabling them to enjoy the best gifts of life. The Utopia is a dream, like Plato's Republic, and offers lively witness of a heart that is torn by the sufferings of humanity. It is properly conceived as a socialist tract, the first ripple of a stream of protest destined in the following centuries to swell to the dimensions of a mighty flood. Unqualifiedly it denounces the ruling classes and their institutions and sketches a new communistic order where men are equal, peaceful, moderately laborious, and — happy. While the program, taken as a whole, is wildly impracticable, it should not escape our attention that it contains a number of humane suggestions which have gradually been turned into realities by the increasing enlightenment of society. Since More's day we reserve the term Utopia for every essentially unrealizable vision of a reconstructed world.

Exactly as in Germany these English humanists helped prepare the way for social and religious reform; but, also like their German congeners, when the movement called the Reformation came, they protested against its violence as well as against its theo- **The English** logical tendencies and, generally speaking, repudiated it **Reforma-** wholly or in part. The outstanding difference between **tion in its** the English Reformation and its German counterpart is **first phase** the English Reformation and its German counterpart is **a political** that, instead of the former being carried through under **rather than** the leadership of an English enthusiast, it was, at least in **a religious** its earliest phase, championed by the ruler of the land **movement** who, animated by little or no interest in religious reform, was set on scoring a political victory over the pope. Indeed it is doubtful whether King Henry VIII did anything whatsoever for the Reformation considered as a spiritual movement, although he certainly promoted it indirectly by carrying through the separation of his country from the Roman allegiance. How that separation came about is the kernel of Henry's reign which we shall now proceed to examine.

Henry VIII mounted the throne in 1509 in succession to his father, Henry VII, from whom he inherited an authority hardly **The** short of absolutism. He was not yet twenty years old, a **accession of** youth of attractive presence, skilled in gentlemanly sports, **Henry VIII** such as riding and tennis, condescending with all people, free-handed and fond of pageantry, and altogether the idol of his nation which received him with acclamations of joy. Not least exultant over his coming to power were the English humanists, for Henry had been brought into the circle of the new learning by his tutors and was reputed to look upon it with favor.

The joy of the humanists over the accession of Henry was not destined to last long. The king, indeed, distinguished various members of the learned group by offices and emoluments, but he soon showed that he did not seriously share their reforming zeal and that he was bent on following his own lead. Beneath the king's smooth exterior appeared a stubborn will which with the passing of the years tended more and more to indulge exclusively its selfish purpose. A despot by nature, Henry became ever more despotic by habit and success.

Breach between Henry and the humanists

Throughout his reign Henry's main purpose was to make himself and his country a decisive factor in European politics. His father had sat quietly at home, perfecting the administration and amassing a considerable treasure. The son saw at once that with France and Spain holding each other in check and engaged in permanent enmity over Italy, there was a splendid opportunity for an ambitious sovereign who felt free to throw his weight into the scales for either party. It is true that the French-Spanish controversy hardly touched the interests of England; still, an English ruler of the sixteenth century could not forget that, less than a hundred years before, a warlike predecessor had been crowned king of France, and that from the port of Calais on the French coast, the last stronghold on the continent which floated the English flag, a descent could be made at any time upon Paris. That Henry therefore kept a sharp lookout across the channel requires neither apology nor explanation. If in the perpetual warfare between France and Spain England threw in her lot with Spain, she might reasonably hope to have restored to her a part of France. This speculation determined Henry's general attitude. But though leaning by preference toward Spain, contingencies might arise which would make it advantageous for him to comport himself for a time as the ally of France. In that case he could demand some convenient territory in payment for his services or, if territory was refused, he might let himself be placated with a handsome subsidy of ready money.

Henry's foreign policy

Such in outline was Henry's shrewdly calculated foreign policy, modified, however, by one factor — Scotland. Henry VII had in-

augurated a policy of reconciliation with Scotland, which he hoped
would lead in the course of time to a complete union.   In this
expectation he had married his oldest daughter, Margaret, to the
Scottish king, James IV.   But matters did not progress Relations of
as favorably as he had planned.   The enmity between Scots England
and English was bred too deep in the bone to be easily and
eradicated, and the Scots, suspicious for centuries of their Scotland
more powerful neighbor, had looked so steadily toward France for
aid and protection that they could not be easily persuaded to
abandon the habit.   A war of England with France had generally
in the past brought Scotland into the field with the object of making
a diversion in favor of France along the English border; and this
traditional alliance, which caught England between two fires, was
usually maintained during the reign of Henry VIII.   Thus the king
was obliged to wage frequent war with Scotland, but only in moments
of intense resentment did he forget what we may name the Tudor
policy, with reference to the northern kingdom, of reconciliation and
ultimate union.

After these general remarks we can dispense with following in
detail the intricate game which Henry played upon the diplomatic
chessboard of Europe.   He joined the pope and Spain in the Holy
League of 1512, the object of which was to drive France Henry's
from Italy.   When Emperor Charles V in 1521 renewed wars
the war against France, Henry again fought shoulder to shoulder
with Spain, until the great victory of Pavia and the capture of the
French king frightened him with the specter of a universal Spanish
domination and drove him for a time into the arms of France.   Late
in his reign, in 1543, he joined the emperor once more in an attack
upon Francis I, in which the chief English success was the capture
of Boulogne.   During these wars Scotland was very troublesome and
several times invaded England, though with small effect, since at
Flodden (1513) and at Solway Moss (1542) her armies were crushingly defeated.   To sum up we may say that Henry won small
profit for England from his diplomacy and wars, but that he had
the purely personal satisfaction of playing a leading role in international politics.

The favorite adviser of Henry in the early period of his reign was
Thomas Wolsey.   Wolsey was a commoner by birth.   Taking orders
as a priest, he rose rapidly by virtue of his talents from post to post,
until the king's favor won for him the archbishopric of York and

at the same time put him at the head of the civil administration of the realm in the capacity of Lord Chancellor (1515). No man in his day accumulated more 'offices and power. His civil position he **Wolsey** filled honorably on the whole, proving himself an able administrator and exercising a check upon the king's martial inclinations; but his immersion in political affairs led him to neglect his spiritual functions and filled him with a sense of importance which induced him to order his life on a scale of munificence altogether out of keeping with the English conception of a churchman. Spurred on by the criticism of the humanists, Wolsey undertook to consider and remove some of the abuses of the English Church, but he was still far from being committed to the humanistic program when Luther's theses against Indulgences (1517) made the Reformation the question of the hour. The development of the English attitude toward the greatest contemporary issue constitutes the most interesting aspect of Henry's reign.

Henry, despot and natural lover of authority in every form, followed Luther's first attack upon the papacy and Catholic doctrine with instinctive aversion. In fact, such was his resentment that he **Henry's attitude toward Luther** did not disdain to descend into the lists in person against Luther, and in 1521 published a vehement pamphlet, wherein he defended both the sacraments and the papal supremacy. In return the gratified Leo X conferred upon Henry the title — still used by English sovereigns — of Defender of the Faith. Of such nature was the understanding between pope and king in Henry's early days. In another ten years the wind had veered and couriers were speeding from Rome not with messages of friendship but with bulls of excommunication. This radical and dramatic change was brought about by the peculiar circumstances of Henry's marriage and his suit for divorce.

Henry's marriage deserves close consideration. The reader will remember that Henry VII, in pursuance of his plan to strengthen himself against the traditional French enemy, had sought to associate himself with Spain. The outcome of this political **Henry's marriage based on a papal dispensation** intimacy was a contract of espousal, by which Arthur, the prince of Wales, was married to Catherine, daughter of Ferdinand and Isabella. Shortly after the ceremony Arthur died, and as the desire for the alliance continued as before, the idea naturally occurred to the families concerned to marry Arthur's widow to his surviving brother, Henry,

However, an obstacle to this project was offered by a law of the Church forbidding a man to marry his deceased brother's wife. In this dilemma Pope Julius II, when appealed to, had recourse to his dispensing powers, by virtue of which he could make a law non-operative in a particular case. He issued what is called a papal dispensation, and on the strength of this the marriage took place in 1509. Now it will be readily understood that if the pope, as Luther was affirming every day with increasing violence, was an impostor, the exercise of the dispensing power was a usurpation, the law remained inalterably the law, and Henry's marriage was illegal. In addition, therefore, to the natural inclination of a despotic mind to uphold the cause of authority everywhere and at all times, Henry had a very personal reason for wanting to see Luther put down and the sovereignty of the pope raised above reproach and challenge. Thus it happened that Henry crossed pens with Luther and became the Defender of the Faith.

But time brings about surprising changes. Only a few years after Henry had broken a lance in behalf of the papacy, his attitude toward his marriage altered. After having for over a decade shown much attachment to his queen, he now thought he had weighty reasons for divorce from her. He had had several children by her, but only one child, Mary, had survived infancy, and owing to Queen Catherine's advanced years there was little hope of further offspring. Even if Princess Mary had not been a very sickly child, the king might reasonably feel that he was playing a dangerous game to stake the succession upon one fragile life. On dynastic grounds, therefore, Henry felt troubled and desired to marry again. But he had also an incentive of a more personal nature. The aging Catherine had long since lost her charm for him, and he was now madly infatuated with her young and charming maid of honor, Anne Boleyn. In 1527 he first whispered to his confidant, Wolsey, the word divorce.

Henry desires to be divorced

Questions of marriage and divorce belonged, as we have seen, to the exclusive competence of the Church, and because marriage was a sacrament, the Church refused to countenance divorce save in certain exceptional circumstances. Henry professed to believe that his was the exceptional case, resting his plea on the contention that the dispensation granted for his marriage was legally defective. He wanted the reigning pope, who was the worldly-minded Clement VII, to acknowledge that defectiveness, thereby automatically cancelling

his predecessor's dispensation and rendering the marriage null and
void. This simple course Wolsey, who had meanwhile, in addition
to his other dignities, become cardinal and papal legate, undertook
with all his might to urge upon the pope, but without
Henry de- avail. Clement VII proceeded with extreme caution,
sires the
pope to an- partly perhaps from conscientious scruples, certainly be-
nul the dis- cause he did not dare offend the powerful Charles V, who as
pensation head of the Spanish house naturally stood by his aunt, the
English queen. Clement would examine, he would not pronounce.
In 1529 he agreed to send to England a legate, Cardinal Campeggio,
who, together with Wolsey already on the ground, was to hold a
legatine court and ascertain the facts. The king put aside his dignity
so far as to appear before the two cardinals like a common suitor,
but even this humiliating act profited him nothing, for the pope,
still proceeding on his original plan of delay, suddenly transferred
the case to Rome.

Henry was furious at this crumbling of his hopes and in his rage
to make a scapegoat of some one let fall the weight of his displeasure
on the head of Wolsey. He stripped him of his civil honors and
Wolsey's exiled him to the country; still unappeased, he had just
disgrace, ordered his arrest as a measure preparatory to his execu-
1530 tion, when the great cardinal was stricken ill and died
(1530). At the last he cast a regretful backward look upon his life,
using to his attendants words which Shakespeare has employed almost literally in his play of Henry VIII: "Had I but served my
God with half the zeal I served my king, He would not in mine age
have left me naked to mine enemies."

What to do now? Almost any other man would have given up,
but Henry had the kind of autocratic will which grows terrible with
opposition. If the pope could not be got to act in what the king
considered a just and necessary case, he would repudiate
Henry re- the pope altogether and establish the English Church on
solves to
renounce a purely national basis. Further, he would no longer
the pope permit the Church to remain an independent power in
the state, but would reduce it to subjection to the civil power,
which meant, of course, himself. The officers of a church cut off
from Rome on the one hand, and dependent on the king upon the
other, could be trusted to settle the divorce question as the king
desired. Upon this plan Henry proceeded, but not without frequent pauses in order to give the pope time to reflect upon the

dangers he was running. For the royal quarrel with the papacy was a matter of policy, not of conviction, and the king would have avoided it at any cost short of the sacrifice of the divorce. As the pope remained deaf to both the threats and pleas of Henry, the anti-papal enactments succeeded each other without interruption until every cable binding England to Rome had been slipped. Let us tabulate the leading steps in this procedure.

The assembly of the English clergy is called Convocation. In 1531 Convocation was summoned and a decree wrested from the clergy, declaring Henry Head of the Church; owing, however, to the qualms expressed by many of the members the quali- Submission fying phrase was added, "as far as the law of Christ of the clergy allows." The next year the king destroyed the legislative independence of the clergy by requiring them to permit him to revise their statutes and to adopt no new laws without his consent.

By these steps Henry had put the English clergy, so to speak, into his pocket. Now it remained only to repeal the laws by which Rome possessed a foothold in England. These laws being acts of parliament could be repealed only by parliament, which The divorce body Henry accordingly summoned and by mingled pronounced threats and persuasion bent to his will. In 1532 parliament abolished the payment to Rome of First Fruits, which, being the first year's revenues of ecclesiastical benefices, constituted the chief income that the pope drew from England. The next year followed a renewal in more sweeping form of the ancient statute prohibiting the taking of any legal case outside the kingdom. This gave to the English ecclesiastical courts the right to pronounce, and pronounce finally, upon the king's suit. And now longer delay was neither necessary nor possible. In February, 1533, Cranmer, a creature of Henry's and half a Protestant at heart, was made archbishop of Canterbury and primate of England; and three months later he pronounced the desired sentence of divorce in his own court. Henry had already without waiting for this action married Anne Boleyn and now proceeded with her public coronation as queen of England (June 1, 1533).

When the pope heard of these doings he at last recovered his power of unambiguous speech and fulminated at Henry The Act of a bull of excommunication (July, 1533). But Henry was Supremacy, now secure and could meet the pope's wrath as an equal. 1534
In 1534 he had parliament pass a culminating act, the Act of

Supremacy, by which the last traces of connection with Rome were removed, and the king confirmed in the title already voted by the clergy of Supreme Head of the English Church, to which there was now attached no qualification whatever.

Thus while the English Church became national by being cut off from Rome, it also transferred its allegiance and became subject to the crown. Naturally there were many who regretted these changes. If they thoughtlessly crossed Henry's path they were not likely to escape with their lives. His marriage with Anne Boleyn, the Act of Supremacy, and all that hung thereby could only be criticised at the risk of death. When Sir Thomas More, the humanist, although he had been Lord Chancellor for three years following Wolsey's disgrace and although he was the foremost living Englishman, refused to take the oath involving acquiescence in these high-handed measures, he was convicted of treason and hurried to the block (1535).

Henry suppresses opposition

From the first it was an interesting question how far Henry would depart from the accepted Catholic system and approach the Protestant theological position. In his own heart and mind he was as much a Catholic before as after the separation. The sole distinction between Henry then and Henry now was that he had taken, as regards England, the pope's place at the head of the Church. But to a certain extent he could not fail to be influenced by the Reformation, for the pope and the Catholic world had solemnly repudiated him, and at the height of the struggle with the pope he had fallen under the influence of a counsellor, Thomas Cromwell by name, who entertained secret Lutheran sympathies. A number of minor changes, redolent of Lutheranism, were therefore carried through. Every church was ordered to provide itself with an English Bible for general use, indulgences were condemned, pilgrimages forbidden, and a few miraculous images destroyed. But the most incisive innovation adopted was the suppression of the monasteries.

Henry makes Protestant concessions

We have seen on several occasions that monasticism was the feature of the Church which chiefly invited the ridicule and criticism of the humanists. On this account, wherever the Reformation was victorious, monasticism was the institution which was first thrown overboard. Doubtless there was exaggeration in the tales of depravity circulated by such a virulent enemy of the orders as Erasmus; still, where there was so much smoke it is safe to assume there was some fire.   Even during the chancellorship of Wolsey, long before the policy of separation was entertained, a number of smaller institutions had been discontinued; and when Cromwell now suggested a plan of suppression on a much larger scale The suppression of the immense material advantage which would accrue to the monasteries the royal exchequer from the confiscation of the extensive monastic lands.   In pursuit of his bold plot Cromwell sent partisan agents through the land to investigate the monastic houses.   Although their reports were steeped in gross exaggeration, they served the purpose of the unscrupulous minister, since on being presented to parliament, they moved that body, outraged by the thought of so much wickedness, to adopt the desired legislation.   In 1536 a bill was passed ordering the suppression of the lesser houses — the exact provision was of all houses of less than £200 revenue — but Henry and his greedy henchman managed to include gradually the richer institutions as well by bringing personal pressure to bear upon the abbots.   Before five years had rolled by monasteries in England were a thing of the past; and the houses and vast tracts of lands which had fallen home to the king had been either given to greedy courtiers, or sold to meet the royal necessities, or dedicated in a few honorable instances to the support of schools and churches.

As far as it is possible to ascertain the attitude of the English people toward the ecclesiastical revolution inaugurated by Henry, it would seem that in their majority they consented, though somewhat hesitatingly, to the separation from Rome because in The English England, as throughout the continent, the prestige of the people papacy had in recent generations been seriously impaired. accept the However, although they rallied behind the Act of Su- royal policy premacy, they were, like Henry himself, essentially conservative and Catholic in spirit.   Apart from a small band of reformers, influenced from the continent, they had little desire for any change in the familiar features of the Church.   Therefore the suppression of the monasteries went beyond their wishes and in the backward counties of the north, where attachment to tradition was particularly strong, led to a dangerous revolt, known as the Pilgrimage of Grace (1536). Henry, as might be expected, put down the insurrection with vigor, but taking the hint which it conveyed, refused to go farther along the path blazed by the Lutheran princes of Germany.

For the rest of his life Henry was content to stand fast, force the

acknowledgment of his supremacy upon his subjects, and keep
the service and the doctrine of his Church free from the taint of
Protestantism. From time to time, in order to remove all doubt, he
Henry's   condescended to inform his subjects what they were
doctrine   authorized to believe; and these pronouncements, such
remains   as the Ten Articles of 1536 and the Six Articles of 1539,
Catholic   contained very little to which a strict partisan of Rome
might not have set his name. The Six Articles in particular were
eminently Catholic, since they upheld the sacrament of the mass,
auricular confession, the celibacy of the clergy, and, for good measure, made diversity of opinion punishable with death.

Under such a régime there was no peace in England either for
supporters of the pope or for adherents of Protestantism, and both
these groups were vehemently persecuted. Thomas Cromwell
Execution   himself, though his fall was coupled with other causes,
of Crom-   could not be saved by a long record of faithful, if shifty,
well, 1540   service when his support of the religious radicals became
obnoxious to the king. In 1540 he was charged with treason and
beheaded. The only safety for Englishmen lay in the quiet acceptance of the system which their masterful sovereign had imposed and
which was substantially Catholic except for the separation from the
venerable capital of Rome and the suppression of the monasteries.

A personal page in Henry's history demands at least passing
recognition. It presents the story of his marriages. His brutal ruth-
lessness, which served him well in politics in so far as it enabled him
His six   to impose his will triumphantly on his environment,
marriages   stands out in appalling nakedness in the tenderer associations of the family. We have already followed the tragedy of
Catherine of Aragon to the coronation of her coquettish rival, Anne
Boleyn. Anne Boleyn gave birth to a daughter, Elizabeth, and soon
afterward was executed on the charge of unfaithfulness (1536). The
next wife, Jane Seymour, died in childbed, leaving a son, Edward.
The fourth wife, a German princess, Anne of Cleves, did not suit
Henry at all and was married only to be immediately divorced (1540).
As the fifth wife, Catherine Howard, proved unfaithful, her head
too was severed by the axe (1542); and so room was made for a
sixth, Catherine Parr, who managed, by dutiful submission, to out-
live the royal Bluebeard.

Henry died in 1547. Before his death he had been granted by
parliament the right to regulate the succession by will. Accordingly,

he devised his crown to his son Edward, with the provision that it
pass, on the failure of Edward's blood, to his daughters Mary and
Elizabeth, in the order named. As Edward was but a boy nine
years old, his father provided further, during his son's The suc-
minority, a council of regency, at the head of which he put cession
Edward's maternal uncle, the duke of Somerset.

EDWARD VI (1547–1553)

Henry was hardly dead when the council of regency met, and without regard to Henry's wishes practically resigned its powers to
Somerset, who was authorized to assume the title of protector. This
measure was of decided consequence because Somerset The
leaned toward the reforming party. As a majority in the Protector
council held similar opinions, Somerset had no difficulty in Somerset
pursues a
inaugurating an era of Protestant legislation, especially Protestant
as he was heartily seconded in his policy by Cranmer, the policy
archbishop of Canterbury. We have therewith touched upon the real
significance of the rule of the protector. The English Church, which
Henry had zealously kept free from theological innovations, was now
definitely launched upon Protestant waters.

If we admit that it was probably impossible to keep the English
Church, following its initial breach with the Catholic world, exactly
where Henry left it, we shall incline to defend Somerset against the
charge of precipitate change which is frequently made Protestant
against him. In any case his decision was, while keeping changes
the Church national and uniform, to swing wide the door to Protestant influence. English was gradually substituted for Latin in the
services; priests were allowed to marry; the use of holy water was
discontinued; and all images were removed from the churches.
Finally, to lend dignity to the conduct of the new services in English,
there was published in 1549 the First Book of Common Prayer,
which vindicates the sobriety of Somerset's policy, since Archbishop
Cranmer, who is mainly responsible for it, modelled it closely on the
ancient services of the Church.

But Somerset's fall was at hand. Not because of discontent
caused by these religious innovations, at least not in a marked degree,
but owing primarily to prolonged economic misery, the peasantry of
England rose in the summer of 1549 and threatened civil war. The
troubles among the English peasants, who were freemen, bore little

resemblance to the situation which provoked the German peasants, held in galling serfdom, to wage the bloody war of 1525. Instead of being bound to the land and laden with services, the English country folk were so little bound that they found themselves in large numbers driven off the land altogether by a curious procedure known as enclosure. The great English landlords had discovered that, owing to the steady demand for wool in the markets of the Netherlands, their returns were larger from sheep-herding than from agriculture. Therefore, by letting their lands run to pasture and enclosing them, with perhaps the addition of the common lands of which the whole village had once had the use, they threw thousands of peasants out of work and occasioned great misery. This conversion of agricultural land to pasture was not new in Somerset's day. It had been going on for several generations, and many were the laws by which the government had tried to stop the movement and give protection to the humble tillers of the soil. But economic causes, operating like forces of nature, are stronger than legislation, and the peasants had not been relieved. When in 1549 they rose, Somerset, who had a heart that beat for the oppressed, did not hesitate to declare his sympathy with them. The rest of the council, members to a man of the landlord class, waited until the army of the government had scattered the insurgent hosts and then proceeded to rid themselves of the traitor in their midst. In October Somerset was arrested and deposed, and although he was allowed to live for a while, his opponents did not feel perfectly secure until his head had been severed from his body. He was executed in 1552.

The agrarian revolution causes the fall of Somerset

The leader of the landlord party in the council which had caused the overthrow of the protector was Warwick, better known by his later title of duke of Northumberland. He became Somerset's successor as governor of the kingdom, without, however, assuming the title of protector. He was a clever, unscrupulous, ambitious man, who, although he had no particular religious convictions, became an enthusiastic advocate of Protestantism when he discovered that a majority of his colleagues were of that opinion. Not content with Somerset's moderate program, he allied himself with the religious radicals and gave free scope to their passions. Now first occurred violent scenes of iconoclasm in England, when the people, incited by the so-called "hot gospellers," entered the churches and indiscriminately broke

Northumberland introduces radical Protestantism

altars, statuary, and stained-glass windows. Now, too, came persecution of orthodox Catholics, although the government never entirely lost the tolerant quality impressed upon it by Somerset. In
1552 there was issued the Second Book of Common Prayer, which
was again largely the work of Cranmer but differed from the earlier
edition in the more Protestant color of many of its passages. The
Forty-two Articles of Religion — a new confession of faith — followed, and therewith the reconstruction of Henry's national Church
on Protestant lines was completed. An Act of Uniformity imposed
the reformed Church upon the nation.

The Protestant revolution of Edward's reign was, as we have seen,
the work of Somerset and Northumberland. Nevertheless, the king,
who was, as is frequently the case with feeble children, a boy of remarkable precocity, followed the religious changes with **The boy**
intense sympathy. When he was twelve years old the **king**
German reformer, Bucer, wrote of him: "No study enjoys his favor
as much as the Bible." His favorite diversion was a theological discussion, which he would follow with a countenance whence every
touch of childish grace had been banished by an unnatural austerity.

Such a boy was only too likely to exhaust prematurely his low
measure of vitality. Early in 1553 Northumberland perceived that
Edward was dying. By Henry's will the succession would now fall
to Mary, who, like her Spanish mother Catherine, was **Edward**
a devout Catholic. With his Protestant record, Northum- **changes the**
berland had everything to fear from her, and in order to **law of**
secure himself he played upon the young king's Protestant **succession**
conscience with such skill that he persuaded him to devise his crown
away from his sisters Mary and Elizabeth upon his cousin, Lady
Jane Grey, who could trace her lineage back to Henry VII.[1] In
Northumberland's eyes Lady Jane not only had the advantage of
being a Protestant who would presumably sympathize with his

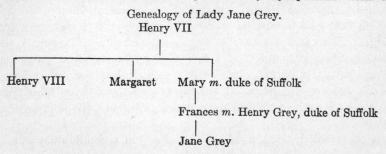

Genealogy of Lady Jane Grey.

Henry VII

Henry VIII   Margaret   Mary *m.* duke of Suffolk

Frances *m.* Henry Grey, duke of Suffolk

Jane Grey

religious measures, but as he had lately married her to one of his own sons, Guilford Dudley, he might hope through these young and inexperienced people to perpetuate his power. It was a base and despicable intrigue without a vestige of legality. For Henry's arrangement of the succession by will was in accordance with an express permission granted by parliament, but Edward, having been accorded no such power, signed an utterly worthless document. Northumberland was still completing the arrangements for his plot when, on July 6, 1553, Edward breathed his last.

MARY (1553–1558)

Edward had hardly expired when Northumberland proclaimed Lady Jane Grey. But if he had any hope of carrying his candidate, he was soon disillusioned. The mass of the people saw through his selfish intrigue and rallied around Mary, their lawful sovereign. They hailed Mary gladly, because not only their sense of law and justice, but also their religious prejudices designated her as queen. For the majority of the people still leaned strongly toward the ancient Catholic usages and had little or no sympathy with the radical Protestantism carried through in Edward's reign. From Mary they expected the return of the mass and the other beloved practices from which they were not yet weaned in their hearts.

Public sentiment declares for Mary

The Lady Jane Grey was, in consequence of this unhesitating devotion of the English people to their rightful sovereign, crowned only to be deposed again. Northumberland, deserted by his followers, gave himself up and was beheaded. His death was a just punishment for his misdeeds, but unfortunately Lady Jane, the unwitting tool of an ambitious man, paid the same penalty. It is true Queen Mary felt compassion for her and delayed the execution, but a rebellion of the following year exasperated her to such a degree that in sudden alarm she gave her consent to her young cousin's death. The gentle and refined young girl, queen of England for nine agitated days, has always excited a pathetic interest. Not having of her own volition sought the crown, she could truthfully call the day on which she gave it back to the commissioners, who arrested her, the happiest day of her life.

Downfall of Northumberland and Lady Jane Grey

It seems likely that if Mary had adopted a moderate Catholic policy, taking her stand upon the platform of her father, Henry, her reign would have met the wishes of her people. But Mary had nothing about her suggesting compromise. Her Spanish blood called upon her to be faithful, above all things, to her faith. She therefore planned nothing less than a return of England to the pope's fold — a full Catholic restoration. And that was a delusion. For however the English people were attached to the ancient worship, the Act of Supremacy, proclaiming the English independence of Rome, had the nation almost solidly behind it. *Mary plans a full Catholic restoration*

The first acts of Mary's reign left no doubt about her policy. The parliament, obedient to a word from the throne, rescinded the religious legislation of Edward's reign, thus bringing the Church back to the condition in which it was at Henry's death. The mass was again celebrated in the Latin language, altars were set up, and the married clergy were expelled from their livings. So much was probably acceptable to the nation. *England returns to the Catholic fold* But doubtful and impolitic measures followed. Urged on by Mary, the parliament next abolished all the legislation of Henry's reign pertaining to the pope, and ended by voting the unconditional return of England to the papal obedience. To crown this policy of recantation, Cardinal Pole, an Englishman of royal blood, who had been sent to England as the legate of the pope, in November, 1554, extended absolution to the nation and received it back into the papal fold. Even so, England had not been quite brought back to the religious status that obtained when Henry began his memorable conflict. There were still the alienated monastic lands. Mary in her honest zeal would have restored them to their owners, but here the parliament, made up largely of landholders who had profited by the spoliation of the Church, showed itself intractable.

If the uncompromising Catholic policy of Mary alienated many sympathizers, she hurt herself still more in popular estimation when she rejected marriage with one of her own countrymen and accepted the proffered hand of her kinsman Philip, son and heir of Charles V. Such a union could not but inspire vague fears of a foreign domination, and although every provision was made in the marriage contract to insure the independence of England, the country was nevertheless drawn into the Spanish system. *Mary marries Philip of Spain, 1554* In the summer of 1554 the marriage was celebrated, and although Philip proved himself afterward in his Spanish realm to be an unbending autocrat and fanatic, it must be set down to his credit that during his occasional visits to England he comported himself with much discretion.

Although the religious persecutions which gave the finishing stroke to Mary's dying popularity and won for her from bigoted Protestant enemies the terrible title of "Bloody Mary" date from about the The perse- time of her marriage, they can not be fairly ascribed to cutions her Spanish consort. If Mary persecuted, the incentive was under Mary chiefly furnished by her own fiery enthusiasm. It was she who stimulated the parliament to reënact the old ferocious statutes against heresy and it was she who urged the bishops to carry them out. Soon the prisons were filled with the Protestant leaders of Edward's time, and soon, too, the fires of persecution were lighted over the realm. It is the period of the Protestant martyrs. Less than four hundred died by the fagot — a number inconsiderable compared with the slaughter in France or the Netherlands, but enough to rack the nerves of a people whose religious vacillation, as reflected in the legislation of the preceding decades, led them to favor a more gentle procedure. The stanchness of the victims in death contributed more toward establishing Protestantism than could have been done by the doctrinal fervor of an army of Calvinist preachers. It was even as Bishop Latimer said to Bishop Ridley at the stake: "Master Ridley, play the man; we shall this day, by God's grace, light such a candle in England as I trust shall never be put out." For the stout part they played Latimer and Ridley head the Protestant martyrology. But the persecution struck a more prominent, if not a more noble victim than these, in the person of the deposed archbishop of Canterbury. This was the celebrated Cranmer, who had served under two kings. Cranmer, the perfect embodiment of the religious irresolution of the age, flinched when the trial came and denied his faith. But in the face of death his courage came back to him. He thrust his right hand into the flame, and steadying it there, said resolutely: "This is the hand that wrote the recantation; therefore it first shall suffer punishment."

If Edward's violent Protestantism made his reign detested, Mary's violent Catholicism produced much the same result. She was at bottom a quiet, tender woman, whose intolerance was a habit of her age Her un- shared by Catholics and Protestants alike, and who popularity found it hard to face the hatred her policy aroused. Besides, her marriage was unfortunate. She loved Philip, but Philip cared little for her and did not much trouble to hide his indifference to the sickly and ill-favored woman, twelve years older than himself. To crown her misfortunes, she allowed her Spanish husband to draw her into a war with France, in which Philip won all the honor and Mary suffered all the disgrace by the loss of the last French foothold remaining to England from its former large possessions across the channel, Calais (1558). Doubtless the loss of Calais was for England a benefit in disguise; she was thereby cut off from the continent and directed to her true sphere, the sea. But to Englishmen of that day the capture seemed an insufferable dishonor. No one felt it more keenly than Mary. "When I die," she is reported to have said shortly before her death (November, 1558), "Calais will be found written on my heart."

ELIZABETH (1558–1603)

Elizabeth, Anne Boleyn's daughter and Mary's younger half-sister, succeeded to the throne on Mary's death, and inaugurated a reign which proved to be one of the most glorious in English annals. Under her, Protestantism was firmly established in Eng- *The glori-* land; the great Catholic sea-power, Spain, was challenged *ous reign* and defeated; and English life flowered in the poetry of *of Queen* Shakespeare and his contemporaries more exuberantly *Elizabeth* than ever before or since. To the national greatness to which England suddenly raised herself in the sixteenth century, Elizabeth has lent her name. She appeared to the English people, and still appears, mirrored in a great time; and their generous loyalty, which gave her in her lifetime the title of Good Queen Bess, has also encouraged them in the view that she was the fountain and the sum of all the glories of her day. Modern historians have modified this judgment. They have separated the woman from her time, and it is a very human Elizabeth who appears to the eye now that the curtain of the myths which concealed her from view has been withdrawn.

Elizabeth had few of the graces of womanhood and many of its customary weaknesses. Her vanity was so great that, though a very plain-featured person, she conceived herself to be a beauty of a particularly rare type. She could not live without flattery *Elizabeth as* and flirtations, and accepting the compliments of the *woman and* courtiers for true coin, allowed herself to be persuaded to *statesman* dance and sing in her maladroit manner before a brilliant court of gentlemen and ladies, who could hardly hide their amusement behind their handkerchiefs. Her manners were rude, especially at the council board, and her ministers were frequently annihilated by language which would have done honor to the camp and the fishmarket. However, if Elizabeth failed to meet the stereotyped ideal of feminine perfection, she certainly possessed what are usually called masculine talents, for she had an inflexible will and an exceptional intelligence. Above all, she loved her country to the point of completely identifying herself with its interests. Her statesmanship, supreme of its kind, took the form of consistently promoting, though less by martial than by diplomatic means, the greatness of England.

One of the qualities by which she rendered England perhaps her greatest service her contemporaries would have been quick to condemn if they had been more clearly informed about it: she was Elizabeth's lukewarm in matters of faith. Regardless of our theoretic religion view of this state of mind, we can not but agree that in the England of that day, shaken by religious passions, the sovereign's religious indifference was an undisguised blessing to the commonwealth. By reason of it Elizabeth was delivered from the destructive radicalism of both Edward and Mary, and being unusually disinterested, was peculiarly fitted to play her royal part of mediator between antagonistic faiths. Let us not forget that the sixteenth century was the century not only of the Reformation but also of the Renaissance. Elizabeth had been brought up to read Latin and Greek and was not unacquainted with the languages and literatures of the continent. It is, therefore, not so very strange that, like Shakespeare, Jonson, and the poets of her time generally, she gave more heed to the voices coming from Italy than to the messages of Luther and of Calvin. In sum, she is a Renaissance rather than a Reformation personality.

The chief organ of Elizabeth's government was the Privy Council, the advice of which she regularly heard before she arrived at a decision. In this body was gathered the best political talent which The Privy the country boasted. It is no small credit to Elizabeth to Council have exhibited such discernment in the choice of her and the ministers. Most prominent among them was William parliament Cecil, Lord Burghley, who devoted a life of exemplary service to advance the twin causes with which England came to be identified: Protestantism and sea-power. But, though Elizabeth was willing to consult in her affairs the Privy Council, which was a body of her own choice, she was not inclined to grant much political influence to parliament, composed of the representatives of the people. Parliament remained, therefore, what it had been under the other Tudors, an obedient recorder of the royal will. During the queen's life the undivided sovereignty of England rested on her shoulders.

As might be expected, the leading question of Elizabeth's reign proved to be the question of religion. Edward had followed a policy of radical Protestantism and Mary a policy of radical Catholicism; after these two uncompromising programs it was plain *Elizabeth* that extremes were dangerous. Elizabeth showed her *steers a* sound judgment by steering deliberately and from the *middle* first a middle course. When her first parliament assembled *course* in 1559 she had it pass a new Act of Supremacy, asserting the English independence of Rome and declaring the sovereign the highest authority in the realm in religious as well as in civil matters. This she had followed up by an Act of Uniformity which imposed upon every minister the forms of worship laid down in a new Book of Common Prayer. The new book was nothing but the second Prayer-Book (1552) of Edward's reign with some few revisions. The plan was to make the national Church thus reëstablished a rallying-ground for average men and women averse to the zealotry of either party. Such was Elizabeth's politic and shifty moderation that for a time even the pope nursed the fond hope of her return to the fold; but after waiting for ten years in vain, he lost patience and issued a bull excommunicating and deposing her (1570).

From that moment Elizabeth became definitely pledged to the Protestant cause and was forced into a more active hostility against Catholicism. As a result severe measures were passed against the adherents of the pope, but never in blind passion or without *Her perse-* recognition of varying degrees of culpability. Catholics *cution* who refused to attend service in the national Church were *political* visited with money fines, while heavier fines, culminating *rather than* in imprisonment, were inflicted for saying or attending *religious* mass. Finally, those Catholics, whose enthusiasm led them to engage in political plots, were repressed by special treason bills authorizing the seizure and execution of conspirators and sufficiently elastic to strike down any inconvenient Catholic fanatic. Under this repressive legislation a considerable number of Catholics were put to death, and all of them, by the system of fines, were gravely molested; but compared with the contemporary persecutions in Spain, France, and the Netherlands, Elizabeth's methods may truthfully be said to bear an unmistakable imprint of moderation.

A church built on these broad foundations must have met the wishes of a majority of Englishmen for they gave it their adherence in increasing numbers, accepted its worship and government, and gradually forgot the Latin mass. Proceeding in her deliberate manner, Elizabeth could, therefore, gradually complete her structure by new legislation. The most important of the supplementary acts is the publication of a confession of faith under the name of the Thirty-nine Articles of Religion (1563). These, too, like the Book of Common Prayer, were based upon the enactments of Edward's time and mark a considerable departure from Catholic doctrinal tradition. The Acts of Supremacy and Uniformity, the Book of Common Prayer, and the Thirty-nine Articles are still in our own day the essential features of the Anglican or English national Church, which may, therefore, claim Elizabeth much more truly than Henry as its founder.

Elizabeth is the real founder of the Anglican Church

Throughout Elizabeth's reign the Roman Catholics decreased in numbers. But as they diminished, there rose into prominence another body of religious opponents, Protestant radicals, who were dissatisfied with what they called Elizabeth's half measures and clamored for a thorough Protestant revolution. These radicals, it soon developed, were of two kinds, Puritans and Separatists. The Puritans were the more moderate opponents, who, while accepting the national Church and attending its services, hoped to eliminate from it certain ceremonial features, such as the elaborate vestments of the clergy, which they despised as "Romish" trappings. Their demand for what they called a purer worship won them as a nickname, in the first instance, the party designation of Puritans. The Separatists, on the other hand (also called Brownists, after their founder Robert Brown), were radicals of the most thorough-going sort. The national Church with its bishops, its surplices, its ceremonies, was hardly better to them than the Roman Church, and they refused to attend it. As their propaganda spread, they were sharply persecuted, while the Puritans, who in the main yielded obedience and worshipped as demanded by the law, were left comparatively undisturbed.

Puritans and Separatists

On turning to the foreign developments of Elizabeth's reign we are immediately struck by the fact that they are so intimately associated with her religious policy that we are forced to conclude that one can not be understood without the other. Exactly as in matters of religion the whole tenor of her conduct in the foreign field was caution, a daring caution if one may venture the expression. Caution the In consequence, she remained for a surprisingly long time chief note of on reasonably good terms with both the pope and Philip Elizabeth's of Spain. But in measure as her Protestant policy took a foreign policy more definite shape, a coolness sprang up which the bull of excommunication of 1570 converted into open hostility. Turn as Elizabeth would in her shifty manner, there was now no way by which she could avoid being identified with the general Protestant movement. With the closing of the ranks effected by the Council of Trent (1563) the Catholic Counter-Reformation, waxing stronger every day, became more resolutely set on winning back the lost ground; and unless the Protestants closed their ranks in their turn, it was only too likely that their forces would be broken and routed. The great fact of the last quarter of the sixteenth century is that inexorably Catholicism and Protestantism were drawn into a world struggle, in which Philip of Spain eagerly stepped forward as the champion of Rome and Elizabeth with characteristic manifest reluctance became the paladin of the newer faith.

Every event of Elizabeth's reign contributed to precipitate the inevitable struggle, notably the queen's relation with Scotland and Scotland's sovereign, Mary Stuart. Scotland had been England's foe for centuries. We have seen that Henry VII, with a The affairs view to a better understanding and possible union of the of Scotland two countries, had married his daughter Margaret to James IV. But war was not thereby averted. James IV and James V both sympathized with France and both died while fighting England, the latter (1542) when his successor, Mary, was but a few days old. As the royal Scottish infant grew to maidenhood, owing to her descent from Henry VII, she came to be regarded as a possible eventual successor to the English throne; and when in 1558 Elizabeth, the last direct heir of Henry VIII assumed the scepter, the opinion was generally entertained that unless Elizabeth married and had children, the crown would in due course devolve on the Scottish queen. Nor should it be overlooked that to passionate Catholics, Mary Stuart had a claim that took precedence even over that of Elizabeth, since to them the daughter of Anne Boleyn was an illegitimate child. Out of this relation of the two women to the English throne sprang their instinctive aversion for each other and the long and bloody drama of their rivalry, ending in Mary's death upon the scaffold.

When Mary succeeded to the throne of Scotland, she was, as has been said, a child in arms. Her mother, another Mary, of the French family of Guise, assumed the regency, and in order to withdraw her

Queen Mary sent to France when a child
child from a threatening English control sent her over to France, where she was soon betrothed to the heir of the throne, who bore the title dauphin. Thus in spite of all the Tudors had been able to do, the interests of France and Scotland had become more closely knit than ever.

Mary of Guise, as Scottish regent, soon met with the difficulties which beset every government in her time. Toward the middle of the century the voices of the Reformation began to be heard in the

The Protestant movement in Scotland
land. Conversions grew apace, and presently the struggle between the old and the new faiths was joined with the customary vehemence. But nowhere was it so brief and nowhere was the victory of the new teachings so decisive. Scotland was still a backward, feudal land, where the chief power rested with a lawless nobility. The clergy, too, had considerable wealth and power, but the religious indifference and luxurious living of the prelates had undermined the affections of the people. So slight was the hold of the Church on Scotland that the fiery Calvinist preachers, among whom John Knox (1505–72) was the leading spirit, had only to spread their propaganda for a few years in order to draw the common people completely to their side. When the nobility, lured by the bait of the rich Church lands, threw in their lot with the preachers, the success of the Reformation in Scotland was assured.

The French gentlewoman who held the regency of Scotland viewed these developments with consternation. She had lost her hold on the country and could think of no other way of getting it back than by

The regent calls in the French to put down Protestant- ism
the aid of French troops. At her request France sent soldiers, who had put themselves in possession of a number of important places and were on the road to repressing the Protestant movement altogether at the very moment when Elizabeth had given a Protestant turn to English affairs by establishing her national Church. The wisdom of aiding the northern Protestants as a means of ousting France from Scotland was so obvious that Elizabeth resolved to send men and ships to their aid. These forces succeeded in bringing the French to terms, and by the treaty of Edinburgh (1560) the latter agreed to abandon

Scotland. As at this juncture, the regent fell ill and died, and as Queen Mary was still in France, the Protestants suddenly found themselves masters of the situation. In a parliament composed of the friends of Knox they abolished the papal supremacy, forbade the mass, and laid the foundations of a new church of their own (1560).

The church that thus came into being only a year after Elizabeth had set up her Anglican establishment was based, like it, on independence from Rome; but this general Protestant feature apart, it bore little resemblance to its southern neighbor. John Knox, the chief organizing genius of the Scottish church, had sat at the feet of Calvin at Geneva, and was resolved to model it, as nearly as the differences between a small city-state and an extensive kingdom permitted, according to Calvin's theory of church organization. In consequence each congregation governed itself democratically, that is, was ruled by the pastor in connection with elected laymen called presbyters, while the national church, being the sum of the separate congregations, was ruled by a body of delegates representing the local groups and called the general assembly. Together with these self-governing features the doctrines and worship of Geneva were taken over by the new institution practically without a change. Because of the important place conceded to the presbyters (or elders) the new church came generally to be known as the Presbyterian Kirk of Scotland.

Calvanism dominates the government, doctrines, and service of the new church

Up to the time of this religious revolution the absent Queen Mary had not concerned herself much with the doings of rude and far-away Scotland. By the accession (1559) of her husband, Francis II, to the French throne she had recently become queen of France; and ever since the death of Mary Tudor (1558) she had, supported by a good part of the Catholic world, looked upon herself also as the rightful queen of England. But the year 1560 perceptibly darkened her outlook. The feeble sovereign, Francis II, died, and Elizabeth made herself tolerably secure at home. Scotland alone seemed to be left to Mary, and as Scotland needed its sovereign, she suddenly (1561) hurried thither.

Mary returns to Scotland, 1561

When Mary landed in Scotland she was only nineteen years old and no better than a stranger. Add to this fact the circumstance that she was confronted by a lawless nobility, and, as a Catholic, was an object of intense suspicion to her Protestant subjects, and one has the elements of a problem that even a better and wiser person than Mary might not have solved. But though she proved unequal to the situation, she was a woman of many admirable **Her diffi-** gifts. Grace of body and spirit were joined to a nimble **culties and** wit and a keen intelligence. The chance that tossed her **character** to France had furnished her with a rare opportunity for development, for the court of the Valois had become the home of all the exquisite influences of the Renaissance, and the people she met there, the very air she breathed, tingled with the joy of living. She soon became the ruling genius of a bright circle and the hours revolved for her amid dancing, music, and poetry. Her contemporaries never tired of praising her beauty; but better than formal beauty, she possessed a subtle charm which appealed to the chivalry of men and raises partisans for her even in our day. Thus endowed, she was called to be a great queen, on one condition: she must subordinate her personal wishes to her duty as a sovereign. And here it was that she failed. Her cousin Elizabeth, who did not fail in this particular, proved herself thereby, if not the better woman, at least the greater queen. Comparing the two cousins, who inevitably force a comparison upon us standing as they do on the stage of history flashing challenge at each other, we are moved to subscribe to the familiar judgment: Elizabeth was first a statesman and then a woman, Mary was first a woman and then a statesman.

Mary began well enough. She made no difficulties about the Presbyterian Kirk, merely reserving to herself as sovereign the right of **Mary mar-** Catholic worship. For four years Scotland enjoyed an **ries Lord** unusual degree of peace. But in the year 1565 Mary **Darnley** married her cousin, Lord Darnley, and by that event she and all Scotland were plunged into troubles involving a succession of climaxes unique in history.

Lord Darnley, who was hardly more than an over-grown boy, turned out to be proud, silly, and dissolute. He was no sooner married than he became the tool of the party of nobles opposed to **The** Mary. They represented to him that if he did not enjoy **murders of** full authority with the queen, it was due to one of Mary's **Riccio and** foreign secretaries, an Italian, David Riccio. Darnley, **Darnley** egged on by the nobles, resolved to have revenge. One night while Mary was sitting at supper, the conspirators burst into the room, fell upon Riccio, and in spite of the queen's frantic efforts to save him dragged him from the chamber and slew him at the door

(1566). Much of what followed is uncertain. Certain it is that such love as Mary may have had for her husband was henceforth turned to hate. She planned revenge. For the moment Darnley and his friends held the reins in their hands and she was forced to resort to dissimulation. By cleverly feigning an affection which she did not feel, she brought her husband to his knees before her, separated him from her enemies, and quickly reacquired control. Thenceforth she took few pains to hide her loathing for the wretched prince. In February, 1567, the house where Darnley was staying just outside the walls of Edinburgh was shattered by an explosion of gunpowder and Darnley was found dead the next morning. We know beyond a doubt that the murderer was the earl of Bothwell, a dare-devil nobleman of evil repute who was in love with the queen, but we should also like to know whether or not the queen was his accomplice. Historical investigation has not yet supplied a definite answer to this question, but certainly by what followed the murder Mary has compromised her good name beyond help. Not only did she permit Bothwell's trial for the death of her consort to degenerate into a farce, but shortly after the earl's acquittal she married him.

Obliged to defend her hasty nuptials, Mary alleged that in marrying Bothwell she had not consulted her free will but had yielded to violence. The apology has little inherent probability and was rejected with scorn by her subjects. Filled with horror **The revolt** and resentment, they revolted against her, and although **against** she rallied repeatedly from defeat, by the year 1568 she **Mary** found herself without further resources. Despairing of success without English help, she crossed the border to appeal to Elizabeth. She would have done better to have risked the perils of the sea, for she became her cousin's prisoner and won her release only after nineteen years by laying her head upon the block.

Before we take up Elizabeth's conduct, let us take note that, tragic as Mary's fate was, her country profited by her downfall. Her infant son was crowned king as James VI, while her half-brother, the earl of Moray, assumed the regency. Moray rep- **James VI** resented the Protestant party, and his rule meant reli- **king and** gious peace for Scotland on the basis of the complete **Moray** triumph of the Presbyterian church. **regent**

It is not difficult to account for the harsh policy which Elizabeth adopted toward her royal cousin. In fairness to the English queen we must acknowledge that imperative considerations of state left no other course open.　Looking out from London over Europe she beheld a perplexing situation.　She saw Philip II in arms against the Netherlands, resolved, if necessary, to drown Protestantism in

Explana-
tion of
Elizabeth's
severity
with regard
to Mary

blood; in France she took note of a civil war, in which the Catholic party, in order to achieve its end, did not balk at such revolting measures as the massacre of St. Bartholomew; she was in frequent peril of her life through the plots of her own Catholic subjects who aimed to raise Mary to the throne; and she saw a threatening general concentration of the whole Catholic world for a supreme blow against the Protestant schismatics.

Under these conditions her conduct could not but be regulated primarily with reference to the Catholic movement now plainly mounting to a climax.　By the beginning of the eighties, Philip,

Prospect of
war between
England
and Spain

through his famous general, Parma, had gone far toward reducing the Netherlands to subjection, while through his alliance with the French Catholic party he so dominated France as to be reasonably sure that that kingdom would not strike him from the rear.　He could therefore concentrate his attention upon the dangerous and elusive Elizabeth.　But in measure as the blow from Spain became more imminent, the patriotism of her subjects mounted, causing them to rally with increasing enthusiasm about her throne.　Without waiting for the Spanish attack, certain bold spirits, such as John Hawkins and Francis Drake, fitted out ships at their own expense and, ranging the Spanish main as pirates, plundered his most Catholic majesty's treasure fleet or burned his trans-Atlantic settlements.　While Philip and Elizabeth, cautious spirits both, slow to decide for war, were still protesting friendship in official notes, their subjects had already engaged in combat on their own account.　Only when, in 1585, the queen went the length of giving open and armed aid to the revolted Netherlands, did Philip resolve to show his hand.　He prepared against England the greatest armament his means permitted.

It was the rumor of Philip's invasion of England, coupled with the renewed activity of the English supporters of Mary, that cost the unfortunate queen of Scots her life.　Probably it had little value

Execution
of Mary

for her, since, grown old and gray behind prison walls, she knew herself beaten.　Elizabeth's ministers succeeded in convincing her that Mary was party to a conspiracy which a man by the name of Babington had directed against the life of the sovereign, and though hypocritically feigning reluctance, she signed her cousin's death-warrant.   With the Spaniards about to descend on the country it was dangerous, nay, suicidal, not to scatter every Catholic nucleus and rallying-point within the kingdom.   That at least was the settled view of Burghley, Walsingham, and the strict Protestant group which dominated the Privy Council.   In February, 1587, Mary was executed at Fotheringay as a sacrifice to Protestant and national security.

The next year the war between Spain and England came to a head. Philip having at length got together over one hundred ships, celebrated as the Invincible Armada, despatched them toward the English coasts.   The plan was that the Armada should The Armada sail first to the Netherlands and by putting itself at the 1588 disposal of the duke of Parma, who commanded the Spanish land forces, should enable that great captain to transport them to England. The island-realm was thoroughly alive to its danger.   In the face of the foreign invader religious differences were forgotten and replaced by a flaming national enthusiasm, temporarily uniting all parties. In fact, the Armada, more than all the repressive legislative acts put together, weakened the English Catholic ranks, for, from the opening of the war, to be a Catholic meant to be a friend of Philip and but few Englishmen cared to expose themselves to so revolting an imputation.   A navy filled with the spirit which is ready to do and die was put at Elizabeth's disposal.   With such leaders as Lord Howard, Sir Francis Drake, and Sir Martin Frobisher, many of whom had spent a lifetime fighting the Spaniards on all known seas, the English were not likely to fail for want of bravery or skill.   Nor were they likely to fail for want of ships.   They mustered even more vessels than the Spaniards, which, although not so large as the galleons of the enemy, by virtue of their speed, the size and number of their guns, and the capable seamanship of officers and men held the Spaniards at their mercy.   Hardly had the slow-sailing Spanish fleet appeared in the English channel (July, 1588), when the more expeditious English vessels fell upon its rear and flank.   The injuries suffered by the Spaniards during a running sea-fight lasting eight days forced them to lie off Calais for repairs.   Here a number of fire-ships sent among them drove them from their shelter into the arms of the English lying in wait outside the port, and in the ensuing combat they suffered so much additional damage that the expedition lost its last breath of offensive vigor.   Finding the channel blocked behind him, the discouraged Spanish admiral tried to make for home by the coast of Scotland. But he encountered storms, even more devastating than the English; his ships were shattered miserably by waves and rocks; and only an insignificant remnant ever returned to Cadiz to tell the story of the great disaster.

England was safe, and more than England, the cause of Protestantism in the Netherlands and throughout Europe. The English admirals now transferred the scene of action to the Spanish coasts, and Elizabeth's soon the disheartened Philip sued for a peace which his last years triumphant foe would not allow. As for Elizabeth, the overthrow of the Spanish Armada was the climax of her reign. Thenceforth her people identified her with the national triumph and worshipped her as the very spirit of England. But her private life slowly entered into eclipse. She was old, childless, and lonely. Her last attachment, of which the earl of Essex was the object, brought her abundant disappointment and sorrow. Essex had been put at the head of an army destined to subdue Ireland, which was just then agitated by the famous rising of O'Neill, but as he mismanaged his campaign and came home without leave, he was dismissed in disgrace. Full of resentment, he now engaged in a treasonable plot, for which he was arrested and executed (1601).

Elizabeth's relations to the handsome earl were hardly as romantic as historians of a sentimental turn have tried to make out. The tiny seed of romance implanted in her nature was suffocated at an Her stunted early age by the accident which had tossed her to the affections throne. Obliged from that moment to regard marriage not as an end in itself but as an affair of state, she deftly fished, with herself as bait, in all the matrimonial waters of Europe only to remain single to the last. Since marriage with a foreign prince would have bound England to the interests of some other country, her refusal to wed promoted English independence, besides making possible the union of England and Scotland through the accession at her death of the son and heir of Mary Stuart. For this wise restraint in the public interest she sought compensation by numerous flirtations with her courtiers such as the earl of Leicester in her youth and the earl of Essex in her old age. But these by no means filled her life which, occupied with the ceaseless agitations of politics, was passed so largely with state business that there was left neither much time nor inclination for the cultivation of the affections. In her last phase she presents the tragic picture of a great and glorious queen who, amidst the acclamations of a grateful people, could not conceal that she was a lonely and embittered woman.

Passing in review the whole Tudor period from the accession of Henry VII in 1485 to the death of Elizabeth in 1603, the observer is struck by the remarkable transformation effected in English politics, society, material well-being, and culture. The unchal- The lenged authority of the sovereign coupled with the weak- progress of ness of representative institutions is the outstanding the age political feature and defines the essence of the Tudor system. Largely through this vigorous Tudor leadership the nascent nationalism was so greatly stimulated that it welded the people into a single unit which, marshalled solidly behind Elizabeth, constituted the real secret of her strength. Full of a new confidence thousands of Englishmen ventured upon the seas in search of fortune and, on being thwarted by the maritime preponderance of Spain, began a buccaneering attack, which in due time dragged their reluctant government into a life-and-death struggle with the world power of Philip II. If at Elizabeth's death England had not yet replaced Spain as a colonial power, at least a way had been cleared which the succeeding generations would only have to follow with energy in order to gain an assured success. In short, the English, who, in view of their island position, had hitherto rather strangely neglected the sea, discovered that it was their true element, opening the possibility not only of adventure and colonial conquest but of an enriching trade with all the peoples scattered over the face of the earth. Already by Elizabeth's time a rapidly expanding commerce had greatly increased the wealth of the country and raised the standard of living especially among the gentry and merchants, while the court was distinguished by a splendor and luxury which recall Renaissance Italy and signify an open and complete break with the frugal tradition of the Middle Age.

But proud navies, numberless merchant ships, abundant trade, and a splendid court are only material manifestations of the underlying human spirit, which is the real achievement of any age. The Tudor spirit was the English version of the energy The spirit which poured itself through the occident with the Renais- of the age sance and signified the seizure of the earth as an untrammeled field of opportunity. Emboldened by this fresh faith, men conceived of themselves as gods with no perceptible limit to their progress along the upward line of realization of themselves and of their world. And when they turned to the arts, as men always do on having their imaginations set aglow, they perforce accumulated a varied and memorable creative product. However, while all the arts registered the stimulating effect of the new outlook, it was, as is well known, chiefly literature, and in literature more particularly the drama, which served as an outlet for the visionary hopes which poured like an electric current through the minds of men. In the plays of Shakespeare, Jonson, and their contemporaries we have the abiding imaginative expression of "the spacious times of great Elizabeth."

REFERENCES

P. SMITH, *Age of the Reformation*
A. L. CROSS, *History of England and Greater Britain*, chs. 18–26
B. S. TERRY, *History of England*, pp. 494–617
E. CHEYNEY, *Industrial and Social History of England*
Cambridge Modern History, I, ch. 14, II, chs. 13–16, III, chs. 8–11
H. O. WAKEMAN, *History of the Church of England*, chs. 10–14
T. M. LINDSAY, *History of the Reformation*, II, Bk. 3, chs. 6, Bk. 4
F. SEEBOHM, *Oxford Reformers*
F. A. GASQUET, *Eve of the Reformation*, chs. 1–4
T. F. TOUT, *Advanced History of Great Britain*
A. D. INNES, *England under the Tudors*
A. F. POLLARD, *Henry VIII*; *Political History of England, 1547–1603;* *Factors in Modern History*
H. GEE, *The Reformation Period*
A. LANG, *John Knox and the Reformation*
A. B. HART, *John Knox* (in Amer. Hist. Rev. XIII, 259–80)
R. S. RAIT, *Mary Queen of Scots*
E. S. BEESLEY, *Queen Elizabeth*
M. CREIGHTON, *Queen Elizabeth*
W. C. ABBOTT, *Expansion of Europe*, I, ch. 15
R. BAGWELL, *Ireland under the Tudors*
SIR T. MORE, *Utopia*
H. FROUDE, *History of England from the Fall of Wolsey to the Death of Elizabeth*
R. H. TAWNEY, *Agrarian Problems in the Sixteenth Century*
E. F. GAY, *Inclosures in England* (in Quart. Journal of Econ., vol. XVII)

CHAPTER IX

THE REVOLT OF THE NETHERLANDS AND THE FOUNDING OF THE DUTCH REPUBLIC

Stadtholders of the House of Orange-Nassau

William I, the Silent (*d.* 1584)

Maurice (*d.* 1625)   Frederick Henry (*d.* 1647)

William II (*d.* 1650) *m.* Mary, daughter of Charles I of England

William III (*d.* 1702) *m.* Mary, daughter of James II of England

The section of Europe known as the Netherlands or Low Countries lies at the mouth of the Rhine and Meuse rivers and in the Middle Age belonged in the main to the Holy Roman Empire (Germany). As, however, the western coastal area, called Flanders, was a part of the kingdom of France, it followed that France had an interest in this area and kept a watchful eye upon it. The Lowlands were divided among many lords, such as the duke of Brabant, the count of Holland, the count of Hainault, and the bishop of Liège, who made it their business to become increasingly independent of their suzerain and who, owing to the steady decline of the imperial fortunes, largely succeeded in their object. By the fifteenth century the authority of the emperor over these territories had become quite shadowy. But there were other reasons than the emperor's feebleness for the growing independence of the Netherlands. Favorably located on the sea and along rivers that permitted an easy penetration to a populous hinterland, they had developed a blooming trade and industry which in their turn gave birth to prosperous towns bent on controlling their own destinies through charters guaranteeing the right of self-government. Hence municipal life flourished and a

The Netherlands become independent of the Holy Roman Empire

191

spirit of communal independence was abroad which, while openly flouting the weak and distant emperor, was strong enough to oblige the local lords to treat the republican system with respect. In short, the Netherlands, teeming with commercial enterprise and headed away from feudalism, gradually lost mental contact with the state of which they were geographically and politically a part.

But still another cause for the gradual failure of imperial authority must be recounted. It has to do with the remarkable political experiment inaugurated in the fourteenth century by the duke of Burgundy. The duke, a younger member of the French reigning house enfeoffed with the duchy of Burgundy, conceived the ambitious project of adding the Netherlands to his native duchy, thereby building up a great, independent power between France and Germany and at the expense of both. By marriage, treachery, and force the successive dukes achieved a notable triumph and were visibly on the way toward realizing their ultimate hope when Duke Charles, called the Bold, perished in battle against the Swiss (1477), leaving his rich inheritance to his only child, his daughter Mary. Taking advantage of this situation, Louis XI of France quickly seized the duchy of Burgundy on the ground that it had with the death of the last male duke escheated to the crown; but the other Burgundian lands, constituting substantially the Netherlands, were kept intact by Mary's marriage with Maximilian of Hapsburg. From Mary and Maximilian the Netherlands passed to their son Philip (d. 1506) and from him to his son, Charles, who ruled them to his abdication in 1555. Naturally enough the long association of these provinces and cities under a single line of rulers contributed not a little to a sense of separate statehood.

Charles, heir of the house of Burgundy, was, as we are aware, heir also of the houses of Spain and Austria and the dominating figure of his age under the title Emperor Charles V. Born and brought up in the Netherlands, he always retained an affectionate regard for this territory, although in his later life, owing to the exigencies of his great position, he only paid it an occasional visit. As his chief purpose was to carry through as far as possible the policy of his Burgundian ancestors, he tried to round off his possessions territorially and to bring them into an effective political union. In both these respects his success was notable. By acquiring Friesland and other lordships he found himself at the

The building up of the Burgundian state

Charles forms the Netherlands into a federal state

head of seventeen provinces, which he tried to draw more and more closely together by strengthening the federal institutions created by his predecessors. He instituted as central governing agencies for the whole Netherlands three councils of appointees, of which the Council of State was the most important; he raised Brussels, centrally located in the province of Brabant, to the dignity of federal capital; and he provided that the common interests of the provinces, especially in so far as they concerned taxation, should be looked after by a common parliament, called the States General and made up of delegates from the provincial parliaments. But though Charles did much toward consolidating the seventeen provinces, he at best overlaid and in no sense destroyed the older system of self-government native to this area. In consequence each province fully retained its own government composed of officials and a legislature called the Provincial Estates, while the chartered liberties of the many flourishing towns remained as exuberant as ever, practically constituting them municipal republics.

Speaking summarily, one need not hesitate to call Charles's reign a success. The life of the Netherlands was based on commerce and industry which prospered so prodigiously that this small area easily maintained its reputation as the bee-hive of Europe. Its busy cities, such as Lille, Valenciennes, Antwerp, Ghent, Bruges, Amsterdam and a score of others, were the wonder and envy of the rest of the world not only because of their wealth but also by reason of the intellectual culture of their citizens. The sovereign drew heavily on their resources for the support of his Spanish and imperial program, scrupulously respecting however the financial privileges of the people by collecting and spending only such monies as had been previously authorized by a vote of the States General. There was a fundamentally amiable relation built on mutual understanding between Charles and his Netherlanders which was only slightly disturbed by their growing discontent over the obligation to contribute to the many far-reaching enterprises of their ruler in which they had little or no concern. Nevertheless when in 1555, in connection with a ceremony conducted at Brussels with much pomp and splendor, Charles abdicated in favor of his son, Philip, he was the object of a spontaneous demonstration of general affection. While this may have owed some of its fervor to the suspicion with which his successor, brought up in Spain and incapable of speaking the language of the people, was regarded, it is safe to accept it as a popular endorsement of his reign.

However, from one source, the Reformation, a deepening shadow had begun to fall across the land.   The religious agitation which centered about Luther was naturally disrespectful of landmarks and at an early point in its history invaded the Low Countries. Charles, whose dependence upon the German princes forced him, as we have seen, to a dilatory policy toward Lutheranism in Germany, was not the man to hesitate where he had the power to act.   In the Netherlands therefore the Protestant heresy was from its first appearance met by a relentless hostility which waxed more and more fierce as Charles's reign proceeded.   The Inquisition, with its bloody record of triumphs in Spain, not unnaturally appealed to the Spanish monarch as the best way of meeting heresy everywhere.   Accordingly it was established in the Netherlands, special inquisitors being appointed for each of the seventeen provinces and the civil authorities being held to a strict execution of the sentences imposed.   The usual violences followed; confiscations, imprisonments, burnings at the stake became common occurrences.   The edicts of Charles against heresy finally went so far as to impose the penalty of death on persons discovered to have in their possession forbidden writings, as well as on those who conducted secret prayer-meetings or who ventured merely to discuss the Holy Scriptures.   The Protestants in the Netherlands were long hardly more than a fraction of the population but Charles's rigor did not exterminate them.   The persecution served but to illustrate once again the famous observation that there is no seed like martyr's blood.   To the original Lutherans were presently added anabaptists and other extravagantly revolutionary sects, who found the intelligent and liberal society of the Netherlands a fertile soil for the propagation of their tenets; and from the middle of the century the faith of Calvin, destined to give the Prostestantism of the northern Netherlands its peculiar mold, found admission, by way of France, into all the leading cities.   The Inquisition, therefore, was enabled to gather a rich harvest.   Contemporary guesses placed the figure of its victims during Charles's reign at fifty thousand.   This is doubtless an exaggeration; but it is sufficiently correct to testify to Charles's intolerance and to establish his partial responsibility for the disaster which overtook his successor.   However, as Charles was regarded by the Netherlanders as one of themselves and as his reign

Charles ruthlessly suppresses Lutheranism

was in other respects happy, his policy of persecution did not during his life arouse any notable resistance.

Such was the country and such were the questions which were agitating it when the cold, bigoted, and Spanish-bred Philip took up the reins of government. The old heartiness which had obtained between ruler and ruled vanished almost over night to be Philip and succeeded by a deepening chill, of which the first stage the Inquisi-was reached when Philip's demand for money was severely tion curtailed by the States General. Unable to hide his resentment, he withdrew into himself, haughtily underscoring more than ever his foreign and Spanish character. If after this exhibition of the democratic resolution of his subjects there remained a single feature of the Netherlands which aroused his spontaneous enthusiasm it was the Inquisition. In fairness we must not forget that this institution owed its presence in the land to his father Charles. Philip felt no need of increasing its already abundantly hideous severities. But, on the other hand, mentally endowed as he was, he was utterly incapable of departing from the system of persecution, even in the face of a growing opposition. And unmistakably such an opposition was beginning to make itself felt. The uninterrupted flow of blood was getting on peoples' nerves and voices began to be heard in favor of a more humane and rational treatment of the current heresies. As Philip sternly sealed his ears to all such appeals the discontent already abroad in the land seized upon ever new elements of the population.

But during these early years, while he was still residing in the Netherlands, Philip had to meet other problems besides the domestic grievances of the Lowlanders. The greatest issue which, as king of Spain, he had inherited from his father was the ancient feud with France. Charles's last war, largely precipi- A new war tated by the help conceded by Henry II of France to the between German Protestants, had recently (1556) been brought to France and an unsatisfactory close. With so many matters unsettled Spain fol-lowed by between them both Philip and Henry were ill inclined the Treaty to peace and looked forward to an early resumption of the of Cateau-irrepressible conflict. Accordingly, in 1557 a new Cambrésis (1559) Franco-Spanish war broke out in which, as on several previous occasions, England took part on the Spanish side. On this occasion, however, the most pressing reason for England's Spanish partisanship was that the English sovereign, Mary, was the wife of Philip and that Philip was able to persuade her to cast her lot with him.

Philip's well-trained armies won two brilliant victories over the French forces, the first at St. Quentin (1557), the second at Gravelines (1558), thereby disposing the French to come to a settlement. It took the form of the celebrated peace of Cateau-Cambrésis (1559). As Queen Mary died during the negotiations, Philip refused to concern himself further about allied England and bought, at least in part, the favorable terms conceded by the French by leaving in their hands the port of Calais, the last English possession on French soil. Cateau-Cambrésis is a European landmark. It closed for the present the long rivalry between France and Spain; it once more confirmed Spain in the possession of Italy and the Netherlands; and it assured the Spanish ascendancy in Europe for another generation. With this feather floating from his cap, the proud victor resolved to end his residence in the Netherlands and to return without delay to his native Spain. Leaving behind as regent his half-sister, Margaret of Parma, he sailed away (1559) never to return.

His departure rapidly brought the threatening domestic crisis to maturity. While the government had been nominally entrusted to the Regent Margaret, a woman of some sagacity as well as popularity, the real power was vested in the Council of State and fell, within the Council, into the hands of a single individual, Cardinal Granvelle, a trusted servant and confidant of Philip. What Philip expected of Granvelle was strictly to carry out the orders received from Madrid, and as these insisted on maintaining every established measure no matter how hateful, the harassed cardinal was soon the object of a general hatred. The great nobles were particularly vociferous against him, in part no doubt on public grounds, but also because they saw in him the personal favorite whose political omnipotence signified the destruction of that influence in the administration which the politic Charles had been ever prompt to concede them. The most prominent members of this powerful class were Prince William of Orange and the Counts Egmont and Hoorn, who, drawing together in their common disappointment, became the nucleus of an active opposition party. But the waxing discontent made numerous converts also among such other classes as the lesser nobles and the burghers. These latter, the real bearers of the peculiar urban civilization of the country, were exacerbated by a long list of ills which they did not hesitate to bring to Granvelle's notice with the request to forward them to the king. In the main the burghers concentrated on three

The growing discontent with Philip's rule

grievances. Following the recent war with France, the Spanish troops, remaining in the Netherlands much longer than was necessary, were quartered on the inhabitants against the express terms of the country's liberties; further, there was the ecclesiastical reorganization which by increasing the number of bishoprics aroused fear not only of new public burdens but also of the increased power of the unbending ecclesiastical element; and finally, the burghers were insulted by the grievance, now a generation old and borne with less and less patience, of the Inquisition and its judicial murders.

Repeatedly the great nobles, acting as spokesmen for the country, undertook to send emissaries all the way to Spain to plead with Philip for a change of system with no result whatever except that the Spanish troops were withdrawn and that the person The protest of Granvelle was at last sacrificed (1564). Thereupon the of the lesser nobles, among whom there was an impoverished, "beggars" madcap, and avowedly Protestant element, took the bit between their teeth and resolved to stage a more effective protest of their own. Probably they were secretly encouraged by Prince William of Orange, although he did not for the present join them outright. In 1565 they formed a league among themselves for the object, among other matters, of securing the abolition of the Inquisition, operating as they put it, "to the great dishonor of the name of God and to the total ruin of the Netherlands." Though voicing their grievances in no uncertain terms, they also affirmed their continued allegiance to their rightful ruler. Plainly they were not yet prepared to resort to open rebellion. On April 5, 1566, three hundred of their number took the fateful step of proceeding in a body to the palace of the Regent Margaret at Brussels to put their petition, formally called the Request, in her hands. In spite of her rage at the impertinent demonstration she promised to forward the Request to the king. At a banquet held by the nobles some days later they were informed that one of the regent's courtiers had slightingly referred to them as beggars (gueux). Amid a scene of frenzied excitement they adopted the term as their party name and assumed as honored badges the beggar's wallet and wooden bowl.

The picturesque act of the "beggars" set the match to the tinder-heap and the whole country flamed up in spontaneous rebellion. The government of the regent was set at naught under the impression that the auspicious moment was at hand for ridding the country of the monstrous incubus of the Inquisition. Its prisoners were forcibly released and its persecution interdicted, while the Protestants openly avowed their faith and, gathering in bands and multitudes, listened with greedy ears to the revolutionary addresses of fanatic pastors. The icono- At length the excitement culminated in a form of mad- clastic fury ness. The Catholic churches were invaded, their pictured of 1566 windows, their saintly images were broken, their crosses and altars were shattered to fragments. The ruin of art wrought by these iconoclasts was incalculable. It was weeks before the fury spent itself, and months before the government, rallying the orderly elements about it, succeeded in repressing the insurgents. And now the question rose spontaneously to every tongue: how would Philip treat this outrage on his sacred authority?

It is possible that the abolition of the Inquisition, coupled with the proclamation of the religious tolerance which public sentiment demanded, would have rescued the situation. But these ideas were The coming foreign to the rulers of that day and seemed nothing less of Alva than deadly sin to a fanatical Catholic like Philip. In- stead of rejoicing at the restoration of civic peace, he planned a fearful vengeance. One of his best generals was the duke of Alva. Soldier and bigot, he was the typical Spaniard of the day, animated with blind devotion to his king and faith. This man of iron was ordered to supercede the regent and to ferret out and punish the participants in the late rebellion. In 1567, accompanied by 10,000 Spanish veterans, he made the long trip from Spain to Brussels via the Mediterranean, Italy, and the Alps. The Spanish troops were the best in Europe and had proved their invincibility on many a battlefield. They were bound for the Netherlands, which coun- try, though Philip was its sovereign, was, we should never forget, not a Spanish province but a separate commonwealth. Alva's coming was therefore an invasion and terror flew before him. It did not require much intelligence to foresee a period of coercion and violence and William of Orange, with a host of those who felt themselves compromised by the recent events, crossed the border into safety.

Alva did not long leave the anxious Netherlanders in doubt as to the meaning of his coming. He set up a special council, called the Council of Troubles, for the discovery of all those who had taken part The Council in the late excesses and who were tinged with disloyalty of Blood and heresy. Operating at Alva's pleasure and without the shred of a constitutional warrant, the new governing body soon received from the people the more ominous name of the Council of Blood. It signified a redoubled Inquisition, freed from the delays of law and the promptings of human pity. Hundreds and probably thousands perished at its order; tens of thousands from among the best of the land fled from the country. Among the more illustrious victims of the executioner were Egmont and Hoorn, whom neither their Catholic faith nor their conspicuous services to the king could save. As the greatest men within the reach of Alva's arm they were sent to the block as a warning to their countrymen. Paralyzed by the violence of the attack, the people meekly suffered the atrocious persecution.

Against this monstrous tyranny one man did not cease to protest — Prince William of Orange. William belonged to an ancient German family which had its seat in Nassau in western Germany. At an early age he had inherited from a cousin the tiny princi- William of pality of Orange on the Rhone, which he never thought it Orange worth while even to visit. However, as he did not scorn the title inhering in his French possession, it has become inseparably attached to his name. His connection with the Netherlands sprung from the fact that he was possessed of large estates there, chiefly in Holland and Brabant, and had been drawn by his early patron, the Emperor Charles V, into the service of the provinces. Disinclined from the first to Philip's policy, he passed gradually from secret to open opposition until he stood frankly on the platform of his country's liberties. Brought up a Catholic, though his parents had turned Lutheran, he abominated the violences of the Inquisition and focussed his attack on this ferocious institution. Throughout his life he never ceased pleading for tolerance, a plea to which all parties alike of that passionate age were deaf. Out of hatred of Philip and his methods, he gradually passed over into the Protestant camp, casting his lot at last with the Calvinist faith as commanding the most numerous following among that Dutch element of the Netherlands with which, as the struggle developed, he chose more and more to identify himself.

The fame of William rests on his risking life, wealth, and happiness in the cause of a people oppressed by a monstrous tyranny. As a general he was mediocre; even as a stateman, though he played the political game as skillfully and subtly as any of his The char-contemporaries, he has superiors among the great names acter of of history. Clearly his chief distinction is his stout, William courageous heart. Sometimes almost single-handed and at best with but the divided support of his little people, he braved the world power of Spain and through defeat piled on defeat persisted in his purpose. Famed for his eloquence and the most courteous of gentlemen, he became, somewhat inappropriately, known as William the Silent; but if the expression conveys the idea of a fortitude unwearied and uncomplaining, no title could be imagined more aptly defining his peculiar distinction.

In the spring of 1568 William, having turned all his available possessions into money and having summoned the most daring exiles around him, began gathering an army for the purpose of invading **William** the Netherlands. His resolution was tantamount to a **levies war** declaration of war against Philip. As coming from him-**upon Philip,** self such a proceeding was an act of sublime folly. Only **1568** in case it succeeded in rousing the Netherlanders against their oppressor would it acquire the altogether different aspect of the rebellion of an outraged people to secure their inalienable rights. To fill the provinces with his own spirit of resistance became William's supreme object, and gradually, although not without grievous disappointments and delays, he succeeded. As a result a small people challenged the greatest power of Europe and, after a dramatic struggle of eighty years (1568–1648), issued from the fight as victor. No more remarkable war than this has ever been waged in the history of the human race.

The first campaign proved the complete superiority of both Spanish generalship and the Spanish soldiery. William's army, largely composed of ill-paid mercenaries, was defeated and scattered. Alva, in **William** consequence, made light of the invasion. It had not been **and Alva** supported, as William had hoped, by an internal rising. To all appearances the country, crushed under the Spanish heel, had fallen into a torpor. But if this was what Alva counted on, he was destined before long to a harsh awakening. The Netherlands had indeed failed from fear to respond to William's first call, but unfortunate as the campaign of 1568 proved, it had had its effect; it had excited the people for a moment with the hope of deliverance and so stiffened them for resistance. Alva's own folly did the rest. Not only did he continue to suspend a pitiless terror over the country, but, in perpetual need of funds to pay his soldiers, he resorted to an extortionate taxation. However, when he attempted to introduce the Spanish *alcabala*, the so-called Tenth Penny, consisting of the levy of ten per cent upon every commercial transaction including the

purchase of daily necessities, he ran into adamant. Though the tax
was abandoned because uncollectable, the whole urban population
was henceforth solidly arrayed against this reckless representative of
military despotism.

At last after years of alert and patient waiting the rebels scored
their first notable success. If Spain held the land in her iron grasp,
she could not in the same unchallenged way hold the sea, peculiarly
the element of these coast-dwellers. Ever since William had The seizure
given the signal for resistance freebooters, proudly calling of Brill, 1572
themselves "beggars of the sea" in imitation of the first brotherhood
of the enemies of Spain, had done great harm to Spanish trade. At
length, rendered bold by the stern battle with wind and wave and in
sore need of shelter, they swept down upon their native coast and,
braving the terror of Alva's soldiery, stormed the small port of Brill
(April 1, 1572). A score of towns, especially in the northern provinces,
felt suddenly encouraged to drive the Spaniards out, and Alva unexpectedly found his power limited to Brussels and the south. Thereupon the liberated province of Holland elected William the Silent
stadtholder or governor, and Holland and Zealand together, both
situated on the sea, became from this time forth the heart of the
resistance.

Thrown into the fiercest mood by this new phase of the struggle,
Alva prepared to win back the lost ground. Pity henceforth was
excluded from his thoughts. Malines, Zutphen, Naarden, and many
other towns which he recaptured were delivered to the Barbarous
unbridled excesses of the Spanish soldiery. Women and character of
children were slaughtered in cold blood. In 1573, after the war
a heroic resistance of eight months, Haarlem was retaken amidst
scenes of unbelievable ferocity. The war entered upon a new stage,
in which oppressors and oppressed thirsted for each other's blood like
wild beasts and neither sought nor gave quarter. It was a fight to
the last ditch and of unexampled fury.

The costly and exhausting struggle shook even Philip's faith, if
not in himself at least in his agent, and he resolved on Alva's recall.
A serious reverse suffered by the Spaniards before the walls of Alkmaar clinched his resolution. In December, 1573, the The recall
man who six years before had come to the Netherlands to of Alva
sow the dragon-teeth of war took his departure amidst the execra-
tions of both friend and foe.

The arrival of a new governor-general, Requesens (1573–76), was marked by a belated effort at negotiations. .But as Requesens was not authorized to offer any substantial concessions and as William insisted as his minimum on the withdrawal of the Spanish troops and on religious toleration, nothing came of these exchanges and Requesens had perforce to proceed with the reduction of the still unsubdued province of Holland. The outstanding event of his governorship was the siege of Leyden (1574). When, owing to the failure of provisions, the city was on the point of surrender, William, who had made futile efforts to succor the inhabitants, resolved on an extreme measure: he ordered the cutting of the dykes built to protect the land against the invasion of the sea. To those who objected to this stern measure he answered with a shrug: "Better to ruin the land than lose it." As the water rushed over the fields, the "beggars of the sea" pressed on in their ships, sailing past trees and houses till they reached the walls of the city. For the drowning Spaniards there was no alternative but retreat. Thus was famished Leyden saved. Wishing to reward the brave inhabitants for their heroism, William founded a university in their midst which rapidly rose to the front rank and has made the name of Leyden illustrious in the history of modern learning.

The unsuccessful siege of Leyden, 1574

With the sudden death of Requesens in 1576 came a notable extension of the revolt, to understand which we must examine for a moment the peoples inhabiting the seventeen provinces. Acquired by the house of Burgundy more or less by haphazard and subjected to a partial centralization, the Netherlands none the less lacked the main qualification of a successful union, the consciousness of a common nationality. The seven northern provinces, of which Holland and Zealand were the chief, together with the two central territories of Brabant and Flanders, were inhabited by a people of Teutonic stock. The southern provinces, such as Namur, Hainault, and Artois, were inhabited by Walloons, a Celtic people using the French language. The population of the Netherlands was therefore predominantly Teutonic, though with a notable Celto-French admixture. But the Teutonic group was to its misfortune not fused into a solid mass, for the inhabitants of Flanders and Brabant were Flemings, while the people of Holland and the neighboring provinces were Dutch. The differences between Flemings and Dutch in speech, customs, and mentality were inconsiderable and would, under favorable circumstances, have proved no

The people of the Netherlands

obstacle to close political association. Nationalism, as we are aware, was as yet a relatively new force in the world. Certainly it had thus far hardly made itself felt in this area nor had it interfered with the Burgundian-Hapsburg program of uniting Walloons, Flemings, and Dutch in a single state. However, awakened by religious and economic differences, nationalism might easily prove a source of serious division.

Up to 1576 the revolt had been confined to the northern or Dutch provinces, which had steeled their rebel spirit by immersion in the Calvinist faith. However, it had also penetrated to such occasional cities of the Flemish area as inclined to the same or to a related form of Protestantism. Plainly revolt from Spain and from the Catholic Church showed a tendency to go hand in hand. The purely political grievances of the central and southern provinces were as great as those of the north, but as they clung to the Catholic faith, they never gave up the hope of an ultimate accommodation with their Catholic ruler, Philip. For a brief moment however, following *The common declaration against Spain in the Pacification of Ghent, 1576* the death of Requesens, north, center, and south, Dutch, Flemings, and Walloons — in a word, the United Netherlands — presented a single and unbroken front to the oppressor. The occasion for this extraordinary display was furnished by the general horror inspired by the Spanish soldiery, which, left on the death of Requesens without a leader and without pay, indulged in a wild orgy of theft, murder, and pillage. The "Spanish Fury," as the mutinous outbreak was called, reached its peak at Antwerp. In this, the greatest trading city of the Atlantic seaboard, some seven thousand inhabitants were put to the sword while property of untold value was carried off or wantonly destroyed. At these outrages a vast indignation against the Spanish rule swept the whole country and in an agreement of November, 1576, called the Pacification of Ghent, representatives of all the seventeen provinces declared that they would not rest until the foreign troops had been withdrawn from the land and all the old liberties restored.

This, the most auspicious moment of the revolution, held out a glorious promise which was never realized. True, the successor of Requesens, who was Don John of Austria, the famous victor of Lepanto, found himself so isolated on his arrival that he accomplished nothing in his governorship (1576–78). But with the coming of Alexander Farnese, duke of Parma (1578–92), the situation gradually changed. Son of the former regent, Margaret of Parma, and a nephew of King Philip, this Italian prince possessed military and diplomatic gifts of a high order and may without hesitation be accepted as one of the greatest men of his generation. If the historian Motley ironically acclaims him the equal in deceit and double-dealing of Queen Elizabeth, against whom, as well as against William of Orange, he was perpetually engaged in matching his wits, this left-handed compliment must not be taken too seriously, for subterfuge and concealment were the stock-in-trade of diplomats then as now. The quality possessed by the duke of Parma which was of the very essence of statesmanship was that he could set himself a goal for his onward march and never lose it from sight even when he stood still or temporarily retreated. With regard to the Netherlands he resolved to save what he could from the wreck left by his predecessors and to use force or cajolery according to the situation. Above all, he relied on the suspicions inevitable between Protestants and Catholics in that day, sure that if he for his part firmly identified himself with the Catholic cause, he would sooner or later find the Catholic provinces behind him. The only basis on which the program of the Pacification of Ghent of a free and united Netherlands could have been realized would have been religious toleration. While William of Orange never ceased advocating this broad measure, he was in his enlightenment far ahead of his age and stood, a helpless arbiter, between venomously contentious groups. By establishing himself in the French or Walloon provinces, in the midst of a solidly Catholic population, the clever duke of Parma once more gained a foothold in the Netherlands and was not long in breaking up the harmony represented by the Pacification of Ghent. In January, 1579, he persuaded Artois, Hainault, and Douay to sign the treaty of Arras whereby they undertook to defend the Catholic religion and, in return for a guarantee of their ancient rights, to renew their allegiance to Philip.

As soon as the Union of Arras, as the Catholic league was called, had created a rallying-ground for Catholicism, it became necessary for William of Orange, however reluctantly, to draw the Protestants together into a counter-league. This was effected in the same year (1579) at Utrecht, where the northern provinces established a union in their turn. Holland and Zealand, as the centers of the rebellion, led the way but were joined by their immediate neighbors finally five

The tactful policy of the duke of Parma enables him to create a Catholic league in the southern Netherlands

in number, Utrecht, Gelderland, Overyssel, Groningen, and Friesland. The Union of Utrecht was substantially a declaration of independence, although the sovereignty of Philip was not definitely renounced till two years later. The new state took the *The Union* modest name of the Seven United Provinces, but before *of Utrecht* the world it became known under the more sonorous title *(1579)* of the Dutch Republic, representative of what henceforth *marks the birth of the* figures in history as a distinct nation. The articles of the *Dutch* Union of Utrecht served as the constitution of the new- *Republic* born state. This constitution had a typically federal character, that is, while leaving the self-governing powers of the seven member-provinces intact, it created a certain amount of central machinery to handle the common interests. As these were rather narrowly interpreted to embrace nothing more than defensive action against Philip, and as, moreover, the provinces were hotly jealous of their traditional rights, the new federal institutions were not given sufficient strength to make them effective. This becomes clear when we discover that, instead of a single federal head, the executive power was vested in a weak Council of State, and that the central legislative body, called the States General, could impose taxes only with the consent of the several Provincial Estates. This cumbersome machinery slowed up federal business considerably and could, on occasion, bring it to a dead stop. For the present, however, the personal ascendancy of William of Orange, who was stadtholder of both Holland and Zealand and who exercised a broad influence in all the other provinces as well, made up for the imperfect and impracticable federal arrangements.

In this new form, expressive of a definite Catholic-Protestant schism in the Netherlands, the struggle went on. Parma, planted in the Walloon south, faced William of Orange established in the Dutch north, while between them lay the rich Flemish *The struggle* provinces of Flanders and Brabant, which, flattered and *between* assaulted by both sides, wavered irresolutely and might *William and* fall either way. However, the skill of Parma, backed by *the duke of* the resources of Spain, began gradually to tell. In his *Parma* deliberate way, sometimes by a successful siege, sometimes by negotiations, he increased steadily the area under his control. To all the world, and more particularly to Philip and his governor-general, it seemed that only William's leadership and resolution stood between Parma and ultimate success. Often the prayer must have risen to Philip's lips that some happy chance might clear his path of his determined enemy.

Finally, since fate seemed reluctant, Philip resolved to come to its assistance and in 1580 published a ban against his rebellious subject, offering gold and a patent of nobility to whoever "should deliver The murder this pest to us, dead or alive." William justified himself of William, against Philip's charges in a pamphlet called the "Apol-1584 ogy," wherein he drew a stinging portrait of the patron of assassins. Nevertheless, the ban proved to be William's death-warrant. Many abortive attempts had already been made upon his life, when a Burgundian, Balthasar Gérard by name, one of those unflinching religious fanatics in which the age abounded, pierced his breast with a bullet. The murder occurred on July 10, 1584, as the prince was descending the stairway of his palace at Delft. The victim's last thoughts turned toward the struggle in which his country was engaged. "Lord have pity on my soul," he said, "and on this poor people." Gérard was executed amid atrocities against which every act of William's life was a protest, while Philip exulted in the deed and rewarded the heirs of the murderer according to his promise.

While William's death did not break down the resistance of the Dutch, as Philip had calculated, it encouraged the Catholic party and shook the resolution of the merely half-hearted defenders of indepen-The Dutch dence. Parma was able to occupy most of the disputed Republic area of Flanders and Brabant, capping the climax with appeals for the capture (1585), after a long and memorable siege, of help to France and the great port of Antwerp. It now only remained to con-England quer the indomitable provinces of Holland and Zealand. If, in the face of so many disasters, they were able to continue their resistance, it was for the single reason that, as from the beginning of the conflict, they still commanded the sea with their navies. But obliged to face the forces of Spain under an extraordinarily versatile general, the Dutch were often despondent. Their dead leader had held that independence could be won only with the help of foreign powers and had long directed passionate appeals for assistance to France and England. But these states, fearful of the power of Philip, had hesitated. Although Elizabeth occasionally sent secret encouragement in the form of money, she would not commit herself openly. France, too, vacillated, but shortly (1582) before William's death, went the length of permitting the duke of Anjou, brother of the king, to come to the aid of the insurgents. Anjou was offered the crown of the Netherlands on the understanding that he would rid the country of the Spaniards; but he proved a broken reed, intrigued and quarrelled with everybody, and happily for all concerned died exactly one month before William's tragic end. There was now no chance of help except from Elizabeth, and the Dutch, at the end of their tether, made her a pressing tender of the young republic. Although the prospect was inviting, moved by her customary caution she declined the dangerous honor. Nevertheless, she could no longer with due regard to her own safety refuse to grant substantial help. Spain and England had already begun to clash upon the sea, while the sentiment of the English people had declared vehemently for the hard-pressed Protestants of the Netherlands. For years Sir Francis Drake and others had been engaged in piratical raids, which they maliciously called singeing the beard of the king of Spain. Philip was nursing a just grievance in silence, but if ever he recovered the Low Countries, it was certain to go hard with England. Ungenerous as Elizabeth was where others were concerned, she had a sharp eye for her own interests, and therefore in December, 1585, signed a treaty with the Dutch, whereby she promised to send 6,000 soldiers to their aid.

When the Englishmen came, under the command of the earl of Leicester, the queen's favorite, they did perhaps more harm than good, for Leicester seemed to consider it his chief business to create divisions among the Dutch themselves (1586–87). His Philip's entrance upon the war none the less marks an epoch, for attack by this step England definitely took sides in the struggle, directed against and Philip came to the conclusion that the conquest of England the island-kingdom was an unavoidable preliminary to the and France reduction of his revolted provinces. Therefore he began to collect all his resources for an attack upon the English. Parma did not cease to warn him against this diversion of his energies and to plead for the support that would enable the Spanish armies to give the finishing blow to Dutch resistance. His eloquent exhortations were not listened to by Philip, who, stubbornly bent on his own purpose, in the year 1588 sent the Invincible Armada against England only to have it ruined by Elizabeth's valiant fleet and scattered by the tempests. Almost at the same time the Protestant Henry of Navarre succeeded to the French throne (1589), and Philip, alarmed at this new peril, resolved to move heaven and earth to save the neighbor-kingdom for Catholicism. Thus fate, or chance, or a too unbridled ambition led him to direct his power on enterprises which carried him far afield and obliged him to relax his hold upon the Netherlands. His exhausting wars, on the water against England, on the land against the Huguenot king of France, weakened him to such an extent that he pursued the struggle against the Dutch with less and less vigor; and when, in 1592, the duke of Parma died, worn out even more by his disappointments than his labors, the Spanish game was up.

The respite due to the wars waged by Spain against England and France was fully utilized by the Dutch. They found in John of Oldenbarneveldt, trained in the school of William of Orange, a statesman not unworthy of the master. As chief official of Holland, the province which was the real backbone of the republic, and as a representative of the great merchant class, he was enabled to impress that unity of purpose on the nation which it had lost with the passing of its first great leader. To supplement the diplomatic work of Oldenbarneveldt there rose to the front, in the military field, William's son and heir, Maurice of Nassau. Only seventeen years old at his father's death, he exhibited such intelligence and dedicated himself to the study of war with such whole-hearted zeal that at the age of twenty-one he was made captain-general and admiral of the republic. Aware of the decline of the Spanish monarchy through the wanton dispersion of its strength, he boldly took (1590) the offensive and was soon able not only to clear the Dutch soil of the enemy by successful siege operations but also occasionally to defeat the Spaniards in the open field. At the same time the Dutch fleets, riding the waters more triumphantly than ever, drove the Spanish merchantmen like frightened birds before them.

Thus matters stood, with the Spaniards now clearly fighting with their backs to the wall, as Philip II neared his end. He tried to open negotiations with the enemy, but too proud to acknowledge defeat, he made no headway toward an accommodation. On his death in 1598, his successor, Philip III, persisted in his father's wasteful and impracticable course. Only when utterly exhausted, did he humble himself sufficiently to agree (1609) not to a peace, but to a Twelve Years' Truce. Incomplete as the truce was, it contained a veiled acknowledgment of the Seven United Provinces as a free and independent state. At the same time, however, it confirmed the hold of Spain on the ten central and

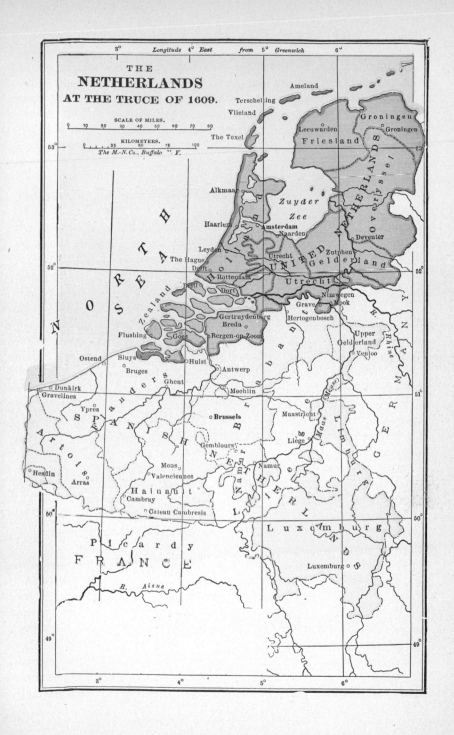

THE
NETHERLANDS
AT THE TRUCE OF 1609.

SCALE OF MILES.
0   10   20   30   40   50   60   70   80

KILOMETERS.
0   25   50   75   100
The M.-N.Co., Buffalo N. Y.

Longitude 4° East from 5° Greenwich 6°

3°

Ameland

Terschelling
Vlieland

Groningen

The Texel

Leeuwarden   Groningen

Friesland

53°   53°

NORTH

Alkmaar

Zuyder
Zee

UNITED NETHERLANDS

Overyssel

Haarlem

Deventer

Amsterdam
Naarden

Leyden

The Hague

Utrecht   Zutphen

Delft

Gelderland

SEA

Rotterdam

52°   Utrecht   52°

Delft

Dort

Nimwegen

Grave   Mook

Zealand

Gertruydenburg   Hertogenbosch

Breda

Goes   Bergen-op-Zoom

Flushing

Upper
Gelderland

Ostend   Sluys

Hulst

Venloo

Bruges   Antwerp

Ghent

Flanders

Brabant

Mechlin

Dunkirk

Rhine

Gravelines

GERMANY

Ypres

Brussels   Maastricht

SPANISH

51°   51°

Artois

NETHERLANDS

Gemblours

Liège

Limburg

Hesdin

Mons

Namur

Valenciennes

Meuse

Arras

Hainault

Namur

Maas

Cambray

Cateau Cambresis

50°   50°

Luxemburg

Picardy

FRANCE

Luxemburg

R. Aisne

49°   49°

3°   4°   5°   6°

southern provinces, which henceforth figure in history as the Spanish Netherlands. When the Spanish branch of the house of Hapsburg failed in the year 1700, its Netherland possessions, as we shall see in due time, were transferred to the Austrian Hapsburgs to become in the nineteenth century, after many interesting vicissitudes, the independent kingdom of Belgium. Thus out of the Netherlands, birthplace and pride of Emperor Charles V, issued eventually two distinct European states.

If the truce of 1609 was not the end, it signified the beginning of the end. When it expired (1621), the Thirty Years' War was raging in Europe, and although Spain tried to make the confusion serve her purpose and again attacked the Dutch, the firm resistance *Futile renewal of the war by Spain* of the hardy little nation rendered the second effort at subjugation even more vain than the first. When the Peace of Westphalia (1648) put an end to the long German war, Spain at last declared herself ready for the great renunciation and signed a peace with the Dutch Republic which acknowledged its unqualified independence.

Returning to the landmark of the Twelve Years' Truce, let us throw a glance at the problems of the new state. Maurice of Nassau and John of Oldenbarneveldt, to whose excellent teamwork the recent triumph had been largely due, developed a dangerous *Factors making for domestic disharmony* rivalry closely expressive of the many difficulties and divisions that characterized the country. Although some of these have already been mentioned, it behooves us at this juncture to get a fuller view of the Dutch internal situation. First to consider is the poor adjustment between the federal machinery, of which the States General was the leading feature, and the sovereign provinces represented by the Provincial Estates. As already noted, such was the power of these latter local bodies that they could at their pleasure paralyze the States General. The second disturbing element was the superiority in resources of the single province of Holland with its many flourishing municipalities, such as Amsterdam, Haarlem, Leyden, and Rotterdam, over the other six provinces put together. This circumstance accounts for the fact that the decision of Holland was usually the decision of the country and that its very name came to be synonymous with the Dutch Republic. The third factor causing trouble was of a social order and acquaints us with the circumstance that the control in the great municipalities rested exclusively in the hands of the leading merchant oligarchs or "burghers," who alone possessed the franchise. As Oldenbarneveldt was identified with Holland on the one hand, and with the burgher oligarchy on the other, it followed that his rival, Maurice of Nassau, received the backing of the other provinces as well as of the disfranchised and disgruntled masses.

Perilous as these divisions were, they might not have led to civil war if a religious issue had not poured oil upon the fire. The Reformed church of Calvin had been made the sole legal religion of the country, while the Catholics, though after a time no longer persecuted with fire and sword, were denied the right of public worship. But the dominant and domineering Calvinists were themselves not an unbroken unit. In the days of Maurice and Oldenbarneveldt a sect arose among them which refused to subscribe to the doctrine of predestination with its many harsh implications and which, because of a remonstrance issued on this head, became known as the Remonstrants. Because the strict constructionists answered with a prompt and vigorous counter-blast, they received the name of Counter-Remonstrants. The quarrel, abstruse and irrelevant to our present-day way of thinking, rocked the country and led to the demand for a national synod to decide the issue. Such an assembly Oldenbarneveldt, who was identified with the tolerant party of the Remonstrants and who feared the rock-ribbed intolerance of the fierce Calvinists, opposed with the result that both parties finally appealed to force. But before the struggle had fairly begun, Maurice by a quick stroke disarmed the opposition. He arrested Oldenbarneveldt, who, tried on trumped-up charges of treason, was found guilty and beheaded (1619). At the same time a national synod called at Dort (Dordrecht) condemned the lax views of the Remonstrants and imposed the most unbending definition of predestination on the Dutch Reformed church.

Thus Maurice and the elements behind him, forming the Orange party, had triumphed, while the burgher oligarchs suffered a complete eclipse. Had Maurice been recklessly ambitious — which he was not — he might now quite probably have made himself king. But he died (1625) like his father before him, a mere stadtholder. His titles and honors passed to his younger brother, Frederick Henry, who proved himself a leader of the Orange party as capable and even more moderate and conciliatory than Maurice. However, from the nature of the case the Orange party with its acknowledged single head had a monarchial tinge, while the defeated burgher oligarchs formed what they called the republican party. For the following generations, in fact as long as the Dutch Republic lasted, these two parties faced each other with the result that sometimes one and sometimes the other seized and exercised the power.

In conclusion, a word must be said of the remarkable commercial expansion of the Dutch Republic. It was as if the heroic effort against tyranny had released an unmeasured energy, for, in spite of the exhausting war with Spain, the country multiplied its *The commercial* merchant-vessels and found occasion through its daring *mercial* traders to inaugurate a profitable commerce with all the *ascendancy* countries of the world. The Dutch became *the* carrier *of the Dutch* nation of Europe, commanding the North sea, penetrating the Baltic, and boldly crowding the Spaniards and Portuguese in the East and West Indies. In 1601 was founded the Dutch East India Company, which, in return for the risks it assumed, was granted a monopoly of trade in the Far East and which gradually succeeded in building up a Dutch colonial empire in the Malay archipelago. When industrial Flanders was reoccupied by Spain, many manufacturers emigrated to the free soil of Holland, where they created linen and woolen works employing thousands of workmen. At the same time the herring industry, which had from of old been a leading occupation of this seaboard people, continued to provide a livelihood for a large fraction of the population. It was the wealth won in the herring trade that gave rise to the saying that the great city of Amsterdam was built on the carcasses of herrings. During the first half of the seventeenth century the upward movement of this prosperity hardly suffered interruption and it was not till the second half of the century that the powerful neighbors, England and France, long filled with jealousy of the Dutch success, took commercial and political measures which inaugurated a gradual Dutch decline. But this belongs to a later chapter as does also a consideration of the contribution to European culture made by the remarkable little nation which for a short time acted as the pace-maker of the western world.

REFERENCES

P. SMITH, *Age of the Reformation*, chs. 5, 10
Cambridge Modern History, III, chs. 6, 7, 19
T. M. LINDSAY, *History of the Reformation*, II, Bk. 3, ch. 5

J. E. BARKER, *Rise and Decline of the Netherlands*, chs. 3, 5–8

E. M. HULME, *Renaissance and Reformation*, ch. 25

P. J. BLOK, *History of the People of the Netherlands*

F. HARRISON, *William the Silent*

R. PUTNAM, *William the Silent*

J. L. MOTLEY, *The Rise of the Dutch Republic*, Pt. 4

CHAPTER X

THE REFORMATION AND THE CIVIL WARS IN FRANCE

Before following the course taken by the Reformation in France let us catch up the threads of French pre-Reformation history in respect first, of the strengthening of the monarchy and second, of the participation of the country in the affairs of Europe. The king's Regarding the monarchy we have learned that the power increased of the king had become very great because, enjoying a control of permanent revenue (the *taille*) not subject to the control and the of the States General, he was enabled to maintain there- Church with a professional army dependent wholly on himself. His steadily increasing stature had brought it about that he more and more decisively overshadowed his two medieval rivals, the nobles and the Church. Although the danger to his authority from either of these agencies was now much reduced, we shall presently have evidence that they retained considerable influence and that the nobles in particular were far removed from giving up the hope of regaining their ancient feudal independence. As for the relation of the king to the French or Gallican Church an important mile-stone had been reached with the Pragmatic Sanction of Bourges (1438). The ostensible purpose of this famous declaration was to eliminate the control of the pope; but instead of gaining its independence, as it hoped, the national Church merely slipped by gradual stages under the domination of the king. While Louis XI (1461–83) and Charles VIII (1483–98) still made an occasional show of respecting the liberties of the Church, Francis I resolved to bring it definitely under his control. As he and Pope Leo X were politically dependent on each other owing to their common hostility to Spanish domination in Italy, the monarch succeeded in persuading the Holy Father in the Concordat of Bologna (1516) to renounce the ancient papal claim to the nomination of the French bishops and abbots in favor of the crown. Therewith, in a formal sense at least, the Gallican Church had passed under the yoke of the civil ruler.

In recapitulating the part played by France in European politics

we shall be doing well to start with Charles VIII and to remind ourselves that, encouraged by the consolidation of the royal power, he
resolved to turn his attention to the conquest of the kingdom of
Failure of Naples. In 1494 he invaded Italy and by arousing the
the per- jealousy of Spain inaugurated the struggle with that power
sistent over the control of the Italian peninsula which was not
drive to
conquer concluded for over half a hundred years. What a kaleido-
Italy scopic succession in that period of time of wasteful wars,
shifting leagues, and fragile peace-treaties! Charles VIII conquered
and lost Italy in the course of a single year. His successor, Louis
XII (1498–1515), returned triumphantly to the attack (1499) but
before his death had to let everything he had won slip again from
his grasp. On the accession of Francis I the assault on the much-
prized peninsula was renewed and, following the victory over Spain
at Marignano (1515), brought the French back into possession of
the Milanese lands. But the Spaniards would not rest content with
this increase of French power and, returning to the attack under
Emperor Charles V, once more drove the French out. Though
captured at the battle of Pavia (1525) and carried a prisoner to Spain,
King Francis had no sooner gained his liberty by signing a humiliating peace with his foe than he reopened the struggle; in fact he reopened it three times without dislodging his stout opponent from
Milan and Naples, the two points, the possession of which enabled
Charles to hold all Italy as with a pair of giant nippers. Francis's
five wars with Spain over Italy constitute a leading feature of his
reign but they failed egregiously to achieve their purpose. At the end
of his rule Italy was more completely under Spanish domination than
at its beginning. However, Francis's unceasing struggle against the
mighty Charles V was not wholly without effect. It hindered the
emperor from becoming the undisputed master of Europe and maintained that balance of power which was just beginning to emerge as
the ruling principle of the political organization of Europe.

During the three reigns just glanced at the Renaissance began its
irresistible conquest of the leading minds of France. Since it was by
origin an Italian movement, the close contact established with Italy
The Ren- by the recurrent French invasions considerably stimu-
aissance lated the flow of trans-Alpine influences into the kingdom
comes to of the Valois. Particularly under Francis I humanism
France and the arts made rapid progress since the king delighted
to exercise a liberal patronage of both scholars and artists. The new

learning unfurled its banners at Paris and at other university centers throughout the country, and great humanists like Budé (Budaeus, 1467–1540), second only to Erasmus in his command of Latin and Greek, held aloft a torch of irresistible attraction for the younger generation. During his Italian visits Francis cultivated the friendship of such leading artists as Leonardo da Vinci, Titian, and Andrea del Sarto, and rejoiced not a little when he succeeded in carrying some of them away to his own country. By this means a direct stimulus was applied to the followers of the arts in France which led them to break away from the older Gothic inspiration and to found a new school of Renaissance architecture, sculpture, and painting. The literary and artistic initiative of Francis, who was a gay, light-hearted worldling, counted for much in the cultural transformation of his country but should not be exaggerated. On the whole our judgment must be that France, like Germany and England, had reached a point of development which made it eager to fling wide its doors to the new message.

When the Reformation followed on the heels of the Renaissance Francis I (1515–1547) became greatly puzzled. Prizing social merriment, refinement of dress and dwelling, and all the other elements of a pleasant, mundane existence, he lacked the moral seriousness which would enable him to understand the deep indignation at the bottom of the Reformation protest; and as for the theological subtleties raised by the reformers they lay wholly outside the circle of his mind. In consequence the Reformation did not touch his spirit, and his indifference in regard to it was not shaken until he made the disconcerting discovery that the religious agitation had a political side and involved him in difficulties with the pope and the fervently Catholic element of his people. Then indeed he struck at the reformers from what were clearly not motives of religious enthusiasm but cold reasons of state.

King Francis indifferent to the Reformation

The Reformation in France, as everywhere else, developed from small beginnings. The new learning, acting as its forerunner, had spread a longing for the reform of both state and Church, and at the opening of the sixteenth century, exactly as in every other country of Europe, certain select spirits began to cast their protest against existing conditions into more precise terms. One of the humanistic leaders was Jacques Lefèvre (1450–1537). After studying in Italy and occupying himself eagerly

The Reformation comes to France

with the classics, he made the swing toward Christian learning so
characteristic of northern scholarship, and in 1512 published a
translation of St. Paul's Epistles with a commentary, wherein he
promulgated the doctrine of Justification by Faith and certain other
positions afterwards championed by Luther.   When one of Lefèvre's
pupils, Briçonnet by name, became bishop of Meaux, he summoned
his old master and other kindred spirits about him and with their
help made the town of Meaux the center of the new religious movement and the diocese of Meaux its seed-bed.   When after 1517 Luther's writings began to appear they were welcomed, at least at
first, as corroborative of the criticism aimed by the Meaux circle at
the ecclesiastical abuses of the day.   Only when Luther took a radical
course and broke entirely away from the Church did his French sympathizers hesitate, for in their majority they were, like the humanists of Germany, firmly opposed to separation.   However, as a
handful of the more youthful and fiery spirits followed Luther's lead
through thick and thin, Lutheranism gained a following in France
which showed a tendency of slow but steady growth, chiefly, it would
seem, among the artisan class.   But that the higher classes were not
left entirely unaffected is proved by the case of Margaret of Navarre,
sister of the king.   Although she never abandoned the Catholic
Church, she became the friend and patron of the reforming group
and as openly as she dared professed her sympathy with the new
ideas.   Her attitude, vacillating between the old and the new but not
definitely committed to either, is typical of many people in France
during the next generation.

From the first the theological faculty of the university of Paris,
which was known under the name of the Sorbonne and which had
enjoyed an immense reputation in the Middle Age, undertook to
Francis   combat the movement of criticism and reform.   The
adopts a   learned doctors prided themselves on their orthodoxy and
policy of   raised a great outcry over the spread of heretical ideas.
repression   Nevertheless their opposition was not likely to count for
much unless they could draw the king to their side.   That, owing to
the cultured tolerance of Francis, proved difficult until the disastrous
battle of Pavia (1525) made him a prisoner and reduced the country
to serious straits.   The mother of Francis, Louise of Savoy, who acted
as regent during his captivity, was ready to go down on her knees
for help to almost anybody; and when she discovered that she could
have the support of the Catholic clergy only at the cost of persecu-

tion, she gave her consent. On his return from Madrid Francis straightway quashed the heretical proceedings, but as his need of ecclesiastical support continued, he saw himself obliged to return, at least intermittently, to the policy of repression. It was in one of these periods of persecution, in 1533, that there was banished from France a young man who was destined to make the world resound with his name — John Calvin. On the whole the severity of repression grew steadily with the passing of the years, for though Francis continued to be personally reluctant to punish the heterodox, in connection with his life-long struggle against Spain it became simply indispensable to him to command the alliance of the pope as well as the money and influence of the French clergy.

The climax of this repressive violence was reached in the famous Waldensian massacre. The Waldenses were a simple and thrifty peasant people who dwelt among the western Alps and who, because they were half-forgotten in their remote valleys, had re- **The Waldensian massacre** mained in undisturbed possession of certain doctrines spread by one Peter Waldo as far back as the twelfth century. Evangelical and anti-clerical, the Waldensian teachings bore a manifest resemblance to Lutheranism. The waxing intolerance of the sixteenth century discovered the neglected and harmless heretics and the king, yielding at last to long-continued pressure, signed the order for their extermination. In 1545 the snow-capped Alps witnessed a terrible scene. Three thousand innocent villagers were butchered, hundreds were dragged from their homes to wear out their lives in the king's galleys, and many other hundreds were driven into exile. It was a repetition of the fierce crusade against the Albigenses without the excuse alleged by the earlier crusaders that they had been obliged to strike in order to save the Church from destruction at the hand of active enemies.

Francis was succeeded by his son, Henry II (1547–1559), who had little in common with his engaging, if somewhat weak and frivolous predecessor. If Francis persecuted from political necessity, Henry did so from deliberate choice. He had a somber streak in **The systematic persecution of Henry II** his character, indicative of the shadow which the approaching Catholic reaction was casting before. On the day of his coronation he took with gusto the traditional oath that he would exterminate from his kingdom all whom the Church denounced. True to his word, he labored incessantly throughout his reign to put an end to heresy. He went so far as to desire to set up the Inquisition after the Spanish pattern with its vigorous machinery of courts, prisons, and police. But here he met with opposition from his supreme law-courts, the *parlements*. Having extended their jurisdiction to heresy on the ground that heresy, being directed as much against the state as against the Church, was a regular statutory offense, they resented the attempt to have their power clipped by means of a new and rival tribunal. Hence the Inquisition was never established in France, but the several parlements, and more particularly the parlement of Paris, urged on by the zealous king, did such thorough work in inflicting death and confiscation of goods on suspected persons that it is not easy to see how an Inquisition on the Spanish model could have been more energetic. When the existing organization of the parlement of Paris no longer sufficed to handle the business, a special criminal section, popularly given the ominous name of *Chambre Ardente* (Court of Fire) was instituted and soon won a deserved infamy as an instrument of persecution.

But neither thoroughness nor ferocity were of avail. The startling success won by the exiled Calvin at Geneva had an incalculable effect on the fellow-believers of his native land. In him they found a leader ever ready to hearten the wavering ranks; in his writings they discovered an ever-flowing fountain of inspiration. In spite of the risks involved, dozens of preachers prepared under Calvin's instruction secretly entered France as missionaries and by the middle of the century had succeeded in giving a uniform Calvinist imprint to the French reform movement. While the chief adherents of the new faith continued to be supplied by the artisan class, the phenomenon was noted that conversions were growing apace among the nobility, particularly among the small nobles of the countryside. Presently an underground organization of the Protestant churches was effected which in 1559 succeeded in holding its first national synod. Its most important act was to adopt a confession of faith prepared by Calvin himself. In the teeth of the law and its brutal champions the French Reformed church had become a fact!

A French Protestant church organized in 1559

If Henry was largely occupied with fighting Protestantism, he did not on this account neglect the foreign interests of France. As the heir of his predecessors he found himself involved in the eternal rivalry with Spain over Italy. As stubbornly determined to contest the issue as his father Francis, he made as little impression on his stalwart adversary and in 1559 signed the treaty of Cateau-

Cambrésis which solemnly acknowledged the Spanish mastery of the peninsula. None the less the wars of Henry brought certain distinct advantages to France. It will be remembered that, fiery Catholic though he was, he did not scruple to join with the German Protestants in their struggle (1552) against Emperor Charles V and that he was enabled by virtue of his intervention in the German civil war to occupy the three border bishoprics of Metz, Toul, and Verdun. Again, *Henry's failure and success in the foreign field* though in the war (1556–1559) which ended in Cateau-Cambrésis he was repeatedly defeated by the forces of Philip II of Spain, he scored a triumph over the English, who had joined the war as Philip's allies, by capturing the port of Calais. The acquisition of Calais and the three bishoprics is an interesting indication that French political ambition, balked of its Italian objective, had uncovered a more promising field of expansion toward the east and northeast. But before the monarchy could take further advantage of this discovery it became involved in civil broils and was obliged to give up an active foreign policy for many a year.

When Henry signed with Philip of Spain the treaty of Cateau-Cambrésis, it was with the resolve to adjourn the foreign issue until he had settled the baffling problem of the Reformation. In a close Catholic partnership with Philip he purposed to extirpate heresy, root and branch. The new alignment was *Death of Henry II* to be signalized by the marriage of his daughter Elizabeth with the Spanish king. At a tournament, which was a feature of the sumptuous nuptial celebration, Henry rode into the lists against the captain of his guard. A chance splinter from his antagonist's lance entered his eye and he died before he could realize his dream of cleansing his realm of the Protestant infection.

On the death of Henry, his son Francis, who was but sixteen years old and physically and mentally feeble, succeeded to the throne. When the power in an absolute monarchy, such as France was at this time, is not exercised by the sovereign, it is inevitably seized by some ambitious man or faction. The conditions *Francis II* in the court which surrounded the boy-king have therefore an unusual interest.

The wife of the feeble Francis was a queen in her own right, Mary of Scotland. Although a woman of parts, she was only a little older than her husband and too inexperienced to assume control in his name. Her presence on the throne, however, offered an opportunity for the ambition of her two uncles, brothers of her mother and heads of the noble house of Guise. The older was Francis, duke of Guise; the younger was a churchman, Cardinal Lorraine. They seized the reins, and because they were ardent Catholics continued Henry II's policy of Protestant persecution.

Queen Mary and the Guises

There were those, however, who looked with jealousy upon the rule of the Guises and called it usurpation. They were the princes of the house of Bourbon, a younger branch of the royal family. The head of the house was sovereign of what was left of the kingdom of Navarre in the Pyrenees and was known as King Anthony. The younger was Louis, prince of Condé. They contended that, as princes of the blood royal, they had a better right to rule for the feeble king than the family of Guise, and naturally everybody at court who had a grudge against the Guises came to their support. Thus the Bourbon princes headed a party of "malcontents" ready to seize every opportunity to rid themselves of their rivals. In casting about for supporters they could not but observe that the Guises were hated also by the Protestants whom they persecuted. Out of this common enmity there soon grew an intimacy and an alliance. Anthony in a faithless, vacillating manner, Condé more firmly, accepted the Reformed faith, and many of the "malcontents" — highplaced courtiers and noblemen for the most part — following their example, it came to pass that French Protestantism became inextricably involved with political intrigue. It was at this period that the party name of Huguenots, a term of uncertain and disputed origin, was fixed upon the French Protestants.

The Bourbons

Between the rival court factions of Bourbon and Guise, and belonging to neither, stood a person not highly regarded at first but destined to become famous — Catherine de' Medici. She was a Florentine princess, widow of Henry II and mother of the young king. Protestant contemporaries came to look upon her as an incarnate fiend, but one of her chief antagonists, who afterward became King Henry IV of France, judged her more leniently and correctly. He once silenced an over-harsh critic by asking what was she to do, an anxious mother, torn hither and thither by the fierce party feuds and with no adviser in whom she could trust. In this apology of the great king lies probably the key to Catherine's career. She was, above all, a mother, a mother of royal children, for whom she desired to preserve the throne of France. Doubtless, too, after she had once tasted the

Catherine de' Medici, the queen-mother

sweets of power, she clung to them with selfish tenacity as men and women will. Armed only with her woman's wit she plunged into the conflict of parties, and like other rulers of her time intrigued, bribed, and prevaricated to keep herself afloat. Only a very biased historian would ascribe to her a code of political conduct essentially different from that of Philip of Spain or Elizabeth of England.

Out of these factions around the throne grew the intrigues which led to the long religious wars in France. It is needless to try to put the blame for them on one or the other side. Given a weakened royal executive, the implacable religious temper which marks the society of the sixteenth century, and a horde of powerful, turbulent, and greedy nobles, and civil war is a necessary consequence. We can notice only the more prominent symptoms of the coming outbreak. The path *The Guises defend their grip upon the government* of the Guises was beset with conspiracies, instigated or connived at by the Bourbon princes. A rising was set for March, 1560, but the Guises, getting wind of it, pounced upon their adversaries before they were ready, scattered them to the winds, and as a warning hanged those they succeeding in catching to the battlements of the king's castle at Amboise or drowned them in sacks in the river Loire.

But the downfall of the Guises was at hand. In December, 1560, King Francis died, and his widow Mary, finding her role in France exhausted, prepared to leave for Scotland. Thus the props upon which the power of the Guises depended broke under them. The successor of Francis was his brother Charles IX, a weakling like his brother and a minor but ten years old. King Anthony of Navarre, as nearest of kin, might have *Death of Francis; Catherine in control* put forward a claim to the regency, but in a fit of pusillanimity yielded the honor to the queen-mother. For the first time Catherine held the reins. Desirous, above all, of maintaining her son's authority and filled with the sense of the difficulty of her position between Guise and Bourbon, she hit upon a policy of balance and moderation, called representatives of both hostile factions into her council, and issued a conciliatory edict by which she ordered the parlements to put an end to religious persecution. Finally, in January, 1562, she went the length of conceding to the Protestants a limited right of worship.

Here was a decided change of policy, exhibiting Catherine in the light of a promoter of the cause of religious liberty! But her good intentions, inspired by her desire to avoid civil war, came to naught, were bound to come to naught among men who, like the Protestants and Catholics of the sixteenth century, were passionately set on realizing their own religious system without the abatement of one jot or tittle. While the Catholics were embittered by the extent of Catherine's concessions, the Protestants grumbled at the remaining limitations, and among the more fanatical followers of the two parties, sometimes without provocation, there occurred sharp conflicts, frequently ending in terrible excesses.

<small>Catherine resolves on toleration</small>

One of these conflicts, the massacre of Vassy (1562), put an end to hesitation and led to war. The duke of Guise was passing through the country with a company of armed retainers, when he happened, at Vassy, upon a group of Huguenots assembled in a barn for worship. Sharp words led to an encounter, and before the duke rode away sixty persons lay dead upon the ground and more than two hundred had been wounded. Fierce indignation seized the Protestants throughout France, and when the duke of Guise was received by Catholic Paris like a hero returning from a successful war and Catherine declared herself unable to call him to account, the prince of Condé, acknowledged head of the Huguenots, issued an appeal·and took the field.

<small>The massacre of Vassy, 1562</small>

Thus were inaugurated the religious wars of France which were not brought to a conclusion until 1598 by the Edict of Nantes, and which in their consequences continued to trouble the country well into the next century. For our purpose it is sufficient to look upon the period from 1562 to 1598 as one war, though it is true that there were frequent suspensions of arms supporting themselves upon sham truces and dishonest treaties.[1] The war, like all the religious wars of the century, was waged with inhuman barbarity, and incendiarism, pillage, massacre, and assassination blot every stage of its progress. Protestants and Catholics alike became brutes and vied with each other in their efforts to turn their country into a desert.

<small>Character of the war</small>

When the Treaty of St. Germain (1570), granting the Protestants a somewhat larger measure of toleration than any earlier concession, temporarily closed the chapter of conflicts, many of the original leaders had passed away. King Anthony of Navarre had been killed

[1] Eight wars have been distinguished as follows: First war, 1562–1563; second war, 1567–1568; third war, 1568–1570 (ended by the Peace of St. Germain); fourth war, 1572–1573; fifth war, 1574–1576; sixth war, 1577; seventh war, 1579–1580; eighth war (called the War of the Three Henries), 1585–1589, which continued in another form until the Edict of Nantes (1598).

(1562) in battle against his former friends, the Huguenots, whom he had deserted with characteristic lack of scruple; the duke of Guise had been assassinated (1563); and Condé had been treacherously slain after surrender in the field (1569). The official head The Peace of the Huguenot party was now Anthony's young son, King of St. Henry of Navarre, but the real leadership devolved on Germain the gifted and trusted admiral of France, Gaspard de Coligny.

The new leader was one of the few high-born noblemen who had joined the Protestant ranks for other reasons than political rancor. While fighting with conviction for the religion of his choice, he never forgot, in the wild broils of partisanship, that he was a Admiral Frenchman and owed a duty to his country. He belonged Coligny to the great family of Châtillon, was allied through his mother with the still greater family of Montmorency, and without going to sea held, anomalously enough, the honorary post of admiral of France. All things considered, he rose both by character and ability above all the faction leaders of his time.

The most interesting feature of the Peace of St. Germain was that it expressed the attitude of a group of moderate men desirous to reach a genuine pacification. To them it was only too clear that the bloodshed, which was draining the country of its strength, Effort at ruined both parties and brought profit to none except the peace after enemies of France. For the time being King Charles St. Germain, 1570 himself, who was now of age and ruled in his own name, inclined to the same view. And yet so persistent were the suspicions and animosities that the effort to remove all cause of quarrel precipitated the most horrible of all the incidents of the war, the massacre of St. Bartholomew.

After the Peace of St. Germain, Coligny joined the court and, being a man of unusual force of character, rapidly acquired great influence with the king. The young monarch seemed to be resolved to put an end for all time to internal dissension, to enforce Marriage of strictly the terms of the new peace with its provision of a Henry and limited right of worship for the Protestants, and to weld Margaret the opponents together by turning their united strength against the hereditary enemy of France established in the Netherlands. For this purpose he arranged, as a preliminary step, a marriage between his sister Margaret and young Henry of Navarre. Joyfully responding to the invitation of King Charles, the Huguenots poured in swarms into Paris to attend the wedding of their chief, which was celebrated on August 18, 1572.

The wedding seemed to inaugurate a period of national harmony based on religious toleration and the ascendancy of Coligny in the councils of the king. That was more than the extreme Catholics under the leadership of the Guises could bear. Besides, the head of the house of Guise bore a virulent grudge against Coligny, whom he regarded, probably quite unjustly, as the instigator of his father's murder in 1563.

The attempted assassination of Coligny

In his desperate mood he hired — at least all the probabilities point that way — an assassin who on August 22 fired at Coligny, as he was leaving the king's palace, and wounded him severely in the arm. The young sovereign, who left a game of tennis unfinished to hurry to the bedside of his councillor, felt or shammed a deep indignation. "Yours the wound, mine the sorrow," he said and swore to bring the assassin and his accomplices to justice.

Much of what followed is to this day wrapped in mystery. Was there a long-prepared and deep-laid Catholic plot to massacre the Huguenots conveniently assembled in Paris for the wedding of their chief? Was the assassination of Coligny to serve as the signal for the general attack? Or rather was the attempted murder of Coligny the act purely of the faction of the Guise extremists and was the subsequent massacre

The massacre of St Bartholomew

an improvisation due to their alarm that the Protestants would rise to avenge their chief? Why did the queen-mother, whose voice had been generally on the side of moderation, now throw in her lot with the Guises? And how did she persuade King Charles to abandon the course of reconciliation to which he was committed by his own free act? As space is lacking for the discussion of these vexing questions, we must content ourselves with a bare narrative of events. It is certain that on the day following the attempt on Coligny's life the details of a general massacre of the Huguenots were arranged under Guise inspiration; it is also certain that Catherine took part in the plot and that it was she who wrung his consent to the crime from the feeble king. In the early morning hours of August 24, which was the feast of St. Bartholomew, the bells rang from all the church steeples of Paris. At the signal the fanatically Catholic inhabitants of the capital slipped from their beds, attacked the houses which had been previously designated with a chalk mark as harboring Huguenots, and slaughtered as many of their opponents as they could get into their hands. The wounded Coligny was one of the first victims of the bloody conspiracy, Duke Henry of Guise presiding in person at the butchery of his rival. That day the streets ran with blood and for many days after the provincial towns, encouraged by the example of the capital, indulged in similar excesses. The grim saying went the round that the wedding of the king of Navarre must be enlivened with a touch of crimson. The bridegroom himself, now Charles's brother-in-law, was in danger of death till he saved himself by declaring his readiness to renounce his faith. The victims of this horrible orgy numbered some two thousand in Paris and probably double that number in the rest of France. We reach some understanding of the depth and ferocity of the religious division of the time when we hear that at the news of the massacre the jubilant Pope Gregory XIII ordered a *Te deum* to be sung and that the somber Philip of Spain emitted his only recorded laugh.

War with all its dreary incidents straightway flamed up again. In 1574 Charles IX died from natural causes, though the Huguenots were pleased to ascribe his death to remorse for his share in the great crime of St. Bartholomew. His brother, Henry III, **Henry III,** succeeded him on the throne. A new element of interest **1574–1589** was introduced into the struggle only when the death of Henry's youngest brother, the duke of Anjou (1584), and his own failure to have heirs, involved, with the religious dispute, the question of the succession.

By the law of the realm the crown would have to pass upon Henry's death to the nearest male relative, who was Henry of Navarre, head of the collateral branch of Bourbon. But Henry, converted to Catholicism in 1572 in order to save his life, had long ago **The ques-** relapsed and was the enemy of the faith of the vast ma- **tion of the** jority of his future subjects. When his succession became **succession** probable, Henry of Guise and his followers formed the Holy League, which pledged itself to maintain the interest of the Roman Church at all hazards, to crush Protestantism utterly, and never to suffer a heretic on the throne of France. While the Catholics were forming a partisan organization regardless of their obligation to their country, the Huguenots showed a spirit no less narrow and sectarian. They planned to form themselves into a federal republic, practically independent of the kingdom. It was plain that party was counting for more and more, country for less and less, and that the outcome of the wasteful civil strife would be the ruin and disruption of France. In consequence of the growing exacerbation Henry III found himself in evil straits. As head of the state he was pledged to the interests of the country and in a weak, shambling way was inclined to pursue a policy of reconciliation and peace. But the League and the Huguenots would have no peace except on their own terms, and the king, trying to hold his course between Scylla and Charybdis, was finally deserted by all except the handful of men who refused to share in the madness of partisan fury. In the new turn of the civil struggle three parties, each championed by a leader of the name of Henry, disputed the control of France.

The new phase, called the War of the Three Henries (1585–1589), steeped the country in such confusion that men soon indulged in every form of lawlessness without punishment. King Henry, an effemi- War of the nate dandy with a fondness for lapdogs and earrings, was Three reduced to such depths that he was unable to maintain Henries even the appearance of authority except by resigning all real power into the hands of Henry of Guise as head of the League. In December, 1588, he indignantly resolved to put an end to this humiliation. Inviting Henry of Guise to an interview in his castle at Blois, he had him treacherously despatched by his guard. Cowardice and rancor could go no further, and the League turned in horror from the murderer, Paris and Catholic France declaring loudly for his deposition. In his despair the royal culprit fled to the camp of Henry of Navarre, and was advancing with his Huguenot subjects upon his capital, when a fanatical Dominican monk forced admission to his presence and slew him with a knife (August, 1589). With him the house of Valois came to an end. The war was now reduced to an issue between Henry of Navarre, the rightful claimant to the crown, and the League, which would have none of him.

The new Henry, Henry IV, first king of the house of Bourbon, was a brave soldier, an intelligent politician, and a courtly gentleman. He had his faults, springing from a sensuous and mercurial tempera- Accession of ment, but intensely human as they were, they actually Henry IV contributed to his popularity. He was confronted on his accession by the disconcerting fact that his followers were only a small part of France. The attachment of the Catholic majority he knew could only be won slowly, and force, he suspected from the first, would be of no avail. Therefore, he undertook patiently to assure the Catholics of the loyalty of his intentions in order to win their recognition. If the League could only have found a plausible rival for the throne, Henry might have been annihilated; but his claim was incontrovertible and that was his strength. Besides, the circumstance that the League leaned upon Spain caused the large body of those who, though Catholic, hated Spain more than their Huguenot fellow-countrymen to rally to Henry's banner. However, for the present no one thought of disarming. Henry won a number of engagements, notably the battle of Ivry (1590), but the League, still managed by the Guise faction in the person of the late leader's younger brother and supported by the resources of Philip of Spain, could not be scattered.

For four years Henry waited for his subjects to hail him as their sovereign; then he took a step which, though much debated, is not incomprehensible. The universal misery caused by the endless struggle wrenched his heart; he was in constant alarm Henry returns to the Catholic fold lest the League or Philip II or both in agreement should impose on France a Catholic ruler of their own choice; finally, with his bubbling southern vivacity Henry, who was a typical Gascon, was not really one at heart with the rather grim and austere Calvinists constituting his political following. In the light of such considerations, it is not to be wondered at that he should have come gradually to the conclusion that since only his conversion would reunite and restore France, he would have to abandon an unpopular cause. His much quoted remark: Paris is well worth a mass, reveals by its flippancy his purely political appraisal of the situation. In July, 1593, after cautious preliminary negotiations with the Catholic clergy, he solemnly abjured the Huguenot faith and was readmitted to the Roman communion.

The effect of the king's action was remarkable. Cities and provinces made haste to recognize him, the League fell apart, and the civil broils came to an end except for a few lingering fires. By February 1594, Henry could proceed with his coronation at Chartres, End of the civil war and when, a month later, he approached Paris, the gates were thrown open and he was received like a hero and savior by those same Parisians who in their intense Catholic fervor had during his apostacy spewed him out of their mouths.

To complete the work of unifying the country two things remained to be done: to punish Spain for interfering in the domestic affairs of France and to give the Huguenots the security to which they were entitled if they were ever to become contented citizens. As soon as he felt reasonably secure in his position, Henry declared formal war on Spain (1595), bringing the united Catholic and Protestant forces into the field against the ancient foe. Since the Dutch and the

English were already at war with Philip, Henry allied himself with
these peoples, and Philip, beset by three governments, was swiftly
reduced to serious straits. However, the Spaniards possessed a
War with   brave and veteran army and the attack of France, owing
Spain fol- to the terrible exhaustion of the country, lacked a consis-
lowed by   tent vigor. Though Philip was not crushed by any means,
the Peace
of Vervins, he saw the necessity of giving up his far-ranging schemes
1598   of control and presently indicated to Henry his willingness to treat. The result was the Peace of Vervins (1598), in which
Henry received formal recognition as king of France and the relations of the two countries were reëstablished on the terms laid down
in the Treaty of Cateau-Cambrésis (1559).

With the country at peace with its neighbors Henry could turn
to the Huguenot problem. In April, 1598, he issued from the city of
Nantes, where he was temporarily residing, an edict by which he
The Edict   hoped to satisfy his Huguenot subjects. The edict
of Nantes, granted to the Protestants, still, it should be remembered,
1598   a very small minority of the nation, considerable rights
classifiable as religious, civil, and political. Let us be clear that the
edict contained no such thing as a sweeping individual toleration of a
modern kind for the simple reason that Europeans of the sixteenth
and seventeenth centuries were not yet ready for this idea. As to
religious rights, Protestant worship was authorized at two places
in each bailiwick (*bailliage*, a political division approximately equivalent to a county) as well as — with certain restrictions — in the
castles of Huguenot noblemen. As a concession to the uncompromising Catholic fervor of the Parisians the reformed service was expressly excluded from the capital. Remarkably full *civil* rights were
conceded by the edict since the Huguenots were guaranteed the
protection of the law and declared eligible to all public offices. So
far the settlement was intelligible and intelligent and, in spite of its
restrictions, far more liberal than any solution found anywhere else
up to that date. But in the sections dealing with *political* rights concessions were made to the Huguenots which to the modern student
must appear amazing and which, in point of fact, were incompatible
with the interests and even the existence of the monarchy. Not only
were the Huguenots permitted to hold assemblies in which they might
legislate for themselves like an independent power but, as a guarantee
of the execution of the treaty, they were put in possession of a certain
number of fortified towns, of which La Rochelle was the most im-

portant. They were thus constituted as an armed minority within and yet outside the state.

From the first it was doubtful whether such an arrangement could last. Owing to the great authority which Henry enjoyed in all circles as the pacifier of France and owing to the lingering trust placed in him by his former comrades in the faith, the Edge of Nantes proved fairly satisfactory so long as the amiable and magnetic Gascon held the reins. But the king's tolerant spirit was shared by only a handful of men and the mass of Protestants and Catholics continued to eye each other with contempt and suspicion. Once more we may see how in that age of religious passion intolerance was not so much the work of the governments as of rival ecclesiastical organizations and their popular following, and how with them it was a thing as spontaneous and uncontrolled as the love of kin or the fear of fire. Hence when the strong hand and even temper of Henry were withdrawn, the religious tension almost at once led to a new outbreak.

Continuance of the religious passions

But that was as yet some years off, and while life smiled at him Henry gave himself with zeal to the task of utilizing the peace in order to heal the wounds of his stricken country. One of his gravest concerns were the finances which were in hopeless disorder. Since for years taxes had been only intermittently collected, the debts of the crown had reached alarming proportions. By putting a friend of his Huguenot days, the duke of Sully, in charge of the treasury he had the satisfaction of seeing how by the vigilance and honesty of his enlightened servant the royal debt was greatly reduced and the annual deficit converted into a surplus available for further debt reduction. Personally Henry was much interested in agriculture and did all in his power to encourage this fundamental activity, then as now the chief source of French prosperity. In addition he improved the system of communication by building roads; he encouraged new industries, especially the manufacture of silk; and he made a modest beginning in the direction of a colonial empire by furthering French enterprise in the basin of the St. Lawrence.

Henry begins the reconstruction of France

With all these constructive labors to occupy his time Henry did not neglect to keep a sharp eye on Europe and the inter-national situation. As to all his immediate predecessors so also to him the house of Hapsburg, reigning through its two branches in Spain and Austria, seemed the enveloping power which paralyzed the expansion of the

French monarchy. In the period after the Peace of Vervins he therefore cultivated the friendship of all the smaller powers of Europe — the Dutch, the Swiss Confederation, the states of Italy, His foreign such as Venice and Tuscany dwelling under the shadow of policy Spain, and the German Protestant states fearful of their Catholic emperor — until he exercised an informal protectorate over them. Having thus fortified himself with a ring of political outposts, he considered the time to be ripe once more to summon the house of Hapsburg to the field. A quarrel over the succession to a small German state on the Rhine was about to furnish him with the necessary pretext for a general war against the Austro-Spanish power when on May 14, 1610, on the eve of his departure for the army, he was laid low by the dagger of a fanatic who had become persuaded that Henry was a secret traitor to the Catholic cause.

No sooner had the strong pillar of domestic order fallen than France was threatened with the resumption of the dissension from which she had just recovered. Henry's successor was his son Louis XIII Regency of (1610–1643), a lad but nine years old. That circumstance Marie de' signified a regency which might easily lead to such broils Medici as had marked the days following the demise of Henry II. Largely to clear the atmosphere and concentrate the power in a single hand the young king's mother, Marie de' Medici, was proclaimed regent as soon as the court had recovered from the consternation into which it had been thrown by the sovereign's assassination. A Florentine like the former regent, Catherine de' Medici, Queen Marie was Henry's second wife, to whom he had been joined (1600) on the grant of a divorce from Margaret of Valois, his bride of the stormy period of St. Bartholomew. The new governor of France was a large, coarse-featured woman without distinction of either character or intelligence and therefore wholly incapable of consistently asserting her authority. In consequence the supreme power became the football of favorites and interested groups. Perhaps without her knowing it but no less successfully for all that, Marie was manipulated by some of her Italian fellow-countrymen constituting her personal following; and this situation naturally enough aroused the resentment of the great French nobles who had hoped to gain the controlling influence for themselves. Among the turbulent nobiliary elements the Huguenot aristocracy constituted a specially dangerous group since they had been permitted by the Edict of Nantes to maintain an army and several fortified places. On meeting with less consideration from the regent than they felt to be their due, they issued a call to arms; and though letting themselves, it is true, be bought off with honors and pensions, they continued to suspend the threat of a new religious war over the country.

If France was saved from this confusion, it was due, and solely due, to one man, Armand Jean du Plessis, known to fame as Cardinal Richelieu. When he entered the royal council to become before long, by the natural ascendancy of his intellect, the lead- Richelieu ing minister (1624), the authority of the queen-regent saves the had already been replaced by that of the king; but state under the king, who had much more of his mother than of his father in him and was dull and slothful, the affairs of the realm had not been in the least improved. Richelieu, therefore, found himself confronted by a heavy task. Only the unique authority which he succeeded in accumulating enabled him to meet it. As a boy he had been destined for the Church, and at a ludicrously early age he had, by reason of his noble birth and the favor of the king, been made bishop of Luçon. On his talents making themselves felt, he was honored by the pope with the cardinal's hat. Thus it happened that when he became the king's chief minister, he united in his person a sum of dignities that raised him above attack so long as his sovereign supported him. And this Louis XIII did to the fullest extent. That is this dull ruler's greatest merit in the eyes of history. While Richelieu lived, he retained, in spite of intrigues and conspiracies, the power in his hands and was the real king of France.

Richelieu was one of those rare statesmen who can form and carry through with an iron will a policy suited to the needs of the country. His program, which dovetails accurately with that of Henry IV, falls into three sections. In the first place, he inherited Henry's His tolerance, a circumstance the more remarkable as he was program a leading dignitary of the Roman Catholic Church. He would grant the Huguenots the civil and religious rights laid down in the Edict of Nantes, but their political rights, which made them almost independent of the state, he would ruthlessly destroy. His second aim was to clip still further the wings of the turbulent nobility; and his third, to overthrow for the glory of France the power of the house of Hapsburg.

Richelieu first attacked the pressing problem of the Huguenots. Following the death of Henry IV, who enjoyed their trust, they had become restless and hung on the horizon like a thunder-cloud ready

to burst at any moment. Richelieu proceeded cautiously, treated with them as long as negotiation was feasible, and suddenly, when the opportunity came, invested their chief town, La Rochelle. A
The long siege followed, wherein the endurance of the
Huguenot beleaguered citizens proved no match for the skill of the
problem tireless cardinal, who conducted the operations in person. In vain did the English fleet, sent by King Charles I at the solicitation of the Huguenots, try to relieve the town. In 1628 La Rochelle, having lost 16,000 inhabitants through hunger and pestilence, surrendered at discretion. The next year the remnant of the Protestant forces in the south was likewise disarmed and Richelieu became master of the situation. And now his remarkable moderation came to light. The average ruler of the time would have compelled the beaten minority to conform to the religion of the majority or else be burned or banished. Not so Richelieu, who cherished a toleration far in advance of his time. He confirmed to the Huguenots the civil and religious rights granted by the Edict of Nantes and merely cancelled their right to hold a number of fortified towns and constitute an *imperium in imperio* (a state within the state).

The turbulent nobles intrenched in the provinces, where they constituted to a certain extent the local government, gave the cardinal much food for thought. With his clear eye he saw that they were an
The taming anomaly in a state aspiring to exercise an exclusive au-
of the thority. They carried on a veritable private warfare by
nobility their duelling habits and defied the authorities from behind their fortified castles. Hence Richelieu threw himself upon duels and castles, declaring by edict that the time for them was past and executing a few of the most persistent duellists as an example to their class. But the great cardinal must not be credited with miracles. Battlemented castles and duels did indeed gradually disappear but less, on the whole, because Richelieu frowned upon them than because of the great change which gradually came over the upper classes and which moved them to surrender their crude medieval independence for the pleasures and luxuries associated with the more courtly forms of the new age. In the matter of the feudal strongholds more particularly it is not recorded that Richelieu destroyed many of them. More usually they were voluntarily abandoned in favor of open, villa-like mansions better suited to the softer manners of this and especially of the succeeding century.

With the measures aimed at undermining the prestige of the nobility there went hand in hand an effort to create a centralized administration over which the nobles should have no power and which should be responsible exclusively to the king. That this was no new idea originating with Richelieu becomes sufficiently clear *Richelieu* when we recall that the vigor of the French king had *strengthens* been intermittently growing for many generations. But *the central* in spite of the increasing influence of the crown, the royal *administration* officials had not yet been able to make their power felt over all departments of government in a consistent way. Following a lead taken by former rulers but again abandoned, Richelieu appointed agents, called *intendants*, whom he despatched to the provinces to take supreme charge of police, justice, and finance. He selected them exclusively from the commoners (the third estate), because commoners might be expected faithfully to carry out orders and to keep aloof from the intrigues of the local nobles. The intendants set the coping-stone on the historical structure of French administrative centralization, which however, far from inventing, Richelieu merely brought to a logical completion.

In the face of this increase of the royal power what became of the States General and the parlements, two institutions which had thus far in some part shared in the government of France and which the king regarded as more or less dangerous rivals? That *Richelieu's* their position would be impaired by Richelieu's policy of *relation to* making the king the exclusive arbiter of the French des- *the States General and* tiny was highly probable. Though the States General, *the parle-* composed of the three estates, clergy, nobles, and com- *ments* moners, had not succeeded in achieving a place in the French political system comparable to that occupied in England by the parliament, they had been irregularly consulted as late as the sixteenth century and had served to maintain a certain valuable contact between king and people. Summoned in 1614, during the regency of Marie de' Medici, the three groups had quarreled impotently with the government and with each other and had been dismissed not to be summoned again for one hundred and seventy-five years. For this shelving of an ancient institution Richelieu was largely responsible since, owing to his suspicion of everything that might challenge the omnipotence of the king, he carefully refrained during his control from issuing a call for a new session. In this way he set an example which was followed by the rulers after his day until the breakdown of absolutism in 1789 forced a resort to the barely remembered institution which had proved such an insufficient pillar of popular liberties. The parlements, supreme courts of justice, ten in number in Richelieu's day, could not be shelved like the States General, since they were the apex of the system of national justice. While Richelieu gave full support to their claims as judicial bodies, he vigilantly quashed every attempt on their part to interfere in politics; and this attitude too became characteristic of the French monarchy until its bankruptcy under Louis XVI. In sum, Richelieu exalted the royal prerogative until the power of the crown seemed to depend on itself alone and the king appeared as an irresponsible agent ruling by Divine Right.

With the Huguenots pacified and the selfish nobility held in check, Richelieu could take up with vigor his foreign plans, looking to the humiliation of the house of Hapsburg. It was a most convenient

Richelieu and the Thirty Years' War circumstance that Germany was convulsed at this time with the religious conflict known as the Thirty Years' War. With the instinct of a statesman Richelieu felt that if he interposed to help the German Protestants against the Catholics, represented by the emperor and Spain, he would sooner or later acquire some permanent advantages for France. That he was helping Protestants against Catholics did not disturb him in the least since he was a Frenchman first and a Catholic afterwards. His gradual interference, developing from occasional subsidies of money to the recruitment of large armies, finally secured to his king the balance of power in the German war and made France practical dictator of Europe when the peace of Westphalia (1648) ended the struggle. Richelieu did not live to see this result (he died 1642), but the advantages which France secured in that document may be written down to his energetic conduct of the government.

Many criticisms might be urged against Richelieu's ministry. Having no talent for finance, he permitted the government accounts to fall into confusion and all sorts of abuses to creep into the ad-

Debit and credit account of Richelieu's rule ministration. Then again he exaggerated the centralization of power with consequences that brought heavy disasters in the following century. Finally, his aggressive foreign policy produced an endless harvest of wars for both France and her neighbors. However, when all is said, it was he more than any other single individual who welded France into a solid political unit and prepared the way for her supremacy in Europe.

REFERENCES

P. SMITH, *Age of the Reformation*, ch. 4
H. O. WAKEMAN, *Europe 1598–1715*, chs. 2, 6, 7
T. M. LINDSAY, *History of the Reformation*, II, Bk. 3, ch. 4
L. BATIFFOL, *The Century of the Renaissance*
E. ARMSTRONG, *The French Wars of Religion*
A. TILLEY, *Modern France*, pp. 1–42
E. M. HULME, *Renaissance and Reformation*, chs. 16, 26
J. N. FIGGIS, *From Gerson to Grotius*, chs. 4–7
J. R. M. MACDONALD, *France*, II, chs. 20–23
C. HEADLAM, *France*, chs. 16–19
G. W. KITCHIN, *History of France*, vol. II
G. B. ADAMS, *Growth of the French Nation*, chs. 11, 12
Cambridge Modern History, III, chs. 1, 20, IV, ch. 4
C. M. WHITEHEAD, *Gaspard de Coligny*
W. BESANT, *Coligny*
E. SICHEL, *Catherine de Medici and the Reformation; The Later Years of Catherine de Medici*
E. ARMSTRONG, *Political Theory of the Huguenots*
H. M. BAIRD, *History of the Rise of the Huguenots; The Huguenots and Henry of Navarre*
P. F. WILLERT, *Henry of Navarre*
R. LODGE, *Richelieu*
J. P. PERKINS, *Richelieu*

THE KINGS OF FRANCE

Charles VIII, 1483–1498
Louis XII (nearest male relative of Charles VIII), 1498–1515
Francis I (nearest male relative of Louis XII), 1515–1547
Henry II (son of Francis I, *m.* Catherine de' Medici), 1547–1559
Francis II (son of Henry II, *m.* Mary Stuart), 1559–1560
Charles IX (son of Henry II), 1560–1574
Henry III (son of Henry II) 1574–1589
    (Line of Valois extinct; crown passes to head of house of Bourbon, descended
    from Louis IX, 1226–1270)
Henry IV, 1589–1610
Louis XIII (son of Henry IV), 1610–1643
Louis XIV (son of Louis XIII), 1643–1715

CHAPTER XI

THE THIRTY YEARS' WAR

The Peace of Augsburg of 1555 must undoubtedly be construed as a victory for German Protestantism. But it was also, since it took the control of religion out of the hands of the central authority, the emperor, and gave it to the princes, a victory for the principle of decentralization. The significance of such a development in a Europe whose states were becoming daily more powerful through the opposite movement of centralization must not be overlooked. Weakened and disunited Germany would draw the covetous gaze of her stronger neighbors and would henceforth be exposed to their attack.

The Peace of Augsburg a victory for Protestantism and decentralization

However, though a victory for Protestantism and decentralization, the Peace of Augsburg did not prove to be a final settlement of the German religious conflict. Unfortunately it left many important matters in suspense. For instance, it recognized Lutheranism without extending any rights whatever to the followers of Calvin. But after the middle of the century Calvinism increasingly gained adherents among individuals of a radical and energetic type and was even formally adopted by some princes and free towns. Not only did such converts fail to enjoy any protection from the law but they encountered the vindictive hostility of Catholics as well as of their Protestant rivals, the Lutherans. Even more important as a source of public disturbance were the features of the peace dealing with Church property, and, more particularly, the article called the Ecclesiastical Reservation. In regard to these and all other disputed matters the Catholics took the position that the limit of concession had been reached. Refusing to be impressed by this attitude, the Protestants continued to secularize monasteries and to appropriate bishoprics whenever the opportunity beckoned. In consequence a very considerable body of territory in the actual possession of the Protestants was angrily declared by their adversaries to be illegally held. If we add to difficulties such as these the hot passion which

The Peace of Augsburg does not heal the religious divisions of Germany

236

every question of religion excited in the sixteenth century, we shall easily persuade ourselves that the country was threatened with an early renewal of the civil war.

That the domestic conflict was not resumed for over half a century is fairly remarkable and may be ascribed to a variety of causes. In the first place, the immediate successors of Emperor Charles V, Ferdinand I (1556–1564) and Maximilian II (1564–1576), were moderate men, who did their utmost to mediate among the factions. Their peaceful policy was seconded by the leading Lutheran princes, inclined by the natural conservatism of successful men to rest content with what they had won. Besides, these princes entertained the hope that without war, by gradual infiltration into all classes of society and through all districts, Protestantism might make a clean sweep of Germany. And, really, for some years following the Augsburg settlement the outlook for the religious revolution was brilliant. It possessed youth and confidence, and, in the Lutheran form at least, had acquired a legal sanction. It continued to mount, like a tide, until it had covered the whole center and north of Germany and threatened the great bishoprics along the Rhine and the hitherto staunchly Catholic dominions of Austria and Bavaria in the south. To a dispassionate observer it must have seemed not improbable that the Roman Church, undermined in these, its last strongholds, would soon altogether disappear from Germany. But this culminating catastrophe never took place. For one thing, the dominant Lutherans, in distinction from the Calvinists in Holland and elsewhere, were too self-satisfied and unenterprising to make the best of their opportunities; and in the second place, in the very nick of time the Catholic revival reached Germany and completely reinvigorated an apparently dying cause.

Adjournment of the issue between the rival faiths

We have already taken note of how the Counter-Reformation fortified by the Jesuits and the Council of Trent steadied the wavering Catholic ranks throughout the world. Its effect did not make itself felt in Germany until the last quarter of the sixteenth century, when Rudolph II (1576–1612) was upon the throne. Breaking away from the conciliatory policy of his immediate predecessors, Rudolph resolved to put the Catholic Church again in the saddle and to make use to this end of the Jesuit order. Operating from the court of Vienna as a center, and also from that of Bavaria, whose ruling family was, if possible, even more

The Catholic reaction

fervently Catholic than the Hapsburgs, the devoted followers of Ignatius Loyola gradually spread in every direction. Their churches multiplied, and their schools, conducted with energy and intelligence, were largely attended. Before long the Protestant advance was checked all along the line and an energetic Catholic propaganda began to score triumphs in those doubtful regions, chiefly of the south, where Protestantism having but recently gained a foothold was still feeble.

By the beginning of the seventeenth century the tension between the religious parties was nearing the danger point and every new incident increased the probability of a rupture. A glance at the Increasing affair of Donauwörth will show us from what quarter tension the wind was now blowing over Germany. Donauwörth, on the upper Danube, was a free imperial city (*freie Reichstadt*) and as such enjoyed representation in the Reichstag. Overwhelmingly Protestant, it had a Protestant town council which, though permitting Catholic worship, refused to tolerate Catholic public demonstrations. In spite of this prohibition some Catholic zealots organized (1606) a religious procession which caused a riot. In hot indignation they appealed to Emperor Rudolph, who, maintaining that Catholic rights had been curtailed, put the city under the ban of the empire and at the same time commissioned Duke Maximilian of Bavaria to occupy it with an armed force. Not content with carrying out the imperial orders, the duke, regarding Donauwörth as conquered territory, forcibly reconverted it to Catholicism.

This decidedly high-handed act greatly excited the more radical Protestant elements, chiefly adherents of Calvinism. They came together for conference and in 1608 formed a union to hinder a The Protes- repetition of the Donauwörth outrage. Thereupon Duke tant Union Maximilian, considering himself threatened by this move, and the Catholic joined with other Catholic estates, chiefly bishops, in a League, similar association which took the name of the Catholic 1608-1609 League (1609). When people among whom no love is lost begin to go about armed the chances of a bloody clash become excellent. Nevertheless so general was the dread of civil war that, in spite of ever increasing animosity, the peace was preserved for another decade.

The occasion that finally precipitated the long-expected conflict was furnished by Bohemia. Bohemia was a kingdom which in 1526 had come into possession of the house of Hapsburg, partly through inheritance and partly through election by the Bohemian diet. Its inhabitants were Germans and Czechs, the Czechs, a Slav people, being decidedly in the majority. In the fifteenth century Bohemia had risen into European prominence through its great citizen John Hus, who initiated a reform movement in the Church and met (1415) a heretic's death at the stake. The wild rebellion of the Hussites, as the reformer's followers were called, was put down after a tremendous struggle. None the less the province continued to seethe under the surface with revolutionary agitation. When, a century after Hus's death, Luther lifted his voice in Saxony, his words raised an answering echo across the Bohemian border. The Reformation made slow but steady progress nor was it seriously resisted by the Hapsburg government until Emperor Rudolph came to the throne. Devoted son of the Church that he was, he tried to put it down, but, crotchety and more than half insane, he only botched matters and was in the end constrained to grant the Protestants a limited toleration in a charter issued in the year 1609. However, both Rudolph and his successor Emperor Matthias (1612–1619) carried out the terms of the charter grudgingly and by a number of irregular acts renewed the animosity of the Protestants. On May 23, 1618, resolved to get rid of the Hapsburg dynasty and give themselves a ruler of their own faith, they rose in revolt. The emperor resided at Vienna and was represented at Prague, the capital of his Bohemian kingdom, by a body of governors. These the insurgents attacked, invaded their castle, and summarily tossed two of them, with a secretary for good measure, out of the window into the moat below. It was a fall of some sixty feet but, wonderful to say, beyond the shock to their bones and the more enduring shock to their feelings, had no evil consequences for the victims. The rebels crowned the day's work by setting up a revolutionary government. While their act was no more than a local Bohemian occurrence, in its consequences it set fire to the inflammable German house and precipitated the struggle known as the Thirty Years' War.

The outbreak in Bohemia, 1618

Whoever makes a study of the Thirty Years' War will be struck by the fact that it is really not so much a single war as an aggregation of related wars. It therefore falls naturally into different periods, designated by the issue which is uppermost at the time. Five such periods are clearly distinguishable: the Bohemian Period (1618–1620), the Palatine Period (1621–1623), the Danish Period

(1625–1629), the Swedish Period (1630–1635), and the French Period (1635–1648). These divisions indicate how the struggle, beginning in Bohemia, spread like a contagion until it included all Europe.

The periods of the Thirty Years' War From Bohemia, where, we have seen, it had its origin, it ate its way into southern Germany into the region known as the Palatinate—this is the Palatine Period. Then slowly northern Germany and its nearest Protestant neighbor, Denmark, were drawn into its sphere — this is the Danish Period. And finally one and another foreign country was moved to take part, until the war, while continuing to be a German civil struggle, acquired something of the aspect of a world-clash between Protestantism and Catholicism, and something, too, of a duel between the two greatest reigning houses of Europe, Hapsburg and Bourbon.

THE BOHEMIAN PERIOD (1618–1620)

The revolutionists at Prague had hardly set up their government when they appealed to the German Protestants for help. The Lutherans of the north denied them even their sympathy, while the Calvinists, inhabiting chiefly the south and constituting the leading element of the Protestant Union, offered advice but little help. The fact was that the Bohemians were in rebellion, and rebellion is a matter which conservative men will always treat with caution. There were, however, in the Union a number of flighty, sanguine characters who were bent on striking, through the Bohemian situation, a blow at the Hapsburgs and Catholicism. Chief of these was the president of the Union, the Elector Frederick, ruling over the region which, loosely strung across southern Germany, was called the Palatinate and boasted as its capital the city of Heidelberg, located on the Neckar not far from its confluence with the Rhine. The Elector Frederick was a Calvinist — a circumstance which helps explain his readiness to take the offensive against Catholicism. From the first he gave the Bohemian rebels secret aid and at the same time attempted to commit the Union to an active policy. In this latter purpose he frankly failed. The Union temporized, adopted a few useless measures, and on the approach of danger dissolved itself (1621). Its record is an unmitigated fiasco.

Meanwhile hostilities had begun between the emperor and his revolted subjects. They had not advanced far when the feeble Matthias, brother and successor of the hare-brained Rudolph, died (March, 1619), and the Hapsburg dominions passed to a better man, Ferdinand II. He had been brought up by the Jesuits and filled by them with their devotion to the Church. He was small and feeble, with hooked nose, weak eyes, and thin hair — plainly not a captain of men who shakes the world with his great purposes. Nevertheless, where his convictions were involved this frail sovereign proved himself more immovable than men of a more heroic mold. Having raised an armed force and secured his capital, Vienna, against attack by the Bohemian rebels, he set out for Frankfort, where the assembly of German electors was convened, after the usual fashion, to name the successor of Matthias. Although three of the seven electors were Protestants, the electoral college so far accepted the time-honored ascendancy of the house of Hapsburg as to raise Ferdinand to the imperial dignity. With the German crown resting on his head, the Hapsburg ruler felt that he must strain every nerve to recover Bohemia. The case seemed to him the more urgent as almost at the same moment that he was acclaimed at Frankfort, the Bohemian struggle had entered a new and more dangerous phase: the revolutionists had made an offer of the crown to the Elector Frederick. Frederick hesitated, torn between anxiety and hope, but in the end, spurred by ambition, set out for Prague, and on November 4, 1619, was crowned king.

Emperor Ferdinand II (1619-37) and the Elector Frederick of the Palatinate

In the course of his preparations for a vigorous campaign, Ferdinand naturally approached the Catholic League for aid. This organization, which was destined to play a very considerable role in the Thirty Years' War, was, in distinction from its rival, the Union, most efficiently managed by its president, Maximilian, duke of Bavaria. He proved himself in the course of the war to be the most capable of the princes of Germany. Brought up, like Ferdinand, by the Jesuits, he shared the new emperor's devotion to the Church but tempered it with a political intelligence wholly foreign to the imperial dreamer and bigot. From the moment of his accession to his Bavarian duchy, he prepared for the coming German crisis by laying up money and drilling an army. In the hard struggles of this world it is generally such men as Maximilian who succeed, men who exercise foresight and energetically carry through well-laid plans. Thoroughly aroused over what he considered the Elector Frederick's usurpation, Maximilian did not require much coaxing to put his forces at Ferdinand's disposal.

Maximilian of Bavaria

In the year 1620 there followed the campaign which decided the fate of Bohemia. Was the country to remain Protestant under its new king, Frederick, or to be won back by the Catholics and handed over to Ferdinand? If the Protestants had had a different champion, their outlook might have been more brilliant. Frederick was a man of little brains and such spirit as he had was largely instilled into him by his ambitious spouse, Elizabeth, daughter of James I of England. What further made greatly against his chances was that he was politically isolated. The Union, in spite of his appeals, did next to nothing, while among the Lutherans one man, the powerful elector of Saxony, went the length of actually coöperating with Ferdinand. The forces of the League, controlled by Maximilian but under the immediate command of General Tilly, penetrated into Bohemia until they came within sight of the towers of Prague. They found Frederick's army drawn up on the White Hill to the west of the town, and the ensuing battle was a crushing defeat for Frederick, who fled for his life across Germany to Holland. The Jesuits had mockingly foretold that he would prove but a winter king, a man of snow who would vanish at the first ray of the sun, and they were right. Ferdinand, followed by an army of priests and Jesuits, took possession of Bohemia, confiscated the immense estates of the revolted nobles, and proscribing every shade of Protestantism, imposed the Roman faith as the sole religion of the country.

The decisive Bohemian campaign of 1620

THE PALATINE PERIOD (1621–1623)

The Bohemian episode was closed and lovers of peace hoped that the war would now end. They were disappointed chiefly because the elated Catholics could not resist the temptation to make the most of their victory. The war entered a new phase when the emperor, egged on by his Jesuit advisers, put Frederick under the ban of the empire and commissioned his two allies, Duke Maximilian and the Spaniards — these latter operating from the Spanish Netherlands as their base — to take military possession of the Palatinate. This was a direct and wanton provocation since the Palatinate was recognized Protestant territory. But Ferdinand and Maximilian reckoned with the incurable divisions among the Protestants and they were fully justified by the event. Although the Protestants gave free rein to their indignation, when it

Seizure of the Palatinate

came to helping the Elector Frederick to defend his inheritance against the adversary they backed away. In consequence the Palatinate fell completely into Catholic hands. Victorious beyond his dreams, the emperor now undertook to reward his main supporter. He transferred (1623) the electoral dignity from Frederick to Maximilian, duke and henceforth elector of Bavaria, and in addition made over to him that part of the Palatinate (the upper Palatinate) which was contiguous to Bavaria. At the same time the Catholic army drove the Protestant preachers out of the Palatinate and gradually forced Catholicism upon the inhabitants.

These Protestant disasters alarmed the other Protestant powers of Europe, such as England, the Dutch, Sweden, and Denmark, and started a correspondence among them in favor of a concerted intervention. In any such movement the leadership would naturally fall to England, first, because since the days of Queen Elizabeth England had been the greatest bulwark of the new faith, and second, the reigning sovereign, James I, was, as we have seen, the father-in-law of the Elector Frederick. James, to be sure, had not encouraged Frederick's disastrous Bohemian ambitions; but when his son-in-law lost his inherited territories too, he could not fail to be disturbed. Wisely wishing to avoid war, he developed a plan to compose the German troubles in close association with Spain; and in furtherance of this policy he tried to effect an Anglo-Spanish alliance to be clinched by the marriage of his son and heir, Charles, to a Spanish princess. The Spaniards willingly negotiated in order to keep the English king from actively interfering in the struggle; but as soon as the German prizes were safely in Catholic hands, they made it plain to the duped James that they had no interest in either a matrimonial or a political alliance. *The policy of James I of England*

At this discovery James fell into a rage and made up his mind that only war would readjust the German balance. To this end he planned a great Protestant alliance. But here, too, as in so many of the measures of his reign he was pursued by ill-luck. His possible allies were the Dutch, Sweden, and Denmark. As to the Dutch, the Truce of Twelve Years having just expired (1621), the war with Spain had been resumed, and the country, fully occupied with its own problem, had no resources to spare for Germany. The case of Sweden was similar. Gustavus Adolphus, the very capable ruler of Sweden, was involved in difficulties with Russia and Poland which constituted as great a burden *James pushes Denmark into the war* as his shoulders could for the time being bear. There remained Denmark, whose king, Christian IV, declared himself willing to strike a blow for Protestantism, provided James supplied him liberally with money. This James agreed to do, but as he had foolishly involved himself in a quarrel with his parliament — a quarrel which under his son led to civil war — he could not get the funds which he required. The upshot was that James pushed the Danish king into a conflict with triumphant German Catholicism and then deserted, his promises of financial support proving to be broken reeds.

THE DANISH WAR (1625–1629)

With the entrance into the war of Christian IV in the role of champion of threatened Protestantism, the scene of action was transferred from the south to the north of Germany. Tilly, still in command of the army of the League, moved against him, but Christian had for a time the advantage of position and numbers. Just as he thought he had the situation well in hand, a second Catholic army appeared and threatened his flank. Raised in the name of the emperor, this force was the first *imperial* army of importance put forward in this war — Tilly, it must always be remembered, was employed by the League — and was commanded by Wallenstein. Wallenstein was a Bohemian nobleman who, having remained faithful to Ferdinand in the crisis of 1618, had been rewarded with immense estates taken from the defeated rebels. In order to free his sovereign from military dependence on the League, he had counselled him to raise an army of his own; and when the emperor pleaded poverty, Wallenstein lured him on with a plan which would make the army self-supporting. The general commissioned by the emperor would simply oblige the magistrates of the districts which the army happened to be occupying to furnish him with the supplies and ready money of which he stood in need. Such a system of forced contributions was not exactly plunder, but it was the next thing to it, and without urgent necessity the legal-minded and scrupulous Ferdinand would never have given his consent to anything so irregular. Wallenstein at first exercised some restraint upon his men; but in measure as the country grew poorer and it became harder to squeeze support out of it, the general took without asking whatever he could find. Naturally his rivals were not slow to imitate him, with the result that there now began that awful harrying of Germany, the cold facts of which remain incredible to our ears and confirm the concise saying of a famous American general that war is hell. And this was only the beginning, for there were destined to be twenty and more years of this slow torture. A French historian has declared the fact that Germany did not become an out-and-out wilderness to constitute one of the most extraordinary endurance tests which humanity has furnished.

A word at this point concerning the armies of this age will not come amiss. To begin with, they were not national but mercenary. A sovereign, wishing to raise a force, first commissioned a number of officers, who hired men at a fixed price wherever they **The organ-** were to be found. In consequence, an army was likely to **ization of** look more like an international congress than anything **an army** else — all races, costumes, and languages were represented. The pay of both officers and privates was liberal, and the cost of an army rose, at least in salaries, to a relatively much higher figure than today. A well-balanced force would be composed of infantry and cavalry in about equal numbers; the artillery was in process of development and did not yet constitute a decisive factor. The infantry was in part armed with rude muskets, but owing to the fact that a general still counted on winning a battle by the push of solidly massed men, the more usual weapon of the foot-soldier was a pike, some eighteen feet in length. In preparation for a battle the cavalry was drawn up on the wings, while the infantry, with the clumsy and ineffective artillery corps in front of it, held the center. All this looks rude and primitive from the twentieth century point of view, but it remains a notable fact that great advances were made in this period, chiefly under the stimulus of Gustavus Adolphus of Sweden. He increased his artillery pieces, turned them to better use, and developed in his troops a greater mobility both on the march and under fire.

To return to the Danish War, Christian IV proved no match for the combined forces of Tilly and Wallenstein. A single campaign settled his fate. In 1626 Wallenstein defeated Christian's lieutenant, Mansfeld, at the Bridge of Dessau, and in the same year **Christian** Tilly crushed Christian himself at Lutter. Not only was **defeated by** the king obliged to retire from Germany, but he was pur- **Tilly and** sued into his own dominions and had finally to take refuge **Wallenstein** in the Danish islands. He had every reason to be thankful when, in the year 1629, the emperor signed the Peace of Lübeck with him, whereby, in return for the abandonment of his German claims and projects, he got back his Danish territories.

Even before the Peace of Lübeck was signed, Wallenstein had overrun the whole Protestant north. Nothing seemed able to resist him. Capable, unscrupulous, and ambitious — the type of the mili-

The revolu- tary adventurer — his remarkable mind began to nurse
tionary designs so vast and intricate that they have never yet
plans of been entirely fathomed. In the main his plan appears to
Wallenstein have been to overawe the princes, both Catholic and Protestant, and once again to make the emperor the real master of Germany. As such a revolution in the German political system could be effected only by means of the army of which he was head, he foresaw that in the event of the reëstablishment of German unity the dominant role would be secured to him. However, the plan was bound to encounter powerful obstacles. In the first place Ferdinand soon showed that he had no taste for the part of conqueror which Wallenstein assigned to him; and, further, all the princes, regardless of religion, arrayed themselves in one solid phalanx against the man who tried to diminish their importance.

If we survey the German situation in the year 1629, the Catholic success seemed to be complete. In the Bohemian and Palatine stages of the war the Union had been scattered and south Germany occupied,

Zenith of while in the Danish stage, the victorious Catholic soldiery
the Catholic had penetrated to the shores of the North and Baltic
triumph and seas. In the length and breadth of Germany there was
Edict of no force able to resist triumphant Catholicism. Therefore
Restitution, it was now or never if a decisive blow was to fall on the
1629 Protestant enemy. In March, 1629, Ferdinand published the Edict of Restitution, by which the Protestants were dispossessed of all Church territories seized by them since the preliminary Peace of Passau of 1552. The measure was a revolution. At a stroke of the pen two archbishoprics, twelve bishoprics, and hundreds of monasteries were reappropriated by the Catholics. The emperor had hitherto cajoled the Lutherans in order to keep them quiet while he crushed the more radical Protestants, but by this step he removed the mask. It was not Calvinism at which he aimed but at Protestantism of every variety. The Edict of Restitution marks the peak of the Catholic tide.

The policy laid down in the Edict of Restitution meant violence perpetrated upon every Protestant prince and city in the land and could be carried through only by an army. But almost simultaneously with its publication the emperor was guilty of the fatal inconsistency of reducing his strength. In the year 1630 a meeting of the electors was held at Ratisbon (Regensburg) where the long repressed indignation of the German princes against Wallenstein found a voice. His misdemeanors were legion: his army exhausted the country, weighing on Catholic and Protestant alike; his imperial plans were revolutionary; his personal ambition was dangerous and boundless. A unanimous cry went up for his dismissal which the timid emperor could not face. Repudiating the policy of Wallenstein, he deposed his trusty lieutenant at the very moment when the Edict of Restitution for the first time welded the Protestants into a solid mass and when a new and threatening power appeared upon the scene.

Imperial inconsistency. Wallenstein dismissed, 1630

THE SWEDISH PERIOD (1630–1635)

In July, 1630, Gustavus Adolphus, king of Sweden, landed on the Baltic coast at the head of an army. We have seen that some years before, when James I of England attempted to create a great Protestant combination, Gustavus had declined to be a party to it. He was at the time engaged in securing his position in the Baltic area against the Poles. Since then Wallenstein's astonishing triumph against Denmark had filled the mind of the Swedish king with apprehension and alarm. He entertained the ambition of securing for himself the first place on the Baltic, of making, in fact, the Baltic a kind of Swedish lake, and here was Wallenstein apparently reviving the defunct Empire, carrying its banners into the north and talking of launching a fleet upon the sea with a view to reviving the German naval power. Concerned about his safety, Gustavus slowly made up his mind to enter the war for the purpose of driving the imperial forces out of northern Germany. But there was more than this in his bold enterprise. As an ardent Protestant he had sympathized from the first with the Protestants of Germany, but not till the publication of the Edict of Restitution did he feel that, unless a blow were struck for it, Protestantism in Germany was doomed. Thus Swedish patriotism as well as devotion to his faith spurred him to action. Did he act selfishly or unselfishly? An idle question, since human actions can only rarely be classified under such simple categories as good and bad,

Gustavus Adolphus lands in Germany, July, 1630

selfish and unselfish. Naturally he acted as was demanded by his conception of the interests of Sweden. To have done otherwise would have been a disavowal of his responsibilities as Swedish king. But it was perfectly compatible with a broadly national policy to believe that Swedish Protestantism was tied up with German Protestantism and that if the new faith were destroyed in the latter country it would sooner or later be doomed also in the former. Be that as it may, it is clear that he invaded Germany in order to strengthen the Swedish position on the Baltic; but it is also true that, while serving his own country, he rescued German Protestantism from destruction and became a hero in the eyes of Protestants the world over.

Gustavus is the outstanding figure of the Thirty Years' War and succeeded during his brief presence on the stage in bringing into the barren struggle something of an epic movement. Let us follow his brilliant course. His first concern on landing in Germany was to secure the alliance of the Protestant princes, whose salvation, together with the safety of his Swedish kingdom, formed the double object of his coming. And here he straightway encountered difficulties. The Protestant princes had, on account of the Edict of Restitution, little or no affection left for the emperor, but they naturally hesitated about allying themselves with a foreigner and aiding him in getting a foothold in their native land. While Gustavus was in turn coaxing and threatening them, help came to him from another quarter, from France. The French government, since 1624 in the extremely capable hands of Cardinal Richelieu, had followed the German developments with close interest, but owing to domestic troubles with the Huguenots had thus far not been able to interfere. By the year 1629 the Huguenot difficulties had been ironed out and Richelieu became free to pursue a more vigorous foreign policy. Though a great prelate of the Church, he was, above all, a Frenchman eager to advance the power and influence of his country. Clear in his mind that a strong Germany would be a disadvantage to France, he resolved not only to aid the successful plot which at Ratisbon brought about the dismissal of Wallenstein but to welcome with open arms every avowed enemy of the emperor. Expressing therefore from the first his approval of Gustavus's German enterprise, he presently (January, 1631) concluded the Treaty of Bärwalde, wherein he agreed to pay the king of Sweden a considerable annual subsidy toward the prosecution of the war. It was a measure preliminary to entering the conflict in person.

The first operations of Gustavus were directed to the reduction of the strongholds of Pomerania for the purpose of acquiring a secure base for his campaign. While he was thus engaged, Tilly, who since Wallenstein's dismissal was at the head of the combined Sack of forces of the League and emperor, stormed and utterly Magdeburg sacked the great Protestant city of Magdeburg on the May, 1631. Elbe. In the course of the assault a fire started, and when Saxony and Branden- the smoke and fury had passed away only the cathedral burg join was discovered standing among the blackened ruins. Sweden Fear and horror turned Protestant sentiment more strongly than ever toward Gustavus, and when, shortly after, Tilly threatened to invade Saxony, its ruler, who was the traditional head of the Lutherans, put an end to his indecision. Together with the elector of Brandenburg, and followed by many minor princes, he came to terms with Sweden. These German alliances so far secured the hold of Gustavus on the north that he was at last able to seek out Tilly for a decisive encounter. In September, 1631, a great battle took place at Breitenfeld, near Leipzig, in which Swedish generalship and discipline astonished the world by utterly defeating the veteran army of Tilly.

The victory of Breitenfeld laid all Germany at the feet of Gustavus. Never was there a more dramatic change. The Catholics, who a year before had held the reins in their hands, were now in exactly the same helpless position in which the Protestants had Gustavus found themselves. Gustavus, received everywhere by takes winter his co-religionists as a deliverer, marched without oppo- quarters on sition straight across Germany to the Rhine. In the the Rhine episcopal town of Mainz he took up his winter quarters. What more natural than that under the stimulus of a triumph exceeding all expectations, his plans should now have soared higher? With Sweden safe and German Protestantism rescued, his expedition had secured its original objects. But as he looked around and saw Germany helpless at his feet, visions arose of himself as champion and permanent head of the Protestant section of the country. The program was tempting but much work remained to be done before he could carry it out. As long as Bavaria and Austria were unconquered, he could not hope to be the arbiter of German destiny.

In the spring of 1632 he again took the field, aiming straight at the country of his enemies. At the river Lech, Tilly tried to block his passage into Bavaria. Again unsuccessful against his more versatile opponent, the veteran general of the League chanced to receive a wound from which he shortly died. Bavaria was now at the great Swede's mercy, who entered its capital, Munich, in triumph. His Gustavus in next and last objective was Vienna, residence of the Bavaria, emperor. If he could enter the Austrian capital, resistance 1632 would collapse and Germany be his acknowledged prize. But long before the situation had taken this critical turn, Ferdinand had turned to the one man capable of averting the final doom — Wallenstein. That general, since his dismissal, had been sulking on his Bohemian estates. When Ferdinand's ambassador besought him for aid, he affected indifference, but at length allowed himself to be persuaded to collect an army upon conditions calculated to raise him to a military dictatorship. Protected, as he thought, by the terms secured against a new dismissal, he floated his standards to the wind, and once again the adventurers of all nations and creeds flocked around the famous leader.

In the summer of 1632 Wallenstein and Gustavus, the two greatest generals of their day, took the field against each other. After long, futile manœuvring around Nürnberg, the two armies met for a deci-

The battle sive encounter at Lützen, not far from Leipzig (November, of Lützen 1632). After the trumpeters had sounded the hymn of (1632) and Luther, "A Mighty Fortress is our God," and the whole death of army had knelt in prayer, Gustavus ordered the attack. Gustavus The combat was long and furious, but the Swedes won the day; they won, but at a terrible cost. In one of the charges of horse, the impetuosity of Gustavus carried him too far into the ranks of the enemy and he was surrounded and slain.

With the death of the king of Sweden the war degenerated into an abominable scramble for the meanest material advantages. Gustavus's great achievement had been that he had turned back the Degenera- Catholic tide and saved the German Protestant cause. tion of the But he left Germany in hopeless confusion. The rage war between Protestants and Catholics, now almost unappeasable, was complicated by the wild territorial greed of the princes; and as if such misery were not enough, foreign powers took advantage of the impotence of the nation to appropriate its fairest provinces.

On the death of Gustavus, Wallenstein was the greatest figure left among the leaders of the war, and Wallenstein, a man not without large views, resolved to aim at a general pacification on the enlightened basis of toleration for the Protestants. As he was persuaded that he could never win the emperor and his Jesuit councillors to such a plan, he opened secret negotiations with his Protestant adversaries and thus laid himself open to the suspicion of Wallenstein's treason. If his army would have followed him through thick and thin, he might have defied the emperor and treason and become the restorer of Germany; but his officers fell death, 1634 away from him on his renewed dismissal by his master, while some of their number went the length of forming a conspiracy against his life. In February, 1634, in the Bohemian town of Eger, they put an end to him and his grandiose plans.

Meanwhile the Swedes did not relax their efforts to retain the dominant position which Gustavus had won for them. The political direction fell into the capable hands of the Chancellor Oxenstiern, who ruled in the name of Gustavus's infant daughter Swedish Christina, while the military affairs were on the whole interests very creditably managed by various generals whom directed by Gustavus had trained. None the less, in September, 1634, Oxenstiern the Swedes were signally defeated by the Imperialists at Nördlingen and had to evacuate southern Germany. With fortune smiling once more on the emperor, he resolved to take his first sincere step toward peace. Calamity had taught him to moderate his demands, and he declared to the elector of Saxony, still the recognized head of German Protestantism, his willingness to sign with him a treaty of peace, to which all Protestants should be invited to accede, on the basis of a virtual withdrawal of the obnoxious Edict of Restitution. The peace proposal had many imperfections, prominent among them being the failure to make express legal provision for the Calvinists. In spite of these drawbacks, in May, 1635, it was in the city of Prague converted into a treaty by the two German principals, and such was the longing for peace in the exhausted country that before many weeks had passed nearly all the princes and free cities had signified their acceptance.

Had Germany been left to itself peace might now have descended upon the land already tormented by seventeen years of civil warfare. Unfortunately the decision between peace and war no longer lay in the hands of the Germans. It now rested with those foreign powers whom the unhappy divisions of the Germans had drawn across the border. Securely ensconced in the heart of the country, the Swedes laughed at the idea that the war was over, especially as France, which had hitherto supported the Scandinavian power only with money, now entered into a new alliance (April, 1635) providing for full participation in the conflict. The death of their great king

France comes to the aid of Sweden followed by the disastrous battle of Nördlingen and the resumption of amicable relations between the Catholic and Protestant factions of Germany were doubtlessly heavy blows to the Swedes, but the French resolution to fight henceforward at their side made up for all these losses. The favorable hour which Cardinal Richelieu had been patiently awaiting to deliver a deadly blow at the house of Hapsburg had struck at last. With the domestic troubles of France allayed, Richelieu issued a declaration of war against Spain (May, 1635) and at the same time entered the German war by dispatching an army to the Rhine to coöperate with the Swedes.

THE FRENCH PERIOD (1635–1648)

The war now entered a new and last phase characterized by the effort of the allied powers of France and Sweden to effect a permanent lodgment in Germany. That religion was no longer an issue

The world struggle between the houses of Bourbon and Hapsburg of any consequence is sufficiently indicated by the circumstance that of the two invaders of Germany one was Protestant and the other Catholic. They and the German princes still bandied the word religion when they imagined something might be gained by it, but their intimate thought was all about territorial advantages. From year to year following Richelieu's decisive step of 1635 the French policy tended to fall with increasing weight into the balance, chiefly owing to the broad outlook and concentrated resolution of the great cardinal. Taking in with statesman-like vision the whole European scene, he sought the friendship and help of every power, great or small, capable of being mobilized against either of the Hapsburg houses, though it was the Spanish house which his interpretation of French history prompted him to honor with a particular aversion. His most immediate object was to weaken the hold of Spain on the Spanish Netherlands, since from this vantage-ground, as the map will show, a perpetual threat was suspended over the French capital. At the very time (1635) that he drew closer to the Swedes, he entered into alliance with the Dutch, who in 1621, when the Twelve Years' Truce expired, had renewed their war of independence. Joined to Sweden and the Dutch Republic, he prepared to meet the Austro-Spanish armies. Thus in its last phase the Thirty Years' War is less a German conflict than an immense international struggle for supremacy between the house of Bourbon, on the one hand, and the two branches of the house of Hapsburg, on the other.

The fighting in Germany during the last or French Period took the form of a stubborn forward thrust across the Rhine on the part of France and a steady movement southward from its Baltic base on the part of Sweden. The object of the allies was to crush the emperor between them. It remains a matter of astonishment that that sovereign, exhausted as he was and ill-supported by the German people, who had fallen into a mortal languor, should have made so stubborn a resistance. *The Franco-Swedish plan of campaign* In the early years he even won some notable successes. But year after year the French and Swedes fastened upon his flanks and with each season he found it more difficult to shake them off. The nation meanwhile, sucked dry by a soldiery which had grown insensible to every appeal of justice and pity, was dying by inches. The cities fell into decay, the country became a desert. In view of the certainty that the product of labor would become the booty of marauders, nobody cared to work. Hence the people fell into idleness, were butchered, or died of hunger or of pestilence. The only profession which afforded a semblance of security was that of the soldier, and soldier signified robber and murderer. Armies became armed bands organized for pillage and marched up and down the country, followed by immense hordes of starved camp-followers, women and children, who hoped, in this way, to get a sustenance which they could not find at home.

Accumulated disaster finally brought the emperor to terms. The forces of France had been growing gradually stronger and at last, under the leadership of the fiery prince of Condé and the gifted strategist Turenne, penetrated far into southern Germany. The honors of the last campaigns rested chiefly with them, though the Swedes also added to their laurels. *French and Swedish victories bring the emperor to terms* Seeing that it was useless to attempt to turn these strangers from the gates, the emperor finally accepted the decree of fate. But it was not Ferdinand II who bared his head to receive the blow. He had been succeeded, on his death in 1637, by his son, Ferdinand III (1637–1657), who opened negotiations with

France and Sweden, and after wearisome and sheer interminable delays, brought them to a successful termination in 1648, in the Treaty of Westphalia.[1]

The Peace of Westphalia is, from the variety of matter which it treats, one of the most important documents in history. First, it determined with what territorial concessions in Germany France and Sweden were to be persuaded to retire from the war; second, it laid a new basis for the peace between Protestants and Catholics; and third, it authorized an important political and territorial readjustment within Germany. Let us consider these heads in the order named.

The main subheads of the Peace of Westphalia

As to the first point, Sweden received the western half of Pomerania and the bishoprics of Bremen and Verden. By these possessions she was set as guardian at the mouths of the rivers Oder, Elbe, and Weser and put in substantial control of the German seaboard. As to France, she was confirmed in the possession of the bishoprics of Metz, Toul, and Verdun, already occupied since 1552, and received, in addition, the greater part of Alsace, which acquisition carried with it the inestimable advantage of a foothold on the upper Rhine. The free city of Strasburg and a number of other Alsatian towns and lordships were not included in the cession.

Cessions made to Sweden and France

Touching the German religious difficulties, the great question was how to settle the seizures of Church property which the Protestants had effected since the Peace of Augsburg. The Catholics, it will be remembered, had always held that these seizures were illegal, and by the Edict of Restitution of 1629 the emperor had peremptorily ordered their surrender. In the peace negotiations the Protestants demanded that they be restored to all the possessions which they had held in 1618, the year when the war broke out, but they compromised at last on 1624. Such former Catholic possessions as were in Protestant hands on the first of January of that year were to remain Protestant; such as were in Catholic hands were to be reserved to the Catholics. This arrangement settled the question of the disputed lands, in the main, in the Protestant interest, but included a concession to the emperor in so far as it gave the sanction of

Dispute about Church lands settled in favor of the Protestants

---

[1] The Peace of Westphalia receives its name from the province of Westphalia on the Rhine, embracing the two cities of Münster and Osnabrück, in which the plenipotentiaries of the powers met.

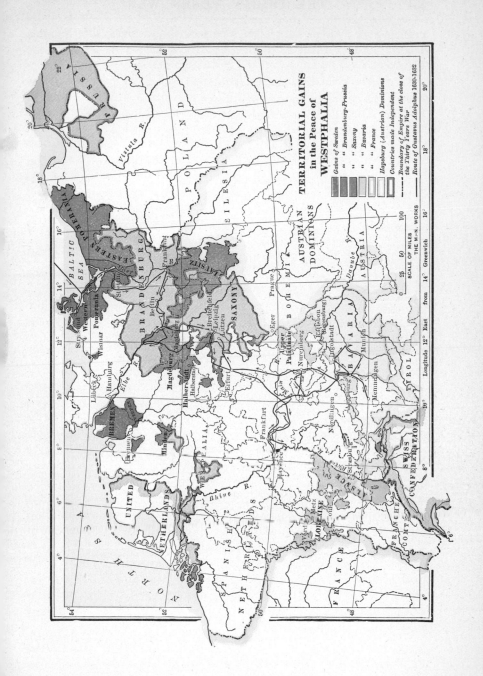

TERRITORIAL GAINS
in the Peace of
WESTPHALIA

Gains of Sweden
  "   "   Brandenburg-Prussia
  "   "   Saxony
  "   "   Bavaria
  "   "   France
Hapsburg (Austrian) Dominions
Countries made Independent
------ Boundary of Empire at the close of
        the Thirty Years War
—— Route of Gustavus Adolphus 1630-1632

SCALE OF MILES
0   25   50   100

THE M~N. WORKS

law to the Counter-Reformation carried out after 1618 in the hereditary possessions of the Hapsburgs. In the matter of Calvinism a reasonable solution was found by giving it the same legal standing as Lutheranism.

Under the third head it is necessary to note a variety of political and territorial changes within Germany. First, the princes were given a number of new sovereign rights, among others the right of forming alliances with each other and with foreign powers. Political Therewith the decentralization of Germany became com- disruption plete and the single states were made as good as inde- of Germany pendent. If the emperor was weak before, he was now no more than the honorary president of a congress of sovereign powers. Of four of these constituent states of the Empire, the Palatinate, Bavaria, Saxony, and Brandenburg, a word remains to be said. The Palatinate, confiscated by the emperor in the early stages of the war, was restored in a mutilated condition to the son of Frederick, ex-king of Bohemia, who had died in the course of the conflict. At the same time this son was recognized as the eighth elector, for Maximilian of Bavaria was left in possession of the electoral dignity as well as a part of the Palatine territory (the upper Palatinate). It admits of no question that under Maximilian Bavaria had played a very effective part and deserved the recognition which it received. From this time on Bavaria aspired to the leadership in southern Germany, while the leadership of northern Germany, exercised since Luther's day by Saxony, passed, largely in consequence of the Peace of Westphalia, to the elector of Brandenburg. This prince received additions of territory — eastern Pomerania and four secularized bishoprics — constituting a possession so considerable as to enable him gradually to replace Saxony as the leading state of Protestant Germany. In 1648 Germany lost the last vestige of its claim to be considered an effective European state. It was broken into about three hundred fragments, of which the four electorates named and Austria alone possessed sufficient power to command a modicum of respect. With Germany no longer a political factor of consequence, interest in German political development centers henceforth in the large principalities and more particularly in Brandenburg and Austria.

As a last curious detail of the Westphalian treaty it may be added that the Swiss Confederation and the Dutch Netherlands A curious (Seven United Provinces), once members of the Empire detail but long since practically independent, became formally sovereign.

Germany, after her insufferable crisis, lay insensible and exhausted.
While the contemporary stories of the ruin done by the war contain
an element of exaggeration, it is certain that the country took more
Effect of   than a hundred years to recover from its disasters. From
the war on   its disruptive political effects it did not recover till the
Germany   nineteenth century. The simple fact is that the material
edifice of civilization, together with most of the moral and intellectual
savings of an ancient society, had been destroyed, and what was
left was barbarism. The generation which survived the war had
grown up without schools, almost without pastors and churches,
and to its mental and moral degeneracy it added, owing to the long
rule of force, a disdain for all simple and honest occupations. Touching the injury wrought by the war, a few data may help us to realize
the desolate situation. Augsburg, the great southern center of trade,
had had 80,000 inhabitants; the war reduced it to a provincial town
of 16,000. Practically all other towns declined in the same ratio.
Thousands of villages were destroyed, whole districts were depopu-
lated. In Brandenburg one could travel for days without meeting a
peasant; in Saxony bands of wolves took possession of the empty
villages. In general, the population of Germany declined from one-
half to one-third of the numbers before the war.

The Peace of Westphalia dealt with so many matters not only of
German but also of international interest that it may be looked
upon as the basis of European public law till the French Revolution.
The Peace   We may also take it to mark a turning-point in the re-
of West-   lation to each other of hostile Christian faiths. From the
phalia   time of Luther the chief interest of Europe had been the
closes the question of religion. Europe was divided into two camps,
period of
religious   Catholicism and Protestantism, which opposed each
wars   other with all their might. In the Peace of Westphalia
the two parties recorded what they had gradually been learning —
which was, that their quarrel was as futile as it was cruel and that
since neither adversary could extinguish the other, it was the part
of wisdom to ground arms. Almost imperceptibly men's *minds* had
grown more tolerant, even if the *laws* maintained as tenaciously as
possible the old exclusive viewpoint. The best proof of the improved
state of the European mind toward the middle of the seventeenth
century is offered by the practical application of this very peace
instrument. The toleration therein granted was merely of the old
kind — each prince or free city could choose among the legally

recognized religions without any obligation of tolerating dissidents — yet, persecution of individuals was henceforth the exception, not the rule. It would be an exaggeration to say that the principle of toleration was henceforth dominant in Europe or that squabbles for religion's sake ceased, but it may be asserted, without fear of contradiction, that toleration had won with the Peace of Westphalia a standing among thinking and liberal-minded men. During the next one hundred and fifty years the principle filtered gradually, through the literary labor of many noble thinkers, to the lower strata of society and became in the era of the French Revolution a possession of all mankind.

REFERENCES

E. M. Hulme, *Renaissance and Reformation*, ch. 27
E. F. Henderson, *Short History of Germany*, I, chs. 16, 17, 18
E. R. Turner, *Europe, 1450–1789*, pp. 227–237, ch. 9
E. Richard, *German Civilization*, chs. 26–29, 31
J. Bryce, *The Holy Roman Empire*, ch. 20
Cambridge Modern History, IV, chs. 1–3, 6, 7, 13, pp. 395–425
H. O. Wakeman, *Europe 1598–1715*, chs. 3–6, pp. 112–128
C. R. L. Fletcher, *Gustavus Adolphus* chs. 4–7, 9–16
S. R. Gardiner, *Thirty Years' War*
J. H. Sacret, *Bourbon and Vasa*
C. R. M. Macdonald, *France*, vol. II
A. Gindely, *History of the Thirty Years' War*
C. E. Maurice, *Bohemia from the Earliest Times*

EMPERORS OF THE HOUSE OF HAPSBURG IN SUCCESSION TO CHARLES V

Ferdinand I, 1556–1564
Maximilian II (son of Ferdinand I), 1564–1576
Rudolph II (son of Maximilian II) 1576–1612
Matthias I (younger brother of Rudolph II), 1612–1619
Ferdinand II (cousin of Matthias I), 1619–1637
Ferdinand III (son of Ferdinand II), 1637–1657
Leopold I (son of Ferdinand III), 1658–1705
Joseph I (son of Leopold I), 1705–1711
Charles VI (younger brother of Joseph I), 1711–1740
    (House of Hapsburg extinct in male line)

CHAPTER XII

EUROPEAN CIVILIZATION TOWARD THE MIDDLE OF THE SEVENTEENTH CENTURY

After bringing the politico-religious movement among the European states down to the middle of the seventeenth century, we may pause to have a look over the whole expanse of western civilization.

The European man breaks with the limitations imposed on him during the Middle Age

We have seen that, beginning with the Renaissance, the European man gradually broke away from his medieval heritage with its primitive social organization, with its backwardness in the arts, and with its emphasis, in the daily affairs of life, on God's marvelous plan of salvation. By imperceptible stages he developed a new viewpoint involving a more experimental existence than had been countenanced by the Middle Age together with the healthy exercise of functions hitherto either forbidden or subject to strict control. A stirring as of stagnant waters followed. Man engaged in trade on an ever enlarging scale, he recovered the ancient art and literature, he reorganized his economic activities, resting them on individual enterprise and capital, he crossed the perilous seas to discover Asia and America, and he did a score of things besides, which revealed to him the earth, the heavens over the earth, and finally, himself.

Then from the new ground gained Luther challenged the authority of the Church and precipitated the great struggle of the Reformation and the Counter-Reformation. Judged by its purely mental content,

Did the Reformation smother the Renaissance?

the Reformation had undoubtedly a reactionary flavor since it once more brought theological controversies to the fore. On the other hand, by attacking the prestige of the great institution which sanctioned the medieval scale of values it promoted the liberation of the human spirit by asserting, though often with timid hesitation, the all-important right to private judgment. In the view of certain modern critics by no means moved by Catholic partisanship, the Reformation proved to be, on the whole, a misfortune for Europe since it put an end to the broad, humanitarian promise inherent in the Erasmian philosophy. A more just and sober judgment would seem to be that the religious revolution did indeed apply the brakes to some of the liberating tendencies of the Renaissance; but that it signified a reversion to the Middle Age is a prejudiced contention in hopeless conflict with the facts. In this chapter we shall review the evidence which proves that the expansive forces of the Renaissance, considered in the mass, continued steadily to gather strength behind the theological controversies which filled so much of the foreground of the age's consciousness. We shall show conclusively that Europe continued with very little interruption its march upon the paths cleared for it by the alert and enterprising spirits who broke through the medieval barriers.

Let us begin with the Fine Arts. As we have already followed their course in Italy, we are aware that they swung through a cycle of development which registered no sudden break at the coming of the Reformation. Such leading figures as Michael Angelo and Gradual Titian did not disappear from the scene until well after decline of the middle of the sixteenth century, and from them the art in Italy artistic movement traveled on in perfectly intelligible stages to ever new communications. True, these later Italian phases, rated by critics as manifestations of decline and designated by the name baroque, reflect, particularly in their altarpieces the rather theatrical devotion of the Counter-Reformation; but they also indicate by their continued attachment to scenes from common life that the naturalistic impulse of the Renaissance was slow to exhaust itself. If art declined in Italy — which can not be denied — it was primarily because the wretched political and economic conditions sapped the vigor of the nation.

Elsewhere the Fine Arts showed a similar persistent tendency toward realism. In Germany Albrecht Dürer (d. 1528) and Hans Holbein (d. 1543) exhibit in their altarpieces much of the old devotional feeling, but their saints and Holy Virgins are mani- Renaisfestly steeped in the earth-loving spirit of the time. In sance art in their many admirable portraits of contemporary worthies Germany of all ranks of society this immediacy of living reaches its and Spain most varied and unhampered expression. Since Dürer and Holbein had no notable successors, it might in their case be contended that the Reformation controversy served to dampen the artistic impulses in Germany, if one could not, as in the case of Italy, point to the do pressing effect of an intolerable politico-economic situation. Besides, in Spain, where the narrowest type of religious bigotry prevailed, artistic expression was apparently hardly stifled by it at all. In the Iberian peninsula we are confronted with a remarkable development of painting which, drawing its vigor from a Renaissance tap-root, came to a head in the seventeenth century. Its greatest figure, Velasquez (d. 1660), belongs to the era of Spanish national decline identified with King Philip IV. His extraordinary vitality, which makes Velasquez one of the most enduring influences of pictorial art, must be accepted as evidence of the presence in Spain of liberating and vivifying forces persisting under the pall of the blackest Counter-Reformation achieved anywhere in Europe.

The small northern folk, the Dutch, who ventured to challenge the majesty of Spain, experienced simultaneously with their turning to what to our generation may seem an arid Calvinism, a remarkable

Renaissance art in Holland and Flanders expansion of the Fine Arts, and again, in accordance with what appears to be a Renaissance rule, chiefly in painting. Aware that the Renaissance was passionately earth-directed, we are not surprised to learn that the inspiration of Dutch painting was a realism frankly redolent of its native soil. Dutch canvases revel in scenes of every-day life and constitute an unsurpassed record of contemporary activities on land and water, in shop and tavern. In Frans Hals of Haarlem (d. 1666) and Rembrandt of Amsterdam (d. 1669) these tendencies reached their supreme expression, although the labor of a score of artists, hardly inferior to these masters, should be borne in mind if we wish to be just to the multiplication of artistic genius in the heroic age of the republic. And, as if to dissuade us from making too much of the theological din of the period, the southern provinces of the Netherlands, which remained faithful to Catholicism and Spain and therefore, according to current stereotyped judgment, suffered their light to be extinguished, put forth hardly less notable flowers of art, as the distinguished names of Rubens (d. 1640) and Van Dyck (d. 1641) sufficiently attest.

These swift indications will have served their purpose if they have convinced the reader that the spirit of the rebirth did not perish with the Reformation, at least so far as the Fine Arts are concerned. The same is true of literature. In France Rabelais (d. 1555) produced *Gargantua* and *Pantagruel*, tales which deal satirically with struggling and deluded man and of which it may be said summarily that rarely has there been more zest of life crowded within the covers of a book. A little later Montaigne (d. 1592) expressed in his *Essays* an attitude toward life which, if more temperate and sceptical than that of Rabelais, is none the less a noble assertion of man's intellectual freedom. True, both of these writers were impatient of the barren dogmatism touching predestination and similar matters which threw a spell over their contemporaries; but their case would seem conclusively to prove that neither their country nor their time ever wholly succumbed to the absorbing folly of doctrinal warfare. And when in the days of Richelieu the religious pettifogging began to go definitely out of fashion, French literature took a fresh start and in the works of Corneille (*Le Cid*, 1636) asserted the characteristic Renaissance theme of the dignity of life. There followed on the heels of Corneille the great outburst connected with the reign of Louis XIV. It lies outside the scope of this chapter, but that it is a delayed expression of sixteenth century energy hardly admits of doubt.

The Renaissance spirit in French literature

The case of Spanish literature, like that of Spanish art, is peculiar for no other reason than that we are disinclined to admit that Spain was at all touched by the Renaissance spirit. But as soon as we agree that in Spain, too, the modern spirit found entrance, though always in subordination to certain dominant national ideas, we have smooth sailing ahead. The great figure of Spanish letters is Cervantes (d. 1617), who in his romance of *Don Quixote* aimed a dart compact of humor, satire, and pathos at the declining chivalry of the Middle Age and drove it, a contemptible wraith, out of the world of living men. Lope de Vega (d. 1632) and Calderon (d. 1681) devoted themselves chiefly to the drama, which, in spite of the ever watchful Inquisition, served as the outlet of a mental life remarkably alert within a narrow compass. Richer however, and of far wider range than the Spanish drama was that of Spain's chief foeman, England. In the "spacious times of great Elizabeth" the English drama achieved its full stature almost at a single leap. If it was Christopher Marlowe (d. 1593), who in such plays as *Tamberlane* and *Faustus* first sounded the majestic note to which the English stage was destined to be keyed, it was William Shakespeare (d. 1616), who in an incomparable succession of tragedies and comedies measured all the heights and depths of life. We are sometimes inclined to forget that Shakespeare made his appearance amidst a galaxy of lesser but

The Renaissance spirit in Spanish and English literature

still brilliant luminaries, such as Ben Jonson, Webster, and the usually inseparable collaborators, Beaumont and Fletcher. The English drama was therefore a general and national assertion of the love of life. But even while these singers were lifting their triumphant voices there slowly rose and gathered round them the somber mists prophetic of that Puritanic eclipse which in the succeeding generation blotted the theater from view and caused Shakespeare himself to become for a time hardly more than a myth. In England more sweepingly perhaps than anywhere else the Reformation, when it conquered, stifled that free and untrammeled self-expression which is the soul of art; but even in England the Puritanic righteousness proved only a phase which before the seventeenth century came to a close was already passing.

Another art, destined to become an especial glory of the Modern Age, owes much to the enlivening touch of the Renaissance, even though its origin and youth fell within the medieval period. Music **The Renais-** is the daughter, certainly not the least noble, of the **sance de-** Catholic Church, and was developed, beginning as far **velopment** back as the seventh century, in order to lend to the **of music:** **opera and** service of the Lord the solemn dignity of the organ and **oratorio** the moving expressiveness of the human voice. Its technical means, such as counterpoint and harmony, were so gradually perfected that it was not till the Italian, Palestrina, wrote (1565) his famous *Mass of Pope Marcellus* that ecclesiastical music attained the full command of its resources. A little earlier a development of another kind among the Protestants, under the direct inspiration of Luther, was destined to produce notable consequences, particularly in Germany. This was the publication (1524) of the first hymnal, a collection of admirably simple melodies for congregational singing. But at the very time that these new prospects opened to music in respectively the Catholic and the Protestant Churches the religious exclusiveness of this art, so long maintained, broke down. How could it have been otherwise in an age that lavished all its resources on its love of earthly and familiar things? Far and away the most important turn taken by music in the sixteenth century was that it was gradually appropriated as a vehicle for the common feelings of men and women in their purely human relations. It was characteristically in Italy that this broadening and secularizing were inaugurated by the invention of two new forms, the opera and the oratorio, the opera being conceived as a musical accompaniment to a strictly worldly tale and the oratorio as a tonal setting to a sacred theme embodying a spiritual conflict. While the oratorio, religiously inspired, sought to retain an ecclesiastical connection, the opera frankly abandoned itself to entertainment. It was in the year 1600 that the first productions in both kinds saw the light, simple and tentative sketches which in the subsequent decades were steadily elaborated. So great was the favor that both new forms, but especially the opera, elicited that they quickly established themselves throughout Europe. Even so, toward the middle of the seventeenth century the secular expansion of music had no more than begun. The great conquests of the art in the field both of technical equipment and of subject matter do not take place till the eighteenth and nineteenth centuries. However, the step here indicated, taken under Italian prompting, deserves to be set down since it opened still another path to the adventuring spirit of the modern man.

Owing to the undisputed preëminence of science in our time there are those who would be content to evalue the successive advances of western civilization by the phases of this single factor. Although the application of so simple a measuring rod is not in accord with the views propounded in this book, we may admit that science is so determining a feature of our modern life that we must give the closest scrutiny to its unfolding through the centuries. Having learned that **Progress in geography and the related sciences** the scientific beginnings made in the Renaissance affected chiefly geography, medicine, and astronomy, we are prepared for further conquests, first of all, in these fields. Geography was particularly favored by the new outlook and activities. So continuously was it enriched by the voyages of discovery that by the time of the Thirty Years' War the main land-masses of the earth had been located and their contours determined with reasonable accuracy. As the cartographer's art eagerly kept pace with these acquisitions of new material, Europeans enjoyed the advantage of maps and globuses of a steadily improved quality. Presently a movement of specialization set in which has continued uninterruptedly down to our own day. The geographers found themselves in possession of such immense masses of information covering the plants, animals, and minerals of the different continents of the earth that their efforts at the mastery of their data necessarily led to the staking off of the fields of botany, zoölogy, and mineralogy. Many other studies, such as chemistry and pharmacology, began to outline themselves and claim each one its own particular band of devotees. In this way an intensification of nature study, prompted by the abundance of new facts, was indicated in more refined subdivisions of knowledge, without however leading to the discovery of any great classificatory principles within the time embraced in this chapter.

The imposing anatomical advance, due to the practice of dissection and brought to a high level by the work of Vesalius, gave, as we are aware, medicine its first scientific foothold. The increased

Progress in surgery and physiology knowledge of body-structure redounded to the advantage, in the first instance, of the surgeons, as the case of the Frenchman, Ambrose Paré, would seem to prove. Living in the second half of the sixteenth century, Paré was enabled to publish a book (with illustrations), which, dealing with his actual practice in amputation, put the surgeon's art on a broad and promising basis. Before long anatomy stimulated the related study of physiology, where slow accumulations of discovery culminated at last in the notable disclosure made (1628) by Harvey, a London doctor, of the circulation of the blood. Fruitful as these advances were, they were slow to affect that department of medicine which is called therapy and deals with the actual treatment of disease. A stubborn traditionalism moved the physicians to cling to the remedies and procedures of the Greek authorities and accounts for the persistence of barbarous practices, such as cupping (blood-letting), which offer reasonable ground for the suspicion that the physicians were a leading cause of the disconcertingly high European death-rate.

However, the really memorable and decisive advance made by science in this period was in astronomy and the related subjects of mathematics and physics. The bold achievement of Copernicus, of

Progress in mathematics which we have already spoken, proved to be tremendously stimulating to the imagination. As the Copernican hypothesis needed for the confirmation of its propositions the support of mathematics, the work, already inaugurated in the fifteenth century, of recovering the mathematics of the Greeks and Arabs was continued until there had been completely mastered not only the geometry of Euclid but also the arithmetic and algebra invented by the Moslems. The incorporation in the Arab arithmetic of that ingenious device, the decimal system, made possible much more accurate calculations than had ever been dreamed of by the Greeks. On these borrowings, as a foundation, the Europeans proceeded to build up their own mathematical structure with the result that by the middle of the seventeenth century they had greatly improved upon the algebra and geometry of their teachers, besides adding wholly new tools to their resources such as logarithms and trigonometry.

When all is said it is the remarkable development of physics and astronomy, the Siamese twins of science, which lends a particular luster to this period; for out of the occupation with these fields came that invaluable conquest, a scientific method, the applica- **Primacy of** tion of which in later times to other fields has procured us **physics and** that amazing control of nature which is in our day our **astronomy** chief pride. The main advances made are connected with the great names of Kepler and Galileo, the scientists, and Bacon and Descartes, the philosophers. Not that this classification is to be taken too literally, for the former pair had philosophic inclinations and the latter were certainly concerned with natural science. In the seventeenth century, when specialization of knowledge was just beginning, no one as yet dreamed of confining himself to a single type of study and investigation. In respect, however, to the main contribution, on the one hand, of Kepler and Galileo, and on the other, of Bacon and Descartes, their classification respectively as scientists and philosophers is incontrovertible.

John Kepler (1571–1630), a German, was called at an early age to Prague, where the Danish astronomer, Tycho Brahe, had, at the bidding of the Emperor Rudolph II, created the most scientifically equipped astronomical observatory then in the world. **Kepler and** Before long Kepler had elaborated the celebrated three **Galileo;** laws of planetary motion which bear his name and fittingly **birth of a** complete the system of Copernicus. It will serve our **scientific** purpose if we reduce these laws to the simple statement **method** that Kepler, taking advantage of the new mathematical resources, proved that the planets describe not a circle but an ellipse around the sun and that their distance from the sun is in a determinable relationship to the time of their revolution. While the German scholar was making these discoveries, Galileo, an Italian, (1564–1642) was carrying on experiments in physics which so fully established his command of a practicable scientific method that it could be described and recommended to others. With Galileo science shook off the last medieval and ancient chains and stood forth like an athlete stripped and ready for the race. Galileo's most famous achievement in the immediate realm of physics was his discovery and formulation of the laws of falling bodies. That he invented or shared in inventing the telescope is hardly less interesting, since it shows that he was throughout his life concerned in perfecting mechanical devices capable of supplementing man's limited powers of observation. But his most valuable contribution was, as already noted, a scientific method of universal applicability in dealing with natural phenomena. Its outstanding parts or features are four in number: (1) observation brought to perfection by special training; (2) the isolation of phenomena in laboratories for the purpose of experimentation; (3) the appeal to precision instruments such as scales, barometer, telescope etc.; (4) the hypothesis as an avenue for penetrating into the unknown but conscientiously treated as merely a hypothesis until fully confirmed by the evidence. This method proved so fruitful and generally valid that it needed only to be refined in its details in order to revolutionize in the course of time the whole body of human knowledge. And indeed the enormous advance since the seventeenth century in our command of scientific fact may unhesitatingly be declared to have its source in the Galilean method.

In turning to the Englishman, Francis Bacon (1561–1624), we take up a many-sided man who, although he practised law and rose to the highest office under the king, the office of Lord Chancellor, remained Francis animated all his life by a passionate interest in purely Bacon intellectual problems. To Bacon it became clear that the old method of treating human experience followed by the medieval philosophers and enjoying the weighty sanction of Aristotle, was essentially barren because it began with metaphysical assumptions, from which it descended to the particular phenomena of nature by a process of logical deduction. Instead of such an unprofitable subjection to general propositions, Bacon recommended in his *Novum Organum* that the searcher for knowledge begin modestly with his personal experience, that is, with the objects close at hand, in order, on the strength of accumulated instances, to rise at last to general conclusions. He advocated an inversion of the thinking process familiar to the logic of his age, the process of *deduction*, by the adoption of the *inductive* method. This was tantamount to the proposal slowly and patiently to accumulate minute evidence in the hope that the abundance of instances might stimulate Nature, as it were, to explain herself. That this was exactly what Galileo had been actually doing in his work in physics Bacon never even took the trouble to learn, for he was a philosophical thinker rather than a professional scientist and therefore not abreast of the discoveries of his day. Nevertheless the advocacy by a Lord Chancellor of England of a new, the inductive method in the sciences — a method essentially that of Galileo — was enormously helpful in securing for it an authoritative standing among the intellectual classes of Europe.

The effect of the new discoveries in the world of nature together with the elaboration and adoption of a new method which could not be waved aside because it was so extraordinarily fruitful was to discredit the inherited medieval philosophy based on the articles of the Christian faith. Not that the truths of Christianity themselves became subject to doubt — for so fundamental a challenge the seventeenth century was not yet prepared — but the old intellectual props hewn and set in place by the scholastic carpenters began to give way. In fact the time was ripe for a new philosophy which would take account of the new scientific data; and the significance of the Frenchman, Descartes, lies in the circumstance that he was moved to act on this situation, thus fairly earning the title of the first modern philosopher. In distinction from his philosophical predecessors as well as from the theologians of his own day, Descartes (1596–1650) based his philosophical system, the purpose of which was to explain the universe in accordance with contemporary intellectual criteria, not on Christian revelation but on what was to him simple, incontrovertible experience: *the reality of the individual*. Of this reality Descartes claimed every man has ample assurance on the strength of the simple proposition: *cogito ergo sum* (I think, therefore I am). On this (seeming) rock set in an uncertain sea, he built up by the deductive resources of the human reason the essential truths of life, which, it was found, in no way quarreled with the recent discoveries of natural science. Since he boldly exalted reason, he was not so far removed from the despised scholastics as he thought, for they also had exalted it within its proper sphere; notwithstanding it is certain that by frankly abandoning the basis of the old philosophy and by detaching his system entirely from the dogmas of faith, which however he did not dream of disputing, he enabled European philosophy to keep abreast or nearly abreast of the movement of science.

Descartes and the birth of modern philosophy

We have seen that the agency which brought flux into the stationary medieval society was the town and that the town remained a fundamental phenomenon of the Renaissance. We have looked into its commerce and industry and noticed how these activities, gradually multiplied, led, on the one hand, to the voyages of discovery and, on the other, to the more effective economic organization denoted by capitalism. That the urban movement was in any way halted by the spirit of the Reformation would be ridiculous to pretend. The contrary is clearly indicated by the fact that it was the towns which chiefly took up the Reformation, largely no doubt because this movement, especially in its Calvinistic form, favored the increased power of the townsmen by transferring the control of religion from the ancient order of the clergy to themselves. The towns, meaning particularly the leaders of trade and industry, the burghers, rose throughout the period here under consideration to an ever-expanding importance.

The Reformation largely a town movement

In turning to the vast social-economic changes, which belong to the Reformation period and chiefly turn about the towns, we may profitably look first at the colonial movement. As a result of the conditions under which the oceanic discoveries took place, only two European states succeeded, in the first instance, in building up colonial empires, Spain and Portugal. First on the ground, they actually succeeded for a time in their plan of dividing the new world between them. From their earliest fortified outposts in the West Indies, Mexico, and Peru, the Spanish adventurers, supported by the armed power of their government, radiated in every direction until the vast area lying between the Gulf of Mexico and the southern tip of South America was substantially in their hands. They settled at important points bodies of their own people sufficient not only to keep the natives in subjection but also to assimilate them gradually to Spanish speech and culture. While Emperor Charles V and his son, Philip II, were with an enormous political and military apparatus asserting their primacy in Europe, their Spanish subjects, a picturesque company of sea-rovers, soldiers of fortune, gold-seekers, and adventurers of every sort, laid the foundations of an empire beyond the Atlantic, beside which the mother-country shrunk to Lilliputian dimensions. In sharp contrast to this territorial empire, Portugal, which the momentum supplied by Prince Henry the Navigator and his successors had carried steadily eastward, was content with a purely commercial enterprise. It claimed and held as its own the fortified route around the Cape of Good Hope to India and the Spice Islands (Moluccas), and by the

The colonial empires of Spain and Portugal

exercise of a jealous monopoly of the rich oriental trade harvested enormous profits. True, by planting a chain of settlements along the Brazil coast, the kingdom engaged also in the territorial game of Spain and no doubt particularly annoyed its larger neighbor by forcing a wedge between the northern and southern settlements of Spanish South America. Though trouble often threatened between the two Iberian rivals, it was in general avoided by each sticking to its own vast and well-marked zone. Besides, for a period of sixty years (1580–1640) Portugal was absorbed by Spain and all rivalry was suspended. And when, in 1640, the smaller state reasserted its independence, the European situation had become so profoundly altered that, instead of Portugal and Spain crossing swords with each other, the two declining kingdoms had their hands full defending their too vast possessions against the youthful impertinence of the English, French, and Dutch.

It was in the days of Philip II that the colonial monopoly so long maintained by the Spaniards and Portuguese began to give way. The two countries owed the control which they had exercised to their overwhelming sea-power, and when this broke down — the failure (1588) of the Invincible Armada supplies us with an approximate date — the English, Dutch, and French were prompt to take advantage of the discomfiture of their Iberian antagonists, rolled into one since 1580 by accession of Philip II of Spain to the Portuguese throne. The problem for the three assailants was to penetrate either into the Portuguese sphere of the east or into the Spanish sphere of the west in order to seize and, if possible, keep a firm hold on whatever of value came to hand. As the Dutch were fighting for their lives with Philip, it is not surprising that they gleefully took the lead in this invasion. Behind them followed the English and behind the English the French, slowed up by their disastrous civil wars, which were not wholly terminated till the days of Cardinal Richelieu.

The Dutch, English and French break down the Spanish-Portuguese colonial monopoly

With sound commercial logic the Dutch threw themselves first upon the oriental trade, in which they had long been interested since, though the spices were brought in Portuguese bottoms to Lisbon, they were distributed over Europe from the Netherlands, notably from Antwerp. In the first phase of Dutch expansion numerous merchant-adventurers made their way into Asiatic waters in competition with one another and at their own risk; but when this was found to lead to disorder and even mutual destruction, the Dutch government consolidated the various existing enterprises, issued a charter to them under the name of the Dutch East India Company (1602), and promised the company all the naval protection in its power. The Dutch Shortly after, the Dutch fleet drove the Portuguese navy build up a from the waters of the eastern archipelago and at the world trade same time cleared the paths of the Atlantic by administer- and a colonial ing a signal defeat to the Spanish navy near Gibraltar. empire By these two victories the Dutch acquired an effective, though constantly challenged, mastery of the oriental route and bit by bit picked up the Portuguese posts and commerce in the Far East. Not content with this triumph, they presently organized (1621) a Dutch West India Company which, while cruelly raiding the Spanish settlements in America, won its greatest glory in wresting, though only for a time, a part of Brazil from its Portuguese masters. Nor was this all. Taking advantage of a North American claim which owed its origin to a voyage, under Dutch auspices, of the famous seaman, Henry Hudson, the West India Company promoted colonial enterprise along the majestic American river to which Hudson had given his name, and in 1626 founded, on the strategic island of Manhattan, the settlement of New Amsterdam. In a word, the Dutch roamed the Seven Seas and when, at the signing of the Peace of Westphalia, their republic achieved its unqualified independence, it had also reached the acme of its power, for it had supplanted Spain as mistress of the seas and created a carrying trade which brought the Dutch flag to every known port and made the Dutch metropolis, Amsterdam, the focus of the world's commerce.

Aware of the potentialities of the eastern trade, Queen Elizabeth had chartered (1600), two years before its Dutch rival, an English East India Company; but the Dutch pursued their opportunities The English with more unflagging vigor and, having ousted the and French Portuguese from the East Indies, refused to split their East India profits with their neighbors from across the channel. companies deflected to Successful in crowding both the English and French the main- competition out of the islands where the spices chiefly land (India) grow, they organized them as their exclusive dominion with the capital at Batavia on the island of Java. The English East India Company and, later, a similar French concern were obliged to give up the East Indies as a field of exploitation and to content themselves with edging their way into the Portuguese trade with the Asiatic mainland, more particularly with India. In this way they gradually built up the respective Indian interests which in the eighteenth century came into fatal conflict.

The successful preëmption of the eastern spice trade by the Dutch persuaded England and France to compensate themselves by turning westward. They were the more readily persuaded to this course since they had already in the age of discoveries established France and vague claims to the certain coast areas of North America England and since, further, the still powerful arm of Spain hardly establish themselves interfered with projects so far north of actual Spanish in North interests. With the new, the seventeenth century the America two powers at last seriously set themselves the task of securing some part of the American shore for colonial development under their auspices. As though propelled by a secret impulse, both moved almost simultaneously. In 1608 the great explorer, Champlain, founded Quebec as the first permanent settlement of France in the New World and by this act staked off the huge basin of the St. Lawrence as prospective French territory. The year before a company of English adventurers, chartered by James, King of Great Britain, had cast anchor off the mouth of a river, which in their sovereign's honor they called the James, while to the settlement they planted on the river they gave the name of Jamestown. During the difficult period when this colony was engaged in getting a firm foothold on Virginian soil, King James's persecution, in the interest of the Anglican Church, of the radical Protestants called Puritans, assumed more serious proportions and drove many of them to consider the advisability of deserting their native land. In 1620 a small vessel, the *Mayflower*, brought the first group of these exiles to the inhospitable shore of Massachusetts, where amidst incredible hardships they established the colony of Plymouth. From these two slender beginnings, Jamestown and Plymouth, there came a relatively rapid development which secured to the English ever new sections of the coast. Inevitably the continued extension of English colonial enterprise would sooner or later lead to a clash with the Dutch settlement at Manhattan as well as with French posts distributed along the St. Lawrence. If during the early formative period, here considered, the conflict was avoided, it was none the less certain that a future age would ring with a colonial struggle of the three vigorous northern nations with one another as well as with their oldest competitor, Spain, provided with more territory than it could properly utilize.

From the colonial expansion here rapidly indicated there flowed tremendous consequences for Europe, some of which must be imperatively enumerated. Most immediately apparent was a change in Effect of the goods brought to the European market. What Europe colonial had in the Renaissance chiefly got from the orient was trade on European spices, silks, and objects of art which, essentially luxuries, diet and were neither heavy nor of great bulk. As soon as the habits European ship made an unbroken journey from India, it became possible, on the one hand, to import such quantities of spices that their price was reduced sufficiently to bring them within the reach of the common man, and, on the other hand, to carry bulky goods like rice, sugar, tea, and coffee. Gradually these articles of consumption, unknown in the older, simpler days, became so firmly incorporated in the European diet that, taking rank almost as necessities, the demand for them experienced an unbroken increase. As compared with these cherished eastern or Asiatic articles, the western products furnish by America were at first few. In fact the gold and silver of the mines of Mexico and Peru constituted for a long time the only notable importation, although sugar from the West Indies became an item as soon as the transfer of African slaves to the American soil secured a reliable supply of plantation labor. From approximately the beginning of the seventeenth century tobacco, which with the more useful, if not more esteemed, potato represents the most famous contribution from America's native herbarium to European civilization, leaped into prominence, and in measure as Europeans acquired the tobacco habit, led to a greater and ever greater import trade.

American gold and silver, if indicative of a rather undiversified stream of commerce, had at least the startling effect of setting European economy almost on its head. The continent was only Influx of just emerging from the system of barter and exchange in bullion and kind, and the sudden influx of specie greatly hastened revolution the decline of this primitive system. It did more. ∣ Flow- of prices ing in great quantities into Europe, especially after the middle of the sixteenth century, exactly like any other over-produced commodity it declined in value, causing a rapid appreciation of all articles of use measured in terms of money. No one could remember that any such amazing inflation had ever occurred before. Having not yet taught themselves to think scientifically about economic processes, men were a good deal dazed and manifested considerable social unrest, specially among the lower orders, until in response to an inevitable adjustment, wages had been advanced sufficiently to meet the increased cost of living.   All these phenomena taken together — the new quantity wares from the east, the influx of American bullion, the more general use of money in place of barter and services, the universal rise in prices — have been often represented as constituting a Commercial Revolution coincident with the invasion of Asia and America.   It is a serviceable suggestion, provided we are not led to regard the Commercial Revolution of the sixteenth century so much in the light of an isolated event as a perfectly natural consequence of the tremendous economic reorganization inaugurated in the Renaissance and signalized preëminently by the advent of capitalism.

In treating of capitalism in its Renaissance phase we noted that it was heralded by such outstanding features as these: the coming of the merchant-adventurer and the merchant company; the breakdown of medieval town economy by reason of a growing Growth of dominance of the national and world market; and the capitalist dissolution or at least weakening of the gild system. enterprises All these tendencies continued to make themselves felt in the era of the Reformation, strengthened and accelerated by the contemporary Commercial Revolution.   Manifestly the waxing trans-oceanic trade conducted by merchant-adventurers would cause this class and the trading and banking companies through which they operated to bulk more largely than ever in the daily affairs of men.   The capital which they commanded grew by leaps and bounds.   If the Medici of Florence represented the richest company of the last half of the fifteenth century with resources equivalent in our money to about $8,000,000, they were in the first half of the sixteenth century completely outstripped by the Fuggers of Augsburg, who operated with a capital calculated at about $40,000,000.   While these latter formidable figures reflect the larger dimensions of the Reformation world, they do much more since they also attest that the center of world trade and finance had moved across the Alps to southern Germany.   Before the middle of the sixteenth century it shifted again, this time to the Netherland seaboard and, more particularly, to Antwerp.   This Flemish city, favorably located on the Scheldt, at a point where important river, sea, and land routes converged, assumed around 1550 an unchallenged trade primacy until, toward the end of the sixteenth century, it suffered an eclipse through its conquest at the hands of Alexander of Parma (1585). It was then replaced by the near-by Dutch metropolis of Amsterdam, to be succeeded in its turn, but not within the period here considered, by London.

By the time business had reached the development indicated by the ascendancy of Antwerp and Amsterdam, the form in which the original merchant-companies had been cast was found to be no longer New organ-serviceable. The old companies had been a family ization of partnership, which, subject to sudden dissolution through business; death or withdrawal, lacked that security and perma-the Joint Stock nence which capital instinctively covets. To replace Company the family partnership there was invented the joint stock company, which, based on negotiable shares, secured continuous operation and was entrusted to a manager of outstanding business talent chosen by a board of directors. After 1600 all the great trading companies, as, for instance, the Dutch and English East India Companies, were joint stock concerns. The negotiability of shares gave birth to that eminently modern institution, the stock exchange, while the small size of the individual shares made it possible for men with even trifling savings to become stock-holders and so contribute their part toward turning the mills of capitalism.

By the first half of the seventeenth century it had become clear that it was the Dutch, the English, and, to a somewhat less extent, the French, who were taking full advantage of the new economic Growing developments. The Latin countries, Italy, Spain and control of Portugal, had been left behind, as was also the case with the business Teutonic Germany, where fatal divisions precipitated element in England, the destructive Thirty Years' War and almost wiped the France, and nation off the earth. It is therefore to the group of three Holland powers around the English Channel and the North Sea that we must turn if we would study at close range the economic aspect of the most advanced section of European society. Here capitalism had become most firmly rooted, and here a body of men, called burghers in Holland, bourgeoisie in France, and middle or upper middle class in England, came to the front, who, no longer merchant-adventurers of the earlier type but increasingly specialized as wholesalers, bankers, and shippers, handled all business of a national and international character, employed thousands of clerks, seamen, stevedores, and other laborers, and wielded a tremendous, if indefinable, social influence. That this could at need be converted into political power was conclusively proved first, in the case of the Dutch Republic and afterwards, during the Puritan Revolution, in England. In the following century, in the great upheaval of 1789, it was also proved in France. That the established governments of the three countries under consideration would not find it easy, with their lingering feudal and ecclesiastical traditions, to adjust themselves to the demands of the rising business class was no more than to be expected. The point to note is that in every instance they either came to terms with the representatives of capital or lived to see themselves overthrown by revolutionary action.

But let us guard against exaggerating the importance either economic or political of the "big" business men. They were in the seventeenth century still in process of formation and from long habit looked upon themselves as inferior to the landed gentry. England Besides, the landed gentry often possessed a political replaces the experience which the bourgeoisie lacked. And the men gilds with of "big" business faced another, by no means insignificant ist system rival in the "little" business men (shopkeepers and crafts- of produc- men) organized in the gilds. To the new men, the great tion merchants and capitalists, the gilds with their charters, their privileges, and their regulations touching every phase of production and sale, represented so many economic shackles which would have to be got rid of if enterprise was ever to become free. The masters and other beneficiaries of the gilds, however, wished to retain the system and were everywhere influential enough to gain their point with the single exception of England. In England alone the free contract system came into vogue and gradually reduced the gilds to hollow shells. By the new system, also called the *domestic* or *putting-out* system, the capitalist gained control by buying the raw product, let us say, wool, and *putting it out* among workmen on terms mutually acceptable. Plainly such workers, though owning their tools and utilizing their homes as a workshop, were wage-earners, much reduced from the status and dignity of medieval gildsmen. But as the new system, because conducted by trained and responsible specialists, produced more and cheaper goods than the gild system with its conservative attachment to time-hallowed methods and with its elaborate restrictive regulations, it was destined to win out everywhere, though in the seventeenth century it was victorious only in England. The advantage gradually acquired by England over the continent in all departments of manufacture (an advantage patent even to casual observers by the eighteenth century) must be ascribed to the virtues of the new system, which put at the disposal of the English capitalists a mass of free labor entirely unprotected by the gild or any other form of workingman organization. On the continent, in sharp contrast to England, the gild system, although showing many evidences of dissolution, continued to weigh upon production until the coming of that hurricane called the French Revolution, which, destructive to so many vested interests, shook also to the ground the long since hollow edifice of the gilds.

The Europe of the seventeenth century, dedicated to the rapid multiplication of wealth and dominated increasingly by the middle classes, continued to be constantly and terribly devastated by wars, **War a permanent feature of European civilization** the immediate effect of which was to destroy wealth and to deliver authority into the hands of professional soldiers. Here was a striking anomaly which would not fail to trouble the middle and intellectual classes, chiefly identified with the forward movement of civilization; and, as might be expected, they raised their voices in moving lament over the political disorganization which kept the sword of Damocles suspended over the unfolding and promising society of their time. While they were ready to admit that an advance had been made by the development of treaties of peace and commerce constituting a growing body of international law,[1] they were distressed to discover that the international system proved so little effective. Undeniably it had a makeshift character and often crumbled suddenly and without warning because it rested on no principle of right enjoying a general European recognition. The first step to formulate such a universal principle was taken by Hugo Grotius.

Grotius (1583–1645) was a Dutchman identified by birth and interest with that burgherdom which had beaten the might and majesty of Spain. A philosophical and legal thinker of rare genius, **Grotius and the modern revival of international law** he was enabled to transcend his class and nation and to raise himself to a level from which he could survey Europe as a whole and ponder its mutually destructive rivalries. Thus prompted to broad thinking, he took over from the ideology of the Middle Age the concept of a united Christian society living in peace and concord. That leading school of humanists which claimed Erasmus as its head had championed the same dream. But since both the medieval and

[1] See p. 89.

Erasmian programs were to be realized through the authority of the universal Church, they had with the Reformation, if not already with the Renaissance, become utterly impracticable. For, let us again remind ourselves, as soon as Europe had abandoned the medieval transcendentalism and turned to earth and man, it set itself the task of elaborating a worldly type of civilization which would refuse to accept revelation and the Bible as the basis and presupposition of international amity. The formulation of a new basis in better accord with the modern outlook on life is the merit of Grotius's famous work, *De jure belli et pacis,* published in 1625. Its chief proposition is that there exists behind the appearances filling the foreground of experience an immutable law of nature, to which all men are subject and which, so far as the relations among states are concerned, operates as the law of nations. Grotius was cautious about drawing conclusions of too sweeping a nature from his doctrine but he did envisage a European and even a world society, the constitutive units of which pursued their ends in mutual forbearance on the basis of a universally valid system of natural rights. In the eyes of the great jurist these natural rights were the moral counterpart of the body of physical laws discovered by the astronomers from Copernicus to Galileo and equally binding and unescapable. Reducing his achievement to its simplest terms, we may say that Grotius attempted to provide a modern and generally acceptable sanction for those longings of unity and concord which had been eclipsed but not extinguished with the passing of the ideas and institutions of the Middle Age. The mere proposal of a new sanction was an important step forward; but let us in this connection observe that "just measure" extolled by the Greek philosophers and agree that, in spite of a general and unbinding theoretical acceptance, the new principle of natural rights did little toward bringing Europe to a practical realization of fraternal living. So great at all times has been the chasm yawning between the visaged ideal and the hard and cruel facts of life!

REFERENCES

E. M. HULME, *Renaissance and Reformation,* chs. 19, 29, 30
P. SMITH, *Age of the Reformation,* chs. 10–13
A. TILLEY, *Modern France,* pp. 400–492; chs. 13–15
L. BATIFFOL, *Century of the Renaissance*
W. C. ABBOTT, *Expansion of Europe,* I
A. L. CROSS, *History of England and Greater Britain,* chs. 26, 35

Cambridge Modern History, III, chs. 11, 14, 22, IV, 26, 27
P. S. ALLEN, *Age of Erasmus*
A. D. F. HAMLIN, *A Text-book of the History of Architecture*, chs. 20–24
A. MARQUAND AND A. L. FROTHINGHAM, *A Text-book of the History of Sculpture*, chs. 21, 22, 23
J. C. VAN DYKE, *A Text-book of the History of Painting*, chs. 9, 10, 11, 12, 15, 16, 17, 18
F. H. GARRISON, *Introduction to the History of Medicine*
W. T. SEDGWICK AND H. W. TYLER, *Short History of Science*
W. R. BALL, *History of Mathematics*
H. W. BRYANT, *History of Astronomy*
J. OWEN, *Skeptics of the Italian Renaissance; Skeptics of the French Renaissance*
A. C. MCGIFFERT, *Protestant Thought before Kant*
H. O. TAYLOR, *Thought and Expression in the Sixteenth Century*
W. WINDELBAND (tr. by Tufts), *History of Philosophy*
W. CUNNINGHAM, *Progress of Capitalism in England; Western Civilization in its Economic Aspects*
A. P. USHER, *Industrial History of England*
J. N. FIGGIS, *From Gerson to Grotius*
H. D. FOSTER, *Political Theories of the Calvinists* (Amer. Hist. Rev. 21, pp. 481 ff.)
W. A. DUNNING, *Political Theory from Luther to Montesquieu*

THE ABSOLUTE MONARCHY FROM 1648 TO 1789

CHAPTER XIII

THE STUARTS AND THE PURITAN REVOLUTION

The House of Stuart

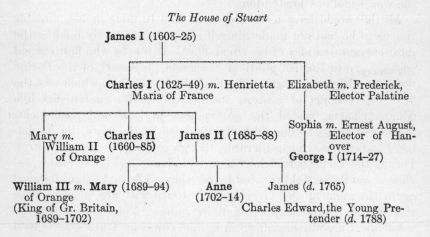

James I (1603–25)

Charles I (1625–49) *m.* Henrietta Elizabeth *m.* Frederick,
Maria of France   Elector Palatine

Mary *m.*   Charles II   James II (1685–88)   Sophia *m.* Ernest August,
William II   (1660–85)   Elector of Han-
of Orange   over
                                       George I (1714–27)

William III *m.* Mary (1689–94)   Anne   James (*d.* 1765)
of Orange   (1702–14)
(King of Gr. Britain,   Charles Edward, the Young Pre-
1689–1702)   tender (*d.* 1788)

When Elizabeth died in March, 1603, she was succeeded by the son of Mary Stuart, who had been king of Scotland almost from his birth under the name of James VI and who figures among English monarchs as the first of that name. James's accession opened the prospect of that union between England and Scotland for which several far-sighted statesmen beginning with Henry VII had carefully prepared the ground. However, the plan still encountered opposition. So deep-rooted were the long-standing antagonisms and jealousies of the two nations that they refused to consolidate their institutions and fortunes, though James himself gave his ardent adhesion to the project. In consequence, Scotland kept its own parliament, laws, and officials, and the accession of James did little more for the present than give England and Scotland a common sovereign.

The Scottish king becomes king of England

It was unfortunate that at a time when the sovereign exercised enormous power the crown should have descended to such a man as James. He had an ungainly figure, a shuffling gait, distasteful
Character personal habits, and was obstinate, weak, and cowardly.
of James A person less royal to look upon had not sat upon the English throne in many a century. He had crammed himself with a considerable stock of knowledge which had not matured into wisdom and which his vanity prompted him to exhibit on every occasion in order to hear himself acclaimed by the flattering courtiers as the British Solomon. His display of pedantic information brought down upon him from Henry IV of France the remark that he was the wisest fool of Christendom.

All this would have merely exposed him to more or less amiable ridicule if he had not made himself really dangerous by holding the most exaggerated idea of his royal office. It was he who first carried
His concep- into English political discussion the theory of the Divine
tion of his Right of kings. The English constitution, which was the
office product of custom and certain specific enactments like Magna Charta, vested the government in king and parliament. While the king was undoubtedly the head of the state, the parliament had exercised a considerable, though varying amount of control. During the Tudor period its rights and claims had considerably declined; but it was highly probable that they would be brought forward again the moment the sovereign lost touch with the nation. And that is exactly what happened under James. Not content with the *substance* of absolutism inherited by him from the Tudors, he craved its open acknowledgment and asserted his claims in terms so boundless that he seemed almost to be set on rousing opposition. On one occasion he edified his hearers with the following typical pronouncement: "It is atheism and blasphemy to dispute what God can do; . . . so it is presumption and high contempt in a subject to dispute what a king can do, or say that a king cannot do this or that." The Tudors, as has been said, held this identical theory; but they came at the time of a great national crisis and acted in the main in close accord with the people. Should the first Stuart undertake to act against the people and their real or supposed interests, it might well be that he would find his power challenged and the nation prepared to fall back on that older conception of the role of parliament which the Tudor absolutism had supplanted. This is the precise turn James brought about, thereby precipitating a struggle between

himself and his people destined to put an end to the "strong" monarchy of the Tudors and to inaugurate a parliamentary régime.

The accession of James occurred amid circumstances which augured a happy reign. The defeat of the Spanish Armada had placed the independence of England beyond question, and subsequent events on the sea and in the Netherlands had so The foreign weakened Spain as to remove all danger from that and quarter. In consequence, James wisely enough nego- domestic tiated with Spain a treaty of peace (1604). In domestic James's affairs the chief interest revolved around the Anglican accession Church established by Elizabeth on the basis of the Acts of Supremacy and Uniformity (1559). By the time of her death her creation had acquired an air of permanence. The Catholics were a waning power and the Puritans, influenced but not yet dominated by Calvinism, demanded certain concessions, based chiefly on their aversion to the surplice, kneeling in service, and similar externals. It must be remembered that they were as yet, in overwhelming majority, friendly to the national Establishment, accepted the religious headship of the sovereign and the episcopal form of government, and merely advocated the simplification or purification, as they called it, of divine service. If James would know how to conciliate them, the religious troubles of England might be accounted as over.

But James did not know how to conciliate them. Shortly after his accession, in 1604, he called a religious conference at Hampton Court for the purpose of discussing a Puritan document, called the Millenary Petition from the fact that almost a thousand James and clergymen had given their adhesion to it. Unfortunately the Puritans he lost his temper during the debate and flared up wildly against the petitioners. He declared that they were the enemies of episcopacy — which was not yet the case — and affirmed with unnecessary emphasis that that system of church government had his unwavering support. His personal spite becomes explicable when we remember that he had been brought up in Scotland, where he had made the acquaintance of the Presbyterian system, by which the church was withdrawn from the control of the king and bishops and put in the hands of the ministers and the people. Having made the pleasing discovery that in England the sovereign ruled the church through the bishops, he was jealously on the lookout against the importation of Presbyterian ideas. He went the length of identifying episcopacy with monarchy and formulated his opinion in tho

epigrammatic assertion, "No bishop, no king." Acting on the unjustified assumption that the English Puritans were Scotch Presbyterians in disguise, he dismissed the Millenary petitioners gruffly
and shortly after issued a proclamation ordering every clergyman
who refused to meet exactly and literally the prescriptions of the
Book of Common Prayer to be removed from his living. In this way
the king made it clear that, instead of conciliating the Puritans, he
intended to drive them from the church.

Toward the Catholics, whom James to his credit regarded with a
tolerance much in advance of his time, he initiated a temperate but
unsuccessful policy. He began by lightening some of their burdens
The gun- of persecution, but when, owing to the pressure brought
powder to bear upon him by his Protestant subjects, he faltered
plot, 1605 in his resolution, a group of disappointed and desperate
Catholics resolved to destroy the whole Protestant government —
king, Lords, and Commons — by one gigantic stroke. They heaped
gunpowder in barrels in the cellars beneath the parliament buildings
and set November 5, 1605 — the day of the opening in state of a
new session — for the monstrous crime. Suspicion, however, had
been awakened by hints thrown out by some of the conspirators;
and luckily, on the eve of the planned disaster, Guy Fawkes, the
hardiest of the conspirators, was discovered keeping watch among
the explosives. While he and his associates were hunted down and
executed with all the barbarity characteristic of the period, a much
more regrettable consequence of the plot was that the English
people were confirmed in that intense distrust and hatred of the
Catholic faith which long remained the leading article of their religious and political creed.

Such was the relation of James to the religious question — the
ritualistic wing of the national Church was vigorously sustained, the
Puritan or reform wing was opposed and actively repressed, and
James and the Catholics, not without a decent reluctance, were per-
the parlia- secuted and crushed. However, the religious situation
ment might of itself not have provoked a crisis, if James had
not created a second difficulty by antagonizing his parliament. To
understand this new development we have but to recall to mind that
to the practical absolutism of the Tudors he wished to give the force
of theory and of law.

The quarrel began almost immediately. James needed money,
partly for legitimate reasons due to the mounting costs of govern-

ment, partly because he was extravagant. The required revenues had, of course, to be voted by parliament, and if that body had been managed after the Tudor fashion, it might have granted supplies as readily as in the days of Henry or Elizabeth. But The ques- James's talk about a monarch being above the law had tion of the aroused suspicion and moved the parliament to ask in finances return for a redress of grievances. The king, thereupon, in a huff, began to help himself to funds by arbitrarily increasing the impositions on certain articles of import and export. Undoubtedly the legality of the measure was open to question. When a merchant, named Bate, refused to pay the imposition on a consignment of currants from the Near East, he was tried and sentenced by the judges. Thus, technically, James triumphed, but the victory only added a limited amount to his revenue, did not settle his financial difficulties, and exasperated the parliament so greatly that it prepared to oppose every demand, reasonable or unreasonable, which the king might make. On the angered James dissolving one parliament, he found its successor still more unwilling to bow to his dictation. Out of what was originally a simple matter of supplying revenue for the crown's legitimate outlay had grown by James's arrogance and tactlessness an issue, at the core of which was the all-important question as to who had the last say in matters of taxation: king or parliament.

Over impositions and related revenue issues James quarrelled with his parliament throughout his reign, with the result of an increasing irritation on both sides. In the year 1621 the wrath of the Commons reached the point of a savage attack on the whole Impeach- administration, culminating in the impeachment of the ment of highest official of the realm, the Lord Chancellor. This Bacon, 1621 was none other than the philosopher, Francis Bacon, one of the greatest Englishmen of the period. By taking fees from suitors while their cases were still pending in his court, he had become technically guilty of bribery. His excuse was that the acceptance of gifts was a long-established custom of his office, but with a disarming candor he avowed that the practice was indefensible. "I beseech your Lordships," he added, "to be merciful to a broken reed." Bacon was fined and dismissed from office, the sentence being declared by himself "just, and for reformation's sake fit"; but he would not have been attacked at all if the parliament had not been set on vicariously striking the king through his leading official and intimate political adviser.

Bacon's trial took the form of an impeachment, in itself an ominous sign that the parliament was raising its claims as the best answer to the king's attempt to exalt his own position. Impeachment was The revival a means by which, in earlier times, the parliament had of impeach- exercised control over the king's advisers, but which had ment become obsolete under the Tudors, when the humbled parliament was obliged to abandon all influence upon the royal ministers. Its revival at this juncture meant that the parliament was furbishing up the old weapons with which it had once held the monarchy in check. An impeachment was a somewhat complicated process. The house of Commons appeared at the bar of the house of Lords to present to it the offender against the commonwealth, and the house of Lords, after listening to the charges, declared them founded or unfounded and pronounced sentence accordingly. The significance of the impeachment of Bacon was not lost upon James, who vaguely divined that a serious struggle was at hand.

The unpopularity caused by his harsh treatment of the Puritans and his violent quarrel with the parliament was increased by the foreign policy of James. We have remarked that shortly after his James's accession he had concluded peace with Spain. His gen- foreign eral program was to further the cause of religious peace policy in Europe by maintaining a close relationship with his late enemy. But such a policy, creditable to his Christian temper, would depend for its success on Spain's willingness to meet him half-way. The test came in the year 1618. In that year occurred the Bohemian incident which led to the Thirty Years' War. James was interested in the struggle from the first not only because Protestantism had once more locked horns with Catholicism, but also more immediately because Frederick of the Palatinate, elected king of the Protestant faction of Bohemia, had married his daughter Elizabeth. None the less James looked feebly on when Frederick was driven from Bohemia; and only when Frederick was expelled from the Palatinate, too, was the British sovereign roused sufficiently to make an appeal to Spain to help restore his son-in-law to his inheritance. That power was delighted to find him so docile, made temporizing proposals, but too thoroughly approved of the Catholic success in Germany to do anything to check it.

Thus matters dragged on until the year 1623, when the young and handsome duke of Buckingham, who was the king's all-powerful favorite, proposed to take a last step to bind Spain to England in a

close alliance and to secure the settlement of the Palatinate question
without war.   He developed the plan of a secret journey with
Charles, the prince of Wales, to Madrid in order to take the Spanish
court, as it were, by storm. By an impetuous attack he
hoped to persuade it to affiance the Spanish Infanta to the
English heir and at the same time to sign the desired
treaty of alliance.   It was a plan as hare-brained as it
was impolitic, but James, teased and wheedled by the
Charles and Bucking-ham journey to Madrid
two young men, at last gave his blessing to the enterprise. After
many adventures Charles and Buckingham arrived at Madrid, but
their reception was very different from what they had anticipated,
and their hosts, although scrupulously polite, met them with eva-
sion at every point.   Utterly disgusted, they came back resolved to
break with the king's timid policy. James was vigorously plied till
he consented to essay the reconquest of the Palatinate by war.
Though the parliament voted supplies, the monies were insufficient
and the expedition, entrusted to a German adventurer, Count
Mansfeld, proved a disastrous failure.   In the midst of these fresh
difficulties, the distracted king died (March, 1625).

REIGN OF CHARLES I (1625–1649)

The new king, Charles I, was outwardly very unlike his father.
His face, familiar to us from Van Dyck's many portraits of the
English royal family, was handsome and his manner
kingly.   Unfortunately he was liberally endowed with
the Stuart traits of perversity and obstinacy and shared his father's
Charles I
exaggerated views of the royal prerogative.

The two main difficulties created by James bore immediate and
dangerous fruit in the new reign.   By antagonizing the Puritans
James had driven them into open opposition to the national Church
and by quarreling with parliament he had raised the
question as to who controlled taxation.   Determined to
follow in his father's footsteps, Charles succeeded in an
incredibly short time in arousing such opposition to himself that the Commons, who had been servilely docile
Charles continues to antagonize Puritans and parlia-ment
under Elizabeth and had, even while protesting, been deeply re-
spectful under James, plainly put the question: Who was sovereign
in England, parliament or king?

Shortly after his accession Charles married Henrietta Maria, a sister of Louis XIII of France. This marriage with a Catholic, extremely unpopular on its own account, was rendered doubly so by the suspicion, only too well founded, that Charles had entered upon

The rising tide of Protestant fervor an agreement with Louis to relax the penal laws against the English Catholics. When parliament assembled, it showed immediately signs of restlessness, and presently grew still more excited on discovering that a small party of churchmen, closely associated with the court, was advocating views that savored of Romanism. Not only did they defend an elaborate, ritualistic service but they also attacked some of the teachings of Calvin and in particular the doctrine of predestination. As the king felt the same way about these matters, he naturally gravitated toward them, while they for their part adhered to his theory of the royal prerogative. To the Puritans, whose fervor and numbers were steadily increasing, such an association looked very much like the alliance of popery and tyranny. Maintaining that the Church of England was, in point of doctrine, Calvinist, they permitted themselves to be carried away by their feelings to the point of declaring that the High Church advocates were innovators embarked on a dark intrigue to carry England back to Rome. Heatedly opposed to Charles on ecclesiastical grounds, the Puritans naturally joined forces with those individuals and groups who resented his political claims; and thus it came about that the absolutist and High Church parties had no sooner united than the two oppositions, Puritan and parliamentarian, fused in their turn. Under this alignment Charles's tumultuous reign began; and under it, after fierce and prolonged controversy, the country plunged disastrously into civil war.

In view of the strained relations between king and parliament, it is intelligible why the parliament took a most unusual course with regard to the chief revenue of the crown, called Tonnage and Poundage.

Tonnage and Poundage age. Tonnage and Poundage was the name given to the customs dues on wines and merchandise commonly voted at the beginning of each reign for the whole period of the sovereign's life. Partly from occupation with other business, partly from desire to bring pressure to bear upon the king, the parliament now failed to make the usual life grant; but Charles, who could not well carry on the government without Tonnage and Poundage, continued, through his officials, to collect it.

With the heavens darkening over him by reason of these domestic infelicities, Charles invited additional criticism by his extraordinary mismanagement of foreign affairs. The war with Spain furnished the occasion. Since it was he who had forced it on his father, he was bent on prosecuting it with vigor. Inclined to give him support, for the war with Catholic Spain was popular, the parliament did, however, expect that the money which it granted would be spent in giving the Spaniards a sound beating. But Charles, with his customary lack of insight, entrusted the conduct of the war to the duke of Buckingham, his father's favorite and his own; and the duke of Buckingham, a handsome, dashing, and romantically minded individual unfit for weighty affairs of state, reaped nothing but disaster. We have already noted that the first campaign, aimed at the immediate object of contention, the Palatinate, was a complete failure. Nothing daunted, Buckingham resolved to level a blow directly at Spain by an expedition to Cadiz. It ended in an ignominious retreat (1625). Thereupon the Commons refused to make additional grants until the blundering duke had been removed; and as the king resented as an impertinence the attempt to dictate to him his policy and his advisers and angrily dissolved (1626) the parliament, the threatening deadlock became definite.

Disastrous management of the war with Spain

In the year 1627 matters grew worse. The king, not content with the unsuccessful war with Spain, allowed himself to be dragged into conflict with France in behalf of the French Huguenots, who were being besieged by Richelieu in La Rochelle. As the Huguenots were hard pressed and there was no other way of getting money for a rescuing expedition, Charles adopted a perilous device: he asked first for voluntary gifts; and when the nation failed adequately to respond, he levied a forced loan. When citizens would not pay their quota, he quartered troops upon them, and in order to spread a general terror, threw some of the more conspicuous recalcitrants into prison. Not only were these measures dangerous, but the sums thus extorted brought no blessing. A relief expedition which sailed for La Rochelle under Buckingham failed as miserably as the attack upon Cadiz, with the discouraging total result that fresh disgrace was added to the ignominy already incurred in the war with Spain.

War with France

The new parliament, which Charles, hard pressed for supplies, was obliged to call in 1628, was amply justified in its outbreak of wrath against the government. Before granting another penny, it insisted that the wrongs of the nation be redressed, and in a docu-

ment called the Petition of Right it enumerated the most outstanding grievances. The Petition of Right declared gifts, loans, and taxes not voted by parliament illegal; it insisted that no freeman
The should be imprisoned without cause shown; and it con-
Petition demned the use of martial law in times of peace as well as
of Right the quartering of troops upon householders. As there was no other way of getting money, the king had to swallow the bitter morsel. The Petition of Right, celebrated as a renewal of Magna Charta, was accepted by him and became the law of the land (June, 1628).

Unfortunately the Petition of Right did not settle all questions at issue between sovereign and legislature. In the first place Charles continued to collect Tonnage and Poundage, although it had not
Murder of yet been voted, on the ground that it belonged to the
Bucking- sovereign by right of custom. Secondly, he persisted in
ham showering favors upon the High Church element and in supporting the obnoxious Buckingham. Proof of the unassuaged hatred engendered by the party strife was offered soon enough. While a new expedition to La Rochelle was being prepared at Portsmouth, a fanatic patriot, John Felton by name, assassinated the hated duke (August, 1628). Though deeply shocked by the murder, the king did not for a moment swerve from a policy for which he was passionately enlisted.

The parliament had no sooner met in the following year (1629) than it reopened the combat. Vehemently the members complained that the king was collecting Tonnage and Poundage, though the
The memo- duty had not been voted; and they were no less wroth
rable at his continued support of the ritualistic churchmen. In
session of mingled alarm and disgust, Charles determined to break
1629 up their session; but before his command to adjourn was read in the house, resolutions expressing the general indignation were put, and, while the speaker was forcibly detained in his chair, carried by acclamation. The resolutions (often called from their proponent the Eliot resolutions) declared that whoever introduced innovations savoring of popery into the national Church, and whoever paid or advised the payment of Tonnage and Poundage, was an enemy of the English people.

Thus, over the two questions of the ceremonial character of the Church and the control of Tonnage and Poundage, war was virtually declared between king and parliament. All prospect of an amicable

settlement had disappeared. Either the king would impose his system
and crush the parliament or the parliament would do The hope-
the same by the king. Immeasurably embittered, lessness
neither side was in a mood for compromise. of peace

For the next eleven years (1629–1640) the victory or seeming
victory was with the king for the simple reason that by not summoning the parliament he gave it no opportunity to contest his preëminence. In this proceeding custom played into his hands, Charles
for a king was not obliged to summon parliament at governs
stated intervals and usually did not summon it at all without the
unless he wanted a money grant. In fact, it should be parliament
clearly understood that Charles always prided himself upon acting
within his rights as defined by the constitution: not he, but the
parliament, had broken with English law and tradition. But his
plan of getting along without the parliament necessitated extreme
economy and demanded the immediate termination of the expensive
wars with France and Spain. Before the end of 1630 Charles had
made his peace with both these powers. His outlook was now, on
the whole, not unhopeful. Tonnage and Poundage, although condemned by the Commons, was regularly paid into the exchequer by a
people not yet ready to renounce their king; and Tonnage and Poundage, with a number of other revenues appertaining to the crown or
scraped together by hook or by crook, was found to be sufficient or
almost sufficient for ordinary current expense.

Charles's chief advisers during this eleven years' interlude of
practically absolute government were Thomas Wentworth, for civil
matters, and William Laud, for ecclesiastical affairs. As the king's
person was still hedged about with something of divinity, Wentworth
all the unpopular measures carried in Church and state and Laud
during this period were laid at the door of these two men, who, as the
years came and went without a parliament, became the target of
a wild, unreasoning hatred.

Laud stood for the tendency in the English Church which emphasized dignity and ceremony — the same tendency with which the
king had already identified himself. In fact, it was because of his
inborn love of ceremony and order that the king had The ecclesi-
bestowed his favor upon the inflexible and earnest church- astical
man, had made him, first, bishop of London, and finally, policy of
in the year 1633, archbishop of Canterbury and primate Laud
of all England. Therewith Laud was in a position to put his own

and the king's ecclesiastical convictions into practice. By means of
visitations which brought every parish of the kingdom into line
and by penalties imposed by the ecclesiastical court, the Court of
High Commission, controlled by him, the fiery archbishop forced on
all Anglican ministers a strict adherence to prescribed forms. Indeed
he did not hesitate to favor the return to partially abandoned features
of an older time. At his instigation the communion table was assigned a fixed position in the east end of the church, and by being
surrounded with an iron railing was given, at least in Puritan eyes,
something of the appearance of a Catholic altar. As part of the
same policy the Declaration of Sports was issued authorizing and
encouraging games on Sunday. To the strict Sabbatarianism of the
Puritans the reëstablishment of the frolicsome medieval Sunday was
a tremendous moral shock. The consequence of all these measures
was to drive the remaining Puritan ministers from the Church and to
bring about the final estrangement of the Puritan population from
the national Establishment.

Wentworth was a man of far greater intellectual powers than either
Laud or Charles. His theory of government was that a king who
governs well is better than a babbling, distraught parliament. As a
The political system of Wentworth natural corollary, he held that the executive power
should be strong, efficient, and large-minded, and that it
should steer its course without fear or favor. This system
of a forward-driving, enlightened despotism he designated
by the name of "thorough." Admitted to the Privy Council, he
uniformly encouraged the king to keep up a bold front; but it would
be a mistake to make him responsible for all the measures, many of
them ill-advised, which followed the dissolution of 1629, for as early
as 1633 he was sent as Lord Deputy to Ireland and was for some
years out of touch with English politics.

Certainly Wentworth can not be charged with the great blunder
committed in connection with ship-money. We have seen that
Charles's system left him in constant need of funds. So slim were his
Ship-money revenues that he could not even maintain a navy large
enough to enforce respect for the English flag upon the
waters of the channel. The legal remedy for the inconvenience would
have been to call a parliament and ask for supplies, but that step
Charles refused to consider. He hit upon a subterfuge. In former
times monarchs had, when the country was in danger, ordered the
ports and seaboard counties to furnish ships. In issuing such an

order in 1634 he therefore had a measure of legality on his side. It was against all precedent, however, when in the two following years he ordered the *inland* counties to contribute money to the same end.

Although a navy might be good in itself, plainly Charles's way of getting it was a piece of very sharp practice. Indignation swelled like an advancing tide, and when a country gentleman, John Hampden by name, preferred, rather than pay his assessment, The case to suffer arrest and trial, he made himself the hero of the of John hour. When the case came up in court, the judges by a Hampden bare majority decided against Hampden, but so general was the disaffection following upon his trial, that it required only an occasion to show that the loyalty which had bound England for ages to her sovereign had suffered fatal impairment.

That occasion was furnished by Scotland. We are aware that the northern kingdom had established the Presbyterian kirk, which, resting on the combined action of clergy and laity, was virtually an independent power free of control by the state. While Charles this situation had been highly displeasing to the auto- stirs up a cratic self-importance of King James, he had contented Scotch himself with a few measures giving the sovereign a larger hornet's nominal influence over the Scottish system. Desiring the nest substance as well as the name of power, Charles made the foolhardy attempt to foist the episcopal and ceremonial features of the Anglican Church upon the northern establishment. His measures, gradually introduced, culminated in 1637 in the imposition on the kirk of a new service book fashioned largely on the English Book of Common Prayer. At once a hurricane was loosed. The Scottish people, radical Presbyterian Protestants almost to a man, not only refused to bow to the royal decree but answered it with a solemn National Covenant which every Scotsman rushed to sign and which pledged the utmost resistance to any attempt to force religious innovations on the kirk. The unanimity and enthusiasm of the people gave them an irresistible power. In the face of it Charles was moved to open negotiations; but on discovering that he must either completely reverse his policy or fight, he chose the latter.

There followed the campaign of 1639 against the Scottish Cov- enanters, known as the First Bishops' War in derisive reference to the bishops whom Charles planned to put over the northern estab- lishment. The campaign was a miserable fiasco. Owing to lack of funds, the king led northward an undisciplined rabble, and when he came upon the Scots, found himself compelled to sign a truce. Between his Scottish and his English subjects whom he had alike alienated, his position was now thoroughly humiliating. In order to War with avenge himself upon the Scots, he required effective Scotland money-help from England, and effective money-help from England involved calling a parliament. In one direction or the other he had, therefore, to make concessions. Charles fought a hard battle with his pride, but finally, feeling that the Scottish matter was more pressing, he summoned the English parliament (1640).

Thus the long period of government without a parliament had come to an end. When, however, the parliament, known as the Short Parliament, began, instead of voting money for the enslave-The Second ment of the Scots, to remind the king of the nation's Bishops' grievances, Charles flamed up as of old and dismissed it. War, 1640 Once more, in spite of his lack of funds, he conducted a campaign, known as the Second Bishops' War, against the Scots (1640). But when the second experiment failed more completely than the first, he had to acknowledge himself finally and irrevocably beaten.

In November, 1640, he summoned another parliament, which he knew would have him at its mercy. It has received the name of The Long the Long Parliament and is the most famous legislative Parliament body in English annals. It sat, though not without an important interruption, for two decades, witnessing, and itself initiating, the transformation of England.

The Long Parliament had no sooner assembled than it practically took the whole government into its own hands. The king's innings were over and it was now the turn of his offended rival. Burning Revenge for revenge, the Commons turned first upon Laud and taken on Wentworth and ordered them both under arrest. Went-Strafford worth, who had lately been created earl of Strafford, was and Laud impeached for treason, but when the case against him threatened to break down because the evidences of treason were insufficient, the Commons simply legislated him out of the world by a bill of attainder.[1] The dismayed king reluctantly signed the act, which on May 12, 1641, sent the most energetic defender of the throne to the scaffold. The aged Laud was spared for the present,

[1] "An impeachment followed, in some sort, legal rules; a bill of attainder was an act of power for which no reasons need be given" (Gardiner).

but in 1645 he too paid with his life for having aroused the relentless hostility of the Puritans.

At the same time the Commons threw themselves on the accumulated grievances of the past. As the Scots, who had invaded the northern counties, would not leave England till their expenses had been made good to them, Charles, to get money, had to accept every proposal. Filled with exultation, the parliament resolved to leave the swollen power of the king no single leg to stand on. The special courts, such as the Star Chamber and High Commission, which had furnished arms to the tyranny of Charles and Laud, were abolished. Star Chamber, it will be remembered, had been created by the first Tudor in order to curb the lawlessness which the common law courts were unable to reach, but Charles had employed it chiefly to punish the too free expression of Puritan opinions. With act following deliberately on act parliament condemned the king's position relating to Tonnage and Poundage; declared ship-money illegal; and provided against the future elimination of the legislature by the Triennial Act which made it obligatory on the king to summon parliament at least once every three years. As a crowning measure it decreed that the present parliament should not be dissolved without its own consent. If Charles in his abasement accepted these intolerable chains, it was perfectly certain that he would attempt to cast them off at the first opportunity.

The king is stripped of his authority

That opportunity dawned for the king on the appearance in the ranks of the Commons of the first serious division. Admirably united on the *political* measures at issue between them and the sovereign, the Commons ran into difficulties from the moment they proceeded to debate the *ecclesiastical* settlement. The inevitable consequence of the Laudian tyranny and the concomitant growth of a vengeful, persecuted Puritanism was that a decisive majority of the Commons desired to destroy episcopacy and all its works. No sooner, however, had this project been bruited than it was found that a minority, cherishing a natural sentiment of loyalty toward the Church of their youth, deprecated sweeping changes. Alarmed at the wild agitation which threatened to turn the country topsy-turvy, they manifested a certain conservatism and prepared to defend not only the remaining rights of the king but, first and foremost, the national Establishment. The emergence of a royal-

The Commons split over the religious issue

ist and Episcopalian party within the Commons not only delighted the king but moved him to resume his former policy and to engage in plots against the parliament. Such dangerous manœuvres that body resolved at last to crush by a frank disclosure of them to the nation. It drew up (December, 1641) the Grand Remonstrance, wherein it enumerated article by article all the abusive and deceitful acts by reason of which Charles had lost the confidence of the people's representatives. It was ominous 'that the Grand Remonstrance passed the Commons only by a small majority. That fact seemed to indicate that at the close of its first year of power, parliament and the nation which it represented were hopelessly and almost evenly divided.

This knowledge was enough to spur the incautious king to the attempt to force the parliament to its knees. On January 4, 1642, he marched at the head of his guard to Westminster Hall, the *The king's* meeting-place of the parliament, and entering the house *attempted* of Commons, attempted to seize the five leaders, Pym, *coup d'état* Hampden, Hazelrigg, Holles, and Strode, in order to bring them to trial on the charge of treason. But forewarned, the intended victims had fled and the king was balked. London rose clamorously to express its indignation, and fearful of their safety, the king and royal family withdrew into the country.

The dramatic invasion of the house of Commons by the king was tantamount to the declaration that rather than continue to wear the yoke of the Puritan majority he would resort to force. That diplo-*The civil* matic relations were not at once broken off blinded no *war begins,* one to the fact that the die had been cast. On August 22, *1642* 1642, Charles, unfurling the royal banner at Nottingham, bade all loyal Englishmen rally to their king. The parliament in its turn gathered an army and prepared to take the field.

The parties thus about to engage were at first rather evenly matched. The king's party, known by the proud name of the Cavaliers, held most of the northern and western counties, while *Early* the adherents of the parliament, derisively dubbed Round-*successes* heads because many of them, in order to show their con-*of the king* tempt for the fashionable curls of their opponents, cropped their hair close, held the south and the east, with London for their center. Neither side was really prepared for war; but the fact that the slashing, fox-hunting country gentlemen crowded into the king's service gave the royal side at first the advantage. In the early cam-

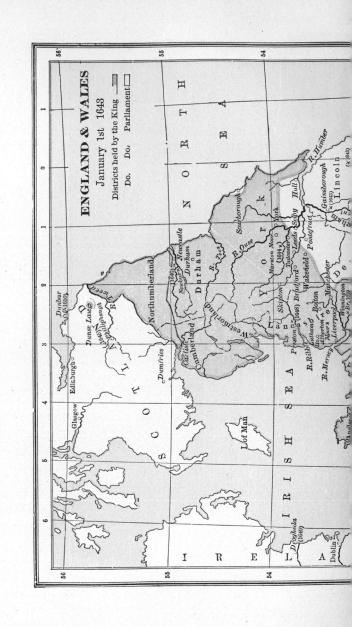

ENGLAND & WALES
January 1st 1643
Districts held by the King
Do. Do. Parliament

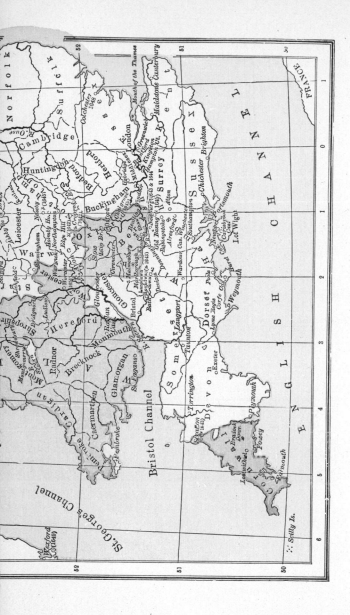

paigns the armies of the parliament suffered many reverses, and on one occasion London, the chief parliamentary stronghold, almost fell into the king's hands. It was really not until the year 1644 that the parliament began to develop anything resembling an efficient army. Simultaneously there rose into prominence the man who was destined to overthrow the king and bring the war to a conclusion — Oliver Cromwell.

Oliver Cromwell is one of those surprising characters who sum up in themselves a whole period of their nation's history. He was a country gentleman of the east of England whose life had become bound up in the Puritan cause. With moral firmness Oliver and religious enthusiasm he combined an extraordinary Cromwell amount of practical good sense, which enabled him to see things exactly as they were. When everybody else was in consternation over the victories of the king, he went straight to the core of the military problem with which the Commons, in which he sat, was vainly wrestling. He thus expressed himself to his cousin, John Hampden: "Your troops are, most of them, old, decayed serving-men and tapsters. . . . Their troops are gentlemen. Do you think that the spirit of such base fellows will ever be able to encounter gentlemen? You must get men of spirit or else you will be beaten still." His sound judgment had discovered the thing needful and his love of action urged him to go about it without delay. He took the field and gradually collected about himself a special cavalry troop of men of his own mind — earnest Puritans who had their hearts in the cause; and his troop soon won for itself the grim title of Cromwell's Ironsides.

In the campaign of 1644 Cromwell's Ironsides first prominently showed their metal. On July 2, 1644, at Marston Moor, near York, was decided the fate of the northern counties, and here for the first time Cromwell's troopers broke the charge of the hitherto The Iron-invincible royal cavalry commanded by Prince Rupert, sides at the king's nephew. When night descended upon Marston Marston Moor, the king had lost his hold upon the north. At the Moor battle of Newbury, which took place a few months later, it is probable that the king himself would have been captured, if Cromwell had not been thwarted by a sluggish and incapable superior.

That winter Cromwell fiercely denounced in parliament the lax method of carrying on the war which had hitherto prevailed; and so convincing were his criticisms that both houses agreed at last to

vote a sweeping military reform. By means of two ordinances, the Self-denying Ordinance and the New Model, the army was completely reorganized. By the Self-denying Ordinance all members of parlia-
Army ment agreed to surrender their commands in favor of men
reforms exclusively concerned with the conduct of the war; and by the New Model the army was adequately financed from national revenues and put on a strictly professional basis. The spring of 1645 found Sir Thomas Fairfax at the head of the reformed forces and the fiery Cromwell in command of the horse.

The effect of the change made itself felt at once; the campaign of 1645 proved decisive. At Naseby, in the heart of England, the king made his last formidable effort. The gallant Rupert plunged,
Naseby, as so often before, through the squadrons of horse op-
June 14, posed to him, but his reckless pursuit took him miles
1645 away from the battlefield, and before he could return, Cromwell had broken the king's left and center and won the day. For almost a year the king still held out, vainly hoping for relief from this or that small circumstance. In May, 1646, judging that all was over, he surrendered to the Scottish army in possession of the English north.

How had the Scots been drawn upon the scene? Aware of the king's continued secret opposition to the Presbyterian system, they had followed with sympathy the struggle of the English Puritans,
Alliance of and in September, 1643, yielding to the solicitations of
England the parliament, had signed a treaty of alliance called the
and Solemn League and Covenant, and taken the field. How-
Scotland ever, in return for their help against the king, they had exacted a grave concession: the parliament was obliged to promise to reorganize the English Church on a Presbyterian basis. Since the outbreak of the civil war, the situation in the parliament in respect of the religious settlement had in so far suffered a change as the Episcopalian minority had surrendered its seats and deserted to the king. Hence the Puritans were in now unchallenged control, and as a religious solution other than episcopacy had to be found, many looked with favor on Presbyterianism. Others inclined the same way on the purely political ground that a Presbyterian England was the only certain guarantee of continued Scottish support. A majority of the Commons therefore was ready to come to the Presbyterian solution; but a minority, calling themselves Independents, voiced a determined protest on the ground that the possibili-

ties of tyranny under a Presbyterian establishment were every whit as great as under Episcopalianism. What the Independents desired was the authorization of free, congregational units under an act of toleration covering all Protestant sects — a project frankly repulsive to the Presbyterians, who were as little inclined as their Episcopalian rivals to tolerate the slightest departure from their system.

Though the Independents were at first no more than a handful in the Commons, they enjoyed an influence out of proportion to their vote through the circumstance that they commanded the powerful backing of Cromwell and the army. As a result the Presbyterian majority was obliged to proceed with cau- *Presby-terians and Independ-ents* tion, especially so long as the war continued and the troops had to be kept in fighting humor. But no sooner had the battle of Naseby been won and the enemy scattered than the quarrel asserted itself with irrepressible vehemence.

When the king surrendered to the Scots he was well informed of these differences of opinion among the victors, and hoped, in his shifty way, to find his profit in them. Let the army, representing the Independents and their view of tolerance, only fall *The king's calculation* to quarrelling with the majority of parliament, repre- senting the Presbyterians and their system of religious uniformity, and his turn would come. As soon as his enemies took each other by the throat, he would step in and seize the spoils.

Herein Charles calculated both well and ill. In the year 1647 the Scots, after trying in vain to bring him to a settlement with themselves, surrendered him, on the payment of their campaign expenses, to the parliament. When the Commons, *The Second Civil War* having him in their power, tried to hurry through a Pres- byterian settlement with him, the watchful army plucked him from the hands of parliament and negotiated with him on the basis of an Independent program. Meanwhile the Scots resumed negotiations on their own behalf and in their resentful anger with the anti-Presby- terian army plotted with the king to invade England in conjunction with a new royalist rising. As a result of all these intrigues, of which Charles was alike the cause and manipulator, a second Civil War broke out in the summer of 1648 with the Scots perversely fighting for the king. If this support seemed to promise success to the royal cause, the Stuart trickster none the less fared ill, for the army had be- come an irresistible power which it was folly to arouse. In a brief campaign Cromwell scattered the invading Scots like chaff, while

Fairfax suppressed the unimportant rising of their allies among the English royalists.

Unquestionable masters of the situation, Cromwell and his friends resolved to tolerate no further negotiations with "that man of blood," Charles Stuart, but to bring him to his trial and death; and when the Presbyterian majority, incurably addicted to compromise, again resumed negotiations with the perfidious monarch, the army leaders no longer scrupled to attack the parliament. On December 6, 1648, they stationed a troop under the command of Colonel Pride at the door of Westminster Hall with orders to exclude one hundred and forty-three Presbyterian members from the Commons. The "Rump" that remained was no longer a truly representative body and continued its enfeebled existence at the mercy of the army.

Pride's Purge and the triumph of the army

With the army in unchallenged control the trial of the king could have begun at once, except for the fact that the army leaders desired to give their proceedings the appearance of legality. They had the servile Rump pass an act redefining treason in such manner as to embrace the misdeeds of the king, and followed this up with the creation of a special High Court of Justice. Its sentence was a foregone conclusion. It found the king guilty of treason as defined for this particular occasion, and, on January 30, 1649, he was executed on a scaffold erected in front of his own palace of Whitehall. He had never been shaken in the conviction that the right, during the whole course of the civil war, had been with him, and he died not without dignity in that belief. No sooner had he been laid in his tomb than his partisans invested him with the halo of a saint and martyr, who had come to his tragic end through devotion to the cause of the true Church and the true constitution.

Trial and death of the king

The violent events connected with Charles's death had dispersed the English government. King and Lords had disappeared, the Commons were a fragment. The power lay exclusively with the army, and the burning question of the day was whether the military leaders would be able to build a new constitution grounded in sound principles and acceptable to the country.

The army in power

For eleven years the army and, more particularly, Cromwell attempted with unquestionable zeal and sincerity to realize their ideal of government. That ideal was born of the deep religious conviction that every man must indeed be a follower of Christ, but that he should be allowed to worship after his own fashion. In consequence, Cromwell and his friends desired a government of upright Puritan men which tolerated every belief but popery. Unfortunately the vast majority of contemporary English- The ideal of men were either Episcopalian or Presbyterian and royalist the Puritan to the core. Therefore the Puritan experiment, though republicans not ignobly inspired, was doomed to end in failure.

THE COMMONWEALTH AND THE PROTECTORATE (1649–1660)

On the death of the king, the Rump voted that England was a Commonwealth without king or Lords, and appointed, The Com- provisionally, a Council of State to act as the executive monwealth branch of the government.

There was work enough ahead for the young republic. In Ireland, which had been in rebellion since 1641, the rebels refused to recognize the new government, while in Scotland Charles II, the oldest son of the dead sovereign, had been proclaimed king. In the Cromwell clear recognition that the Commonwealth could not live conquers with Ireland and Scotland ranged against it, Cromwell Ireland and was despatched to reduce the neighboring kingdoms to Scotland submission. In an irresistible campaign of the year 1649, he disposed of the Irish, not scrupling to break their spirit by two bloody massacres at Drogheda and Wexford. Then a rule of force was established such as Ireland had not seen before, while a project was set afoot which confiscated vast tracts of land for the benefit of the conquerors. This done, the victor turned to Scotland. At Dunbar (1650) Crom- well's soldiers, whose tempers were like the steel with which they smote, scattered the Scottish army; and when a second army, with Charles II in its midst, struck across the border in the hope of stirring up an English rebellion, Cromwell, starting in pursuit, met it at Worcester, in the heart of England, and won the crowning victory of his life (1651). Charles II escaped after many romantic adventures to the continent; but the Scots, with whose kirk Cromwell was too wise to meddle, were compelled to align themselves politically with the victorious Commonwealth.

With peace reëstablished throughout the British isles, the question of a permanent government became more pressing than ever. Every- body clamored for a settlement and the termination of the long disorder. Only the Rump was in no hurry, and the fifty or sixty members who composed it not only clung to office, but even planned to perpetuate their power. With the characteristic impatience of soldiers the army grew ever more restive over the long delay. In Dismissal April, 1653, Cromwell, despairing of good from so narrow of the and legalistic a body of men, resolved to have done with Rump them. He invaded the Rump with a detachment of troops and ordered the members home. "Come, come," he shouted in indignation, "we have had enough of this. It is not fit you should sit here any longer." Thus the last fragment of the old constitution vanished from the scene.

A new parliament, freely elected by the nation, would have been the normal solution of the difficulties which now confronted Cromwell. But such a parliament would have immediately called back Barebone's the Stuarts, and Cromwell was ready to try all other Parliament, means before he declared that the great Puritan cause, 1653 which to his fervid mind was that of God Himself, had failed. In conjunction with a number of officers he, therefore, nominated an assembly of Puritan partisans who were to discuss the bases of a new government. In an opening speech he told them that they were called to service because they were godly men. Undoubtedly well meaning, they were inexperienced and crotchety. The town wags, immensely amused at their provincial manners and ideas, called them Barebone's Parliament, from a certain worthy member whose excessively evangelical name of Praise-God Barebone invited their ridicule. Luckily, after a few weeks a party among the nominees recognized its own unfitness and brought about the end of the session (December, 1653).

It was now the turn of the officers to try their hand with a plan. Accordingly, they drew up a constitution in forty-one articles, called the Instrument of Government, which placed the chief power in the The Pro- hands of Oliver Cromwell under the title of Lord Protector. tectorate By the new constitution the Lord Protector, together with a Council of State, was to exercise the executive power, while a parliament of a single house, from which all partisans of the Stuarts were excluded, was to perform the legislative functions of government. The Instrument of Government came nearer to being a workable scheme than anything tried by England since the outbreak of the civil war; but it must not be overlooked that it was grounded on the disfranchisement of the royalists and that such success as it achieved should be attributed to the fact that it placed in supreme control a man of extraordinary natural gifts.

The five years (1653–1658) of Oliver's rule as Protector were beset with ever-recurring difficulties. His very first parliament insisted on revising the Instrument of Government. As that was tantamount to calling the whole settlement in question, Oliver in high dudgeon dissolved the parliament (January, 1655). For over a year following this disappointment he ruled without a legislature. There were frequent attempts upon his life, republican conspiracies, royalist risings, the cares and annoyances inseparable from rule. The Protectorate, with its one-man power, was, if possible, even more offensive to the strong republican element which had come to the front in England than to the royal adherents of the Stuarts. Oliver confessed with sorrow that "it was easier to keep sheep than to govern men." But his brave spirit was undaunted and he met every difficulty as it arose. In the year 1656 he called a second parliament and with this he got along more smoothly for a while. The traditional English conservatism came to the front in this assembly and it tried to get back to the forms of the old constitution. It created a second house to take the place of the abolished house of Lords and offered to make Oliver hereditary king. But Oliver, who had no love of baubles and who, besides, already exercised a virtual kingship as Protector, wisely declined a title repugnant to the republican sentiments of his army adherents. When this same parliament came up to London for a second session and attempted to limit the powers of the executive, Cromwell reproachfully dismissed it, like its predecessor (February, 1658). His bitter experience with his successive parliaments must have convinced him, if he stood in need of proof, that the nation was not with him. Disguise the fact as he might, his rule rested upon the army and was a military despotism.

The domestic difficulties of the Protector

In all this time the great principle of toleration, which Oliver had mainly at heart, made no progress. His original plan, laid down in the Instrument of Government, was to give to all Christians, except such as adhered to "popery or prelacy," the protection of the law. That meant state support for the whole diversified body of Protestant sects. He even conceded the private use of the Prayer Book and, while excluding the Catholic mass, greatly relaxed the penalties in force against the Catholics. But he could not put out the fierce religious fires that, in accordance with the temper of the time, kept flaring up all over the country. Like all who march too far ahead of the mass of mankind he was left without

The failure of toleration

support, and long before his life closed he had the bitter conviction that the government of his beloved Puritan Commonwealth rested on no single principle that had taken root in the nation.

At best but moderately successful at home, Oliver heaped triumph upon triumph abroad. From 1652 to 1654 there was a war with the Dutch, caused by English jealousy of the immense commerce of the rival republic. In a measure passed by the Rump in 1651 and known as the Navigation Act this English attitude found vigorous expression. As this act declared that foreign ships were permitted to bring to England only such goods as were produced in their own country, the Dutch, who were carriers for the whole world, were dealt a severe blow. In the course of the war the English, after a few preliminary losses, got command of the channel, thus enabling Cromwell to sign (1654) a favorable peace which greatly strengthened his credit in the eyes of the world.

War with the Dutch, 1652–1654

Soon after, in 1655, Oliver engaged in a war with Spain, finally joining in an alliance with France against the common foe. By the seizure of Jamaica England gained a firm foothold in the West Indies, and by defeating, in conjunction with the French, the Spanish forces in the Netherlands, the English army was enabled to occupy Dunkirk,[1] one of the best ports in Flanders (1658). Not since the days of Elizabeth had England held so lofty a position in the councils of Europe. Oliver's arm reached even to the Alps, and at his command the duke of Savoy ceased persecuting the Protestant peasants and herders of the upper Alpine valleys.

Oliver makes war upon Spain

Thus to the end the Protector held the rudder firmly. But his health was broken by his great responsibilities and on the third day of September, 1658, he passed away. It had been his "fortunate day," the day of the great victories of Dunbar and Worcester, and was to his mind, heavy with the disappointments of office, perhaps no less fortunate because it brought the end of tribulation. His last prayer, which breathes his peculiar Puritan fervor, has been recorded for us. "Lord," ran a part of it, "Thou hast made me, though very unworthy, a mean instrument to do Thy people some good. . . . Pardon such as desire to trample upon the dust of a poor worm, for they are Thy people too."

The death of Oliver

Cromwell's death was followed by a year of anarchy. As the Commonwealth was founded on the power of the army and not on the

[1] Dunkirk was held only till 1662, when Charles II sold it to France.

consent of the people, its continuance depended on the army's finding a successor of the same metal as the great Protector. But that was impossible. Oliver was succeeded in the protectorate by his inoffensive and incapable son, Richard, who in May, 1659, resigned an office calling for powers which he did not possess. Then the Rump came back, arrogantly insisting that it was the true and authentic English government. At the same time the generals, who with the death of their leader had lost their cohesion, quarreled with the Rump and with each other. Clearly the only way out of the intolerable confusion was to call back the son of the dead king. The people themselves were more than willing, but to insure success a resolute man at the head of an armed force would have to take the enterprise in hand. Anarchy

The savior wanted was found in General George Monk, one of Cromwell's most capable lieutenants and his representative in Scotland. At the head of his army Monk marched to London and, recalling the Long Parliament, obliged it to dissolve after issuing writs for a new election. With the way thus cleared, Charles II from his exile in Holland issued a general pardon, and when the new parliament met was enthusiastically invited to mount the throne of his ancestors. The new parliament declared that "the government of this kingdom is, and ought to be, by king, Lords, and Commons." When Charles entered London on May 28, 1660, the houses emptied their eager population upon street and square and the reimpatriated king was cheered like a conqueror. General Monk brings back the Stuarts

THE RESTORATION. CHARLES II (1660–1685)

Charles II was one of the most popular monarchs England ever had, but, as has happened before and since in history, his popularity was due not so much to his virtues as to his vices. In this connection let us remember that the Restoration signified a sweeping general reaction. Not only did it mark the abandonment of the republican political experiment but also a sharp revulsion from the austere and somber scheme of life which the Puritans had imposed upon society. Like one who had thirsted a long while, the Englishman of the Restoration threw himself greedily upon splendor and distractions. As for the restored Stuart, he had lived long in France, where his self-indulgent nature had drunk its fill of the Character of Charles II

gayety and licentiousness which characterized the sumptuous court of Louis XIV. Upon his return to England he became the advocate of French manners and, making profligacy fashionable, added to his constitutional function of sovereign the far more congenial role of master of the revels. The country, out of sorts with the Puritan ideals, applauded, admired Charles's witty sallies and studied courtesy, and joined the dance and sounded the pipe around the "Merry Monarch" of an England passionately resolved to be likewise merry.

Charles, though endowed with a good deal of natural sagacity, had little mental energy and not the faintest suspicion of that rectitude which we define as character. His pleasures went before everything His political else, and when a conflict threatened with either ministers opportun- or parliament, he was in the habit of giving way, with the ism jocose fling that whatever happened he did not care to start again upon his travels. Intelligent, supple, and unencumbered with either the obstinacy or the principles of his father, he succeeded in making himself both popular and secure.

No sooner was the monarchy restored than the desire seized the victors to be revenged upon their Puritan adversaries. The king's general pardon issued from Holland was subject to parliamentary The re- revision, and the parliament, far more vindictive than action the sovereign, resolved to punish all who had been instrumental in bringing Charles I to death. Thirteen regicides were executed, and a contemptible and revolting vengeance was wreaked upon the body of the great Cromwell. Dragged from the tomb, it was for the length of a day suspended with iron chains from the gallows on Tyburn hill.

Such scenes apart, the Restoration was far less violent than similar reactionary occurrences in history, owing largely, it must be admitted, to the lack of rancor of the king. Yet to the defeated and dejected The revolu- Puritans, whose leading survivor was the great poet tion not Milton, it looked as if the return of Charles had closed in vain upon them the gates of paradise and rendered vain both the civil and religious struggle of the past generation. But such was not quite the case. As the Petition of Right and most of the early enactments of the Long Parliament had received the royal assent, they remained in vigor, thereby substantially reducing the royal prerogative. Never again did an English king dispute the right of parliament to control taxation. Nevertheless, the royal power was still so great that an energetic monarch might feel encouraged to carry through a personal program in the teeth of the opposition of both parliament and people. In that case a new conflict was certain. But that so unenterprising a reveller as Charles II would undertake, and having undertaken, would sustain such a conflict was far from probable.

The Cavalier Parliament, as Charles's second parliament, convened in 1661 and allowed to hold power for eighteen years, was significantly called, exuberantly expressed the reaction which had taken hold of the country. It was, at least so far as the The expression of its sentiments went, more royal than the Cavalier king. One of its earliest acts was to vote that no one Parliament, could lawfully take arms against the sovereign, that is, 1661-1679 it proclaimed the late civil war a felony and a rebellion and affirmed an unqualified doctrine of non-resistance. The most pressing issue which confronted it was the question of religion. During the last twenty years every conceivable form of Protestant dissent had sprung into existence and Presbyterians, Congregationalists (Independents), Baptists, and Quakers disputed the ground with Anglicans and Catholics.

Were all these denominations to be tolerated or was England to go back to a uniform national Church? In the Cavalier Parliament — a body of royalist reactionaries — there was only one Intolerance opinion: the Church of England and nothing but the of the Church of England. It undertook, therefore, to restore Cavalier the historical Church and persecute every deviation from Parliament it with relentless severity.

In the year 1662 the parliament imposed a new Act of Uniformity on the reëstablished Church. By its provisions the Prayer Book was made obligatory, and two thousand clergymen who would not bend their necks to the yoke were ejected from their livings. A new Act Among the dismissed ministers were many zealous and of Uni-honorable men of all denominations who were henceforth formity; classed together as Dissenters. In the religious history the Dis-senters of England this formal and definite ejection of the Puritan element from the Church marks a notable mile-stone. It will be remembered that the Puritans in general had not wished to separate from the national Church, but desired rather to modify its forms in such a way that it might include or "comprehend" them. From now on all hope of comprehension was given up. Accepting their exclusion from the national Church as an irrevocable fact, the Dissenters henceforth directed all their efforts toward acquiring toleration for their own distinct forms of worship.

But the Cavalier Parliament was the last body in the world to give ear to a request for religious liberty. As in its opinion the proper way to treat Dissenters was to suppress them, it developed a highly perfected system of persecution. Already in 1661 it had enacted the Corporation Act, providing that no man could hold office in a corporate town unless he took the sacrament according to the Church of England. In 1664 the Conventicle Act was passed, by which the meetings of Dissenters for religious purposes were punished with fines culminating in transportation; and a year later (1665) there followed the Five Mile Act, by the terms of which no Dissenting minister was allowed to live within five miles of any corporate town unless he made submission in a form which, as an honest man, he was bound to reject.

Repressive legislation against Dissenters

It is not probable that the Cavalier Parliament would have insisted on the national creed with such vehemence, if it had not been persuaded that toleration granted to the Dissenters would open a loop-hole for the Catholics. And just then the suspicion against Catholicism was stronger in the land than ever because of the machinations of the king and his intimates in its behalf. Indeed with each passing year the atmosphere of the court became more markedly Catholic. Before long many courtiers, with the king's younger brother, James, duke of York, at the head, openly avowed their return to Rome, while Charles was restrained from taking the same step by nothing more noble than his fear of what might happen to him at the hands of his people.

Catholicism is the enemy

A monarch who identified himself so little in religious matters with his people was not likely to serve them in the foreign field. In fact, his guidance of England was of a piece with his superficial and selfish view of life. Disliking the bluff, republican Dutch and admiring the sumptuous Louis XIV of France, he permitted this question of taste to play a large part in determining his public conduct.

The foreign policy of Charles

We have noticed the growing commercial rivalry between the Dutch and the English. The Navigation Act, passed in 1651 by the Rump, and the short war that followed gave ample evidence of it. When to conflicting colonial claims in the East Indies and along the American coast going back to the beginning of the century was added the animosity created by the reënactment (1660) of the obnoxious Navigation Act, war could not long be averted. For three years (1664–1667) the adversaries engaged each other upon all the seas; but when peace was signed, the Dutch were obliged to cede their American colony with its capital of New Amsterdam. Renamed New York in honor of the duke of York, head of the English navy, it soon gave evidence of commanding one of the most favorable commercial sites in the western world. *First Dutch War of the Restoration, 1664–1667*

This was the time of the ascendancy of France in European politics. The leading fact of the general situation was that Louis XIV was planning to extend his territory and power at the expense of his neighbors. The logical policy for England, as the rival of France, would have been to support the victim against the aggressor; but it was the peculiarity of Charles that he looked at the situation from a personal rather than a national angle. *Charles leans toward France* Since he led a riotous and disordered life, flinging fortunes away on entertainments and mistresses, he was in perpetual financial straits. To get money, therefore, and more money became his great object in life; and Louis XIV, who was not without a shrewd streak amid his lavishness, was perfectly willing to oblige his brother of England, if he could by this means buy England's aid, or even her neutrality in the conflicts he anticipated. Now the French king began his systematic aggression in the year 1667 by invading the Spanish Netherlands; but after taking a few towns he was forced to desist, chiefly owing to the energetic protest of the Dutch, supported temporarily by England and Sweden. No wonder that the haughty Louis resolved to have revenge on this nation of traders and republicans. By the Treaty of Dover (1670) he won over Charles by means of an annual grant to join him in his projected war against the Dutch; and Charles, in his turn, stipulated to avow himself a Catholic, as soon as the occasion served, and to call on Louis for military aid in case his subjects, on the news of his conversion, rose in revolt.

When, in the year 1672, everything was at length ready, Louis and Charles fell suddenly like two highwaymen upon the Dutch, engaging in what in England is known as the Second Dutch War of the Restoration. Just as the war was about to break out, Charles, not yet daring to go the whole length of announcing his return to Rome, published a decree of toleration, the so-called Declaration of Indulgence, which, overriding the statutes of parliament, suspended the execution of all penal laws against both Catholics and Dissenters. While the measure was a movement in behalf of a broad toleration, it is necessary to remember, in judging it, that its motives were impure and that it nullified the laws of England by an arbitrary royal act. The outcry was general; and when parliament met it vehemently insisted on the king's withdrawing his Declaration. Reluctantly Charles yielded (1673), but with this retreat the war had lost its interest for him; and as at the same time the English people were learning to feel more and more strongly that their real enemy was France and not the Dutch, he further gave way to popular pressure and concluded peace (1674). Thus the treason hatched out in the Treaty of Dover came to nothing, except in so far as it involved the Dutch in another heroic struggle for life and liberty. So stubborn was their defense under their stadtholder, William III of Orange, that Louis XIV, baffled and discouraged, finally followed Charles's example and ended the war (Peace of Nimwegen, 1678).

Second Dutch War of the Restoration, 1672-1674

Though triumphant in the matter of the Declaration, parliament was not satisfied with its victory. Thoroughly suspicious of the pro-Catholic policy of the court, it added (1673) a crowning act to its intolerant religious legislation, the Test Act, which provided that all persons holding civil or military office under the crown should publicly receive the sacrament according to the national Church. In consequence, only avowed adherents of the Church of England could henceforth hold office, and no less a person than the duke of York, the king's brother and prospective successor, had to resign the post of Lord High Admiral because he was a Catholic.

The Test Act

Unfortunately the specter of Catholicism, aroused by the king's secret cabals, continued to stalk through the land, leading at times to outbreaks which would have been ludicrous, if they had not been so profoundly tragical. The most famous of them belongs to the year 1678 and is known as the "Popish Plot." A certain Titus Oates, a discredited adventurer and confessed scoundrel, told a rambling story before a magistrate to the effect that he had discovered a conspiracy on the part of the Catholics to institute in England a second and more terrible massacre of St. Bartholomew. Although Oates's story was palpably absurd, it won general credence; and as a result of the frantic agitation which seized the country a score of prominent Catholics were executed on

The "Popish Plot"

false and trumped-up charges, while a corollary was added to the Test Act by which Catholics were barred from sitting in either house of parliament.

Charles died in the year 1685 after a reign of twenty-five years. On his death-bed he received first, privately the sacrament according to the Church of Rome; and then, keeping up his life- The death long comedy to the last, died, as it were, publicly and a of Charles second time according to the prescriptions of the Anglican Church of which he was the official head.

The reign of Charles is marked by an advance in the political life of the nation which merits close attention. The gushing loyalty which accompanied the first acts of the Cavalier Parliament did not last. The distrust engendered by the Catholic tendencies Whigs and of the court had already impaired it, when the prospect Tories of the succession of the Catholic James, duke of York, gave it a staggering blow. A party, called the Whigs, arose which aimed to exclude the king's brother from the throne on the ground of religion; a second party, called the Tories,[1] stood stanchly by the principle of legitimate succession. By adroitly taking advantage of the extreme violence of the Whigs, Charles managed to arouse a strong Tory sentiment in the country which made him more powerful at the close than at any time during his reign. While the king undoubtedly on this occasion secured a personal triumph, the real historic import of the succession controversy lies in the circumstance that for the first time in English experience two opposed parliamentary parties came into being with a definite program and something like a permanent organization. For over two hundred years after their appearance the Whigs and Tories (latterly under the names of Liberals and Conservatives) were destined to dispute the government of England between them. As for the succession issue, over which the two parties originated, its intimate connection with the question of religion will not escape the reader's attention. The Tories, defending the succession of the Catholic James, drew their strength from the uncompromising supporters of the Church of England, while the Whigs, standing for an exclusively Protestant succession, found it profitable to lean upon the Dissenters and to advocate religious toleration

[1] These names were originally taunts, flung by excited orators at the heads of their opponents. Tory is derived from the Irish and signifies robber. Whig comes probably from Whiggam, a cry with which the Scotch peasants exhorted their horses. Applied as a party name, it was intended to convey the idea of a rebellious Covenanter.

for every variety of Protestant. If ever the Whigs came to power the Dissenters could count on something being done for them, while as long as Tory opinion ruled the state they were sure to be oppressed.

JAMES II (1685–1688)

James II, who succeeded his brother Charles, was not only an open and avowed Catholic, which, of course, raised an impassable barrier between him and his subjects, but he was resolved, if possible, to bring England back to the Roman fold. Sincere and honest, he scorned to resort to the political trickery of his predecessor. He was cordially acclaimed on first mounting the throne but by a succession of rash and ill-judged measures was with extraordinary rapidity reduced to a state of icy isolation.

James II

As James was a Catholic among suspicious and embittered Protestants, he would have been wisely inspired at the very least to let sleeping dogs lie. But his conscience prompted him to move heaven and earth in behalf of the Catholic cause. He did not even trouble himself to proceed cautiously. Overriding the Test Act, he put his co-religionists into important positions in the army and civil service. Soon after, in 1687, he published, in imitation of an earlier act of his brother's, a Declaration of Indulgence suspending all penalties against Catholics and Dissenters alike. He justified his action in these matters by the *dispensing power* inhering in the kings of England which was supposed to confer the right to suspend in a given case the execution of a law. Regardless of the universal discontent, he published, in 1688, a second and more sweeping Declaration which he ordered to be read from all the pulpits. By this ill-judged measure he mortally offended the Anglican clergy, the main supporters of obedience to the king's will and the backbone of Tory opinion through the country. An overwhelming majority of ministers refused to communicate the royal order to their flocks and seven bishops went the length of presenting a written protest to the king. James's answer was an order that legal proceedings be taken against them. Immense excitement gathered around the trial of the seven bishops which occurred in June, 1688.

Catholic measures of James

Meanwhile other irregularities and violences of the king had added to his unpopularity. In the year of his accession, the Protestant duke of Monmouth, an illegitimate son of Charles II, had invaded England with a small force, but was defeated, captured, and executed. James might have been satisfied with this success. He preferred to institute a general persecution. He sent into the west, among the people who had supported Monmouth, the savage and infamous Judge Jeffreys for the purpose of ferreting out the adherents of his Monmouth nephew. The mockery of justice engaged in by Jeffreys and "the is known as "the Bloody Assizes." The inhuman monster Bloody was not satisfied until he had executed three hundred Assizes " and twenty victims, mostly poor peasants, and transported eight hundred and forty to the West Indies. The odium of these misdeeds fell, of course, upon the king.

The distressing situation was for a time put up with by the people because the next heir to the throne, James's daughter Mary, who was the child of his first marriage and the wife of William of Orange, was a Protestant. The nation looked forward to her succes- Birth of sion with the more pleasure as her husband, too, was, a son through his mother, of Stuart blood. When, however, James's second wife gave birth, in June, 1688, to a son, who by the English law would take precedence over Mary, consternation seized the whole people. The son, it was forseen, would be educated in the Catholic religion and thus the Catholic succession would be perpetuated. As the birth of the son and the trial of the seven bishops befell at the same time (June, 1688), England was filled with excitement from end to end. Forgetting their differences, a group of Whig and Tory leaders sent a secret letter inviting William of Orange and his wife Mary to come to England's rescue.

In November, 1688, William landed in England, and joyously and spontaneously the people of all classes rallied around him. When some of James's officers went over to the enemy and the whole army wavered in its allegiance, the wretched king could no William longer close his eyes to the fact that he stood alone. Sud- lands in denly and utterly discouraged, he sent his wife and child England to France and shortly after followed in person. All history hardly reports a more swift and bloodless revolution.

When parliament met it was confronted by the difficult task of harvesting the fruits of the popular success. Declaring that the throne had become vacant through desertion, it offered the succession conjointly to William and Mary. By this act it plainly committed itself to the view that the king did not rule by hereditary Divine Right but was the choice of people and parliament. Henceforth a king of England could boast no better claim to the crown than a statute of the realm. With the succession disposed of, the victorious parliament proceeded to complete the edifice of its power. Throughout the seventeenth century the conflict had raged between The reor- king and parliament over their respective spheres of con- ganization trol. The Petition of Right (1628) was the first act which of the had effectually clipped the wings of the monarchy. The monarchy. The Bill Long Parliament was engaged in completing the work of of Rights royal subjection, when the civil war intervened and buried the issue beneath the din of arms. At length the flood of loyalty, once again set in motion by ten years of military rule, brought Charles II back to the throne, without, however, restoring him to the ample prerogative of his grandfather, James I. The only means of tyranny left in his hands was the claim that, as a divinely appointed king, he was above the laws and could suspend their execution at his pleasure. While Charles, a cautious and timorous man, had invoked this traditional right only occasionally, the infatuated James erected on it a sweeping Catholic policy. This last remaining loop-hole of arbitrary rule the parliament now proceeded to stop up by means of a Bill of Rights (1689), wherein the royal dispensing power was declared abolished and the king was in every respect subjected to the law. Further, the Bill of Rights enumerated and condemned all the illegal acts of James and formally and solemnly excluded Roman Catholics from the throne. One may say summarily of this famous measure that it terminated the long constitutional struggle by giving the victory and the fruits thereof to the parliament. With the Bill of Rights England entered on a new era, the era of parliamentary government.

If the revolution of 1688 closed the long political conflict by seat-ing the parliament in the place of power, it also led to a measure which pointed the way toward a solution of the religious troubles. The Tolera- Chiefly with the support of the Whigs, parliament passed, tion Act almost simultaneously with the Bill of Rights, a Toleration Act conceding to the Dissenters the right of public worship. Though the intolerant legislation of Charles II's reign was not repealed, non-Anglican Protestants could henceforth serve their God as they pleased, and that, after the long persecution they had suffered, was a very sub-stantial blessing. But to the adherents of the pope the current Angli-can bigotry refused to make the slightest concession. Against them tests and penal laws continued in full force. None the less by molli-fying the strong Puritan element the Toleration Act greatly promoted religious peace and, taken together with the Bill of Rights, defines the historical significance of the "Glorious Revolution."

REFERENCES

C. H. Hayes, *Political and Social History*, I, ch. 8
A. L. Cross, *History of England*, chs. 27–37
B. S. Terry, *History of England*, pp. 618–805
E. P. Cheyney, *History of England*, chs. 14–16
R. S. Rait, *History of Scotland*, chs. 7–9
G. B. Adams, *Sketch of English Constitutional History*, chs. 6–8
Cambridge Modern History, III, chs. 17, 18, IV, chs. 8–12, 15, 17–19, 26, V, chs. 3, 5, 8–10, VI, chs. 1–3, 23
J. R. Green, *Short History of the English People*, chs. 8, 9
W. C. Abbott, *Expansion of Europe*, I, ch. 22, II, ch. 23
T. B. Macaulay, *History of England*, I, ch. 3, II, chs. 4–10
G. M. Trevelyan, *England under the Stuarts*
J. N. Figgis, *The Divine Right of Kings*
G. P. Gooch, *English Democratic Ideas in the Seventeenth Century*
P. H. Brown, *Scotland*, II, Bk. 6, chs. 3–7
S. R. Gardiner, *History of England from the Accession of James I; Oliver Cromwell*
C. H. Firth, *Oliver Cromwell*
J. Morley, *Oliver Cromwell*
T. Carlyle, *Cromwell*
A. T. Mahan, *Influence of Sea Power*, chs. 1, 2
H. D. Traill, *Social England*, IV, chs. 13–15
E. Dowden, *Puritan and Anglican*
A. S. Green, *Irish Nationality*, chs. 8–10
G. Edmundson, *Anglo-Dutch Rivalry*
R. Dunlop, *Ireland under the Commonwealth*
E. Jenks, *Parliamentary England*
O. Airy, *Charles II*
A. Hassall, *The Restoration and the Revolution*
S. Pepys, *Diary and Correspondence*
J. Evelyn, *Diary and Correspondence*

CHAPTER XIV

THE ASCENDANCY OF FRANCE UNDER LOUIS XIV

Louis XIV (1643–1715) *m.* Marie Therese, oldest daughter of Philip IV of Spain
|
Louis, the dauphin
|
|————————————————————|
Louis, duke of Burgundy   Philip, duke of Anjou, who, as Philip V be-
| comes founder of the Spanish line of
Louis XV (1715–1774)   the house of Bourbon

The work of Richelieu, as we have seen, cleared the way for the supremacy of France in Europe. By destroying the political privileges of the Huguenots, by reducing the power of the nobility, and The work of by discontinuing the States General he had freed the royal Richelieu authority from the last restraints which weighed upon it and had rendered it absolute. At the same time the great minister had engaged France in the Thirty Years' War and had reaped for her the benefits of the Peace of Westphalia (1648). But just at this point, as France was about to assume a dominant position, she was threatened once more, and as it proved for the last time under the old monarchy, by civil war.

Richelieu's king, Louis XIII, died only a few months after him, in 1643, leaving behind a five-year-old son, in whose name the queen, Anne of Austria, assumed the regency. At the same time the post The regency of leading minister, which had been occupied by Richelieu, of Anne of fell to the confidant of the regent, another churchman and Austria an Italian by birth, Cardinal Mazarin. Trained under the eyes of Richelieu, the new minister tried to carry out faithfully his predecessor's program, and though he achieved fresh and startling successes in the foreign field, he gained them by such reckless expenditures that the financial confusion inherited from Richelieu became intolerable. At last the parlement of Paris resolved to make itself the spokesman of the popular discontent by protesting against the ever new taxes which the government was prolific in inventing in order to meet its crushing obligations. It will be remembered that it was an issue of taxation which had led to the civil war in England,

314

just then coming to a close with the complete defeat of the self-willed king. Doubtless the parlement was encouraged to resist financial oppression by the English example, but it did not stop to reflect that it was not suited either in respect of its personnel or its functions to play a truly popular role. For the parlement was not only a supreme court, that is, a judicial body, but its officials were irremovable and hereditary, that is, they constituted a close, privileged corporation. In spite of these drawbacks the parlement in January, 1648, boldly opened the struggle with the monarchy by demonstrating against a fresh series of tax edicts. Encouraged by the acclaim of the Parisians, the members thereupon took the further step of drawing up a sweeping reform program which aimed at nothing less than the conversion of France into a constitutional monarchy. To Regent Anne and her minister Mazarin this meant a revolution to which they would submit only under duress. In consequence a civil war resulted known in French history as The Fronde.

The Fronde lasted five years (1648–1653) and ended in the complete triumph of Mazarin for chiefly two reasons. The first has already been indicated in the fact that the parlement, being neither a legislative nor a representative body, was not the natural rallying-point of the French people in a constitutional *The Fronde* struggle. It never furnished more than a half-hearted leadership and in a surprisingly short time permitted the control of the movement to slip into the hands of the nobles. Here lies the second reason for Mazarin's success. For since this turbulent order cared not a straw for either the people or constitutional government and fought only to recover its ancient power, the citizens rather than see the return of feudal disorder rallied once more around the throne. In short, if Mazarin came out on top it was because when the revolution was deflected from its original purpose, the nation, left to choose between king and nobles, declared unequivocally for a single master. The Fronde turned out to be the last rebellion of the nobles, who henceforth accepted the loss of their political influence. True, they retained their great landed estates, their immunity from direct taxation, and their immense social prestige, but they degenerated more and more into a body of docile courtiers content to squander their time and resources upon the games, intrigues, and entertainments of the court. Their story as a proud, self-willed feudal order ends with the Fronde to be succeeded by their record as a soft, pleasure-loving, and purely ornamental aristocracy.

The Fronde was only a few months old when Mazarin signed the Treaty of Westphalia (1648), which, by concluding triumphantly the war with the Austrian branch of the house of Hapsburg, brought immense advantages to France. However, as the Spanish branch was unwilling to accept Mazarin's terms, the war between France and Spain continued after as before 1648. Owing to the embarrassments caused by the Fronde, the French were for a number of years obliged to stand on the defensive. Under these circumstances the Spaniards regained much of the lost ground. But as soon as the Fronde was broken, the energetic cardinal pushed the fight with fresh vigor and soon forced his proud neighbors to come to terms. Borne down by foreign wars and internal revolutions, Spain was in fact at her last gasp. On signing (1659) with France the Peace of the Pyrenees, she signed away with it the last remnant of the supremacy which she had once exercised in Europe. France, the victor, took the place of Spain and signalized her triumph by acquiring certain Spanish territories. These were Roussillon, lying on the north or French slope of the Pyrenees, and Artois, which gave the monarchy a more favorable boundary toward the Spanish Netherlands.

The war with Spain concluded by the Peace of the Pyrenees (1659)

With the glory of the Peace of the Pyrenees still lingering in the skies of France, Mazarin's life turned to its setting (1661). The skillful Italian will always be remembered among the great ministers of his adopted country. On his disappearance from the scene the young king, Louis XIV, assumed the government in person; but when he announced with quiet pride that he would henceforth be his own prime minister, many smiled and doubted. However, he kept his word, and while he lived the government rested squarely on his shoulders. He is said to have boasted once: *l'état c'est moi* (I am the state). Even if he never employed the phrase, as is now generally admitted, it expresses admirably the spirit of his reign, for he held himself to be the absolute head of the state, source of every authority exercised throughout the country. No wonder that even his ministers were in his view no better than clerks who met daily in Council to receive his orders. He chose the sun as his emblem, because he was pleased to imagine that as the earth drew its sustenance from the central luminary, so the life of France emanated from his person. *Le roi-soleil* (sun-king) was the title given him by idolizing courtiers. Absolutism, that is, monarchy strengthened by the ruin of the feudal

The system of Louis XIV

ACQUISITIONS OF
LOUIS XIV AND LOUIS XV

Acquisitions of Louis XIV
Acquisitions of Louis XV

SCALE OF MILES
0   50   100   150   200

THE MATTHEWS-NORTHRUP WORKS.

powers, had existed in France and Europe long before Louis XIV; so had the theory of Divine Right which had been invoked by sovereigns ever since the Middle Age. But Divine Right seemed to have acquired a new glamour when the French sovereign carried his absolutism to a completeness and splendor never seen before. Louis himself spared no pains to minister to his own exaltation. It is here that Versailles comes in, the court or rather the royal city which he built for himself to the southwest of Paris. By withdrawing to Versailles, he removed himself from contact with the common herd and lived surrounded, like a pagan divinity, with acolytes and worshippers. It is remarkable to what degree Versailles aroused the admiration of the world. That was not so much because of its, after all, trivial splendors as because, first, it symbolized the new absolutism, envy of all the other monarchical governments in the world, and second, because its central figure, to borrow the words of a contemporary, undoubtedly was "the greatest actor of majesty that ever filled a throne."

But strong and omnipresent as the ceremonial element was in Louis's conception of his office, he had a sense of duty which obliged him to attend strictly and regularly to business. To this unflinching acceptance of responsibility must be added a remarkable Improved feeling for symmetry and system which enabled him to administra-add the finishing touches to the rather haphazard govern- tion mental organization which had been put together during several previous generations. With administrative centralization carried through, in principle, by the royal agents of Richelieu's invention, the intendants, the next step was to rearrange and energize the central departments destined to serve as the brains of the system. Of incalculable value in this work of unification were the devoted officials trained in the school of Richelieu and Mazarin. To Lionne must be given credit for the effective organization of the foreign office under an unequaled staff of diplomats, while the tireless Louvois, minister of war, created a standing army not only considerably larger than any seen in Europe since the Roman Empire, but, what was still more important, supplied from government arsenals and stores and completely dependent on the king. In fact, Louvois may be regarded as the man who gave the standing army its modern form and who by causing it to be generally imitated imposed it on Europe.

However, Louis's most important collaborator was without doubt the controller general (minister of finance), Jean Colbert. On being put in 1661 at the head of the French treasury, he found himself flung into a veritable Augean stable choked with the accumulated Colbert, refuse and disorder of the previous half century. By minister firmly eliminating peculation and by establishing a system of finance of strict accounting he succeeded, without the aid of new taxes, in liberating the government of its burden of debt and in converting the annual deficit into a surplus. Colbert might even have proceeded to a reduction of taxation, if after a few years of a welcome peace the country had not been again plunged into war. War became the very breath of Louis's nostrils and long before his end threw the country back into the financial abyss from which Colbert had rescued it. Since the great minister died in 1683, he was spared the pain of facing the worst consequences of his master's military mania.

But Colbert was more than a good financier, much more, for he was also an economic thinker. With the science of political economy not yet formed, it was a step toward its creation when Colbert ar-
The rived at the conclusion that the question of revenues
economic must be considered in connection with the whole problem
policy of of production, and that the primary object of a good
Colbert minister of finance should be the increase of the total
wealth of the nation. Colbert therefore undertook to foster agriculture, manufactures, and commerce to the best of his ability. His
system, often called Colbertism, except for the severer logic of its
application, hardly differs from that mercantilism which dominated
the policy of all European states in his day. Mercantilism favored
home industries by a heavy tariff on imported manufactures and encouraged exports in the hope of creating a favorable balance of trade.
In spite of its many fallacies, mercantilism must not be regarded as
wholly barren even from a strictly economic angle. Of the mercantilist, Colbert, more particularly it may be said that he succeeded
in promoting the manufacture of certain articles suited to the French
genius such as silks, brocades, laces, furniture, and glass. Also he
improved communications by the building of roads and canals; and
he unfolded a considerable colonial activity in Canada, India, and the
West Indies. True, his commercial companies (East India Company, West India Company), formed on the Dutch model, failed to
achieve much success; and even many of the manufactures which
he called into existence by means of special privileges went under

when France plunged deeper and deeper into war. But fair-minded critics will incline to ascribe these and other failures in the economic field less to Colbert and his system than to the unfortunate militarism of his lord and master, Louis.

While the king took pleasure in ample revenues and was of course by no means averse to bourgeois prosperity, he was none the less particularly eager for military fame, the fame beside which every other kind of reputation seemed to him to shrink to Louis nothing. Though only twenty-two years old at Maza- resolves on rin's death, he was already the cynosure of Europe. In a career of all truth he could regard himself as the leading power of conquest the western world. But in measure as he found that his neighbors were no match for him, he began to be tempted by the thought of making himself their acknowledged master. A questionable ambition, this, but like other rulers, before and since, grown arrogant with power, Louis succumbed to it. Accordingly, in 1667 he formally inaugurated a career of conquest which, after a few brilliant results, led to such a succession of disasters that the man whose early actions had been attended by clouds of incense wafted by admiring courtiers, closed his career under a deepening shadow.

Four great wars substantially filled the rest of Louis's life. They were: (1) The War with Spain for the possession of the Spanish Netherlands (1667–1668); (2) the War with His wars the Dutch (1672–1678); (3) the War of the Palatinate (1688–1697); (4) the War of the Spanish Succession (1701–1714).

When Louis, in the year 1667, surveyed the political situation, and noting his own resources and the weakness of his neighbors, resolved on a career of conquest, he must have debated carefully where to deliver the first blow. He decided finally to Louis push the French boundaries toward the east. Spain, certain intrenched in the Spanish Netherlands, seemed moribund, to unite and, besides, France needed from a purely military view- against point to be strengthened, most of all, on this side. By himself choosing to expand eastward, however, Louis was bound to antagonize the three countries which were directly threatened by this move — Spain, the Dutch, and Germany. Sooner or later, too, he was likely to arouse the jealousy of the ancient rival of France, England. Did Louis, when he began war so lightly, reckon with the chance of a European coalition against him? Probably not. He saw only the contemporary divisions of Europe and his own brilliant opportunity, and like every other adventurer he let the future take care of itself.

In 1667 Louis suddenly and frivolously invaded the Spanish Netherlands. The fact that he tried to justify himself by putting forth some wholly irrelevant claims of his Spanish wife, daughter of Philip IV, to these territories, only added hypocrisy to violence. His magnificent army, brought to an unrivalled pitch of perfection by the labors of Louvois, took place after place. Decadent Spain was unable to offer resistance, and if the Dutch, frightened at the prospect of such a neighbor as Louis, had not bestirred themselves, Louis would have overrun the whole of the Spanish Netherlands. The Triple Alliance of the Dutch, England, and Sweden, formed by the rapid ingenuity of the republican patriot, John de Witt, just then the controlling member of the Dutch government, bade Louis halt. He was still at the beginning of his career and not yet stubbornly set on having his way regardless of consequences. In answer to the threat of the Triple Alliance, he declared himself satisfied with a frontier strip and abandoned the struggle. The Peace of Aix-la-Chapelle (Aachen) formally secured him in his bold acquisition (1668).

The War of the Spanish Netherlands, 1667–1668

For the next few years Louis seemed to be dominated by a single thought — revenge upon the Dutch. The Dutch had been the soul of the Triple Alliance; the Dutch primarily hindered his expansion eastward. The plan he now formed was to sever the Dutch from all their friends and allies and then fall upon them unawares. The diplomatic campaign preliminary to the declaration of war was a masterpiece. Sweden and the emperor were lulled into security by special treaties, while the despicable Stuart, Charles II, was by an immense bribe drawn into an active alliance with France (Secret Treaty of Dover, 1670). In the spring of 1672 everything was ready. While the combined French and English fleets engaged the Dutch fleet under the celebrated Admiral Ruyter in the channel, the French army, led by Condé and Turenne, invaded the territory of the Seven United Provinces by following the course of the Rhine.

Louis isolates the Dutch and then falls upon them

In a few weeks most of the provinces, owing to the decay into which the too secure de Witt had permitted the army and fortresses to fall, were in the hands of the French. And now one of those panics to which men are but too unfortunately heir took possession of the alarmed people. They fell upon and murdered de Witt, and would be satisfied with nothing less than the triumphant reinstatement of the house of Orange, which some twenty years before, following the successful conclusion of the war with Spain, had been excluded from the public service. In an outburst of enthusiasm William The house III of Orange was made stadtholder and supreme com- of Orange mander on sea and land. William, a young man but to the front twenty-one years of age, was far from being a genius, but he was sprung from heroic stock, and the responsibility for a nation's safe-keeping, put upon him in a stern crisis, brought out his best qualities. The English ambassador invited him to look about him and submit, urging that it was easy to see that the Dutch were lost. "I know one means of never seeing it," he replied, "to die on the last dyke." It was this spirit that now steeled the temper of the little people and enabled them to emulate the deeds of their ancestors against Spain.

Before Louis could take the heart of the Netherlands, the city of Amsterdam, the Dutch had, at the order of William, cut the dykes and restored their country to the original dominion of the waters. Louis was obliged to retreat; his opportunity was lost. The Dutch Moreover, the fear of France now became general, and war be-before many months had passed Spain as well as the comes emperor and a large number of German princes had rallied general to the cause of the Dutch. In the year 1674 the position of Louis was still further weakened. In that year the angry state of English feeling forced Charles II to abandon Louis and make his peace with the Dutch. Thus Louis found himself faced with a great continental coalition with no ally but remote Sweden. The odds in such a struggle were patently against Louis, and although the continued superiority of the French army both in organization and leadership enabled him to win every pitched battle with his foes, he was glad onough to end the war when peace was offered. By the Treaty of Nimwegen (1678) he had to acknowledge his failure in his main purpose, for the Dutch did not lose a foot of territory; but he was permitted, in recognition of his military successes, to incorporate with France the Franche Comté (Free County of Burgundy), a detached eastern possession of the king of Spain.

The second war, too, although it had roused a European alliance against Louis, had brought him its prize of a new province. Louis was now at the zenith of his glory. The adulation of his court became more and more slavish, until the flattered monarch imagined that he could do everything with impunity. His imperious temper is well exhibited by his resolve to continue his aggressions in time of peace. He submitted the interpretation of the Treaty of Westphalia, an international instrument, to the French law-courts, subject to his dictation, and on the strength of their one-sided verdict insolently occupied a number of districts of the German border with an armed force. His most considerable acquisition made in this manner was the Alsatian city of Strasburg. Seized (1681) in open disregard of the public law of Europe, it was promptly incorporated in France.

Louis
seizes
German
districts
in time
of peace

A no less high-handed treatment was accorded to a group of his own subjects, the Huguenots. Since the suppression of their political privileges by Richelieu they had been satisfied with the civil and religious liberties guaranteed them by the Edict of Nantes and had consistently conducted themselves as faithful subjects of their king. But the Catholic clergy never ceased to protest against the presence of a tolerated heretical minority among the orthodox majority.

Persecution
of the Hu-
guenots and
Revocation
of the Edict
of Nantes

Unable to bring such wise statesmen as Richelieu and Mazarin to their point of view, they achieved a better success from the moment they began to deal with Louis. It is undeniable that even Louis, bigoted believer though he was, hesitated at first to take vigorous measures against the Huguenots; but surrounded by Catholic zealots and under the influence of Jesuit confessors, he adopted gradually a policy of petty annoyances expressive of his instinctive aversion for the dissident minority. The next, more serious step was a succession of illegal encroachments which deprived the Huguenots of their printing-presses, schools, and temples; and when, finally, the king authorized the seizure of their children in order to hand them over for training to Catholic priests and teachers, the royal protection guaranteed by treaty had become a mockery. By the early eighties it remained only to apply the last indignity in the form of a forceful conversion of those who still clung to their faith. Rude soldiers were quartered in their houses to torture them at pleasure until they murmured their willingness to be confessed by a priest. When in 1685 his councillors reported to Louis that all or nearly all the Huguenots had returned to Mother Church, Louis revoked the Edict of Nantes on the ground that it no longer served any useful purpose. By a unique mixture of hypocrisy and violence approximately one million people had been deprived of their religious rights and, in so far as they did not succeed in winning security by accepting Catholicism, became outlaws.

The responsibility for this monstrous and inhuman policy rests squarely on the shoulders of Louis and the Catholic clergy of France. The outraged Huguenots, however, were inclined to throw much of it on Madame de Maintenon. A remarkable woman brought **Madame de** up as a Huguenot, she had become a convert to Catholi- **Maintenon** cism and, like many another convert, distinguished herself by a passionate devotion to the Church. By being appointed governess of some of Louis's illegitimate children, she made his acquaintance and by the natural ascendancy of her character quickly gained a remarkable influence over him. When his first wife, Marie Therese, a Spanish princess, died, he married Madame de Maintenon (1683) and at the same time surrendered his loose and libertine habits in favor of her severe and impeccable moral code. The woman who could work this miracle with an habitual rake was naturally credited with an inordinate influence over his policy. The suspicions of the Huguenots, already ill-disposed to her as a renegade from their faith, are therefore comprehensible. However, when we remember that the policy of persecution considerably antedates Madame de Maintenon's time, we are obliged to declare that her share in the Huguenot tragedy has been exaggerated and that she figures in it with certainty only in the last act. That tragedy, revoltingly inhuman, brought loss and sorrow not only to the immediate victims. In a very true sense the heaviest loser was France herself, for several hundred thousand active and resolute people, chiefly of the artisan class, made desperate by their ruler's cruelty, fled across the border and carried their industry, their culture, and, above all, their unflinching spirit to the rivals and enemies of their country.

The seizure of Strasburg and the Revocation of the Edict of Nantes befell in a period of nominal peace. They spread such a feeling of uneasiness and insecurity that William of Orange resolved to prepare for the worst by a new coalition, and by 1686, he had **England** persuaded Spain, the emperor (Austria), and a large num- **joins the** ber of German states to join him in a league of mutual **coalition** protection. The war between Louis and this new com- **against** bination had already become inevitable, when a happy **Louis** accident brought England into the fold of the allies. In 1688, James II, who, like his brother, Charles II, cultivated friendly relations with France, was overthrown by the "Glorious Revolution" and William of Orange became king of England. As the temper of the English people had at the same time become thoroughly anti-

French, William found no difficulty in persuading them to join Europe against the French monarch. Thus in the new war — called the War of the Palatinate from the double fact that with his usual effrontery Louis put forth an unfounded claim to the Palatinate and that the war began with a terrible harrying by fire and sword of that poor Rhenish land — Louis was absolutely without a friend.

This third war (1688–1697) is, for the general student, thoroughly unmemorable. Battles were fought on land and on sea, in the channel, in the Netherlands, and along the Rhine, and, generally speaking, the French proved their old superiority; but they were no longer strong enough to reap any benefit from their successes against the rest of Europe, and in 1697 all the combatants from mere exhaustion were glad to sign, on the basis of mutual restitutions, the Peace of Ryswick.

The War of the Palatinate, 1688–1697

The War of the Palatinate was the first war by which Louis had gained nothing. That and the circumstance that England had now definitely joined the ranks of his enemies, should have served him as a warning that the tide had turned. And indeed he must have felt less secure than had once been the case, since he gave a most anxious consideration to the problem of the Spanish succession just then looming before Europe. The king of Spain, Charles II, had no direct heir, and at his death, which might occur at any time, the vast Spanish dominion — Spain and her colonies, Naples and Milan, the Spanish Netherlands — would fall no one knew to whom. The Austrian branch of Hapsburg naturally put forth a claim, but Louis fancied that his descendants had a still better title in right of his first wife, who was the oldest sister of the Spanish king. The inheritance was so involved by a long succession of treaties and renunciations that even at this day no scholar would venture authoritatively to declare who, in a strictly legal sense, was the heir of Charles II.

The Spanish inheritance

Old enough to have grown cautious, Louis approached his chief adversary, William of Orange, as soon as the Peace of Ryswick had been signed, with the sensible proposal to come to some arrangement with him over the Spanish inheritance by which war might be averted. Accordingly, the two leading sovereigns of Europe pledged themselves to a plan of partition as the most plausible settlement of the impending difficulties. But when, on the death of Charles II, November, 1700, it was found that the Spanish king had made a will in favor of Philip, duke of

Louis signs and rejects the Partition Treaty

Anjou, one of Louis's younger grandsons, Louis, intoxicated by the prospect, forgot his obligations and threw the Partition Treaty to the winds. He sent young Philip to Madrid to assume the rule of the undivided dominion of Spain. The house of Bourbon now ruled the whole European west. "The Pyrenees have ceased to exist" were, if we may believe Voltaire, Louis's exultant words.

It was some time before Europe recovered from the shock of its surprise over this bold step and nerved itself to a resistance. The hoodwinked and angered William was indefatigable in arousing the Dutch and English and by 1702 had succeeded in creating The Grand the Grand Alliance, the reconstituted coalition of the Alliance previous war. Before the conflict had fairly begun, however, William, the stubborn, lifelong enemy of Louis, had died (March, 1702). In the new and supreme struggle against the ambition of Louis, a struggle familiar under the name of the War of the Spanish Succession (1702–1714), it is not merely fanciful to imagine his indomitable spirit marching with and heartening the hosts of the allies.

In the new war the position of Louis was more favorable than it had been in the preceding struggle. He commanded the resources not only of France but also of Spain; his soldiers carried themselves with the assurance of troops which had never been beaten; The combatants and his armies had the advantage of being under his single direction. The allies, on the other hand, were necessarily compared divided in council and interest. What advantages they had lay in these two circumstances, which in the end proved decisive: they possessed greater resources of money and men and they developed superior commanders. The brilliant generals of Louis's youth, men like Condé and Turenne, had long since died, and their successors, with the exception of Vauban, the inventor of modern military engineering, and the intrepid Villars, were all, like Louis himself, without a spark of fire and originality. In the highest commands, where France was weak, England and Austria on the other hand proved themselves particularly strong. They developed in the duke of Marlborough and in Eugene, prince of Savoy, two eminent commanders.

Not even the Thirty Years' War had assumed such proportions as the struggle in which Europe now engaged. It was literally The War of universal and raged, at one and the same time, at all the the Spanish exposed points of the French-Spanish possessions, that is, Succession in the Spanish Netherlands, along the upper Rhine, in a world struggle Italy, in Spain itself (where the Hapsburg claimant, the

Archduke Charles, strove to drive out the Bourbon king, Philip V), on the sea, and in the colonies of North America. The details of this gigantic struggle have no place here. We must content ourselves with noting a few striking military actions and the final settlement.

For the first few years the French showed their strength by maintaining an offensive which aimed at nothing less than the termination of the war by the capture of the Austrian capital, Vienna. In 1704 this over-daring plan led to a great catastrophe.

The victories of Eugene and Marlborough Securely planted on the upper Danube, the French were proceeding eastward, when to their great surprise they were confronted with the combined armies of Marlborough and Eugene. Against all expectations the two audacious generals had carried their forces, one from the lower Rhine, the other from Italy, to throw a sudden barrier across the French advance. In the resulting battle of Blenheim the allies administered a crushing defeat to France, which not only broke the long chain of French victories but demoralized both army and government. Following up their success at Blenheim, the allies scored triumph on triumph. In 1706 Marlborough won a splendid victory at Ramillies, in the Netherlands, and in the same year Eugene defeated the French at Turin and drove them completely out of Italy. The victories of Oudenarde and Malplaquet, won in 1708 and 1709 respectively, seemed to complete the discomfiture of France, for they exhausted the country and cleared the road to Paris.

The road to Paris, however, owing to a number of unexpected occurrences which utterly changed the face of European politics, was never taken. In 1710 the Whig ministry, which had supported Marlborough and advocated the war, was shaken by a number

A Tory ministry succeeds the Whigs of English domestic developments; and gradually Tory ministers, strongly in favor of peace, displaced their Whig rivals. Marlborough, no longer receiving support from home, found his actions in the field paralyzed. No sooner had the Tory cabinet, early in 1711, opened secret negotiations with Louis than another event occurred which put an end to what little harmony still existed among the allies.

In April, 1711, the head of the Austrian branch of the house of Hapsburg, Emperor Joseph I, died, and in default of a direct male heir, was succeeded by his brother, Charles VI. As Charles was also the candidate of the Grand Alliance for the Spanish throne, his accession to the crown of Austria held out the prospect of the reunion of

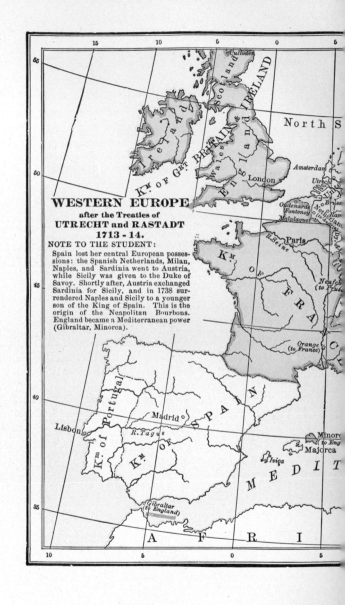

WESTERN EUROPE
after the Treaties of
UTRECHT and RASTADT
1713 - 14.

NOTE TO THE STUDENT:
Spain lost her central European posses-
sions: the Spanish Netherlands, Milan,
Naples, and Sardinia went to Austria,
while Sicily was given to the Duke of
Savoy. Shortly after, Austria exchanged
Sardinia for Sicily, and in 1738 sur-
rendered Naples and Sicily to a younger
son of the King of Spain. This is the
origin of the Neapolitan Bourbons.
England became a Mediterranean power
(Gibraltar, Minorca).

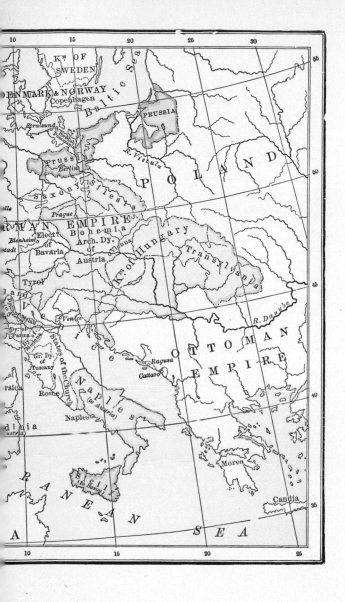

the vast Hapsburg dominions in one hand, as in the time of Charles V. As such a development did not accord with the interests of the two sea-powers, England and the Dutch, they were moved — and we have seen that England at least needed no spurring — to come to an agreement with the French over the head of Austria. The exhausted Louis eagerly seized the hand unexpectedly held out to him. In 1713 the Peace of Utrecht ended the War of the Spanish Succession. *The death of Emperor Joseph*

In the Peace of Utrecht it was agreed that the vast Spanish empire was not to be kept intact. Every state, great or small, wanted a part of the booty and by insistent clamor managed to get something for its pains. First, Philip V, Louis's grandson, was recognized as king of Spain and her colonies, on the strict condition that France and Spain should remain forever separated. *The Peace of Utrecht, 1713* In a limited sense, therefore, Louis's policy had triumphed, for a Bourbon sat upon the Spanish throne. Next, the emperor was provided for; he received the bulk of the Italian possessions of Spain (Milan, Naples, and Sardinia), together with the Spanish Netherlands (henceforth Austrian Netherlands). The Dutch were appeased with a string of border fortresses in the Austrian Netherlands to serve them as a military barrier against France; and England took certain French possessions in the New World, Newfoundland, Nova Scotia (Acadia), and Hudson's Bay, together with the two Spanish strongholds, the island of Minorca and the rock of Gibraltar. These latter gave her a powerful grip on the Mediterranean. The dissatisfied emperor, who continued stubbornly to regard the whole Spanish inheritance as his, refused at first to accept this peace; but, deserted by his allies, he was forced to give way and confirm its arrangements by the Peace of Rastadt (1714).

Shortly after the Treaties of Utrecht and Rastadt, Louis XIV died (September 1, 1715). The material prosperity of his early years had vanished, and in their place his failing eyes rested upon a famished peasantry, an impoverished middle class, a discontented aristocracy, and a government breaking down under its burden of debt. *Louis's death* The disastrous end was the answer of fate to his overweening ambition. When his little five-year-old successor was brought to his bedside, the dying man said to him with great seriousness: "Do not imitate me in my taste for war." But, regardless of the many and patent ills produced by a policy of military conquest, Louis and his court exercised an enormous influence in their time. French manners, French fashions, French art, all curiously and closely expressive of the magnificent Louis himself, came to dominate the taste of Europe. In these manifestations of the French spirit it is impossible not to recognize something rather grand and splendid. At the same time they leave us more than a bit suspicious that they have an excessive artificiality and do not rest on very solid foundations.

REFERENCES

C. H. HAYES, *Political and Social History*, I, ch. 7
J. H. ROBINSON AND C. A. BEARD, *Development of Modern Europe*, I, chs. 1–3
R. M. MACDONALD, *History of France*, II, chs. 24–25
C. HEADLAM, *France*, ch. 20
G. W. KITCHIN, *History of France*, III, pp. 58–360
Cambridge Modern History, V, chs. 1, 2, 13, 14
H. O. WAKEMAN, *Ascendancy of France*, chs. 7–11, 13–15
M. A. S. HUME, *Spain*, chs. 9–13
A. TILLEY, *Modern France*, pp. 42–73, 242–271
R. LODGE, *Richelieu*
F. C. PALM, *The Economic Policy of Richelieu*
A. J. SARGENT, *The Economic Policy of Colbert*
J. B. PERKINS, *France under Richelieu and Mazarin*
A. HASSALL, *Mazarin; Louis XIV*
J. P. BLOK, *People of the Netherlands*, Pt. 4
R. N. BAIN, *Scandinavia*, chs. 10–12

CHAPTER XV

BALTIC AFFAIRS: THE RISE OF RUSSIA AND THE DECLINE OF SWEDEN

It was not till the sixteenth century that Russia swung decisively into the ken of Europe. During the Middle Age the Russian people, who constitute the easternmost branch of the Slavs, spread slowly in peasant colonies over the great east-European plain; and during all that time they remained steadily outside the circle of west-European civilization. In this early period of their history they experienced successively three influences from without of enduring significance. Russia, a non-European state during the Middle Age

In the ninth century they were conquered by a band of Germanic Northmen under a leader, Rurik by name, who gave them a military organization and a taste for conquest. Predatory expeditions under Rurik's successors brought them into contact with the Byzantine Empire which, putting the same spell on them as the Roman Empire of the West exercised on the barbarous German tribes, persuaded them (in the tenth century) to give up paganism and adopt the Christian religion of the eastern or Greek Orthodox type. While they were digesting this Mediterranean influence and slowly raising themselves from barbarism, they were (in the thirteenth century) overrun by a wild Asiatic people, the Tartars, and subjected to a crushing servitude. The military spirit of the Northmen, the civilizing effect of Greek Christianity, and the hard subjection imposed by the Asiatic Tartars constitute the main ingredients from which was brewed the early Russian destiny.

After two hundred years of Tartar subjection, that is, toward the middle of the fifteenth century, there occurred a national revival championed by the ruler of the Moscow area. The Tartar yoke was gradually shaken off and the prince of Muscovy, as leader of the movement, was enabled to adopt a title indicative of complete liberation: he called himself tsar of Russia — tsar, derived from Cæsar, being equivalent to king or emperor. Although the first tsars present themselves to Accession of the Romanov dynasty

329

view as autocratic rulers of a distinctly Asiatic order, they were not so autocratic as not to be obliged to reckon with rival agencies, for they were confronted with a body of nobles (boyars) with a tradition of military power and a Christian clergy with an almost magical influence over a down-trodden and superstitious peasantry. Toward the close of the sixteenth century the extinction of the first dynasty led to civil disturbances which, taken advantage of by the neighboring state of Poland, almost brought about the renewed ruin of the barely resuscitated state. From this evil epoch, known in Russian history as "the time of troubles," the country was saved by a popular assembly which, prompted by the instinct of self-preservation, conferred (1613) the tsarate on a leading boyar, Michael Romanov. Michael was the first ruler of the dynasty which maintained an uninterrupted ascendancy in Russia for three hundred years.

The most pressing business of the new dynasty was to drive back the western neighbors of the Russians, the Poles, who had attempted to extend their power all the way to Moscow. Between Russia and Poland, themselves countries of the plain, interposed itself the flat expanse of the Ukraine, loosely ruled by bands of war-like Cossacks. Hard fighters though they were, the Cossacks, squeezed between two great states and protected by no natural barriers, were not strong enough to preserve their independence. In 1667 the Tsar Alexis, the second ruler of the Romanov line, forced Poland to a division of the Ukraine, by which the Russian boundary was pushed to the left bank of the river Dnieper. The treaty was an indication that the days of Polish aggression had come to an end and that in its stead the westward expansion of Russia had begun. More important still was the fact that Tsar Alexis vaguely glimpsed the thought that the time had come to end the intellectual stagnation of Russia by multiplying the contacts with Europe. But unable to detach himself from an ancient and overmastering tradition, he stood irresolutely in his tracks, looking at Europe, as it were, across an impassable stream. It was his grandson Peter who boldly took the plunge and planted his feet on European soil.

Tsar Peter is that rare and stirring combination, autocrat and revolutionary in one. Together with an older brother, Ivan, he was proclaimed tsar on the death of his father in 1682. As the two lads were too young to rule, a regency was established under an older

The westward movement of Russia begins

sister, Sophia. Peter, a wide-awake and masterful youth, accepted this situation until 1689, when, being seventeen years old, he took the government into his own hands and relegated Sophia to a nunnery. As the co-tsar, Ivan, was a feeble, half-witted creature, he did not, during the few years still conceded to him, interfere with Peter's sole control. *Accession of Tsar Peter, 1689*

In order to grasp Peter's epochal activity it is necessary to have in mind the chief factors of the situation. At Peter's accession the Russians were still essentially an Asiatic people, connected with Europe solely by the two bonds of race and faith: they were both Caucasians and Christians. Their state was of vast extent, comprising the great plain lying between the Caspian and the White seas and extending across the Ural Mountains — a largely imaginary barrier — into northern Asia. *The situation of Russia at Peter's accession* In fact, the tsars had already established a loose control over a large part of the thinly populated mass of snow-bound Siberia. In the opposite direction, however, toward the west, Russian action was hampered, as we have already seen, by rival Poland. Nor was that all, for Sweden blocked the access to the Baltic sea, while the vast Mohammedan state, the Ottoman Empire, owned or controlled the whole circuit of the Black sea. Enormous as Russia was, embracing an area greater than that of all the west-European states put together, it suffered from being a land-locked empire without an approach, except by the frozen White sea, to the oceans which are the open highways of the world. It was this emphatically inland character of Russia which alone explains its long delay in establishing contact with European civilization. Its prolonged isolation accounts also for the existence of a government so peculiar and indigenous that, though absolute, it was looked upon by European visitors as having little or no resemblance to the familiar absolute governments of Europe. Representing a mixture of Byzantine autocrat and Mongolian khan, the tsar was the product of an entirely different tradition from, say, Louis XIV of France; nevertheless he was, if an Asiatic as distinct from a European despot, not without checks upon his power. The assembly of the boyars counted for something; the patriarch, head of the Russian Church exercised the authority inherent in a numerous and richly endowed clergy; and the *Streltsi*, a sort of national militia, had acquired a great, if indeterminate, power by reason of their being the main organized force of the state and a privileged one besides.

From the very outset of his rule Tsar Peter set himself, in the main, three aims and clung to them to the end of his life with an incomparable tenacity. (1) He resolved to make the culture con-

Peter's three aims nection between Russia and Europe strong and intimate and not to rest until he had carried his country into the circle of western civilization; (2) he labored to open a physical way to the west by gaining a foothold on the Baltic and Black seas; (3) he planned to rid himself of the restraints put upon him by boyars, patriarch, and Streltsi not so much because they seriously hampered him as because they were the conservative instruments of a hateful Russian past, which he was minded to obliterate.

Peter is a difficult person for a modern man to understand. At one time he seems to be no better than a common murderer; again he strikes us as a monster in the grip of revolting violences and sensu-

The charac- ter of Peter alities; and on a third occasion we see him as manifestly one of nature's noblemen. We have the key to his character when we remember that he was a barbarian of genius — never anything more. Civilized standards applied to him are unjust and futile. Barbarity was an element of his blood, and all his strenuous, life-long aspiration for the nobler possessions of the mind never diminished his natural savagery. Therefore, his life is full of the strangest contrasts. With barbarian eagerness he appropriated everything that he encountered, good and evil alike, and surrendered himself, for the time being, to its sway with all his might. Certainly his distinguishing characteristic is an indomitable energy: his life burned at a white heat.

Peter's first chance to realize his foreign program came in the year 1695. The Emperor Leopold was at that time waging war against the Turks, who were beginning to show the first symptoms of

Peter's first conquest, Azov collapse. Peter saw that the embarrassment of the Mohammedans might serve him to gain a foothold on the Black sea, which the sultan arrogantly looked upon as his private domain. In 1696 he conquered the port of Azov. The future now opened more confidently to him, and before taking another step he determined to visit the west and study the wonders of its civilization with his own eyes.

Peter spent the year 1697-1698 in travel through Germany, Holland, and England. The journey, undertaken with a large suite of fellow-students like himself, was meant purely as a voyage of instruction. Throughout its course Peter was indefatigable in his efforts to get at the bottom of things, at the methods of western government, at the sources of western wealth, at the systems of western trade and manufacture. "My part to learn," is the motto encircling the seal which he had struck for this voyage. Peter's In Holland he hired himself out for a time as a common journey of ship-carpenter, ships having been a passion with him from instruction his boyhood. In addition he attended surgical lectures, visited paper-mills, flour-mills, printing-presses, in short was untiring in his efforts to assimilate, if not the deep-down secrets, at least the more obvious features of western civilization. The uncouth Peter, a giant who towered to the height of about six and a half feet, was the joke of the day among the courtiers and dandies, but simple folk were stirred to interest in this implacable worker, who balked at no drudgery to fit himself for the task of uplifting his backward people.

The tsar had reached Vienna on his return trip when he heard that the Streltsi had revolted. He set out post-haste for home, and although order had been restored before he reached Moscow, he took a fearful vengeance. Over a thousand of the luckless Peter dis-guards were executed with unimaginable tortures. In bands the his savage fury Peter, splashed with blood, presided in Streltsi and organizes a person at the butchery. Sovereign and executioner — standing such an accumulation of offices in one hand clearly exhibits army the chasm that then yawned between Europe and Russia. But no one will deny that there was method in Peter's madness. The Streltsi, a privileged national militia, were the spokesmen of the discontent aroused by the policy of Europeanization, and Peter felt that in striking them he dealt a blow to the forces of conservatism. The Streltsi were totally dispersed and in their place the tsar created an army on the European pattern, which before the close of his reign had become an efficient instrument of war. As the assembly of the boyars was, like the Streltsi, a center of Russianism, he rid himself of it by the cunning device of never calling it together.

With the opposition trampled in the dust, Peter's reforms crowded thick and fast. Every barrier was levelled to facilitate the invasion of western influences. He invited colonists, mechanics, and ship-wrights to settle in Russia. He introduced western dress Peter's by making it obligatory for the court. He discouraged reforms the wearing of beards, an ancient, almost a religious custom of his people, and, armed with a pair of scissors, occasionally with his own imperial hand practiced the barber's art upon his subjects. By such measures he clashed with many cherished habits, and the clergy, the natural center of conservatism, became increasingly suspicious of his policy. As their discontent was a danger to the throne and a hindrance to reform, the tsar resolved to make them more dependent on himself. When the patriarch died in 1700, Peter committed his functions to a Holy Synod which he himself appointed and controlled, and thus the tsar became the head of the Church as he already was the head of the state.

Following his return from the west, Peter was more desirous than ever of gaining an outlet on the Baltic. Azov, on the Black sea, was worth little to him as long as the Turks held the Dardanelles. The inevitable clash with Sweden Peter's paradise, the west, it was clear, could be best gained by the northern route. But the enterprise was far from easy. At every point convenient to Russia the Baltic coast was held by Sweden, and Sweden, the leading power of the north, was prepared to resist with energy any attempt to displace her.

The rise of Sweden to the position of the leading Baltic power dates from the heroic time of Gustavus Adolphus (1611–1632). In his early years Gustavus successfully extended the Swedish The greatness of Sweden territory along the eastern shore of the Baltic; and when, later, he plunged into the Thirty Years' War, in which he met his death, he gained such triumphs that his daughter, Christina, who succeeded him, was enabled to demand, as her share in the German booty, western Pomerania and the land at the mouth of the Weser and the Elbe (Treaty of Westphalia, 1648). For a short time now Sweden took rank with the great powers of Europe. Unfortunately for her, her greatness was the result not of her wealth, population, and culture, but solely of her military prowess; and, as experience proves, a purely military greatness rests on precarious foundations. A weak, unmilitary ruler, or a military adventurer who overstrains the bow, may undermine it. Although the immediate successors of Gustavus possessed more than the average human endowment, they injured and antagonized so many interests that it was only a question of time when their neighbors would combine against them. Denmark to the west, Brandenburg-Prussia and Poland to the south, and Russia to the east, had all paid for Sweden's greatness with severe losses and nursed a corresponding grudge against her. The long-awaited opportunity for revenge seemed at length to have arrived, when in the year 1697, Charles XII, a boy of fifteen, came to the throne. His youth and inexperience appeared to mark him as an easy victim, and Denmark, Poland, and Russia formed a league against him to recover their lost territories (1700). The allies had, however, made their reckoning without the host. Charles XII turned out, in spite of his youth, to be the most warlike member of a warlike race — a perfect fighting demon. Aside from his unflinching courage and his Spartan code of conduct, he lacked, however, every virtue of a ruler. Of a proud and *Charles XII* obstinate nature he was never governed by a consideration of the welfare of his people, but always shaped his policy by his own romantic notions of fame and honor. He was Don Quixote promoted to a throne, and though he could fight with admirable fury against windmills, he could not govern and he could not build. In the year 1700 his full character was not yet revealed, and people stopped openmouthed with wonder as he went up in splendor, like a rocket, in the north.

Before the coalition was ready to strike, young Charles gathered his forces and fell upon the enemy. As the armies of Denmark, Poland, and Russia were necessarily widely separated, he calculated that if he could meet them in turn, the likelihood of vic- *His* tory would be much increased. He laid his plans accord- *marvelous* ingly. In the spring of 1700 he suddenly crossed the *campaign* waters from Sweden and besieged Copenhagen. The king *of 1700* of Denmark, unprepared for so bold a step, had to give way and sign with Charles the Peace of Travendal (August, 1700), in which he promised to remain neutral during the remainder of the war. The ink of his signature was hardly dry before Charles was off again like a flash. This time he sailed to the gulf of Finland, where Peter with 40,000 men was besieging Narva. Charles, at the head of only 8,000, advanced straightway to the attack, and his well-disciplined Swedes soon swept off the field the ill-trained army which Peter had built upon the ruins of the Streltsi. Free to turn upon his last and most hated enemy, August the Strong, king of Poland, Charles now moved southward and in the course of another year signally defeated August's forces.

Thus far the war had been managed admirably. Charles might have dictated terms favorable to his country and gone *He spoils* home. But passionately obstinate, he was set on humil- *all by his* iating August, whom he regarded as the instigator of the *Polish* alliance and whom he determined to drive out of Poland *policy* altogether. The attempt necessitated getting Poland into his hands and proved so difficult that it led to the undoing of his first successes and, finally, to the ruin of his life.

Poland was at this time in a condition hardly better than anarchy. The nobles exercised all the power and were sovereign, each on his own lands. The only remaining witnesses of an earlier unity were The anarchy a diet, which never transacted any business, and an elected of Poland king, who, being deprived of all power, was impotent. In the year 1697 the Poles had even elected to the kingship a foreigner, August the Strong, elector of Saxony. When in the course of the Northern War, as the Baltic struggle was generally called, King August met with repeated reverses at the hands of Charles, the majority of the Poles were glad rather than sorry, for August had engaged in the war without the consent of the diet; but when Charles began to harry Poland with an armed force and, in addition, insisted on forcing a monarch of his own choosing on the country, a national party naturally gathered round August, who, although a foreigner, was the legally elected king.

For many years following his brilliant opening campaign Charles hunted August over the marshy and wooded plains of the Slav kingdom, and, though victorious, could never quite succeed in utterly Charles and crushing his enemy. Even the capture of Warsaw and the August elevation of his own candidate, Stanislaus Lesczinski, to the Polish throne, did not change the situation. Finally, in 1706, Charles desperately plunged after August into Saxony and forced him to sign a humiliating peace, including his abdication of the Polish crown.

The vindictiveness of its sovereign was destined to cost Sweden dear. While Charles was chasing a mere will-o'-the-wisp, the practical Peter was making excellent and solid use of his time. The lesson of Progress of Narva had not been lost upon him. While continuing Peter on the reconstruction of his forces with the victorious Swedthe Baltic; ish army as his model, he at the same time wedged his Pultava way into the Swedish territory along the Baltic coast. To show his confidence in the future, he founded in 1703, on the banks of the Neva, a new capital and named it St. Petersburg. Not till 1707, when he had, as he thought, conclusively disposed of August of Poland, did the king of Sweden undertake to check the Russian aggressions. To let the impertinent tsar feel the full weight of his sword, he marched against Moscow; but long before he reached that distant capital his ranks were thinned by the rigors of the Russian winter and decimated by disease. When Peter came up with Charles at Pultava (July, 1709), the Swedes fought with their accustomed bravery, but their sufferings had undermined their strength. And now Narva was avenged. The Swedish army was literally destroyed, and Charles, accompanied by a few hundred horsemen, barely succeeded in making his escape to Turkey. The verdict of Pultava was destined to be final. Sweden stepped down from her proud position, and a new power, Russia, henceforth ruled in the north.

As for Charles, the sultan received the famous warrior hospitably and offered him Bender (on the Dniester) for a residence. There Charles remained five years — long enough to make Bender the name of one of the maddest chapters of his adventurous career. Charles in No sooner at Bender, his one aim in life came to be to drag Turkey Turkey into a war with Peter; and after two years of importunate pleading war actually resulted (1711). Peter, who impetuously carried the struggle into Turkish territory, manœuvred so unhappily that he found his army completely surrounded by the enemy and faced with the necessity of surrendering. From this imminent disaster the tsar was saved by the action of the Ottoman commander-in-chief, the grand vizir, who in return for Azov on the Black sea and a munificent personal bribe, allowed the Russian army to escape. The disappointed Charles raved like a maniac on seeing his foe elude his grasp; and when the sultan, disgusted with the meddling stranger within his gates, at last requested him to leave, Charles obstinately refused to budge. It took a regular siege to bring him to understand that his entertainment in Turkey was over, and even then he fought with Berserker fury until he fell senseless amidst the ruins of his burning house. Only after wasting five years in the sultan's dominions did he consent to turn his face homeward (1714)

Charles returned too late to stem the ebb of Swedish power, for the surrounding states had taken advantage of the king's long absence to help themselves to whatever territories they coveted. Although he met his foes with his accustomed valor, Sweden his country was exhausted and his people alienated. steps down In 1718, during his siege of Frederikshald in Norway, he from her was shot while riding out to reconnoiter the position of Baltic throne the enemy. His sister, Ulrica Eleanor, who succeeded him, was compelled by the aristocratic party to agree to a serious limitation of the royal prerogative. Then the tired Swedes proceeded to negotiate a peace with their enemies. The German states of Hanover and Prussia acquired most of the Swedish conquests in Germany, Hanover getting Bremen and Verden, Prussia part of Pomerania; August the Strong was recognized as king of Poland; but Peter, who had contributed most to the defeat of Charles, got, too, by the Treaty of Nystad (1721), the lion's share of the booty. He received from the foe Carelia, Ingria, Esthonia, and Livonia — in fact, all the Swedish possessions of the eastern Baltic except Finland.

The Treaty of Nystad set a crown upon Peter's life-long efforts. But as he gazed into the future he was faced by serious perplexities. Would Russia, after he was gone, persist in the policy of Europeaniza-

The death of the tsarevitch
tion? His son and heir, Alexis, refused to accept his father's guidance in this all-important matter and leagued himself with all the forces of reaction among the clergy and nobility. For many years the tsar did his best to win his successor over to his views, but when his efforts proved without avail, he resolved for the sake of the cause he represented to get rid of his son. The resolution we may praise, the method was terrible. The tsarevitch died (1718) under the blows of the knout administered, we have reason to believe, under the very eye of the implacable parent.

When Peter died in 1725 there was reason to suspect that the beaten conservative forces would gain the upper hand and once more turn Russia away from Europe. The crown passed to Peter's second

Peter's policy survives his death
wife, a former Lithuanian serf, who ruled for two years as Tsarina Catherine II. To the close of the century the scepter was tossed capriciously about with little or no regard to any recognizable rule of succession and in sole response to the pressure of the faction temporarily dominant at court. It was chiefly women who were elevated to the throne and who need not detain us further than to note that, though they maintained a conspicuously profligate and corrupt rule, they did not abandon Peter's work. The Russia of the period after Peter's death may be thought of as a ship helplessly drifting in the currents released by the tsar-reformer till the accession (1762) of another woman, one of the most masterful figures of history, Catherine II, put the helm in a firm hand. Catherine, by birth a petty princess of Germany, came to Russia as the wife of the heir-apparent, Peter. Extraordinarily intelligent and determined, she was also wholly unscrupulous, and shortly after her husband, who was crotchety and half-insane, had

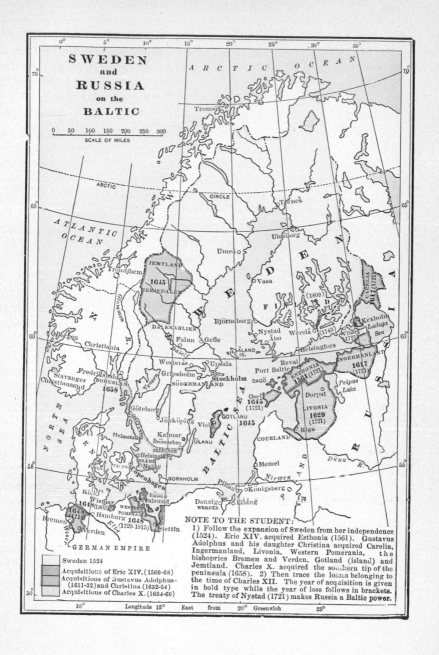

SWEDEN
and
RUSSIA
on the
BALTIC

0   50   100   150   200   250   300
SCALE OF MILES

ARCTIC   OCEAN

Tromsö

ARCTIC

CIRCLE

Torneå

ATLANTIC
OCEAN

Uleåborg

Umeå

JEMTLAND

1645

Vasa

HERJEDALEN

Trondhjem

(1809)

CARELIA
1617 (1721)

DALEKARLIEN

Björneborg

Kexholm
Ladoga
Sea

Wiborg
(1721)

Falun   Gefle

Nystad   Werelä   (1743)
Åbo

Helsingfors

Christiania

Dalen

Westeräs   Upsala

Reval
Port Baltic

INGERMANLAND
1617
(1721)

Fredrikshald
Stavanger
Christiansand

BOHUSLÄN
1658

Gripsholm
SÖDERMANLAND

Stockholm   DAGÖ

ESTHONIA
1561 (1721)

Peipus
Lake

Göteborg

Jönköping

Osel
1645
(1721)

GOTLAND
1645

Dorpat

LIVONIA
1629
(1721)

Halmstad

Kalmar
Brömsebro

ÖLAND   Visby

Riga

COURLAND

Düna   F.

Helsingborg
BLEKINGE
SKÅNE   Malmö
Copenhagen

BORNHOLM

Memel

Niemen

Pillau   Königsberg

GERMAN EMPIRE

Wismar
1648 (1803)
WESTERN
POMERANIA

Hamburg   1648
(1720-1815)   Stettin

Danzig
WERDER

Elbing

Bremen
(1719)

Verden

NOTE TO THE STUDENT:
1) Follow the expansion of Sweden from her independence
(1524). Eric XIV. acquired Esthonia (1561). Gustavus
Adolphus and his daughter Christina acquired Carelia,
Ingermanland, Livonia, Western Pomerania, the
bishoprics Bremen and Verden, Gotland (island) and
Jemtland. Charles X. acquired the southern tip of the
peninsula (1658). 2) Then trace the losses belonging to
the time of Charles XII. The year of acquisition is given
in bold type while the year of loss follows in brackets.
The treaty of Nystad (1721) makes Russia a Baltic power.

Sweden 1524

Acquisitions of Eric XIV. (1560-68)

Acquisitions of Gustavus Adolphus
(1611-32) and Christina (1632-54)

Acquisitions of Charles X. (1654-60)

Longitude 15°   East   from   20°   Greenwich   25°

ascended the throne (1762), she led a revolution against him, in the course of which he was dethroned and murdered. Although she won the scepter by a crime, once in possession of it she wielded it not only with remarkable skill but also with single-minded devotion to the policies mapped out by Peter. Herself of western birth, she naturally favored western civilization. The transfusion of somnolent Russia with European ideas and institutions continued with unabated vigor in her day. Since she accepted also Peter's foreign policy, she of course resumed the movement intended to carry the Russian boundary westward.

Owing to Peter's overthrow of Sweden, the Tsarina Catherine faced a problem which, if different in detail from that which had confronted her great predecessor, was in point of principle the same. With Sweden removed from the scene, Catherine's western neighbors, the only ones with which she had seriously to reckon, were Poland and the Ottoman Empire. Although they were, territorially, imposing states, neither of them was likely to offer a successful opposition to a persistent Russian drive. None the less a difference is to be noted between them. Poland, reduced to what has been expressively called a legalized anarchy, was as open to Russian attack as a flock of sheep to a predatory wolf, while Turkey, though brought by internal corruption to a lamentable decay, still had the appearance and, to a certain extent, the resources of a dangerous foe. During a long and brilliant reign (1762–1796) Catherine trampled both these neighbors, though not with the same degree of completeness, in the dust.

Catherine turns her attention to Poland and Turkey

To consider first the case of Poland, we have noted that at the time of the great Northern War it was already so negligible a power that Charles XII of Sweden was enabled to occupy it for a number of years with a mere handful of troops and to impose on it a king of his own choosing. The political misery of Poland was the result of a historic process, in the course of which the feudal nobles had usurped the power of the king and reduced the national parliament, the diet, to impotence. The gradual exhaustion of the central government brought it about that by the eighteenth century king and diet, although still existent, had become a mockery. To prove the assertion it will suffice to recall the famous parliamentary provision called the *liborum veto*. This conferred on every member of the diet, that is, on every noble, for only nobles attended the diet, the right to

The Polish anarchy

forbid by his single veto the adoption of a resolution. By *liberum veto* one man could at his pleasure throw a wrench into the machinery of government. Under these circumstances Poland was necessarily the victim of factions which in their strange infatuation did not hesitate to call upon the foreigner for aid. It is therefore undoubtedly true that Poland has chiefly herself to thank for the ruin that overtook her in the days of Catherine. But that does not of course free from responsibility Catherine as well as the rulers of Prussia and Austria, who threw themselves on the Polish quarry and rent it asunder.

The complicated political and diplomatic circumstances which led to the partition of Poland can not be treated here. If we remember that Poland was reduced to helpless anarchy and that its neighbors, Russia, Austria, and Prussia had undergone a monarchical reorganization and were steadily waxing in strength, we shall agree that it was a biological certainty that sooner or later the decadent organism would disappear from the scene. After extended negotiations between Berlin, St. Petersburg, and Vienna, a preliminary measure disposing of Poland was signed in the year 1772. The partition of that year — called the First Partition — did not wipe Poland off the map; it merely handed over convenient sections to the leagued brigands. The land east of the Dwina and the upper Dniester (White Russia) went to Russia, Galicia to Austria, and the province of West Prussia to Prussia. With partition admitted in principle, the logic inherent in events pushed the three powers to a Second and a Third Partition (in 1793 and 1795 respectively), by which the fate of Poland was sealed. It ceased to exist as a political entity when its last army, gallantly led by Kosciusko, went down before the Russians; but the Poles themselves, though apportioned among their enemies, became increasingly conscious of their separate nationhood and never ceased nursing the hope of liberation.

Catherine's signal success in Poland served to excite her to multiply her efforts against the Turks. In two triumphant wars (first war, 1768–1774; second war, 1787–1792) she succeeded in breaking through the cordon which the Mohammedans tried to maintain around the Black sea and in establishing herself along the sea of Azov and in the Crimean peninsula. In fact, before she died the Russian boundary had been extended to the river Dniester. The exultant tsarina nursed the hope of seeing the Russian banners float from the minarets of Constantinople, but, death overtaking her, she was obliged to leave her dream as a heritage to her successors. With, on the whole, a remarkable consistency, they have ever since striven to convert it into reality.

When Catherine died in 1796, Russia not only had been incorporated in the European state system but was one of its most powerful members. As in the case of Peter, it is difficult to concede her a whole-hearted admiration. Sadly deficient in many directions, these two must none the less be credited with the extraordinary achievement not only of having carried Russia into the fold of European civilization but also of having won for her within that fold an eminent political position.

Russia a great European power

REFERENCES

J. H. ROBINSON AND C. A. BEARD, *Development of Modern Europe*, I, ch. 4

C. H. HAYES, *Political and Social History*, I, pp. 366–387

H. O. WAKEMAN, *Ascendancy of France*, chs. 8, 13

Cambridge Modern History, II, ch. 17, IV, chs. 5, 20, V, chs. 16–19

R. N. BAIN, *Scandinavia*, chs. 2–9; *Slavonic Europe*, chs. 1–4; *The First Romanovs; Charles XII*

W. MORFILL, *Story of Poland*, chs. 7–10; *Story of Russia*, chs. 5–7

J. MAVOR, *Economic History of Russia*, I, chs. 1, 4, 7

A. RAMBAUD, *History of Russia*, II

S. PLATONOV, *History of Russia*

E. R. TURNER, *Europe 1450–1789*, chs. 20, 21

O. BROWNING, *Peter the Great*

K. WALISZEWSKI, *Peter the Great*

K. GJERSET, *History of the Norwegian People*, II, pp. 160–322

H. H. BOYESEN, *History of Sweden*

R. H. LORD, *Second Partition of Poland*

Sovereigns of Sweden (House of Vasa)

Gustavus II Adolphus, 1611–1632
Christina (daughter of predecessor), 1632–1654
Charles X Gustavus (cousin of Christina), 1654–1660
Charles XI (son of Charles X), 1660–1697
Charles XII (son of Charles XI), 1697–1718

Sovereigns of Russia (House of Romanov)

Peter I (the Great), 1689–1725
Catherine I (wife of Peter I), 1725–1727
Peter II (grandson of Peter I), 1727–1730
Anne (niece of Peter I), 1730–40
Ivan VI (grandnephew of Anne), 1740–1741
Elizabeth (daughter of Peter I), 1741–1762
Peter III (nephew of Elizabeth), 1762
Catherine II (wife of Peter III), 1762–1796
Paul I (son of Peter and Catherine), 1796–1801

CHAPTER XVI

GERMAN AFFAIRS: THE RISE OF PRUSSIA AND
THE REBIRTH OF AUSTRIA

Prussia is a German state created in the Modern Period from inconsiderable beginnings reaching far back into the Middle Age. The cradle of Prussia is the *mark* or march of Brandenburg, founded in the tenth century, that is, at a time when Germany which was itself just beginning to take shape as a distinct political entity, was confined in the main between the rivers Meuse and Elbe, and was constantly threatened

Rise of the mark of Brandenburg

on the exposed Elbe frontier by the incursions of loosely organized tribes of Slavs. The mark of Brandenburg was created as a German outpost against the hostile raiders, who, besides being of a different race, bore in the eyes of the recently Christianized Germans the added stigma of blind and stubborn heathens. The head of the frontier post, an appointee and servant of the emperor, was a military-feudal official of large authority, whose title, *markgraf* or margrave, signified ruler of the mark. Standing at first on the defensive, the margrave presently carried the struggle across the Elbe into enemy territory and by gradual steps took possession of all the land between the Elbe and the Oder, ultimately penetrating even beyond that river toward the Vistula. The lowland character of the north-German plain, entailing the absence of serious natural barriers, gave from the first a powerful impetus to the eastward expansion of the mark. One result of this development was that the margrave, looming larger and larger in the affairs of Germany, was recognized as one of its leading princes, entitled with six other magnates of the highest order to the designation of elector.

But the growth of the mark of Brandenburg must not be thought of as proceeding on a steadily upward-moving line. There were grave setbacks, in consequence of which some of the territory gained was again lost; and the periodic extinction of the ruling house was regularly followed by a social confusion which threatened to submerge

342

the whole youthful organism. The fourteenth century was a particularly distressing period when, with the succession in dispute between rival candidates, the feudal nobles seized the opportunity to enrich themselves at the expense of The Hohen-burghers and peasants. From this intolerable anarchy zollerns in the mark of Brandenburg was saved when, in the year Branden-1415, the Emperor Sigismund conferred it on Frederick burg of Hohenzollern, a south-German nobleman of the Nürnberg area, to whom he had fallen under personal and political obligations.

The new margrave and elector proved to be the founder of a dynasty which reigned uninterruptedly in Brandenburg for five hundred years and which under its later representatives rose to distinction by acquiring the kingship of Prussia and ultimately the Slow imperial dignity in a reconstituted Germany. In fact growth of it is nothing less than this expansion of the house of the house Hohenzollern from its territorial base of Brandenburg of Hohen-zollern which constitutes in modern times the central thread of German history. The first ruler of the new line, Frederick, energetically took in hand the difficult situation before him, overawed the knights by battering down their castles with cannon, and made the highways safe for commerce. His son and successor, Frederick II, imposed his law upon the recalcitrant cities, particularly on Berlin, where he established his residence, while his successors in their turn slowly and steadily extended the newly gained authority. In that period of storm and stress, the Reformation, the Elector Joachim II passed in 1539, shortly after his accession, into the Lutheran camp; but as he had been preceded in this transfer of allegiance by the elector of Saxony, who moreover boasted the distinction of being the immediate ruler and protector of Luther, he failed to win the leadership of the Protestant party. It is undeniable that the role of the Brandenburg electors continued throughout the sixteenth century to be distinctly mediocre and that it was not till the seventeenth century that the line rose into general view. Even so the decisive impulse came to the house of Hohenzollern less from the initiative of one or more of its members than from the accident of two lucky legacies. The elector who stood at the head of the state on the eve of the Thirty Years' War bore the name John Sigismund, and reigned from 1608 to 1619. When in 1609 the last duke of Cleves and Juliers passed away, John Sigismund claimed the territory on the ground of kinship and successfully occupied about half of it; and a decade later (1618), on the demise of another relative, the duke of Prussia, he succeeded to the duchy of that name. Thus by two happy strokes occurring almost simultaneously, the elector of Brandenburg found himself endowed with valuable lands in the west of Germany on the lower Rhine, and with a promising strip of Baltic shoreland beyond the Vistula.

But before taking up the story of what happened to the enlarged Hohenzollern territories, it will be necessary to have a look at the inheritance of 1618, the duchy of Prussia. Far back in the Middle Age the name Prussia was applied to the Baltic coastal area lying east of the mouth of the Vistula and inhabited by a heathen Lithuanian tribe called Prussians. In the thirteenth century the Teutonic Knights, one of those monkish-military orders which owed their origin to the prevalent crusading spirit, undertook to serve the cause of religion and the Church by conquering Prussia and converting its habitants to Christianity. The enterprise was successful. Either the Prussians accepted the cross or were wiped out in bloody encounters and replaced by German colonists; and the Grand Master of the Knights, as head of the order, became a great potentate ruling over a large area on either side of the Vistula river. A hundred years later his glory began to fade. The state carved out by the Teutonic Knights bordered on Poland; frequent wars took place with that powerful kingdom; and at last the Knights, crushingly defeated, were obliged to accept an ignominious peace (Treaty of Thorn, 1466). By its terms the king of Poland divided the Teutonic territory into two parts, East Prussia and West Prussia, and while keeping West Prussia for himself, returned East Prussia to the Knights on the understanding that they were to hold it as a fief of the Polish crown.

Henceforth completely overshadowed by Poland, the diminished and dependent state of the Knights led a precarious existence. Plainly the changed times were no longer favorable to medieval military orders. In the days of Luther the then Grand Master, one Albert, a younger member of the house of Hohenzollern, became convinced that the order had outlived its usefulness. He joined the Protestant ranks, dissolved the institution of which he was the head, and converted East Prussia into a secular duchy with himself as hereditary duke (1525). A hundred years later (1618), on the failure of Albert's direct heirs, the duchy fell, as we have seen, to the Hohenzollern relatives of Brandenburg. A valuable acquisition indeed, but coming to them on the old terms: they held it as a fief of the Polish crown.

No sooner had the house of Hohenzollern experienced this fortunate increase than the terrible Thirty Years' War broke out in Germany. The waxing might of the ruler established at Berlin, at the center of the broad north-German plain, might, under favorable circumstances, have assured him a considerable role in the struggle. But the reigning elector, George William (1619-1640), was a timid man; *Brandenburg and the Thirty Years' War* and with his lands interposed between the leading combatants, Sweden and Austria, he lived to see them invaded and ruined by both sides, by Protestants and Catholics, by friend and foe. On his death amidst unutterable confusion, he was succeeded by his twenty-year-old son, Frederick William, who, a man of a bold and unscrupulous initiative, not only saved Brandenburg from impending destruction but carried its name for the first time into European politics.

It is because Frederick William, who ruled for nearly half a century (1640–1688), is the real founder of the state of Brandenburg-Prussia that he has been acclaimed as the Great Elector. Without doubt he is one of the constructive statesmen of the seventeenth century, not unworthy to be put into a class with Richelieu, Cromwell, and William III of Orange. But in the face of the hopeless disorder engendered by the endless *Advent of the Great Elector, 1640–1688* war, he could not at once show his metal. So far as circumstances permitted he tried on his accession to withdraw from a world struggle in which he was but a helpless pawn; and to support his peace policy he gradually organized from his meager resources a small but effective army dependent on himself. The result was that when the negotiations which ended in the Peace of Westphalia (1648) began, he could insist on attention being paid to his demands. These were by no means modest and led to his receiving as his share of the general spoils four secularized German bishoprics (Halberstadt, Camin, Minden, and Magdeburg) as well as the eastern section of the duchy of Pomerania on the Baltic. He had, by virtue of ancient agreements between his ancestors and the Pomeranian ducal house, a legally valid claim to all of Pomerania; but as, in the course of the Thirty Years' War, conquering Sweden had gained a firm footing in Pomerania and insisted on keeping the western section of the Baltic duchy in its own hand, the Brandenburg claim had perforce to be cut down.

The breathing-space granted to exhausted Germany by the Peace of Westphalia found Frederick William in a relatively favorable position. He was at the head of a rather extensive territory distributed Frederick in three separate groups across the northern plain of William Germany, the central unit of Brandenburg-Pomerania converts the being flanked on the east by the duchy of Prussia and on feudal into an absolute the west by the Rhenish lands of Cleves-Mark. That the state three groups were unconnected with one another constituted, of course, a serious weakness. On the other hand, the lack of contiguity was sure to prove a constant stimulus to remedy the evil by filling in the territorial gaps. Turning to another, the constitutional angle, we find the Great Elector's situation most embarrassing. Brandenburg, Prussia, and Cleves were three separate states, each with its own laws and customs, and each with a diet, made up in feudal fashion of representatives of the nobles and the cities and controlling the taxes and administration. On developing his army policy, which required a steady stream of subsidies, Frederick William encountered so much ill-will on the part of all his diets that he was forced to the conclusion that, in order to maintain a standing army at all, he would have to break the power of these feudal parliaments which considered only their own class interests and cared not a fillip for the good of the whole community. Let us remember in this connection that the feudal state was at this time giving way everywhere to a modern reorganization, notably so in France. The French example seemed conclusively to prove that a feudal reform was possible only by means of a centralization which suppressed the too exuberant local rights in the interest of a larger unity and raised the sovereign aloft to an absolute position on the shoulders of a royal standing army and a royal civil service. Proceeding on these lines, Frederick William gradually undermined the power of his parliaments and gained control of taxes as well as legislation. Simultaneously he endowed his three dominions with a common army and administration. In short, he fused his several territories into a single unit and for the first time created a political organism in northern Germany with the essential aspects of a modern state. No wonder that he was enabled to unfold both a domestic and a foreign activity which won for the new creation of Brandenburg-Prussia European consideration.

To examine in more detail the domestic developments, we note that the Great Elector regarded himself as the father of his country, called to reign in order to advance it along all lines of human endeavor.

He encouraged industry and agriculture, built roads and canals to facilitate communication, and called colonists from near and far in order to bring again under the plough the lands which the Thirty Years' War had turned into a wilderness. In the main, Inner solid and creative labors, these, but hampered in certain labors of instances by the well-meant but obstructive legislation the Great with which, under the same mercantilist inspiration as Elector guided his contemporary, the Frenchman Colbert, he undertook to "regulate" economic processes. His most notable single achievement as economic legislator is associated with the name of the Huguenots. When by reason of Louis XIV's folly and bigotry the Edict of Nantes was revoked (1685) and the Huguenots began to abandon their native land, Frederick William invited them by public proclamation to take shelter with him. Some thousands, largely skilled craftsmen, responded, and, settled advantageously in the towns of Brandenburg-Prussia, by their industry and intelligence communicated a powerful stimulus of mind and hand to backward northern Germany.

In the field of foreign affairs the Great Elector cut, if not a more important, certainly a more spectacular figure. From a military viewpoint, his state, distributed in three separate sections, was so open to attack that he was bound to seek to strengthen The Great himself by acquiring additional territory. As matters Elector stood after the Peace of Westphalia the chief source of between danger to him was Sweden, which, a great power firmly Sweden and planted in western Pomerania, threw a shadow all the Poland way to Berlin. This situation would of itself have sufficed to arouse resentment, even if there had not been the additional reason that Frederick William considered western Pomerania to be by claim of right his own. Luckily for him Sweden had other enemies, far more formidable than himself — Denmark, Russia, Poland, in fact the whole ring of the Baltic powers. The paramount position which Sweden had won was distasteful to them and they were ready to seize upon the least occasion for lowering her pride. In 1655 war broke out between Sweden and Poland, during which Frederick William, whose territories lay between the hostile states, was alternately coaxed and bullied by both to oblige him to take sides. In these difficult circumstances he steered his course between the combatants with such dexterity that he came out of the war with profit and prestige, having forced the king of Poland to surrender to him the suzerainty of East Prussia (Peace of Oliva, 1660). Although the elector gained no territory, he henceforth possessed East Prussia in full sovereignty. This success would of course have been impossible without that standing army which was the starting-point and remained the core of his policy.

More than a decade later an opportunity presented itself to drive Sweden out of Pomerania. It came by way of the Dutch War inaugurated in 1672 by Louis XIV of France. Frederick William, War with followed by the emperor and other German states, rose Sweden, in defense of the threatened Dutch Republic and thus 1675-1679 made the war general. Thereupon the angered Louis persuaded the Swedes, who were bound to him by treaty, to invade Brandenburg. This unexpected move obliged the elector, who was operating on the Rhine, to hurry home. Approaching by forced marches and with great stealth, he fell in June, 1675, upon the invader at Fehrbellin and beat him signally. Fehrbellin brilliantly opens the independent military annals of the new state. What followed showed that the victory was not merely a lucky stroke, for the elector pursued the Swedes into Pomerania and actually conquered the province. But to his deep chagrin he got no good from his victory, for when Louis XIV closed by the Treaty of Nimwegen (1678) the Dutch War, he stood faithfully by his ally, Sweden, and compelled the reluctant elector to disgorge his Swedish conquests. Though Sweden continued to be a threat to Brandenburg, Frederick William was the first to disclose the fact that the colossus rested on feet of clay.

Finding the path blocked toward Pomerania, he tried to advance his interests in the direction of Silesia, where his house had claims to certain districts, to wit, to the four duchies of Liegnitz, Brieg, Wohlau, and Jägerndorf. Since the province of Silesia was The Silesian actually in possession of the house of Hapsburg, and since dispute its head, the Emperor Leopold I, refused to admit the validity of the Hohenzollern claims, Frederick William made no headway with them. At last, in 1686, under the pressure of the deepening menace for Germany extended by the ambitions of Louis XIV, he resolved, drawing close to the emperor, to smooth out all their difficulties. He therefore surrendered, in return for the small district of Schwiebus in Silesia, all his presumptive rights in that province. But Leopold I played a double game. While negotiating this arrangement with the elector, he secretly persuaded the elector's son, who was not on good terms with his father, to promise to give back Schwiebus on his accession. Two years later Frederick William died (1688), and though his son and successor, Frederick, lived up to the bargain, he could and did maintain with much show of reason that the return of the purchase price revived the original claims. This Silesian incident is of importance only because some fifty years later it issued like a ghost from the grave and proved a terrible boomerang for the Emperor Leopold's successor.

The Elector Frederick III (1688–1713) presents a sharp contrast to his imposing, capable father. Physically weak and deformed, he was disinclined to exert himself either in the field or council-chamber. Nevertheless he achieved a certain luster by winning the title king. For almost ten years he solicited humbly for this vainglorious distinction at the court of the Emperor Leopold at Vienna by reason of his view that the title would not be valid unless conceded by the potentate who was officially his suzerain. Since the Emperor Leopold saw no reason for advancing the fortunes of a rival German house, he refused the request and would have continued to refuse it, if a new war with Louis XIV had not loomed in which Leopold's stake was nothing less than the whole Spanish heritage. In return for the promise by Frederick of military aid against the French king, the emperor at last permitted his northern rival to indulge his vanity. On January 18, 1701, Frederick crowned himself king at Königsberg, the capital of East Prussia, and figures henceforth as King Frederick I in Prussia.[1] The title king in Prussia was given the preference over that of king of Brandenburg for the reason that Brandenburg, being a fief of the empire, had an inferior legal status to Prussia, which since 1660 was an independent state held in full sovereignty by the Hohenzollerns. Increasingly applied to the unified Hohenzollern state, the designation Prussia in a surprisingly short time drove from usage the older name of Brandenburg.

The elector acquires the title king

Frederick's son and successor, King Frederick William I (1713–1740) represents a curious, partial reversion to the Great Elector. He had his grandfather's common sense and love of work but conspicuously lacked his mental acumen and keen understanding of European politics. His constructive energy was directed to the army and the administration, the two acknowledged main pillars

---

[1] The first form of the title was as here, king *in* Prussia, in order to forestall any criticism from Poland, which, possessing West Prussia, might have protested against the title king *of* Prussia, as implying the sovereignty over all Prussia. Nevertheless, the simpler form, king of Prussia, came before long into general use.

of the state. By thrifty financial management he succeeded in
raising his standing army to some 80,000 men, thus putting little
Prussia in military matters in a class with the great states of Europe.

The Prus-
sian army
and bureau-
cracy
And what troops they were! An iron discipline molded
them into a precise military machine, to which a corps of
officers, trained in special schools, gave a devoted service.
His main administrative task the sovereign conceived to
be to knit still more closely the domestic unity established by the
Great Elector. Though the state was already served by a professional
bureaucracy, it was possible minutely and intelligently to adjust its
various departments and to fill the whole body of officials with an
unrivalled sense of duty. It is highly probable that for hard efficiency
Frederick William's army and civil service held a unique position in
the Europe of his day.

The only foreign action of importance in which this stalwart, tyrannical ruler engaged befell early in his reign. On his accession
(1713) the War of the Spanish Succession was coming to an end, while

King
Frederick
William I
acquires
Stettin
(1720)
the so-called Northern War, waged against Charles XII
of Sweden, had entered on its last phase. Defeated at
Pultava (1709) by Peter the Great, the wounded Swedish
lion had fled to Turkey; and during his long absence from
the scene of action his neighbors stepped forth to appropriate his lands. Not to be left out in the cold, Frederick William
mobilized his army in his turn against Sweden and occupied Swedish
Pomerania. When Charles XII at last abandoned Turkey and hurried
home, he made a gallant but hopeless effort against his many enemies.
On his death in 1718 the exhausted Swedish government promptly
read the writing on the wall. It began the negotiations in which it acknowledged defeat, those with Prussia ending in a peace (1720) which
gave the victor the bulk of western Pomerania including the river
Oder together with the invaluable seaport of Stettin. The heart of
the Prussian state was now connected by the course of the Oder with
the Baltic sea and the ancient enmity with Sweden gradually sub-
sided.

This sturdy king, who has left such solid memorials behind him,
made himself, through some of the strangest eccentricities which
have ever characterized a human being, the laughing-stock of Europe.

His eccen-
tricities
His conception of his office was a curious compound of
Biblical patriarch and modern drill-sergeant. He had
his eye upon everybody and everything. If he suspected a man of

being wealthy, he would compel him to build a fine residence to improve the looks of the capital. He had a particular abhorrence of idleness; the very apple-women, while waiting in their booths for customers, were ordered to do some useful knitting, while the police were empowered to pick up any random lounger and impress him into the army. But perhaps his wildest eccentricity was his craze for tall soldiers. At Potsdam, his residence some miles from Berlin, he established a giant guard for which he gathered recruits from all parts of the world. He coddled his giants like a sentimental father, and was so completely carried away by his hobby that he, who was thrifty to the point of avarice, offered enormous prices in all markets for tall men and did not scruple to capture them by force when they refused to enlist.

This unpolished northern bear naturally kept his elegant neighbors in convulsions of laughter, though on at least one occasion the comedy ended tragically. The king's son and heir, Frederick, known afterward as the Great, was a self-willed youth who, drawn *His conflict* much more to books and music than to soldiering, grew *with the* up in all respects the very opposite of his bluff, practical *crown* father. Parent and son conceived a strong antipathy for *prince* each other; and when the irate father resorted to corporal punishment the proud prince made a vain attempt to flee to France. Frederick William almost lost his mind from rage. He threw his son into prison, executed one of his accomplices, and spoke wildly for a time of executing also the crown prince. When he at last relented, it was on the promise of the son to submit to a training of unexampled rigor in the civil and military branches of the government. As a result when, on the death (1740) of his Spartan father, the prince at the age of twenty-eight mounted the throne as Frederick II, he knew every branch of the Prussian service like a thumbed book. Owing to his devotion to art and literature as well as to the refinements of a cultivated society, his intimates imagined that he would abruptly terminate the harsh system of his father. They were mistaken. Not only did he jealously maintain and consolidate the inherited traditions, but he showed almost at once that beneath a pleasing exterior he nursed as consuming an ambition as any autocrat of history. A crisis in Austria coming to a head some few weeks after his accession furnished him with a rare opportunity for action.

The name Austria or East Mark adhered originally to the German territory along the Danube between approximately Passau and

Vienna. By absorption of the neighboring Alpine provinces, such as Styria, Carinthia, and the Tyrol, the duke of Austria became in the course of the Middle Age one of the most influential princes of **The rise** the Holy Roman Empire (Germany). In the last quarter **of Austria** of the thirteenth century the house of Hapsburg became the ruling family of this enlarged Austria and with persistent ambition and almost unvarying success undertook to promote the fortunes of the state. We have seen that in the days of Emperor Maximilian and his grandson, Charles V, Austria was so easily the leading German state that the imperial office, although strictly speaking elective, had become virtually hereditary in the Hapsburg line. But we have also seen that the imperial office, if a still much coveted honor, conferred little or no real power on its holder. Whatever influence the emperor of the house of Austria wielded he owed to his hereditary Austrian lands together with such other territories as looked to him as their immediate ruler.

The reader will recall that the Emperor Charles V (1519–1556) completely overshadowed Europe in his day because, in addition to Austria, he commanded the resources of the Netherlands and Spain, **The Aus-** and that on his abdication his vast possessions were di- **trian branch** vided between his son Philip, who received the Nether- **of the house** lands and Spain, and his brother Ferdinand, who acquired **of Hapsburg** the Austrian territories. With Ferdinand therefore the younger branch of the Hapsburgs began an independent career; and in evidence that, in spite of the partition of 1556, the family was still the foremost dynasty of Germany, Ferdinand was invited to succeed his brother Charles upon the German throne. Since for the next two hundred years Ferdinand's heirs regularly won the imperial election, the house of Hapsburg came not unreasonably to look upon the headship of Germany as its prescriptive right.

But we should not fail to note that the power of the Hapsburg dynasty had from the time of Emperor Ferdinand I come to rest on more than its original Austrian foundation, for, in 1526, Ferdinand **Consolida-** had, partly by inheritance and partly by election, become **tion of the** head of the two large neighboring kingdoms of Bohemia **Austrian** and Hungary. Advanced thus to the sovereignty of three **Empire** large groups of territory — Austria, Bohemia, Hungary — occupying the basin of the middle Danube, he may be looked upon as the founder of what came to be known as the Austrian Empire. True, Ferdinand I was obliged to forego the immediate control of

Hungary, for Hungary, or all but its western rim, was in the very year of Ferdinand's acquisition conquered by the Turks under the Sultan Solyman; true also, his successors encountered such difficulties in Bohemia, in connection with the Reformation, that in 1618 Bohemia too slipped from their control. However, following the battle of the White Hill (1620) the troubled Hapsburg fortunes began decidedly to look up and not only was Bohemia recovered in the course of the Thirty Years' War, but half a century later the emerging Austrian Empire was enabled to render its most egregious service to occidental civilization. This brings us to the Ottoman Empire and requires a brief elucidation.

When, in 1526, the Turks overran Hungary, it looked as if all central Europe might fall into their grasp. In 1529 they took their next logical step by advancing against Vienna but were obliged to fall back in defeat. Though threatening repeatedly to renew the attack, their state, which was a pure oriental despotism, was before long overtaken by internal difficulties and thereby deprived of its offensive vigor. With surprising suddenness the sultans lost their warlike character and became content to pass their days amidst the pleasures of the harem; at the same time the army and administration became cankered with corruption. The march on Vienna in 1529 remained therefore the high-water mark of the Turkish inundation of the continent. However, in 1683, owing to a temporary revival due to a spirited family of grand vizirs, the Ottoman Empire resumed its attack on Europe by the Danube route and conducted a second siege of the Austrian capital. The stubborn resistance of the garrison, seconded by a rescuing movement led by the gallant king of Poland, John Sobieski, not only rendered the second siege as futile as the first but converted it into an utter rout of the Mohammedans. From that splendid success Austria took courage and boldly resolved at last to turn the tables on the Turks by assuming the offensive against them. To her great good fortune heaven presented her at this decisive moment with a gifted general in the person of Prince Eugene of Savoy. We have already encountered him in connection with the wars waged by Europe against the aggressions of Louis XIV. Great as were his services to Austria on the western scene, they were completely overshadowed by his achievements in the Danubian area. In two wars (first war, 1683–1698; second war, 1715–1718) the Austrians under the magnetic prince administered such a beating to the Turks that they drove them completely out of Hungary.

Austria liberates Hungary by driving back the Turks

The final liberation of Hungary from the Turkish yoke befell in the reign of Emperor Charles VI (1711–1740). In Charles's time the model state of Europe was France, whose sovereign, Louis XIV, *The prob-* had given a lesson in centralization which astonished his *lem of cen-* contemporaries. The effect of the French example had *tralization* already begun to make itself felt, more particularly in the case of Austria's German neighbor, Prussia, which in the reign of the Great Elector had been converted into quite as effective an absolutism as its French prototype. Austria, too, had felt the need of unifying its many separate dominions and during the wars conducted by Prince Eugene on the Rhine and the Danube had gone so far as to create a central Austrian army supported by the contributions of all the Hapsburg territories. While this was an auspicious beginning, it did not alter the fact that the three main constituent groups, Austria, Bohemia, and Hungary, remained stubbornly distinct, each with its own laws, courts, and finances, and each provided with a vigorous champion of tradition in an assembly of feudal estates. If Charles VI, in spite of his seeing the advisability of breaking down these local barriers, made practically no headway against them, his failure may be ascribed not only to the grave difficulties inhering in the situation but also to a peculiar personal concern which, ruling his mind like an obsession, fell heavily into the scales.

When the older branch of the house of Hapsburg had died out in the male line in the year 1700, the question of the Spanish succession had released a world war. Now the younger branch, of which Charles *Charles VI* himself was the representative, was about to die out in *and the* its male line, owing to Charles's failure to have begot *Pragmatic* other than two daughters. Would his death be followed *Sanction* by a War of the Austrian Succession and the end be, as in the Spanish case, a division of the spoils among the combatants? To forestall such a calamity he determined to make his older daughter the sole heir of his undivided dominions; and this, his will and testament, he laid down in an ordinance which received the name of the Pragmatic Sanction. To make sure that his regulation of the succession would be respected after his death, he persuaded the diets of his many territories to formally accept it; and to make assurance doubly sure he knocked at the door of all the European cabinets to get them likewise to guarantee his program. At often heavy sacrifices he finally secured the endorsement of all the leading states and, reasonably comforted, in October, 1740, laid himself down to die.

Immediately, in accordance with the terms of the Pragmatic Sanction, Charles's daughter, the Archduchess Maria Theresa, assumed the rule of all the Hapsburg lands. It was of course well known that practically all the neighbors coveted some Frederick II part of the Austrian possessions, many of them on the of Prussia basis of claims which the Pragmatic Sanction had nulli- inaugurates fied, others on the ground of older claims which had never (1740) the been brought to a settlement. Among these latter was the War of the Prussian claim to the four duchies of Silesia. While every Austrian claimant was waiting in breathless suspense to see what the others Succession would do, the young sovereign of Prussia, Frederick II, stepped boldly forth and took the bull by the horns. He marched an army into Silesia to secure his claim by force. It was beyond challenge an act of brutal, undisguised aggression. Immediately, as at a signal, every state of Europe that nursed a grudge against Austria followed suit, and regardless of whether it had a claim or not, set its army on foot against the Hapsburg territories. Conspicuous among them were the two German states, Bavaria and Saxony, and the two Bourbon powers, France and Spain. These four together with Prussia formed a great anti-Austrian alliance which planned to strip Maria Theresa of most of her inheritance. Thus did the Pragmatic Sanction, in spite of the abundance of signatures attached to it, prove abortive. The life-long bogey of Charles VI, to lay which he had made so many sacrifices, the War of the Austrian Succession, had become a reality!

It might have gone hard with Maria Theresa if she had not found splendid resources of heart and mind in herself, and if she had not succeeded in arousing a spirit of loyal devotion among her people. Her enemies were descending upon her in two main direc- The spirited tions, the French and their Bavarian ally from the west, conduct of by way of the Danube, and Frederick of Prussia from the Maria north. Unprepared as she was, her raw levies gave way, at Theresa first, at every point. On April 10, 1741, at Mollwitz, Frederick won a victory over the Austrians which clinched his hold upon Silesia. In the same year the French, Saxons, and Bavarians occupied Bohemia. So complete, for the time being, was the dominion of the anti-Austrian alliance that when in January, 1742, the imperial election took place, the combined enemies of Austria were able to raise their candidate, the Elector Charles of Bavaria, to the imperial throne. The elector assumed his new dignity with the title of Emperor Charles VII (1742–1745). For the first time in three hundred years the crown of the Empire rested upon another than a Hapsburg head.

But at this point Maria Theresa's fortunes rose again. Her own magnetic enthusiasm did wonders in injecting new life into her weak and battered forces. Not only was the army of the coalition driven out of Bohemia, but Bavaria, the land of the enemy, was invaded and occupied. The Prussians, who had likewise entered Bohemia in order to coöperate with their allies, saved themselves from imminent disaster by a victory at Czaslau (May, 1742). Thereupon Maria Theresa, who saw that she could not meet so many enemies at one and the same time, declared her willingness to come to terms with her most formidable foe. In 1742 she signed with Frederick the Peace of Breslau, by which she gave up practically the whole province of Silesia. What is known in Germany as the First Silesian War had come to an end.

Maria Theresa makes over Silesia to Frederick, 1742

Maria Theresa now prosecuted the war against her other enemies with increased vigor. England and Holland, in order to redress the European balance, joined her, and with each new campaign the scales inclined more visibly in her favor. When the puppet emperor, Charles VII, had lost every foot of land he owned and the Austrian armies had penetrated triumphantly as far west as the Rhine, Maria Theresa could feel with elation that she was successfully bringing Germany under her heel. Aware that in that case he could not possibly hold his new conquest, Frederick was moved to strike a second blow. In 1744 he began the Second Silesian War, in which his calculations were completely successful. He first relieved the French and the Bavarians by drawing the Austrians upon himself, and then he defeated the enemy signally at the battle of Hohenfriedberg (1745). On Christmas day, 1745, Maria Theresa bought her second peace of Frederick by a renewed cession of Silesia.

Maria Theresa's success and Frederick's second attack upon her

On Frederick's retirement the war, which, once ignited, could not be easily extinguished, was waged chiefly in Italy and the Austrian Netherlands. In the Netherlands the French won a number of brilliant victories which actually put them in possession of this territory coveted by them for so long a time; but discouraged by the successes of Maria Theresa in Italy and of the English at sea, they agreed at last to treat. In 1748 the Peace of Aachen (Aix-la-Chapelle) ended the War of the Austrian Succession essentially on the basis of mutual restitutions and the

The Peace of Aachen, 1748

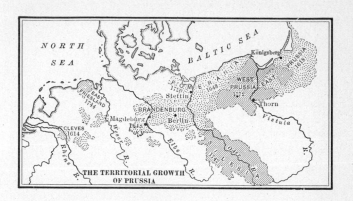

THE TERRITORIAL GROWTH
OF PRUSSIA

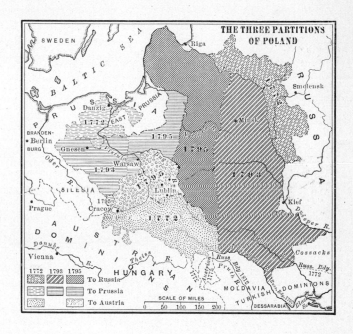

THE THREE PARTITIONS
OF POLAND

recognition of Maria Theresa as the sole heir of her father. Already three years before this consummation the German situation had slipped back into its accustomed form. The Bavarian emperor, Charles VII, having died (1745) after being ignominiously chased from all his lands by the Austrian army, the electoral college offered the crown to Francis of Lorraine, Maria Theresa's husband. Therewith the house of Hapsburg was back in the German saddle; but if it had, with the exception of certain slight cessions in Italy and the one substantial sacrifice of Silesia, emerged triumphantly from its terrible ordeal, it owed its success almost exclusively to the undaunted courage of the fair and spirited sovereign at its head.

When Frederick retired from the Second Silesian War, he was accepted into the select company of the great powers of Europe. He did not owe this improved status to the size of his monarchy, which, in spite of the Silesian acquisition, boasted only a modest circumference, but to the efficient army and sound finances inherited from his father and to the audacity and genius contributed by himself. Alert and intelligent, he was fully aware that only at the cost of unremitting labor could he hope to maintain himself in his precarious position. The ten years of peace that followed the Second Silesian War serve to illustrate his viewpoint and activities. He pursued with added energy and enthusiasm the policy inaugurated by his predecessors of reclaiming waste lands, settling colonists on advantageous terms, building canals, and fostering industries, especially the manufacture of woolen and linen textiles. In these economic labors we recognize the mercantilist teachings which had inspired the governments of Europe since the seventeenth century and which Frederick took over practically without modification. At the same time he reacted strongly to the intellectual influences which sprang into life in his day and which are conveniently summarized under the name of *Aufklaerung* or enlightenment. Championed by advanced thinkers all over Europe, the movement of enlightenment aimed at the overhauling of the body of inherited institutions to the end of bringing them into accord with the new criteria of reason and of science. As their reform would render them socially more serviceable, there was also a distinct humanitarian element present in the movement. From the day of his accession the Prussian king prided himself on standing with the humanitarians and reformers; and by a series of acts, such as the proclamation of religious toleration, the abolition of torture in

Frederick typifies eighteenth century absolutism

criminal cases, and a sweeping reform of the civil courts, he won favor as a leading "enlightened" monarch. By these and similar activities he helped give absolutism that peculiar turn, by virtue of which it presents itself to view as "benevolent despotism." Closely considered, benevolent despotism, mercantilism, and enlightenment are three correlated aspects of eighteenth century government and society.

It is this benevolent and reforming bent of Frederick which explains his close association with so many French literary men and notably with the prince of them all, Voltaire. He long cherished the plan of making his court at Berlin the center from which the new intellectual light was to radiate over the world and to this end gathered around himself men of many nationalities, but particularly Frenchmen because that nation actually furnished the leading spokesmen of the movement. For a while Voltaire condescended to give up France in order to join the circle about Frederick, but the exuberant friendship between the king and the poet-philosopher did not last, and when the golden bubble burst, Voltaire vanished from Berlin in a cloud of scandal. Thanks to an artistic inclination which marked him from his youth and which the cares of office did not succeed in suffocating, Frederick aspired to become in his own person a poet and historian. In his hours of leisure he produced a considerable body of literary work in the French language, but it can not be said that it has materially added to his reputation.

His court a literary and intellectual center

Following the peace of 1748 the political situation in Germany remained remarkably tense for the reason that the high-spirited Empress Maria Theresa refused to forget the violence of which she had been the victim. She hoped to get back Silesia and for years carefully laid her plans. As early as 1746 she entered upon a close alliance with the Tsarina Elizabeth, which the two women consciously aimed at Frederick. Next, the man whom she raised to the post of chancellor, Kaunitz, a most skillful player of the diplomatic game, planned the bold step of an alliance with France. In the eighteenth century an alliance between Hapsburg and Bourbon, the century-old enemies, was generally held to be out of the question. But since the Silesian wars Austria had come to regard not France but Prussia as her leading enemy, and Maria Theresa and Kaunitz were very anxious to have France understand that thenceforth they had no further quarrel

Maria Theresa plans to get back Silesia

with her. Their plan of making friends with France was greatly aided by the circumstance that England and France were at this very time making ready to contest the empire of the sea.[1] Both were on the lookout for allies; and as Prussia, after holding back a long time, was induced at last to sign a convention with England, France, in order not to be isolated, accepted the proffered hand of Prussia's rival, Austria. By the spring of 1756 this diplomatic revolution was an accomplished fact. The two great political questions of the day, the rivalry between England and France, involving the supremacy of the seas, and between Prussia and Austria, touching the control of Germany, were about to be fought out in the great Seven Years' War (1756–1763), and the two northern powers, England and Prussia, were to consolidate their claims and interests against the claims and interests of France and Austria. The remaining great power of Europe, Russia, instead of remaining neutral in a dispute which did not concern it, sided with the cabinets of Versailles and Vienna.

War was formally declared between England and France in May, 1756, and at once the storm broke in America, India, and on all the seas. For a moment Frederick entertained the hope of banishing the conflict from the continent of Europe, more particularly from Germany. It was in fact in the hope of this result that he had bound himself to the English cabinet. If he proved to be mistaken, it was because Maria Theresa held all the diplomatic trumps and was set upon war as the consummation of her dreams. For not only had she bound France and Russia to her cause, but two smaller powers, Saxony and Sweden, were sure to take her side, and with their additional help she might hope to draw a ring around Prussia, which, gradually tightened, would choke to death that hated, upstart power. *The outbreak of the Seven Years' War, 1756*

In this tremendous crisis Frederick's one chance was to move quickly. Therefore before the coalition had perfected its plans against him, he took the offensive and by a lightning stroke occupied hostile Saxony and invaded Bohemia (August, 1756). Thenceforth he could at least utilize Saxony as a southern bulwark against Austria. When the campaign of 1757 began, his enemies, having at length completed their preparations, descended upon him from all points of the compass. His one possibility of escape was to meet them separately. Hurrying into Bohemia to eliminate first his leading enemy, Austria, *Frederick's first and second campaigns*

[1] For France and England see the next chapter.

he was on the point of taking Prague when the defeat of a part of his army at Kolin (June 18) forced him to retreat. Slowly the Austrians followed him and poured into the coveted Silesia. The Russians had already arrived in East Prussia, the Swedes had entered Pomerania, and the French, together with the German troops furnished by the many small states of the Empire, which in this crisis also sided with Maria Theresa, directed their march upon Berlin. Even the friends and family of Frederick were ready to declare that all was lost, while his enemies exulted openly. He alone kept up heart, and by his courage and resolution freed himself from all immediate danger. At Rossbach, in Thuringia, he fell (November 5, 1757), with 22,000 men, upon the combined French and Germans of twice that number, and scattered them to the winds. Then he turned like a flash from the west to the east. During his absence in Thuringia the Austrians had completed the conquest of Silesia and were already proclaiming to the world that they had come again into their own. Just a month after Rossbach, at Leuthen, near Breslau, he signally defeated, with 34,000 men, more than twice as many Austrians, and drove them pell-mell over the passes of the Giant Mountains back into their own dominions. Fear and incapacity had already arrested the Swedes and Russians. Before winter came both had slipped away, and at Christmas, 1757, Frederick could call himself lord of an undiminished kingdom.

In no succeeding campaign was Frederick threatened by such overwhelming forces as in 1757. By the next year his ally, England, had fitted out an army, largely of German mercenaries, which, under Ferdinand of Brunswick, operated against the French upon the Rhine, and so protected Frederick on his western flank. As the Swedish attack, through the incapacity of the decadent government, displayed no energy, Frederick was permitted to make light of his Scandinavian enemy and give all his attention to Austria and Russia. No doubt, even so, the odds against Prussia were enormous. Prussia was a small, barren country of 5,000,000 inhabitants, and in men and resources Austria and Russia together outstripped her many times; but at the head of Prussia stood a military genius with a spirit that neither bent nor broke and that fact sufficed for a while to maintain an equilibrium.

Altered position of Frederick from 1758 on

It was Frederick's policy during the next years to meet the Austrians and Russians separately in order to keep them from smothering him with their combined forces. In 1758 he succeeded in beating the Russians at Zorndorf and driving them back; but in 1759 they beat him in a battle of unexampled carnage at Kunersdorf, which apparently opened the road to Berlin. For a moment Growing now Frederick himself despaired but somehow managed to feebleness raise another force and save the heart of his dominions. of Prussia The end of the campaign found him not much worse off than the beginning. However, he was evidently getting feeble; the terrible strain continued through years was beginning to tell; and when on the death of George II (1760), the English government resolved to come to terms with France and to desert Prussia, Frederick was pushed to the edge of the abyss.

From what to human eyes looked like unavoidable disaster the king of Prussia was saved by a mere accident. On January 5, 1762, Frederick's implacable enemy, the Tsarina Elizabeth, died, and as Russia had no direct interest in the war and had engaged Peace with in it only because the tsarina had a personal dislike for Russia, Frederick, there was no reason why her successor, Peter 1762, fol- III, who was an ardent admirer of the Prussian king, general should not come to terms with him. Peter in his enthu- peace siasm even insisted on allying himself with his country's late enemy; but little came of this plan, as he was overthrown and murdered in July, 1762, and Catherine II, who succeeded him, would not engage further in the war. However, she put Frederick under a heavy debt of gratitude by at least ratifying the peace which Peter had concluded. This same year England and France came to an understanding (Preliminaries of Fontainebleau, 1762) and hostilities between them were at once suspended at all points. Therewith there remained under arms of the great powers only Austria and Prussia; and as Austria could not hope to do unaided what she had failed to do with half of Europe at her side, Maria Theresa, although with heavy heart, resolved to come to terms. In the Peace of Hubertsburg (February, 1763) the cession of Silesia to Frederick received a third and final endorsement.

From the Peace of Hubertsburg Frederick had still twenty-three years before him, which, a practically unbroken stretch of peace, he devoted to the continuation of those inner labors which we have considered under the heads of mercantilism, enlightenment, and benevolent despotism. By promoting the welfare of his people according to the light of his age he became the outstanding sovereign of

Europe. Among the political events of this closing period of his life only those having to do with Poland and Austria call for special comment. His relation to Poland has already been glanced at in connection with the Tsarina Catherine's successful exten-

Frederick's last years. The Partition of Poland

sion of her power westward. It is highly probably that the First Partition (1772) was carried out chiefly at the suggestion of Frederick, who by this arrangement secured a part of a kingdom which the tsarina had already earmarked as her exclusive possession. All three neighbors of Poland, Russia, Austria, and Prussia, shared in the partition, and though Prussia got the smallest slice, it was perhaps the most valuable since it consisted of the province of West Prussia by which the detached territory of East Prussia was at last joined to the Brandenburg nucleus. To comprehend the development in Frederick's last phase of his relation to his German rival we must once more have a look at the Austrian Empire.

Although the Empress Maria Theresa did not succeed in her purpose of regaining Silesia, she played so large a part in the affairs of Europe that she greatly added to the prestige of her empire. How-

Vain attempt of Joseph II to unify the Austrian Empire

ever, permanently to secure it against rapacious neighbors, she would, as she came to recognize, have to make it over in accordance with the current program of centralization. Her very first measures in pursuit of this end aroused such opposition that, seized with discouragement, she

desisted; and it was only when her son, Joseph, became emperor (1765) and at the same time co-regent with his mother of the Austrian state that the work was seriously taken in hand. Joseph II was a typical "enlightened" sovereign, in whose eyes no inherited institution found favor which did not meet the two requirements of reason and utility. If he had had his way he would at once and without hesitation have inaugurated a furious reform movement; but while his mother lived, she effectively applied the brakes, for the last word rested, after all, with her. However, between 1765 and 1780 when he ruled in association with his mother, and much more sweepingly between 1780 and 1790 when, on his mother's death, he ruled alone, he enacted as revolutionary a body of statutes as have ever issued from a royal despot. As an analysis would show, they were devised not only to centralize the Hapsburg dominions but to bring them into harmony with the advanced economic and intellectual program of the day. An unusually informed and kindly soul, Joseph showed in his measures much more good will than tact and foresight; for his dominions, pieced together with so many unrelated provinces and distinct peoples, were bound to demur against this ruthless wiping out of their established customs and historic rights. The most indignant among them, like the Austrian Netherlands (Belgium) and Hungary, even rose in revolution; and before he died the heartbroken sovereign, of whom, if ever of a ruler, it may be said that he desired only the good of his people, was obliged to revoke practically the whole mass of his reform edicts. That Joseph II should have tried to carry out a political reorganization along the lines successfully laid down by France, Prussia, and Russia is wholly comprehensible. His failure proved that the Hapsburg dominions were composed of so many heterogeneous elements that it was madness to hope to recast them into a single uniform mold.

So eager and far-ranging a spirit as Joseph was sure to pursue an active foreign policy. It was he rather than his mother who was responsible for Austria's sharing in the Partition of Poland; and no sooner were his hands entirely freed by his mother's demise than he entered into negotiations with the equally enterprising Tsarina Catherine which, if successful, would have led to the partition of the even vaster area of Turkey-in-Europe. It was largely only because of the domestic revolutions already mentioned in Belgium and Hungary that the great plan miscarried. For no sooner was Austria embarrassed by these inner disturbances than she was obliged to renounce her warlike plans against the Ottoman Empire. In fact, perhaps because of an unfortunate habit of precipitate action, Joseph was about as consistently unfortunate in his foreign as in his domestic ventures. And, as might be expected, when he entered the lists against so deft an adversary as Frederick II of Prussia, he was regularly worsted. Only once, however, in the year 1778, did it look as if the irreconcilable quarrel between Austria and Prussia would precipitate a new war. In that year Joseph made an arrangement with the elector of Bavaria by which he hoped to acquire this important, south-German territory. Increased by an immediately adjoining state, Austria would once more have obtained a clearly dominant position in Germany. Such a consummation Frederick was bound to hinder at all costs. For several months war threatened; and if it was avoided it was not because Frederick yielded but because Joseph renounced his ambitious Bavarian project.

Joseph's ambitious foreign policy

When Frederick II, called the Great, died in 1786 he left behind a Prussia which had grown powerful and famous, but a German Empire which was still the same broken reed as during the four or five pre- ceding centuries. It was something, nay, much that within Germany there was now a strong and vital organism which inevitably communicated a certain vigor to the whole dead mass. Undoubtedly the awakening of Austria under Maria Theresa and her son was to no small extent the result of the Prussian example. If from now on these two states faced each other as enemies, it was not only because of the bitter Silesian memory but, even in larger measure, because each coveted the headship of a new and reborn Germany. Of the official Germany of the eighteenth century the headship rested of course with Austria and its ruler, the elected emperor. But for practical purposes Prussia from the time of Frederick was quite as strong as Austria and, in substantial equilibrium as they were, each watched the other's every move since each hoped to outstrip the other and force its law upon the smaller German states. For that the structure called the Holy Roman Empire would cumber the earth much longer was utterly unbelievable. When three years before the outbreak of the French Revolution Frederick passed away, the German future was undoubtedly as dark as ever; but it was at least clear that it hung upon the outcome of the rivalry of Austria and Prussia.

The German situation dominated by the rivalry of Prussia and Austria

REFERENCES

C. H. HAYES, *Political and Social History*, I, 347–364 and chs. 11, 12
G. M. PRIEST, *Germany since 1740*, chs. 2, 3
A. HASSALL, *Balance of Power*, chs. 6, 7, 8, 9, 11, 13
F. SCHEVILL, *Making of Modern Germany*, Lectures 1, 2; *The Balkan Peninsula*, chs. 16, 17;
J. A. R. MARRIOTT AND C. G. ROBERTSON, *Evolution of Prussia*, pp. 1–165
E. F. HENDERSON, *Short History of Germany*, II, chs. 1–5
R. M. MACDONALD, *France*, II, ch. 27
Cambridge Modern History, V, chs. 12, 20, 21, VI, chs. 8, 9, 11
A. H. JOHNSON, *Age of the Enlightened Despots*, ch. 7
W. A. PHILIPPS, *Poland*, chs. 5, 6
H. O. WAKEMAN, *Ascendancy of France*, ch. 12
R. N. BAIN, *Slavonic Europe*, chs. 5–19
J. F. BRIGHT, *Maria Theresa; Joseph the Second*
F. REDDAWAY, *Frederick the Great*
T. CARLYLE, *Frederick the Great*
H. TUTTLE, *History of Prussia*
History of All Nations: Philippson on Frederick in vol. XV

C. T. ATKINSON, *History of Germany*, 1715–1815
H. TEMPERLEY, *Frederick the Great and Kaiser Joseph*
R. H. LORD, *Second Partition of Poland*

Rulers of Prussia

(House of Hohenzollern)

Frederick William (the Great Elector), 1640–1688
Frederick I (son of the above, first king of Prussia), 1688–1713
Frederick William I (son of Frederick I), 1713–1740
Frederick II (the Great; son of his predecessor), 1740–1786
Frederick William II (nephew of Frederick II), 1786–1797
Frederick William III (son of his predecessor), 1797–1840

Rulers of Austria

(House of Hapsburg)

Charles VI (last male of his line) 1711–1740
Maria Theresa (daughter of the above; *m.* Francis of Lorraine) 1740–1780
Joseph II (son of the above), 1780–1790
Leopold II (younger brother of Joseph II) 1790–1792
Francis II (son of Leopold II; last Holy Roman Emperor), 1792–1835

CHAPTER XVII

GREAT BRITAIN AND FRANCE IN THE EIGHTEENTH CENTURY

We have seen that the Revolution of 1688 had secured the victory in the long civil struggle in England to Protestantism and the parliament. It was without doubt a triumph of the English people but it was not in any modern sense a democratic triumph. If henceforth the parliament was the decisive factor in the English government, let us not fail to observe that, composed of the house of Lords and house of Commons, it represented only the men of property, that is, the class of freeholders, to whom the franchise was limited. While the Revolution, constitutionally considered, definitely and finally displaced the absolute with the parliamentary régime, its social-economic significance lies in its vesting the political control in the landed gentry and the great merchants of the towns. For almost a century and a half, until the Reform Bill of 1832, England was governed by a rarely successful combination between an aristocracy of birth and an oligarchy of wealth.

The sovereign of the Revolution, King William III (1689–1702), soon learned that he was not to have his throne without fighting for it. The deposed James had sought refuge with Louis XIV, and the decision of the French king to espouse the cause of James naturally threw England on the side of the allies, consisting of the emperor, the Dutch, and Spain, with whom Louis had just begun the war known as the War of the Palatinate (1688–1697). This struggle marks a turning-point in the fortunes of the French king. Thus far his policy of continental aggression had met with success to no small extent because the Great Britain of the restored Stuarts had, when not actively aiding him, remained neutral. With the advent of William Great Britain frankly aligned itself with the continental nations against all-powerful France. In fact it was to achieve this very purpose that William, who was a Dutchman before he became an Englishman and who had made it his life-work to defend the liberty of his native land against

366

Louis XIV, had launched the invasion of 1688. But though inspired in the first place by the desire to help the Dutch and Europe, William certainly also served the true interests of his new kingdom, since in arraying England against France he committed it to that maritime and colonial policy by virtue of which it rose in the following century to its peculiar position of world power.

The War of the Palatinate has been dealt with in connection with Louis XIV, except for the phase belonging exclusively to England. Its story carries us to the English dependency, Ireland. In March, 1689, James II effected a landing in Ireland with William in French aid and immediately the native Irish, Catholic and Ireland anti-English in sentiment, gathered around him. Even before his coming the ancient hatred between Celt and Saxon had once more flamed up in war. The Protestant colonists were driven from their homes and for a time it looked as if the island might again revert to its original owners. However, a year later, on July 1, 1690, William, who had come to the rescue of the Protestants, defeated James at the Battle of the Boyne. Thoroughly discouraged, especially since as an Englishman he did not feel happy in an Irish environment, James abandoned his supporters and fled back to France. The measures by which the victorious English now took vengeance on the Irish broke the back of Irish resistance for a hundred years.

Before speaking of these measures it will be necessary to review the relations of Ireland and England during the previous century. When James I mounted the throne in 1603, Ireland had been a dependency of the English crown for nearly five hundred Early years; but for most of that time the English rule had been history of largely nominal since the representative of the king gen- the English erally controlled no more than the district around Dublin in Ireland known as the English Pale. The heart of the island was held by the native Irish, who, divided into tribes and governed by chiefs in accordance with ancient custom, retained a substantial independence. If the Irish could have replaced the perpetual tribal warfare which was usual among them with some form of national organization, they might have rid themselves of their conquerors, for not till the time of Henry VIII did the English take the task of subduing Ireland seriously in hand, and not till the close of Elizabeth's reign was the work completed. Almost the last triumph of Elizabeth was the suppression of the great rebellion in Ulster led by Hugh O'Neill. When James I succeeded to the throne he became responsible for an innovation fraught with tremendous consequences. He resolved to confiscate the northern province of Ulster and colonize it with English and Scotch settlers as the surest means for securing the submission of the island. In 1610 the natives of Ulster were dispossessed of their land with no more said than that they must find subsistence elsewhere. From that act dates a hatred between conquerors and conquered which has proved terrible and implacable.

When the English civil war broke out, temporarily annihilating the power of the government, the Irish fell (1641) upon the colonists of Ulster and murdered them or drove them from their homes. The **England's oppressive policy** English revenge for this outrage was adjourned till 1649 when Cromwell, representing the might of the restored nation, undertook to bring Ireland back to her allegiance. At the head of a Puritan army he relentlessly beat the natives into submission. In this connection it should be remembered that since the Reformation religious differences had sprung up which added new fuel to the ancient quarrel of the two races. On establishing their national or Anglican Church the English had imposed it also, under the misleading name of the Irish Church, on their dependency. However, as the native Irish stubbornly adhered to the Church of Rome, they professed a proscribed religion and laid themselves open to savage persecution. To the Puritan soldiers of Cromwell's army the Catholic Irish were no better than beasts of the field, whom to render harmless was a good deed in the eyes of the Lord. No sooner had the army completed its crushing work of conquest than the parliament resumed and even extended James's policy of seizure and colonization. As a result the title to over half of the land of the island now passed into English hands. The dispossessed peasants were bidden to go find bread or a grave in the bogs and thickets of the yet unconfiscated west. When in 1690 William III overthrew the next insurrection at the Battle of the Boyne, the English parliament, now the real sovereign of England, completed the process of Irish dispossession, thereby reducing the natives to a people without land, without the right of worship, and without a future. Nor was this all. At the demand of the English landlord interest the parliament forbade the importation into England of Irish cattle and dairy products; and in the interest of the English manufacturers the Irish were prohibited from sending any woolen goods out of the country. These prohibitive economic measures struck at the Anglo-Scotch colonists quite as much as at the natives, but the burning memories existing between them kept them from uniting against the oppressor. Injured in their material interests, many of the colonists migrated to America, while the natives, eking out a miserable existence as tenants, day-laborers, and beggars, stolidly awaited the day of deliverance.

We have already noted that William's drawing England into the coalition against France enabled him to bring the War of the Palatinate to a close without conceding any gains to France. He spent the years following the Peace of Ryswick (1697) negotiat- The Act of ing with Louis a feasible division of the expected Spanish Settlement, heritage; but when, in the year 1700, the king of Spain 1701 died, leaving a will in favor of the house of Bourbon, Louis XIV disavowed the negotiations with William by sending his grandson, Philip, to Madrid to assume the rule of the undivided Spanish dominions. Out of this presumptuous act grew the War of the Spanish Succession, for which the great opponent of Louis XIV had hardly prepared by a renewal of the continental coalition, when he died (1702). Since his wife, Mary, had died some years before (1694) without issue, the crown now passed to Mary's sister Anne; but as it was foreseen even in William's lifetime that Anne too would leave no offspring, a special statute had been passed, called the Act of Settlement (1701), for regulating the succession. Supplementing the Protestant provision already incorporated in the Bill of Rights, the Act of Settlement passed over the head of a score of Catholic claimants and established the succession on the demise of Anne in the Electress Sophia of Hanover, granddaughter of James I through his daughter Elizabeth, and her heirs after her.[1]

We have repeatedly insisted that the Revolution of 1688 and the Bill of Rights of the following year consecrated the victory of the parliament in its long struggle with the king. In the course of the next two or three generations the parliament confirmed Slow elaboits hard-won ascendancy by completing the constitutional ration of edifice on its own plan. Without interruption but with- the parliaout haste, act followed act, each enlarging somewhat fur- mentary ther the sphere of the parliament at the expense of the system crown until the entire government came to be vested in the representatives of the people and the monarch was reduced to a position largely ornamental. Let us take note what contributions toward this result were made in the reign of William.

[1] See Genealogical Table at the head of Chapter XIII.

The first subject to be considered is the important matter of supplies. The parliaments of the past had been in the habit of voting certain revenues for the king's lifetime, thereby securing to the sovereign a relative independence and putting it in his power in certain favorable circumstances not to call the legislature at all. William's parliaments now fell into the habit of *annual* grants, which greatly enhanced parliamentary influence since the king, merely to keep the government going, was obliged to summon the parliament every year. This system necessarily led to the drawing up on the part of the government of an annual budget of expenditures, every item of which fell under the lynx-eyed scrutiny of the parliament. Annual budget and annual parliament represent a correlated development which has secured the minute control of the purse, and therewith of the government itself, to the representatives of the nation. Hardly less important was the Mutiny Act, which, along with the revenue arrangements just mentioned, helped assure the annual return of parliament. By this statute military courts for the punishment of mutiny and other acts of insubordination were authorized for one year only. It was a clever device for maintaining the discipline, without which an army can not exist, without permitting the forces to get from under the hand of the parliament. Finally let us note that a step, constituting a magnificent tribute to the modern spirit, was the refusal (1695) to renew the act subjecting all printed matter to official censorship. Henceforth England enjoyed a free and unfettered press, the necessary corollary of a government aspiring to be free.

Annual grants and annual parliaments

The event of the reign of Queen Anne (1702–1714) overshadowing all others was the War of the Spanish Succession. It has been treated elsewhere with due regard to the fact that England won in this conflict a leading position among the powers of Europe. But the applause attending Marlborough's march of victory from Blenheim to Malplaquet was not universal. He depended for support on the party of the Whigs, who in the early part of the war dominated the parliament and increasingly forced their leaders into the ministry. The queen, a narrow-minded woman passionately devoted to the national Church, inclined to the Tories but was dissuaded from supporting them by her friend, the duchess of Marlborough, who had acquired a complete ascendancy over her. However, when the war continued interminably, bringing heavy taxation and a national debt increasing like an avalanche, public

The War of the Spanish Succession

sentiment rallied behind the Tory opposition and encouraged the queen to cast off the Whig yoke. She was unwittingly aided in this design by the arrogant and tempestuous duchess, who carried her tyranny to such a point that the offended Anne at last forbade her the court. Abetted by back-stairs influences, always rife where a weak ruler holds the scepter, the queen became more and more disgusted with the Whigs and in 1710 peremptorily dismissed them from office. There followed a ministry of Tories led by Oxford and Bolingbroke, who dared cashier Marlborough himself and open negotiations with France which in 1713 terminated in the Peace of Utrecht. Although the treaty was concluded somewhat precipitately and without proper regard to Great Britain's allies, the main advantages gained by the Whig conduct of the war even their Tory adversaries did not sacrifice. Great Britain acquired from France Newfoundland, Nova Scotia, and the Hudson Bay territory; from Spain, Gibraltar and Minorca, which secured the control of the western Mediterranean; and, most important of all, she was confirmed by her unquestioned naval ascendancy in that command of the seas which became the basis of her world position.

While the war was at its height an event of great significance occurred in the union of England and Scotland. Although the two kingdoms had possessed a common sovereign ever since the accession in 1603 of the Scottish sovereign, James, to the English throne, from fear of its more powerful neighbor, the smaller state had for over a century jealously guarded its independence. In 1707 the ghost of ancient rivalry and war *Union of England and Scotland* was laid for all time by a measure in which the Scottish parliament voted its own extinction and accepted for the northern kingdom representation in the Lords and Commons seated at Westminster. To mark the fusion of the two governments in one they adopted as their official common designation the name Great Britain.

In the year 1714 Anne died, and the crown fell to the German house of Hanover, whose family name is Guelph (Welf). Since the Electress Sophia, who had been designated by the Act of Settlement as the eventual heir, had preceded Anne in death, her son, George I, now ascended the throne. Some great stroke *Accession of the house of Hanover* on the part of the Pretender, the son of James II, was expected, but when it fell (1715) it turned out to be harmless. The man who claimed to be James III was a weak and unenterprising individual who, having effected a landing in Scotland, was quickly discouraged by the situation confronting him and turned back to France.

George I (1714–1727), who owed his elevation to the Whigs, naturally chose his first advisers from that party. As the Tories were more or less compromised by their support of the Stuart claim, George clung to the Whigs for the rest of his life and thus laid the foundations of that long era of Whig control which puts its stamp upon English history for the next fifty years.

George I leans upon the Whigs

This prolonged power of a single party helped parliament in taking another and practically its final step toward acquiring complete control of the state: with George I is associated the establishment of cabinet government. We have already seen that as far back as the reign of Charles II the parliament fell into two groups or parties, each pledged to a certain course of action. As matters stood at that time, though the majority of the Commons might be Whig, the king, still enjoying a considerable prerogative, was free to choose his advisers from among the Tories. Sooner or later it was bound to appear that such a division of power, enabling the executive to pull one way and the legislature another, was harmful and that to obtain the best results the ministers and the Commons would have to be in some sort of accord. Under the prevailing drift of English constitutional development there was no other conceivable way of achieving this end than for the king to select his ministers from among the majority party. This is what happened under George I, who thus inaugurated a practice which gradually acquired the sanction of custom. The new sovereign was an honest and reliable but mentally sluggish individual. Furthermore, he was more interested in Hanover than in England and did not even trouble to learn the English language. In need of counsel among strange and bewildering conditions and owing his throne to the Whigs, he naturally put his whole trust in them. In consequence the government fell more and more into the hands of a group of Whig ministers, called the cabinet, who collectively governed the country with the support of the majority of the house of Commons. Cabinet rule was of course a gradual development, but when it was at last complete it signified that the ministers, still nominally appointed by the king, were really the agents of the party commanding a majority in the lower house. With cabinet and party rule added to the older features of parliamentary practice the English constitution may be

Cabinet government

said to have reached the form which has distinguished it down to our own time.

The Whig ascendancy is inseparably connected with the name of Sir Robert Walpole, during whose tenure of office lasting for more than twenty years (1721–1742) the cabinet system became a reality. He was a coarse, vigorous, and practical-minded realist, Sir Robert who coupled with a shrewd understanding of the strength Walpole's of his country a desire for peace in order first, to secure the system Hanoverian succession and second, to enable the commercial interests to make the most of their unrivalled opportunities beyond the seas. Himself a country squire, he belonged to a social order which was overwhelmingly Tory and violently antagonistic to the great merchants with whom, organized under the Whig banner, they disputed the control of parliament. It is a tribute to Walpole's breadth of view that, though a member of the landlord class, he identified himself with the urban element and tried in every way to promote its interest. Inspired by the current mercantilist ideas he promoted colonial development, favored the importation of raw products and the exportation of manufactured goods, and by a hundred different devices attempted to achieve that *summum bonum* of mercantilist thought, a favorable balance of trade. If his measures, by which he manipulated production and exchange as if they were pawns on a chess-board, were far from being an unmixed blessing, they probably did stimulate enterprise along certain lines of colonial trade and lead to the establishment of a number of favored industries. In any case they won the applause and incidentally the votes of the merchant class. But let no one imagine that in his trading zeal he neglected the landlords to whom he himself belonged. The solid legislation of earlier days in their favor culminating in the payment of bounties for the export of wheat, he not only refrained from touching but judiciously enlarged from time to time. With such a policy he drew at least a part of the country squires into the Whig camp and was enabled to give the parliament that Whig complexion which it retained for so many years. Walpole's economic measures do not differ essentially from those practiced in other countries of that age dominated by mercantilist doctrines, but it can not fail to strike our attention that in its political implications his legislation appears as a bribe offered to the two classes alone represented in parliament and therefore ruling the elections. If we see him, in addition, employing a vast patronage to maintain his required majority in the lower house, we are prepared for the fact that corruption became an inherent feature of the new parliamentary system and can also understand how the all-powerful minister, made thoroughly cynical about human nature, came to be credited with the bleak saying that "every man has his price." In the governing circles of eighteenth century England it came very close to being true.

Dedicated to a peace policy, Walpole was moved in part at least to favor trade on the theory that a commercially minded people necessarily abhors war. He was destined to a rude disillusionment.

War of Jenkins' Ear, 1739 Among the advantages obtained for England by the Treaty of Utrecht was an invasion of the monopoly maintained by Spain in the western world. By an agreement called the *asiento* England received the monopoly of the African slave trade for the Spanish colonial world and, in addition, the right to send one trading ship each year to Spanish colonial ports. It was a slight wedge which the reckless enterprise of the English traders attempted to convert into a broad breach; and when the Spaniards resisted and seized and punished smugglers, the English trading interests at home raised a resounding clamor. In 1738 a smuggler by the name of Jenkins was paraded through London with a shrivelled ear wrapped in cotton-wool which he declared he had lost seven years before through the assault of a Spanish coast guard. Jenkins' miraculously preserved appendage is the most famous ear in history, for it tipped the scales against peace. Pushed by public opinion and against his better judgment, Walpole began (1739) a war with Spain. It aimed at greater rights in Spanish waters and, in view of its origin, is appropriately named the War of Jenkins' Ear.

Meanwhile George I had been succeeded by his son, George II (1727–1760), like his father in at least the one important circumstance that he meekly acquiesced in the new party and cabinet development. **The War of the Austrian Succession, 1740–1748** The war with Spain had hardly begun when the continental powers, on the heels of the death of Emperor Charles VI (1740), became involved in a struggle over the Austrian succession. As England took alarm at the policy of France, which again visibly aimed at European ascendancy by means of a partition of Austria, the government threw in its lot with Charles's heir, Maria Theresa. Looking with inner displeasure on all these developments, Walpole was at length (1743) forced out of office to be replaced by men more eager than he to fight and more ready, above all, to join with Austria in order to present a united front against the leagued Bourbon powers of Spain and France. Having already dealt with the War of the Austrian Succession we need not linger over it at this point. Its importance lies in the fact that it ended in the Peace of Aachen (1748), in which the French acknowledged the defeat of their anti-Austrian project and recognized Maria Theresa as heir to the dominions of her father with the one substantial exception of Silesia, which was conceded to Frederick of Prussia. In other respects the conflict was without fruit, the treaty being based on the principle of the mutual restoration of conquests. This meant that the colonial issues both as between Great Britain and Spain and as between Great Britain and France were adjourned to a later day.

A memorable incident of the War of the Austrian Succession was the attempt of Charles Edward Stuart, son of the Pretender, and known as the Young Pretender, to win back his lost realms. That he was not lacking in the spirited audacity which has often **Prince** gained a crown is proved by the fact that without help **Charles** from France and with a following of only seven men he **Stuart** secretly landed on the Scottish Highland coast. The **to regain** time, July, 1745, was well chosen since the British troops **his crown** were fighting on the continent. The Highlanders were in this period still divided into clans, at the head of which stood hereditary chiefs. As Celts, with a language and a civilization, albeit backward, of their own, they were by no means friendly either to the Teutonic Lowlanders of Scotland or to the English. Moreover, practically self-governed, they were subjected to King George II in hardly any thing more than name. That Prince Charlie, as the Young Pretender was fondly called, had thrown himself upon their mercy, stirred their imagination and kindled their generous hearts to wild enthusiasm. Flocking around him in crowds, they advanced from point to point until by an irresistible rush they captured Edinburgh. For a moment London itself was apprehensive of capture, but on the troops being recalled from the Netherlands, where they were engaged in fighting the French, it was soon found that the wild courage of feudal clans was of no avail against the discipline of a trained army. On Culloden Moor (April, 1746), the Highlanders were defeated with fearful slaughter by the king's second son, the duke of Cumberland. Prince Charlie, after many romantic adventures, made his escape; but broken apparently by his one capital misfortune, he became an habitual drunkard and lived ever afterward in indolence abroad (d. 1788). His failure marks the last Stuart attempt to recover the throne.

While England, under Walpole's vigorous initiative, was preparing to assume the commercial leadership of the world, France was doing little or nothing to recover from the disasters of the War of the Span-The regency ish Succession. When the aged Louis XIV died in the in France year 1715, he was succeeded by his great-grandson, Louis XV (1715–1772). As the young king was but five years old, the government was exercised in his name by the nephew of Louis XIV, Philip, duke of Orleans. The Regent Orleans, although a man of parts and a celebrated wit, was so passionately given to the pursuit of pleasure that he only plunged France deeper into economic and financial misery. Perhaps the one good point about his rule was that, recognizing the advantage of peace, he maintained amicable relations with England. It was not a sufficient contribution to make him popular; and when he died, in 1723, he was regretted by none but the companions of his wild nights.

Although the boy-king had been declared of age even before the regent's death, he was still too young to exercise the rule, which, taken over by his religious director, the Cardinal Fleury, was re-Cardinal tained for almost two decades (1726–1743). Fleury, too, Fleury and held the view that France needed nothing so much as a the acqui- long peace. Nevertheless, his administration is marked sition of by two wars forced on him by circumstances which he Lorraine was too weak to command. In the year 1733 France became involved with Austria because of the different sides taken by these two powers in the election of a Polish king. The so-called War of the Polish Succession (1733–1735) is unmemorable except for the right conceded to France to take over Lorraine after the death of the defeated king of Poland, to whom it was given during his life in compensation for his loss of the Polish crown. More than a hundred years before this time France had turned its attention to the acquisition of Lorraine and had gradually succeeded in severing the ties which bound it to the Empire. Louis XV therefore did no more in 1735 than gather a piece of ripe fruit. Taken in connection with the territorial gains made by Louis XIV, the duchy of Lorraine satisfactorily rounded off the French eastern boundary.

In the year 1740 the death of the Emperor Charles VI and the accession in Austria of the young girl Maria Theresa so completely turned the head of the court party at Versailles with the brilliant chance which the situation offered of war and conquest, that Cardinal Fleury was obliged once again to yield to pressure and against his better judgment to attack Austria. The War of the Austrian Succession involved all Europe for eight years, as we have seen, but when it was closed by the Peace of Aachen (1748), France recognized Maria Theresa as heir of the Hapsburg dominions and withdrew from Germany without a gain.

The War of the Austrian Succession from the French point of view

As we approach the middle of the eighteenth century it becomes plain that the struggle which Louis XIV inaugurated with the object of making France supreme in Europe had ended in failure. The remedy proposed by William III and consisting of the alliance of Austria, the Dutch, and England had proved successful. By the War of the Spanish Succession Louis XIV had been brought to his senses; and when, in the War

The colonial rivalry of France and England

of the Austrian Succession, Louis XV had revamped the old plan, he too had been obliged to draw in his horns. But in spite of disasters on the continent, perhaps even because of them, French colonial expansion continued vigorously with the result that in India and North America it entered into ever sharper rivalry with Great Britain. Plainly the aim of the French was to compensate themselves for the failure of their European plans by the acquisition of an empire beyond the seas. Comprehensible enough in itself, the plan conflicted with a similar purpose of the English. Accordingly, with the march of the century the gaze of Frenchmen and Englishmen turned across the seas, and slowly the center of interest, which in the long struggle of France for supremacy in Europe had been the continent, shifted to the colonies.

Such a change of interest necessarily involved a subtle change of international relationships in Europe. In measure as France withdrew from her aggression against her continental neighbors, she conciliated her ancient enemies, Austria and the Dutch; and in measure as she emphasized her colonial ambition, she aroused the increased hostility of England. Thus, by the gradual operation of circumstances, England and France had, toward the middle of the eighteenth century, been brought face to face to fight out the great question of supremacy in the colonial world; and in this colonial question Austria, the old ally of England against France, had no immediate interest. Was Austria or any other continental power likely, under the circumstances, to take the side of the English?

England and Austria dissolve partnership

The war between France and Great Britain which followed, called the Seven Years' War (1756–1763), is properly the most important struggle of the century, for it determined whether America and India were to be French or English. But though the other European powers had no direct interest in the colonial question, they nevertheless participated in the conflict. That, as already explained, was owing to the circumstance that the two German powers, Austria and Prussia, had a quarrel of their own to settle, and that by choosing sides in the French-English conflict, Prussia allying herself with England and Austria with France, they brought about a fusion of two distinct issues in a general war.

Prussia sides with England, Austria with France

France did not fail to extend herself in the Seven Years' War in the hope of fastening victory to her banners. She sent an army across the Rhine to coöperate with the Austrians against the Prussians and their British allies, and she made considerable, though uneven, efforts to equip a navy and to support her colonial forces in India and America. It was her great misfortune that the government lay in the hands of Louis XV, than whom there is hardly a feebler and more despicable sovereign in history. As he was selfishly concerned only with his pleasures and at the same time cynical and indolent, he permitted the business of state to slip into the grasp of intriguing courtiers and base courtesans with the result that merit was disregarded in distributing the posts of honor, that one plan of campaign was adopted only to be rejected in favor of another, and that a lavish and corrupt expenditure diverted into private channels huge sums of money which should have been dedicated to the national defense. More than with any other single individual the direction of affairs rested with the king's official mistress, Madame de Pompadour, who, though possessed of a certain light grace of person and of mind, boasted neither the intelligence to grasp the significance of the conflict nor the character worthily to sustain it.

Failure of government under Louis XV

While the absolute government of France thus conspicuously failed to give the country that leadership which is invaluable in a crisis, the parliamentary government of Great Britain brought to the front the one man capable of giving it just that. By a combination of various Whig groups William Pitt, who since Walpole's decline had become the most brilliant figure of the Commons, was in 1757 promoted to be Secretary of State, from which vantage-point he for four decisive years controlled the ministry and directed his country's policy on land and sea. A vibrant personality, he communicated his patriotic energy to the whole body of his countrymen and won their hearty support for his far-sighted plan of utilizing the Pitt, leader favorable situation to eliminate France entirely from the and strate- colonial field. Under these circumstances the victory gist of necessarily fell to the English. In 1757 the French army England was catastrophically beaten by Frederick the Great at Rossbach in Thuringia, and on its reorganization in 1758 was held in effective check by an Anglo-Hanoverian force under Ferdinand of Brunswick, one of Frederick's most reliable generals. So much for the British effort in Germany, which Pitt consistently regarded as a secondary fighting area. With great acumen he reserved his best efforts for the sea and the colonies, since on them, according to him, the struggle really hinged. At the outbreak of the war the French had won a naval action off the island of Minorca (May, 1756), which jeopardized the English control of the sea-routes. Aware that the colonies would fall automatically to him who mastered the sea, Pitt strengthened his navy until, assuming the offensive, it gained in 1759 the two victories of Lagos and Quiberon Bay by which it practically annihilated the French fleet. From 1759 on the French colonies were cut off from the mother-country and therefore doomed.

At the same time Pitt eagerly pushed the war in America and India. In India, with remarkably little help from home, a daring adventurer, Robert Clive by name, first built up a native political and military system enabling him to hold his own against Victories in the French, and then at Plassey (1757) began a series of India and victories which ended with the downfall of the rival America power. In America the struggle lasted longer because more steadily supported by the French home government. One of the crucial American areas was the headwaters of the Ohio which the French claimed as a part of the Mississippi basin and where they had erected a fort to warn off intruders. As early as 1755, that is, a whole year before war was officially declared, the British sent an army under General Braddock to destroy the French stronghold. Refusing to take the advice of a young Virginian officer, George Washington, who twenty years later won immortal fame in a contest of another kind, Braddock's army was badly beaten and he himself killed by the Indian allies of the French. Pitt was of course unwilling to abide by this decision, and in 1758 reëstablished the English prestige by the capture of the French fort. Rebaptized Pittsburg, it still proclaims to the living generation the great minister's share in its foundation. However, it was not the Ohio but the St. Lawrence area which was the real basis of the French empire in America. In 1759 General Wolfe by a daring assault captured the nigh impregnable stronghold of Quebec; and in the following year with the seizure of Montreal the whole province of Canada passed into British hands.

At this juncture, with an unexampled victory in sight, King George II died (October, 1760), to be succeeded by his grandson, George III, who was destined to reign for sixty years. George III, but twenty-two years old at his accession, was passionately resolved to regain for the sovereign that leading influence in the government which had in recent generations passed to cabinet and parliament. "Be a king, George," had been from his boyhood his ambitious mother's constant admonition to him. So he set about to reverse the constitutional movement, and as a preliminary step turned to the Tories and injected his personal supporter, Lord Bute, into the Whig ministry. His plan was by degrees to get rid not only of Pitt but incidentally of the heavy Whig yoke to which his predecessors had been obliged to submit ever since the accession of the house of Hanover. In pursuit of this program Lord Bute, once seated in the cabinet, headed an opposition party which clamored for peace; and when Pitt, learning that Spain was coming to the rescue of France, moved to enlarge the scope of the war by attacking Spain before she was ready, he found himself isolated and obliged to resign (1761). That Pitt was right had to be admitted by Bute himself a few months later when, in January, 1762, he was forced to meet the now open preparations of Spain with a declaration of war. However, such was the impetus which had been given the British armaments by Pitt that in the new struggle the Spanish possessions were invaded and Havana and Manilla, the leading strongholds of the Spanish colonial empire, were captured. In spite of these successes, Lord Bute, supported by the king, did not desist for a moment from his efforts to get peace and, before the year closed, succeeded in reaching an accommodation with the two Bourbon powers. Without any doubt Pitt in Bute's place would have exacted much more crushing terms. Even so it can not be denied that by the definitive Peace of Paris, signed on February 10, 1763, England

Fall of Pitt and the Peace of Paris, 1763

gained every essential point at issue between herself and Louis XV, for France surrendered Canada together with all territory east of the Mississippi, a number of important islands in the West Indies, and all claim to exercise political dominion in India.

If the Seven Years' War is Great Britain's greatest triumph, the country was visited soon afterward with its severest calamity. In the year 1765 the British parliament levied a tax upon the North American colonies called the Stamp Act and therewith *The Ameri-* precipitated an issue of control which had long been *can Revolu-* brewing between the colonies and the mother-country. *tion, 1776* When it became known that the tax aroused discontent, it was wisely withdrawn; but at the same time the principle was asserted and proclaimed that the British parliament had the right to tax the colonies. As the Americans would not agree that they could be taxed by a body in which they were not represented, friction grew apace and soon led to mob violence. The British ministry, dominated by an ambitious and obstinate king, resorted to military force, and the answer of the Americans to this measure was the resolution to revolt (Declaration of Independence, July 4, 1776). In 1778 the colonists, through their agent, Benjamin Franklin, made an alliance with France, and from this time on the British were hard pressed by both land and sea. At last the surrender at Yorktown (1781) of the British army under Cornwallis to the American hero of the war, George Washington, disposed the mother-country to a settlement. In the Peace of Paris (1783) Great Britain made France a few colonial concessions but, in the main, retained the decisive advantages gained in the Seven Years' War. The really memorable feature of the peace was the recognition of the independence of the revolted British colonies under the name of the United States of America.

The American Revolution should have served notice to the British that something was wrong with their colonial system. This it failed to do, at least at the time, although the developments in another dependency, much nearer home, might have enforced the *Ireland* American lesson. We have seen that Ireland received the *wins self-* harshest kind of treatment in that the welfare and wishes *govern-* of the natives were not regarded by the conquerors, who *ment, 1782* finally carried their policy of repression to the point of confiscating the land and distributing it among men of their own race as colonists. As the home government could not deny the settlers, men of English and Scottish blood, certain rights of self-government, Ireland had been conceded a parliament, in which the colonist element was alone represented by virtue of the provision that Catholics were excluded from representation. However, to keep the Irish parliament, even though it was a close Protestant corporation, securely tied to the English chariot, an ancient ordinance was enforced to the effect that no act passed by the Irish parliament should become law until it had received the approval of the British Privy Council. Loyal as the colonists were to England, they resented this limitation of their political rights and, under the stimulus of the American example, demanded its cancellation. In order to avoid a second colonial rebellion the ministry conceded the point with the result that Ireland by the grant (1782) of Legislative Independence became self-governing.

It was a decided gain, though it redounded to the exclusive advantage of the Protestant minority. Inevitably, however, it released an agitation among the Catholic natives for that participation in the affairs of their country of which they had been systematically deprived. Religious coupled with political animosities soon blazed up in civil war. The immediate effect of Legislative Independence was an anarchy which proved that the time was past when a minority could keep a majority in subjection, even though that majority might lack for the present the arms and organization enabling it to wrest the power from the privileged group. The British ministry in London under the energetic control of the younger Pitt, son of the organizer of victory in the Seven Years' War, long watched the Irish confusion with concern before it resolved to interfere. At length Pitt made up his mind that the way out was to merge Ireland governmentally with Great Britain. Partly by persuasion but, much more commonly, by open bribery he induced the Irish parliament to vote its own extinction in return for Irish representation in the British house of Lords and house of Commons. In 1800 this measure, called the Act of Union, became law. Ireland lost its political independence by the action of a minority of its inhabitants composed of Protestant colonists. Was it likely that the Catholic natives, constituting an overwhelming majority, would abide by this decision if the time ever came when they could make their power felt?

Loss of home-rule and Act of Union, 1800

REFERENCES

E. R. TURNER, *Europe 1450–1789*, chs. 17, 18
A. L. CROSS, *England and Greater Britain*, chs. 36–43
T. F. TOUT, *Advanced History of England*
C. H. HAYES, *Political and Social History*, I, chs. 9, 10
R. M. MACDONALD, *France*, II, chs. 26, 27
A. HASSALL, *Balance of Power*, ch. 12
Cambridge Modern History, IV, chs. 16, 25, V, chs. 10, 15, VI, chs. 1, 2, 3, VII, chs. 1–4
G. M. TREVELYAN, *England under the Stuarts*, chs. 14, 15
C. G. ROBERTSON, *England under the Hanoverians*
G. B. ADAMS, *Constitutional History of England*,
P. H. BROWN, *History of Scotland*, III, Bk. 7, chs. 1–3
P. W. JOYCE, *Concise History of Ireland*
W. O. C. MORRIS, *Ireland*, 1494–1905
J. MORLEY, *Edmund Burke; Sir Robert Walpole*
LORD ROSEBERY, *William Pitt*
F. HARRISON, *William Pitt*
A. F. POLLARD, *The Evolution of Parliament*
M. BLAUVELT, *Development of Cabinet Government in England*
F. PARKMAN, *A Half Century of Conflict; Montcalm and Wolfe*
R. MUIR, *The Making of British India*
A. P. INNES, *Short History of British India*
G. B. HERTZ, *British Imperialism in the Eighteenth Century*
Cambridge History of India, vol. I
G. R. GLEIG, *Life of Robert, Lord Clive*
A. T. MAHAN, *Influence of Sea Power upon History*
J. B. PERKINS, *France under Louis XV*
G. B. MALLESON, *Dupleix*
R. G. THWAITES, *France in America*
W. E. H. LECKY, *A History of England in the Eighteenth Century*

CHAPTER XVIII

POLITICAL, SOCIAL, ECONOMIC, AND INTELLECTUAL CURRENTS BETWEEN 1648 AND 1789

We have seen that in the period considered in this section Europe was dominated politically by the absolute monarch. Philosophically considered, his function was to bring all classes of the population **The func-** under a common law in the interest of a larger political **tion of ab-** unit, the nation. This was the ideal, nowhere entirely **solutism** attained, not even in France which served as the model absolutism to the rest of Europe. Reaching his full stature in the seventeenth century, the absolute sovereign of France indulged himself in the eighteenth century in the dangerous luxury of living on his reputation. We have seen what happened under Louis XV. On account of this passivity French absolutism was in Louis XV's time outstripped in effectiveness by some of its imitators, notably by that of Prussia.

The absolute monarchy was created and upheld by the king who became its living spirit after the formula: *suprema lex regis voluntas* (the supreme law is the will of the king). To an age still dominated **Absolutism** by Christian concepts and prepared to refer all human **transformed** situations to an omnipotent Creator this supremacy of **to constitu-** the king would quite normally appear as the law of **tionalism** heaven and the king a sovereign by Right Divine. However, the case might arise that the king, taking his Divine Right too literally, would forget the social service, which was his real justification, and attempt to put through measures strongly repugnant to the nation of which he was the head. His exalted autocratic position, calculated to disturb the always precarious balance of the human reason, would and did tend to make him think that the state existed for his sake and not *vice versa*. In that event, as the case of England proved, he was destined to arouse an opposition which would not cease until it had put an end to the theory of Divine Right by bringing home to the king the realization that he was, the flattery of the courtiers to the contrary notwithstanding, a decidedly man-made instrument. And, as the case of England also proved, the legal form of the subjection of the king to the concept of the public weal would be constitutionalism. The essence of the constitutional system is the bringing of the king in all respects under the law according to the formula: *suprema lex salus populi* (the supreme law is the welfare of the people.)

If absolutism and its English modification, constitutionalism, are the ruling political forms of the seventeenth and eighteenth centuries, they are, like political forms in all climes and ages, an expression of the underlying social-economic situation. Although this varied in detail in every country of Europe, we are aware that its essential features were everywhere the same and that they consisted in a decline of the older privileged orders, the clergy and nobility, and in the rise to constantly greater influence of the business and professional groups. The social dislocation represented by this statement was of course particularly striking among the commercial nations, such as the Dutch and the English; but even among them it was not attended at first by anything more than a gradual penetration of national policy with commercial interests. Such was the authority of the older classes that they wielded a political power considerably out of proportion to their numerical and economic strength. Their authority, which from being an economic had become a moral value, had been built up through the slow action of the centuries and would have to be destroyed, if at all, in the place where it most stubbornly persisted, that is, in the human mind. How this mental undermining of the clergy and nobility proceeded in the period covered by this chapter is a fascinating study and must be briefly indicated, if for no other reason than that it throws a penetrating light on the formation of the modern outlook.

The social-economic basis of government

To begin with the clergy, we are aware that the Reformation, wherever it was successful, deprived this order of its medieval halo by denying that it was a necessary link in the process of salvation. True, even in Protestant countries clergymen continued to maintain a high standing as moral and intellectual leaders, though they were now no longer a special order recognized by the law, a first estate. When in the second half of the seventeenth century interest in theological controversy began to decline, and when at the same time the primacy in matters intellectual passed to laymen, that is, to scientists and philosophers,

Decline both of the clergy and theology

the clergy not only in Protestant lands but also for the first time now in Catholic countries were slowly crowded into the background. Inevitably a non-religious type of thinking gained an increasing body of adherents as soon as the barrenness of theological discussion was contrasted with the positive results obtained by the followers of science. Such was the authority of theology, however, that the whole succession of scientists from Copernicus to Newton paid homage to it, sincerely in some cases, perfunctorily in others with a view to buying immunity from a power which still ruled the universities and looked upon itself as the crown and glory of the edifice of learning. Only very gradually did men become more courageous. At first an occasional rare scholar paraded a certain indifference to theology, to be followed gradually by others who directed a moderate criticism against the various theological systems whether Catholic or Protestant; finally, still bolder spirits advanced to the position that every closed intellectual system was hopelessly incompatible with the perpetual search of science for new truth. What greatly sustained these pioneers in the battle for intellectual freedom was the strong revulsion against dogmatic rigor that followed in the wake of the ruinous religious wars together with the rise of a body of tolerant men interested in mediating between the rival faiths. If the Reformation had already succeeded in more or less fusing the Protestant clergy with the body of common men, after the passing of another century the time had come to drag theology itself from its throne along with the churches built on theological systems. The instrument which chiefly served to carry out this levelling work was deism.

Deism represents a crystallization in the minds of men of the conditions just sketched. In substance therefore it is first, a reaction against theological contentiousness, and second, an enthusiasm for Significance the new scientific universe of eternal law. To be sure, it of deism drew a certain strength also from the "natural rights" philosophy of the ancients, into which the recent discovery of a body of "natural law" had infused fresh vigor. If the universe was ruled by natural law — as the seventeenth century scientists upheld — and human beings were endowed with natural rights — as was maintained by the thinkers of antiquity — it followed that there was also a natural religion, not necessarily in conflict with Christianity but certainly older than Christianity or any existing faith. But what had this original, this natural religion, the essence of which was simple piety, to do with a priesthood, a metaphysical theology, and an institutionalized church?   Plainly all these human constructions smothered much more than they stimulated the glad worship of the pure in heart and would have to be cleared away if mankind was ever again to be set right with its Creator.

Deism first manifested itself in England during the Puritan Revolution and grew strong in measure as men grew tired of the hair-splitting and rancor of the theological controversialists.   The respective exponents of the Tory and Whig political philosophies, History of Thomas Hobbes and John Locke, were already strongly deism in tinged with deism; and among the generation following England the "Glorious Revolution" some of the greatest political leaders, like Shaftesbury and Bolingbroke, openly professed a deistic philosophy.   Full of resentment against the evangelical and emotional tendencies of Puritanism, the upper classes that took over the government after 1688 adopted a hard, common-sense attitude toward life and ridiculed the very mention of miracles, visions, and revelation. In supporting the national Church, as they most earnestly did, they were indeed inconsistent, as practical men often are, but they had an excellent reason for their course since the Anglican Church served in their view as a moral police and helped keep the vulgar herd in check.   So far, however, was the elegant and restrained scepticism of the English upper classes from infecting the lower strata of the population that when the national Establishment threatened to become spiritually dead under the prolonged rule of worldly bishops, a revolt among its own members proved that men will not for long permit religion to be degraded to a round, however dignified, of public ceremonies.   About the middle of the eighteenth century a popular Puritanical revival, connected with the brothers John and Charles Wesley and with their disciple, George Whitefield, made its appearance in the common membership of the Establishment; and although it ended in a schism which produced the Methodist church, it shook the old Church wide-awake, putting an end to its flirtation with the deistic movement.   As for the English intellectual class, however, once won over to a mild scepticism, it was, generally speaking, never again detached from its position; with regard to its members it is undeniable that they had forever freed their minds from the triple domination of theology, the priesthood, and the Church.

When deism crossed the channel to the continent, it made a much greater stir than in England, possibly because it locked horns there with a more formidable adversary, the Catholic Church, and possibly

because it acquired as its spokesman one of the sprightliest and
wittiest writers of all time, Voltaire (1694–1778). This gifted
Frenchman, who began life as a purely literary artist with an
Voltaire as ambition to succeed to the great heritage of Corneille
exponent of and Racine, presently found himself caught up by the
continental intellectual currents of the day and launched upon a
deism campaign for the reform of the institutions of society.
Among these the Catholic Church occupied of course a preëminent
position. Coming by virtue of a two-year exile in England under the
empirical and deistic influences ruling that country, Voltaire on his
return to France made himself their spokesman. But he added important features of his own to the English borrowings. From the
rather mild English deism, for example, he fashioned a mighty sword
or rather a swift-glancing rapier with which to slay the champions of
revealed religion. For every revealed religion organized as a church,
and therefore not only Catholicism, was to Voltaire a lie which he
was resolved to laugh out of the world with the unanswerable logic
of his caustic wit. Naturally the churches met his light raillery
with the heavy theological artillery which was their familiar weapon,
but though they subjected him to much personal inconvenience,
they failed to reduce him to silence. We may take the drawn battle
as evidence that the power of the churches was waning and that a
considerable percentage, perhaps a majority of the educated element throughout Europe, had, toward the middle of the eighteenth
century, rallied, if not to Voltaire's extreme deistic position, at least
to some form of rationalist outlook which freed them from the
domination of the clergy.

A further indication that the fortunes of the day were going
against the churches may be seen in the fact that they were threatened and in some cases overtaken with divisions in their midst.
The signifi- The case of Methodism, an offshoot of the Anglican
cance of the Church, has already been mentioned. So far from being
struggle unique, it is rather a typical instance. Within both the
between Lutheran and Calvinist churches similar tendencies came
Jansenism to the fore, producing schismatic movements on the part
and of those sincere spirits who, cherishing religion as a
Jesuitism transforming inner experience, protested against having their enthusiasm stifled by a dead professional routine. The equivalent
movement in the Catholic Church is indicated by the name of the
Jansenists, a sect which had its center in France and which stressed

spiritual illumination as against an excess of outward ceremonies. Under the powerful Jesuit influences, which had been predominant in the Church from the period of the Council of Trent, Jansenism was formally condemned as heretical by Pope Clement XI in the famous Bull, *Unigenitus* (1713); but before the century closed the Jesuits were themselves overtaken with disaster. This overthrow of the followers of Loyola is peculiarly significant. The free spirits, of which Voltaire was the acknowledged leader, had made the famous order the objective of a concentrated attack on the ground that it not only dominated the papacy and the higher clergy but by means of its extensive school system ruled also the Catholic laity. When the governments of the thoroughly Catholic states of Portugal, France, and Spain added their protest to that of the liberal-minded publicists, the pope came to the conclusion that the much vexed ship of St. Peter could only be saved by tossing the Jesuits overboard. In 1773 the mighty order was dissolved by papal command — clearly an act which was forced on the Catholic Church by Catholic public opinion and which we may accept as the high-water mark of anti-clerical agitation in the eighteenth century.[1]

The decline in authority of the nobles was not less real than that of the clergy, though a considerable variation may be observed in their regard among the different countries of Europe. In England there was an actual increase of upper class influence be- The variable case of cause the victory of the parliament delivered the power largely into their hands. But two observations are in the nobles place in this connection: (1) as the gateway to power after 1688 was not so much birth as property, the line of division between the landed gentry and the captains of industry tended to disappear; and (2) in view of their subjection to the law and the excellent public service which they undoubtedly rendered, the nobles were accepted as an integral and useful element of the nation. In sharp contrast to their eminence in England is their decline in France and in many other continental countries. Absolutism from its very nature was bound to aim at the political depression of its feudal rival. As this point has been repeatedly elaborated, it will suffice here to instance the case of France, where the victorious monarch built up a royal administration exclusively of commoners, though he was at pains to

---

[1] The restoration of the Jesuit Order by the pope in 1814 is evidence of the revived clericalism connected with the general reaction following the downfall of Napoleon.

placate the subjugated nobles by reserving to them the officer grades in the army and navy. At the same time he summoned them to his court at Versailles to dance attendance on his person, thus divorcing them from the land which was their ancient source of strength and encouraging their transformation into a butterfly aristocracy. Without doubt the Bourbon absolutism disastrously undermined the moral credit of the nobles by converting them into a class of social sycophants and economic wastrels. And in so doing it suffered the familiar lot of the corrupter, it became itself corrupt. However, in certain other countries, in Poland and Hungary, for instance, the influence of the nobles rose rather than declined. The reason for this reversal of the usual development must be found in the circumstance that in these countries the nobles held the monarchy in successful check, thereby keeping intact or even increasing their medieval authority. Prussia is in this matter a half-way house. In Prussia there was no class of great nobles and, in their absence, the land was largely distributed among small country gentlemen, called *Junker* and corresponding approximately to the English squires. Privileged in the matter of taxation as well as in the reservation to themselves of the officer positions in the army, they invite comparison in these respects with their fellows of France; but as they avoided the court and dwelt on their estates, which they personally superintended, they remained a body of active agriculturists integrated with the state and nation in a manner which became entirely obsolete in France.

While an examination of clergy and nobility seems to justify us in insisting on an actual decline of their authority in the moral sphere, it may well be that the movement was relative rather than absolute

The inevitable projection of the middle classes into politics

and is incontrovertible only when confronted with the growth of the middle classes, around which, as we have seen, the movement of civilization since the Renaissance chiefly turned. These classes had been steadily becoming numerically stronger as well as more complex in their composition. Among them were not only the representatives of big and little business but the professional groups of lawyers, physicians, teachers, artists, and writers of every sort whom we may bring together under the convenient label of intelligentsia. Without any interruption the whole movement of European evolution continued to play into their hands. Wherever the king built up the absolute state, he entrusted its administration to the hands of his commoners;

if he needed money, he was obliged to follow an economic policy calculated to multiply commerce and industry; and the vast colonial movement which made Asia and America the footstool of Europe was carried on by the middle classes and redounded primarily to their benefit. Only slowly, however, were they moved to aspire to political control. With the decline of respect for the feudal orders they became indeed correspondingly self-assertive, but as long as the king rendered the national service which might be reasonably expected of him they were pleased to stick to their ledgers and counting-houses. In England occurred the first instance of their overthrowing a king who consistently and continuously offended them. It was a startling manifestation of power but ended in a compromise with the landed gentry whose superior political intelligence could not yet be dispensed with. Would the English Revolution be lost on the middle classes of the continent? It was not likely, provided they ever reached the same economic strength in the community, and provided, further, they encountered a similar provocation at the hands of the absolute king. It did not require a prophet to foresee that the continent, too, was moving toward a political adjustment of the kind inaugurated by England and involving the assertion by the middle classes of a claim to the scepter of state.

An outstanding characteristic of man is that he feels impelled to justify on philosophic grounds every act which marks a departure from established practice. Not until he finds what seems to him a moral and intellectual sanction for his breach with law and custom will he rest content. It was on this account that the English Revolution had no sooner begun than a stream of books and pamphlets issued from the press defending the parliamentary position. That stream, indicative of the deep mental agitation of Englishmen, continued to broaden through the seventeenth century; and when the Revolution at last crystallized in the historic form of 1688, the man at once appeared who wrote its apology and formulated its theory. That was John Locke (1631–1704), a Whig in English party strife, the founder of what in the history of philosophy is usually called empiricism, and, finally, a keen political theorist. In his *Treatise on Government* (1689) he broke with the ancient Tory idea of a king instituted by God in favor of a purely human and earth-born doctrine. It represents the ruler as issuing from an agreement by the terms of which he serves as the executive agent of the ruled.

Locke voices the political theory of the emerging middle classes

Called the contract theory of government, it justifies the deposition of the monarch as soon as he breaks the terms imposed on him or consistently runs counter to the good of his subjects. It is a doctrine of popular sovereignty which, carried to its logical conclusion, might easily lead to frequent upsets and revolutionary excesses. These implications of his theory Locke, like the possessing classes which he represented, wished of course to avoid. In consequence the "people" of his theory of sovereignty are really only the property holders; and it was made particularly easy for Locke to arrive at this limitation since in the actual instance under his observation it was indeed the property holders who instigated the revolution and insisted on becoming its beneficiaries. The philosopher represented the reasonable, compromising temper which was asserting itself in England as a result of a long succession of evil experiences with political extremes and which was destined to become the characteristic note of political-minded, middle class Englishmen. For this temper the only proper road is always the *via media*, and under its doctrine of reasonableness, meaning nothing other than a confirmed habit of accommodation, it identifies itself with property, toleration, utility, common sense, individualism, that is, with all the forces represented by the developing middle classes. Well into the nineteenth century Locke has remained the vaunted oracle of these groups not only in England but throughout the world.

If Locke's political science has a manifest flaw, it is to be found in the deduction of his position from general principles without the least reference to the actual facts of government through the ages.

Montesquieu and the scientific method
Whatever sanctions it may possess, it can not claim the sanction of history. But as in Locke's day the collecting of data for the purpose of applying the inductive method of the natural sciences to the study of society had not yet been inaugurated, the learned Whig had no choice but to employ a deductive and rationalist proceeding. By the following century, however, scholars had developed more of a taste for facts and a Frenchman, Montesquieu, was able to present a study of government which may be said to have founded political science in its modern genetical aspect. It was in 1748 that Montesquieu published his *Spirit of the Law* (*Esprit des Lois*). It is a work of description and comparison which reaches the conclusion that there is no single "perfect" form of government but that every people normally works out a juridical and constitutional system suited to its particular situation

in the world. While it is true that Montesquieu, as a scientific pioneer, awakened a great interest in problems of government, it is improper to look upon him as a propagator of revolution. Revolution, meaning resort to swift and headlong change, accorded neither with his aristocratic temper nor with his factual, observational method.

The leading apostle of revolution was Rousseau (1712–1778), a strange, wayward son of the republic of Geneva, who, after dabbling in a score of occupations only to abandon them in turn, at last tried his hand at literature and, like other literary men of his age, Voltaire for instance, came face to face with social reform. But much more radically inclined than Voltaire, he became the hot advocate of an entirely new political order, finally setting forth his views in a manual of government called the *Social Contract* (1762). To understand the Social Contract we must first know personally about Rousseau that he carried the longing of his century for emancipation from inherited bonds to the last possible point since he craved to be emancipated from civilization itself by a return to an assumed state of nature. It is by his glowing evocation of the simple life freed from all the familiar conventions of human intercourse that he became the father of the romantic movement. Of this more anon. At this point it will suffice to make clear that when a man of this radical outlook sat himself down to sketch an ideal government, he was bound to start with a generalization commensurate in its sweep with his contempt for the existing order. That generalization rings up the curtain of the Social Contract, sounding a clear trumpet call to war: "Man is born free and everywhere he is in chains." Since under these circumstances — offered as facts needing no proof — all existing governments are bare usurpations without moral sanction, why trouble to examine and compare them? Casting Montesquieu's historical method scornfully aside and using the above postulate as a spring-board, Rousseau bounded off into the empyrean where he engaged in the exciting occupation of constructing a society of truly free men. His ideal state of the Social Contract is based on the sovereignty of the people, election and recall of magistrates, the right of insurrection, majority rule, in fact, on all the principles constituting the substance of present-day democracy. It should be noted that the Genevan philosopher's plan, radical though it is, nowhere proposes to substitute community of goods for private property. Indeed a certain caution about Rousseau restrained him from following his arguments through to their

Rousseau, the prophet of democracy

inevitable logical goal. And yet since in this, and more violently still in other writings, he preached a fanatical equality, that body of modern political extremists, whose doctrine is an unqualified communism, do him no particular wrong in worshipping him as one of the idols of their temple. Locke, Montesquieu, Rousseau mark three important stages of political theory. Locke, the advocate of reason, toleration, utility, that is, of middle courses, became the darling of the middle classes; with Montesquieu we get the application to government of the historical method, which, interesting chiefly to scholars, gained only a small following in the author's day since it promised at best no more than a gradual amelioration of human conditions; and with Rousseau we reach the liberator of the disfranchised masses, the arch-revolutionist, the prophet of an unlimited democracy.

Economic theory in this period developed along lines which run strikingly parallel to political theory. We are already aware that such economic thinking as is recorded for the Middle Age centered about the towns as the foremost economic units. Not **Rise and domination of mercantilism** till the absolute monarchy united the nation was there created even the possibility for economic thinking on a really national scale. But as the very existence of the new central power turned on the problem of revenue, the earliest and most imperative kind of thinking done by and for the strengthened monarchy was what we may call fiscal thinking. There being nothing the absolute king needed and desired so much as money, he supported a bullion policy, taking particular pains to prohibit the exportation and to favor the importation of gold and silver. From this position it was only a step to the program of a favorable balance of trade vigorously advocated on the assumption that an excess of exports over imports secures a flow of bullion to the exporting country to make up the difference. Further deductions commonly made from the bullion principle we have already encountered in connection with mercantilism, which is the name usually given the complicated economic system finally elaborated from the original fiscal premise. We have seen that mercantilism dominated every country of Europe, and that if Colbert the Frenchman, Walpole the Englishman, and Frederick the Great of Prussia are notable representatives of the economic system represented by this name, the men who preceded and followed them in office held to very much the same views and practices. Other features of mercantilism are that it favored the export of manufactures while trying to hinder their importation; that it encouraged ocean-borne commerce carried exclusively in native bottoms; and that it believed in colonies on the ground that they furnished desirable raw products while serving as a market for goods manufactured in the mother-country. Mercantilist governments were moved to favor here, prohibit there, regulate and control everywhere on the theory that this interference was socially necessary and economically advantageous.

Such a system the eighteenth century, supremely interested in liberating itself from every kind of bondage, was not likely to leave unchallenged. Toward 1750 there came to the front in France a group of students who began the application of the scientific method to the economic field and thereby as certainly became the fathers of the science of political economy as their contemporary, Montesquieu, was the father of the science of politics. They called themselves physiocrats and of course made only a beginning since they did not succeed in entirely clearing their brains of all the old metaphysical cobwebs. But they did grasp that there existed a body of economic laws with something of the sweep and dignity of the natural laws of the astronomers and that it was suicidal to attempt to interfere with their operation. Above all, they pointed out that the government's regulating and checking the economic processes at every turn was in substance no more than mischievous meddling which hindered enterprise and was mainly responsible for the curse of poverty. They coined the slogan, *laissez faire* (let alone!), and agitated in favor of a complete abandonment of government supervision in order that the creative energy of the individual might unfold itself without let or hindrance.

While the French physiocrats were still groping their way toward a new economic philosophy, their cause was taken up by a masterful champion across the channel, the Scotsman, Adam Smith. In 1776 he published his famous *Wealth of Nations*. Smith is not only the advocate of the removal of all trade restrictions (for which reason he has remained identified with free trade), but he reaches the conclusion that the basic factor in production is human labor and that if man is to bring his highest energy into play he must needs enjoy the greatest possible degree of freedom. By this philosophic line of argument the keen Scotsman showed that he moved in the line of middle class thought and possessed the key to middle class evolution. Already Locke had broken a lance for utility and reasonableness in government; and now Smith argued in their behalf in economics, his whole exposition culminating in the demand for the free untrammeled individual. A society of liberated men and women would need no regulative principle beyond their enlightened self-interest and, with state interference withdrawn, would soon produce wealth on a scale undreamed of in the period of economic bondage. If ever the middle classes, who have so largely made the modern world, build a Pantheon to their great men, they owe it to themselves to reserve a prominent niche for Adam Smith.

With the thought of this period directed so largely to emancipation we are prepared for the great forward strides of that arch-emancipator, science. Already the previous period had culminated, with the Physical work of Galileo, in the discovery of a successful method science: for penetration into the physical world. Its adoption by Newton investigators of every conceivable variety coupled with a certain amount of necessary accommodation to each particular field of study would be certain to unlock in ever increasing measure the secrets of Nature. Hardly a generation after Galileo's death the crown was set on his and Kepler's labors by the Englishman, Sir Isaac Newton, who combined all the discoveries of his predecessors into one of the most startling as well as simple generalizations that have ever been elaborated by the human mind. In 1686 Newton in his *Principia* announced the law of universal gravitation which showed that the apple dropping to the ground was part of the same general force which held the planets in their courses. The discovery of the laws of gravitation brought to a noble close a group of related labors covering almost two hundred years.

While continuing its exploration of the physical world, the spirit of human curiosity guided by the new method now turned its attention to the plants and animals of the earth and for the first time produced The dawn of a botany and zoölogy that rested on a solid observational chemistry basis. Space is lacking to describe these and other advances, but our main purpose will be served if it becomes clear that every department of knowledge registered and was bound to register conquests of bewildering scope the moment it threw overboard the old petrified learning and made a fresh start trusting to the new tools. Certainly an outstanding achievement was the creation of modern chemistry. This was the work of the Frenchman, Lavoisier (1743-1794), after a number of valiant predecessors had in the usual manner blazed a trail for him. Lavoisier was the first chemist to resolve water into its elements; thereafter, with the aid of others, he provided his science with a serviceable nomenclature. From the end of the eighteenth century chemistry went forward with amazing rapidity. Its intensive cultivation indicated that men were passing from the consideration of problems dealing with matter in motion to the subtler problems of the constitution of matter. The next great step would logically be the passing from chemistry to biology, that is, to the mysterious processes of life itself. That step with its revolutionary consequences was duly taken in the nineteenth century.

Among the varied interests bound to attract the attention of a keen physical observer like Galileo was the problem of the pressure of gases. Numerous experiments conducted by the great Tuscan and his Italian followers and finally carried on throughout Europe led to a concentration on the most obvious of all gases, water-vapor. Some crude engines, utilizing the expansive power of steam, were constructed until a serviceable engine for pumping water had been put together. *Science and invention: Watt's steam engine*
By adding a number of improvements the Scotsman, James Watt, was at last enabled to build an engine capable of driving a machine. In 1769 he patented his invention, which with subsequent alterations by himself and others was taken over by the textile industry of England, thus inaugurating one of the most momentous movements in the history of mankind, the movement known as the Industrial Revolution. However, since this revolution got only slowly under way and did not work its magic transformations till the nineteenth century, we are content at this point to note the relation between science and invention and to indicate the probability that, in measure as science extended its dominion, its discoveries would be appropriated by men of an inventive turn and utilized for the creation of machines and other devices calculated by making life less laborious for the human race to make it gradually more generally enjoyable.

The movement of modern philosophy starting with Descartes continued for some time along his general line. Other philosophers arose who, like him, both took account of the new world picture due to modern scientific discovery and held to the inherited view that it was possible to fuse all knowledge into a logical system dominated by a group of coherent concepts. *Philosophy comes down to earth with Locke*
The habit of system-building had been contracted in the Middle Age and in consequence of a firm faith, which nothing had

yet shaken, in one God, Creator and Sustainer, men fairly thirsted for majestic metaphysical constructions. Spinoza (d. 1677) and Leibnitz (d. 1716) may be cited as illustrative of this comprehensible and long continued philosophic trend. But it also came about that a certain revulsion set in against these over-bold philosophies as being too pretentious in view of the limited powers of the human mind; and characteristically it was in matter-of-fact, deistic England of the Restoration Period that the protest first made itself clearly heard. John Locke, the same man who endowed the Whigs with their political doctrine, is largely responsible for drawing Dame Philosophy from her ancient habitat among the clouds and setting her feet upon the earth. He achieved this result by diverting attention from the unfruitful discussion about God and immortality which had been going on for ages to the fundamental, though perhaps no less vexatious, problem of knowledge. In his *Essay on Human Understanding* (1690) he undertook to show that we acquire knowledge in two ways, first, through our senses, and second, through that mysterious entity, the human mind. In substance Locke declared that before we wrestle with problems that have balked the wise men of every generation, we would be doing well to study the means at our disposal for penetrating the darkness all around us. He thus achieved a shift of emphasis and inaugurated a practical, observational study of the mind which tended to convert metaphysics into psychology. Turning from heaven to earth, he is correctly characterized as an empiricist.

Plainly the tendency of Locke is sceptical so far as the purposes and claims of traditional philosophy are concerned. In the generations after Locke this scepticism grew until with the Scotsman Hume

Kant and the autonomy of science it dropped to a level close to complete negation. Substantially what Hume said was that we have no certainty about anything and are helpless to achieve it. Under these circumstances not only philosophy but science itself became enveloped in a cloud of doubt, which was not cleared away till Emanuel Kant, a native of Königsberg in Prussia (1724–1804), spoke his weighty word. What Kant chiefly did in his *Critique of Reason* and other works was to disentangle from one another science, philosophy (metaphysics), and theology and to assign to each a definite province and technique. Throughout the Middle Age these three studies had been considered as inseparable parts of a single empire of knowledge in which theology ruled as lord and dictator. Although that conception had been breaking down in recent generations, it still held sufficiently in influential circles to hamper seriously all three disciplines since they were too intimately bound together to secure to each its requisite degree of freedom. Kant's achievement was to prove by his deductions that in its own particular world, the world of appearances (phenomena), science was not a dependent but an absolute master. In this way he freed the pursuit of practical, mundane knowledge from the control of either the theologian or the philosopher. But in liberating science Kant did not depress the status of theology and philosophy. For them too he staked out independent realms where each was as free of the other as both were free of science. Not improbably this division of knowledge into air-tight compartments was a specious procedure which may ultimately break down; coming when it did, it rendered a great service to a still trammeled science by cutting its remaining chains and clearing the road for its unimpeded onward march.

To sketch even hastily the literary and artistic currents of this period would require a separate chapter for which there is unfortunately no room. Doubtless it would add its touches, important touches too, to the picture of the age for the reason that The literature and art are particularly sensitive to changes romantic of opinion and feeling and never fail to reflect them in movement their creations. For information on the varied and many-voiced message of the artists and writers the student will have to be referred to the special histories devoted to these matters and to be content in this swift review of a given period of culture with the consideration of a single novel agency which, projected into literature and art in the eighteenth century, almost as completely revolutionized them as the parallel movement of science revolutionized knowledge. I am referring to romanticism. It can be traced back to many distant sources and burst on Europe only after a long gestation; but as Rousseau is commonly accepted as its father and admittedly was its chief promoter, we shall find our task somewhat simplified if we attempt to understand romanticism in the light of his activity. We have already seen that Rousseau reacted passionately against the elaborate conventions of society and dreamed of a life of simplicity and innocence which, in certain extravagant moods at least, he imagined to be identical with an original and long since vanished state of nature. The real secret of his violent rejection of the contemporary world was that its social, literary, and artistic leaders had fallen more and more under the domination of a dry, ultilitarian intellectualism which aimed at improving man by stifling the untamed energy of his instincts and emotions. As these were to Rousseau the most precious thing in life, he heatedly asserted their inalienable right against the tyranny of the controlling mind. In his novel, *La Nouvelle Héloise* (1759), he disclosed the world of feeling from which his contemporaries had become estranged and which they received back at his hands with extravagant expressions of delight. In this novel and in other works as well he invited men to give themselves whole-heartedly to love — to love of God, nature, woman, and the whole wide gamut of creation. Romanticism, considered as a historic movement, signifies the recovery of these deepest well-springs of our being coupled with the rejection of purely intellectual norms of living. By effecting a release of our neglected basic energies it opened a new chapter in literature and art among all the peoples of Europe.

But romanticism did more than quarrel with the pedantic self-satisfaction and intellectual arrogance which characterized the dying, eighteenth century phase of the Renaissance movement; it took issue also with the frozen *forms* of literature and art, which, approved by long practice, claimed the high distinction of being sacrosanct and "classical." Forms of this character, whether of the drama and the lyric poem or of the portrait and the mural decoration, are not very serviceable for the expression of spontaneous feeling, and Rousseau and his romantic contemporaries tried their best to modify and even to replace them with new forms. In the end a new pulsating literature (and art) came to the fore which in casting off the formalism of the past incidentally provided itself also with fresh subject-matter. Than this nothing was more natural since in strict keeping with its narrow outlook classicism had taken account of life only at its highest social level. The French drama of the seventeenth and even of the eighteenth century will bear witness to this contention and the same situation may be observed in English literature from Addison to Pope. A review will show that the writers of the period named dealt chiefly with kings and queens, with lords and ladies. Starting as a movement of rebellion against an established aristocratic prejudice, romanticism reached out until it embraced within its scope the whole of humanity. The poets and painters of the movement therefore quite naturally turned for inspiration to the

The romantic movement not only a literary but a moral and social movement

peasant, the sailor, the carter, and other representatives of the common man; in fact they discovered the democratic masses and by declaring them worthy of artistic treatment added to their prestige and contributed powerfully to the advent of nineteenth century democracy. While it is usual to consider romanticism as a movement purely of the arts of expression, it should be clear from this exposition that it is much more than that. It is a sweeping moral and social revaluation, of which the outstanding features are first, a protest against the priggish domination of an upper class and its literary henchmen, and second, a flaming demand of freedom and justice for the humble and submerged.

In looking back over the matters treated in this chapter we receive the unmistakable impression that European civilization was entering on a new phase in which the middle classes with their increased wealth and improved mental equipment would play a *The stage* dominating role. While they give evidence of a steadily *cleared for* mounting self-assurance, they have as yet only in the *the middle* Dutch Republic and to a lesser degree in England reached *classes* out for political power. When in the year 1789 the French middle classes took a famous revolutionary step and wrested the scepter from the enfeebled hand of their Bourbon sovereign, they really did no more than give effect to a movement which had been maturing in the womb of time for several generations. And when the middle classes of the neighboring countries were fired by the French example to similar ambitions, this too was to be expected in view of the essentially identical conditions prevailing throughout the west-European area. Even the fact that the democratic masses projected themselves into the French Revolution, thereby deflecting it from its bourgeois ends and producing a frightful chaos, can be accounted for on the basis of the previous popular awakening effected by the romantic movement. But the masses failed; their inexperience and lack of organization proved fatal to them. Plainly their day had not yet come. It would dawn, if it dawned at all, only after the Industrial Revolution had packed the machine workers by the thousands into manufacturing centers and with their numbers had given them a sense of irresistible power. Conceding that already on the stage of the eighteenth century, the city mob, raising an indistinct, raucous murmur in the background, is a disquieting phenomenon, we can not escape the impression that the central space, the place of honor, has been cleared for the entrance of the middle classes. They were at last to achieve the full fruition of their arduous labors of the past.

But before the action of the triumphant middle classes unfolds itself, let us take note that the dimensions of the European stage had tremendously expanded. At the very outset we laid down certain Impressive predications touching European civilization. We in- spread of sisted that it inhered by origin in a limited area identical European with the dominion of the Latin Church in the Middle civilization Age; that within this area it had everywhere essentially the same physiognomy; and that, starting from the platform of a common religious faith, the various peoples constituting western Europe had without exception been shaped by the same outstanding experiences. However, that does not mean that innovations and new attitudes manifested themselves evenly throughout the occident and at exactly the same time. They usually originated in a limited group, radiating thence till they had been brought to all the others and been woven into the stuff of life. The Renaissance, an Italian movement, is a case in point, as is also the Reformation, incubated in Germany. As for the great contributions of the seventeenth and eighteenth centuries which we have just reviewed, they originated chiefly in England and France, where the middle classes were most alert and the specific middle class mentality was first formed. But in accordance with the usual practice and because western Europe had a long established cultural unity, the new ideas gradually filtered through the whole area, though by no means evenly since in some countries the middle classes, on whom the issue turned, were still weak and under feudal domination. But if in the light of the past it was reasonably clear that the occident would, though perhaps with uneasy fluctuations, continue to behave as a unit, it now for the first time became apparent that such was the vigor of occidental civilization that it would crowd upon the domain of rival civilizations and gradually supplant them. That the very primitive culture of the American Indians would go down before Europe had been demonstrated from the first moment of contact following the discoveries. By the eighteenth century both South and North America, at least in so far as they were under colonial rule, already represented a material as well as a spiritual extension of Europe. It was far more expressive of the strength of Europe that even relatively advanced civilizations could not resist the European onslaught. In the days of Peter the Great Russia surren- dered to it bag and baggage; and though the great Slav empire long remained in what we may call the apprentice class, its whole-hearted acceptance of western methods and objectives gave it an irresistible push and prepared the way for the Europeanization of half of Asia. When the English at last ejected the French from India and in all seriousness took in hand the government of their vast new dependency, another civilization, one of the oldest and most subtle the world has known, registered the impact of a more vital movement and slowly retreated before it. In short, if Europe in the sixteenth century, with the voyages of discovery, inaugurated a period of physical expansion, this by the close of the eighteenth century had led not only to the economic exploitation of large subject-areas throughout the world but also to the mental conquest of numerous peoples endowed often with a by no means negligible civilization of their own. It is not too much to say that a civilization of a very definite character and hatched in a circumscribed section of Europe was reaching out to take possession of every continent. If it imposed itself often by war and related violent means, it just as often was taken over voluntarily on the strength of its indubitable superiority. In either case it was busy making the world over in its image. In the difficult adjustments necessitated by these far-reaching developments lay the assurance of tremendous and prolonged disturbances in the time to come, but also the promise, no more than the shadow of a hope perhaps, of the ultimate drawing together of all the peoples of the earth on the basis of a common understanding.

REFERENCES

E. R. TURNER, *Europe, 1450–1789*, chs. 22–26
A. TILLEY, *Modern France*, pp. 242–71
Cambridge Modern History, VI, chs. 13, 19, 23, 24
C. H. HAYES, *Political and Social History*, I, chs. 13, 14
A. L. CROSS, *England and Greater Britain*, ch. 44
J. B. BURY, *The Idea of Progress*
J. N. FIGGIS, *Divine Right of Kings*
H. HIGGS, *The Physiocrats*
W. W. STEPHENS, *Life and Writings of Turgot*
H. E. BOURNE, *Revolutionary Period in Europe*, chs. 1–5
W. A. DUNNING, *Political Theories from Luther to Montesquieu*
J. MORLEY, *Rousseau; Voltaire*
A. H. JOHNSON, *Enlightened Despots*, ch. 10
H. M. STEPHENS, *Portugal*, ch. 16
F. A. OGG, *Economic Development of Modern Europe*, ch. 4
H. L. LASKI, *Political Thought in England from Locke to Bentham*
J. M. ROBERTSON, *Short History of Free Thought*
W. WINDELBAND (tr. by Tufts), *History of Philosophy*

W. T. Sedgwick and H. W. Tyler, *Short History of Science*
O. Lodge, *Pioneers of Science*
A. Berry, *Short History of Astronomy*
F. Cajori, *History of Physics*
W. A. Shaw, *History of Currency*
E. Cheyney, *Industrial and Social History of England*
W. C. Webster, *General History of Commerce*
C. Day, *History of Commerce*
H. de B. Gibbins, *Industry in England*

REVOLUTION AND DEMOCRACY FROM 1789 TO OUR OWN DAY

CHAPTER XIX

THE FRENCH REVOLUTION AND NAPOLEON

The long reign of Louis XV (1715–1774) was disastrous not only to France but also to the monarchy. The disgraceful termination of the colonial struggle with England fell like a blight upon the state, while the system of taxation which favored the old feudal orders and rested with extortionate severity upon the common people tended to spread discontent and maintain a perpetual sense of injury and injustice. In these circumstances the court, supported at Versailles on a scale of wanton magnificence, became a favorite target of criticism. Its lavish expenditure was not in the least reduced when the long drawn-out wars impoverished the country and exhausted the treasury; and what was even worse than its splendor maintained amidst the general misery, its moral tone declined under a voluptuary like Louis XV until with the advent to power of the official mistress, Madame de Pompadour, it seemed as if vice and frivolity had usurped the scepter of the kingdom. A modern French historian has strikingly voiced his sense of the situation by declaring that Louis XV "gangrened" the monarchy. *(Louis XV discredits the monarchy)*

The most significant effect of this open and flagrant failure of government was the formation of a hostile public opinion which was fed by the spoken word and, in spite of a vigorous censorship, uninterruptedly found its way into print. Indeed long before Louis XV's reign came to an end a criticism had sprung to life as clamorous and many-voiced as a frog-pond in spring. *(Growth of a critical opinion)* Voltaire was its leader and, although he threw himself with particular glee upon bigotry and unreason in the Church, he never failed to discharge his biting shaft at any abuse whatever in society and government which came under his notice. Around Voltaire gathered scores of lesser lights, all set on spreading the doctrine of "enlightenment" and bringing the traditional institutions to the test of reason. At the side of these swift skirmishers, who called themselves philosophers and really were a band of sublimated journalists, stood men of a more serious turn — physiocrats, like the elder Mirabeau, who studied the phenomenon of wealth; political scientists, like Montesquieu and Rousseau, who probed into the mysteries of government; and natural scientists like Buffon and Lavoisier, engaged in conquering new continents of knowledge. In sum, during her eighteenth century degradation under Louis XV France produced a unique array of writers and thinkers who furnished her with a wholly new equipment of ideas. And since every government ultimately rests on opinion, we may safely conclude that changes were impending in the French system expressive of the altered state of the public mind. The dissolute old king was himself occasionally visited by forebodings of disaster. He would then relieve his mind with the cynical remark: "Things will hold together till my death," while his friend, Madame de Pompadour, would add cheerily, "After us the deluge!"

On his death in 1774 Louis XV was succeeded by his grandson, Louis XVI. The new sovereign, not quite twenty years old, was a shy, awkward man, prone to corpulence and irresolution. To confirm the alliance with Austria he had been married to Marie Antoinette, daughter of the famous Empress Maria Theresa and a woman — or rather a girl, for she was only eighteen — of unusual vivacity and charm. Had she possessed the political intelligence of her mother, she might have been of considerable help to the bewildered young man who was her husband; but as she lacked the seriousness necessary to wrestle with the problems of government, such influence as she exercised was prompted by personal bias and usually harmful to the public interest. Mixed into Louis's average endowments was a measure of good will, also average, which he was resolved to exercise in behalf of his people. The clamor of enlightened opinion had penetrated the secluded precincts of Versailles and made the young king hesitantly desirous to become a benefactor and reformer. Besides, the finances were in such confusion that something had imperatively to be done about them. There was a large debt inherited from the past, an obstinate annual deficit, and a critical, exacerbated public unwilling to bear additional taxation. Responding to this situation, Louis began his reign by dismissing the whole body of the discredited ministers inherited from his grandfather

The accession of Louis XVI

and by putting the treasury into the hands of Turgot as comptroller general.

He could not have made a better choice, for Turgot was not only a thoughtful economist, a physiocrat, but a practical administrator as well who had served for over a decade as intendant of Limoges, where he had successfully introduced a number of local reforms. He took from the first a large, statesmanlike view of the situation and, instead of losing himself in financial details, developed a broad program of national renovation. What France needed, according to him, was to cancel the privileges enjoyed by the feudal orders in the matter of taxation, to put an end to the monopolistic system of industry identified with the gilds, and to reduce and perhaps finally to abandon entirely the intimate control of trade exercised by the state in obedience to the old mercantilist philosophy. It was a program which aimed at lifting from the country the dead-weight of tradition and unifying the nation on the basis of economic liberty and equality of taxation; moreover, as it accorded with enlightened public opinion, it would, if successfully carried through, have modernized France without the necessity of a revolution.

Louis calls Turgot to office

But the program failed. Inaugurated in 1774, it scored a number of successes, such as the establishment of free trade in grain, the abolition of the *corvée*, the hated obligatory service of the peasants in connection with the maintenance of the public highways, and the destruction of the gilds, whereby the crafts were opened to whoever chose to exercise them. After two years, with his work only just begun, Turgot was dismissed (1776). The reason is not far to seek. As soon as the comptroller general, instead of indulging in the usual window-dressing of ministers of finance, laid the ax to the French upas-tree and attacked the parasitical system of privileges, all the groups which had any interest in the maintenance of abuses combined against him. Clergy, nobles, gild-masters, and the hordes of speculators who grafted on the corrupt finances were equally aroused and were immeasurably delighted to have their opposition voiced in the parlement of Paris. This, like the twelve other provincial parlements, was an integral feature of the privileged régime, since it consisted of a judiciary which was irremovable and hereditary. Enjoying by custom the right of refusing to register the king's edicts, the parlement was moved to throw itself across Turgot's path, but was pushed aside by the royal command communicated in a

Turgot's attack on privilege

formal session (*lit de justice*). If Louis had continued to stand resolutely by his reforming minister, it might well have been that the opposition, though only after a prolonged and bitter struggle, would have broken down; however, Louis was weak and, to make matters worse, he lived his life in the exclusive company of high-born gentlemen and ladies who daily poured their irritation over Turgot into his ears. Tired of the sour faces of the courtiers, he at last yielded to their pressure and sent the great statesman away. Thereupon frenzied cheers from the representatives of privilege, withdrawal of Turgot's edicts, and a prompt return to the old abuses!

However, as the financial problem could not be evaded, Louis now submitted it for solution to Necker, a native of Geneva, who, as a young man, had come to Paris where he had made his fortune as a **Necker,** banker. Necker, a fairly good administrator but certainly **1776–1781** not a statesman, contented himself with introducing a certain degree of thrift and efficiency into the public service. Doubtless he thus somewhat reduced the deficit, but whatever advantage he secured was completely sacrificed when the government resolved (1778) to make an alliance with the rebellious American colonists in order once more to try conclusions with Great Britain over the issue of colonies and sea-power. The enormous war expenditure could only be met by loans, the heavy interest on which continued after the war and embarrassed the treasury more than ever. But even the very modest reform program of Necker angered the privileged intriguers at court and in 1781 they persuaded the king to let him go.

It was now perfectly clear that the clergy, the nobles, and the court formed a cabal which would continue indefinitely to paralyze the feeble volition of the sovereign and keep things as they were. Reform **The nation** form from above was therefore a chimæra and the only **demands** certain way to clean up the Augean stables was for the **the States** nation itself to take the work in hand. In this way the **General** reform sentiment gradually mounted to a revolutionary pitch, manifesting itself at last in a demand for the States General. That was the old feudal assembly, which, having met for the last time in 1614, had perished from disuse. To the ill-informed and romantically minded generation which lived under the scepter of Louis XVI the States General looked like a body genuinely representative of the nation and thoroughly capable of legislating the country back to health. First here, then there the call was heard for this national council until the demand rose finally as from a single throat.

Meanwhile the utterly helpless king charged one man after another with the task of disentangling the royal finances. New loans could not be raised because the credit of the state was ruined, while new taxes could not be levied because the parlement refused to register the edicts and the king's authority had declined to such a point that he could no longer successfully impose his will on the recalcitrant members. When the government, staggering like a drunken man, at last returned to the sweeping reform program of Turgot, public opinion, now become a fiery flood, refused to take the announcement seriously. The reform of France was no longer considered to be the business of the king but of the nation. By the summer of 1788 the monarchy was absolutely paralyzed; there was no longer either authority or obedience and the only possibility of avoiding immediate bankruptcy — the forerunner of a general collapse — was for Louis to surrender to the popular will. He did so in characteristic listless despair. Because Turgot was dead and because of all the names connected with the cause of reform Necker's enjoyed the greatest currency, the king recalled Necker to office and at the same time issued a call for the States General for May, 1789.

Beside themselves with joy, Frenchmen at first hardly stopped to consider what sort of an assembly the resuscitated States General were. But presently as the antiquarians, grubbing among the dusty records, recovered its physiognomy, the nation learned Necker that the three groups, the clergy, the nobility, and the concedes commoners, called in French usage respectively the First, double representation Second, and Third Estates, met as three separate houses to the Third and that the privileged orders were always able to out- Estate vote the representatives of the people by two to one. At this information public sentiment gave evidence of disappointment and alarm. To conciliate it Necker took the half-step of ordering that the Third Estate should send twice as many delegates to Versailles as either of the other orders, that is, the commoners should have approximately six hundred delegates to the same number divided equally between nobles and clergy. On the one really crucial point as to whether the assembly should be constituted in three houses, as tradition required, or merged in a single house, as public opinion insisted, the minister wrapped himself in an enigmatic silence.

In the spring of 1789 France was stirred by the wholly unfamiliar phenomenon of a general election. In each bailiwick the electors met in three assemblies according to their legal status, and after drawing up a list of grievances (*cahier*) to be presented to the government, elected their respective delegates to the States General. On May 5, 1789, Louis XVI opened the session with a few words of welcome and Necker followed with a wearisome exposition of the financial chaos. It is indicative of the minister's feeble grasp of the situation that he imagined the States General were going to vote the government a few new taxes and humbly retire from the scene. Any one but a tyro would have sensed that, sustained by the people, they would be content with nothing less than a complete reorganization of the administration. The glaring difference of viewpoint brought an immediate clash. The first meeting over, the government expected the three estates to constitute at once their separate organizations. The two privileged orders were in their majority not in the least averse to the suggestion, but the commons were firmly set on a single house, since only in this way could they get the full benefit of their numerical preponderance. The result was a deadlock. The First and Second Estates organized as the king commanded, but the Third Estate refused to take the least step toward the same end. Assembling each day informally, the members declined to proceed with business until the other two estates had joined them.

Opening of the States General and recalcitrancy of the Third Estate

Over this issue a tremendous crisis was precipitated, which was decided by an irresistible public opinion. Since the favor of the people massed itself like a tidal wave behind the Third Estate, the delegates simply waited till they felt strong enough to go ahead without regard to the royal wishes. On June 17th they for the last time summoned the other two estates and then voted themselves the National Assembly with or without their colleagues of the clergy and nobility. It was a revolutionary act destructive alike of the old constitution and the authority of the king. Spurred on by the courtiers to defend his rights, Louis now closed with troops the hall where the Third Estate met. To this challenge the undaunted commoners responded by meeting on a near-by tennis court and taking a solemn vow to continue their sessions until they had given their country a new constitution (June 20th). A more frank avowal of their revolutionary purpose was impossible. The king met their defiance by calling a formal session wherein, after lecturing the delegates on their misconduct, he reiterated his inalterable resolution of maintaining the old States General in its tricameral form. As agreement seemed out

The States General becomes the National Assembly

of the question, civil war would certainly have followed if one side had not given way. Of course it was the king who yielded. On June 27th he announced a new inalterable decision in the form of an order to the two privileged estates to join the commoners and complete the happy family. On that June day the monarchy, manifestly a broken reed, saw its authority slip into the hands of the National Assembly which in effect took over the government.

THE NATIONAL ASSEMBLY (1789-1791)

The National Assembly, thus raised aloft over the nation, boasted among its members many of the most alert and intelligent men of the country. In spite of the fact that the Assembly contained a party of clerical and noble irreconcilables who vigorously re- Preponderance of the homogenous body in respect of the great matter of the commoners sented the turn affairs had taken, it constituted a fairly renovation of France, since a group of liberal nobles and an even larger group of liberal clergymen frankly took their stand with their fellow-citizens of the Third Estate. The division in the two upper orders greatly weakened them and in the end proved even more of a blow to the traditional rights of the clergy than to those of the nobility. Within the clergy, in spite of its being legally one estate, there existed really two distinct social strata, for the great prelates (bishops and abbots) were men of noble birth, whereas the parish priests, generally speaking, belonged to the urban group and to the peasantry. In the great political issues debated in the National Assembly the priests, constituting a majority of the clerical membership, sided with their kin of the Third Estate, thus contributing considerably to the numerical preponderance of the commoners.

In consequence of these circumstances and particularly because of its victory over the king the National Assembly began its labors in an atmosphere of extraordinary exultation. Without any doubt whatever the members were in overwhelming majority Enthusiasm animated with a noble enthusiasm to give their country and the best service that was in them. It was no negligible theoretical matter that this spirit of magnanimity presided, generally bias of the speaking, over their sessions. And yet what good it may Assembly have done was largely neutralized by a momentous defect. Educated theoretically but not practically in the affairs of government, the members were prone to treat all questions as occasions for the display of an emotional eloquence and to formulate decrees, beautiful in the abstract but hopelessly out of relation to the concrete facts. When the Assembly convened there existed as yet no political parties. But gradually parties began to form about individuals who championed a program of some sort and who by virtue of their talents forged to the front. Only a few of these can be pointed out here. The Marquis de Lafayette had won a great name for himself by the magnanimous offer of his sword, when a young man, to the cause of freedom in America. Though a nobleman by birth, he sympathized with the people, rallied the liberal wing of the nobles about himself, and was accepted by a large section of the bourgeoisie as its leader. No man during the early months of the Revolution had a greater following within and without the Assembly. The best representative of the current dogmatic and philosophical spirit was the Abbé Sieyès. He carried to absurd lengths the idea that government was a clever mechanism, capable of being constructed in accordance with preconceived ideas. When one constitution failed, he was always ready, political conjurer that he was rather than organic thinker, to shake another out of his sleeve. Then there was the lawyer Robespierre, who hailed from the small town of Arras. Sharing with a handful of other members democratic sentiments which he had drawn from his idol, Rousseau, he never spoke without parading a patriotism of an incorruptible Roman grandeur. However, the member who without doubt towered head and shoulders above the rest of the Assembly was Count Mirabeau. Mirabeau was a born statesman, perhaps the only man in the whole Assembly who instinctively knew that a government could not be fashioned at will by a committee of philosophers, but to be worth anything must be the natural expression of the moral, economic, and historical forces ruling the nation. He wished, therefore, while preserving the monarchy, to *nationalize* it by injecting into its enfeebled arteries the fresh blood of the commoners. If he had had his way he would have abolished all privileges in order to create a unified people, the members of which would be equal before the law; and he would have given the king a considerable measure of authority on condition that he exercise it in coöperation with a legislature elected by the people. Unfortunately he never succeeded in acquiring a guiding influence. In the first place, he was a noble and therefore subject to suspicion on the score of birth; and, further, his early life had been a succession of scandals, which had filled the public prints

The leaders (margin note)

for more than a decade and kept him under a moral cloud which
never lifted.

In strict accord with the Oath of the Tennis Court of June 20th
the National Assembly considered its main function to be the making
of a new constitution. It was of the highest importance that this
work should be done in perfect security, free from the Calamitous
interference of popular passion and violence. But, owing influence of
to the excitement permeating the whole population, the the masses
Assembly soon fell under the domination of the street. The growth
of the influence of the lower elements, who, while desiring reform,
created anarchy, is the most appalling feature of the great events of
1789. If we understand this fact, we have the key to the extraordinarily rapid descent of French society to complete dissolution.

For this degeneration the king and the Assembly were both responsible, as well by reason of what they did as of what they did
not do. It goes without saying that the sudden failure of absolutism
in 1789 demoralized the government and threw France Failure of
into unutterable confusion. Parisian and provincial mobs the author-
frequently fell upon and murdered the royal officials, ity of the
while the excited peasants everywhere burned and plun- king and the
dered the castles of the nobles. In view of these danger- Assembly
ous and unprofitable excesses king and National Assembly should
have united to maintain order; but unite they would not, because the
king, who was under the domination of a reactionary court, looked
askance at the triumphant Assembly, and because for its part the
Assembly feared the designs of the court and the king. Mutual suspicion ruined harmony and played into the hands of the anarchists
and agitators.

Early in July the court party engaged in a plot which only too
fully justified the suspicious attitude of the Assembly. His intimates
persuaded the king, who as usual was not hard to persuade (though
hard to keep persuaded), to reëstablish his authority by The fall of
means of troops. Soldiers were accordingly concentrated the Bastille,
around Paris to overawe the citizens as the necessary July 14,
step preliminary to dismissing the popular ministers, 1789
such as Necker, and to dissolving the Assembly. At the sight of the
soldiers a tremendous excitement took hold of the people; and although, to calm the populace, the troops were again withdrawn, vast

¹ For this reason the National Assembly is known also as the Constituent
Assembly.

crowds, seizing what weapons came to hand, gathered in the streets. Savagely resolved to teach the court a lesson, they at last threw themselves (July 14th) upon the Bastille, a royal fortress and state prison in the eastern section of the capital. After a brief encounter involving not a little bloodshed, the small garrison of ancient invalids, who held the gloomy stronghold, surrendered to the multitude. They were butchered almost to a man and the fury of the enraged mob did not subside till it had begun the work of razing the hated fortress to the ground.

Like the famous shot fired at Lexington in 1775, the fall of the Bastille was heard around the world. Everywhere excited opinion interpreted it as signifying the end of tyranny and the dawn of a new era of brotherly love. We must in this connection remember that the Bastille was more than an ordinary fortress. Because the French kings had employed it as the living grave of those of their subjects who ventured to criticize their policy, it had become the outstanding symbol of their absolutism. Arrested on the private order of the sovereign by what was called a *lettre de cachet*, the bold critics disappeared behind the solid masonry of the Bastille to be held in confinement without trial subject to the royal pleasure. It was this system that was levelled to the earth with the Bastille; it was arbitrary power culminating in arbitrary arrest that stood condemned. Small wonder that France and the neighboring countries, too often cursed with the same system, should have rejoiced and prophesied a millennium in which the triple blessing of liberty, equality, and fraternity would hold undisputed sway. Of course it need hardly be expressly said that the storming of the Bastille did not bring the fulfilment of this Utopian dream; but because it did put an end to an immediate tyranny, it is at least intelligible that French republicans should ever since have cherished the fourteenth of July as the birthday of a new era.

The most immediate consequence of the Bastille uprising was that the plan of turning back the revolutionary tide by force was abruptly abandoned. Plainly the court party was beaten and its most violent members, with the count of Artois, the king's younger brother at its head, resolved to show their disgust by leaving the uncongenial soil of France. In this way began the so-called emigration, which, continuing in the following years, soon collected in every country of Europe, but chiefly in Germany along the Rhine, many thousand members of the old privileged orders.

While most of these *émigrés* were warlike nobles, there was a fair sprinkling of clergymen among them.   In their various places of retreat the exiles were not only spared the hateful sight of a triumphant people but were also free to spin plots calculated to restore them to the fleshpots of "the good old days."

By administering a rebuke to the king the storming of the Bastille helped fill the National Assembly with a renewed sense of its ascendancy.   To recover a little of his popularity Louis paid (July 17th) a formal visit to Paris during which he put the seal of his approval on everything the people had seen fit to do. *Lafayette and the* He was received with transports of joy, for his subjects *National* had not yet plucked the old loyalty to the hereditary *Guard* dynasty from their hearts.   He also endorsed two political creations by which the bourgeoisie had attempted to restore order to the disturbed capital.   Since all government had broken down and every man's goods were at the mercy of his neighbor, the property owners of Paris had set up, first, a new municipal government and second, a militia or National Guard pledged to maintain the peace.   Nuclei of order in a dissolving society, they were imitated throughout France and contributed not a little to hinder the country from going completely to pieces.   The popular Lafayette was elected head of the Parisian National Guard; and when the militia of the capital affiliated itself with that of the provincial towns Lafayette was accepted as commander-in-chief of the whole organization.   His headship of so considerable an armed force made him a preëminent figure in the political world, more particularly because the regular army, owing to the desertion of the noble officers and the impact of revolutionary sentiment on the rank and file, had largely dissolved.   In the summer of 1789 Lafayette was undoubtedly the most powerful individual in the country, on whom rested almost exclusively the maintenance of internal peace.   And yet such was the excitement stirring the country from end to end and such were the violences manifesting themselves in ever recurring fits of fever that even had Lafayette been less of a dilettante than he was, it is extremely doubtful whether he would have been able to keep the situation firmly in hand.

The test of Lafayette's control of the elements of disorder did not have to be long awaited.   In October the rumor of another plot on the part of the remnant of the court party ran through Paris.   Excited men and women told one another that at a banquet of officers, held at Versailles, the new national cockade of red, blue, and white, the passionately adored emblem of the Revolution, had been trampled under foot and the health of the king and queen drunk amid scenes of wild enthusiasm. What really happened was an act of homage, The events perhaps unnecessarily demonstrative, on the part of of October officers toward their sovereign; but suspicion of the king 5th and 6th and court had sunk so deeply into the hearts of the Parisians that even the most senseless invention was sure to be believed. To further blow upon the flames demagogues circulated the whispered news that the king was the cause of the famine in the city and that he and the court intercepted the grain-carts outside of Paris in order to reduce the capital to starvation. These allegations served to arouse the fear of a new military plot and precipitated a fresh explosion. On the morning of October 5th 10,000 women, fierce and haggard from long suffering, set out for Versailles to fetch the king to Paris. As they straggled over the muddy roads in a steady downpour of rain all the male riff-raff of the suburbs joined them. In the face of this tremendous danger Lafayette, the commander of the militia and guardian of the civil order, did nothing. If, as has been supposed, he remained inactive in order to let the king feel once more the power of the multitude, he may be fairly charged with political trickery. Certain it is that it was only when the National Guard refused to wait longer that he consented to conduct it to Versailles in order to preserve the peace. When he arrived there in the night, some hours after the Paris rabble, he found everything in the greatest confusion; but by his timely intercession he did at least save the lives of the royal family and could with some justification pose as the preserver of the monarchy. But if the rioters spared the king and queen, they declared firmly at the same time that they would be satisfied with nothing short of the removal of the royal family to Paris. What could the king do but give his consent? On the 6th the terrible mænads, indulging in triumphant song and dance along the road, escorted to the palace of the Tuileries "the baker, the baker's wife, and the baker's little boy," from whose presence in their midst they promised themselves a reign of plenty. The National Assembly, of course, followed the king and was quartered in the riding-school near the palace. Paris was again in fact as well as name the capital of France.

The events of October 5th and 6th undermined the last remnant of authority enjoyed by the monarchy and Lafayette can not escape the charge of having contributed to the result. The king at the

Tuileries was now practically Lafayette's prisoner, if that was what Lafayette wanted; but Lafayette himself, even though it took him some months to find it out, was henceforth the prisoner of the Parisian populace. The October days had allowed "the patriots," as the agitators euphemistically called them- selves, to realize that they could break through every obstacle in their path; and having repeatedly eaten of the poisonous fruit of violence, they would require more than Lafayette's energy to bring them back to a respect for the established order. Henceforward clever and unscrupulous demagogues, utilizing the uncontrolled Paris mob as their instrument, acquired an ever broadening influence until they were able to defy the king, Lafayette, the National Assembly, and every constituted authority in France.

The "patriots" henceforth supreme

What greatly contributed to the power of the democratic politicians was the excitement and vague enthusiasm which possessed all classes alike. Would we understand the tremendous pace at which the Revolution developed, we must never forget that the year 1789 marks an almost unparalleled agitation of public opinion. Leading symptoms of this general excitement were the innumerable pamphlets and newspapers which accompanied the events of the day with explanatory comment and which not infrequently assumed the form of fanatical exhortation against the existing institutions. But the most picturesque witnesses of the disturbed state of opinion were the clubs. Clubs for consultation and debate became the great demand of the hour; they arose spontaneously in all quarters; in fact, every coffee-house acquired, through the passion of its frequenters, the character of a political association. Two clubs in particular, the Cordeliers and the Jacobins, were destined to become famous. The Cordeliers recruited their members from among the Paris extremists and boasted Danton as their leader, a capable young barrister in whom there burned a submerged volcanic fire. Another radical much seen among them was Marat, whose journalistic effusions were a perpetual call to violence and betokened a mind more than a little cracked. The Jacobins, destined to become a name of general dread, began their existence in a much higher social stratum than the Cordeliers. The Jacobin club was formed as a place of meeting for the moderate and educated elements and rapidly spread in numerous branches or so-called daughter societies over the length and breadth of France. Before long, however, the Jacobins too succumbed to the extreme revolution-

Pamphlets, newspapers, and clubs

ary tendencies which had become the very breath of the country's nostrils. Lafayette, Sieyès, and Mirabeau, whose power was at first dominant in their councils, were gradually displaced by men like Robespierre who skillfully used the club as a means of binding together the radical opinion of the country.

It was against this agitated background of opinion that there was projected between 1789 and 1791 the new governing body, the National Assembly. To its acknowledged task, the making of a constitution, the breakdown of the monarchy had obliged it to add also the practical rule of the country. In consequence it was overburdened with business and faced situations and enacted decrees, some of which it will be necessary to examine. And first of all we may consider its handling of the great question of privileges and monopolies which had proved unsolvable in the early years of Louis's reign. So far had opinion progressed since the time of Turgot that it now took but a single night to dispose of an issue, the mere broaching of which in his day had caused his downfall. On August 4, 1789, the liberal nobles renounced voluntarily their feudal rights of the chase, manorial justice, and a vast variety of petty feudal dues, while liberal-minded clerics followed the example set them by the nobles by giving up their claim to the general ecclesiastical levy called the tithe. Naturally the Third Estate could not let itself be outdone and magnanimously laid the trade monopolies conferred by the gild charters on the altar of the fatherland. When the various renunciations of an intoxicated session had been swept into a summary decree it was seen that the whole feudal edifice had been levelled with the ground and the road cleared for complete legal equality. Examined from whatever angle one chooses, August fourth was and will remain one of the great days of the Revolution.

Fall of the system of privilege on August 4th

Another burning question left over from the old régime was the problem of the finances. To save the country from imminent bankruptcy had been, it will be remembered, the immediate cause for summoning the States General. An inevitable consequence of the confusion attending the overthrow of the absolute system was that the treasury was reduced to the last extreme of misery. People very generally ceased to pay taxes, while the manifold disturbances on the highways, besides making the provisioning of Paris uncertain, precipitated an industrial crisis which caused wide unemployment. Confronted with an absolutely depleted money chest, the National

Financial jugglery. Confiscation of Church property and assignats

Assembly was moved to rescue the situation by an extreme measure and on November 2, 1789, voted to confiscate the vast property of the clergy valued conservatively at several hundred million dollars. Against this real estate it presently authorized the issue of paper money, called *assignats*, and with these resources enabled the government to meet its most pressing expenses. The assignats were a perfectly safe financial device on one condition: that with mere real estate as security, they should not be multiplied indefinitely and thereby undermine the confidence of the holders in the ability of the government to redeem them. But indefinite multiplication was the very policy actually adopted. Though the National Assembly must be credited with an effort to apply the brakes, it none the less authorized paper money in sufficient quantities to cause it to drop with each month farther and farther below par. Presently, since bad money always drives good money out of sight, the standard gold and silver coins either were exported or disappeared in the stockings of the peasants while the steadily declining assignats came more and more into exclusive use. At the close of the Assembly in 1791 the paper inflation was already well under way; but when the legislatures which followed the first assembly found no other solution of the country's financial needs than the running of the printing presses, it became certain that the flood of assignats would terminate in a colossal bankruptcy. Staved off till 1797, the financial cataclysm, one of the sorriest chapters of the French Revolution, must in part at least be ascribed to the National Assembly, which not without strong forebodings of evil launched the country on the treacherous sea of an insufficiently secured and recklessly multiplied paper currency.

In the intervals of the discharge of current business the Assembly undertook to rear the structure of that new constitution which was to be the crown of all its labors. By the spring of 1791 the work was nearing completion. If we remember that it was the prod- *Leading* uct of men who had suffered from an absolute executive *features of* and were under the spell of the liberal and romantic *the consti-* thought of the eighteenth century, we shall understand *tution* its principal feature. This was that the royal executive was made purposely weak and political power distributed as widely as possible among an innumerable body of elected officials. The system culminated in a national legislature. This assembly, it was provided, should consist of but a single house elected for two years by all the active citizens of the kingdom. Active citizens were those who paid a small direct tax enabling them to qualify as property owners. This limitation of the franchise to the well-to-do was a bourgeois triumph which was deeply resented by the democratic masses. It meant that the masses, as a disfranchised body, were classified by the constitution as passive citizens. Although the bourgeoisie scored a victory in the matter of the franchise, it was a dangerous triumph since it tended to render the Assembly extremely unpopular with the common people.

Throughout the long discussions on the constitution, Mirabeau fought hard to secure to the king that measure of power which an executive requires in order to maintain the unity and tranquillity of the country; but he was unappreciated by his colleagues and distrusted by Louis and in almost all important matters met defeat. Broken by disappointment and reckless excesses he died (April, 1791), prophesying in his last days, with marvellous accuracy, all the ulterior stages of the Revolution.

Death of Mirabeau, April, 1791

Though the death of Mirabeau was generally lamented, no one had more reason for regret than the king, since, in spite of his refusing to take Mirabeau's advice, he possessed in him an invaluable supporter. Ever since October 6th Louis had been a virtual prisoner in the Tuileries and had lost all influence in the shaping of events. The constitution, which in the spring of 1791 was nearly ready and would soon be forced upon him, he regarded as impracticable. So long as Mirabeau lived, Louis might entertain the hope of some slight changes being introduced calculated to strengthen the executive; but when the great orator's death robbed him of this prospect, his thoughts turned definitely to flight as the only means of escaping from a position which he regarded as untenable and which put his queen, his children, and all who were dear to him at the mercy of his jailers.

The unsatisfactory position of the king

The flight of the king and royal family was arranged with the greatest secrecy for the night of June 20th. But too confident of his disguise as a valet, Louis exposed himself needlessly at a post-station, only to be recognized by the son of the postmaster, who galloped through the night to give the alarm. At the village of Varennes the bells sounded the tocsin, and the excited people, summoned from their beds, refused to permit the royal carriage to proceed. With safety almost in view the flight came to an end. The fugitives were brought back to Paris, where once more they had the key turned on them in their palatial prison.

The flight to Varennes, 1791

The flight of the king divided opinion in Paris sharply. It gave the constitutional monarchists, who had a clear majority in the Assembly, their first inkling that they had gone too far in weakening the executive. A monarch was necessary to their constitutional fabric and now they beheld their chosen representative embracing the intended honor by running away from it. They began in consequence to exhibit suddenly for the captive and discredited Louis a consideration which they had refused him in his happier days. Many popular leaders, on the other hand, with Danton and Robespierre at their head and with the support of the radical Cordelier and Jacobin clubs regarded the flight as an abdication and a welcome pretext for proclaiming the republic. For the first time therefore since the beginning of the Revolution there was a clear-cut issue between monarchists and republicans. A struggle followed (July, 1791), the most ominous which Paris had yet witnessed; but the monarchists were still a majority, and by ordering out against the republican agitators the National Guard under Lafayette won a victory. The Assembly, on hearing from the king the doubtful statement that he had never meant to leave the soil of France nor employ force against his subjects, solemnly welcomed him back to office; and Louis, in return, to mark his reconciliation with his subjects, accepted and swore to observe the constitution. By its bloody repression of the republican malcontents coupled with the magnanimous forgiveness extended to the king for his many lapses, the Assembly was pleased to imagine that it had solved all the difficulties of the situation. By September 30, 1791, it had added the last touches to its work, and, dissolving itself, retired from the scene. Its strenuous labors of two years, from which the enthusiasts had declared would date the renovation of old Europe, culminated in the gift to the nation of the completed constitution. The question now was: Would the constitution prove workable and inaugurate the expected era of liberty, equality, and fraternity?

The monarchical majority of the Assembly reinstates the king and closes the session

THE LEGISLATIVE ASSEMBLY (OCTOBER 1, 1791, TO SEPTEMBER 21, 1792)

The First Legislative Assembly, elected on the basis of the new constitution, met the day after the National Assembly adjourned. By a self-denying ordinance, characteristic of the mistaken magnanimity which pervaded the National Assembly, that body had voted the exclusion of its members from the succeeding legislature. The seven hundred and forty-five new rulers of France were, therefore, all men without experience. That alone constituted a grave danger. It was still further increased by the fact that most of the members were young enthusiasts, who owed their political fortune to the oratorical vigor displayed by them in their provincial Jacobin club.

Character of the Legislative Assembly

The radical disposition of the Assembly became apparent as soon as the members fell into party groups. Only a minority, called the Feuillants, undertook heartily to support the constitution. Opposed to them was the Gironde [1] which frankly favored the establishment of a republic. The majority, attached neither to the monarchists nor to the republicans, inclined none the less to accept Girondist leadership. Under the circumstances the work of the Assembly was from the first day directed at the destruction of the monarchy. The stages by which it accomplished its purpose we need not here consider; but as the supreme blow against the king was delivered when he was forced to declare war against Austria, we may, except for this declaration, which marks a new mile-stone in the Revolution, dismiss the Legislative Assembly from consideration.

Hostility to king and monarchy

The declaration of war against Austria resulted first, from the rising indignation in France over the *émigrés*, who had gathered in armed bands along the Rhine, and second, from the increasing fear and hatred of monarchical Europe for the Revolution. Frenchmen generally supposed that Emperor Leopold II, brother of Queen Marie Antoinette, was planning a war to punish them for their opinions. This we now know was not the case; but in August, 1791, Leopold held a conference with the king of Prussia and together with him issued a document which threatened an eventual interference in French affairs (Declaration of Pillnitz). Ceaselessly ringing the changes on the armed émigrés and the impertinent brother of the French queen, like her the enemy of the Revolution, the Girondist orators gradually worked up a public sentiment for war. They were sincere republican enthusiasts who had brought themselves to the belief that only by means of war would the republic triumph in France and ultimately

France declares war upon Austria, April, 1792

---

[1] The Gironde owed its party designation to the circumstance that many of its leaders hailed from the department of Gironde (Bordeaux).

throughout the world. Making bolder and bolder demands on Leopold, which of course stimulated him to increasingly vigorous replies, they at last ended discussion by launching on April 20, 1792, a declaration of war against the Hapsburg monarchy.

Unfortunately Leopold, who was a moderate and rarely capable man, died a month before war was declared, and it was his dull-witted son, Francis II, who was called to battle with the Revolution. But the far-sighted Leopold had not died without making provision for an eventual war with France. In February, 1792, alarmed by the hostile attitude of the French people, he had persuaded the king of Prussia to league himself with him in a close alliance. Austria is joined by its ally, Prussia The declaration of April 20th, therefore, though directed only at Austria, brought Prussia also into the field. Under these circumstances began the wars which were destined to carry the revolutionary ideas around the world, to sweep away landmarks and traditions, and to lock young France and old Europe in death-grapple for over twenty years.

It is probable that the republican Girondists, who more than any man or party were responsible for the war and proudly looked upon it as their work, expected an easy victory. They saw in a vision the thrones of the tyrants crumbling at the irresistible onset of the new democracy and themselves hailed everywhere as the liberators of the human race. The first engagement brought a sharp disappointment. It occurred in the Invasion and terror; the Brunswick proclamation Austrian Netherlands (Belgium) which the French undertook to invade. But the French army, which had been completely undermined in its discipline by the radical propaganda, had no sooner established contact with the Austrians than it scampered away without risking a battle. Thereupon the Austrians and Prussians prepared an offensive in their turn and with the coming of summer undertook the invasion of France. At this unexpected turn wrath and terror filled the republicans in Paris. They began to whisper the word treason and soon their orators dared to denounce the king publicly as the author of the national calamities. In August the allies crossed the border and proceeded on their march to the capital. Excitement rose ever to new heights, and when the duke of Brunswick, the allied commander-in-chief, threatened, in an extravagant proclamation, to wreak an unexampled vengeance on the capital if but a hair of the king's head were injured, the seething passion burst in a wave of uncontrollable fury. In the early morning of August 10th the mob, organized by the republican leaders, marched against the Tuileries to overthrow the man whom the radicals of the press and clubs represented as in league with foreign despots against the common mother, France.

When, shortly after midnight, the bells from the steeples rang out the preconcerted summons over the city, the king and his family knew that the supreme struggle had come. Dispersed about in August 10, small groups, the palace inmates passed the hours of dark- 1792 ness and dawn discussing the chances of the coming day. Of all the soldiers of the king the Royal Guard of Swiss mercenaries could alone be counted on. That fact tells more vividly than words the pass to which the ancient monarchy of France had come. Even so, if Louis XVI had now resolved to conquer or die at the head of this faithful regiment, he might have rallied the moderates and constitutionalists, still without any question a majority, around the throne. But from this king no such action was to be expected. He could be patient, tolerant of ideas beyond his grasp, and even generous to his enemies, but he could not form a heroic resolution. At eight o'clock in the morning, seeing that the mob was about to storm the palace, he abandoned it to seek shelter with the Legislative Assembly. The Swiss Guard, deserted by their leader, made a brave stand. Only on the king's express order did they give up the Tuileries and attempt to effect a retreat to their barracks. But the odds were against them; and the enraged populace, falling upon them, butchered most of them in the streets.

Meanwhile, the Legislative Assembly was engaged in putting its official seal to the verdict of the mob. In the presence of Louis and the royal family the members voted the suspension of the king End of the from office and ordered the election of a National Conven- monarchy tion to constitute a new government. The present As- and of the sembly agreed to hold over till September, when the new constitution body was expected to meet. Thus perished miserably, after an existence of ten months, the constitution which had filled so many generous hearts with the highest hopes for mankind.

The suspension of the king left the government nominally in the hands of the Legislative Assembly and a committee of ministers appointed by that body. But as the capital was in the hands of the radical leaders supported by the multitude and nobody paid any attention to the authorities, the real power fell into the hands of the men who had been most active in striking down the king. In

preparation of their success at the Tuileries they had, in the early
morning hours of August 10th, overthrown the municipal government of Paris and now lay intrenched in the city hall or *hôtel de
ville*. Robespierre, Marat, and others of their complexion The govern-
acted from this local center; but they were completely over- ment seized
shadowed by Danton, who had been made a member of by the
the ministry by the Legislative Assembly and who by his victors
extraordinary energy completely dominated the situation. In fact it
is hardly an exaggeration to say that Danton was the self-appointed
dictator of the country during the interlude from August 10th, the
day of the overthrow of the monarchy, to September 21st, the day
of the meeting of the National Convention.

As Danton saw the critical situation the first and imperative need
was to beat back the invasion. He therefore made himself with his
allies of the city hall the champion of the national defense. He
strove to infuse into the hearts of the citizens an indom- Danton
itable courage. "What do we require in order to con- saves
quer?" he shouted: "to dare, and dare, and dare again!" France
The fatherland was declared in danger; all occupations ceased but
those which provided for the necessities of life and the manufacture
of weapons; finally, steps were taken to bring the whole male
population under arms. Whatever we may think of this government by violence and frenzied enthusiasm, it certainly accomplished
its purpose, for it put an army into the field composed of men who
were ready to die and so saved France.

If we now turn to the invasion of France, which had been the
compelling cause of the tremendous events in the capital, we must
imagine it proceeding in the deliberate manner of eighteenth century
strategy. The French armies, hurriedly reconstituted as The
a republican force by Danton and his helpers, were for invasion
some weeks incapable of offering any effective resistance. checked at
However, on September 20th, at Valmy in the Argonne Valmy, Sep-
forest, the republican general, Dumouriez, threw himself tember 20,
across the path of the Prussian army under Brunswick and brought 1792
it to a halt. Inordinately discouraged by the check administered
to him, Brunswick ordered a retreat which became almost a rout. In a
few weeks not a Prussian or Austrian soldier was left upon French soil.

Just before this really remarkable success had been achieved by
improvised troops a series of frightful crimes committed in Paris
had shocked the sensibilities of an attentive world. To understand

how they could have occurred we must have a vivid comprehension
of the general French situation. With the country in unutterable
confusion the monarchy had broken down under the impact of a
The relatively small group of republicans, resolute to save
September their country from the foreigner. To this band, with
massacres Danton at its head, the great work was to organize the
defense of France; and since it could not afford to let itself be disturbed in its preparations by monarchist uprisings at home, it resolved to cow its opponents, as yet far from converted to republican
principles, by means of terror. As a preliminary step thousands of
citizens, suspected of being devoted to the king, were put under
arrest; the next measure, taken in the early days of September,
was to relieve the pressure on the prisons by a deliberate massacre
of the inmates. An armed band of assassins went the round of the
places of detention and did not suspend its bloody work until it had
despatched nearly two thousand helpless victims. Not a hand was
raised to stop the hideous proceedings. Paris, to all appearance,
looked on stupefied.

THE NATIONAL CONVENTION (SEPTEMBER 21, 1792, TO OCTOBER 26, 1795)

The short interlude of government by an irresponsible radical
faction came to an end when the National Convention met (Sep-
The tember 21st) and assumed control. Its very first measure
National was to declare the monarchy abolished. By a happy
Convention coincidence the victory of Valmy, which had occurred
abolishes on the previous day, freed France from all immediate
monarchy danger from without. The Convention began its career
in an atmosphere of patriotic exultation.

In the precarious situation obtaining in France much depended
upon the composition of the new governing body. It was made up
of nearly eight hundred members, who, because the monarchists
Parties either from terror or indolence had absented themselves
in the from the polls, were solidly republican. But attachment
Convention to the same fundamental principle did not hinder the
rise of important differences of opinion. The outstanding republican
group was the Gironde, already known to us from the previous
assembly. Its most active competitor was the Mountain,[1] composed

[1] So called from the fact that the members took their seats upon the highest
tiers of benches.

of individuals like Danton, Robespierre, and Marat who inclined to extreme views and who had shown their caliber in the recent extraordinary events. Men given more to action than to words, they desired that the war be kept to the fore until it had been concluded by a victorious peace. The Girondists, too, were for the war; in fact they had been largely instrumental in bringing it about. But high-minded idealists given to speculative thought, they detested the violences of the radicals and were revolted by the September massacres. Between these two groups, and permanently attached to neither, was the great bulk of the deputies, designated as the Plain. Whichever, Gironde or Mountain, could sway the Plain, would possess a majority and rule France.

The sessions were no sooner opened than a hopeless rift was created by the demand of the Gironde for the punishment of the perpetrators of the September massacres. To divert attention from itself the Mountain proposed instead to bring the king to trial. Ever since August 10th Louis and his family had been closely confined in prison. In December the deposed monarch was summoned before the Convention acting as a court of justice. The Girondists, amiable dreamers for the most part, would have spared his life, but the Mountainists, backed by the threats of the mob, carried the Plain with them. By a very small majority the former Louis XVI, degraded to the rank of citizen Louis Capet, was condemned to death, and on January 21, 1793, was beheaded by the newly invented machine, called the guillotine. On that eventful day no hand was raised to save the monarch, who, a feeble creature with no single action to his credit commanding our respect, must none the less be regarded in the main as the helpless victim of a tragic chain of circumstances. *Trial and death of the king*

The execution of the king raised a storm of indignation throughout monarchical Europe, and a great coalition, which every state of importance joined, sprang to life for the purpose of punishing the regicides of the Convention. The republicans, nothing loath, accepted and even anticipated the challenge. In this way the war with Austria and Prussia promised to assume immense proportions in the coming year. The members of the great coalition planned — in so far *The first European coalition against France*
as a loose association of states may ever be said to have a plan — to attack France from every side and humble her pride in one rapid campaign. The English were to sweep down upon her coasts, the

Spaniards to cross the Pyrenees and attack from the south, the Piedmontese to pour over the Alps, and the Austrians and Prussians to operate along the eastern border from the direction of Belgium and the Rhine. Under these circumstances the question of the defense of the French soil became again, as it had been in the summer of 1792, the supreme question of the hour. It was plain that in order to meet her enemies, who were advancing from every point of the compass, France would have to be united and display an almost superhuman energy.

The new crisis quickly developed the animosities between Gironde and Mountain into implacable hatred. There can be no doubt that both sides were equally patriotic; but the immediate issue was Overthrow not love of country so much as the most practical means of the for meeting the threatening invasions. The philosophers Gironde of the Gironde insisted on pressing their scruples about the September massacres and on rejecting every war measure which implied an encroachment on the new-won liberties of the individual. But since the situation would not wait either on debate or moral scruple, the fanatical leaders of the Mountain resolved to rid themselves of their rivals. Mobs were regularly organized by Marat and other minor henchmen in touch with the Parisian masses to invade the Convention and howl at its bar for the heads of the Girondist leaders. On June 2, 1793, the Convention finally yielded to pressure and excluded from its midst and put under arrest thirty-one Girondist leaders, among whom were the brilliant orators Vergniaud, Isnard, Brissot, and Gensonné.

The fall of the Girondists meant the removal of the last check upon the fierce determination of the Mountain. The power now lay in its hands to use as it would; and the most immediate end of The power, the Mountain had from the first maintained, Mountain was the salvation of France from her enemies. To acsupreme complish that great purpose the party now deliberately returned to the successful system of the summer of 1792 — the system of terror. This new phase of the Revolution, famous as the Reign of Terror — it could appropriately be called the Long Reign of Terror, in order to distinguish it from the Short Reign of Terror of August and September, 1792, which it closely resembles — begins on June 2nd, with the expulsion from the Convention of the moderate republican element, represented by the Gironde.

THE REIGN OF TERROR (JUNE 2, 1793, TO JULY 27, 1794)

The Short Reign of Terror of the summer of 1792 was marked by two conspicuous features: first, an energetic conduct of the war and, second, a bloody repression of the monarchical opposition. The Long Reign of Terror reproduces these elements A strong developed into a system. What is more likely to secure executive: an energetic defense than a strong executive? The the Committee of Mountain, therefore, created a committee, finally, of Public twelve members, called the Committee of Public Safety, Safety which it endowed with almost unlimited powers. While it is true that the Committee of Public Safety was established some weeks before the Girondists fell, the fact that it did not acquire its sovereign influence until the summer of 1793 proves how intimately it was associated with the Mountain scheme of government.

Of the famous Committee of Public Safety the most conspicuous figure was Robespierre, for which reason the whole period of the Terror is sometimes identified with his name. But Robespierre, if most in view, was by no means the most active of the Robespierre members of the Committee. He was indeed the hero of the and Carnot populace and the Jacobins and swayed the Convention by his oratory, but the man who provided for the defense of France was Carnot, aided by such capable administrators as Prieur and Lindet. During the prolonged internal convulsions these men kept as far as possible aloof from politics and quietly and unostentatiously attended to business. It was they who carried out the universal conscription voted by the Convention; it was they who equipped the armies, appointed the generals, and mapped out the campaigns. If France was able to confront the forces of the coalition by armies which soon exceeded the enemy in numbers and are sometimes set, though with evident exaggeration, at 1,000,000 men, this great achievement, on which hung the salvation of the country, may be written down primarily to Carnot and the other working members of the Committee. But why was not that fiery titan, Danton, a member of the executive? In view of the fact that the creation of the Committee of Public Safety was largely his work, he had been originally appointed a member, but in the course of the summer of 1793, owing, it is surmised, to an intrigue of Robespierre, he was dropped from its roll. Of course he remained a powerful political factor, with a strong following in and outside the Convention, but that he should have allowed himself to be crowded, without a struggle, from the seat of power was and remains a mystery.

With the conduct of the war provided for by means of a powerful executive, it remained to systematize the repression of the anti-revolutionary elements. The machinery of the Terror, as this sys-

The machinery of the Terror tematization may be called, presented, on its completion, the following features: first, there was the Law of the Suspects. By this unique measure the authorities were authorized to imprison anyone soever who was denounced to them as "suspect," a term that could be stretched to mean almost anything. It was afterward said by a wit that all France went about in those days conjugating the verbal expression, "I am suspect," through all its moods and tenses. In consequence, the prisons were crowded from garret to cellar with thousands of victims. To empty them was the function of the second element of the terrorist machinery, called the Revolutionary Tribunal. This was a special court of justice created for the purpose of trying the suspects without the delays incident to the ordinary courts. However, even the Revolutionary Tribunal at first provided certain safeguards for the accused. With the passing of time these were more and more eliminated until merely to be brought to trial was tantamount to condemnation. On sentence of death being pronounced by the judge there remained for the luckless victim the third and last step in the process of the Terror: he was carted to an open square, called the Square of the Revolution, and amid staring and hooting mobs, who congregated to the spectacle every day as to a feast, his head fell under the stroke of the guillotine.

Before the Terror had well begun, one of its most revolting agents, Marat, fell victim to that violence which he had so sedulously preached. Marat was the mouth-piece of the utterly ragged and

Marat and Charlotte Corday lawless element of Paris. He had lately developed a thirst for blood that can only be accounted for on the ground of disease. Yet this degenerate impudently published his frothings under the name of "the Friend of the People." The blow which finally put an end to his wild declamations was delivered from an unexpected quarter. Many of the Girondists, on being proscribed, had succeeded in making their escape to the provinces. At Caen, in Normandy, the fugitives aroused the sympathies of a beautiful and noble-minded girl, Charlotte Corday. Passionately afflicted by the divisions of her country which she laid at

Marat's door, she resolved by a bold stroke to free France from the oppressor. On July 13, 1793, she succeeded in forcing an entrance into his house and stabbed him in his bath. She knew that the act meant her own death, but her exaltation did not desert her for a moment, and she passed to the guillotine a few days after the deed with the sustained calm of a martyr.

The dramatic incidents associated with so many illustrious victims of the Terror can receive only scant justice here. In October Marie Antoinette was summoned before the Revolutionary Tribunal. She faced the court with noble dignity and on receiving her death-verdict mounted the scaffold with the courage befitting a daughter of the Caesars.[1] A few days after the death of Marie Antoinette, twenty-one Girondists, representing the total number at that moment in the hands of the victorious Mountain, travelled the same road. They were followed by the duke of Orleans and Madame Roland, each intensely hostile to the other but charged alike with complicity in the Girondist plots. The duke of Orleans, head of the secondary branch of the house of Bourbon, awakened few regrets either then or afterwards. An ambitious intriguer, he had from his youth plotted against Louis XVI. To save his miserable life he had joined the Jacobin club and, dropping his hereditary titles, invited eternal ridicule by reintroducing himself to the world as Mr. Equality (*Egalité*). When in 1792 he was elected to the Convention, he unblushingly committed his final act of infamy by voting for the death of the king. His very antipodes was Madame Roland.[2] Her honest but bookish enthusiasm for a regenerated public life naturally drew her to the Girondist party. For a time her house had been their meeting-place, and she herself, with the emotional extravagance characteristic of the period, had been worshipped as the muse, the Egeria, of the republican philosophers. In spite of her political immaturity, her mind had the

Execution of Marie Antoinette, October, 1793

---

[1] Marie Antoinette left two children, a princess of fifteen years and the dauphin, Louis, aged eight. The princess was released in 1795, but before that mercy could be extended to the boy, he had died under the inhuman treatment of his jailers. The systematic torturing to death of the poor dauphin is one of the dark blots upon the men of the Terror. The dauphin is reckoned by legitimists as Louis XVII.

[2] Madame Roland owed her influence in part to her husband, who was a prominent member of the Gironde and a minister during the last months of the reign of Louis XVI and again in the summer and fall of 1792. Roland made his escape from Paris when the Gironde was proscribed, but committed suicide on hearing of the death of his wife.

imprint of nobility and sustained her in her hour of trial. On mounting the steps of the guillotine, she paused to contemplate a statue of Liberty which had been erected near by. Her last words were addressed to the impassive goddess. "Liberty," she said, "what crimes are committed in thy name!"

But it would be a mistake to suppose that the Terror was limited to Paris or was directed merely against prominent individuals. By means of Deputies on Mission, clothed with the powers of the Committee of Public Safety, and of so-called revolutionary committees set up in every community it was carried into the provinces on the ground that all France would have to be inspired with the same martial sentiments if the war was to be won. The departments, inhabited for the most part by men of moderate means and moderate opinions, had from the first shown signs of restlessness under the violences of the Terror; and when the Gironde, a provincial party, fell victim to the Mountain, identified with Paris, the situation straightway became strained and led to the raising here and there of the standard of revolt. Thus the great city of Lyons refused to recognize further the authority of the Convention, while the important naval station, Toulon, went a step farther and actually surrendered to the foreign enemy, the English. Here was matter for thought but it was as nothing compared with the great rising in the west. The peasants of the region called *La Vendée* gathered in armed bands under the leadership of priests and nobles, and inflamed by the attacks upon the Catholic Church and the attempt of the Convention to conscript them for war, refused to bow their necks to the revolutionary régime.

This difficult situation the Convention, or rather its agent, the Committee of Public Safety, met with unflinching resolution. It sent an army against Lyons, and in October, 1793, after a brave resistance, the city was taken. Then the Convention resolved to inflict an unexampled punishment, happily only partially carried out: it ordered the destruction of the city and the erection on the ruins of a pillar with the inscription, "Lyons waged war with liberty; Lyons is no more." In December, 1793, a French army regained Toulon, chiefly through the skill of a young artillery officer, Napoleon Bonaparte; and, in the same month, another army scattered the insurgents of the Vendée. But discontent continuing to smoulder among the peasants of the agricultural west, the Committee of Public Safety was moved to despatch thither as Deputy on Mission one Carrier, armed with full powers to stamp out the embers. The vengeance wreaked by this madman upon the hostile priests and peasants makes the infamies of the Revolutionary Tribunal at Paris look like nursery pastimes. Dissatisfied with the slow process of the guillotine, Carrier invented new methods of wholesale execution. The most ingenious, the *noyade* (drowning), consisted in loading an old vessel with one hundred, two hundred, and even eight hundred victims — men, women and children — floating it down the Loire, and then scuttling it as it approached the sea. By such means the Terror penetrated to every corner of the land and held all France in subjection.

But its rule was, by its very nature, exceptional. Sooner or later there was bound to occur a division among its supporters; and when division came the revolutionists were sure to rage against each other as they had once raged in common against the aristocrats and moderates. The supreme statesman of the period, Mirabeau, had foreseen that development. In a moment of prophetic insight he had declared that the Revolution, like Saturn, would end by devouring its own offspring.

Disruption of the Terror inevitable

Ominous signs of the disintegration of the Mountain, the party of the Terror, began to appear in the autumn of 1793. The most radical wing, which owed its strength to its hold on the government of the city of Paris and which followed the lead of one Hébert, had turned its particular animosity against the Catholic faith. To replace this ancient cult, despised as aristocratic and superstitious, the Hébertists invented, in the spirit of reckless atheism, the so-called religion of Reason, and presently forced its acceptance upon the city of Paris by means of a decree which closed all places of Catholic worship. Although this extravagant measure was soon withdrawn and religious toleration, identified with the Revolution, reasserted in principle, Robespierre took alarm. He was further annoyed with the Hébertists because they leaned toward communism and dared launch an attack on private property. Disinclined to such extravagances, Robespierre, who, though a republican, was a characteristic bourgeois, denounced Hébert and his ilk before the Jacobins, and in March, 1794, abruptly sent them *via* the Revolutionary Tribunal to the guillotine.

End of the Hébertists, March, 1794

The overthrow of Hébert was followed by that of Danton, a man of a better and nobler stamp, who, falling, carried his friends and satellites down with him. A rude son of the soil, with a claim to real statesmanship, he had exercised a decisive influence in more than one great crisis: France had primarily him to thank for her rescue **The fall of** from the Prussians in the summer of 1792; and, again, the **Danton,** establishment of the Committee of Public Safety was **April, 1794** largely his work. But now he was growing weary. The uninterrupted flow of blood disgusted him and he raised his voice in behalf of mercy. Mercy, to Robespierre and his young follower, the arch-fanatic Saint Just, was nothing less than treason, and in sudden alarm at Danton's "moderation" they hurried him and his friends to the guillotine (April 5, 1794). Thus Robespierre was rid of his last rival. No wonder that it was now whispered abroad that he was planning to make himself sole dictator.

And between Robespierre and a dictatorship there stood, in the spring of 1794, only one thing — his own political incapacity. That he had the Jacobins, the municipality of Paris, the Convention, and **Supremacy** the Committee of Public Safety in his hands was proved **and fall of** by their servile obedience to his slightest nod. On May **Robespierre** 7th he had the satisfaction of wresting from the Convention a decree after his own heart, for that body made solemn affirmation to the effect that the French people recognized a Supreme Being and the immortality of the soul. It sufficiently characterizes the solemn pedantry of Robespierre that he never in his life took anything so seriously as this ludicrous declaration and that he had no inkling of the absurdity of the festival of June 8, 1794, at which he presided as high-priest and proclaimed the gospel of the Supreme Being to the heathen. Two days after the ceremony he revealed the spirit of fanaticism which animated his religious leadership. In order to facilitate the condemnations of the suspect the Revolutionary Tribunal by the law of June 10th was quadrupled and its procedure stripped of the last vestiges of legal form. Then only did the executions in Paris begin in a really wholesale manner. During the six weeks before the adoption of the new measure, the numbers of those guillotined in Paris amounted to 577; during the first six weeks after its adoption, the victims reached the frightful figure of 1,356. No government office, no service rendered on the battle-field secured immunity from arrest and death. At last, the Terror invaded the Convention itself. Paralyzed by fear that body submitted for a time to the desperate situation. But when the uncertainty connected with living perpetually under a threat of death had become intolerable, the opponents of Robespierre, men of his own party, banded together in order to crush him. It is only fair to say that he took no personal part in the indiscriminate slaughter of these last weeks. He had a certain fastidiousness distinguishing him favorably from many of his associates in the governing clique, low informers such as Billaud, Collot, and Fouché, who covered themselves with every infamy. With his immense following among the people he could doubtless have anticipated his enemies, but instead of action he wrapped himself in a mysterious silence. On the 9th of Thermidor (July 27th) [1] he and his adherents were condemned by the Convention and executed the next day.

THE RULE OF THE THERMIDORIANS (JULY 27, 1794, TO OCTOBER 26, 1795).

The fall of Robespierre put an end to the Terror, not because Robespierre was the Terror, but because the system had, after a year of wild extravagance, become so thoroughly discredited, even among its own supporters, that the Convention saw itself *The reac-* obliged to discontinue the methods of tyranny. The *tion in the* Thermidorians, many of whom had been the vilest in- *Convention* struments of the Terror and had dipped their hands into every kind of crime, bowed, therefore, to the force of circumstances. Supported by the Plain, the men of the middle ground in the Convention, they studiously heaped all the blame for the past year on the dead Robespierre and hypocritically assumed the character of life-long lovers of law and order. Slowly the frightened bourgeoisie recovered its courage and rallied to the support of the Thermidorian party; and finally a succession of concerted blows swept the fragments of the

---

[1] The Convention, guided by its hatred of the royalist past, had introduced a new system of time reckoning. Since the birth of the republic was regarded as more important than the birth of Christ, September 21, 1792, the day when monarchy was formally abolished, was voted the beginning of a new era. The whole Christian calendar was at the same time declared to be tainted with aristocracy and a new calendar devised. Its chief feature was the invention of new names for the months, such as: Nivose, Snow month; Pluviose, Rain month; Ventose, Wind month, for the winter months; Germinal, Budding month; Floréal, Flower month; Prairial, Meadow month, for the spring months, etc.

It is worthy of notice that the Convention, a body of men unhampered by tradition, discussed many laudable reforms and carried some of them into effect. One change has invited imitation. The ancient and conflicting systems of weights and measures were supplanted by the uniform metrical system.

Terror from the face of France. The municipality of Paris, the citadel of the rioters, was dissolved; the Revolutionary Tribunal dispersed; the guillotine dismantled; the functions of the Committee of Public Safety restricted; and, to make victory sure, the Jacobin Club, the old hearth of radicalism, was closed. During the next year — the last of its long lease of power — the Convention ruled France in substantial accord with the moderate opinion of the majority of the citizens.

But if the Terror fell, its overthrow was due not only to the horror it inspired but also to the fact that it had accomplished its end. Its cause, as well as its excuse, was the danger of France; and whatever else be said, it had really succeeded in organizing the resources of the country against the forces of a tremendous coalition. On this defense the reader must now bestow a rapid glance. In the campaign of 1793, during which the Committee of Public Safety was engaged in creating its republican armies on the basis of a general conscription of the youth of the country, the French had been obliged to yield ground at certain points. But by 1794 the work, largely due to Carnot's organizing talents, had been done, and the armies, numerous, well-equipped, and commanded by young men of ardent spirit, were enabled to carry the war into the territory of the enemy. Thus the tables were turned and monarchical Europe, instead of invading republican France, found itself invaded. In the course of this year (1794) an army under Jourdan conquered Belgium; and, shortly after, Pichegru seized Holland. Belgium, which ever since the Treaty of Utrecht had been a dominion of Austria, was promptly annexed to France, but Holland was left independent, though reconstituted as a republic and subjected to French influence. During these stirring events the ancient animosities between Prussia and Austria had flared up anew and proved of incalculable benefit to France. Suspicious of each other over the final partition of Poland, they refused to act whole-heartedly against the French, who were in consequence enabled to occupy the whole left bank of the Rhine. Thus incurable jealousies, coupled with the demoralizing effect of the revolutionary victories, undermined the coalition; and as the Thermidorians had no reason for continuing the war indefinitely they entered into negotiations with Prussia and Spain and in the spring of 1795 concluded peace with them at Basel. By these treaties, which acknowledged the French conquests, France began

The Terror successfully defends France

to emerge as victor.   None the less fighting was by no means over, since England and Austria remained in the field against her.

While these successes were being won abroad, the Convention took up the long-neglected task for which it had been summoned and in the course of the year 1795 completed a new constitution for republican France.   This constitution was ready to be promulgated, when the representatives, fearful that a *The Convention completes a republican constitution* free election might bring the royalists back to power, re- solved to provide for the perpetuation of the republic to which they were devoted.   They accordingly passed a law by which they virtually perpetuated themselves on the strength of a provision declaring that two-thirds of the new legislature must be composed of men who had sat in the Convention.   Over this high-handed measure the monarchists, who, favored by the powerful reaction against the Terror, had become both numerous and bold, waxed so exceeding wroth that in October they organized an armed rebellion and swept down on the Convention in order to force it to rescind its action.   After a long succession of riots instituted by anarchical radicals France now witnessed the strange phenomenon of an uprising of conservatives.   Nothing could have shown more convincingly the recent sharp turn-about of opinion.

However, the Convention was sufficiently in earnest about its republicanism to resolve to defend itself and entrusted with the task one of its members, Barras, who had come to the front in the Thermidorian period.   But Barras, who was no soldier, *Napoleon Bonaparte saves the Convention* conferred the command of the troops upon a young officer and acquaintance of his, Napoleon Bonaparte. Bonaparte had already creditably distinguished himself at Toulon and elsewhere and wanted nothing better than this opportunity.   When the rioters marched against the Convention on October 5th he received them with such a volley of grape-shot that they fled precipitately, leaving hundreds of their comrades dead upon the pavement.   It was a new way of treating armed popular uprisings and it had its effect.   Henceforth, in the face of the firm resolution of the government to defend itself, partisan groups lost their taste for overawing those in power by means of insurrections.   Bonaparte and his volley of grape-shot meant the return of *authority* and proclaimed with brazen tongue that violence masquerading as liberty had seen its day.

The Convention could now without fear complete its remaining

business. On October 26, 1795, its stormy, cowardly, and yet, in some respects, highly creditable career, came to an end, and the new constitution went immediately into effect. It is called the Consti-
The Consti- tution of the Year III from the year of the republican
tution of the calendar in which it was completed. Its main provisions
Year III mark a return from the loose liberal notions of the constitution of 1791 to a more compact executive. Nevertheless, the tyranny of the *ancien régime* was still too near for the objections against a too-powerful executive to have vanished utterly. Therefore a compromise was found in a multiple executive of five members, called the Directory. The legislative functions were entrusted to a lower house, called the Council of Five Hundred, and to a senate of two hundred and fifty, called the Council of Ancients. This bicameral legislature, too, represented a departure from the constitution of 1791, whose single legislative chamber had proved a failure. Exactly as in the earlier constitution, however, the suffrage was limited by a property qualification with the result that the Directory signified a strictly bourgeois régime.

THE DIRECTORY (1795-1799)

The Directory wished to signalize its accession to power by terminating the war with a brilliant victory over the remaining enemies of France, Great Britain and Austria. But an attack upon Great
The Britain was, because of the insufficiency of French naval
Directory power, out of the question. Austria was more vulner-
plans a con- able, and Austria the Directory now resolved to strike
centrated
attack upon with the combined armies of France. In accordance
Austria with this intention, "the organizer of victory," Carnot, who had been elected a Director, worked out a plan by which the Austrians were to be attacked simultaneously in Germany and Italy and forced back upon Vienna. Two splendid armies under Jourdan and Moreau were assigned to the German task, which was regarded as by far the more important, while the Italian campaign, undertaken largely to divert the attention of the Austrians from Germany, was intrusted to a poorly equipped army of 30,000 men, which, through the influence of the Director Barras and in reward for services rendered in connection with the October insurrection, was put under the command of General Bonaparte. But the unexpected happened. By the force of his genius Bonaparte upset completely

the calculations of the Directory and gave the Italian campaign such importance that he, and not Jourdan or Moreau, decided the war.

Bonaparte's task was to beat, with his army, an army of Austrians who, together with their Piedmontese allies, considerably outnumbered him. Resolved to meet them separately, he managed by a swift and secret movement to wedge his way between the allies, and by forcing the Piedmontese away from the Austrians toward Turin to hold them at his mercy. As a result the king of Sardinia-Piedmont sued for peace and retired from the war (April, 1796). Demoralized by these successes of the enemy, the Austrians fell back toward Milan. But Bonaparte, who broke every rule of the old deliberate strategy and moved with the stealth and swiftness of a beast of prey, outflanked them and, before May was over, had by a series of engagements driven them out of Lombardy. The pope and the small Italian princes, in alarm, hastened to buy peace of France by the cession of territories and of works of art, while the Austrians tried again and again to recover their lost position. But at Arcola (November, 1796) and Rivoli (January, 1797), Bonaparte, by his astonishing alertness, beat signally the forces sent against him. Then he crossed the Alps to invade Austria and dictate terms under the walls of Vienna.

This bold stroke of Bonaparte's determined the Emperor Francis II to sue for peace. Although his brother, the Archduke Charles, had, at the head of the Austrian forces in Germany, beaten Jourdan and Moreau in the campaign of 1796, the emperor was not prepared to stand a siege in his capital. His offers were met half-way by Bonaparte, and out of the negotiations which ensued there grew the Peace of Campo Formio (October, 1797). By this peace Austria ceded her Belgian provinces as well as Lombardy, recognized northern Italy as a sphere of French influence, and accepted for herself the principle of the Rhine boundary, the details to be arranged later with the diet of the Holy Roman Empire. In return for these concessions she received at Bonaparte's hands the ancient republic of Venice, which the young general had just seized with more than a soldier's usual absence of scruple. In spite of Austria's becoming established in this way at the head of the Adriatic, the Peace of Campo Formio virtually delivered all Italy into French hands. True, the ceded Lombardy became the Cisalpine Republic and the former city-

state of Genoa was transformed into the Ligurian Republic, but as
both of these creations were modeled on the French Republic and
submitted to control from Paris, they became, like Holland, timid
clients of the triumphant Directory.

When Napoleon returned to France he was hailed as the national
hero, who out of the bramble war had plucked the jewel peace. And
what a peace he brought, a peace which French rulers had dreamed
Bonaparte   of for generations and which, while establishing France
the hero   firmly in northern Italy, carried her also into western
of France   Germany by giving her the whole left bank of the Rhine!
Undeniably by these acquisitions the republic reverted to the war-
aims of the Bourbon monarchy and turned its back on the eloquent
declarations against conquest with which it had begun the struggle
with Europe back in 1793; but in the exhilaration of victory these
idealistic professions were conveniently forgotten and the conqueror
himself received with all but divine honors.

That Napoleon Bonaparte should become the foremost man of
France before he had reached the age of thirty would never have
been prophesied by the friends of his youth. He was born at
Youth of   Ajaccio, on the island of Corsica, in 1769, of a poor but
Napoleon   noble family. The inhabitants of Corsica, Italians by
Bonaparte   race, had long been under the rule of Genoa but had
latterly asserted their independence. Disgusted at their inability
to again subdue the islanders, the Genoese had in the year 1768
ceded Corsica to the neighboring kingdom of France. At the time
of Napoleon's birth, therefore, the French were occupied in establishing their rule over a people who resisted them heroically but without success. In the midst of the patriotic indignation caused by his
country's overthrow the young Corsican grew up. When he was
ten years old, his father took him to France to enter him as a cadet
in the famous royal military school at Brienne. In due course of
time he became a lieutenant of artillery, and it was while he was
holding this commission, among a people whom he still detested as
the oppressors of his country, that the French Revolution broke out
and opened a career to all possessed of talent and ambition. The
irresistible current of events caught up and bore the young Napoleon
along until he forgot his narrow Corsican patriotism and merged his
person and his fortunes with the destinies of France. We have
noted how, at the age of twenty-four, he performed his first great
military feat at Toulon. The four years of warfare which lay be-

tween Toulon and Campo Formio had carried him by rapid stages
to the uppermost round of the ladder of success.

In 1797, after two years of existence, the Directory had reason to
congratulate itself. Belgium, Holland, Italy, and the Rhine boundary sounded a catalogue of brilliant achievements and assured
France a preëminent position on the continent. Unfor- Foreign
tunately, the domestic situation continued to give trouble success,
since the country was still bleeding from the wounds in- domestic
flicted by the divisions of the past years. The religious failure
situation was particularly troublesome because the schism produced
by the persecution of the Catholic Church was farther than ever
from solution. If we add that financial embarrassments threatened
positively to overwhelm the government, we can understand why,
in spite of Bonaparte's victories, the royalists steadily grew stronger.
As the national finances actually plunged into the abyss in 1797, a
word about them becomes absolutely imperative. We have seen
that the Revolution from the very first turned to paper money
(*assignats*) as the way out of the wilderness. Since then the printing-
press had served as the chief source of French revenue; billions of
francs had been issued with the result of a disastrous decline in their
purchasing power; and when all this paper at last ceased to have
any value at all, it was simply repudiated (1797). That meant
bankruptcy, which, though hardly with strict justice, was laid at
the Directory's door. Doubtless the wisest course would have been
to make peace and give France a chance to breathe. But the
Directory had a different idea and chose to divert attention from
the domestic woes by launching an attack upon the last remaining
foreign enemy, Great Britain.

For the year 1798 the government planned a great action in order
to bring Great Britain to terms. As the lack of a fleet put a direct
attack upon the island-kingdom out of the question, it was resolved
to strike at Great Britain indirectly by threatening its France
colonies. With due secrecy an expedition was prepared attacks
at Toulon and Bonaparte given the command. Nelson, Great
the English admiral commanding in the Mediterranean, Britain in
was of course on the lookout, but Bonaparte succeeded Egypt
in evading his vigilance and in starting unmolested for Egypt
(May, 1798). Egypt was a province of the Ottoman Empire
(Turkey) and the key to both the Near and the Far East. By
establishing himself on the Nile, Bonaparte calculated that he could

sever the connection of Great Britain with India and the regions beyond. Nelson gave chase as soon as he got wind of the movements of the French; and although he arrived too late to hinder them from landing near Alexandria, he just as effectually ruined their expedition when on August 1 he attacked and destroyed their fleet anchored in Abukir Bay. Bonaparte might now go on conquering Egypt and all Africa — he was shut off from Europe and as good as imprisoned with his whole army.

In this way the Egyptian campaign, certainly from every angle an extraordinarily hare-brained enterprise, was lost before it had fairly begun. Bonaparte could blind his soldiers to the fact but he hardly **Bonaparte** blinded himself. Of course he did what he could to re-**in Egypt** trieve the disaster to his fleet by his successes on land. By his victory over the Egyptian soldiery, the Mamelukes, in the battle of the Pyramids (1798), he made himself master of the basin of the Nile; and in the year 1799 he marched his men to Syria. The seaport of Acre, which he besieged in the hope of establishing communication with France, repulsed his attack, while the plague decimated his brave troops. Sick at heart over his failure, Bonaparte returned to Egypt and, despairing of a change in his fortunes, resolved to desert his army. Contriving to run the English blockade, he landed on October 9, 1799, with a handful of friends, on the southern coast of France. Though the army he had deserted was irretrievably lost,[1] that fact was forgotten amid the rejoicings over the return of the national hero.

The enthusiastic welcome of France, which turned Bonaparte's journey northward to Paris into a triumphal procession, was due largely to the new dangers to which the country had been exposed dur-**The Second** ing his absence. Bonaparte was hardly known to have been **Coalition,** shut up in Egypt, when Europe, hopeful of shaking off the **1798, 1799** French ascendancy, formed a new coalition against the hated Republic. Austria and Russia, supported by English subsidies, renewed the war, and the year 1799 was marked by a succession of victories which swept the French out of Italy and Germany. At the time when Bonaparte made his appearance in Europe, an invasion of France had narrowly been averted by the heroic defense put up by General Masséna.

No wonder that the hopes of the nation gathered around the dashing Corsican. What other French general had exhibited such

[1] The army surrendered to the English in 1801.

genius as Bonaparte, had won such military glory for himself and France? Moreover, after the ceaseless agitations of the past ten years people were tired to death of revolution, the party spirit, the financial and economic embarrassments, and the con- The French tinued uncertainty of all social relations. Discontent was public is so general that optimistic royalists predicted the early weary of return of the legitimate king. In short, France was in revolution hopeless confusion and everybody turned spontaneously to Bonaparte as toward a savior.

The general was no sooner apprised of this state of the French mind than he resolved to act. With the aid of some conspirators in power and urged by public opinion he overthrew the gov- Bonaparte ernment. The only resistance of note was offered by the overthrows Chamber of Five Hundred and was overcome by military the Directory, force. The ease with which the *coup d'état* of November November, 9, 1799 (18th Brumaire), was executed proves that the 1799 Constitution of the Year III was dead in spirit before Bonaparte destroyed it in fact.

THE CONSULATE (1799–1804)

The successful general was now free to set up a new constitution in which an important place should be assured to himself. Instinctively he divined that what France desired was a strong executive, for ten years of anarchic liberty had disposed the people A new to be again in love with authority. The result of Bona- constitution parte's deliberations with his friends was the Constitution of the Year VIII, by which the government was practically concentrated in the hands of one official, called the First Consul and appointed for ten years. To hoodwink the democratic enthusiasts still abroad in the land the appearances of popular government were carefully preserved. The legislative functions were reserved to two bodies, the Tribunate and the Legislative Body, but as the former discussed bills without voting upon them, and the latter voted upon them without discussing them, their power was so divided that they necessarily lost all influence. Without another *coup d'état*, by means of a few minor changes in the new constitution, the Consul Bonaparte could, when he saw fit, evolve himself into the Emperor Napoleon who would govern France as its absolute master.

With his position at home secured, the First Consul gave his

attention to the war with the Second Coalition. Very opportunely for Bonaparte Russia, disgusted with her Austrian ally, retired from the struggle at the close of the campaign of 1799. As the enemies of
Bonaparte France were thus reduced to Great Britain and Austria, a
again in situation presented itself to view closely resembling that
Italy, 1800 of 1796. Not unnaturally Bonaparte resolved to meet
it by an analogous plan. Neglecting England as inaccessible and concentrating his attention upon Austria, he sent Moreau into Germany, while he himself went again to meet her in Italy. By a strenuous and picturesque march in the early spring over the Great St. Bernard Pass, a feat which rivalled the performance of Hannibal in the days of antiquity, he was enabled to strike unexpectedly across the Austrian line of retreat and force the enemy to make a stand. In the battle of Marengo, fought June 14, 1800, he crushed the Austrians and recovered all Italy at a stroke. Again Francis II had to admit the invincibility of French arms. In the Peace of Lunéville (1801) he reconfirmed all the cessions made at Campo Formio, and as the Holy Roman Empire became a party to the treaty, there was no longer any legal defect in the cession of the left bank of the Rhine. It is this feature of the Rhine boundary, perfected in every detail, which gives the Peace of Lunéville its importance. As the treaty, furthermore, redelivered Italy into Bonaparte's hands, he straightway reëstablished the Cisalpine and Ligurian Republics in their old dependence upon France.

Again, as in 1798, the only European state which held out against France was Great Britain. How reduce the great sea-power to submission? The French naval resources were as inadequate now as ever,
Peace with and as for striking at the British colonies, the recollection
Great of Egypt quickly disposed of the idea. Sated for the time
Britain, with success and glory, Bonaparte opened (1801) negoti-
1802 ations with the British government, and in March, 1802, concluded, substantially on the basis of mutual restitutions, the Peace of Amiens.

After ten years of warfare, France was now at peace with the world. The moment was auspicious. But it remained to be seen
France at whether the country would heartily take up the labors of
peace with peace and, while healing its wounds, would at the same
the world time remove the justifiable apprehension with which it was regarded by cowed and defeated Europe.

Certainly the First Consul showed no want of vigor in attacking the domestic situation, though the picture which unrolled itself before his eyes was frightful. After the wholesale destruction and careless experimentation of the last decade, France needed, above all, a season of constructive statesmanship. Not that the Revolution had not scattered plentiful seeds; but because the harvest had not been awaited with patience, the seeds had failed to mature. The work before the First Consul during the interval of peace which followed the treaties of Lunéville and Amiens was, therefore, nothing less than the reconstruction of the whole social order. He shouldered his responsibilities with his usual ardor. In a public proclamation he announced that the disturbances had been brought to an end and that he considered it his special task to "close" the Revolution and to "consolidate" its results.

Bonaparte undertakes the reconstruction of France

One of his first cares was to bring back material prosperity. The national bankruptcy of the Directory now proved a help, for by wiping out the worthless paper money it enabled the new ruler to make a fresh and wholesome start based on the resumption of specie payments. With the currency stabilized, confidence again began to prevail in business circles and industry and commerce quickly recovered from their long depression. Surely the country had reason to be proud of its "man of destiny." Sustained by an unexampled popularity, he now undertook to create a number of fundamental institutions, which, in spite of the revolutions of the nineteenth century, exist, in the main, to this day, and are his best title to fame. Let us give these institutions a brief consideration.

Return of prosperity

The administration of France had, during the Revolution, fallen into complete anarchy. The constitution of 1791 had divided France into eighty-three administrative units, called departments, and had supplanted the old royal appointees by a highly decentralized system of local self-government. Practically every office was made elective, requiring a political activity of which the electors, unaccustomed to the exercise of such duties, became weary. They refused to attend the polls and permitted the power to drift into the hands of a few professional politicians connected with the Jacobin club. Even under the Terror, which favored a strong executive, local self-government had been abandoned; and now with Bonaparte's advent a deliberate return was made to the traditional policy of centralized control. As a result

A new centralized administration

every department received an official head, called prefect, who was appointed by the First Consul and reported back to him. By means of the prefects the whole country was bound together by threads which met in the hands of the chief executive. With his wonderful sense of precision Bonaparte so perfected his system that no monarch by Divine Right has ever in an equal degree made his will felt through the length and breadth of his dominion. Democracy, the will-o'-the-wisp pursued through blood and fire for ten agitated years, was sacrificed, but the weary people were content for the present with the order and security assured by the new administration.

Religion, which lay in as bad a tangle as the administration, engaged Bonaparte's attention from the first. To understand his action it will be necessary to review the whole history of the Catholic Church during the Revolution. That the French intelligentsia, which dominated the National Assembly, had developed a decided hostility toward the ancient institution was indicated by the confiscation of Church property which occurred as early as November, 1789. A much more serious measure followed in July, 1790, which under the name of the Civil Constitution of the Clergy ordained a complete reorganization of French religious life. The Civil Constitution of the Clergy was in essence an attempt to set up a French national Church, separated or all but separated from the universal Catholic Church and served by priests and bishops dependent on the state, from which they drew their salaries. When the overwhelming majority of the clergy on order from the pope refused to accept the new national Church, a schism was produced which gradually led to persecution and, in the period of the Terror, to the wholesale slaughter of orthodox priests and prelates. It was the lively animosity against Catholicism which accounts for such extravagant episodes as Hébert's worship of Reason and Robespierre's cult of the Supreme Being. But in spite of banishment and guillotine, Catholicism at the dawn of the new century was still alive. Though Bonaparte, like the bourgeoisie in general of his age, possessed no positive religious views, he had a splendid sense of reality and divined the superior vigor of the persecuted faith. Having also a clear appreciation of the support which the reconstituted Church might furnish his reorganized state, he presently entered into negotiations with Rome. The result was a treaty of peace, called the Concordat (1801): the Church resigned its claim to its confiscated estates and the state undertook the main-

The religious tangle solved by the Concordat

tenance, on a liberal basis, of priests and bishops; these latter were to be nominated by the state and confirmed by the pope. If the Catholic Church was reëstablished in France by the Concordat, it can not be denied that it was reduced to a much closer dependence on the state than formerly.

With the administrative and religious snarls unraveled, Bonaparte next gave his attention to the department of justice. The legal confusion reigning in France before the Revolution is indescribable, for everything had been left to chance, and radically The new different systems of law were in force in the various sec- judicial tions of the country or, often enough, in the same section. system The Revolution had made an attempt to clarify the confusion but had not got far when Bonaparte came to power. With his usual energy he soon had a commission of experts at work upon the creation of a precise and uniform system; and in 1804 he was enabled to publish the result of their labors in the Civil Code, called afterward the *Code Napoléon*. No legal labor of similar scope had been undertaken since the distant days of Justinian. While the Roman law was made the basis of the Napoleonic code, modifications were freely introduced dictated by the progress of the centuries and the principles of the French Revolution.[1]

Bonaparte also planned a general system of state education, consisting of the primary, secondary, and university stages, but he made headway with only the more advanced elements of the program and was obliged through the pressure of events to Bonaparte postpone entirely the project for a much needed system at the of primary schools. From his various achievements, parting of however, some idea can be gained of his constructive and the ways methodizing genius. Let us again note that his labors of peace have survived [2] the subsequent revolutions, while the conquests of his sword have been "swept in fragments to oblivion." Bonaparte as First Consul stood at the parting of the ways. He might continue the labors of peace so happily inaugurated or he might return to the

[1] In enumerating the elements of the new France mention must imperatively be made of the peasantry, even though their improved status was not due to any action of Napoleon. The confiscation by the Revolution of the property of the clergy and nobility led to the numerous peasants becoming freeholders on their farms and therewith the most powerful and stabilizing element of French society down to our day.

[2] The religious settlement laid down in the Concordat was rejected a century later by the French government (1905) under circumstances which will be examined in their place.

policy of aggressive war lately closed with the treaties of Lunéville
and Amiens. We must remember that he was primarily a soldier,
animated with restless energy and spurred on by boundless ambition,
and that continued civil labors probably failed to satisfy an imagination which embraced the ends of the earth. Besides, he was the
heir of the Revolution which with the apparent approval of the
whole French people had turned its back on idealist professions and
accepted conquest as the logical end of war. With conquest adopted
as a national policy who could bring it to a halt or prescribe metes
and bounds for it?

Prompted by these personal preferences and general conditions,
Napoleon Bonaparte irresistibly lifted his vision to embrace Europe
and the neighboring continents and girded himself for a role like
Napoleon, that of Julius Cæsar or Alexander the Great. Therewith
emperor of the Revolution entered upon its last or Napoleonic stage,
the French in which France becomes the tool for the realization of
the ambition of the most remarkably endowed man of modern times.
He took the initial step upon this path of self-aggrandizement when
he modified the consular constitution in his own interest. In 1802 he
had himself appointed consul for life; and in May, 1804, he dropped
the last veil of republican pretense by the assumption of the title
emperor of the French. The final step in this transformation occurred
in December of the same year, when in the presence of the pope and
with all the formality and pomp of the ancient régime, he crowned
himself and his wife Josephine before the high altar of the cathedral
church of Paris.

THE EMPIRE (1804–1815)

The Consul Bonaparte, become Emperor Napoleon I, immediately
turned his attention to the subject-republics with which France had
surrounded herself. Republics no longer accorded with the new
Napoleon's imperial style. At a nod from the emperor the Batavian
action in Republic bloomed forth as the kingdom of Holland and
Holland thankfully accepted Louis Bonaparte, a younger brother
and Italy of Napoleon, as king. In like manner the Cisalpine
Republic became the kingdom of Italy and offered the crown to its
powerful protector. In May, 1805, Napoleon crossed the Alps and
crowned himself king at Milan. The Ligurian Republic now had no
further reason for existence and, like Piedmont some years before,
was quietly incorporated with France.

Even before these signal acts of aggression had been carried out, the last grain of confidence with which the European governments regarded Napoleon had disappeared. Unescapably it dawned on them that he was an insatiable conqueror, who was Renewal of awaiting only an opportunity to swallow them all. As the war early as 1803 continued disputes over the Peace of Amiens with Great had led to a renewal of the war with Great Britain. Britain Napoleon now prepared a great naval armament at Boulogne, and for over a year England was deeply agitated by the prospect of a descent upon her coasts; but the lack of a fleet of warships powerful enough to protect his convoys against the English navy under Nelson made Napoleon's project chimerical from the first, and in the summer of 1805 he unreservedly gave it up.

He gave it up because Great Britain had succeeded in playing upon the fears of Austria and Russia until they joined her in a new coalition to curb the alarming power of France. No sooner had Napoleon got wind of this state of affairs than he abandoned his quix- The Third otic English plans and threw himself upon the practical Coalition: task of defeating his continental enemies. His military England, genius presently celebrated new triumphs, for at Ulm he Austria, surrounded and captured the whole Austrian advance Russia guard; and on December 2, 1805, he followed up this advantage by administering a crushing defeat to the combined Austrians and Russians at Austerlitz in Moravia. With his capital, Vienna, and much of his territory occupied by the enemy, the Austrian emperor was reduced to bow down before the invincible Corsican and sign the Peace of Pressburg (December 26, 1805). By this document he gave up his Venetian acquisitions to the kingdom of Italy and the Tyrol to Bavaria, which German state had acted as Napoleon's ally.

These provisions introduce us to a very characteristic feature of Napoleon's policy of conquest. He did not plan to incorporate all the provinces which he might conquer directly with France but rather from France as a center to rule over a ring of Napoleon's dependent territories governed by princes under his con- German trol. Especially in regard to Germany, his policy was to policy reduce the influence of the two great powers, Austria and Prussia, by fattening the smaller states at their expense. Therefore, Würtemberg as well as Bavaria received some of the Austrian spoils and both were at the same time raised by him to the rank of kingdoms. Napoleon was now prepared for a still bolder step; he negotiated with the many small German states with a view to bringing them into a special union under his presidency. As they had neither the power nor the moral stamina to resist his persuasions, the world was presently informed of the organization of a new German confederacy, composed of Bavaria, Würtemberg, Baden, and in its final form of all the states of Germany except Austria and Prussia. Of this union, called the Confederation of the Rhine, Napoleon became sovereign under the title of Protector. A glance at the map will show how this triumph made him master alike of Germany and central Europe.

Naturally, the creation of a new German organization administered the death-blow to the Holy Roman Empire, deserted by its members. It had been an unconscionable time a-dying, and now End of the Napoleon, the product of a revolution which made sport Holy of tradition, bade it begone. Emperor Francis spoke Roman a last service over its remains when he resigned (1806) his Empire now empty title, and in order not to suffer loss of dignity adopted the new designation, emperor of Austria. Certainly no German, however much he might regret the manner of its taking off, had any cause to shed a tear at the passing away of this decrepit government. Though such was not his intention, Napoleon really did the German people an enormous service by lifting an incubus of centuries from their backs. With the Holy Roman Empire out of the way the path was cleared to a happier national future.

But that future was as yet hidden behind the clouds of the gathering storm which threatened to destroy every vestige of German independence. For with Austria humbled and the small states re-Napoleon duced to subservience in the Confederation of the Rhine, turns upon Napoleon now turned his attention to the remaining factor Prussia in the German situation, to Prussia. Ever since 1795 (Treaty of Basel) Prussia had remained steadily neutral, and all the persuasion and threats of the rest of Europe had not induced her to renew the war against her western neighbor. Even after Napoleon became emperor, the government of Berlin pursued an amicable course, weakly hoping for all kinds of advantages from a close association with France. But as soon as Napoleon had disposed of Austria and secured the support of the small German states, he showed his true hand and inaugurated toward Prussia a policy of provocations, which the obsequious government of the incompetent king, Frederick William III (1797–1840), refused for a long time to resent. However, by the autumn of 1806 Napoleon's acts had grown so flagrant that Prussia, to save the poor remnant of her self-respect, had to declare war.

Again Napoleon had an opportunity to show that the old military art of Europe could not maintain itself against his methods. As we examine these now, they surprise us by their mathematical simplicity. To get ready earlier than the enemy, to march Napoleon as more rapidly than he, and, finally, to strike him at the a strategist weakest spot with concentrated energy — these were the principles of Napoleon's military science which he combined with personal qualities of such hot daring and cool foresight that they have perhaps never been equalled.

The campaign of 1806 against Prussia brought Napoleon's genius into view more clearly than any that had preceded it. But if the emperor won, his soldiers shared the honors with him. For the Prussian troops, well-drilled mercenaries without any enthu- The siasm for the cause they represented, were as little the Prussian equals of the great national French armies, fighting for campaign, fame and country, as the Prussian commander, the an- 1806 cient duke of Brunswick, who had been trained in the antiquated school of Frederick the Great, was a match for the fiery young emperor. On October 14, 1806, old and new Europe clashed once more, and at the battles of Jena and Auerstädt, fought on that day, the military monarchy of the great Frederick was overwhelmed. With a bare handful of troops King Frederick William fled toward his province of East Prussia in order to put himself under the protection of Russia; and before the month of October had passed, Napoleon entered Berlin in triumph.

Practically all Prussia now lay in Napoleon's hand. Another man would have preferred to rest before continuing his march of triumph, but Napoleon was unsatisfied as long as there was anyone who dared brave his legions. In order to humble Tsar Alex- The ander, who had presumptuously allied himself with Prus- campaign sia and was bringing an army to her aid, Napoleon set out against from Berlin on a winter campaign which proved indeci- Russia, 1807 sive. However, in June, 1807, he met the Russians supported by the remnant of the Prussian army at Friedland and won a brilliant victory. Convinced that it was dangerous to penetrate farther east at that time, he now offered peace to Alexander and to the surprise of the world the enemy of yesterday became the bosom friend of today.

Tsar Alexander was a mercurial young man, easily elated and easily discouraged, and when Napoleon in a succession of personal interviews developed political plans to him in which a considerable part was assigned to Russia, he lent a willing ear. The consequence of the deliberations of the two emperors, of which the disgraced king of Prussia was for the most part a silent witness, was the Peace of Tilsit (July, 1807). By this peace Russia lost not a single village, but Prussia was thoroughly humiliated and condemned to the sacrifice of half her territory. The Prussian provinces between the Elbe and Rhine were made the nucleus of a new kingdom of Westphalia for Napoleon's youngest brother Jerome; and the Prussian spoils of the later Polish Partitions were constituted as the grand-duchy of Warsaw and given to the elector of Saxony. Prussia became a third-rate power with nothing more to boast of than that she still lived.

Treaty of Tilsit and humiliation of Prussia

But more than by the peace the world was agitated by the close alliance with which Alexander and Napoleon capped their Tilsit negotiations. By its terms the tsar promised, in case Great Britain refused to accept a mediation aiming at a general peace, to become Napoleon's ally against her. In return for this favor the French sovereign agreed to support Russia in her projects on Sweden and Turkey; and by way of good measure he diverted the impressionable Alexander with the picture of a Europe divided, as in Roman times, between an emperor of the west and another of the east.

Alliance of Napoleon and Alexander

The Peace of Tilsit carried Napoleon to the zenith of his career, for with Russia as his ally the rest of the continent was subject to his will and obliged to wear his yoke. Let us for a moment with the map before us review his position. He held directly in his hand an enlarged France which overflowed into Germany and Italy. This central nucleus he had surrounded with a host of dependencies where subject-princes ruled according to his will. As he could count with greater certainty on the members of his family than on strangers he had freely promoted his relatives to dependent thrones. While his brothers Louis and Jerome served as kings of Holland and Westphalia respectively, his brother Joseph had been assigned to the kingdom of Naples and his brother-in-law, the brilliant cavalry general, Murat, had been made grand-duke of Berg. Berg, like Westphalia, was an artificial creation out of the German spoils; both states were of course incorporated in the

Napoleon at the height of his power

Confederation of the Rhine and helped to keep it faithful to its mighty Protector. As his most capable relative was probably his step-son, Eugene Beauharnais, son of the Empress Josephine by her first marriage, Napoleon employed him as viceroy in his kingdom of Italy. Even in the Swiss Confederation he exercised control under the title of Mediator. If we now add that by a succession of unparalleled strokes, delivered between 1805 and 1807, he had humbled Austria, Prussia, and Russia, we shall agree that he had nothing further to fear upon the continent. He could therefore resume the struggle with his most inaccessible and elusive foe, with Great Britain.

This struggle is the most momentous chapter in Napoleon's career. Adjourned at the Peace of Amiens (1802), it had broken out again the next year and led to the armament of Boulogne and the plan to invade the island. The project proved to be unrealizable *The war* because Great Britain controlled the waters with a superior *with Great* fleet; and such slight chance as it may have had of being *Britain* carried out at a later time was completely blasted while Napoleon was fighting the Austerlitz campaign. For in October, 1805, Nelson encountered the French fleet off Cape Trafalgar on the Spanish coast, and though he paid for his victory with his life, destroyed the hostile armament. Since Napoleon commanded no further naval resources, effective fighting on the seas came to an end with this disaster. The Corsican might march with his invincible army from capital to capital; his control stopped with the shore.

Undismayed by his inability to attack England directly, Napoleon now resolved to strike at her indirectly by ruining her commerce and sapping her wealth. He devised an elaborate commercial war which has received the name of the Continental System. In *Commercial* this new war he fired his opening gun when in November, *war: the* 1806, he issued from Berlin a decree by which he ordered *Continental* the seizure of all British goods in his own or allied terri- *System* tories and rigorously excluded from their ports all British ships. His calculation was that the requisite supplies of non-European articles, such as sugar and coffee, would be furnished by the vessels of neutral powers, primarily by the United States. To destroy this hope the British answered the Berlin Decree with an Order in Council whereby, under penalty of seizure, they forbade neutral ships to visit ports from which the British were excluded unless they had first put in at British ports to take on a consignment of British goods. To this Napoleon's counterblast was to declare every neutral vessel which obeyed the British order subject to confiscation. Plainly neutrals were between the devil and the deep sea and were welcome only if they rendered service to one or the other combatant. On signing the alliance with Russia Napoleon was able to carry his commercial war to its logical conclusion. This was hermetically to seal the whole continent of Europe against British trade. His dependencies had of course no voice in the matter and were simply expected to obey the orders they received; Austria and Prussia, having been defeated, had already been obliged to meet the imperial wish and close their ports to British ships; and at Tilsit Russia, too, was persuaded to acquiesce in the Napoleonic policy. Nay, more, the tsar agreed to join the emperor in forcing the closure of ports to British goods on every state of Europe which still yearned for British trade. No continental neutrals were to be tolerated on any pretext whatsoever and the mass of Europe was to be flung into the struggle as an economic whole.

With Napoleon and Alexander standing together no state in Europe could resist the program. By persuasion or threats they all came in with the exception of little Portugal, which, being far away and de-
Continental pendent for its living on English trade, ventured to re-
System a fuse. Thereupon Napoleon sent an army across the
main cause Pyrenees which drove out the Portuguese royal family
of and successfully occupied the country (November, 1807).
Napoleon's
ultimate The seizure looked like the final triumph of Napoleon's
failure system but appearances are frequently deceitful. At the
moment indeed Napoleon's will was law from St. Petersburg to Lisbon, but in the long view of the emperor's career Tilsit and the Continental System mark, if a culmination, also the beginning of decline. In the first place his new purpose involved him in new and ever new wars; and secondly, by dislocating and ruining commerce and industry throughout Europe he created a discontent which lost him his popularity and proceeded at last from sporadic rebellions to a general revolt. It is necessary to remember in this connection that the emperor's astonishing successes had been won over old-fashioned, absolute monarchies, set at such a height above their peoples as to be out of direct touch with them. In Italy and Germany more particularly the masses to a considerable extent had sympathized with Napoleon, for he represented the principles of the French Revolution and his armies brought in their train the overthrow of such feudal evils as serfdom and the reign of privilege. But this precious support

the emperor sacrificed when he paralyzed the economic life of Europe and carried exasperation into every city and village. Greeted at first as a liberator, he was gradually cursed as a scourge and reaped the harvest of his policy in a series of national revolts which swept himself, his throne, and his family off the face of Europe. It is of course questionable whether Napoleon's cosmopolitan empire, based on the subjection of so many ancient and spirited nationalities, would have endured under any circumstances; it is certain that by means of the Continental System he himself made adequate provision for his failure.

If the occupation of Portugal was an act of unjustifiable violence, it dwindled to blue-eyed innocence compared with what happened immediately after in Spain, for there the emperor struck a friend and ally. The history of Spain during the French Revolution is a miserable tale, largely because of the despicable character of the Bourbon king, Charles IV, and the rank corruption of the court. Having made war upon the Revolution in its first stage, the king had as early as 1795 signed a peace, which in the period of the consulate had ripened into an alliance with the late enemy. For the sake of his good friend Napoleon, Charles IV had joined his fleet to that of France, and also for the sake of that friend he had sacrificed it at Trafalgar, where, acting in support of the French fleet, it had been all but destroyed. As a return for these good offices, Napoleon now deliberately planned to seize the country of his ally, probably in the first instance because he did not feel secure in Portugal unless he had Spain absolutely in his hands. Taking advantage of a quarrel between Charles IV and his son Ferdinand — two clowns as disgusting as any that have ever masqueraded in a royal mantle — he invited the pair to Bayonne, just across the border, in order to lay their quarrel before him. There the trap closed on them and the two simpletons were forced to resign their royal rights to the wily arbiter (May, 1808). Spain was thereupon given to Joseph Bonaparte, who before assuming his new dignity was obliged to surrender the kingdom of Naples, held since 1806, to Caroline Bonaparte's husband, Murat. For not quite two years Murat had served as grand-duke of Berg in Germany. These exchanges of territory were a part of the system by which the omnipotent ruler impressed their servile status upon his political puppets.

The shameless violence and duplicity by which Napoleon seized the crown of Spain sent a thrill of horror through the Spanish

The policy of Spain during the Revolution

people. By disposing of them as if they were a nation at auction he had wounded their pride, and instead of a peaceful occupation he found himself confronted with an insurrection. It was a new The insur- phenomenon upon the emperor's path of which he utterly rection of failed to catch the significance. Convinced, soldier-Spain like, that there was no obstacle in the world which would not yield to force, he rapidly diagnosed the Spanish situation as requiring a little treatment by cold steel. If the Spaniards had met in the open field the regular army which he now launched against them, it is plain that their ineffective forces would have gone down before the French eagles like the rest of Europe. But wisely they assembled only in small guerrilla bands, swept from ambuscades upon French detachments and rear-guards, and were gone again before they could be punished. The summer of 1808 brought Napoleon through these tactics his first serious military disasters; and to make things worse England at once took notice of the situation and projected herself into it. Having waited in vain for Napoleon to seek her on the sea, she found and seized this opportunity to seek him on the land. In the summer of 1808 a British army disembarked in the peninsula for the purpose of supporting the Spanish revolt. When Napoleon, angered by the check received by his political system, appeared in person on the scene (autumn, 1808), he had no difficulty in sweeping the Spaniards into the hills and the British to their ships, but he was hardly gone when the scattered guerrillas ventured forth from their retreats and the British forced a new landing.

Napoleon had now to learn that a people resolved to live free can not be conquered. The Spanish war swallowed up vast sums and immense forces, but the emperor, as stubborn in his way as the Napoleon Spaniards, would give ear to no suggestion of concession. can not put Slowly, however, circumstances told against him. The the Span- revolt showed no signs of abating; and when, in 1809, a iards down capable general, Sir Arthur Wellesley, better known by his later title of duke of Wellington, took command of the British forces, and, using Portugal as his base, foot by foot forced his way toward Madrid, Napoleon's Spanish enterprise became hopeless. Of course that was not at once apparent; but what did very soon become clear was that the enslaved states of central Europe were taking the cue from the Spaniards and making ready for a similar struggle with their oppressor.

In the year 1809 Austria, encouraged by the Spanish successes, was inspired to arouse the Germans to a national revolt. But the effort was premature, for as Prussia was still occupied by French troops and the whole territory of the Confederation of the Rhine was pledged to Napoleon's interests, only detached bodies in the Tyrol, in Jerome's kingdom of Westphalia and elsewhere, responded to Austria's call. At Wagram (July, 1809) Napoleon laid Austria a fourth time at his feet. In the Peace of Vienna, which followed, she was forced to make fresh cessions of territory not only to France but also to Napoleon's satellites, such as Bavaria and the duchy of Warsaw. The territory yielded to France included Austria's only sea-port, Trieste, and, joined to Dalmatia, was constituted as the Illyrian Province. It was but a trunk shorn of its boughs which the conqueror left; and it is not improbable that he would have felled the trunk, too, if he had not been forced at this time to provide for a complete change of his political system.

Austria tries to organize a German insurrection

The fact was the Tsar Alexander was growing tired of the alliance of Tilsit for many reasons, but chiefly perhaps because his adherence to the Continental System proved ruinous to his country. Napoleon noticed the diminishing heartiness of the tsar and resolved to secure himself against defection by means of an alliance with Austria. That state was, after the war of 1809, in no position to refuse the proffered hand; and when Napoleon further demanded the emperor's daughter, Marie Louise, in marriage, that request, too, had to be granted. That he had ever since 1796 been married to Josephine Beauharnais was a slight annoyance which could be and was removed by means of divorce. Although various reasons were alleged in support of his suit, the only genuine one was that the union had remained childless and that Napoleon imperatively needed a son to perpetuate his dynasty. In April, 1810, the military upstart, for that is what Napoleon was from the point of view of the drawing-room and the court, celebrated his union with a daughter of the ancient imperial line of Hapsburg; and when, in the succeeding year, there was born to him a son and heir to whom he gave in his cradle the resounding title of king of Rome, he could fancy that his empire had acquired a secure dynastic foundation.

Napoleon changes his political system, Russia being replaced by Austria

And surely never did Napoleon's power exhibit a greater outward splendor, never did his behests meet with more implicit obedience

than in the year 1811. The spoiled son of fortune had now acquired the imperious habit of falling into a rage at the slightest sign of opposition. Imposing the Continental System with increas-
Review of ing rigor, he punished the pope and his own brother
Napoleon's Louis with the loss of their territories when they seemed
position to him to slacken their vigilance toward British goods. One
in 1811 cloud would not disperse and that was the Spanish
rising; but with the help of a little illusion that struggle could be comfortably minimized to an outbreak of bandits and guerrillas. As Napoleon looked about conquered Europe, he might not unreasonably imagine that now was the auspicious time to put an end to the last independent state of the continent, the eastern colossus, Russia. He had made a friend of that nation largely for the purpose of European solidarity against Great Britain; but now that the tsar was secretly opening his ports to British goods, he was adjudged to have broken the alliance and to have merited an exemplary punishment.

The breach between Napoleon and Alexander became definite in the course of the year 1811. Both powers began preparations for war, and in the spring of 1812 Napoleon set in movement toward
Invasion of Russia the greatest armament that Europe had ever
Russia, 1812 seen. A half million men, representing all the nationalities of Napoleon's cosmopolitan empire, French, Germans, Italians, Poles, seemed more than adequate to the task of bringing the tsar under the law of the emperor. And the expedition was at first attended by many superficial successes. The Russians, retreating before Napoleon, drew him ever farther from his supplies; and when they at last made a stand suffered a defeat which cleared the road to Moscow. On September 15th Napoleon entered the Russian capital. It was his view that the submission of Alexander would now follow automatically.

But he had underrated the spirit of resistance which animated the empire of the tsar. Here, as in Spain, a determination to die rather than yield possessed every inhabitant, and Napoleon had
Napoleon at already received ample evidence of the national aversion
Moscow in the deserted villages through which he marched. Any lingering doubt on this head was dramatically settled at Moscow. Rather than have their capital fall into the hands of the French, the retreating Russians set fire to it, leaving to the victorious emperor nothing but a smoking heap of useless ashes.

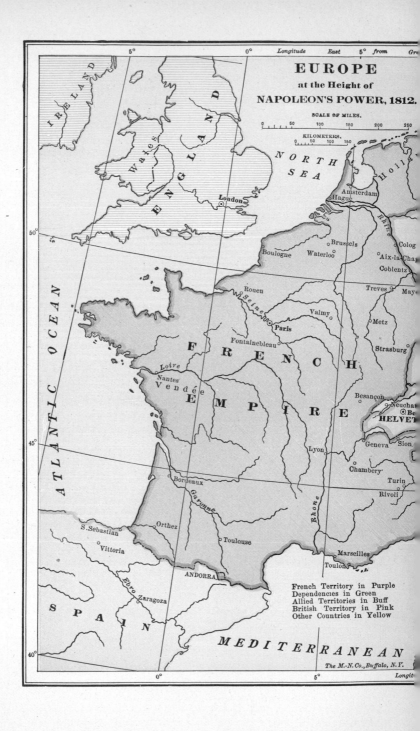

EUROPE
at the Height of
NAPOLEON'S POWER, 1812.

SCALE OF MILES.

French Territory in Purple
Dependencies in Green
Allied Territories in Buff
British Territory in Pink
Other Countries in Yellow

The M.-N. Co., Buffalo, N.Y.

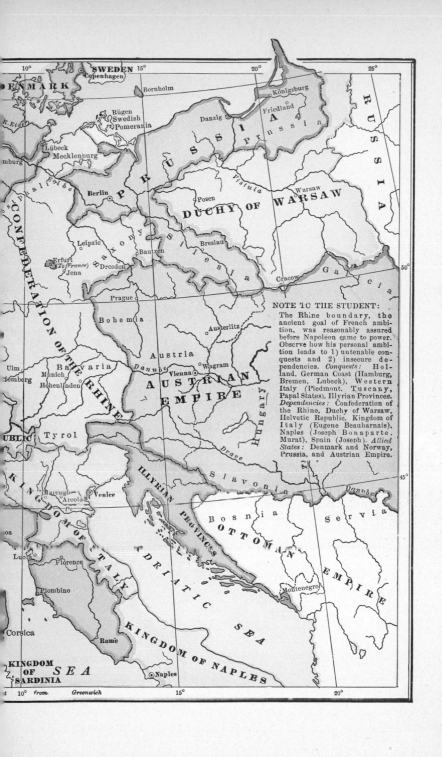

NOTE TO THE STUDENT:

The Rhine boundary, the ancient goal of French ambition, was reasonably assured before Napoleon came to power. Observe how his personal ambition leads to 1) untenable conquests and 2) insecure dependencies. *Conquests:* Holland, German Coast (Hamburg, Bremen, Lubeck), Western Italy (Piedmont, Tuscany, Papal States), Illyrian Provinces. *Dependencies:* Confederation of the Rhine, Duchy of Warsaw, Helvetic Republic, Kingdom of Italy (Eugene Beauharnais), Naples (Joseph Bonaparte, Murat), Spain (Joseph). *Allied States:* Denmark and Norway, Prussia, and Austrian Empire.

In the vain hope that the tsar, unnerved by the invasion of his country, would offer to make peace, Napoleon lingered among the ruins of Moscow for over a month. But as for once Alexander was firm, their delay overwhelmed the French with dis- The aster. For since the retreat, unavoidable in a country Russian eaten bare of supplies, was not begun till October 19th, disaster the troops were overtaken by winter in a vast country with impassable roads and were buried under its blasts. To the misery of cold were added hunger, disease, and the constant raids of the swift-moving Cossacks until the formidable Grand Army of the spring had melted into a few scattered bands of struggling fugitives. Napoleon directed the retreat through the first stages, but early in December he set out for Paris, realizing that he had sacrificed the greatest army ever united under his command in an impossible enterprise. In his absence Marshal Ney, "the bravest of the brave," fighting like a common soldier, did what valor could to save the honor of the French Empire and the remnant of its military power. Late in December a few thousand starved, broken, and half-crazed men, whose brothers strewed the frozen plains of Russia, tottered across the Niemen into the comparative safety of an area held by French reserves.

The loss of his splendid army was, in any case, a serious calamity for Napoleon. But it would become an irremediable catastrophe if it encouraged Germany, long throbbing with suppressed indignation, to rise in revolt and create new complications at a juncture The revolt when he required all his strength to repair the supreme of Germany disaster of his life. Unluckily for Napoleon the growing body of German patriots felt this fact instinctively and were uplifted with the consciousness that never again would such an opportunity be offered them. They wanted a general and national rising; but they saw that its success would be best assured if it could be organized around Prussia as a nucleus. And Prussia, which Napoleon had trampled in the dust at Jena and shut in a tomb at Tilsit, did not deceive their expectations and raised the standard of revolt.

Prussia since her overwhelming disasters had gone through a renovation which is one of the remarkable revivals of history. Her leading men had come to see that her overthrow was the inevitable consequence of her backward conditions and reached the The renais- conclusion that new foundations would have to be laid by sance of a series of sweeping reforms. Temporarily silenced by Prussia his disasters, the stiff and reactionary king, Frederick William III, hesitatingly yielded to their importunities. Stein, a man of broad vision, was appointed chief minister, and with Scharnhorst in charge of the war department and with other audacious spirits in high places, a number of important reforms were carried through. Serfdom was declared abolished; and together with serfdom all the old feudal class divisions were swept aside in favor of a united citizenry equal before the law. Further, the old mercenary and professional army defeated at Jena was replaced by a national army based on the principle of universal military service first applied by the French republicans in 1793. Plainly such fundamental changes gave Prussia many of the advantages of the French Revolution. And with the new institutions was born a new spirit, unknown hitherto in this feudal and military state, which bound high and low together in a common passionate love of country. When this revived nation heard of Napoleon's ruin on the Russian snow-fields, all classes alike were seized with the conviction that the great hour of revenge had come; no debate, no delay on the part of the timid king was suffered; and resistlessly swept along by the rising tide of enthusiasm, he was forced to sign an alliance with Russia and declare war (March, 1813).

The disastrous campaign of 1812 would have reduced any other man than Napoleon to complete exhaustion. But he faced the new situation as undaunted as ever. By herculean efforts he succeeded **The campaign of 1813: first part** in mustering and training a new army, and in the spring of 1813 appeared suddenly in the heart of Germany, ready to punish the new coalition. Everything hinged for him on his defeating Russia and Prussia before the Confederation of the Rhine, already simmering with revolt, and Austria, only waiting for a chance to recover her own, had declared against him. At Lützen (May 2) and at Bautzen (May 20) he maintained his ancient reputation by driving the allies from the field. But clearly the day of the Jenas and Friedlands was over, for not only did he capture no cannon or men, but the enemy fell back in good order on Silesia, while Napoleon had to confess that his victories had been paid for by such heavy losses that to win, at this rate, was equivalent to ruin. On June 4th he agreed to an armistice in order to reorganize his troops and to take stock of the political situation.

Both parties now became aware that the issue of the campaign depended upon Austria, for so delicately adjusted were the scales between the contestants, that the side upon which she would throw her influence would be sure to win. In these circumstances

Metternich, Austria's unscrupulous and juggling minister, undertook, at first, the role of mediator; but when Napoleon indignantly rejected the conditions for a general peace which Metternich proposed, Austria threw in her lot with the European coalition, which by this addition came to embrace the three continental powers and Great Britain.   In August, 1813, at the expiration of the truce, there followed a concerted forward movement on the part of the allies, now for the first time since Napoleon's advent to power firmly cemented together.   Prussians, Russians, and Austrians crowded in upon Napoleon, who sat ensconced in the heart of Germany, in Saxony, where he defended the strategic line of the Elbe river.   Having the smaller force, he saw his outposts gradually driven in, himself outmanœuvred, and his dissolving army crushed utterly in a savage three days' battle at Leipzig (October 16–18).   With such remnants as he could hold together he hurried across the Rhine.   Germany was lost beyond recovery.   The question now was: Would he be able to retain France?

The campaign of 1813: second part

If the great conqueror could have seen a future for himself in France in the role of a beaten man, he might have ended the war by the acceptance of the Rhine boundary, which the allies now offered.   But he believed that he could not afford to end the war with a defeat and by rejecting the proffered peace obliged his enemies to continue the struggle.   In the winter they invaded France, resolved to annihilate him before he had recovered his strength.   His defensive campaign, conducted in the cold of winter with slender forces, is regarded by military men as among his most brilliant achievements; but he was now hopelessly outnumbered, and when, on March 31, the allies forced the gates of Paris, even Napoleon's confidence received a shock. As he looked about him he saw the whole east of France in the hands of his enemies, while the south was as rapidly falling into the power of Wellington, who in the two victorious campaigns of 1812 and 1813 had finally pushed the French completely out of Spain and was now engaged in pursuing them across the Pyrenees.

The winter campaign of 1814

On April 6, 1814, at his castle of Fontainebleau, Napoleon acknowledged that all was over and offered his abdication.   The allies conceded him the island of Elba (off the coast of Tuscany) as a residence, and then gave their attention to the problem of the future of France.   Not from any enthusiasm for the house of Bourbon, but

merely because there seemed to them to be no other way out of the difficulties, they finally gave their sanction to the accession to the throne of Louis XVIII, brother of the last king. As re-
Abdication of Napoleon; return of Bourbons
gards the extent of the restored kingdom, it was agreed in the Peace of Paris that France was substantially to receive the boundaries which she enjoyed at the outbreak of the revolutionary wars in 1792.

This important preliminary matter arranged, a general congress of the powers assembled at Vienna to discuss the reconstruction of Europe. The modern age has rarely seen a more brilliant gathering of notabilities. All the sovereigns and statesmen who
The Congress of Vienna
had stood in the center of public attention during the last momentous years were, with few exceptions, present, and a single drawing-room sometimes held the mobile Tsar Alexander, the grave Wellington, the ardent German patriot Stein, the courtly Frenchman Talleyrand, and that passionate enemy of revolutionary change, the Austrian chancellor Metternich. But before the Congress of Vienna had ended its labors, the anti-Napoleonic coalition, which the congress represented, was once more called upon to take the field. For in March, 1815, the startling news reached the allied statesmen at Vienna that Napoleon had made his escape from Elba and had once more landed in France.

The resolution formed by Napoleon, after only a few months of exile, to try conclusions once more with united Europe, was the resolution of despair. Without doubt it was folly on the part of the
Napoleon returns from Elba
allies to expect that a man like him, with a burning craving for activity, would ever content himself with the island-realm of Elba, especially as France, his willing prize, lay just a few leagues across the water. However, it was even greater folly on the part of Napoleon to fancy that he could thwart the will of united Europe. A gambler by nature, he waited till he saw what seemed to him a rift in the coalition and plunged into a new adventure. On March 1st he landed unexpectedly near Cannes, accompanied by eight hundred of his old veterans, who had been permitted to attend him in exile as a guard of honor; and no sooner had he displayed his banners than his former soldiers streamed to the standards to which they were attached by innumerable stirring memories. Marshal Ney, who was sent out by Louis XVIII, the restored Bourbon king, to take Napoleon captive, broke into tears at sight of his old leader and folded him in his arms.

There was no resisting the magnetic power of the name Napoleon. The familiar *"Vive l'empereur!"* rang through France till the luke-warm partisans of the Bourbon dynasty fell away from it with feverish alacrity. Discouraged by the diminishing ranks of his supporters, Louis presently fled across the border, while, hailed by the soldiers and common people but hardly by the bourgeoisie whom his perpetual wars had estranged, Napoleon once more entered Paris.

The Hundred Days, as Napoleon's restoration is called, form a mere after-play to the great drama which began with the coronation at Notre Dame, reached its climax at Tilsit, and had the curtain rung on it at Fontainebleau. Napoleon's empire was a **The Hun-** thing of the past and it was hopeless to revive it against **dred Days** the will of a united Europe. The proof is furnished by the action of the members of the coalition at Vienna as soon as they heard of Napoleon's return from exile: unhesitatingly they renewed the war and prepared for a fresh invasion of France. The issue was decided with spectacular suddenness in Belgium. There Wellington stood at the head of a composite Anglo-Dutch-Hanoverian army, and thither marched to his assistance from the lower Rhine, where he had been in winter-quarters, Marshal Blücher with his Prussians. These enemies, because they were closest at hand, Napoleon resolved to meet first. With his usual swiftness he fell upon Blücher on June 16th at Ligny, before this general could unite with the forces of Welling-ton, and beat him roundly. Leaving Marshal Grouchy with 30,000 men to pursue the Prussians, Napoleon next turned, on June 18th, against his remaining adversary.

Wellington, who had taken a strong defensive position near Waterloo, resolutely awaited the French attack. All the afternoon Napoleon hurled his infantry and cavalry against the "iron duke's" positions without dislodging his tough opponent, and **Waterloo,** when in the late afternoon the Prussians unexpectedly **June 18,** made their appearance on his right he was caught between **1815** two fires. Blücher had evaded his French pursuer and by a forced march had reached the battlefield. Unable to disentangle itself, Napoleon's army was completely ruined. Precipitately the em-peror fled to Paris and there abdicated a second time. Deserted by all in his misfortunes, he now planned to escape to America, but finding the coast guarded by English cruisers, was obliged to take passage on the British ship *Bellerophon* to be carried first to Eng-land, and thence, in accordance with the verdict of his victorious enemies, to the remote and rocky mid-Atlantic island of St. Helena. There, six years later (1821), he died, a lonely and embittered exile.

At Paris, meanwhile, the allies once more restored Louis XVIII to his ancestral throne by virtue of a new instrument called the Second Treaty of Paris. It differed from the document of the previous year in nothing more than that France was obliged to pay for her renewed acceptance of Napoleon by having imposed on her a few border rectifications and a considerable money indemnity.

Second restoration of Louis XVIII

. . . .

With Napoleon's elimination a reaction seized upon Europe which was as natural as it was irresistible. For not only was revolutionary conquest discredited when Napoleon fell, but no less so were the revolutionary principles in which he had his origin and with which he had been more or less identified to the end. The victory of the coalition was interpreted as a victory of monarchy by Divine Right as well as of the old feudal classes, the clergy and nobility, historically identified with monarchy. Through their triumph the monarchs and the old ruling classes gained a new and arrogant self-assurance, while the middle classes, which in 1789 had acted in the confident belief that their hour had at last struck, received a set-back. Plainly France and all Europe were about to experience a period of reaction.

The reaction

Before narrating the incidents of that reaction it may be well to assure ourselves that the eclipse of the middle classes could not in the nature of things be other than temporary. As their vigor had been steadily ripening for generations and was fundamental to the whole European structure, it was inconceivable that they should be permanently barred from political influence. Partly in consequence of the recent Revolution, but chiefly because of a long evolutionary process, they had become reasonably clear in their minds as to their program and did not dream of abandoning it when the reaction temporarily triumphed. In fact, in so far as that program had already become an integral part of the social and legal system of France and her neighbors, the reaction itself did not dare to disturb it. This program, formulated with a view to undermining the conservative tradition in the state, drew much of its sustenance from eighteenth century enlightenment; in the nineteenth century it has usually sailed under the summary

Persistence of the political program of the middle classes

name of liberalism. Although we are anticipating, its leading features deserve enumeration at this point, since by means of them we learn not only what united the liberals throughout Europe after 1815 but also what conferred upon the civilization of the new century its leading political characteristics.

1. *Equality before the law.* Incensed against the feudal orders with their privileges and honors, the middle classes insisted on a leveling to be effected by means of a common citizenship involving equal rights and burdens for the whole population.

2. *Religious toleration.* For the middle classes a dominant church, which undertook to dictate what men were to believe and which threatened to punish every departure from its standards, had become both an absurdity and a nuisance. Their growing sense of personal freedom made them insist on liberation from clerical control coupled with toleration of all reasonable beliefs and cults.

3. *Sovereignty of the people.* To discredit monarchy by Divine Right it would have to be replaced by another principle. This in an age which was turning from dogmatism to empiricism, from gods to men, could only be the sovereignty of the people. That signified in effect that the Divine Right of kings was replaced by the more credible Divine Right of the people. It is true that the bourgeoisie meant by sovereignty of the people the sovereignty of *their* people, that is, of the property holders. The proof is supplied by their unfailing attempt to limit the franchise. However, in theoretic discussion at least the sovereignty of the people could not be held to signify anything else than the sovereignty of the whole citizen body; and the unassailable character of this logic always served to undermine bourgeois exclusiveness and to favor the larger definition.

4. *Nationalism.* The bourgeoisie in fusing all classes into a single legal class made possible the nation in the modern sense. Henceforth under middle class guidance all groups which felt a common impulse due to community of race, language, customs, and institutions were certain to aspire to the leveling of accidental class and state barriers in order to effect a close political fusion. This self-assertion of the national mass came to be called nationalism.

In these four features of the middle class program is indicated the order of liberal ideas with which the conservative reaction of 1815 was met and finally overcome. Realized for the first time in the French Revolution, they served on their revival as the basis for the political reorganization of Europe.

REFERENCES

R. M. JOHNSTON, *The French Revolution; Napoleon*
S. MATHEWS, *The French Revolution*
C. H. HAYES, *Political and Social History*, I, chs. 15, 16
E. FUETER, *World History*, chs. 1, 2, 4–6
C. D. HAZEN, *The French Revolution and Napoleon*
E. R. TURNER, *Europe 1789–1920*, chs. 3, 4
C. M. ANDREWS, *Historical Development of Modern Europe*, I, chs. 1, 2
C. A. FYFFE, *History of Modern Europe, 1792–1878*
H. E. BOURNE, *Revolutionary Period in Europe*
H. M. STEPHENS, *Revolutionary Europe*
F. S. MARVIN, *Century of Hope*, ch. 1
J. R. M. MACDONALD, *France*, II, ch. 28, III, chs. 29–34
Cambridge Modern History, VIII, IX
H. TAINE, *The Ancient Régime*
E. LOWELL, *Eve of the French Revolution*
J. H. ROSE, *The Revolutionary and Napoleonic Era; Life of Napoleon I*
L. MADELIN, *French Revolution; Consulate and Empire; Life of Danton*
A. TILLEY, *Modern France*
J. A. R. MARRIOTT, *The Remaking of Modern Europe*, chs. 1–11
A. L. CROSS, *History of England*, chs. 45, 46
E. F. HENDERSON, *Short History of Germany*, II, chs. 6, 7; *Bluecher and the Uprising of Prussia*
G. M. PRIEST, *Germany Since 1740*, ch. 7
J. H. CLAPHAM, *The Abbé Sieyès*
H. BELLOC, *Robespierre*
NAPOLEON, *Letters to Josephine, 1796–1812*
A. FOURNIER, *Napoleon I*
J. C. ROPES, *The First Napoleon*
H. A. L. FISHER, *Studies in Napoleonic Statesmanship in Germany; Napoleon*
A. T. MAHAN, *Influence of Sea Power upon the French Revolution and Empire*
LORD ROSEBERY, *Life of William Pitt*
J. R. SEELEY, *Life and Times of Stein*
G. S. FORD, *Stein*
C. T. ATKINSON, *A History of Germany*, chs. 18–35

CHAPTER XX

THE CONSERVATIVE REACTION

The Congress of Vienna, which met to arrange the affairs of Europe after the unparalleled storms of the past generation, gathered the agreements reached among the powers regarding the many matters in debate in a summary document called the Final Act. The Taken in connection with the Peace of Paris, this docu- principles ment traces the political geography of reconstructed which governed the Europe. It also conveys an idea of the principles and Congress sentiments which animated the victors. Although ve- of Vienna hemently condemned by the following generation, they can not fail to be recognized as the logical expression of the conservative triumph. Since the Viennese diplomats felt that by erasing the old boundaries and toppling over the old dynasties the French Revolution had created a general unrest, they persuaded themselves without much difficulty that the surest way to achieve security and permanence would be to reëstablish as far as possible all the states, great and small, in existence before the late disturbances. These states were said to be "legitimate," as against the illegitimate creations of the Revolution and Napoleon. The desirability of separating the sheep from the goats on the score of this distinction of legitimacy, was, in the interest of his master, the restored Louis XVIII, first championed by the supple French diplomat, Talleyrand, and gradually imposed itself as a piece of divine wisdom upon the congress. But while legitimacy made for a general restoration, the four victor powers did not forget to compensate themselves territorially for their past losses and labors. Their hunger for land modified the plan of a restoration pure and simple; and that plan was further affected by the desire to check all possible future aggressions on the part of the feared and hated disturber, France. Legitimacy, territorial compensation for the victors, and hostility to France are the main forces out of the interaction of which grew the new map of Europe.

The greatest interest at the congress gathered around central Europe as the region which had been subjected to the most sweeping territorial changes by the Revolution. In Italy restoration met with few obstacles and was carried through with two notable exceptions. Instead of being restored as an independent state the republic of Genoa was given to the king of Sardinia in order to strengthen him against France; and the republic of Venice was delivered to the emperor of Austria as a compensation for the loss of Belgium. The German settlement caused much more trouble since a return to 1789 would have meant the reëstablishment of the Holy Roman Empire, which everybody was glad to be rid of. But how to replace it? On this head there were wide differences of opinion. A small group of fiery patriots clamored for a strong united Germany, but the German princes were so attached to their separate sovereignty that they would agree to nothing but a loose federation, which was finally accepted. Great was the agitation when the question of territorial compensation for Prussia, one of the four victor powers, came up, for Prussia desired to incorporate Saxony, a small German neighbor. The right of Prussia to an indemnity was admitted in principle on account of its surrender to Russia of most of its Polish territory; and Saxony was in some quarters regarded as reasonable payment, on the ground that its king, having exhibited an exceptional attachment to Napoleon, had forfeited whatever claim to be restored he might have had under the theory of legitimacy. The truth was Prussia and Russia had come to a private agreement over the heads of the congress by which Russia, in return for the bulk of the Prussian Polish spoils, agreed to support Prussia in her effort to gain Saxony. Over this issue the congress was rocked as a boat by a storm, for Austria, Great Britain, and France firmly declared themselves against the Russo-Prussian bargain. Nor was the conflict adjusted by a compromise until both sides had begun to make preparations for war. By the final agreement Prussia got half of Saxony, the remainder being returned to the "legitimate" sovereign. For the part she gave up she received in exchange territory on the left bank of the Rhine (the Rhine province), which brought her into direct contact with France and imposed on her the defense of Germany against its western neighbor. In the final settlement of the Polish-Saxon crisis the tsar received Napoleon's creation, the so-called grand-duchy of Warsaw, with the exception of the province of Posen which was left in the hands of Prussia. This Polish acquisition Alexander agreed to constitute as the kingdom of Poland with himself as king.

Restoration and compensation in Central Europe

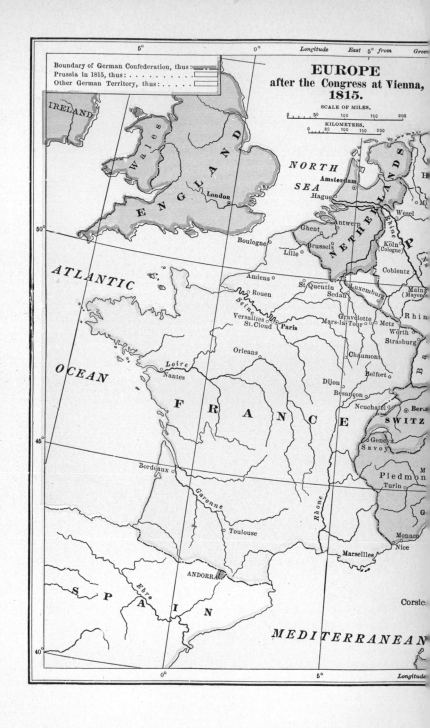

Boundary of German Confederation, thus:
Prussia in 1815, thus: . . . .
Other German Territory, thus: . . . . .

EUROPE
after the Congress at Vienna,
1815.

SCALE OF MILES.
50   100   150   200

KILOMETERS.
50   100   150   200

IRELAND

Wales

E N G L A N D

London

N O R T H
S E A
Amsterdam
Hague

N E T H E R L A N D S

H

Wesel

Köln
(Cologne)

P

Coblentz

A T L A N T I C

Amiens
Rouen
Seine
Versailles
St. Cloud
Paris

Boulogne
Lille

Ghent
Brussels

Antwerp
Rhine

St. Quentin
Sedan
Luxemburg

Mainz
(Mayence)

R h i n

Gravelotte
Mars-la-Tour
Metz
Wörth
Strasburg

O C E A N

Loire
Nantes

Orleans

Chaumont

Dijon
Besançon

Belfort

B

Neuchatel
Ber.

F   R   A   N   C   E

SWITZ

Geneva
Savoy

40°

Bordeaux

Garonne

Piedmon
Turin

M

G

Rhone

Toulouse

Monaco
Nice

Marseilles

ANDORRA

S   P   A   I   N

Ebro

Corsic

M E D I T E R R A N E A N

40°

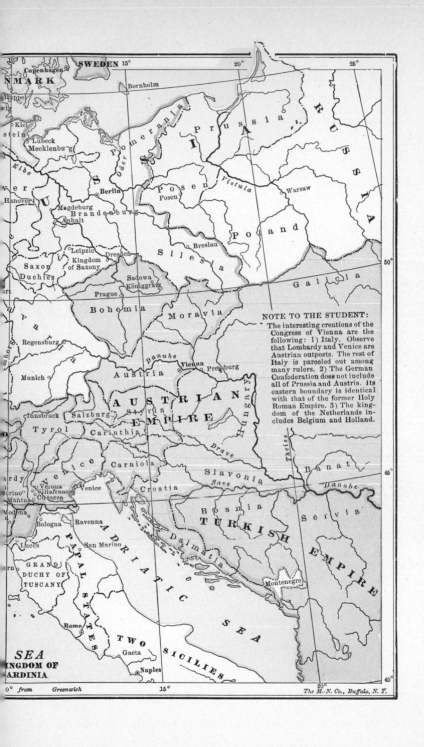

SWEDEN 15°   20°   25°

Copenhagen
NMARK
Düppel   Bornholm
Kiel   R
stein   P
Lübeck Mecklenburg o   S   I   P r u s s i a   U
Elbe   m   S
ver   Hanover U e Oder E S I A   S
                r
            Berlin   Posen   Warsaw   I
        Magdeburg Brandenburg Posen Vistula   A
        Anhalt
                                        P o l a n d
        Leipzic Dresden Breslau   50°
Saxon Kingdom of Saxony S i l e s i a
Duchies   Sadowa   G a l i c i a
        Prague Königgrätz

        B o h e m i a   M o r a v i a

Regensburg   Danube   NOTE TO THE STUDENT:
                          Vienna Pressburg   The interesting creations of the
Munich   A u s t r i a   Congress of Vienna are the
                                                 following: 1) Italy. Observe
        A U S T R I A N   that Lombardy and Venice are
Innsbruck Salzburg Styria E M P I R E   Austrian outposts. The rest of
T y r o l   Carinthia   Italy is parceled out among
                                        Hungary   many rulers. 2) The German
                                                 Confederation does not include
        V e n i c e Carniola   all of Prussia and Austria. Its
                                        Drave   eastern boundary is identical
ardy   with that of the former Holy
erino Verona Villafranc Venice Croatia Slavonia Theiss Banat Roman Empire. 3) The king-
Mantua Custozza   Save   Danube dom of the Netherlands in-
Modena   cludes Belgium and Holland. 45°
Bologna Ravenna   B o s n i a   Servia
Lucca   T U R K I S H
        San Marino   Dalmatia   E M P I R E
GRAND
DUCHY OF   Montenegro
TUSCANY   A D R I A T I C
Rome   S E A
        T W O
SEA   Gaeta   S I C I L I E S
NGDOM OF
ARDINIA   Naples   40°
0° from   Greenwich   15°   20°   The M.-N. Co., Buffalo, N. Y.

Between France and Germany lay Belgium and Holland, both incorporated with France during the period of French ascendancy. In order to establish a strong bulwark against France the congress consolidated these two territories and placed them under the rule of the house of Orange. The new creation received the name of the kingdom of the Netherlands. Great Britain, the oldest and the most successful of the enemies of Napoleon, was paid in ample colonial territory, receiving South Africa (the Cape), Ceylon, Malta, and the North sea island of Heligoland.

Belgium and Holland united; gains of Great Britain

The most serious danger to the permanence of these territorial arrangements arose from the fact that they disappointed the national hopes of the Italian, the Polish, the German, and the Belgian peoples. Let us examine the agreements from this point of view, beginning with Italy. The Bourbon Ferdinand was recognized as king of Naples and Sicily, joined under the name of the Two Sicilies; the pope was restored to the State of the Church; a younger branch of the house of Hapsburg to Tuscany; the king of Sardinia to Piedmont, increased, as we have seen, by Genoa; and Austria was given back her former possession of Lombardy, enlarged by the addition of Venetia. The lesser states, like Modena and Parma, we may leave out of consideration. Italy was thus in effect parceled out in five independent blocks; and since no attempt was made to bind the parts into a whole, and since further, ancient jealousies hindered united counsels, Austria, a foreign power, by taking advantage of the inner divisions, acquired an easy paramountcy. That this ascendancy would give offense to the national sentiment goes without saying. As for the Poles, they remained distributed among the three partitioning powers, Austria, Prussia, and Russia; and even though the mass of them was now united under Tsar Alexander in the kingdom of Poland, they had every right to feel that they had been auctioned off like cattle. In turning to the Belgians let us note that they had been united with the Dutch and placed under a Dutch king without the least account being taken of their wishes. Finally, German nationalist disappointment issued from a situation so complicated that it requires a detailed explanation.

The rearrangements of Vienna disappoint national hopes

When Napoleon first undermined in order finally to destroy the Holy Roman Empire, he carried through an important domestic reorganization. With his military love of order and hatred of confusion he abolished the many useless small entities, such as the free knights, the free cities, and the prince-bishops, left over from the Middle Age. In general he simply incorporated them in the larger dominions. As The a result of this ruthless extinction of absurd survivals German there were, when the Congress of Vienna met, instead of situation some three hundred, only thirty-eight sovereign German states. These may be divided, for the sake of convenience, into three groups: first, the two great powers, Austria and Prussia; second, the five middle-sized states, to wit, the kingdoms of Bavaria, Saxony, Würtemberg, and Hanover, with the grand-duchy of Baden; and third, Weimar, Hesse, and other petty principalities which, together with the city-republics of Hamburg, Bremen, and Lübeck, constituted the numerous group of the small states. Now the national party, headed by the Prussian statesman, Stein, had on Napoleon's fall demanded a close federal union of the thirty-eight existing states; but the Austrian chancellor, Metternich, who feared all novelties as revolutionary, played upon the dynastic sentiments of the German princes until they had been brought over to his program of a loose association to be called the German *Bund* (Union). The Bund was authorized to transact business in a diet, which was composed of delegates of the thirty-eight member states and which sat at Frankfort-on-the-Main; but as the heads of the states yielded none of their sovereignty to the common parliament, it will be seen — and such was Metternich's plan — that the Bund, as a means of effective union, was a farce. As a consequence of this futile organization Germany remained a mere geographical expression and the disappointment of the nationalists was keen.

But there was another sentiment besides that of nationalism offended at Vienna. We have already noted the set-back given to liberalism but perhaps we have not sufficiently emphasized the amaz-

The ing vigor of the current political reaction. Indeed more political than political, it was also religious and swept all the ruling reaction; circles of Europe fairly off their feet. Evidence of this Holy Alliance religious exaltation is furnished by a document drawn and up by Tsar Alexander, in which he pledged himself to Quintuple govern his state in accordance with the New Testament Alliance and which he induced all his brother-potentates either to sign or give their assent to. This mystical profession of Christian principles has become famous under the name of the Holy Alliance.[1]

----

[1] See the text in Translations and Reprints (University of Pennsylvania), Vol. I. "It is verbiage," said the cynical Metternich.

It owes its reputation less to what it contains (for it is a mass of hollow, well-meant platitudes) than to the circumstance that its name of Holy Alliance came to be applied to the actual and effective league maintained after 1815 by the victors over the Revolution and Napoleon. They achieved such a league by perpetuating their war-time coalition under the name of the Quadruple Alliance. In 1818, when the restored Louis XVIII of France was admitted to membership, the Quadruple became a Quintuple Alliance. Since the Quintuple Alliance embraced all the great powers, it may without exaggeration be held to be the first attempt made in modern times to give the western world a permanent political organization. To give the experiment still greater significance it was agreed that the five powers should meet from time to time in congress. In the light of these facts it may with some show of reason be contended that the Quintuple Alliance, which the average man, incapable of fine distinctions, confused with Tsar Alexander's Holy Alliance, was a shadowy League of Nations. Only we should remind ourselves that it was not designed as a means of directing the ever-changing life of Europe, but that it was constituted solely to defend the arrangements of 1815 against even the minutest change. This immobility was, above all, the obsession of the Austrian chancellor, Metternich. It was he who became the leading champion of the policy of holding congresses but always and exclusively in order that any revolutionary activity might be crushed by concerted action as soon as it arose. In other words, Metternich was in favor of intervening, in the interests of conservatism, in the internal affairs of the European states; and congresses and intervention became the chosen tools of the leagued reactionaries of Europe. Let us, since it has been hallowed by custom, continue to call this system by the name of the Holy Alliance; but let us also agree that such efficacy as it had rested on a definite political agreement laid down in the Quintuple Alliance and not on the mystico-bombastic pronouncement of Tsar Alexander which has approximately the importance of a magniloquent newspaper editorial.

We should now be in a position to understand the nature of the opposition aroused by the triumphant conservatism of 1815. For several years the Holy Alliance operated successfully under the direction of its guiding spirit, Metternich, and actually The quelled a number of revolutions. We shall presently revival of examine the particular incidents. But before we do so, liberalism let us agree that it was probably impossible to maintain for long that

unanimity among the five powers necessary for success. It was to
be expected that Great Britain, which had less cause than the continental powers to uphold an extreme conservatism, would presently
grow cold to the Holy Alliance. The first rift would encourage others
until at last the whole system would violently fall apart. That is indeed what happened; but even before the collapse came, the reactionary program had aroused against it throughout Europe those natural
favorers of change, the middle classes. Admittedly their political
ideas, already summarized by us as the program of liberalism, had
suffered an eclipse in 1815. But under the rough trampling of an
unrestrained conservatism, liberalism experienced a revival and soon
joined battle with its foe all along the line. It is from this struggle
of a resuscitated liberalism against an arrogant and triumphant
conservatism that European history largely takes its color and atmosphere from 1815 to 1830 and even to 1848.

The first serious test of Metternich's policy of a Europe held in
an unalterable mould by means of a conservative league of guardians
came when certain Mediterranean countries were swept by a revolution. The beginning was made by Spain. On the fall
of Napoleon Spain had experienced a restoration in the
person of the Bourbon monarch, Ferdinand VII, whom
Napoleon had deposed and exiled. The sovereign showed
his true face at once by committing a perjury. Although he had
sworn to maintain the constitution which had been drawn up during
his exile by the heroic defenders of the Spanish soil and which from
the year of its completion was known as the Constitution of 1812,
he not only set it aside as soon as he had his hand once more on the
helm, but encouraged a cruel and wholesale persecution of the patriots on the ground that they bore the terrible taint of liberalism.
Spain slipped back to eighteenth century conditions and was governed for the exclusive benefit of a corrupt and incompetent court,
an overbearing nobility, and a clergy which did not scruple to revive the repressive rigors of the Inquisition. Before long signs of
disaffection appeared everywhere but with particular insistence in
the army. This was primarily due to the fact that the army was
being despatched to South America to subdue Spain's revolted
colonies and that the enterprise, which carried the soldiers thousands
of miles from home, was highly unpopular. In January, 1820, some
companies about to be embarked at Cadiz raised the banner of rebellion and proclaimed the Constitution of 1812. Instantly garrisons

in other parts of Spain took up the cry. At last Madrid itself rose and refused to be appeased until the cringing sovereign had made his bow to the people by taking the oath to the constitution.

This Spanish success created imitators. In Naples the fall of Napoleon had brought back another Bourbon, also named Ferdinand, who bore a remarkable moral resemblance to his relative of Madrid. On receipt of the happy news from Spain the Neapolitan army raised the banner of revolt and with the aid of the people forced the king to accept for his realm of Naples the now popular Spanish constitution. Nor did this complete the tale of revolution. The contagion spread to Portugal. In the absence of the royal family, which was still in Brazil, whither it had fled on Napoleon's invasion in 1807, a provisional government was hurried into office which tried to conjure the storm by a profusion of liberal promises.

Revolution in Naples and Portugal

Against these popular movements in the Latin south the indignant Metternich resolved to set in action his machinery of congresses and intervention. But if he hoped for unanimity among the powers for the maintenance of the conservative system, he soon saw his mistake. A meeting in the Austrian town of Troppau (1820), called for the discussion of the Neapolitan revolution, which from its nearness to Austria was particularly pressing, revealed that England and France had no desire to share in the proposed intervention. But as the Austrian's counsel prevailed with Russia and Prussia, intervention was accepted in principle, though it was agreed that it should not be undertaken until King Ferdinand himself had been heard in the case. The congress was therefore adjourned to Laibach, another Austrian town near the Italian border, and the mendacious Bourbon had no sooner appeared (1821) and denounced his late liberal acts as wrung from him by force than Austria accepted the mandate of her friends and marched an army into Naples.

The Congresses of Troppau and Laibach

Unfortunately the Neapolitan liberals had not been able to call a strong government into being. They lacked experience, and worst of all, by falling out with the island of Sicily, which asked for home rule, were obliged to send a part of their army across the straits to maintain their authority. The mere approach of the Austrian forces served to scatter the undisciplined Neapolitan soldiery and break all opposition to the restoration of Ferdinand as absolute king. When the patriots in

Intervention of Austria in Naples, 1821

the Italian north, more especially in Piedmont, tried, in aid of the liberal movement in the south, to raise an insurrection in the Austrian rear, Austria marched an army into Piedmont also. Thus did Metternich by the exercise of a police power, for which he found authority in his own principles and in the mandate of the eastern potentates, make Italy safe for the Holy Alliance.

This first success only stimulated the appetite of the three eastern courts; and when the court of Paris, which had been wavering, now came over to their side, they could take another important step. At a congress held at Verona (1822) they commissioned France to interfere in Spain. A French army under the duke of Angoulême, the king's nephew, crossed the Pyrenees and entered Madrid practically without opposition. The downfall of Spanish liberalism was as swift and ignominious as that of Naples and for substantially the same reasons. The body of liberals in these two backward countries was small and inexperienced and failed to attach the impoverished and ignorant masses to its program. Priest- and beggar-ridden Naples and Spain were not good soil for an immediate constitutional development. The consequence of French intervention was the restoration of an absolutism, marked, as in the case of Naples, by a cruel persecution of the liberals. The Spanish sovereign, as revolting a combination of imbecility, ignorance, and duplicity as ever disgraced a throne, now hoped that the European monarchs would extend their services to America. The Spanish colonies, embracing the vast regions of Central and South America, were in revolt, and Ferdinand argued that to put down rebellion across the seas was quite as holy work as repressing it in Spain.

Intervention of France in Spain, 1823

The rebellion of the Spanish colonies had run a curious course, for it had begun not with a movement against the mother-country, but with the patriotic refusal to accept the usurper, Joseph Bonaparte, imposed on the peninsula by his all-powerful brother. While Napoleon was engaged in fighting a losing war against the Spaniards, the colonies governed themselves and, acquiring a taste for independence, had, on Ferdinand's restoration, declared their unwillingness to return to the old allegiance without some provision for home rule. This the stubborn Ferdinand had rejected, with the result that the colonies, one after another, had renounced the Spanish connection. He at once levied war upon them but with such

Intervention in South America blocked by Great Britain and the United States

poor success that in his despair he appealed at last to the Holy Alliance. Metternich and his friends duly took up the question thus brought before their bar. However, they had hardly begun to debate the issue when Great Britain and the United States thrust themselves into the situation. The British foreign minister, Canning, had recently succeeded Lord Castlereagh; and in place of the passive attitude taken by his predecessor in regard to the Neapolitan and Spanish interventions, Canning resolved actively to oppose the extension of the system of the Holy Alliance to the Spanish colonies on the purely practical ground that it would injure British trade. The insurrection of the South American colonies had proved a great boon to Great Britain since the war against the mother-country had delivered the South American markets into British hands. As the proposed restoration of Ferdinand VII would indubitably bring in its wake the revival of the ancient Spanish trade monopoly, Canning, in order to avoid that contingency, was ready to risk a breach with the continental powers. In 1823 he boldly adopted the course of recognizing the independence of the South American republics. In this policy he was ably seconded by the United States, prompted to be sure less by trade advantages than by pressing considerations of national security. Through the mouth of President Monroe the Washington government declared (Dec. 1823) in ringing tones that it would not look with equanimity on the attempt of an European coalition to subjugate the South American republics. The message of President Monroe is memorable not only because it marks the entry of the United States upon the stage of world politics but also because it formulates a policy of opposition to European enterprise in the western hemisphere which, under the name of the Monroe Doctrine, has served the government of the United States as a guiding principle down to our own time.

The upshot of the energetic action of Great Britain and the United States was that the Spanish colonies made good their independence and that the leagued champions of reaction, to the joy of the liberal parties the world over, met their first serious check. Shortly after, they became aware that there were regions, even in Europe, which they could not control. For with Naples and Spain won back to absolutism, conservative logic demanded that Portugal be served the same way. But Portugal, a coastal state, was accessible to Great Britain; and when Canning prepared to protect it from interference by the use of force, the allies saw fit to abandon the enterprise.

Intervention in Portugal blocked by Great Britain

Reviewing the events in the Mediterranean countries, we observe that, after winning a number of important successes, the reaction headed by Metternich was obliged to relax its principles in at least **The Holy** two instances, owing to the veto of Great Britain supple-**Alliance** mented by that of the United States. Such strength as **goes to** the conservative program mustered resulted from union; **pieces** and the defection of Great Britain under the direction of Canning showed that union, on the absurd and unhistorical basis of political immobility, could not be maintained for any considerable length of time. It is sometimes said that Canning destroyed the Holy Alliance. A more correct statement would be that Great Britain under Canning deserted the Holy Alliance, and that, weakened by defection, it was reduced to all but complete dissolution by another event to which we now turn — the Greek revolution.

At the very moment when the eastern powers were formulating their policy against popular movements at the Congress of Laibach, the news reached them that the nefarious spirit of revolt had raised **The revolt** its head also in southeastern Europe and that the Greeks, **of Greece,** subjected for centuries to the sultan, demanded inde-**1821** pendence. The Greek movement was the result of a nationalist revival coupled with the progressive decadence of the Ottoman Empire. The government of the sultan, exercised by venal and capricious agents called pashas, pursued the policy of squeezing every possible penny from its Christian subjects, besides treating them socially as an inferior group wholly at the mercy of their Mohammedan masters. If since their conquest in the fifteenth century the Greeks had meekly bowed their necks to the alien yoke, beginning with the second half of the eighteenth century, they showed signs of an ominous unrest due to the coming among them of a new spirit. They again turned with enthusiasm to their great past; representative Greeks traveled and studied in Europe and on their return disseminated western ideas; and Greek traders, taking advantage of the long revolutionary wars which drove French commerce from the Mediterranean, prospered to a degree unknown for centuries.

By the beginning of the nineteenth century the Greeks felt encouraged to prepare for a revolt against an intolerable tyranny and founded toward this end a secret political society with branches throughout the eastern Mediterranean. True, the mass of the Greeks lived in the restricted territory of ancient Hellas, that is, in the southern extremity of the Balkan peninsula, but scattered communities of their people might be encountered throughout the Balkan area as well as in Asia Minor. North of the lower Danube lived the mass of the Rumanians, while the heart of the **The racial** peninsula was held by two Slav groups, the Bulgars and **and** the Serbs. As these three non-Greek peoples had been **religious** Christianized in the days of Greek ascendancy, they were **situation among the** members of the Greek Orthodox Church which recognized **Balkan** as its head the patriarch of Constantinople. It further **Christians** contributed to Greek prestige among the non-Greek Christians that a large part of the clergy, especially among the prelates, was of Hellenic blood and speech. This being the situation which the leaders of the secret society, the *Hetairia Philiké*, had under their eyes, it is not strange that they should have laid their plans for an insurrection against the sultan which, though under Greek guidance, should embrace all the various Christian peoples. To their surprise they discovered they had made a miscalculation. Their fellow Christians refused to accept their leadership because the Greek control of the Slav and Rumanian Churches was almost as much resented as the political control of the Turks. The division among the Christian subjects of the sultan appearing thus early in their period of awakening must under no circumstances be overlooked. Not only did it delay the process of Balkan liberation from the Turk by hindering united action, but after freedom had been gained it became the source of a succession of disastrous conflicts which will engage our attention in due time. At this point it will suffice to note that when the Greek leaders unfurled the banner of revolt in the spring of 1821, they met with no response from either the Slavs or the Rumanians. The movement would have been a complete fiasco, had not the Greeks in ancient Hellas heroically resolved to go on with it, even though they were unsupported by their fellow-Christians of the other races. By sudden concerted action they succeeded in clearing almost all of the Morea (the ancient Peloponnesus) and central Greece of the Ottoman enemy.

Thoroughly alarmed by the rebellion, the sultan made formidable efforts to recover the lost territory. His armies penetrated (1822) into the revolted districts but failed to break the resistance of the little people conducted chiefly in the form of guerrilla warfare. Balked of their prey, the Turks committed abominable atrocities, to be followed presently on the part of the Greeks by acts of similar fury. The tale of mutual butchery between the two races surpasses belief and becomes intelligible only when we remember that the animosity, usual between slave and master, was here blown into an unquenchable flame by wild religious fanaticism. In the year 1824 the sultan, recognizing the exhaustion of his resources, invited the coöperation of his powerful vassal, Mehemet Ali, pasha of Egypt; and the arrival on the political scene of this capable and unscrupulous ruler soon gave another complexion to affairs. The Egyptian mobilized an army and a navy under his son Ibrahim against the Greeks, and Ibrahim, using the island of Crete as a base, gradually penetrated into the Morea. By 1826 he had made such forward strides that to the casual view the Greek cause seemed doomed. But at this point Europe, hitherto painfully indifferent, interposed, and Greece was saved.

The sultan fails to subdue the Greeks

As long as Metternich's influence prevailed among the powers it was clear that Europe would quietly look on while the sultan waded in the blood of his Christian subjects. The *peoples* of Europe, it is true, in contrast to the *governments*, made from the first no secret of their sympathy with the cause of freedom. Bands of volunteers, among whom was the famous poet, Byron,[1] gathered under the Greek banners; but though they rendered welcome assistance, they could not hinder the triumph of the Egyptian forces. In these desperate curcumstances nothing was likely to prove of avail short of the action of one or more of the powers. Great Britain was already pondering intervention, when in 1826 she received welcome support from Russia. In the previous year Tsar Alexander, who in his later days had fallen completely under Metternich's influence, had died to be succeeded, in default of direct heirs, by his brother Nicholas I. Nicholas was as fanatical a reactionary as Metternich, but he was also a Russian nationalist and therefore hated to see the sultan, the age-old enemy of Russia, strengthen his hand by subduing the Greeks to obedience. Approaching the London cabinet, he discussed a modest program of intervention, which, by the admission of France, led in 1827 to the Treaty of London. Therein the three signatories agreed to put an end to the bloodshed on the basis of Greek autonomy. Here then was intervention but not of the Metternichian kind! That it was

Great Britain, Russia, and France agree to interfere in behalf of Greece, 1827

[1] He died of fever, a martyr to the cause, in 1824 at Missolonghi.

actually to be exercised in favor of rebels gives the measure of the completeness of the shipwreck of the Holy Alliance.

The Treaty of London had no sooner been signed than the three powers ordered their fleets to concentrate in the Mediterranean and sail to the bay of Navarino, Ibrahim's base in the Morea. They came to announce the end of warfare; and when Ibrahim, The battle outraged at the interference, failed to comply promptly of Navarino with the request to suspend hostilities, a battle ensued the Turco- in which the whole Turco-Egyptian fleet was shot to Russian war driftwood (Oct. 20, 1827). The roar of the guns at Nava- of 1828-29 rino announced to the world the birth of a new Christian state, but the sultan was not yet ready to concede the point. Profoundly irritated by the Navarino disaster, he opened a heated correspondence with his chief enemy, the tsar, which Nicholas shrewdly utilized to issue a declaration of war. Thus the Greek rebellion culminated in another Turco-Russian conflict, in which the Russians more signally than in any earlier instance exhibited an easy superiority. Their forces crossed successively the Danube river and the Balkan mountains and in 1829 reached Adrianople, only a few days' march from the Turkish capital. At this juncture the sultan's resistance collapsed; he offered to treat and in the Peace of Adrianople accepted all the Russian demands. Not only did he concede to the three powers the right to settle the affairs of Greece as they saw fit, but he renewed and enlarged his former promises of home rule to Serbia and to the two Rumanian provinces, Wallachia and Moldavia, besides acknowledging the tsar as the guarantor of these concessions. The effect of the Treaty of Adrianople was nothing less than to make the tsar co-sovereign with the sultan over considerable parts of his Balkan dominions.

After prolonged discussions touching the settlement of Greece the three powers agreed at length on these points: (1) that Greece was to be not merely autonomous under the sultan but an entirely independent kingdom; (2) that its northern boundary against The Greek the Ottoman Empire was to be ungenerously drawn from settlement Arta to Volo, thus leaving large numbers of Greeks outside the kingdom; and (3) that the crown of the kingdom was to be given to a young Bavarian prince, Otto by name. It was not till 1832 that these conclusions were finally arrived at. The long delay was due to the fact that shortly after the Peace of Adrianople Europe was shaken by a new revolution in the old center of disturbance, France.

REFERENCES

C. H. HAYES, *Political and Social History*, II, chs. 17, 19
J. S. SCHAPIRO, *Modern and Contemporary Europe*, chs. 2, 4
C. M. ANDREWS, *Development of Modern Europe*, ch. 3
C. D. HAZEN, *Europe Since 1815*, I, chs. 1–3
E. FUETER, *World History*, chs. 5–14
E. R. TURNER, *Europe 1789–1920*, chs. 5, 7, 10, 11
F. J. HEARNSHAW, *Main Currents of European History*, chs. 4, 5
F. S. MARVIN, *Century of Hope*, ch. 2
W. A. PHILLIPS, *Confederation of Europe*
C. K. WEBSTER, *Congress of Vienna*
Cambridge Modern History, IX, chs. 18, 19, 21, X, chs. 1, 2, 4–8, 11–14, 20, 21
G. B. MALLESON, *Life of Prince Metternich*
G. M. PRIEST, *Germany Since 1740*, ch. 8
E. F. HENDERSON, *Short History of Germany*, II, ch. 8
K. FRANCKE, *Social Forces in German Literature*, ch. 9
A. W. WARD, *Germany 1815–1890*
G. P. GOOCH, *Germany and the French Revolution*
F. SCHEVILL, *Making of Modern Germany*, Lect. 4; *History of the Balkan Peninsula*, chs. 19–21
W. R. THAYER, *Dawn of Italian Independence*
B. KING, *History of Italian Unity*, I, chs. 1, 2, 6, 7
H. D. SEDGWICK, *Short History of Italy*, chs. 34–36
W. J. STILLMAN, *The Union of Italy*
M. A. S. HUME, *Modern Spain*, ch. 5
C. E. CHAPMAN, *Spain*
W. R. SHEPHERD, *Latin America*

CHAPTER XXI

THE BOURBON RESTORATION IN FRANCE AND THE REVOLUTIONARY MOVEMENTS OF 1830

The restoration of the Bourbons in 1814, and again in 1815, was the work of the victorious allies, for the old royal family was as good as forgotten in France and aroused no enthusiasm among the people. Its position, therefore, was precarious and its success would depend on the wisdom with which it used its opportunity. Louis XVIII, the most moderate and intelligent member of his family, made a not unpromising beginning when he published a constitution (*la charte constitutionelle*), which recognized the institutions of Napoleon — his administration, his legal system, his church, his army, and even his nobility — and conceded to the people a share in legislation by two houses, an appointed chamber of Peers and an elected chamber of Deputies. The system bore a certain resemblance to that of England, except that the ultimate control remained vested with the king, inasmuch as the ministers were responsible to him and not to the chambers. The constitution made a strong bid for middle class support by recognizing that those objects of eighteenth century criticism, the feudal privileges and the absolute monarchy, had departed never to return.

Louis XVIII grants a constitution

Having wisely inaugurated a policy of conciliation, the king next turned to the task of creating confidence and allaying suspicion. But this was difficult in view of the fact that he was surrounded at court by the *émigrés*, who had returned with the fall of Napoleon and fatuously imagined they had brought the old times back with them in their traveling-kits. At their head was the count of Artois, the king's fanatic brother, who in twenty-five years of exile had learned nothing and forgotten nothing. These courtly gentlemen thought chiefly of revenge and repression. Selfishly animated with the desire to recover their confiscated estates and to restore the Church to power, they compassed, after a few ephemeral triumphs, their own ruin and that of the royal family. Their party policy — they were known as ultra-royalists — was not,

The ultra-royalists

481

at least for the present, to overthrow the constitution, but to insist on a sharp control of the press and to insure themselves a majority in the lower chamber by manipulating the elections. This was relatively easy because, the franchise being dependent on a high property qualification, there were roughly only 100,000 citizens entitled to vote. It is on account of this limitation of the suffrage that the monarchy rested in last analysis on the small body of the well-to-do.

Louis XVIII, with laudable common-sense, at first resisted the clamor of the ultras and leaned upon the constitutionalists. However, he was too weak to maintain his position in the face of continued pressure. The assassination in 1820 of his nephew

Louis, at first liberal, yields to the ultras

and ultimate heir, the duke of Berri, shook him profoundly. Although the murder was the deed of a fanatic, who acted only on his own prompting, the courtiers declared that the real responsibility rested with the liberal ministry, which was accordingly replaced with a ministry of ultras. Thus at last the conservatives had triumphed, and controlling the king, the ministry, and the chambers, muzzled the press, passed restrictive electoral laws, and identified France with the Holy Alliance by accepting in 1822 the mandate to suppress the Spanish revolution. With the ultras floating on the tide of power Louis XVIII died (1824). He was succeeded by the count of Artois, under the title Charles X. His accession added the finishing touch to the triumph of the forces of reaction.

Events now rapidly traveled toward the inevitable crisis. By passing an act which distributed one billion francs among the ancient nobility as an indemnity for their estates confiscated during

Charles X carries out a coup d'état

the Revolution and by other measures of like tenor, the ministry deeply offended the bourgeoisie, who made up the bulk of the voters, and in the election of 1827 suffered a signal defeat. Though Charles X now changed his ministers, he clung with such stubborn infatuation to his reactionary policy that the chamber of Deputies was more and more moved to withdraw its support. With the courage of the self-righteous he resolved to break the resistance of his legislature by an illegal act, a so-called *coup d'état*. On July 26, 1830, he issued four ordinances by which, in the hope of getting a docile chamber, he arbitrarily changed the laws governing the elections and the press.

The four ordinances sounded a challenge which was immediately

taken up by bands of republican workmen and students. Parading
the streets with loud cheers for the constitution, they presently
raised the ominous cry, "Down with the Bourbons!" The king
himself was at St. Cloud, just outside the capital, and the The revolu-
few thousand troops in Paris were not adequate to keep tion of July
the insurgents in hand. Occasional conflicts soon led to 1830
a pitched battle, in which the soldiers, outnumbered and fighting
without enthusiasm, yielded ground until their commander ordered
them to evacuate the capital. On the night of July 29th, the people,
brimful, after three days of fighting, of the old republican spirit,
rested from their bloody and triumphant work.

In spite of Charles's misrule there was a large monarchical party
of liberal tendency still in France, and this party now stepped forward to save the country from anarchy. In contrast to the republican workmen who had done the street-fighting, its The middle
members were recruited from the bourgeoisie. In a class turns
gathering of leaders it was decided that what France to Louis
wanted was a genuinely constitutional monarchy and Philip
that the person to secure it was Louis Philip, duke of Orleans. The
duke was head of the younger branch of the house of Bourbon and
had a revolutionary record, for he had served for a time (1792–1793)
as a volunteer in the republican army. This, and the fact that his
father was the unsavory Egalité of Jacobin fame, had dug an unbridgeable chasm between him and the elder branch of his house.
At the invitation of the moderates he left his country-place to come
to Paris and by an adroit conciliation of the republicans, who had
accepted the aged Lafayette as leader, took the reins into his hands,
practically without opposition. The first business of the improvised government would in all likelihood be a struggle with Charles X.
But the frightened king agreeably disappointed expectations. In a
fit of despondency he resigned in favor of his little grandson, son of
the murdered duke of Berri, and fled to England; but the chamber
of Deputies chose to take no further note of his acts and, on
August 7th, proceeded to proclaim Louis Philip king of the French.

The substitution of the younger for the older branch of the house
of Bourbon, which at first blush seems to measure the whole achievement of the so-called July revolution, does not fully express the
change which came over France in 1830. In the first place, although
the old constitution remained in force, it was liberalized somewhat
by a slight revision and, more particularly, by the passing of a law

which sufficiently lowered the property qualification for the franchise to bring about a doubling of the number of electors; and, second, the accession of Louis Philip signified nothing less than a complete change of system. Charles X represented legitimacy, was identified with the *émigrés* and the Church, and ruled by grace of God. Louis Philip, a revolutionary and illegitimate sovereign, was cursed and avoided by the convinced royalists, and in order to secure his throne had to lean upon the monarchical middle class. For this reason the July monarchy is often called the reign of the bourgeoisie and Louis Philip himself the king of the middle class (*roi-bourgeois*). Caricatures habitually represented him as a thickset, comfortable grocer, armed with a huge umbrella. The final touch to this change of system was communicated by the replacement of the lily banner of the Bourbons with the famous tricolor of the Revolution.

Results of the revolution

Meanwhile the report of the revolution in Paris had traveled abroad, producing joy among the progressive groups and consternation among the governments. Since the work of the reaction had been so easily undone in France, there was good reason to think that the national and liberal sentiment, outraged by the Congress of Vienna and persecuted by the mean-spirited police-control of Metternich and Tsar Alexander, might assert itself with success in other regions of Europe. France, since the Revolution the acknowledged leader of progressive opinion, had given a signal to which her imitators and admirers everywhere joyfully responded.

Effect of the revolution on Europe

The first people to be seized with the French infection were the Belgians. The reader will remember that by the Congress of Vienna the old Austrian Netherlands had been annexed to Holland in order to create a strong state on the French border. But the union was unfortunate, for the Belgians felt that they were not admitted to complete equality by the Dutch, while the fact that one people was Protestant and the other Catholic kept up a constant irritation, very cleverly fostered by the Belgian clergy. Besides, there was the question of race; while one-half of the Belgians were Flemings and, as a Germanic people, closely allied to the Dutch, the other half were Walloons, that is, Celts who used the French language. Lastly, Flemings and Walloons alike were imbued with French civilization and looked rather toward Paris for intellectual guidance than toward The Hague.

The causes of Belgian discontent

In August, 1830, a revolt, begun in Brussels, spread so rapidly that the Dutch army had to abandon the whole country with the exception of a few fortresses. King William, who had at first treated the Belgian national movement with contempt, now offered concessions, but it was too late. Nothing short of complete independence would satisfy the revolutionists, and since the Dutch king resisted this demand, war seemed to be unavoidable. *The Belgian revolt, August, 1830*

When a conference of the powers met at London to deliberate on the issue it was seen that the Holy Alliance was dead, for the conference actually decided to yield to the will of the Belgian people and sever their lot from the Dutch. The truculent King William was cowed into acquiescence and, not without many difficulties and delays, a Belgian assembly declared Belgium a constitutional monarchy and elected a small German prince, Leopold of Saxe-Coburg, king. The boundary of *Europe interferes in behalf of the Belgians* the new realm caused a prolonged dispute with the offended king of the Netherlands, but this matter, too, was finally disposed of, and Belgium, a new state under a new dynasty, was added to the fraternity of nations.

In central Europe, in Italy and Germany, the revolution was not received with such enthusiasm as might be expected, when we consider that in these countries the progressive groups had been balked of their dearest hopes by the treaties of 1815. In Italy there was no outbreak outside the papal states, where the government, exclusively in the hands of the *The revolution of 1830 in Italy* pope and his clergy, was about as unprogressive as that of Turkey. Of course the pope called in the Austrians, who quickly extinguished the revolutionary fire. The fact was that Italy, in consequence of the defeat of its liberal hopes in 1821 and its experience of Austrian omnipotence, was unwilling for the present to risk an uprising. The total result of the year 1830 for the peninsula was an increased sense of enslavement to Austria and an increased hatred of the master.

In Germany political activity had been reduced to very meager proportions between 1815 and 1830. The Bund, as its projectors planned, was treated as a nonentity by the thirty-eight member states and soon became a general laughing-stock. The only occasion on which it showed signs of life was when, at the instance of Metternich, it adopted severe police measures to bridle the expression of liberal opinion in the press and universities and to hunt the sporadic democrats to their holes (Carlsbad decrees, 1819). In the middle-sized states of South Germany — Bavaria, Württemberg, Baden — constitutions were granted by the rulers; and here all that Germany could show in the nature of popular political activity during this period took refuge. The two great states, Austria and Prussia, and almost all of the small North German states, were, in respect of popular participation in politics, as dead as extinct volcanoes. Throughout this area absolutism flourished unchecked. In Austria the reaction presented to view no single redeeming feature; Metternich's hand seemed to have paralyzed the national energies. In Prussia the case was somewhat different. The king had indeed not fulfilled his promise to his people, given at the height of the struggle with Napoleon, to create a representative government, but he offered some compensation for this omission by a rigidly honest administration and a progressive economic policy. A really notable achievement was the German Customs-Union, called *Zollverein*. Inaugurated by Berlin in 1818 and completed after patient efforts continued through a generation, it gathered around Prussia, under a uniform tariff system, all the German states except Austria. The student can not fail to see that by unifying Germany economically the Zollverein promoted prosperity, strengthened the middle classes, and pointed the way to German political consolidation under that same Prussian guidance which had proved effective in the economic field.

Germany during the dominance of Metternich

Such was the general situation — except for the fact that the Zollverein was as yet in an early, experimental stage — when the news of the revolution in Paris reached Germany. For a revolutionary movement to be really significant it would have to be initiated in the great states, Austria and Prussia; but as these remained quiet, the outbreaks in Germany never acquired more than a local character. In a number of the absolute states of North Germany — Hesse-Cassel, Brunswick, Saxony, Hanover — there were risings which were quickly quelled by the grant of a restricted form of representative government. Phlegmatic Germany, unused to the exercise of political rights, had not acquired the revolutionary habit, and the sole result of the action of 1830 was the establishment of constitutionalism in some of the lesser states. In Austria and Prussia the absolute system seemed to rest on granite, though it was as clear as daylight that the rise of a powerful liberal opinion could not be long delayed.

The revolution of 1830 in Germany

It deserves special notice that the German movement of 1830 was not only a scattered and local disturbance but also exclusively concerned with liberal aims. No cry was raised for a more effective national organization and no hand was lifted against the feeble and despised Bund. In the light of the unimportant happenings of 1830 we are forced to the conclusion that while the liberal movement in Germany was more developed than the national one, both alike, hardly yet out of their swaddling clothes, awaited the development of a more powerful middle class.

The German movement of 1830 liberal, not national

If the year 1830 saw hardly more than storm-signals in Germany, there was a fierce tempest of the east of her, in Poland. We have seen that at the Congress of Vienna the Tsar Alexander, to whom had been assigned the grand-duchy of Warsaw, converted it into the kingdom of Poland with himself as king. At the same time he gave it a constitution, by which it became a separate entity from Russia with a Polish administration and army and with a Polish diet enjoying a consultative voice in internal affairs. That this constitution represented an act of unusual liberality for the times can not be denied, but it did not satisfy the Poles. They chafed under the remaining restrictions on their independence and could not forget the time when the parts were reversed, and they, and not the Russians and their tsar, ruled eastern Europe.

Alexander creates the kingdom of Poland

The discontent was kept under control as long as Alexander, the giver of the constitution, lived; but Nicholas I had no sooner succeeded his brother (1825) than the signs of conflict multiplied. The excitement spread through Europe by the July revolution applied the torch to the accumulated discontent, and in November, 1830, the capital, Warsaw, rose in insurrection. The country took the cue from the metropolis; the few Russian troops in Poland retired with all possible speed; and not without surprise at the ease of the achievement, the Poles discovered that they were free under a revolutionary government.

The Poles rise in revolt, November, 1830

Plainly the success of the movement would depend on united, intelligent action. But that was hard to obtain, owing to the political inexperience of the leaders and to the lamentable social divisions inherited from the past. For one thing the great nobles, who as owners of vast estates were the most powerful group in the country, found it difficult to agree with the democratic element in the city of Warsaw which was largely responsible for the revolution; and second, the bulk of the nation were agricultural laborers in a condition **Reasons for** little above that of brutes. Serfs for centuries, they had **the Polish** indeed been declared free by Napoleon (1807); but as noth-**failure** ing was done to convert them into peasant-proprietors, they lived from hand to mouth and were, at least in a material sense, no better off than before. Nevertheless the revolutionary government, aided by the general enthusiasm, managed to create a national army, which with next to no training and a very deficient equipment sustained a most honorable combat when in the spring of 1831 Tsar Nicholas launched his Russian legions against it. However, mere valor was of no avail; at Ostrolenka (May, 1831) the Russians overwhelmed the Poles with their numbers, and a few months later (September) entered Warsaw in triumph. Thus the seal of fate seemed to be set upon the *finis Poloniæ* pronounced in the previous century.

When the Russian autocrat again took hold, it was with the grim resolve to make every possible provision against another Polish revolution. He firmly believed that he had been trifled with because **Poland** he and his predecessor had proved themselves too gener-**crushed by** ous. He would not err in that way any more. He began **the Russian** by abrogating Alexander's constitution not without **autocracy** calling attention to the fact that the Poles had preceded him in abrogating it by rising in revolution. Then he merged the ex-kingdom into Russia as a Russian province and carried through a succession of measures which aimed to break the rebellious spirit of the Poles: a Russian army of occupation was saddled on the country; Russian was made the official language; the press was put under strict supervision; and most of the Polish educational institutions were closed. Poland fell into complete eclipse. Bound and gagged she lay at the feet of Russia, but as long as the blood coursed in their veins the people were determined to cling to their national memories.

Reviewing the revolution of 1830 throughout Europe, we may assert that though its fruits, outside of France and Belgium, were small, a new era was struggling into being. The liberal platform, **Results** as yet indubitably monarchical but affirming the right **of the** of every people to a share in the political direction of **revolution** the state, had called general attention to itself and could **of 1830** never again be treated as a negligible item. Nationalism, too, always more or less allied with liberalism, had asserted itself, successfully in Belgium, unsuccessfully in Poland. Through the movements of 1830 the Holy Alliance received its last blow and expired; and although Metternich and other reactionaries might hope to revive it and actually never ceased trying, their effort was foredoomed to failure because a new day which would not be denied had dawned.

REFERENCES

C. SEIGNOBOS, *Europe Since 1814*, ch. 5
C. M. ANDREWS, *Development of Modern Europe*, ch. 4
C. A. FYFFE, *Modern Europe*, II, chs. 1, 2
E. FUETER, *World History*, chs. 12, 13
C. H. HAYES, *Political and Social History*, II, pp. 14–20, 50–57
C. D. HAZEN, *Europe Since 1815*, chs. 5, 6
J. S. SCHAPIRO, *Modern and Contemporary Europe*, ch. 7
E. BOURGEOIS, *Modern France*, I, chs. 1, 3, 4
J. R. M. MACDONALD, *France*, III, chs. 35, 36
Cambridge Modern History, X, chs. 2, 3, 15–17, XI, 2
J. R. HALL, *The Bourbon Restoration*
W. A. PHILLIPS, *The Confederation of Europe; Poland*
F. J. C. HEARNSHAW, *Main Currents in European History*, chs. 4, 5
W. R. A. MORFILL, *History of Russia*
A. RAMBAUD, *History of Russia*

CHAPTER XXII

THE REIGN OF LOUIS PHILIP (1830–1848) AND THE REVOLUTION OF 1848 IN FRANCE

We have seen that the consequence of the July revolution was that Charles X was obliged to vacate the throne of France in favor of his relative Louis Philip, who owed his elevation to the favor and resolution of the bourgeoisie. He thus represented not the united nation but one of its social divisions, and this identification with a limited group largely determined the character of his reign. Friends and enemies alike referred to him jocosely as the king of the bourgeoisie (*roi-bourgeois*); and the phrase has a double significance since it defines not only his political status but also to a certain extent his personality. Abandoning the traditional pomp of royalty, he exhibited an easy fellowship with men of all classes, lived simply in the midst of his numerous family, and, like his bourgeois subjects generally, was shrewd, thrifty, and obstinate.

King Louis Philip identified with the middle class

The July monarchy never enjoyed a day of complete and unquestioned security. In the legitimists and the republicans it had from the start two uncompromising political opponents. The legitimists, devoted to the older Bourbon branch, worked at all times against Louis Philip, but apart from a single outbreak in that revolutionary home of troubles, the Vendée, were content to bide their time. In the Vendée, the duchess of Berri, mother of the young Bourbon claimant, whom legitimists called Henry V, courageously headed a movement (1832) which, though appealing to the imagination of the royalists, by its failure to arouse the masses proved that legitimism was practically without popular support. Far more serious was the enmity of the republicans. The leaders were stubborn enthusiasts, often of the middle class, who drew their inspiration from the doctrines of the Revolution; and the followers were the workingmen of Paris, Lyons, and other city centers. Prepared to take risks for the cause in which they believed, republi-

Legitimists and republicans

can groups appealed in 1832 and again in 1834 to arms only to be suppressed with bloody consequences. After the second rising the government passed a series of repressive acts (the September laws, 1835), which by special courts for the trial of offenses against the security of the state made republicanism practically a felony, and which by an extraordinarily severe censorship drove all republican agitation underground.

But far more important than all the surface agitations of politics and indeed largely explanatory of them was a social and economic upheaval inaugurated in Louis Philip's reign. The upheaval has been ordinarily called the Industrial Revolution. As it will The be given later a systematic treatment, it will here suffice Industrial to indicate some of its leading aspects. We have already Revolution and the noted [1] that the Industrial Revolution was an offspring origin of of science and that its powerful emblem was the machine. socialism Louis Philip's reign saw the dawn of the modern machine age which signified, in the French as in every other case, the familiar changes associated with factories and tenements and the innumerable problems born of the conflict of capital and labor. Its most immediate effect was to strengthen still further the position of the middle classes since, as the groups endowed with capital, they became the powerful masters of the machines. But the workingmen, too, were strengthened, though at first only in numbers. Since the law forbade them to form trade unions for the purpose of protecting their economic interests, and since it also prohibited their agitating politically through a republican organization, they were wholly at the mercy of their employers. Greatly exasperated by their bondage, they inclined a willing ear to a new type of radical thinker who taught that as long as the bourgeoisie owned the means of production the existing injustice would inevitably continue; the only effective cure, according to the new gospel, was for the working people to overthrow the régime of private capital and to possess themselves of the machines and factories. A journalist, Louis Blanc, was the first to preach in clear terms this doctrine, to which came to be attached the name of socialism. The striking feature of Blanc's program was the proposal that a given body of workmen apply to the state for a loan of capital in order to undertake the coöperative management of a factory under the name of a national workshop. While Blanc and his followers were sincere republicans, their position, envisaging a radical economic

[1] See Ch. XVIII.

upheaval, went far beyond the purely political demands of ordinary republicanism. This difference of purpose between republicans and socialists should be carefully noted, as under Louis Philip a deceptive impression of republican and socialist unity was created because both happened to stand shoulder to shoulder against the common oppressor.

Though the socialist development is interesting in itself and potentially significant, we must not credit it with an important role in the conscious political life of France under Louis Philip. Under the prevailing constitution politics was the exclusive preserve of the middle class and, apart from occasional flurries caused by legitimists and republicans, only the bourgeoisie and their affairs held the stage. Had this middle group remained closely united, it might have continued its rule almost indefinitely. But it fell apart over an issue as irrepressible as life itself. The bourgeois control of the state came to a head in the chamber of Deputies, where one political party took the usual conservative position that the existing system was so entirely satisfactory that it required no change at all, while a minority party scouted this immobility and advocated a moderate program of reform. What the reformers particularly urged was the lowering of the franchise requirement with a view to enlarging the body of the electors. After 1840 the famous historian Thiers assumed the leadership of the progressive minority, while the equally famous historian Guizot served as the head of the conservatives. King Louis Philip leaned strongly toward the conservatives, indeed had so consistently leaned toward them from the first day of his reign that with unimportant intermissions they may be said to have held the power so long as the Orleanist rule lasted. In 1840 the king called Guizot to the ministry, and Guizot steadily maintained himself in office with the support of a majority among the deputies. To be sure he employed highly questionable means to hold his followers together since he rewarded party fidelity with distributions from the vast patronage at his disposal. Though, with a majority behind him, his rule was constitutionally impeccable, it was profoundly corrupt; and this situation led the minority under Thiers to insist with greater and greater vehemence that the only way to break the iron ring of the conservatives was to enlarge the electorate to such an extent as to make bribery by a system of individual favors entirely impracticable.

The division of the bourgeoisie into conservatives and progressives

The method which Thiers chose to carry his agitation for electoral reform among the people was a series of banquets at which the immobility and corruption of the government were denounced by fiery speakers. During the year 1847 these banquets The were in progress throughout the country; and one, set for February Paris on February 22, 1848, was planned to be a particu- revolution larly impressive occasion to be inaugurated with a public procession. Scenting danger, the government forbade the meeting, but crowds gathered nevertheless and began to demonstrate noisily to show their displeasure. The next day the rioters resumed their activity, calling so insistently for reform that the king yielded and dismissed the unpopular Guizot. This met the wishes of Thiers who hoped to step into Guizot's shoes; but the passion of the populace having been aroused, the agitation mounted steadily like a flood until on February 24th it burst all bounds. The morning of that day began with an assault upon the district of the Tuileries by the republican masses, which exhibited such savage determination that the timid king abdicated the throne in favor of his little grandson. While the aged sovereign with his queen sought safety in ignominious flight, his daughter-in-law, the duchess of Orleans, led her young son, the count of Paris, to the chamber of Deputies and had him proclaimed king. But it was already too late to save the Orleanist dynasty. The republican multitude invaded the hall, ignored the deputies, and set up a Provisional Government. Owing to the fact that the socialists had helped in the street-fighting and were in possession of certain strategic buildings, some of their leaders, including Louis Blanc, were absorbed into the government; and the two united factions began their rule by announcing to the world that France was henceforth a republic.

The harmony between the two groups lasted long enough for the Provisional Government to proclaim universal male suffrage and complete freedom of the press. But it was subjected to a great strain as soon as the socialist minority developed its The view that the political revolution was merely a beginning struggle to be followed as promptly as possible by a sweeping between economic upheaval. To keep the government intact and a compromise was arrived at to the effect first, that the socialists state should recognize "the right to work," and second, that in fulfilment of this pledge, which meant that the government agreed to provide labor for every applicant, it should accept Louis Blanc's socialist prescription, the national workshops. The two declarations represented the limit of the concessions which the republicans were prepared to make to their socialist colleagues. And even these were quickly jeopardized. For when early in May the National Assembly, elected to give France a new constitution, met in the capital and took over the powers of the Provisional Government, it was at once seen that it would not tolerate even the mildest socialist experiments. What had happened was that the French people, called to the polls to choose between republicans and socialists, had shown their horror of the unfamiliar tenets of the new school by returning an overwhelming republican majority. Alarmed at this situation, the socialists rose in rebellion (May 15th), on the suppression of which the angered republicans voted to abolish the national workshops. Thereupon in order to save their one valuable concession, the socialists, rendered desperate, made a second attempt to overthrow the Assembly which was only defeated after four days of the bloodiest fighting Paris had ever seen (June 23–26, 1848). Several thousand men were killed defending the barricades they had erected, and other thousands, captured by the victorious soldiers, were either shot or exiled. By this disastrous outcome the socialist party was eliminated for many a day from the political situation.

A great deal of interest has always attached to the national workshops because they represent the first experiment with a frank socialist label made by the government of any European state. But the interest is spurious since the national workshops, as **The national workshops** actually instituted, were socialist only in name. Accepted by the republicans against their conviction and under street pressure, the national workshops plan was put into the hands of an anti-socialist management for the express purpose of sabotaging it. Instead of specially trained and reliable workmen being joined in a coöperative enterprise supported by capital advanced from state funds — the program of Louis Blanc — the republican enemies charged with the execution of the plan indiscriminately sent all men applying at the bureau of labor to work with pick and shovel at the fortifications of Paris. This was a not unfamiliar method in France and elsewhere of meeting the unemployment situation and may be defended on the ground that the public disturbances had closed the factories and thrown thousands of men out of work. However, it was very costly to the national purse as the unemployed grew from week to week until their number threatened to become fantastic.

That the anti-socialist members of the Assembly had no stomach for this type of poor relief is intelligible in view of the fact that they would have to meet the expenditure with increased taxes. That they finally resolved to save the budget by ruthlessly suppressing a very haphazard system of unemployment doles, falsely called national workshops, is also intelligible. But when the socialists for their part then and afterwards contended that their scheme had never been tested, they were undoubtedly supported by the facts. So far as the much vaunted experiment of 1848 was concerned, no light whatever was shed on the workableness of the national workshops proposal.

A safe inference from the savage struggle of the spring of 1848 was that France, although a republic, was not ready to indulge in hazardous experiments. With the socialists out of the way the the republican majority of the Assembly proceeded to *The republican constitution of 1848* fulfil its mission of giving France a constitution. Insisting on the democratic principle that "all public powers emanate from the people," it drew up a document which vested the legislative power in a single assembly of 750 members elected by universal suffrage. The executive power was conferred on a president elected for four years. As to the manner of the president's election, it was agreed after much discussion, that he, too, was to be chosen directly by the people. In order to inaugurate the new system the election was ordered for December 10, 1848, and to the surprise of all unacquainted with the heart of the French people their choice fell, not upon General Cavaignac, the leader of the republicans and the hero of the battles of June, but upon Louis Napoleon.

That this prince should ever be called to the head of the nation by popular vote could hardly have suggested itself to the most prophetic spirit. He was the son of Napoleon's brother Louis, king of Holland, and after the death of Napoleon's only son at *Career of the new president* Vienna (1832) was regarded as chief of the house of Bonaparte. As such he felt it his duty to conspire for his dynasty and made two attempts, in ludicrous imitation of Napoleon's return from Elba, which were greeted by Europe with a burst of Homeric laughter. In 1836 he suddenly appeared in Strasburg, but in spite of his uncle's hat, sword, and boots, donned for the occasion, was only stared at by the amused populace and promptly marched off to prison. Louis Philip felt so secure that he freed the theatrical hero without more ado. Undaunted, the young man made in 1840 another attempt to rouse France by crossing from England to Boulogne; but the boat conveying him and a few helpmates capsized, and wet and dripping he was fished out of the channel by the ubiquitous police. Punished for this second escapade with imprisonment for life, he effected his escape after a number of years and again took up his residence in England. On the proclamation of the republic he became a candidate for the Assembly and easily won the election. Plainly he was outliving the ridicule he had aroused and by his clever trading upon the magic name Napoleon was rallying about him all those classes, especially the peasants, who clung to the traditions of the empire. When some months later his compatriots elected him president, they were thinking less of him, of whom they knew nothing, than of the dead warrior, whose brilliant victories his name recalled. Undeniably, however, the election to the presidency of a prince, who had never let an opportunity pass to declare himself heir to the French throne, was a clear indication that republicanism as a principle was not yet deeply anchored in the national conscience. Under these circumstances it might well be that the republic would prove but a passing phase.

REFERENCES

E. FUETER, *World History*, chs. 21, 23
C. SEIGNOBOS, *Europe Since 1814*, chs. 5, 6
C. M. ANDREWS, *Development of Modern Europe*, chs. 7, 8
C. D. HAZEN, *Europe Since 1815*, I, chs. 7, 10
J. S. SCHAPIRO, *Modern and Contemporary Europe*, ch. 6
C. H. HAYES, *Political and Social History*, II, pp. 116–123
C. A. FYFFE, *Modern Europe*, II, ch. 7, III, ch. 1
J. R. M. MACDONALD, *France*, III, chs. 36, 37
E. BOURGEOIS, *Modern France*, I, chs. 4–9
H. A. L. FISHER, *Republican Traditions in Europe*
G. L. DICKINSON, *Revolution and Reaction in Modern France*
F. J. C. HEARNSHAW, *Main Currents*, ch. 6
J. A. R. MARRIOTT, *The French Revolution of 1848 in Its Economic Aspects*
A. LEBON, *Modern France*, chs. 9, 11
K. MARX, *Revolution and Counter Revolution*

CHAPTER XXIII

THE REVOLUTION OF 1848 IN GERMANY, AUSTRIA, AND ITALY

If the revolution of 1830 produced no great stir in central Europe, it was, as we have seen, because the liberal and national sentiments had not yet become powerful and, more fundamentally still, because the middle classes, the historic carriers of these sentiments, were insufficiently developed to make successful headway against the conservative interests in control of the government. Hence in the period after 1830 the reaction remained in the saddle throughout Germany, Austria, and Italy. Still the areas of popular unrest continued to multiply, while the growing well-being and self-assertion of the business and professional groups was a certain indication that the days of an uncompromising conservatism were numbered. To people in the alert state of mind of the central European liberals the February revolution at Paris came as a challenge to action. Amidst a general outburst of jubilation they rose here, there, and everywhere, declaring for popular government and a national state. While it is undeniable that France had once more asserted the liberal leadership of Europe by setting an example which the other countries imitated, it remains a fact that by 1848 the liberal movement had developed sufficiently in Germany, Austria, and Italy to make an impression by its own inherent vigor.

Central Europe ready in 1848 for a liberal and national upheaval

It is one of the ironical touches so frequent in history that Metternich's own capital, the chief shrine of the spirit of reaction, was among the first to voice the new freedom. On March 13, 1848, Vienna rose and drove the aging prince, who since 1815 had been the not undistinguished mouthpiece of an outworn system, from the chancellery of the Austrian empire and from the capital. With Metternich's ignominious flight the whole government collapsed without more ado: absolutism was renounced, and the feeble Emperor Ferdinand, frightened by the tumult in the streets, speedily promised a constitution, a parliament, freedom of

Revolution at Vienna

497

the press, and whatever else the rioters exacted. With the suddenness of melodrama a new era seemed to have dawned upon the petrified realm of the Hapsburgs.

The news of the fall of Metternich caused exultation throughout Germany, on which his hand had rested with no less heaviness than on Austria. In many of the small capitals riots broke out which were Revolution placated by liberal concessions; and overshadowing these at Berlin disturbances, on March 18th Berlin followed the example of Vienna and rose to protest against the autocratic system. In view of Prussia's failure to respond to the revolution of 1830 this action may seem somewhat surprising. But the last decade had been preparing changes. The old king, Frederick William III, who had endeared himself to his people because of his connection with the War of Liberation against Napoleon, had died in 1840. His successor was his son, Frederick William IV, and the new generation surrounding his throne let it be known in no uncertain tones that, while it approved of the efficient administration maintained by the state, it did not intend to let itself be excluded any longer from a share in legislation. In spite of his firm belief in Divine Right, the new king had, as early as 1847, yielded so far to public opinion as to summon to Berlin the representatives of the several provincial estates. This assembly, called the United Diet, at once assumed the airs of a Prussian national parliament; and although it did not accomplish anything, the fact that the king had been obliged to call it together proves that the revolution of 1848 was more than a sudden popular caprice. As a result of the March days, which did not pass without the spilling of blood, the intimidated king surrendered completely to the people. Not only did he, by withdrawing his troops from the city, hand Berlin over to the agitators, but he promised to call an elected parliament and, in addition, to promote to the best of his ability the cause of German unity.

Thus was all Germany in the course of a few days won over to a thorough-going constitutionalism. But there was also another aspect to the stirring movement: it was animated by a fiery national- ism. The middle class leaders of the revolution were The revo- convinced that the time had come to scrap the ludicrous lution is national as confederation of 1815, the Bund, in order to erect upon its well as ruins a really effective German union. Resolved to strike liberal while the iron was hot, they met informally in March and quickly came to the conclusion to issue a call for a general German parliament to be elected by universal manhood suffrage and to be endowed with full authority to create a strong federal government. To this bold invitation the German people responded with an extraordinary and apparently united enthusiasm.

When the German parliament, elected on these terms, assembled in May, 1848, at Frankfort-on-the-Main, it was found to be by every moral and intellectual standard a very distinguished body of men. But all their learning and high principles did not serve to cancel one fatal defect inherent in their position: so long as they had at their disposal neither an administration nor an army, that is, so long as they possessed none of the realities of power, their status hardly differed from that of a debating society. In the early days of the revolutionary triumph this weakness might be offset by an irresistible public opinion; but if opinion sagged, as it regularly does since it can not be forever maintained at high tension, and if the state governments, panic-stricken by the first glimpse of the revolutionary ferment, recovered breath and courage — what then? The Bund, swept off the stage by the national hurricane, had been established expressly to guarantee the sovereignty of the thirty-eight member states, which would certainly yield their dearest possession only under duress. Austria and Prussia, in particular, proud of their position as great powers, could hardly be expected without some show of resistance to recognize as their superior the democratic and revolutionary body sitting at Frankfort. Sooner or later Austria or Prussia or both together would follow an independent policy, and the clash, testing the question of supremacy, would be at hand. *Strength and weakness of the German parliament*

The clash came over the Schleswig-Holstein complication. This, one of the most confused questions of nineteenth century history, haunted the European chancelleries like a nightmare for more than a generation. But apart from its enormous legal difficulties it is quite simple since it is a characteristic issue of the new nationalist type. The united duchies of Schleswig and Holstein occupied the southern half of the peninsula of Jutland and were inhabited, except for the northern rim of Schleswig, which is Danish, by a German population. By an accident of inheritance the king of Denmark was also duke of Schleswig and Holstein, but the two duchies were otherwise independent, having their own laws and administration. This independ- *The Schleswig-Holstein difficulty* ence of Denmark the two duchies, because they were preponderantly German, were firmly resolved to preserve. Toward the middle of the century an issue dawned which put the Germans on their guard. The royal house of Denmark, about to die out in the male line, was faced by a constitutional difficulty. By the law of Denmark the crown would descend to a female line, while by the Schleswig-Holstein law, at least as interpreted by the German population, the crown of the united duchies would pass to the nearest male relative. This prospect of an early divorce between Denmark and the duchies rejoiced the Germans as much as it grieved the Danes, and in 1846 the king of Denmark took the weighty step of issuing a public declaration to the effect that, come what may, he would see to it that the ancient union was maintained. This declaration the German population regarded as a breach of law and custom; they were thrown into a revolutionary mood and, taking advantage of the general agitation of 1848, they rose in revolt, proclaimed Schleswig-Holstein independent of Denmark, and appealed to the German parliament at Frankfort for support.

The German parliament at once responded with fair words, but when it came to deeds found itself hampered by the fact that it had neither an army nor other resources at its disposal. In consequence it was obliged to appeal to Prussia, which bordered on the duchies, to go to the aid of the rebels. Entering Schleswig-Holstein, the Prussians drove out the Danes, but the latter retaliated by seizing the Prussian merchant vessels in the Baltic. This fact, coupled with the interference in behalf of Denmark of Russia and Great Britain, induced King Frederick William, who had only with reluctance obeyed the German parliament, to sign a truce with Denmark (August 26th). By its terms he practically redelivered the duchies into the hands of the Danes. Thereupon the legislators at Frankfort mounted their high horses, branded Frederick William as a traitor, and declared the truce null and void. On sober second thought, however, they recognized that without an army they could not coerce Prussia and, reversing themselves, endorsed all that Prussia had done. The incident was highly instructive as to the distribution of effective power between Prussia and the German parliament. Greatly humiliated the members turned to the constitutional labors for which they had been summoned, resolved to bring them to a conclusion before the revolutionary tide which had

The German parliament bows to Prussia in the matter of the Danish war

swept them to power had completely ebbed. At this task we shall leave them while we look into the affairs of Austria and Italy.

The Austrian Empire was as strange a patchwork of states and peoples as has ever been pieced together by fortune and policy. Germans in Austria proper, Hungarians along the middle Danube, Italians in the provinces of Lombardy and Venetia an- *Austria falls* nexed in 1815, and at least six different groups of Slavs *into its* chiefly in the northern and southern areas were expected *component* to live together as brothers in a common household. Sur- *parts* prising as it may seem, it is undeniable that the experiment proved fairly successful so long as the emperor at Vienna exercised an unimpaired absolute power and the national sentiments of the component peoples remained in abeyance. But as soon as the March revolution had undermined the emperor's autocracy at the central seat, the nationalist passion of the various peoples was fanned into flame and the whole Hapsburg structure threatened to fly apart with violent centrifugal action. In the course of a few weeks the Italians at Milan and Venice, the respective capitals of Lombardy and Venetia, drove out the Austrian garrisons and declared for independence; the Hungarians, ignoring Vienna, set up their own government; and while the Slavs remained relatively quiescent, some of them, notably the Czechs of Bohemia, inaugurated measures looking, if not toward complete sovereignty, at least toward home rule. To the casual observer the proud Austrian Empire seemed to have reached its end. Let us follow these insurrections in their leading centers.

In Italy the fall of Metternich was no sooner reported than the people of Lombardy and Venetia, long restive under his lash, rose, fell upon the troops, and declared for independence. The Austrian army, yielding to the sudden pressure, retired in good *The Italian* order under its general, Radetzky, to a chain of impreg- *patriots turn* nable fortifications prepared for just such an occasion at *upon Aus-* the foot of the Alps and known as the Quadrilateral. A *tria* Provisional Government at Milan appealed to all Italy for help and especially to Charles Albert, king of Sardinia-Piedmont, the most powerful of the Italian princes and the only one devoted to the general cause. As for the moment the national movement was irresistible even the other rulers, such as the king of the Two Sicilies, the grand-duke of Tuscany, and the pope, who traditionally served only their local interests, agreed to send contingents to fight side by side with the Sardinians for the liberation of the northern provinces. It was Italy's first great national war; its purpose the expulsion of the foreigner.

In this heroic enterprise, originating in the spontaneous action of the people, there was one weakness which no enthusiasm could overcome. Among the motley and undisciplined Italian forces the Sardinian army was the only efficient body and its numbers were too small to resist the Austrian legions. When on July 25th the decisive clash came at Custozza, within the Quadrilateral, whither the king of Sardinia had led his army in order to dislodge the Austrians, the veteran General Radetzky inflicted a complete defeat on the Italians, reconquered Lombardy, and obliged Charles Albert, in order to save Piedmont from invasion, to sue for a truce. When at the expiration of the truce the war was renewed, the Austrians won another great victory at Novara (March, 1849), and the struggle was over. Sick at heart the defeated Charles Albert abdicated, and his son and successor, Victor Emmanuel, made haste to sign a treaty with Austria by which, in return for abandoning the national cause, he received back his undiminished realm. That left the Austrians free to deal with their two revolted provinces of Lombardy and Venetia. Milan, the capital of Lombardy, being already in their hands, siege was now laid to Venice and the city obliged, after a courageous defence, to capitulate.

Austria defeats Sardinia and her allies

Though the struggle in the north against Austria marks the climax in the drama of the Italian revolution, the rest of the peninsula shared in the aspirations and delusions of that year of turmoil. While the revolutionary movement was at its height, the pope, the grand-duke of Tuscany, the king of the Two Sicilies, and the lesser princes had made every conceivable concession to the liberals; but as soon as the tide receded, they hurried to revert to the cherished system of absolutism. The king of the Two Sicilies was the first to cast aside his liberal mask. A despot without a scruple or, rather, a vaudeville sovereign in real life, he overthrew the constitutional system, first in Naples and afterward in Sicily. A reaction worse than that imposed by the Austrians in Lombardy, because its author was more despicable, fastened upon the fair provinces of the south. Far more memorable was the march of the revolution in the central section, in the State of the Church, of which Pope Pius IX was sovereign. In fact the course which the revolution

The revolution in Naples

took at Rome throws so much light on Italian problems that we must examine it somewhat more fully.

Pius IX, elected to the papacy in 1846, was a kind and affable man, with a reputation for liberalism which he owed to nothing more significant than an occasional good-natured word and deed. However, as a born Italian, he did in a measure sympathize The with the Italian national movement; and undeniably revolution when Lombardy revolted against Austria, he gave evi- at Rome dence of approving the action by sending a papal contingent to the rebels' aid. But as soon as he became aware of the consequences of this step he called a halt. To send troops against Austria meant a declaration of war against that power and the adoption of a martial policy hardly consistent with his position as head of the universal Church. He found himself in a dilemma, the inevitable consequence of his dual character; for as pope and successor of the Prince of Peace he had spiritual obligations toward the whole Catholic world, while as secular lord of an Italian territory he had definite temporal interests, the imperative one at the moment being to join with the nation against the foreign conqueror. Obliged to choose between his obligations to Catholicism and those to his temporal state, he naturally preferred the greater to the less and, to the relief of Austria but to immense indignation of his Roman subjects, withdrew from the Austrian war. The incident proved that a pope, who wished to play a consistent international role, could never follow exclusive national ends. But the Romans, who were not philosophers but passionate Italians, showed their disgust with their sovereign by rising in revolution. A strong republican faction pronounced against Pius as a traitor to Italy; and when, alarmed at the situation, he sought refuge (November 24, 1848) with his friend, the king of Naples, the revolutionists took affairs into their own hands and converted the papal dominion into a republic. The leading spirit of the new government was Mazzini, a high-minded, life-long prophet of Italian unity and a tireless conspirator against the selfish reigning houses of his divided country.

The Roman Republic never had more than a fighting chance. Catholics the world over were horrified at the dispossession of the Holy Father and several Catholic governments considered measures looking to his restoration. Louis Napoleon, just elected president of the French Republic, was especially delighted at the opportunity offered to curry favor with the Catholic clergy and peasantry of

France; and intent only on his own advantage and heedless of the fact that he was pitting one youthful republic against another, he sent an army to Rome to sweep Mazzini and his followers out of the city. General Garibaldi, who had been created commander-in-chief of the Roman forces, offered a gallant but hopeless resistance. In July, 1849, the French entered the conquered city. When on the invitation of his rescuers the disillusioned Pope returned to his capital, he was cured of such slight predilection for reform as he may once have felt and reëstablished the traditional autocratic system with all its time-worn abuses.

France overthrows the Roman Republic

Thus with a harvest of disappointments the Italian revolutionary action of 1848–1849 came to a close. Affairs relapsed to their former state; the brave effort had been apparently in vain. But one fact, shining out like a star in the night of their discouragement, was that patriotic Italians had found in the king of Sardinia a sovereign dedicated to their cause and in his army the one substantial hope of a future renewal of the war for independence. True, Charles Albert had been defeated; but not only had he stood by Italy till his overthrow, but his successor, Victor Emmanuel, showed an even more resolute spirit. For though subjected in turn to Austrian threats and bribes, he refused to give up his interest in Italy or to qualify as a reactionary by withdrawing the constitution granted to his country in 1848. Such sturdy attachment to the liberal-national program roused a love and admiration which drew the eyes of the Italians of north and south alike toward Piedmont and the house of Savoy.

Italy looks to the house of Savoy

At the same time that Austria was occupied with stamping out the Italian revolution, she was obliged to attend to rebellions in several other sections of her extended dominions. We have already noted that the March rising of the Germans at Vienna had served as the signal for nationalist upheavals among the Italians, Hungarians, and Czechs, not to mention a number of smaller groups. With chaos ruling in the capital and with the imperial authority paralyzed at its core by the unfortunate circumstance that the Emperor Ferdinand was a harmless imbecile, it is more than likely that the Austrian Empire would have been lost, had it not been for the army. Its ancient traditions and effective discipline held it together in spite of the intolerable confusion at Vienna. In Italy, as we have seen, it furnished incontrovertible

The army saves the Austrian Empire

evidence that it had not gone to pieces like the civil government; and with the Italian example before them the Austrian generals in command in the other rebellious areas became desirous of employing Radetzky's remedy of the sword to the situation under their eyes. An unruly multitude imposing its will by street demonstrations is never a match for trained soldiers under professional command. When, in June, General Windischgraetz, commanding at Prague in Bohemia, came to grips with the insurrection of the Czechs, he snuffed it out without much trouble. His next logical step was to attack the revolution of the Germans in Vienna. Arriving in October before the city, he encountered a resistance which broke when his troops stormed the gates and forced their way into the town. With the Czech and German movements once more under control and the Italian cause on the road to ruin there remained only the Hungarian revolt to crush for Austria to be her accustomed self again.

The Hungarian revolt turned out to be the hardest nut which the Austrian army undertook to crack and which it might not have cracked at all if it had not received help from an unexpected quarter. It was in the sixteenth century, as the reader will remem- *The revolution in Hungary, 1848–1849* ber, that the crown of Hungary had passed into the possession of the house of Hapsburg. The kingdom of the Magyars had an ancient constitution which conceded considerable power to a representative parliament; and although the Hapsburg sovereigns, aiming at the unification of all their territories under their absolute rule, had frequently set the constitution at naught, they had never succeeded in entirely abrogating it. The Magyars for their part clung stubbornly to their political inheritance; and when the Viennese absolutism collapsed suddenly through the impact of the March revolution, they gained at a stroke all that they had been demanding. As a result Hungary to all intents and purposes seceded from the Austrian Empire, although it continued to recognize the Hapsburg sovereign as its king. But with the insurrectionary fires extinguished in Italy, Bohemia, and at Vienna the baffled central government again plucked up courage and ceased to cringe before the Magyars. Disputes over questions of competence between the parliament at Budapest and the Hapsburg sovereign led to a state of war, and in December, 1848, the hitherto victorious Windischgraetz directed his army upon the Hungarian capital. The struggle which followed constitutes a splendid tribute to the undaunted spirit of the Hungarians. Ever since the revolution had begun, it had been under the powerful guidance of Louis Kossuth, who at the approach of the supreme crisis assumed the dictatorship of the country. Kossuth put the army under the command of the capable General Görgei, who by the adoption of a bold strategy succeeded in driving the Austrian army back upon Vienna. Elated by this success, Kossuth, a convinced republican, issued a decree declaring the deposition of the house of Hapsburg. The measure was of doubtful wisdom, for not only did it divide the Hungarians, many of whom, perhaps a majority, were royalists, but it reduced the Viennese court to desperation and persuaded it to accept the proffered help of Tsar Nicholas. The Russian autocrat, long waiting for an opportunity to ride into the lists in behalf of the monarchical principle, promptly sent an army across the Carpathians which took the Hungarians in the flank. Caught between two fires, the rebels gave a good accounting of themselves; but by August, 1849, their forces had been overwhelmed and with Kossuth, Görgei, and the other leaders either captured or driven into exile the movement for Hungarian independence came to a tragic close.

Thus Austria had emerged from the terrible revolutionary crisis feeble and wounded but intact. It remained to dismiss the general Austrian parliament, which had been summoned on the demand of the people, and to shelve the constitution which the parliament had elaborated. A capable and unscrupulous man, Prince Schwarzenberg by name, who was appointed prime minister late in 1848, carried through these measures of reaction. Then with the scene swept clean of the revolutionary débris, Schwarzenberg frankly returned to the pre-revolutionary absolutism, which envisaged the Austrian Empire as a unitary state under a common army and a common administration and took no account of either traditional rights or national claims. As the feeble-minded Emperor Ferdinand was incapable of supporting so vigorous a policy, and as, besides, he was compromised by having given too many liberal pledges, Schwarzenberg, as early as December, 1848, had persuaded him to resign in favor of his young nephew, Francis Joseph.

On returning now to the affairs of Germany, we are immediately struck by the fact that the progress of reaction in Austria greatly encouraged the conservative party in all the German states and more particularly in Prussia. King Frederick William IV, who, though yielding to revolutionary pressure, had remained an unconverted absolutist, was readily persuaded that the time had come to treat revolutionary Berlin as Windischgraetz had treated revolutionary Vienna. By royal order the Prussian parliament, which was engaged in making a constitution for the state, was first prorogued *The reac-* to a provincial city and then dissolved (December 5th). *tion reaches* At the same time the troops reëntered the capital and *Germany* overawed radicals and liberals alike. Riding on a tide *and Prussia* of reaction, the king might now have returned to the old absolutism, but deterred by certain moral scruples, he offered his subjects a constitution of his own making. Most certainly it was a document which failed to incorporate the full liberal demands. In its final form adopted in 1850, it left to the executive the appointment of the ministers, who therefore acted as agents not of the Prussian parliament but of the king. Moreover, in the matter of the franchise the so-called three-class system was adopted, by virtue of which the men of voting age were divided into three classes in accordance with the amount of taxes paid by them. As all the well-to-do were in the first two classes and the rest of the citizenry in the third, and as, further, the representatives of the first two classes by standing together could outvote the representatives of the third the candidate elected to the parliament in a given district was always an agent of the men of property. Nevertheless a Prussian legislature, which made the laws and voted the taxes, secured to the Prussian people henceforth a share in the government and furnished evidence that in Prussia almost alone in central Europe the revolution had not been entirely in vain.

The next body to feel the chill breath of the reaction was the German parliament at Frankfort. We left it at the time of its discomfiture in the Schleswig-Holstein matter, when the proof of its weakness had been furnished by its inability to control *The* the policy of Prussia. Since then it had proceeded, in *German* spite of multiplying signs that the revolution had passed *parliament* its meridian, with its work of uniting all Germany by a *its constitu-* national constitution. The greatest barrier in its path *tion, 1849* was Austria. As this country, a mixture of half a score of nationalities, would cut a strange figure in a German national state, it was finally resolved to exclude it from the proposed union. Unfortunately the action excluded also the Austrian Germans, who, ideally, were of course a part of Germany. However, the elimination of the Hapsburg Empire settled almost automatically the related difficulty of the headship of the new Germany. Not without heated discussion, it was decided that the chief executive should be a hereditary emperor and that the post would be offered to the king of Prussia. In April, 1849, a deputation from the parliament journeyed to Berlin to offer the crown of united Germany to Frederick William.

Their answer was a refusal. Frederick William was too deeply penetrated with ideas of Divine Right to have any sympathy for a popular and democratic honor; he was convinced that the constitu-

The king of Prussia rejects the proffered crown tion was in many of its features unworkable; and — he was afraid of Austria. Under the energetic Schwarzenberg Austria was just effecting a phenomenal recovery and notified Berlin in no uncertain language that the acceptance of the imperial office by a Hohenzollern would be deeply resented. The Viennese view was that if the German crown was to be revived, it must revert to the house of Hapsburg which had worn it for so many centuries. Frederick William was a weak, well-meaning man of mystical, confused ideas, and, like all waverers, ended by yielding to the various pressures brought to bear upon him. The committee of the parliament went back to Frankfort and reported its failure, whereupon the German assembly sadly acknowledged its inability to go on with its work and not without a small flurry of revolt retired from the scene.

Frederick William IV, who, in spite of his refusal of the German crown, felt that he was pledged to do something for the national cause, now made an attempt to persuade the German governments

The Prussian and Austrian plans for a German union to negotiate among themselves about the bases of a new union. His thought was that since the people, acting through their representatives at Frankfort, had failed to solve the German problem, it behooved the princes to try their hands at it. But against this plan, too, because it excluded the Austrian Empire, the Austrian government threw the full weight of its influence. Finally, Vienna came to the front with a German plan of its own, which proved to be nothing other than the Bund of 1815. Of this ludicrous confederation the great attraction was that it left Austria in Germany; that it did not impair the sovereignty of the member states; and that it reduced the king of Prussia to the level of the other German princes. Although in the spring of 1848 the Bund had fallen like a house of cards before the first revolutionary gust, Austria once more boldly set it up at Frankfort. Then it issued an invitation to all the former members to enter and complete the happy German family. With their eyes directed, above all, to their sovereignty, the German princes deserted Frederick William's proposed union under Prussia and gathered under the Austrian standard. Almost before he knew it, the Prussian king found himself alone like an actor on a deserted stage; and when Austria, aware that she was dealing with a timid man, now haughtily ordered him to give up every idea of a closer union and be satisfied with the Bund, he yielded without a struggle (Treaty of Olmütz, November, 1850). The old Bund — that was the ridiculous issue of the two years' labor of the nation for a better union.

In this general collapse of German hopes and illusions the Schleswig-Holsteiners, who had rebelled against their sovereign, the king of Denmark, could not escape disaster. Abandoned by Prussia in August, 1848, they several times renewed the fray, only Schleswig-to be crushed definitely in 1850. A conference of the Holstein powers gathered in London to consider their case and crushed decided the succession question against them. It was agreed (Protocol of 1852) that the union between Denmark and the duchies should be maintained and that on the extinction of the reigning line Prince Christian of Glücksburg should succeed to both inheritances. Although the German population of Schleswig-Holstein protested against the decision, they bowed to the verdict of the powers in the hope of finding a future occasion to reassert their rights.

With the German parliament banished to the shades, the duchies of Schleswig and Holstein redelivered to the Danes, the Bund set up again at Frankfort, and Austria restored under an absolute sovereign, the Metternichian system with all its attendant The miseries and abuses had been given a new lease of life. German National and liberal circles were filled with despair. But situation as no evil is without some grain of good, the confusion of the revolution had shown two things: it had proved that the greatest enemy to German unity was the Austrian court and that a German union, if it ever came, would have to be effected under Prussian leadership. Prussia's prestige, it is true, was, after her many failures, lamentably low. But something remained: it was not forgotten that the national hopes had for a short time turned enthusiastically to her; and by her adoption of a constitution she had begun to divorce herself from eighteenth century forms in order to plant her feet in the present.

REFERENCES

E. Fueter, *World History*, chs. 10, 11, 13

C. A. Fyffe, *Modern Europe*, III, ch. 2

C. D. Hazen, *Europe Since 1815*, I, chs. 8, 9

C. H. Hayes, *Political and Social History*, II, pp. 123–144

C. M. Andrews, *Development of Modern Europe*, chs. 5, 6, 9, 10

Cambridge Modern History, XI, chs. 3, 4, 6, 7

L. Blanc, *Historical Revelations*

K. Marx, *Revolution and Counter Revolution*

C. E. Maurice, *The Revolutionary Movement of 1848–49*

E. F. Henderson, *Short History of Germany*, II, ch. 9

C. Schurz, *Reminiscences*, I

G. M. Priest, *Germany Since 1740*, chs. 8, 9

K. Francke, *Social Forces in German Literature*

L. Leger, *History of Austria-Hungary*

C. M. Knatchbull-Hugessen, *Political Evolution of the Hungarian Nation*, II, chs. 12–16

B. King, *History of Italian Unity; Joseph Mazzini*

W. J. Stillman, *The Union of Italy*

R. M. Johnston, *Roman Theocracy and the Republic*

G. M. Trevelyan, *Garibaldi and the Making of Italy*

H. D. Sedgwick, *Short History of Italy*, ch. 37

W. R. Thayer, *Dawn of Italian Independence*

CHAPTER XXIV

THE INDUSTRIAL AND SOCIAL REVOLUTION OF THE NINETEENTH CENTURY

Again and again it has been emphasized in the course of this book that the leading consequence of the modern social development had been to give an increasing importance to the middle classes, and that up to the time of the French Revolution it was the middle classes of England which had reaped the greatest benefits from an altered world. Among them the abandonment of older attitudes and usages and the experimentation with new ways had gone farther than among the corresponding groups of the continent. It was in England that the absolute monarchy first broke down through an uprising of the middle classes; and it was also in England that the gild system, which minutely regulated the production and sale of goods, first gave way. By the eighteenth century, when the gilds still exercised an unbroken domination over the industry of countries like France and Germany, they had as good as vanished altogether from English soil. In their place had appeared, above all in the flourishing textile industry, a free contract or capitalist system, in accordance with which a small number of wholesalers advanced the raw material (wool, cotton) to individual workers, who converted it into the finished fabric in their homes and on its redelivery to the wholesaler effected a financial settlement. Although the workers labored in their own homes, which were also their workshops, and although they were technically independent producers, it is undeniable that they became more or less dependent on a small group of powerful men with capital and energy, who determined the price to be paid to the workers and dominated the market.

Emergence in England of a middle class, capitalist régime

Such a system attached a wholly novel importance to personal initiative and must have served to stimulate the spirit of invention. In any case it was again in England, after gild obstructionism had become a thing of the past, that men first perfected devices which greatly improved the ancient processes of the textile industry. It

511

is notable that so long as the gild system, whether in England or elsewhere, exercised its conservative sway, these processes followed the same familiar groove for centuries. The two most important operations in cloth-making are spinning and weaving. **New inventions revolutionize the textile industry** Between 1740 and 1790 a number of ingenious individuals, such as Kay, Hargreaves, Arkwright, and Crompton introduced numerous improvements, among which we may note the spinning jenny and the power loom, with the aid of which one man could in the course of a day turn out as much work as had formerly required three, four, and even five men. There was now need of more cotton. It was met by planting a larger acreage with cotton in the southern section of the United States, but also by the invention of an American, Eli Whitney by name, who constructed a cotton gin capable of picking the seeds from the raw cotton more swiftly than several score of negro slaves.

Into the rapidly changing textile situation of the second half of the eighteenth century James Watt projected (1769) his steam-engine. Harnessed to the new spinning and weaving machinery, it replaced the motive power of man with that of water-vapor. It **The revolution wrought by the steam engine** is a work of supererogation to descant upon the significance of this invention to a generation which is in daily and hourly contact with the miracles wrought by the expansive power of steam. Rather must the student, familiar with the present-day uses of steam, be cautioned against seeing the eighteenth century situation in the light of the twentieth century development. He must not indulge his imagination by assuming that the world changed magically within the hour in which Watt stood before his completed model. It took many additional improvements before the first engine could be put economically to use; and even after it had been annexed by the texile industry, the most advanced of English trades, many decades passed before it was adapted to other forms of enterprise. As its application to transportation had particularly important consequences, we should not fail to note that an American, Robert Fulton, was the first man to build a practicable steamboat. In 1807 his side-wheeler, the *Clermont*, equipped with a Watt engine, made the trip up the Hudson river from New York to Albany. Some years later an Englishman, George Stephenson, built a steam locomotive which, being powerful enough to draw a train of cars, encouraged a group of capitalists to construct 1825) the first English railway. On the heels of these two inventions there followed so intensive a building of steamboats and railways that in a few decades the conditions of travel and transportation in the world had been completely revolutionized.

Such are a few indications of the earliest applications made of the steam-engine. Because it was hitched before long to the printing-press, saw-mill, pumping-station, and a hundred other kinds of machinery, it became a commonplace to speak of the nineteenth century as the age of steam. But the century was not yet old when a rival power was discovered in electricity. While it took some decades before the possibilities of this new agent were fathomed, before the nineteenth century came to a close its secrets had been sufficiently mastered to utilize it for running trains and street-cars; in fact every indication pointed to an electrical development which would make the twentieth century as distinctly an age of electricity as the previous century had been the age of steam. However, long before the experiments conducted with electricity as a motive power had been crowned with success, ways and means had been discovered to apply it to the simpler purposes of human communication. In 1832 the electric telegraph was invented; and in 1866 the first submarine cable was laid across the Atlantic. In 1876 followed the invention of the telephone, to be succeeded before the close of the century, in 1895, by the wireless. In how masterful a manner the telegraph and, later, the telephone have facilitated and intensified the communications maintained among modern groups and individuals will appear to any one who tries to imagine his daily life without them. *Electricity revolutionizes the system of communication*

The changes in ways of living effected by innumerable inventions, great and small, but chiefly by the invention of power machinery driven by steam-engines have been so immense that men have agreed they constitute an Industrial Revolution. But if the Industrial Revolution may be conceived of as beginning in England in the second half of the eighteenth century, two features touching its growth must be steadily kept in mind. In the first place, as soon as the Napoleonic wars were over, it leaped across the channel to France and spread thence, though often with conspicuous delays owing to special local conditions, to every country of the continent. In this connection it is well to remember that wherever the French Revolution had forced an entrance, it had destroyed the antiquated gild system, thereby creating the free labor market which already existed in *The Industrial Revolution; its spread and cumulative energy*

England and which had been the chief cause of the ferment leading up to the machine. In the second place, the Industrial Revolution must be thought of as a continuous movement still persisting in our day and bearing along the present generation in an ever broadening and more irresistible stream. As for the countries which it has chiefly affected, doubtless Great Britain, where the revolution began, enjoyed an industrial primacy throughout the nineteenth century. Not till the days of Louis Philip and Napoleon III was neighboring France definitely won to the movement. Under these sovereigns France made great forward strides, acquiring an unquestioned ascendancy in certain specialized lines such as silks, velvets, and the highly diversified articles of female apparel. Somewhat later than France, though not systematically till its unification (1871), did Germany experience the Industrial Revolution. With a mighty effort it then came from behind, quickly outstripping the other continental countries; and as the twentieth century dawned, it was plainly girding its loins to catch up with the industrial leader, with Great Britain itself. At the same time Belgium, although a small state, became highly industrialized, while other countries, such as Italy and Austria, felt indeed the new forces but somewhat less intensely. Generally speaking, the measure of a country's industrial possibilities is furnished by the abundance of its supplies of coal and iron. These have proved themselves the basic raw products of the machine age; and because Great Britain, Germany, France, and Belgium, in the order named, have the largest and most convenient deposits of these minerals, these four countries hold a foremost place in the Industrial Revolution.[1] The rule here formulated for Europe is confirmed by the case of the United States. With iron and coal deposits larger than those of all Europe put together and with abundant other raw materials such as copper, lumber, and fuel oil, hardly less valuable than coal and iron, the United States, although starting later than Europe, was able in recent years to overtake the older continent as a producer of machine goods. Henceforth America's

Social and position as the industrial leader of the world is bound to
economic   become more and more clearly manifest.
conse-
quences of   While it is permissible to pass hurriedly over all the
Industrial external and obvious phenomena of the Industrial
Revolution Revolution — machines, steam-engines, steamboats, railways, telegraph, etc. — because they have become as familiar as

[1] This order reflects the situation as it was up to 1914.

domestic animals, whom indeed they have in part replaced, it is necessary to consider much more carefully, because they are less apparent, the leading social and economic consequences of the new movement. They may be conveniently classified under five heads:

1. *Enormous increase of wealth.* It goes without saying that the Industrial Revolution greatly increased human possessions. Not only were clothes, shoes, hats, china, chairs, and other articles now manufactured quantitatively, but, produced by machines at a lower labor cost, they could be placed more cheaply on the market. The cheaper price in turn attracted a larger number of buyers and greatly stimulated consumption. Statistics prove the rapid increase in the mass of marketable goods, but as we have little space for this type of evidence, let the figures of the British textile industry suffice to illustrate the point. In 1760 the value of British cotton manufactures was $1,000,000; one hundred and fifty years later, in 1910, it was $600,000,000. The ratio of one to six hundred probably gives with reasonable accuracy the increase of wealth, that is, of articles of use, in Great Britain between the above dates.

2. *Accessibility of raw products and of markets.* The new means of transportation — steamboats and railways — made it possible to tap supplies of coal, iron, lumber, etc., which in the days of the horse vehicle and the sailing vessel were practically inaccessible. None the less long hauls continue to mean increased production costs, and therefore the rule has been for great manufacturing centers to develop in close proximity to coal and iron beds. Much more expedient than the transfer of bulky raw materials is the despatch of finished articles; and with the expansion of the new means of transport not only have the European countries been drawn closer together but the other continents have, as it were, been brought to Europe's dooryard and flooded with factory-made goods. In fact, in measure as goods were multiplied beyond the power of the European peoples to absorb them, it became absolutely necessary to find American, African, and Asiatic markets on which to unload the surplus. Thus obliged to look beyond the boundaries of their little continent, the European states entered on a new and more intensive phase of colonial expansion which, toward the end of the nineteenth century, took on the special form called imperialism. In this way the Industrial Revolution has become a lively and even a leading factor in world politics.

3. *Machines and factories bring the triumph of capitalism.* We have seen that capitalism had become a factor in European economics

beginning with the Renaissance and Reformation. The early capitalists were generally wholesalers who organized the expeditions into distant countries and assumed the heavy risks which these entailed. In case a large foreign trade developed, these early capitalists became wealthy and automatically exercised a decisive influence in the affairs of their city and, ultimately, of their nation. When the English wholesalers broke down the prerogative of the gilds and organized production around themselves on a simple contract basis, they climbed another rung or two up the ladder of success. But not till the coming of machines did the capitalist discover the path which led to the domination of society. The reason is not far to seek, for first, machines cost a great deal of money, and second, they have to be housed in specially constructed factories. Plainly these and other advances, such as wages, must be met before there is any return from the sale of goods. In consequence a limited group of moneyed men entered into possession of the means of production and became masters of the situation. While many of them performed immediate, indispensable services in the role of promoters, superintendents, and salesmen, considerable numbers, entirely outside the active management, made a money contribution in return for an interest payment. The investment system predicated on interest gave the new production methods a vast power of expansion, since not only the rich but small individuals also with only petty savings in their stockings were enabled to share in capitalist enterprises. However, the relatively broad participation of the public must not induce us to close our eyes to the fact that in every industrial nation a relatively restricted class of capitalists was created with almost unlimited control of that nation's economic life. The age of machines became synonomous with the age of capitalism.

4. *Growth of population.* Wherever the Industrial Revolution has taken root it has greatly increased population for the simple reason that the production of more goods has enabled more people to live. Statistics would seem to show that the increase is only partially due to an improved birth-rate (or lowered death-rate) and that it most often presents itself to view as migration from the rural districts to the urban centers in possession of the machines. In the case of England, which serves as the industrial type, the total population doubled in the first half of the nineteenth century and has continued to increase since at a scarcely slackened rate. Concomitantly the rural population has in this same period slowly declined until **at**

present fewer people live on the land than in the eighteenth century. It helps us to grasp how the Industrial Revolution has altered the social aspect of England if we recall that fully three-fourths of the inhabitants of the island reside at present in cities. The food deficit resulting from the enormous increase of the urban population is made up by importations from abroad paid for with the export of manufactured goods. No other country is exactly in the English class, since no other took, after grave political conflicts to be noted later, the English course of deliberately sacrificing agriculture to industry. Germany, for instance, has tried to save its agriculture by protective measures; but even with this support, the German agricultural population has at best remained stationary, proving that the considerable German increase of population belongs to the towns and is of industrial origin. However, while giving the machines their due as population producers, let us not forget that science, which has made machines possible, has, chiefly through the revelations of chemistry, revolutionized also the practices of agriculture by causing three, four, and more blades to grow where but one grew before. Conceding that Europe's amazing growth of population is overwhelmingly industrial and urban, we are obliged, in considering the problem of the maintenance of this human increase, to take account not only of the new foreign markets but also of the improved productivity of the soil.

5. *Economic and social depression of the industrial workers.* What the Industrial Revolution meant specifically to the new class of machine-workers is a special story of the greatest importance. Drawn from privately owned looms or lured from the farm to the factory, they found themselves in frankly deplorable conditions. From having been, to a certain extent at least, their own masters, they were reduced to slaves of iron monsters, to whose wants they attended during long hours and at wages arbitrarily fixed by the employer class. Owing to the novelty of the situation they were completely helpless, for with the employers owning the only available means of livelihood the alternative before the hapless immigrants from the country-side was to work or starve. They were unknown to one another, they lacked even the rudiments of an education, and if in self-defense they tried to combine, they encountered rigorous laws which forbade them to form associations to the end of increasing wages or reducing hours of labor. In England such a prohibitive statute was formally renewed as late as the year 1799. And yet the

wages were literally starvation wages and the working day was commonly reckoned at from fourteen to sixteen hours! As though all this were not misery enough, there was in addition the grim, persistent threat of unemployment. Again and again it descended like a bludgeon, sometimes owing to the ever recurring industrial crises, sometimes because of the employer's discovery that much of the machine-work could be done by women and children, ready and eager to sell themselves at a reduced rate. The social degradation resulting from this wage slavery completes the revolting picture. The towns, springing up like mushrooms around the factories, exhibited a disorder which indicated the complete absence of plan on the part of the people in authority. The workers and their families, herded in cheap tenements, constituted a slum with disgustingly filthy streets and the scantiest supply of such hygienic necessities as light, heat, and water. Of course disease was rampant, periodically assuming an epidemic form and mowing down its victims by the hundreds. Even in the most favorable years the general death-rate of the slum was high; among infants and children more particularly, owing to the lack of milk, cleanlinesss, and fresh air, it was so excessive as to reach the proportions of a national tragedy. It is not unusual to attach the responsibility for these conditions to the middle classes; and since the Industrial Revolution occurred under their auspices, they might, it is true, have fairly concerned themselves with its human implications. However, they were fully occupied with a great utilitarian work which absorbed all their energies and won them the applause of the world, and after the fashion of men at all times they proudly drove their chariot forward until a rumble as of a coming storm warned them of their peril. Then with the damage done they gradually faced the problem — with results which we shall presently examine.

An economic and social movement to begin with, the Industrial Revolution necessarily brought in its train a political upheaval because its immediate effect was to strengthen the middle classes,

The political program of the middle classes may be summarized as liberalism — that is, classes which already for generations had been slowly adding to their vigor. We have repeatedly pointed out that they were the leading agency which undermined the feudal system and created the national and absolute monarchy; and we have shown that it was again they who, first in England and then in France and elsewhere, insisted on an immediate share in the government by means of the constitutional system. It was the English middle classes who made up the strength of the Whig, that is, the constitutional party; and in the nineteenth century they and the awakened middle classes of the continent were identified with the various liberal parties which, though separately organized in each country, had, from the point of view of their general purpose, a strikingly international character. In a purely historical sense liberalism, meaning the principles of the liberal party, is not a better or a nobler program than conservatism; it is merely the program by which a powerfully expanding group proposed to secure for itself those benefits and that control which were necessary for the realization of its ends. Wishing to break down the annoying interference of the clergy, liberalism pronounced for toleration; desiring to terminate the political monopoly of the king, it aimed at the constitutional system; and anxious to level the obstructive barriers of a narrow provincialism, it championed the larger cause of nationalism. In other words the liberal program, in spite of its often abstract phraseology, has a very concrete basis in the middle class will to power. And when we now recall that the middle classes built the machines and furnished the capital; that it was they who supplied the engineers, technicians, and financial advisers; that, finally, theirs was the group which organized the educational systems and trained and employed the lawyers, physicians, teachers, and other professional servants, we have the clue to the political upheavals of the nineteenth century and the explanation of bourgeois success. For, although the bourgeoisie met with resistance on the part of the conservative interests in control and, even after a victory, experienced an occasional set-back, its march to power was on the whole uninterrupted. The age of the machine and capitalism is also the age of the middle classes and of their program of liberalism.

Alongside its political philosophy the dominant group developed an economic and moral philosophy in close harmony with it. Always and everywhere can we observe among men the passion to make their outlook on the world consistent in all its *Laissez* parts. We made acquaintance with the beginnings of *faire* the the bourgeois economic philosophy when we glanced at economic the physiocrats of France with their *laissez faire* and at of the mid- Adam Smith with his free trade, that is, trade freed as dle classes much as possible from artificial restrictions. While these thinkers undoubtedly subjected political economy for the first time to scientific organization, they at the same time planted it on characteristic middle class ground, as even a superficial examination will show. For the bourgeoisie was the class which, identified with business enterprise, found itself systematically thwarted by the mercantilist policy of state interference with the processes of production and distribution. *Laissez faire* and free trade alike advocated a policy of "no interference," since, the more the state abandoned its regulative and patriarchal program, the more the bourgeoisie gained the liberty it craved to exercise to the full its initiative in developing the world's natural resources. The extreme middle class ideal of the state came to be an institution of such exemplary modesty that it habitually kept itself out of sight. Should it ever step forth into the light of day, it was to do so hesitatingly in the role of the benevolent policeman quelling a disturbance. Generally speaking, it was voluntarily to leave the stage, on which the great human action unfolded, to the hero of the piece, the bourgeoisie. *Laissez faire* or "hands off" was, when first raised, the cry of an economic opposition intent on breaking down a hostile system of control. No sooner, however, had the middle classes gained control themselves than *laissez faire* changed to an exultant: leave *us* alone, leave everything to us!

While this attitude discloses a vigorous selfishness and materialism, it is indispensable to recognize that it also contains a definite moral core. Let us rest assured that, had they not been supported by a profound ethical conviction, the middle classes could not have pushed so relentlessly to the front and performed their amazing work. The conviction which sustained them and which in their view represented their service to the world was — to put it simply and sweepingly — that theirs was the cause of freedom. They saw, or their thinkers saw for them, that the course of events since the Middle Age had been to deliver man from bondage: the bondage of the Church, the bondage of the feudal law and of dead tradition, the bondage of the absolute state, the bondage of the mercantilist system. Having served a hundred masters, many of them reduced by the wear of time to the merest shadow, man was now to be manumitted and free. The moral philosophers of the bourgeoisie preached *the free man* as the goal of human endeavor. Liberated from the tutelage proper to a ward and a minor, human beings were to be summoned henceforth to assert their manhood. They were to stand on their own feet, to shape their own destiny, and to realize the dignity inherent in them as the crown and glory of creation. It

[marginal note: Freedom and individualism the ethical philosophy of the middle classes]

followed from this view of man's development from an early barbarous plane to ever higher levels that life was considered to be essentially a struggle, a free competitive game in which the unfit perished and the best came out on top. There was of course misery, poverty, and defeat, but they were the unescapable reverse of the medal. One forgot about them over the intoxication induced by the conviction that the world was engaged in a movement of uninterrupted progress, that it was driving onward and upward under the guidance of its natural leaders. It was not the degraded mass that counted but the tested and selected few. And even the degraded mass would benefit in the long run from the increased production resulting from a liberated and multiplied activity. Stated in ethical and philosophic terms this position may be defined as a vigorous individualism.

However, neither the middle class nor its philosophy was left in quiet possession of the field and, as the irony of history would have it, the challenge to their ascendancy issued from the group, which, since it was the child of the Industrial Revolution, the middle class had in a sense called into being. This group was the industrial workers. We have looked at their lowly condition in the first phase of the industrial movement due to the novelty of the situation coupled with their own mental backwardness. The best chance for their social advance lay, on the one hand, in a better education, and, on the other, in the strength to be derived from organization. Turning first to popular education, we note that it was as yet woefully neglected. Of all the great powers of Europe only Prussia possessed in the first half of the nineteenth century a broad public school system that successfully reached the masses. The other countries did not precisely ignore popular education, but they left it to the churches or to private enterprise, and gave it at best a half-hearted support. Not till the second half of the nineteenth century were the European states other than Prussia shamed into establishing public and compulsory systems of primary education. Great Britain made a beginning with the Education Act of 1870; France passed a measure of similar intent in 1881. That these enactments, strengthened by later supplementary legislation, were crowned with success is proved by the fact that the percentage of illiterates in both countries was steadily reduced until at the beginning of the twentieth century it was rapidly approaching the remarkably low percentage which

Reasons for the impotence of the working class: (1) lack of education

Prussia, as the oldest champion of popular education, had already succeeded in attaining.

It is thus clear that the European workers were for a long time grossly uneducated and that in this condition they might easily be dominated by their employers. Still, despite their profound igno-
(2) Lack of rance, they might have counted for something if they had organization stood together and made vigorous, concerted demands on their masters. Therewith we have touched the second factor in their social depression, the lack of organization. Divining the power of purposeful numbers, the forehanded lords of industry had sought to protect themselves by spreading upon the statute books of all the European countries measures forbidding workingmen to unite. It was not until 1824–1825 that bills were passed in parliament making it possible for the British workingmen to combine in order to promote their interests. And as it was not till the revolution of of 1848 that labor unions came out into the open on the continent, it is clear that they were very slow in unfolding their strength, especially as the revolution of 1848 was followed by a reaction which canceled, for a time at least, all that had been won. Not till 1864 did France pass legislation definitely permitting workingmen to form unions. In short, as it was not till the second half of the nineteenth century that laborers became generally free to combine, their inability promptly to help themselves, ascribable in part to their lack of education, becomes wholly comprehensible.

In the absence of self-help the first effective succor was extended to the workingmen by sympathizers of the middle class. Humanely disposed people founded societies for medical aid, for distributing
The prob-   milk among babies, for better housing conditions, and
lem at-   other similar purposes. All such activities may be classi-
tacked in   fied as philanthropy; but while conceding that they
turn by phi-
lanthropy,   alleviate suffering and honor those who sincerely practise
Utopianism, them, let us agree that they do not penetrate to the root
and science of the working class problem. That problem called for
more than a tender heart, much more; it demanded, if it was ever to be solved, a thorough, objective study of all the conditions that surrounded it. Robert Owen (d. 1858) in Great Britain and Saint Simon (d. 1825) in France may be named among those who, though prompted in the first instance by philanthropy, rose in some sort to the exercise of thought and method; and it is interesting that both, different as their proposals were, agreed that the existing system of

free competition and capitalist control would have to be abandoned
if the workingman was ever to have his due. What they offered by
way of cure of the existing evils was so utterly impracticable as to
be plainly Utopian — which goes to prove, if proof were necessary,
that first ventures into complicated social issues are almost certain
to be failures owing to insufficient information. When in the course
of the forties the Frenchman, Louis Blanc (1811–1882), took up the
championship of the workers, he was already in possession of better
data and hence his famous proposal of national workshops represents,
even if it is still rather visionary, a forward step on the hard road of
facts. However, the view generally held that it was not till the appearance of Karl Marx that the working class problem received a
genuinely scientific treatment is probably correct. Marx's approach
may claim to be "scientific" in the sense that it analyzes and classi-
fies the body of economic data in order to let them, so far as possible,
speak for themselves.

Karl Marx (1818–1883) was a German Jew of an intellectual,
revolutionary bent, who first announced his economic position in a
document issued in 1848 under the name of the *Communist Manifesto*.
As the terminology in the new field of thought was still Marxian
very fluctuating, he used the word communist to indicate socialism
something that was later called socialist, and therefore we may accept his Manifesto as the first great pronouncement of modern
socialism. Devoting the rest of his life to the study of political
economy from the working class angle, he laid down his conclusions
in a fundamental work, *Capital*, of which the first volume appeared
in 1867 and the other two after his death. Marxian socialism is not
only an economic theory but also a philosophy of life. Combating
the various bourgeois philosophies with their emphasis on liberty,
it stresses equality and looks to the welfare not of distinguished individuals but of the mass of men. The equality which is its goal is
to be attained by the many taking over from the few the machines,
the railways, the mines, in sum, the total characteristic tools of
modern production. The transfer need not necessarily involve violence and bloodshed. It may, indeed it must result primarily from
the unescapable operation of historical forces, for the laborers are
becoming constantly more numerous as compared with the middle
classes and, sooner or later, will be in a position to assert their economic will. The new socialist society of equals owning in common the
means of production will thus come about by peaceful stages, by

evolution rather than by revolution. However, the workingmen can hasten the happy day by becoming class-conscious, a process involving the absorption of the Marxian philosophy as well as the fixed determination to reorganize the world according to its dicta. To this end they must stand shoulder to shoulder in close ranks like an army marching to conquest. As a class name for the army of workingmen Marx favored the word proletarians. With the idea of winning them to united action he supplied them with an electrifying slogan: Proletarians of all countries, unite! You have nothing to lose but your chains!

Even this bare outline of socialism would be incomplete, if it did not bring out, in addition to the above, that the working class movement was to be not so much national as international. It was to

The Social-democratic party and The International

encircle the earth and ultimately make socialism a new world order. Until that not too distant day it was to lock horns with the bourgeois ruling group, and in order to make an effective fight under existing constitutional conditions, it was to organize as a party and descend into the political arena. In this manner socialism would become under the name of the Social-democratic party a factor in the politics of every country of Europe. While each separate Social-democratic party would make its own fight in its own way and in response to the particular conditions which confronted it, it would recognize its world obligations by periodically despatching representatives to an International Social-democratic congress for an exchange of views. This crowning and world organization of socialism would bear the name of The International.

The immediate business of each Social-democratic party was to persuade the workingmen to enter its ranks and vote its ticket. But that, despite the siren character of the Marxian song, was not so

Anarchism and syndicalism

easy as it looked. Naturally, as soon as the workingmen got the franchise, the older parties, Conservative and Liberal, also made a bid for the support of the workers; and in so far as they persuaded the laborers that the small, solid benefits offered by them were worth more than the immense but vague promises of the Social-democrats, they actually captured the humble vote. And therewith we have not yet exhausted the list of competitors for working class favor. Since socialism set the fashion of reconstructing the world on a new philosophic plan, it was not to be expected that it would remain alone in the field, especially as the realization of its program called for a vast bureaucratic organization of the state in order to administer the tremendous properties to be held in common. This feature of an omnipotent state was intensely repulsive to a group of thinkers who carried the middle class creed of freedom to its last consequence. To them, too, it was a laudable undertaking to break away from the various bondages of the past, but they saw no reason why a halt should be called before the heaviest bondage of all, the state! They declared themselves to be enemies of the state, that is, anarchists, in the hope that by its destruction the individual man might resume his last and most important right and become his own master, acknowledging literally no superior on earth. While anarchism never became popular, and while it but rarely, because detested and persecuted by its enemies, the existing governments, succeeded in establishing itself in any country as a regular political party, it must none the less be acknowledged to represent one of the most revolutionary forces of the modern world. Presently by the side of pure and uncompromising anarchism a type of socialism found advocates which, without abandoning the main socialist tenets, took over something of its anti-government bias from anarchism. Late in the nineteenth century this movement, called syndicalism, saw the light. While aiming, with socialism, at the capture of the great modern trades by the workers, it put its faith, with anarchism, in the violent destruction of the political state.[1] Though syndicalism has made a more powerful appeal to the wage-earners than anarchism and though, above all, in the Latin countries such as France and Italy, it has enjoyed a remarkable success, it has no more than anarchism, pure and simple, been able to undermine the strength of the socialists.[2] So far at least as Europe is concerned, the respective Social-democratic parties may fairly be said to have steadily increased their following among the workingmen from their origin to the present day.

With the dominant state confronted with so many opponents radically opposed to it, it seemed not improbable that the industrialized countries of Europe would face a domestic situation, which under certain conditions might assume the extreme form of civil war. The French revolution of 1848, in which the republicans

---

[1] Syndicalism, on being transplated to America, gained the support of a body of radical workers who call themselves the I. W. W. (International Workers of the World).

[2] Since the Great War syndicalism, in the non-violent form of Gild Socialism, has made considerable headway in England.

(bourgeoisie) and socialists (workingmen) waged a ferocious battle over the national workshops, illustrates the ever present hazards of the social cleavage. Before long other instances, to be examined at Civil war or the proper time, accumulated in other countries. And compro- yet, in the main, civil and class war has been avoided mise? because, while some men will fight at the drop of the hat, most fortunately for the cause of a slow and steady development of society the majority is so constituted that its members are always ready to abate something of their extreme demands in the interest of social peace. They will seek a compromise; and compromise has, on the whole, been the most characteristic feature in the relation of the two classes, employers and employees, carried to the front by the Industrial Revolution.

The most striking evidence of the triumph of compromise is furnished by what is usually called Social or Labor Legislation. The theoretic position of the middle class was, as we have seen, for the Social Leg- state to leave the economic world alone, meaning, in islation practice, to the capitalists. But in no single instance have they been able to maintain this attitude. If we turn to the always typical case of Great Britain, we discover that as early as 1824–1825 the workingmen were accorded the right to combine; and a decade later (1833) parliament passed its first important Factory Act, which protected children and youths against the most extreme forms of current exploitation by declaring that they might be employed in textile factories no more than nine and twelve hours per day respectively. In 1842 followed the Mines Act, which prohibited underground work for boys under ten years and for women of any age. Slight and almost derisory as these earliest protective measures were, they are important as marking a departure from an uncompromising devotion to "industrial liberty." In the second half of the nineteenth century they were succeeded by a rain, which became almost a deluge, of industrial enactments, providing Great Britain with a great labor code. By virtue of it the state once more "interfered," and on a tremendous scale, in the social-economic situation by restricting or forbidding outright the labor of children and women, by reducing and regulating the hours of employment for both sexes, by providing for light, air, and sanitation in the factories, and by appointing inspectors whose duty it was to see that the regulations were strictly enforced.

While this Social Legislation was being drawn up in the earliest home of the machine, the other European countries launched similar measures so that by the end of the century elaborate provisions were spread on every national statute book against the most crying abuses of the industrial system. Then, in the eighties, Ger- Insurance many took the lead in a measure which constituted a Legislation fresh inroad on the unlimited control originally claimed by the capitalists. The Reichstag passed its famous Insurance Legislation, by which it insured the workingmen against some of the worst evils of their lot, such as illness, accidents, and invalidism due to old age. Other countries have copied and, in the case of Great Britain, have even enlarged on the German legislation with the result that Social Legislation culminating in Insurance Legislation may be said to represent the generally accepted program of every modern industrial society and state. This program, let us again note, travels the line of compromise; but while its benefits are unchallengeable, it is certain that it has not succeeded in removing the most striking antithesis of our age, the antithesis between the middle and the working classes, between capital and labor.

REFERENCES

E. Fueter, *World History*, chs. 3, 4, 21, 23, 32
J. S. Schapiro, *Modern and Contemporary Europe*, chs. 3, 24
C. H. Hayes, *Political and Social History*, II, ch. 18, pp. 252–274
C. D. Hazen, *Europe Since 1815*, I, chs. 4, 15
E. R. Turner, *Europe 1789–1920*, pp. 109–145
C. Seignobos, *Europe Since 1814*, chs. 22, 24
Cambridge Modern History, IX, 23, X, 23, 24, XI, 1
F. S. Marvin, *Century of Hope*, chs. 4, 5, 10
F. A. Ogg, *Economic Development of Modern Europe*, chs. 3, 4, 7–11, 19–23, pp. 369–382
D. H. Macgregor, *Evolution of Industry*
C. Taylor, *Modern Factory System*
A. Toinbee, *Lectures on the Industrial Revolution*
E. Cheyney, *Industrial and Social History of England*
A. L. Cross, *History of England*, chs. 48–51, 53
C. Day, *History of Commerce*, chs. 29, 35
J. A. Hobson, *Evolution of Modern Capitalism*, chs. 1, 5, 16, 17
G. H. Perris, *Industrial History of Modern England*
W. J. Ashley, *Economic Organization of England*
G. Slater, *The Making of Modern England*, Intro. and ch. 11
A. P. Usher, *Industrial History of England*
E. W. Bryn, *Progress of Invention in the Nineteenth Century*
J. R. Macdonald, *The Socialist Movement*
L. Levine, *The Labor Movement in France*
W. H. Dawson, *Evolution of Modern Germany*, ch. 22
E. Bernstein, *Evolutionary Socialism*

K. KAUTSKY, *The Social Revolution*
A. BEBEL, *My Life*
O. D. SKELTON, *Socialism*
W. H. MALLOCK, *Critical Examination of Socialism*
W. SOMBART, *Socialism and the Socialist Movement*
J. SPARGO, *Socialism: a Summary and Interpretation*
M. HILLQUIT, *Socialism in Theory and Practice*
J. H. CLAPHAM, *Economic Development of France and Germany*
L. C. A. KNOWLES, *Industrial and Commercial Revolutions of the Nineteenth
Century.*

CHAPTER XXV

THE NINETEENTH CENTURY MOVEMENT IN SCIENCE, RELIGION, AND PHILOSOPHY

The intimate connection of the Industrial Revolution with the natural sciences, on which we have all along insisted, makes it desirable to follow up the picture of the nineteenth century social-economic transformation with the developments in this same century not only in the immediate field of science but also in the general intellectual outlook. Turning first to science, we are better prepared to see the recent phases in their true perspective if we pause to recall the earlier development. In putting out his theory of the ordered movement of the planets around the sun Copernicus stimulated investigation into the whole body of phenomena connected with matter in motion. These researches, conducted by many scholars, among whom Kepler, Galileo, and Newton are the most shining names, culminated in the theory of gravitation and the recognition of an eternally established and majestic universe of law. Hand in hand with these brilliant physico-astronomical discoveries went the development of mathematics, which reached its eighteenth century culmination with the invention of calculus by Newton and Leibnitz. It was calculus that made possible the accurate and complicated measurements demanded by the study of moving objects and it was in mathematical terms that the laws of motion not only of solid bodies but also of such physical phenomena as sound, heat, and light were stated.

Early science investigates matter in motion

These magnificent physico-mathematical achievements encouraged every other kind of scientist to new endeavor. Perceptible advances were made in the eighteenth century in such subjects as botany, zoölogy, and ethnology, but far and away the most promising development occurred in chemistry and is marked by the great name of Lavoisier. Almost at once with Lavoisier's discoveries there was a crowding of investigators into this field, which meant that a new type of curiosity was gaining ground, the curiosity to follow up the knowledge of matter in motion with the study of its composition. What four gene-

Science turns with chemistry to study the composition of matter

rations of chemists since Lavoisier have discovered touching the constituent elements of the universe is one of the wonders of the age but can not be dilated upon here further than to point out that chemistry is founded on the atom and that the infinitesimal atom, instead of being the ultimate, irreducible form of matter, has been recently discovered to be a complicated structure of still minuter parts. Thus with so many triumphs to its credit chemistry faces a still more splendid future; and the same may be confidently said of physics and astronomy. For, in spite of a certain air of finality attaching to Newton's crowning work, the discoveries of physicists and astronomers have continued since Newton's day as before to pour forth in an uninterrupted stream. Rightly or wrongly, however, a hurried sketch like this, primarily concerned with indicating the new orientations of science, claims the right to neglect the old lines of investigation in order to call attention to strictly pioneer labors. Even these, because science, growing ever more confident, has branched out on a hundred new lines, are so numerous and overwhelming in their yield that the baffled writer is reduced to a system of meager short-hand notation.

Under no circumstances may one omit to speak of geology. It was around 1830 that Sir Charles Lyell headed the study of the earth in a new and profitable direction by his *Principles of Geology*. In this book he ascribed the present physical appearance of our earth to the operation through an almost incalculable period of time of causes still busily at work today. This proof of the steadiness and continuity of earth-forces together with the immense stretch of time during which

Science turns with biology to the study of life

they have operated favorably affected the study of living organisms already undertaken by botany and zoölogy. Concerned hitherto chiefly with tabulating the great variety of vegetable and animal forms to be found in all countries and climates, botanists and zoölogists now turned to the problem of their origin, growth, and structure and therewith became biologists. In this entirely new field, in biology, nineteenth century science produced perhaps its most epoch-making work. And it did so, as usual, by slow accumulations. Long before there was an official study called biology an occasional individual like the poet Goethe (d. 1832) had proclaimed on the basis as much of intuition as of precise scientific data that all life was akin; and Lamarck at about the same period declared that species were not fixed from all time and for all time but were derived from a remote common stock. The records of the rocks as read by Lyell and others repeated this tale of immemorial relationships among living things. There was therefore a growing consensus touching the common origin of plant and animal forms, but how formulate a single inclusive principle which would account for the enormous multiplicity of·living shapes? At last in 1859 a book, *On the Origin of Species,* was put out by the Englishman, Charles Darwin, and here, supported step by step by personal observation, the theory was advanced that the factor which explained the great variety of existing species, both vegetable and animal, was Natural Selection. By Natural Selection Darwin wished to signify the tendency of that individual in each species to survive which is endowed with some tiny variation calculated to give it a better chance in its environment. Producing offspring in its turn emphasizing the same variation, the first variable individual might, it was suggested, by imperceptible accumulations through many generations become the ancestor of a new type or species.

Thus biological study and speculation, continued for some decades, converged upon a comprehensive principle which came to be called the theory of evolution. Embracing all life, it made of course no exception of man. Our human kind is of the same essential stuff as the tiger, the rat, the rose, and the jelly-fish; and if it flatters our vanity to put man on a special pedestal, the only scientific justification for our bias lies in the circumstance that man is indeed a higher species making *The theory of evolution; Darwinism, Mendelism* a very late appearance in the evolutionary process. Without doubt there is something beautifully unifying and inclusive about the evolutionary theory. Bred in the hard realm of science and having a solemn scientific air, it yet brings to many people something of the expansive feeling of religion. Though such have welcomed it as a new hope, a modern pantheism, we should not fail to see that to the strict scientist it is no more than an invaluable hypothesis. Or rather, admitting that the evidence in favor of an evolutionary development of animate nature is overwhelming, the method by which the development takes place and which Darwin assumed to be Natural Selection remains hypothetical. As early as 1866 a German Catholic monk, Gregor Mendel by name, adduced evidence in favor of the sudden production of new species through the accidental breeding of "sports"; and by the early twentieth century this Mendelian theory had received wide acceptance. While it did not disprove Darwinism, it caused it to be modified; but the theory of evolution as such, let it be understood, does not depend on the validity of either the Darwinian or the Mendelian hypothesis. These are merely suggestive formulations as to how evolution works; and if the darkness of the process is not yet by any means cleared up, the movement itself may be accepted as certain. In any case it supplies the most magnificent framework conceivable for the whole mass of scientific data making up the universe of the modern man.

The new geology and biology culminating in the evolutionary doctrine and imposing a wholly novel picture of creation profoundly disturbed all the followers of historical Christianity, whether they were attached to the Roman Catholic or to any of the Protestant Churches. For all Christians alike accepted the Bible account of creation, according to which God made the world in six days, and while giving every species its definite, individual form from the start, fashioned man by a special act of grace in his own image. No wonder they were disgusted and enraged with a theory which, while shattering the Bible story *in toto*, seemed intolerably to humiliate man by endowing him with an ape ancestry at the trifling remove of a few hundred thousand years! A crisis rocked the churches which continued for decades and from which some of them have not yet recovered.

The theory of evolution and Christianity

But in the long run a difference made itself felt in the adjustment to the new thought of the Protestant churches, on the one hand, and of the Catholic Church, on the other. Admitting that all Protestant churches rested on the foundation of the Bible, let us take note they had, beginning with Luther himself, insisted also on the right of private judgment. This opened an avenue of escape which the more adventurous Protestants had for centuries back taken advantage of to assimilate the data of science and the various empirical philosophies built thereon. Protestantism in the nineteenth century was therefore no longer what it had been in the sixteenth. It had imperceptibly changed and was, at least in an advanced section of its membership, in some sort of sympathy with an inclusive doctrine of development like evolution. Then, at the beginning of the nineteenth century, Protestant historical scholars, taking up the study of the Bible, made the startling discovery that, far from being the indubitable product of divine inspiration, it was manifestly pieced together by different authors writing under very different conditions. More-

Slow adjustment of Protestantism to modern thought

over, while becoming, according to these same critics, a wholly human document, the ancient book actually gained in dignity and interest! The orthodox elements, everywhere in control, rejected these conclusions as blasphemous and vigorously defended all the old positions; but the fact remained that the new liberal thought slowly captured important elements of both clergy and laity within the various Protestant denominations and, in spite of strong and prolonged resistance, prepared the way for an adjustment between the old faith and the new discoveries. By the first quarter of the twentieth century much of the fury which had marked the struggle in its earlier phases had disappeared. Without doubt important orthodox groups cling to this day to what is to them the security and finality of their divine inheritance; but if to generalize a complicated situation is not too hazardous, the statement may be ventured that the Protestant churches either have already or are about to adjust themselves to scientific discovery, including evolution, and that, should they join the modern standpoint to their ancient ethical purpose, instead of cutting themselves adrift, they are likely to become an invaluable factor in the better integration of society.

The quarrel of Catholicism with the new thought was from the first far more uncompromising and the possibility of an adjustment much more remote. Catholicism was based on an absolute, unalterable body of doctrine and possessed in the Church an Pius IX enormously powerful institution to inculcate and defend attacks the its position. Moreover, this vast organization had at modern world; his its head a single, authoritative official, the pope. When Syllabus of he spoke even great states were obliged to take notice Errors since his views determined the attitude of tens of millions of devoted followers. Ever since the advent of eighteenth century rationalism the papacy had found itself out of sympathy with the direction taken by European thought and had often pronounced itself without reserve on the subject of sceptics and atheists. Then came the French Revolution with its confiscation of Church property and its fanatic persecution of the clergy. Quite naturally Catholicism became violently anti-revolutionary and anti-liberal and identified itself in every country of Europe with political conservatism. In the first half of the nineteenth century the Catholic clergy regularly stood shoulder to shoulder with the forces of the past, with the aristocracy and the absolute monarchy. When the Italian nationalist movement took shape, the pope became its leading victim, being subjected to a long series of acts of spoliation in the name of peninsular unity. To Pius IX, in whose long reign (1846–1878) these misfortunes befell, liberalism and nationalism must have seemed to be indistinguishable evils. And when the theory of evolution was now put forth with its implied refutation of the Biblical version of creation, the pope's cup overflowed and he saw the whole modern movement as a systematic, sinister attack on the Church. Thirsting for the fray, for he was a man of deep convictions, he denounced the age in fiery invectives, culminating in 1864 in an encyclical to which he attached a *Syllabus of Errors* recounting the principal aberrations of our times. Free-thinking scientists, advocates of religious toleration, supporters of lay marriage and lay schools, opponents of the temporal power of the Church — such are a few of the human categories whom the pope solemnly condemns. Indeed it would be difficult to discover a specifically modern movement of thought or politics which Pius IX did not declare to be in conflict with religion.

It is clear that in the eyes of Pius IX the Church was fighting for its life and that it needed to put itself unwaveringly under his supreme command if it desired to survive. This frame of mind **The Vatican** explains his calling an Ecumenical Council of the Church. **Council pro-** The last previous meeting of such a body had taken place **claims** at Trent three hundred years before. He summoned the **(1870) the** **dogma of** new council to his palace of the Vatican and in the course **papal in-** of many sessions, but not without grave difficulty, per- **fallibility** suaded the assembled prelates to promulgate (1870) the dogma of papal infallibility. By virtue thereof it was declared that when the pope speaks *ex cathedra*, that is, when in his official capacity he defines a doctrine regarding faith or morals, his word must be accepted as infallible. If, as Catholic writers have frequently pointed out, the claim of infallibility was not entirely new, it is yet undeniable that the definition of doctrine in the past had in the main been reserved to the Church Councils. This historical function the Vatican Council now resigned into the hands of the pope. Henceforth there could hardly be found a good reason for summoning another Council. The pope, long absolute in political matters, had become equally absolute in matters of faith and doctrine. As with these new powers all the resources of the Church without any exception became concentrated in his sole hand, he had the satisfaction of feeling that he could confront a hostile world with an army, the members of which would respond as one man to his word of command.

When on the death of Pius IX Leo XIII (1878–1903) succeeded
to the throne of St. Peter the struggle with the system of modern
thought as well as with the many European governments which had
curtailed the rights of the Church continued, but soon a Leo XIII
difference made itself noticeable. Inclining, in distinction aims at a
from the emphatic and downright Pius IX, to the subtle truce with
modern
and elastic diplomatic tradition of the papacy, Leo XIII govern-
saw no reason for quarreling with governments merely be- ments
cause of their democratic form. He let it be known that to him the
political form was immaterial; also he took a stand in favor of Social
Legislation. By these means he reëntered the political arena in some
sort of alliance with both the Catholic bourgeoisie and the Catholic
workingmen. That something like a truce with the European governments resulted and that the Church drew recognizable benefits
from this situation is certain. But a politic *modus vivendi* is not a
surrender. Neither Leo XIII nor any later successor of Pius IX
has ever even faintly hinted that he considered it possible some day
to bridge the gap between Catholicism and the general thought
movement of the modern world.

Because philosophy reflects as in a mirror the concentrated movement of life and thought, this book has undertaken to indicate at
least the main philosophic trends within the compass of occidental
civilization. It has pointed out that in the Middle Age Philosophy,
a philosophy (scholasticism) saw the light which ordered the mirror
the leading data of experience under the majestic con- of civiliza-
cept of Christian revelation. In the Renaissance, owing tion
to the vigorous impact of newly acquired knowledge, scholasticism
disintegrated without anything particularly satisfactory and constructive being put in its place. If we celebrate Descartes (d. 1649)
as the first modern philosopher, it is because he attempted a new
integration of experience on another than the traditional and Christian basis. None the less, like the scholastics, he sought an absolute
and eternal truth and brought unity into our multitudinous existence
by reference to an omniscient and omnipotent creator. His successors, like Spinoza and Leibnitz, while following independent lines of
inquiry and drawing a hundred subtle distinctions between themselves and all other thinkers, propounded systems as absolutist and
logically coherent as that of the great Frenchman. It was Locke
who first definitely took a new track by sacrificing coherence and
completeness in favor of a procedure which paid more attention to

the immediate evidence of our senses. He thus became the father of empiricism and, drawing philosophy from heaven to earth, brought or tried to bring it into closer touch with the natural sciences. There followed a conflict between the absolutist and dogmatic tendency, on the one hand, and the empirical and observational movement, on the other, which Kant brought at least to a provisional solution by assigning a particular function to each and thus justifying both.

With the coming of the nineteenth century the issue could not rest where Kant had left it for the simple reason that the enormous expansion of our mundane life hopelessly disturbed the Kantian balance. With a more varied and experimental living in state and society, with the influx of new knowledge along a hundred avenues of investigation, there was a steadily increasing concentration on the problems of our earth together with a more marked withdrawal from the cold and unprofitable peaks of metaphysics. Empirical philosophies tended to flourish, absolute philosophies tended to decline. Not that this was everywhere the case or at least consistently and from the start. In Germany, for instance, the absolute type long continued to dominate the situation, producing in the work of Fichte, Schelling, and, above all, Hegel, a number of world-constructions, which, though brilliant, were also highly romantic in character as might be expected of products of the Romantic Age. Nor need these men, merely because they were metaphysicians, be thought of as living wholly in the clouds, out of touch with contemporary discovery. Hegel (d. 1831), for instance, marched sufficiently abreast of his time to cast the universe and God Himself in an evolutionary mold. Universe and God became under this philosopher's touch as dynamic as the age in which he lived. But Hegel marks a peak. His prophetic exaltation could not last; and Schopenhauer (d. 1860), discouraged by a mechanical universe propelled by the force of a blind Will, plunged into despair and pessimism. It was left to Schopenhauer's follower, Nietzsche (d. 1900), to break with absolutism in all its numerous disguises from the scholastics down to Hegel and to assign to man the task of facing his earth-born destiny with just his earth-born powers. With Nietzsche German absolutism gave up the ghost and German thought resigned itself to the relativity of experience.

The absolutist trend, which, although most conspicuously represented in Germany, found champions in every country of Europe,

Two main philosophic types: the absolute and the empirical or relativist

came, perhaps in order to distinguish it from its Cartesian and other prototypes, to be called idealism. The name has been helped to greater currency by reason of the fact that the followers of the opposite or empirical school, concentrating more and more exclusively on the material furnished by the senses, acquired the title of materialists. Since in some instances they believed that the true test of knowledge was its usefulness to man, they were also often called utilitarians. *Prevalence of philosophies of the empirical type* These must be understood to be hard, scientific classifications, carrying no suggestion of praise or blame. To be an idealist is no merit in itself nor is being a materialist or utilitarian a demerit. It is essentially a question of two attitudes, which, objectively considered, are equally valid and between which the individual makes a choice usually on the basis of that subtle shade of personality called temperament. However, owing no doubt to the success and preponderance of science during the most recent period, there are now more people than was once the case who are so endowed that they instinctively incline toward a materialist and utilitarian interpretation of the world. The materialist schools, broadly empirical, have therefore been particularly active and an examination would show that they have flourished in England, France, Germany, Italy, and in every other country, besides developing within each country a dozen different varieties. In England let us select for illustration the great name of Herbert Spencer (d. 1903). Spencer undoubtedly communicates a very personal message and like every distinguished spirit eludes strict classification; but by virtue of his intense preoccupation with the natural sciences coupled with his use of evolution as a frame for his picture of the universe, he belongs decidedly with the empiricists. So, on the whole, does his older French contemporary, Comte (d. 1857). He founded the so-called Positivist school on the theory that if the method of science, which had given such sure results, were only resolutely applied to human affairs, nature and man would soon be joined in a new and magnificent synthesis. Both Spencer and Comte were system-builders like the idealists whom they despised, but at least their systems purported to rest on the evidence of the senses and to meet the most severe criteria of science.

To more than one reader it may seem that these few generalizations about modern philosophy are so broad that it would be better not to broach the matter at all. Admittedly modern philosophy is a continent which a man may hardly hope to subdue in a lifetime

of effort. And yet, though our superficial procedure fails wholly to do justice to the subject, it may still pass muster if it has succeeded in showing that the natural sciences have with each new genera-
The modern man accepts an experimental world tion tended more and more to dominate philosophic think-ing. A noticeable consequence of this development has been a tendency to abandon such venerable and unsolvable problems as the soul, immortality, the origin of good and evil, the nature and purposes of God. These belong to the realm of final truths, acknowledged even by the Christian saints and doctors to lie beyond the reach of our human powers and frankly and avowedly beyond the reach of the modern scientific method. Devotion to science means to abandon the pursuit of what is remote and absolute in favor of the innumerable tiny data cognizable by our senses and serving to build up an ever changing, relativist world. The modern man, whenever he is oriented in a truly scientific way, accepts as his one great purpose the making of himself and of his kind more completely at home on earth. That means more, much more than the gross materialism with which he is often charged and with which he is, alas, too often content. It means for each one of us an unremitting effort in his fleeting hour to bring mankind to a level of ability and understanding on which the struggle for existence, without ceasing to be a struggle, will take on something of the aspect of a vast, associative enterprise among all the nations and peoples of the earth.

And therewith we have touched on a feature of human thought which constantly recurs in history. It is man's search for unity. The significance of medieval Christianity lies in the very fact that, having
Man and the search for unity realized unity for a considerable part of mankind, it aspired to become nothing less than universal. But Christian unity was built on faith and presented itself to view in a changeless and eternal form. On this account it quarreled with something else working irrepressibly in man and nature, it quarreled with "the law of becoming" which we have just encountered as a principle of science under the modern name of evolution. As this history has shown, from the period of the Renaissance the strong forces of development, identical with life itself, were engaged in undermining Christian unity with such success that by the nineteenth century the one and indivisible Church had been replaced not only by countless Christian sects but also by the numerous bands of disbelievers and agnostics who had put themselves entirely outside the

Christian fold. To many an anxious observer it must have seemed that the growing disorganization could only end by engulfing society in chaos. But almost imperceptibly, even while chaos was still gaining ground, the principle of unity had set to work again, this time following a path in close keeping with the experiential attitudes which were at the root of the Christian disintegration. The early Modern Age (the period just before and after 1500) witnessed exploration and discovery, it brought commerce, industry, and the intensified activity of the new monarchical societies. While it is true that conflicts multiplied and that the whole struggle for existence assumed a fiercer aspect, it is also true that a counter-current aiming at the reduction of disorder was set in motion by the practical needs of men of affairs. They were inexorably impelled by the pressure of their daily interests to put travel and exchange on a basis of security. Hence a treaty of peace closing a war came invariably to include strong guarantees for traders and presently involved so many complicated details touching the inviolability of private property, the safety of persons, tariff regulations, and other similar matters that it was found desirable to negotiate special treaties of amity and commerce. Then, in the seventeenth century, the Dutchman, Grotius, took a further step by setting up a body of international law which aimed to secure certain basic rights to all men and all societies in both peace and war.[1] Although Grotius's deductions met with opposition and were honored more often in the breach than the observance, a body of international practices none the less did gradually emerge which tended to take on the character of compulsion. In this way they materially contributed toward a régime of smoother relations among states in time of peace and toward the elimination of some of the more brutal features of warfare. Slowly, with many set-backs, men were working out rules of universal intercourse.

To this spinning of threads across the boundaries of states the nineteenth century added a tremendous impulse. We have in this connection only to recall the railroad, the steamboat, and the telegraph to realize at once that the old jealous barriers would Accelerated have to be modified and that governments which wished to movement lend support to the most pressing interests of their peoples toward would be obliged to do their utmost to promote travel, unity in the communication, and the exchange of goods and ideas. nineteenth century The rapidity of this movement in recent generations mocks descrip-

[1] See p. 276.

tion. Luckily most of the facts are so much a part of our daily experience that it suffices to tabulate a few of them for purposes of illustration. Nineteenth century governments were obliged to make postal arrangements which logically culminated in a Universal Postal Union. Similar agreements about the telegraph were followed by others, hardly less sweeping, touching railroads and steamboats. At the same time private business groups, especially bankers, entered into negotiations for discounting bills and floating loans until to speak of capital as international became a commonplace. Certainly money has recently flowed without particular concern for political boundaries over all the countries of the world. No less important have been the unifying influences of science. A discovery in any one country was immediately appropriated by the others, and scientists, aware of this interdependence, did not hesitate to come together in international societies of physicists, chemists, engineers, physicians, and finally even of historians and artists in order to exchange views and to organize their search for knowledge on the most effective and harmonious plan. And when in the last quarter of the nineteenth century socialism had succeeded in gaining a foothold among the new classes of industrial workers, it, too, organized itself on an international scale and by a system of international congresses brought the workingmen into line with the efforts of business men and intellectuals toward a better coördination of the forces of the world.

Although the governments, enamoured of their sovereignty and deeply entangled in traditional rivalries and enmities, were reluctant to yield to the growing movement of association, it will not do to

The governments based on conceptions of absolute sovereignty reluctant to give up their freedom represent them as consistently hostile to it. So far, for instance, as improved communications by post, telegraph, and railroad were concerned we have seen that they seized upon them with an almost rapturous eagerness. But when it came to a modification of their selfish pursuit of power in the form of better boundaries and new territories they not only hesitated but resisted. The idea had become rooted in the conviction of all the European peoples that an unlimited sovereignty was the *summum bonum* of earthly happiness and that its essence was a relentless competition with reference, in the last resort, to war. It was for this reason that they had systematically developed their armies and navies; and even when they permitted their regiments and ships to remain idle for many decades together, they kept them in reserve like a pack of hungry hounds, and even while they negotiated in apparent amity they pointedly drew attention to the leash resting in their hands. Undeniably two contrary currents had taken possession of the modern world and the unity promoted by the rapidly expanding practical needs of men was confronted with the old and rooted absolute conceptions of sovereignty. And instead of these latter declining in strength, it so happened that the extraordinary opportunities unfolded before the European governments in the most recent period in Africa, Asia, and other backward areas stimulated and exaggerated their selfish energy. In the last quarter of the nineteenth century the great powers entered upon the most frenzied phase of their agelong rivalry, the phase known as imperialism and which will be treated in due time. One and all without exception steadily enlarged their means of offense. It became a period appropriately called the armed peace. A growing nervousness possessed the world and forward-looking individuals and groups everywhere raised a cry of warning. Even the governments did not close their eyes to the risks they were running; and when in 1898 Tsar Nicholas II issued an invitation to a meeting to consider means for the preservation of peace all the important states sent delegates to The Hague where the assembly took place (1899). Something was done, although in essence it amounted to no more than a beautiful gesture. A court of arbitration was set up to which governments were advised to submit their disputes, and the rules of war were codified in the interests of a more humane prosecution of armed conflicts. A second Hague conference held in 1907 also confined itself largely to a display of eloquence. In such immediately pressing matters as the reduction of competitive armaments and of exorcising the dangerous spirit of imperialism it did as little as its predecessor.

The most one can say touching the interesting attempts of 1899 and 1907 to bring the question of world peace under the competence of a world parliament is that they disseminated through mankind a greater awareness of the perils involved in a conception The terms of sovereignty which acknowledged no limits in its pur- of the world suit of imperialist rewards. No one capable of seeing problem the world as a whole could fail to grasp that the European development had by the beginning of the twentieth century reached a breathless stage. Doubtless the most promising and characteristic forces of the age were at work to bring men together in a new unity based on immediate, mundane, and experimental considerations; at the same time the old governments with their absolute and obsolete ideas of sovereignty hesitated to surrender as much as a jot or tittle of their boasted self-determination. In seeking to express the situation in the language of philosophy, one might be tempted to say that unity and freedom, both desirable and both dominating forces in human history, had been brought into sharp confrontation with each other, and that unless they could somehow be reduced to an accommodation, a catastrophe of world proportions was inevitable.

REFERENCES

E. Fueter, *World History*, chs. 5, 28
C. H. Hayes, *Political and Social History*, II, ch. 21
J. H. Robinson and C. A. Beard, *Development of Modern Europe*, II, pp. 405–422
E. R. Turner, *Europe 1789–1920*, chs. 14, 15
J. S. Schapiro, *Modern and Contemporary Europe*, chs. 25, 26
Cambridge Modern History, XI, ch. 18, XII, chs. 22, 26
F. S. Marvin, *Century of Hope*, chs. 1, 3, 5, 6, 8–10, 12
W. T. Sedgwick and H. W. Tyler, *A Short History of Science*, chs. 14–17
W. A. Lacy, *Biology and its Makers*
J. C. Brown, *History of Chemistry*
J. A. Thomson, *Introduction to Science*
O. Lodge, *Pioneers of Science*
A. Geikie, *Founders of Geology*
R. C. Punnett, *Mendelism*
E. R. Lankester, *Kingdom of Man*
H. F. Osborn, *From the Greeks to Darwin*
A. R. Wallace, *The Wonderful Century*
E. W. Bryn, *Progress of Invention in the Nineteenth Century*
F. S. Marvin, *The Living Past; Recent Developments in European Thought*
F. M. Stowell and F. S. Marvin, *Making of the Western Mind*, chs. 40–43
J. T. Merz, *History of European Thought in the Nineteenth Century*
A. W. Benn, *History of English Rationalism in the Nineteenth Century*
J. M. Robertson, *Short History of Free Thought*
A. C. McGiffert, *The Rise of Modern Religious Ideas*
E. Troeltsch, *Protestantism and Progress*
A. L. Guérard, *French Prophets of Yesterday*
J. T. Hobhouse, *Liberalism*
E. R. Hecker, *Short History of Women's Rights*
F. Nielson, *History of the Papacy in the Nineteenth Century*
H. W. Cark, *History of English Nonconformity*
F. W. Cornish, *History of the Church of England in the Nineteenth Century*

CHAPTER XXVI

FRANCE UNDER NAPOLEON III AND THE
UNIFICATION OF ITALY

The indication furnished by the choice of Louis Napoleon as president, that France did not really want a republic, was converted into positive proof by the elections of May, 1849, to the Legislative Assembly, the first parliament under the new constitution. Louis Napoleon favors the monarchical elements. The country returned an immense monarchical majority; and the only reason the republic was not immediately overthrown lay in the circumstance that the monarchists were divided into three groups: legitimists, favoring the elder Bourbon line; Orleanists, devoted to the family of Louis Philip; and a rising Bonapartist faction, supporting the president. While doing his best to strengthen his personal supporters, Louis Napoleon, desirous above all of weakening the republic, encouraged a combination of all the monarchists to reduce the popular rights secured by the recent revolution. Yielding to its conservative bias, the Assembly limited the freedom of the press, forbade political meetings, and finally (1850) capped this anti-republican legislation by a bill which put an end to universal male suffrage, probably the most important popular achievement of the revolution. By making the suffrage dependent on certain residence and tax requirements, practically the whole body of the workingmen was deprived of the vote. Evidence of the prince-president's close attachment to the conservatives (monarchists and clericals) was at the same time furnished by the military expedition sent in the spring of 1849 against the Roman Republic. While the responsibility for this action, of which mention has already been made, falls upon Napoleon, he could not have carried it through without the support of the reactionaries, who plainly delighted in wrecking republics wherever an opportunity beckoned.

More than a year passed before the monarchical majority of the Assembly perceived that the president was playing their game not for their sake but for his own. In view of his past exploits they looked upon him as a rather comic figure, kicked upstairs by capricious Fortune and not sufficiently intelligent to be a serious threat to the state. Under cover of the Assembly's contempt he was therefore able to pursue unmolested his inalterable course

The president builds up a personal following looking toward an imperial restoration. As it was the time of railroad-building, the president was constantly invited to all parts of France to assist at the formal opening of some new section, and on these occasions he never failed to make a speech. Beginning with railroads and the blessings of industrialism, he rose rapidly to a vision of the past glories of France under his great uncle and with the last sentence of his peroration had the crowd shouting " *Vive Napoléon!* " and a few, perhaps specially planted individuals, forgetting their republican manners to the point of intoning " *Vive l'empereur!* " In this way he built up a powerful personal following; and when the Assembly, at last enlightened regarding his fixed purpose, drew away from him, it discovered that the conservative sentiment had rallied to the president, while the liberals, offended by the stream of anti-popular legislation, had lost interest in the republic. In 1851 Napoleon, rendered confident by the large personal party he had brought together, let fall the last veil from his plans by presenting himself before the Assembly with the request to alter the constitution to his advantage. The constitution fixed the presidential term at four years, without the right to reëlection. As by the operation of this article Louis Napoleon would have become a private citizen in 1852, he urged repeal upon the legislature. When the legislature refused, he resolved, in order to maintain his power, to overthrow the government.

The *coup d'état* was set for December 2, 1851. The most important preliminary step, taken during the preceding months, had been to win over the leaders of the army; and with these secured the success

The coup d'état of December 2, 1851 of the conspirators was certain. While the troops occupied Paris, closed the hall of the deputies, and put the president's leading opponents under lock and key, the president himself announced by placard the return to the system of the great Corsican as embodied in the Constitution of the Year VIII. The country, called upon to express its opinion upon these proceedings, indorsed the *coup d'état* by a large majority. Louis Napoleon thereupon completed his government on the basis of a granted constitution, which he provided with a false façade of liberalism by means of a legislature elected by universal suffrage. But since the legislature was carefully deprived of all effective powers, the control was concentrated in the sole hand of the chief executive. There was nothing left to make the triumph complete but to gather its last fruits, and exactly a year after the *coup d'état* the president assumed the title Emperor Napoleon III.

The new emperor never forgot that he was a usurper, who could retain his throne only if he acquired and kept the good-will of the French people. Clever politician that he was, he therefore tried to curry favor with as many social classes as possible. The policy Hitherto his electoral victories had been chiefly due to of Napoleon the peasants, whose conservative and clerical sympathies III he had systematically flattered. Without ceasing to appeal to them he directed his attention also to the middle classes. He had a sufficiently alert and modern mind to recognize the importance of factories and railways, and by vigorously favoring their multiplication he played into the hands of the bourgeoisie. But chiefly he wished to impress all classes alike with his personal prestige, and in order to increase it, he resolved to embark on an adventurous foreign policy. This was taking a page from the note-book of Napoleon I, who had frequently remarked that what the French people preëminently wanted was military glory. Whither the doctrine led that great man we are aware. Napoleon III, too, at first had his military triumphs, but without ever climbing as high as his exemplar managed in the end to fall much lower.

Napoleon had hardly seated himself on the throne when a brilliant opportunity presented itself for fishing in the ever troubled waters of the Near East. The alarming feebleness shown by the Ottoman Empire in the Greek War of Liberation persisted during Tsar the succeeding decades and prompted Tsar Nicholas of Nicholas Russia confidently to expect the early agony of the rival and the state. He referred to the sultan cheerfully as "the sick Ottoman man," and became convinced that Russia and Great Empire Britain, as the likeliest heirs, should anticipate the sultan's demise by coming to an agreement on the division of the heritage. But as every probable scheme of division would place Russia in possession of Constantinople, and Great Britain, far from wishing to put that strategic point in the hands of the tsar, was delighted to have it held by a sovereign so weak in naval strength as the sultan, Nicholas's overtures were firmly rejected. Other complications, more particularly a dispute between Nicholas and Napoleon as to which of the

two enjoyed the right to protect the Holy Places of Palestine, added
to the bitterness which gradually charged the tsar's soul. In April,
1853, it suddenly and wrathfully overflowed in the form of an attempt to wrest from the sultan an acknowledgment of the tsar's
special position with reference to the Ottoman Empire. In peremptory words the sultan was ordered to concede to the tsar the protectorate over all Greek Christians resident in Turkey. As this
would have made Nicholas co-sovereign with the sultan in the
Turkish dominions, the British ambassador at Constantinople urged
the Ottoman government to refuse. The answer of the Russians was
to occupy Moldavia and Wallachia (the Danubian principalities) in
order to enforce their claim; and after much diplomatic sparring,
in which all the powers took part, another war broke out between
the tsar and the sultan.

But Turkey was not left alone this time as in 1828–1829. Great
Britain, having prompted the sultan to resistance, was in honor bound
to help him; and though no vital French interest was at stake, Napo-
**Great
Britain and
France
support
Turkey** leon, glad and eager to find an occasion to put himself
forward, offered Great Britain his alliance. Together the
two western powers signed a treaty with the Ottoman
Empire (March, 1854) and declared war upon Russia.
What had threatened at first to be merely another Turco-
Russian conflict, thus became a European war, the first on any con-
siderable scale since the Napoleonic struggle.

The first important move of the campaign of 1854 was that the
Russians retired from the Danubian principalities into their own
territory and stood on the defensive. The allies therefore were
**The
Crimean
War,
1854–56** obliged to agree upon some point for attack, and after
much waste of time hit upon the fortress of Sebastopol
in the Crimea. The war practically reduced itself to the
siege of this great stronghold, which the Russians defended
skillfully and vigorously for a whole year. Its fall in September,
1855, discouraged the Russians greatly; and as Tsar Nicholas, whose
pretensions had caused the war, had died during the siege, to be succeeded by his more moderate and conciliatory son, Alexander II,
negotiations were begun which led to a general European congress at
Paris and to the signing in March, 1856, of a peace. As the Ottoman
Empire had been the ally of France and Great Britain, the treaty in
effect registered, even though the fighting had been done by the two
western powers, a victory of the sultan over his ancient foe, the tsar.

As a result of the peace the tsar was obliged to renounce not only his plan of a protectorate over the Greek Christians but also certain special rights secured by earlier treaties with regard to such semi-autonomous territories as Serbia and the Danubian principalities (Rumania). In fact Russia was put on an exact level with all the other powers in regard to the Ottoman Empire, the independence and territorial integrity of which were solemnly guaranteed. As for the Christian subjects of the sultan the treaty affirmed that their proper and natural protector was their Mohammedan sovereign and he alone. To discourage Russia from renewing her attacks on Turkish territory, the conferees, largely at the instance of Great Britain, wrote a provision into the treaty neutralizing the Black sea and obliging Russia to promise to maintain neither a naval base nor warships on its waters. Doubtless the treaty of Paris leveled a heavy blow at Russia; but whether it would have a long life was another question, since it was based on the absurd assumption that the disintegration of the Ottoman Empire, which had been proceeding for centuries, could be stopped by the paper command of interested diplomats. Was it, in the nature of things, possible to decree either the cessation of Turkish decay or the arrest of Russian growth?

The Crimean War, signalized by the spectacular capture of Sebastopol chiefly through the action of French troops, and brought to a close at Paris under the eyes of Napoleon, greatly enhanced the Emperor's influence, though, as already remarked, it would Napoleon's be hard to say what advantage France reaped therefrom. prestige Napoleon III's policy was personal, not national. That is the conclusion which his whole reign confirms, and particularly the steps he now took in the Italian question.

As his career must by now have fully convinced us, Napoleon, in spite of his name, was less a soldier than a clever and juggling politician endowed with a consuming ambition and a few general ideas derived from the age in which he lived. We have Napoleon seen that he supported the Industrial Revolution; at reopens the same time he was so persuaded of the power of nation- the Italian alism that he looked upon a nationalist reorganization of question Europe as inevitable. It is one of the pleasanter sides of his nature that he was occasionally willing to risk something in behalf of a cause which stirred his soul. The spectacle of Italy in chains had excited his sympathy when, as a young exile from France, he had dwelt on Italian soil. It was even popularly held that he had joined the Italian revolutionary society of the Carbonari. His youthful memories now led him to play with the thought of the liberation of the peninsula from Austrian rule — a generous impulse without doubt, but one explained by his personal predilections, not grounded in the necessities of the French state of which he was the official guardian.

Ever since the failure of the rising of 1848 Italy had been again swayed by Austria. In these circumstances the hopes and prayers of the patriots turned with increasing fervor to Sardinia-Piedmont, now a constitutional state under a young and vigorous king, Victor Emmanuel II. In 1852 the king appointed as the head of his ministry a remarkably gifted nobleman, Count Cavour by name, who cautiously and systematically prepared the liberation and unification of the peninsula. In Cavour's view the great national movement was to radiate from Sardinia-Piedmont as its center; but because this state could not by itself defeat Austria, the minister held that one of the great powers would have to be persuaded to lend military help. That could only be France, which had never ceased to regard Austria's hegemony in Italy with a jealous eye and whose sovereign did not conceal his sympathies for the oppressed Italian people. With remarkable skill Cavour manipulated the various elements of the situation. In order to curry favor with both Great Britain and France he took their side in the Crimean War and actually despatched a Piedmontese expeditionary corps to Sebastopol; then having laid Napoleon under obligation, he lured him with the prospect of a greater than the Crimean glory to be won across the Alps; and at last, in 1858, he drew him into an alliance (agreement of Plombières). The Franco-Sardinian alliance was directed against Austria, which was to be deprived of Lombardy and Venetia and driven out of Italy.

Cavour obtains an alliance with Napoleon

The war began in the spring of 1859 and was over in a few weeks. By two victories, at Magenta and at Solferino, the allies — France and Sardinia — drove the Austrians out of Lombardy back upon the Quadrilateral. Italy was ablaze with bonfires and with tumultuous enthusiasm hailed Napoleon as its liberator wherever he appeared. But much remained to be done; the Quadrilateral, one of the strongest defensive positions of Europe, would have to be taken before the Austrians could be said to have been really driven from Italy. Just as everybody was expecting a fresh advance of the allies, the telegraph flashed the news of a dra-

The Italian war of 1859

matic change: Napoleon had met the Emperor Francis Joseph of Austria in private conference at Villafranca and arranged a peace (July 11th). By its terms Austria agreed to give up Lombardy, but was permitted to retain Venetia and therewith a powerful foothold in the peninsula. Disgusted with what he stigmatized as Napoleon's perfidy, Cavour resigned from office — luckily only temporarily — but Victor Emmanuel II accepted the Villafranca arrangements, comforted by the reflection that the cause of Italian unity had for the first time successfully unfurled its banner.

The considerations which moved Napoleon to his sudden turn-about were manifold. He was not a masterful character and easily fell victim to his fears. One of these concerned the military problem of breaking through the Quadrilateral. So strong was this **Napoleon's** position that not improbably the French might bleed **reasons for** themselves to death before it. The second fear concerned **making** Prussia, which, moved by sympathy for Austria, was **peace** preparing to mobilize upon the Rhine and threaten his exposed flank. And finally, he was filled with dismay by the wild nationalist tempest sweeping over Italy from the Alps to the straits of Messina. He gave Lombardy, representing one-half of the stipulated terms, to Victor Emmanuel and hurried home, resolved to wash his hands of the troublesome Italian question. Tempted as much by his own mystic hopes about nationalism as by Cavour's promise of easy laurels, he had plunged into a movement of liberation which he expected to control at every point. In place thereof the self-deceived adventurer faced a national turmoil which broke all bounds and mocked at compulsion.

To this turmoil we must now give attention, for it brings us face to face with the piece-meal method by which Italian unification was brought about. Elated by the war against the national enemy, Tuscany, Modena, Parma, and the Romagna (the north- **Sardinia** ern section of the Papal States), making up together north- **annexes (1)** central Italy, rose against their princes and, driving **Lombardy** them from their thrones, declared for annexation to **(1859); (2)** Sardinia. Victor Emmanuel, pleased though he was, **central** dared not accept these territories without the consent **states** of the all-powerful Napoleon. Feverish negotiations **(March,** followed, which ended (March, 1860) in an agreement **1860)** that permitted the annexations in return for the cession to France of Savoy and Nice. It was a typical political trade based on the principle of give-and-take. The cession of the Alpine county of Savoy deeply hurt the king, for it was the original home of his dynasty; but as Savoy with even Nice thrown in was manifestly worth less than the north-central states, Cavour persuaded Victor Emmanuel to yield. In the course of a single year the kingdom of Sardinia-Piedmont had absorbed first, Lombardy, and second, the remainder of northern Italy with the exception of Venetia. These two acquisitions represent the first and second steps in the process of Italian unification.

The third step was the capture in the summer of 1860 of the kingdom of the Two Sicilies. This was accomplished by a daring buccaneering expedition led by Italy's soldier of fortune, Giuseppe Garibaldi. Secretly encouraged by Cavour, Garibaldi gathered at the port of Genoa one thousand volunteers, called from their conspicuous attire his thousand Red Shirts, and in May suddenly set sail for Sicily. He had only to show himself with the national colors for the Sicilians to toss their hats into the air and abandon the hated Bourbon king. Sicily conquered, Garibaldi crossed the straits to the mainland, and again proof was furnished that the imported, Spanish-minded Bourbon dynasty had never taken root among the people. The victory fell as usual to the courageous heart, and, acclaimed as a savior, the bold conqueror in September entered the unresisting city of Naples. Being a convinced republican, Garibaldi now took up the plan of organizing his conquest as a separate democratic state. The project alarmed and outraged Cavour, who regarded it as the wreck of his unitary policy. He therefore persuaded his king to march the Piedmontese troops through the Papal States into the southern kingdom in order to dispute Garibaldi's possession. In the face of this opposition and, on the further ground, that the south Italians manifestly desired annexation to Sardinia, Garibaldi yielded his position and generously surrendered his power into the hands of King Victor Emmanuel. A plebiscite taken (Nov. 1860) in Sicily and Naples gave a staggering majority for absorption into the northern kingdom. With the defeat and exile of the Bourbon king, Francis II, who made a last stand at the fortress of Gaeta, the Neapolitan incident was brought to a happy close.

Simultaneously with Naples another issue had arisen and become pressing. In driving through the eastern sections of the Papal States, Cavour had become aware that these territories too (Ancona, Umbria) passionately desired annexation to Sardinia. The weak papal forces were easily disposed of and, encouraged by a favorable plebiscite (Oct. 1860), Cavour carried through the annexation of these territories. While these events were proceeding, the Annexation tempestuous Garibaldi attempted to wring from the king of the bulk permission to lead an expedition against the city of Rome; of the Papal but as Rome was held by French troops and the attempt States to capture the capital of the pope would have meant a war with

France, Cavour interposed a firm veto. He was a statesman who knew when to go forward and when to retreat; and although he held with Garibaldi and the impulsive patriots that Italy would remain a torso until Rome and Venice, too, had been joined to the Italian trunk, he took a realist's account of things and forces as he found them. Just as to drive upon Rome would precipitate a war with France, so to descend upon Venetia would certainly cause a war with Austria; and for neither of these conflicts was Italy as yet, according to Cavour, prepared. He resolved to bide his time, convinced that sooner or later incidents would occur which would play into his country's hands and enable it to complete the work of unification so happily begun. It was folly to overlook that for the present the movement of advance was effectively checked.

In view of these elements of the general situation, Cavour resolved to inaugurate a period of rest and domestic consolidation. In consequence of the rapid march of events since 1859 he had upon his hands a kingdom of Sardinia plus a mass of annexations several times its size. In February, 1861, he summoned to Turin, the Sardinian capital, elected representatives from all the recent acquisitions who enthusiastically proclaimed the transformation of the kingdom of Sardinia into the kingdom of Italy. At the same time the Sardinian constitution was made applicable to the new state and Victor Emmanuel took the title king of Italy. It was a proud and uplifting moment in the history of a reborn people. But there was much work ahead; an administration, an army and navy, a modern economic system had to be created, not to mention the necessity of finding a *modus vivendi* with the pope, who, outraged by his spoliation, had excommunicated the king, Cavour, his rebellious subjects — in fact, everybody conspicuously connected with the movement of unification. The important work of domestic regeneration had hardly begun when the great Cavour, worn out by his labors, died (June, 1861), and the cloak of the inspired statesman fell upon the shoulders of well-meaning but humdrum politicians.

Proclamation of the kingdom of Italy

Twice the impatient Garibaldi took the bit between his teeth and charged upon Rome, resolved to repeat his buccaneering exploit of 1860. Both attempts were failures because the government of Victor Emmanuel, true, in spite of temptation, to Cavour's counsels, refused to precipitate a war with France. And exactly as the great leader had prophesied, fortune before long successively produced the two opportunities which enabled Italy to realize her hopes with regard to Venetia and Rome without exposing herself to excessive risks. The first opportunity occurred in 1866. In that year there broke out the long-threatening war in Germany between Austria and Prussia, of which we shall hear in the next chapter. Prussia naturally appealed to Italy for help, and the two powers, upon both of whom Austria rested like an incubus, made an alliance. Austria was obliged to face two enemies at once; and although victorious over Italy, defeating her army at Custozza (June 24th) and her navy at Lissa in the Adriatic (July 20th), was so conclusively crushed by

The Austro-Prussian crisis enables Italy to acquire Venetia

Prussia at Sadowa that she had to sign a peace. In the hope of winning French favor, the emperor of Austria had, on receipt of the news of Sadowa, handed over the Italian objective, Venetia, as a present to Napoleon III; but the French emperor at the conclusion of peace transferred the province to Victor Emmanuel. Venetia was promptly incorporated with Italy, and in November the old republic of St. Mark gave the king a stirring and patriotic welcome in its midst.

The Patrimony of St. Peter (Rome and its immediate environment) now alone remained outside the reconstituted nation. If the question had been submitted to the vote of the Romans whether they wished to be governed by the pope or by the king, The there can be no doubt for whom they would have declared. Franco-But French troops held the city for the pope, and Napo-German leon made it plain that, much as he had done for Italian War en-unity, his complaisance stopped at the walls of the Eternal to acquire City. To snatch Rome from the pope would have pre-Rome cipitated a French war. The upshot was that the Italian government resolved to let time do its work, and when in 1870 a war broke out between France and Prussia, its patience was fully rewarded. Obliged to mobilize his full strength against the Germans, Napoleon III withdrew his garrison from Rome and, shortly after, was rendered wholly impotent by his capture at Sedan. There was now no one to hinder the march upon Rome. In September, 1870, the Italian army appeared before the gates and forced its way into the city amid the plaudits of the citizens. Although Pope Pius IX poured renewed anathemas on his despoilers, he was not disturbed in his vast official residence, the Vatican palace, from which he continued to rule the Catholic world. While Rome is therefore still the head of Catholic Christianity, it has since 1870 been also the secular capital of the Italian state.

Rulers of the House of Savoy

(Sardinia-Piedmont; Italy)

Charles Albert, 1831–1849
Victor Emmanuel II (son of the above; first king of Italy) 1849–1878
Humbert I (son of his predecessor), 1878–1900
Victor Emmanuel III (son of Humbert I) 1900–

REFERENCES

C. D. HAZEN, *Europe Since 1815*, I, chs. 10, 11, 13

C. M. ANDREWS, *Development of Modern Europe*, II, chs. 1, 3, 4

C. A. FYFFE, *Modern Europe*, III, chs. 3, 4

Cambridge Modern History, XI, chs. 10, 14, 17, 20

J. H. ROSE, *Development of European Nations*, I, ch. 1

A. LEBON, *Modern France*, chs. 12–14

E. BOURGEOIS, *Modern France*, I, chs. 9, 10, 11, chs. 1–4

J. R. M. MACDONALD, *France*, III, chs. 37–40

F. J. C. HEARNSHAW, *Main Currents*, ch. 7

H. A. L. FISHER, *Bonapartism*

F. A. SIMPSON, *The Rise of Louis Napoleon*

P. GUEDALLA, *The Second Empire*

P. F. MARTIN, *Maximilian in Mexico*

H. D. SEDGWICK, *Short History of Italy*

J. A. R. MARRIOTT, *Makers of Modern Italy*

R. S. HOLLAND, *Builders of United Italy*

B. KING, *History of Italian Unity; Joseph Mazzini*

J. W. MARIO, *Birth of Modern Italy*

W. R. THAYER, *Life and Times of Cavour*

P. ORSI, *Cavour and the Making of Modern Italy*

E. MARTINENGO-CESARESCO, *Life of Cavour*

G. M. TREVELYAN, *Garibaldi and the Making of Italy; Garibaldi and the Thousand*

R. DE CESARE, *Last Days of Papal Rome*

H. R. WHITEHOUSE, *Collapse of the Kingdom of Naples*.

CHAPTER XXVII

THE UNIFICATION OF GERMANY

Although, following the failure of the German revolution of 1848, Prussia remained a constitutional state, this success offered only a slight consolation to the dejected liberals in view of the fact that a dark reaction spread its shadows over the country. The erratic king, Frederick William IV, once more openly expounded his views of Divine Right, and leaning on the landowners (*Junker*), the army officers, and the Lutheran clergy reduced the action of the Prussian parliament (*Landtag*) to the smallest possible scope. The press was muzzled and political meetings were forbidden. As, in addition to the loss of credit resulting from this domestic situation, Prussia suffered from having at the dictation of Austria (1850) meekly reëntered the Bund, her influence among the liberal and unitarian elements of German society temporarily disappeared. In the year 1858 occurred a change, slight in itself but destined to become significant. In that year, owing to the appearance of symptoms of insanity, the reactionary monarch was replaced by his brother William, first as regent and, on the demise of the patient in 1861, as king.

The advent of William was hailed as the dawn of a new era and attended by a revival of hope among the liberal elements. Endowed, in sharp contrast with his romantic brother, with a matter-of-fact mind and having besides, through long association, a professional interest in the army, the new ruler inaugurated at once what seemed to him an urgent military reform. The Prussian army, a creation of the Napoleonic wars, was based on a law of 1814 which prescribed universal military training in the form of three years' service with the colors and two years in the reserve. At the time this system was adopted some 40,000 recruits reported annually for training and the total standing army was slightly in excess of 120,000 men. Since then the population of Prussia had increased by more than fifty per cent; but as only 40,000 recruits could be annually accommodated on the basis of the existing arrangements, the principle of universal compulsory

555

training had in practice been abandoned. The new sovereign determined to make military training once more general, not only of course because of his devotion to the principle but also because its strict enforcement would provide a larger army and secure for Prussia a greater degree of consideration in the councils of Europe. At the same time he wished to introduce a few minor changes, such as the extension of the service in the reserve from two to four years, which recommended themselves to him on technical military grounds. He had an Army Reform Bill presented to the parliament, which actually voted the recommended changes in a provisional form. Then a hitch occurred. The liberals had acquired a majority in the lower house and, desiring to reduce the military expenditures, demanded certain concessions, above all, the reduction of the service with the colors from three to two years. Angered by this attempt to interfere in the organization of the army, which he looked upon as a government service pertaining to the king alone, William dismissed the lower house only to find that in the new elections the people returned a larger liberal majority than before. The king, who, on the strength of the provisional vote, had already begun the reorganization of the army, persisted in carrying through the work, while his liberal opponents with ever waxing shrillness declaimed against the unconstitutionality of his action. In this way it came about that, beginning with the year 1861, Prussia entered upon a vivacious struggle between executive and legislative, which, while it turned immediately about the Army Reform Bill, involved also the question of the constitution, since the king insisted on giving permanent character to a measure only provisionally authorized by the legislature.

Discouraged but obstinate, King William resolved to make a last attempt to force his measure through the parliament and in October, 1862, appointed Otto von Bismarck as prime minister. Bismarck The was a Brandenburg squire (*Junker*) of ancient lineage, ministry of who had emerged into public life in 1848 as the fearless Bismarck defender of the royal prerogative. On the strength of his militant conservatism he was drawn into the diplomatic service and acted successively as the Prussian representative in the Bund at Frankfort, and at the courts of St. Petersburg and Paris. This experience greatly broadened his outlook. Not only did he gain a masterful grasp of the general European situation, but he reached the conclusion that German unity was feasible only under Prussian leadership and that it would not be attainable except through the destruction of the Bund and the ejection of Austria from Germany. As an efficient army was indispensable to such a program, he was prepared to support the king against the lower house with all the fighting zest at his command.

As soon as he presented himself with his conservative record and his habitual self-assurance before the parliament a tremendous storm broke loose. But he refused to be deflected from his path and with apparent tranquillity faced even the prospect of a Bismark's civil war, which seemed not so remote in view of the un- unshaken compromising position of the two opponents. Before that stand pass was reached, however, a succession of events occurred which drew public attention elsewhither and which enabled Bismarck by a series of brilliant successes to effect a triumphant reconciliation of the sovereign with the parliament and the people.

In the year 1863 took place the long-expected death of Frederick VII of Denmark, the last male of his line. By the verdict of the powers known as the Protocol of London (1852) he was succeeded at Copenhagen by his relative, Christian IX; but the The Danish duchies of Schleswig and Holstein, which had never ac- War, 1864 cepted the Protocol, immediately proclaimed the Duke of Augustenburg, who, according to their view, was the rightful heir. At bottom their action was due less to legal than to nationalist considerations. They wished, as Germans, to break the ties that bound them to Denmark and they counted confidently on the support of German public opinion. Nor were they mistaken. Even the sluggish Bund was sufficiently stirred to plan an intervention in their behalf, but before the measure had got well under way, it was rudely pushed aside from an unexpected quarter. Convinced that the shadowy Bund was unable to meet the crisis but that Prussia could, Bismarck persuaded Austria to join him in settling the issue in a manner conformable with the interests and obligations of the two great German states. Luckily for the Prussian minister, King Christian IX played into his hands. Immediately upon his accession the king had signed a bill, incorporating Schleswig, the northernmost of the two duchies, with Denmark. This was a clear breach of the London Protocol, which recognized Christian as king of Denmark on the strict understanding that he would respect the historical autonomy of the duchies. Prussia and Austria issued an ultimatum to Copenhagen, demanding that the incorporation be withdrawn without delay. When Christian, under pressure from the Danish nationalists, refused to yield, Berlin and Vienna declared war, and in January, 1864, Prussian and Austrian troops entered the duchies side by side. In a swift campaign they brought Denmark to her knees. By a peace signed in August Christian IX ceded Schleswig and Holstein to the victors.

The question now was how to divide the spoils, and this question Bismarck faced without flinching since he regarded it as the convenient door through which to enter on the larger issue of German unity. Preliminary to an effective reorganization of Germany was, as he saw the situation, the exclusion of Austria; and since he foresaw that Austria would never depart voluntarily, he was prepared to resort to war to drive her out. As King William hesitated to accept Bismarck's uncompromising view, the negotiations between Berlin and Vienna were spun out till the spring of 1866, when the Prussian king at last went over to his minister's opinion. In consequence Bismarck sought contact with that other enemy of Austria, the young kingdom of Italy, and signed an alliance which, in the event of victory, promised Venetia to King Victor Emmanuel. As the rulers of the other German states all feared that a renovated Germany under Prussian guidance would impair their sovereignty, most of them, and more particularly those of the larger states such as Bavaria, Würtemberg, Baden, Saxony, and Hanover, sided with Austria. With these arrangements made, in June, 1866, the two apparently well-matched combatants took the field. While the ostensible issue between them was the division of the Schleswig-Holstein booty, Bismarck had succeeded in making it as clear as day that the real issue was the reorganization of Germany on a different and more solid basis than the Bund.

Although a part of the Prussian army had to be detached against the German allies of Austria, the Austrians, too, were hindered from concentration in a single mass by the obligation of sending an army to Venetia to defend that province against the Italians. Weakened only by these subtractions, the Austrians and Prussians, assembled in two great armies, made ready to meet each other in Bohemia. This meeting of the two leading powers, it was evident, would decide the war.

And now it was proved to friend and foe that the reform of the Prussian army was a most timely measure. The Prussians were more quickly mobilized than the Austrians and showed themselves to be much better armed and disciplined. By the admirable arrangements

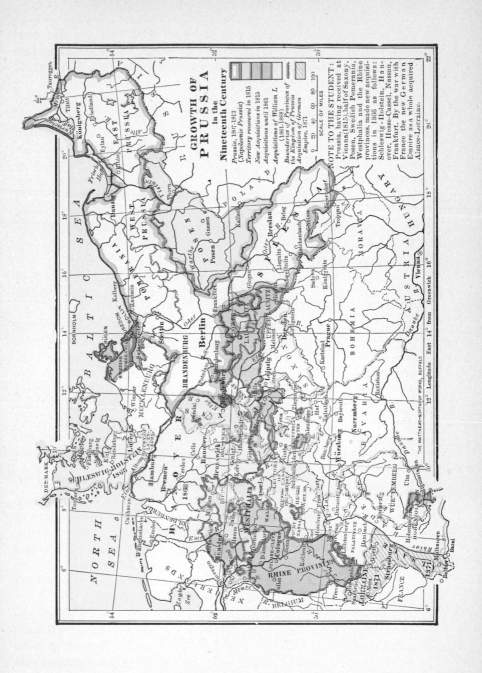

GROWTH OF
PRUSSIA
In the
Nineteenth Century

Prussia, 1807-1813
(Napoleonic Prussia)
Territory recovered in 1815
New acquisitions in 1815
Acquisitions until 1861
Acquisitions of William I.
Boundaries of Provinces of
the Kingdom of Prussia
Acquisition of German
Empire, 1871

SCALE OF MILES
0   20 40 60 80 100

NOTE TO THE STUDENT:
Prussia, having received at
Vienna, (1815), half of Saxony,
Posen, Swedish Pomerania,
Westphalia and the Rhine
provinces, made new acquisi-
tions in 1866 as follows:
Schleswig-Holstein, Han-
over, Hesse-Cassel, Nassau,
Frankfurt. By the war with
France the new German
Empire as a whole acquired
Alsace-Lorraine.

"THE MATTHEWS-NORTHRUP WORKS, BUFFALO"

of the great strategist Moltke, three Prussian columns were made to converge upon the Austrian army, engaged in concentrating near the fortress of Königgrätz in Bohemia, and catching the enemy at Sadowa as in a vise, crushed him utterly (July 3d). The Sadowa (or war had hardly begun when it was over. It was of little con- Königgrätz) sequence that the Austrians in Italy defeated the Italians July 3, 1866 at Custozza, or that the Prussians completed their triumph by defeating the minor German forces. Incapable of continuing the struggle, Austria was obliged to open negotiations. A truce in July was followed in August, 1866, by the definitive Peace of Prague.

By the Peace of Prague Austria agreed to cede her rights to Schleswig-Holstein to Prussia, to accept the dissolution of the Bund, to withdraw from German affairs, and to leave Prussia free to form a confederation of the states of northern Germany. The The Peace four South German states (Bavaria, Würtemberg, Baden, of Prague and Hesse) were accorded the right to form a federation and the of their own. Although Austria made the further sacri- triumph of fice of Venetia, which was surrendered to Italy, in view of Prussia the immensity of her disaster, her territorial losses were not crushing. As soon as these arrangements were assured, Bismarck made peace with the German allies of Austria. In order to ease the animosities produced by the late conflict he let off the four South German states with small indemnities; but certain hostile North German states, like Hanover, Nassau, and Hesse-Cassel, which drove a wedge between the mass of Prussia around Berlin and her possessions on the Rhine, he incorporated with the monarchy of the Hohenzollerns. Without any question the war delivered Germany into Prussia's hands; none the less as long as the South German states remained aloof from reorganized North Germany, the national unity was incomplete. It took another war, the war with France, to fuse North and South Germany and crown Bismarck's national policy.

Meanwhile, the Peace of Prague left Bismarck free to establish a North German Confederation. In the stress of civil war, the old Bund had gone to its reward, with no greater outburst of sorrow than had attended, exactly sixty years before, the demise of the The North Holy Roman Empire. For the first time since the Middle German Age Germany was to have a strong union. The twenty- Confedera- two states which joined it accepted the king of Prussia as tion chief executive under the title president, while the legislative power was entrusted to a Federal Council or *Bundesrath*, representing the participating governments, and a parliament or *Reichstag*, representing the people and elected by universal suffrage. Although the component states preserved a broad measure of autonomy, they lost their leading sovereign rights which were taken over by the new federal institutions, the Bundesrath, the Reichstag, and, above all, the king of Prussia in his capacity of chief executive. While the constitution, drafted by Bismarck, made in the elected Reichstag a considerable concession to liberal opinion, it was so framed that the king of Prussia and the other sovereigns, represented with him in the Bundesrath, retained substantial control of the policy of the new state. The South German states, free to form a confederation of their own, failed to do so, and occupied a very unsatisfactory position as wandering comets of the German system, until a new crisis drew them into the North German Confederation.

This crisis, which constitutes the last step in the unification of Germany, was precipitated by the strained relations resulting from the victory of Prussia between herself and her western neighbor, France. We parted from the Emperor Napoleon on the occasion of his victorious campaign of 1859 in Italy. While contributing immensely to the liberation of Italy, he had not failed to collect a generous fee for services in the form of Nice and Savoy. The Italian campaign marks the last occasion on which his ventures prospered. Owing to his persistent occupation of Rome with French troops for the purpose of protecting the pope, he sacrificed the good will of the Italian nation, won upon the battlefield, and made himself almost as detested as the Austrians. Then in an evil hour he turned his desires upon the New World. In the hope of fresh laurels he interfered in the internal affairs of Mexico, and beginning with the occupation of Vera Cruz, sent an army against Mexico City and overturned the republic. Thereupon setting up a government of his own, he offered the throne to the Archduke Maximilian, brother of the emperor of Austria. His candidate landed in Mexico in 1864. The American Civil War was just then at its height, and the United States was too embarrassed to do more than register a weak protest against this violation of the Monroe Doctrine; but no sooner had the Civil War been brought to a close than the government at Washington gave Napoleon to understand that he must withdraw immediately. Napoleon shuffled awhile, but did not care to face the consequences of a refusal. The French sailed for Europe, and Maximilian, deserted by his protector, was captured and

Napoleon and the Mexican muddle

shot (1867). The victorious Mexicans at once reëstablished their republic.

The shame of this disgraceful ending was not the only hapless feature about the Mexican adventure, for, owing to the absence of the best French troops in the New World, Napoleon could not bring his full influence to bear on the Austro-Prussian crisis of French 1866. Prussia won, established her supremacy in Ger- jealousy of many, and in spite of Napoleon's insistence that France Prussia must receive some territorial compensation along its eastern boundary, refused to yield a single foot of land. Napoleon's position was profoundly shaken. The French people were angry with their sovereign because he had permitted Prussia enormously to increase its strength without utilizing its embarrassment to realize wholly or in part that ancient objective of French policy, the Rhine boundary. To appease the opposition the emperor gradually relaxed the autocratic régime in favor of a truly representative system. The new phase of his government is known as the Liberal Empire. But his discomfitures in the foreign field had been too numerous to revive his popularity, and when, in spite of cunning and constant diplomatic pressure, he was unable to wring from Prussia the slightest concession in the matter of French annexations, the relations of the two governments grew rapidly more and more exacerbated. Inevitably the dangerous frame of mind of the diplomats was reflected in the French and German press and public. Under the circumstances an atmosphere of excitement came to prevail which, with the aid of the blundering and scheming of the leading ministers on both sides, caused a relatively unimportant incident to flare up in war.

In the year 1868 a revolution had occurred in Spain by which the Bourbon sovereign, Queen Isabella, was expelled. Ever since, the Spanish revolutionary leaders had been looking about Europe for a new king, and finally offered the crown to Leopold of The Hohenzollern-Sigmaringen, a distant relative of the king Spanish of Prussia. The prospect of a Prussian prince upon the incident Spanish throne greatly excited French opinion, and Napoleon hastened to protest. Prince Leopold's wise refusal of the crown ended the crisis; but almost at once the French foreign minister, the headstrong duke of Gramont, revived it by insisting that King William should give a promise that he would never permit his relative to renew his candidature. On July 13, 1870, at the order of Gramont, the French ambassador, Benedetti, presented himself before King

William, while he was taking the waters at Ems, with this futile and provocative demand. The king, scenting an effort to humiliate him, gave an unequivocal refusal and then telegraphed a detailed version of the incident to Bismarck at Berlin. The minister, convinced that the refusal by the prince of the Spanish throne was as far as Prussia could in honor go, and prepared and even eager for a war in which France had manifestly put itself in the wrong, gave to the press for general publication a concise version of the Ems despatch. Though it was not a falsification, as has been often charged, it was a conscious act of provocation intended as a counterblast to Benedetti's unjustified demand. The effect in Paris of the Ems message was electric. Press and public declared that French honor had been insulted, and the government, carried off its feet, rushed into war (July 15th).

The advantages in the struggle which now ensued were, from the beginning, with Prussia. The first success was achieved in connection with the South German states. Napoleon was hoping that they The advan- would, out of aversion for Prussia, side with him, but tages are the far-seeing Bismarck had provided for just such an with Prussia emergency. Immediately after the war of 1866 he had signed offensive and defensive treaties with the South German states which obliged them to fight shoulder to shoulder with Prussia. Even without these alliances, however, the South German governments would not have remained neutral, for the people were aroused to explosive enthusiasm and insisted on regarding the cause of Prussia as that of all Germany. From a purely military point of view, too, the preliminary honors were all with the German side. The North German Confederation and its allies were ready sooner and mustered a larger and better-organized army than Napoleon. In consequence, the famous Moltke, who acted as chief-of-staff of the German forces, could assume the offensive and carry the war into France.

The Germans found the French drawn up in two main bodies, one in Alsace under General MacMahon, the other in Lorraine, under Emperor Napoleon himself. A simultaneous attack on August The early 6th was crowned with a double victory, obliging Mac-German Mahon to abandon Alsace and Napoleon to fall back on victories the great fortress of Metz on the Moselle. The combined German armies thereupon concentrated their attack on the French forces covering Metz, and by three bloody battles, culminating in the battle of Gravelotte (August 18th), succeeded in blocking the French retreat and bottling up the best French army in the chief fortress of the eastern frontier. Just before the situation around Metz had become acute, Napoleon made his escape to the army of MacMahon, which he now tried to bring up, as fast as possible, to the relief of Metz. But he was ruinously defeated at Sedan and obliged to surrender with his whole army (September 2d). After a moving interview with King William the fallen emperor was sent to Germany as a prisoner of war.

Thus far the campaign had been managed with extraordinary skill and swiftness on the part of General Moltke. The war had hardly lasted a month, and already Napoleon, at the head of one of the French armies, had been captured, while the second French army, commanded by Bazaine, was locked up in Metz. Apparently, it remained only to march upon Paris and dictate terms of peace. Accordingly, *The investments of Metz and Paris* a German army of 200,000 men proceeded westward and toward the end of September undertook the investment of the French capital.

Meanwhile important developments had occurred in the capital. The calamity of Sedan had hardly become known when the city of Paris rose in indignation against the luckless imperial government. The Empress Eugénie, whom Napoleon had left behind as regent, fled in dismay and, amid scenes of wild disorder, France was declared a republic (September 4th). *France proclaimed a republic* At the same time a number of men, the most prominent of whom was Gambetta, set up, for the purpose of effectively prosecuting the war, the Government of the National Defence.

The siege of Paris marks the last stage of the war. If the Germans entertained the hope of settling things in a few weeks, they were greatly mistaken. Gambetta, supported by the aroused opinion of the country, made a most active and honorable resistance. But his raw levies were no match, in the long run, for the disciplined soldiers of the enemy. The surrender of Bazaine at Metz, on October 27th, withdrew *Capitulation of Paris followed by peace* from the war the last veteran army which France boasted. Undismayed the Parisians held out, until, forced by hunger, they at last, on January 28, 1871, agreed to capitulate. The war was over. In the preliminary Treaty of Versailles (made definitive at Frankfort in May, 1871) France had to buy peace from Germany by paying an indemnity of one billion dollars and by ceding Alsace and a part of

Lorraine. In March the Germans began the evacuation of the French territory.

But it was not the old divided fatherland to which the German soldiers returned. The great victories won by the united efforts of north and south had aroused a boundless enthusiasm. In all circles the feeling prevailed that the present happy military union must take a constitutional form; and, yielding to this sentiment, the South German governments signed agreements with Prussia by which they entered the North German Confederation. It was further stipulated that the completed union was to be called the German Empire, and that its head, the king of Prussia, should take the title German emperor. On January 18, 1871, the completion of the edifice of German unity was proclaimed to the world from the Hall of Mirrors in Louis XIV's sumptuous palace at Versailles. Bismarck, the architect of Germany, was raised to the rank of prince and took the post of chancellor, which, by the terms of the constitution, made him head of the national administration under the emperor.

King William becomes German emperor, January 18, 1871

France, in the weeks following the treaty with Germany, went through a terrible crisis. The peace had been authorized by an Assembly which, elected by the people and convened at Bordeaux, had superseded Gambetta's improvised Government of National Defence. This body gave Thiers, a man of conservative views, the provisional executive authority. Being largely composed of monarchists it aroused suspicion among republicans and radicals as to its ultimate intentions. In March, as soon as peace was assured, the Assembly left Bordeaux and moved to Versailles in order to be nearer Paris. Thoroughly persuaded that the next step would be the establishment of a reactionary régime, the extreme radicals, a mixed group of socialists and anarchists, resolved to block action by rising in revolution. Taking possession of Paris, they set up a government which they called the Commune. Commune in French usage means the town or city considered as a political entity, and has nothing whatever in common with what in English is designated as communism. The Commune had no program worth mentioning apart from the purpose of setting up radical Paris as a political entity in as complete independence as possible of conservative France represented by the National Assembly and its executive agent, Thiers.

The Paris Commune

There followed a bitter civil war which lasted two months (March–

May, 1871). It took the form of a siege of Paris by the national government at Versailles — the second siege sustained by the unfortunate city within a year! The issue was decided by the larger forces and supplies of the national government, and in May the insurgents made their last stand in the heart of the capital. When resistance became useless, a few despera- Victory of the National Assembly does attempted to set fire to Paris and actually succeeded in destroying the Tuileries, the City Hall, and a few other historical structures. The exasperated victors knew no mercy. Thousands of men connected or suspected of connection with the insurrection and representing every shade of radical opinion were shot without trial; thousands more were transported to the colonies or condemned to imprisonment with hard labor. The National Assembly became the unchallenged government of all France. How would it order the future of the country? The year that gave to Germany, which for hundreds of years had been a political laughing-stock, a strong government, brought to France, which for centuries had been the synonym of political strength, a troubled and harassed government faced with the necessity of reconstructing the country from the foundations.

Rulers of Prussia and the German Empire
(House of Hohenzollern)

Frederick William III, 1797–1840
Frederick William IV (son of the above), 1840–1861
William I (brother of his predecessor; first German emperor), 1861–1888
Frederick III (son of William I) 1888
William II (son of Frederick III), 1888–1918

REFERENCES

J. S. SCHAPIRO, *Modern and Contemporary Europe*, ch. 9
C. SEIGNOBOS, *Europe Since 1814*, chs. 14–16
C. A. FYFFE, *Modern Europe*, III, chs. 5, 6
C. D. HAZEN, *Europe Since 1815*, I, chs. 12, 14
C. J. H. HAYES, *Political and Social History*, II, pp. 180–206
E. FUETER, *World History*, chs. 26, 27
C. M. ANDREWS, *Development of Modern Europe*, II, chs. 5, 6
Cambridge Modern History, XI, chs. 15, 16
E. F. HENDERSON, *Short History of Germany*, II, chs. 8–10
G. M. PRIEST, *Germany Since 1740*, chs. 9, 10
J. A. R. MARRIOTT, *Remaking of Modern Europe*, chs. 19, 20
J. H. ROSE, *Development of European Nations*, I, chs. 1–4
F. SCHEVILL, *The Making of Modern Germany*, Lect. 5 and Appendices D to H
H. LICHTENBERGER, *Germany and its Evolution in Modern Times*, Bk. 2, pp. 65–137

M. SMITH, *Bismarck and German Unity*
J. W. HEADLAM, *Bismarck and the Foundation of the German Empire*
C. G. ROBERTSON, *Bismarck*
G. B. MALLESON, *The Refounding of the German Empire*
W. H. DAWSON, *The German Empire*, I
J. A. R. MARRIOTT AND C. G. ROBERTSON, *The Evolution of Prussia*, chs. 9–13
LORD ACTON, *Historical Essays and Studies*, chs. 7, 8
R. H. LORD, *The Origins of the War of 1870*

CHAPTER XXVIII

GREAT BRITAIN AND THE BRITISH EMPIRE FROM
1815 TO 1914

The Great Britain which was victorious over Napoleon and which with its three continental allies undertook in 1815 to reshape Europe was animated by the resentment against the program of the French Revolution common to all the victor powers. This national state of mind found political expression in the domination of the Tory party and in its determination to uphold without change the whole body of inherited institutions. At the core of these institutions was the parliamentary system which, the product of the seventeenth century revolution, transferred the political control from the king to the house of Commons and, more immediately, to the ministry (cabinet) representing the majority party in the Commons.[1] Owing to its astonishing success since its creation this British governmental system enjoyed an enormous prestige not only at home but also among the liberal groups of the continent. And yet it was not really liberal or rather it was liberal only in comparison with the absolutism prevailing everywhere else in Europe. Considered in itself it was a system conferring political rights exclusively on property owners and, more particularly, on owners of landed property. Conclusive evidence on this head is supplied by the composition of the two houses of parliament. While it goes without saying that the Lords, a house of feudal origin and character, consisted predominantly of great landholders, it is less self-evident but none the less true that the landed interests dominated also the house of Commons.

The British parliamentary system reared on a narrow property foundation

The situation in the Commons becomes clear only by an examination of its composition and of the prevailing system of election. There were three classes of constituencies: the *counties* elected 186 members, the *boroughs* 467, and the *universities* 5, making a total membership of 658. Neglecting the university members because numerically unimportant, we may begin with the county members, taking note

---

[1] See pp. 372–373.

that the county franchise was dependent on agricultural property and fairly uniform throughout the country. It was the boroughs with their 467 members that chiefly invited the criticism of reformers.

The anomalous electoral system By boroughs should be understood what in America are colloquially called towns and cities. In the English boroughs the franchise had been conceded not to the inhabitants but to privileged bodies within each borough. While the electoral system showed much variation from borough to borough, it none the less holds that the privilege of the franchise was as a rule so narrowly distributed that the borough members were appointed by no more than a handful of electors. Furthermore, as the list of boroughs having the right of representation had been drawn up in the reign of Charles II and had never since been revised, it happened that not a few had by the vicissitudes of history dwindled to petty villages. Of such reduced boroughs the largest neighboring landowner usually acquired control and sent up to Westminster some near relative or dependent responsible to no one but his patron. Such a borough was picturesquely and adequately described as a pocket borough. As many other boroughs, nay, the vast majority, depended on so restricted a franchise that the few voters could either be bought or delicately manipulated by socially eminent lords or economically powerful millionaires, it followed that the taunt was justified which referred to the boroughs as generally "rotten." While pocket and rotten boroughs sufficiently tell the prevailing tale of injustice and corruption, it should be further noted that the south and east of England were favored at the expense of the north and west. This becomes explicable when we recall that the existing system had taken shape in the seventeenth century when the south and east overshadowed the other sections in point both of wealth and population. But since the middle of the eighteenth century the Industrial Revolution had produced a startling change. It had brought into existence new towns such as Birmingham, Leeds, and Sheffield in the coal and iron districts of the English north. Themselves totally unrepresented in parliament, they had to put up with the irrational and offensive circumstance that vanishing and microscopic communities of the south, carried in his pocket by some powerful magnate, enjoyed an honor to which the newer, flourishing centers aspired in vain. In sum, the house of Commons was not representative of the English people. According to an eminent authority 487 members out of a total of 658 were chosen, in one way or another, by patrons. In their case the election held from time to time was a hollow form. Instead of representing the English people the house of Commons may be truthfully said to have represented a small oligarchy of landlords, bankers, and great merchants.

For the period in which it arose this distracting system was, after all, not so very anomalous, for at the end of the seventeenth century the landed aristocracy and the great merchants undoubtedly were the most vital elements of English society. But since the middle of the eighteenth century a change had been going on due to the revolution connected with machines and factories. A new industrial class had come to the front which with its wealth and energy was sure to insist on more adequate political representation. It is highly probable that it would have been heard from before the century came to a close, if the French Revolution had not broken out and, by involving Great Britain in war, had not produced the usual war-time tightening of the reins of government. When in 1815 the victory fell to Great Britain and its allies, the spirit of reaction, as we are aware, triumphed all along the line. The victory over Napoleon, won under Tory guidance, so heightened the prestige of the conservatives that they were able to extol the inherited system as well nigh perfect, to support their spiritual brethren of the continent linked together in the Holy Alliance, and grimly to set their faces against change.

The struggle with revolutionary France strengthens the conservatives

However, a few years of peace sufficed to blow into flame the justified discontent of the rapidly multiplying middle classes. Most of them, as men of means, possessed a natural caution and asked for nothing more than for political recognition of their type of property (machines, factories, capital); but some of their allies — journalists, pamphleteers, and social students, in short, the important group of intellectuals — went farther and, taking their cue from the French Revolution, proclaimed such extreme demands as universal suffrage and a secret ballot. These men called themselves *radicals* and aroused such fierce indignation among the governing Tories that their agitation was at last suppressed by special laws (Gag Laws, 1819). None the less they made themselves felt in the general realm of opinion. In the altered circumstances of the country a group within the Tory body gradually became convinced of the advisability of offering con-

The Tories themselves inaugurate reform

cessions and with the advent to the foreign office of Canning (1822) succeeded in inaugurating a modest era of reform. It was characteristic of the new spirit that Canning definitely dissociated himself from the Holy Alliance by supporting revolution in Portugal and in the Spanish colonies. The domestic program of himself and friends was as much of an innovation as his foreign policy, for it broke, albeit gently and indecisively, with the inherited economic system by simplifying the customs tariff. The duties on many articles of import were reduced, while a few duties were actually abolished. More particularly the duty on corn (grain), instead of being kept at the established prohibitory figure, was sufficiently lowered to permit a limited importation (1823). All this was not free trade, far from it; but it was a breach with the traditional exaggerated system of protection. In final analysis it was a concession to the new manufacturing interests which needed open avenues of trade and the cheaper foreign food.

Before long another concession to liberal opinion was recorded in the cancellation of the disabilities resting on the remnants of the Puritans, designated by the law as Dissenters. Enjoying since 1689 freedom of worship, the Dissenters had gradually by a process of connivance been admitted to public office, although the so-called Test Acts of Charles II's reign formally excluded them. As there was no use in clinging to laws which were no longer effective, the Test Acts were in 1828 abolished, thus making the Dissenters at last full-fledged citizens in the enjoyment of all the civil rights of Anglicans. While the cancellation of these Acts redounded also to the benefit of the Catholics, certain special laws existed which excluded them from both houses of parliament. In 1829 these special laws were abandoned in their turn and therewith a formal end made to the religious intolerance so deeply embedded in the English and Scottish law and conscience.

Full civil rights granted to Dissenters and Catholics, 1828-1829

With the door thus slowly swinging open to reform it was impossible to avoid the reform of that institution, the parliament, against which criticism aimed its sharpest shafts. As the Tories stubbornly resisted the growing agitation, they were, on the strength of a Whig victory at the polls in 1831, replaced by a Whig ministry; and in the following year a bill for parliamentary reform at last passed both houses and received the signature of the king. Far from being a radical measure, it was manifestly a patch-work concession to the new manufacturing elements. It did, however, destroy the worst abuses of the old system by abolishing the pocket and rotten boroughs and by creating a more uniform franchise; at the same time it admitted the new towns of the north to repre- *The Parlia-* sentation. Its two main provisions were: (1) *A redistri-* *mentary* *bution of seats.* Seats to the number of 143 were taken $\frac{\text{Reform Bill}}{\text{of 1832 and}}$ from the minor boroughs and redistributed in such a way *its signifi-* as to put an end to the most glaring cases of unequal repre- *cance* sentation. (2) *A more uniform electoral franchise.* In the counties the franchise was given to all holders of land worth £10 a year; also to all tenants-at-will (a peculiar English legal category) of lands worth £50 a year. In the boroughs all occupants of houses (whether as owners or tenants) were given the vote, provided the house was worth £10 a year. By this reform the total number of voters was almost doubled. What was more important still the middle classes were on the above basis admitted to full representation and acquired an electoral preponderance which by the mere operation of time was bound to become more and more decisive. It would be an exaggeration to say that by the Reform Bill of 1832 the middle classes leaped at a bound into a position of control; but it would be an entirely fair description of the situation to declare that from 1832 on the middle classes, representing developing industry, were prepared to wrest the power from the older aristocratic interests founded on land tenure. The next generation witnessed a political and social struggle conducted on these lines. In preparation for it the Whigs, who had put through the parliamentary reform and looked to middle class support, reorganized themselves as the Liberal party. Aware that a new time had dawned bringing in its train new problems, the Tories followed the Whig example and presented themselves to the public in the guise of the Conservative party. For several generations to come the parliamentary battle was waged between these two heirs of the old Whigs and Tories.

How in the decades following the reform of parliament the middle classes, acting through the Liberal party, steadily strengthened their position may be illustrated by several outstanding measures. The established method of borough government gave the control to a close or self-perpetuating corporation made up of privileged local families — a typical oligarchical system. Hateful to the new men who found themselves excluded from a voice in town affairs, it was abolished in 1835 by the Municipal Corporations Act, by virtue of which the municipal power was vested in a mayor, aldermen, and councillors responsible to the tax-payers, the whole body of whom was admitted to the franchise. By this measure the expanding middle The middle classes took over the administration of the towns. classes After transferring by various similar acts the influence of complete the aristocracy in other local matters such as poor relief their con- and highways to elective boards and salaried officials, the quest of society and middle classes were finally encouraged to attack the government Tory landlords in their most powerful stronghold. This was the Corn Laws. Planned to give the monopoly of the home market to the British growers of breadstuffs, the Corn Laws put so high a tariff on foreign grain as effectively to exclude it. The very rapid growth of population incident to the Industrial Revolution produced a crisis. Not only did the price of bread rise to a fantastically high figure, but Great Britain was really no longer able to provide the quantity of wheat necessary for the sustenance of its people. It was this consideration which induced even the Tories to favor in 1823 that mitigation of the system of which mention has been made. But the middle classes, identified with manufacture and trade, gradually became persuaded that what the country needed was not mitigation but abolition. They were won to this view by a vigorous agitation for free trade in corn carried on under the auspices of two great leaders, Richard Cobden and John Bright. Finally, a terrible famine in Ireland in 1845 precipitated action; and under the general impression that what the British islands needed was plentiful and cheap food, the parliament in 1846 repealed the Corn Laws. Since with English manufacturing ascendancy an established fact there was, on the abandonment of agricultural protection, no need of maintaining any kind of tariff at all, the parliament gradually swept away the import duties on hundreds of articles. By 1860 there were only 48 dutiable articles left. Of these tea, wine, and tobacco were the most important and even this list was maintained not with a view to protection but solely for revenue purposes. In the course of a few decades Great Britain had thrown the old mercantilist theories overboard and committed itself to free trade!

However, the waxing ascendancy of the middle classes soon encountered an obstacle. An inevitable concomitant of middle class prosperity was that the factory workers multiplied with extraordinary rapidity. As the Liberals, identified with the manufacturing interests and dedicated to a *laissez-faire* philosophy, regarded even the most ruthless exploitation of the workers with equanimity, it depended on the Conservatives if any official note was to be taken of the sufferings of the factory hands. Moreover, as the old ruling order indulged a familiar aristocratic contempt for the newer riches of the Rise of industrial magnates, it was naturally disposed to irritate working them by harping on their social iniquities. An early effect class agitation; the of this upper-class rivalry was the passage under Tory Chartist auspices of the law authorizing trade unions (1824– movement 1825). When in 1832 the middle classes obtained the parliamentary franchise, they were so fully satisfied with their elevation to power that they vigorously opposed every further extension of the suffrage. But the workingmen, egged on by a group of intellectual radicals, thought otherwise. Persuaded that only political representation would enable them fully to protect their interests, they inaugurated the Chartist agitation, so called from a petition, named the People's Charter, around which the movement turned. The People's Charter contained six demands addressed to parliament, the most important of which was universal suffrage. The agitation continued lustily for a decade (1837–1848), but as the government refused to pay any attention to it and the workingmen were not yet very powerful, it ended in failure.

Seeing that their time had not yet come, the workingmen changed their tactics, and taking advantage of the fact that they were now organized in unions, for about a generation they conducted a purely economic struggle, which, chiefly by the weapon of the Disraeli strike, frequently brought them reduced hours of work carries the and increased wages. Then they returned to the assault second Parliamentary of the citadel of politics; and not only because they had Reform meanwhile become a vast army but also because they had Bill, 1867 unified their power by means of local and national trade-union federations, their demands could no longer be overlooked. Both Gladstone, the leader of the Liberal party, and Disraeli, the leader of the Conservatives, recognized the necessity of yielding, but could not immediately persuade their followers to take their view. At length in 1867 Disraeli carried a new or second Parliamentary Reform Bill. Again it was a moderate, conservative measure built along the lines of the earlier Act. It authorized a redistribution of 58 seats in the interests of a more equal representation; but, above all (and here lies the significance of the reform), it widened the suffrage. In the case of the counties it cut the property qualification in half, while in the boroughs it conceded the vote to all householders, regardless of the worth of the house, as well as to lodgers in tenements whose lodgings were worth £10 a year. As the skilled mechanics could meet this last condition, it followed that the reform of 1867 substantially enfranchised the unionized workers.

Conceding that this was a democratic measure, it was not universal suffrage. In their deliberate manner the British preferred to move slowly and to retain as much of their traditional system as possible. **Gladstone carries the third Parliamentary Reform Act, 1884** By 1884 they were ready for a third Parliamentary Reform Act sponsored by Gladstone and the Liberal party. By this measure, in the effort to remove certain remaining inequalities, there was again a partial redistribution of seats, but the outstanding feature of the bill was the application of the borough franchise to the counties. In consequence the agricultural laborers, provided they were £10 householders or lodgers, were admitted to the vote. It was estimated that after 1885 over 1,800,000 grown men were still excluded from the polls because they could not meet the requirements of the law; but as, for the most part, they were uneducated and unorganized casual laborers, they failed to get a hearing for their case.

Under these circumstances there might have been no further extension of the parliamentary franchise if the women had not, toward the end of the century, begun an agitation for political **Female suffrage agitation and the Franchise Act of 1918** emancipation. Despite or perhaps because of the extravagant antics of a militant group among them, humorously called suffragettes, successive ministries long refused to make the slightest concession. Then in 1914 the Great War broke out, and in 1918 the government, obliged to recognize the patriotism shown not only by the women of the country but also by the still disfranchised men, brought in and carried what we may call the fourth Parliamentary Reform Bill. Though it lies beyond the scope of this chapter it must be briefly sketched to complete the story of the evolution of the British franchise. Now at last the old patch-work procedure of the older bills was dropped in favor of universal male suffrage; and not content with the enfranchisement of all men over 21 years of age, the parliament partially at least conceded female suffrage by giving the vote to practically all women over 30.

If its progressive democratization is the conspicuous fact of British political history in the nineteenth century, and if the cause of this transformation may truthfully be discovered in the spread of new ideas and programs, a still more fundamental search will confront us with the social-economic changes brought about by the Industrial Revolution. As this close connection between social and political movements has been developed else- where, as it constitutes indeed one of the persistent assumptions underlying this history, it does not require restatement at this point. The perpetual social-political inter-play may, however, be illuminatingly brought to the reader's mind in connection with the new class of factory workers, to whom we now desire briefly to direct attention. Let us concede that their partial political emancipation in 1867 was a significant manifestation of power and that they owed this triumph chiefly to their having taken their destiny into their own hands by means of their federated trade unions. But long before they had gone thus far on the road of self-help, they had by the mere fact of their presence in the social body drawn attention to themselves, and by virtue of their depressed status had provoked a challenge of the dominant *laissez-faire* philosophy. The view that the state is a cold, detached observer of the activities of its members could not be maintained in the presence of the intolerable miseries piled by the employers on the employees. Courageous men obliged the British ruling classes to see the brutal industrial facts, and slowly, reluctantly even, parliament undertook to ease the lot of the workers by protective legislation. In 1833 it passed the first Factory Act. A more moderate interference with the "freedom of contract" proclaimed by the middle classes can hardly be conceived, for the law fixed a maximum working day of 9 hours for children under 13 years and a maximum of 12 hours for young persons from 13 to 18 years. In 1842 followed the Mines Act. It had been preceded by a parliamentary investigation which laid bare to view the almost incredible conditions in the mining industry. Under the shock of this information the Mines Act became a law, thenceforth forbidding underground work for women as well as for boys under 10 years of age. Slight restrictions indeed! But they inaugurated a new policy of governmental watchfulness and were followed by ever new acts which, after still further reducing hours of labor, provided for heat, light, and fresh air, instituted protective devices against dangerous machinery, and subjected all factories to rigorous inspection. By 1878 this industrial legislation had grown to such proportions that it had to be coördinated by being fused into a single Act; and with

[margin note: Labor agitation]

protective measures dropping after 1878 at an even accelerated rate from the legislative mill a new general labor code had to be drawn up in 1901.

By the beginning of the twentieth century very few people were left in England who were prepared to uphold the old unimpaired *laissez-faire* doctine. The right and duty of the state to protect its **The Insurance Legislation of 1906–1911** weakest members, that is, something like a return to the patriarchal views of the Middle Age, had firmly established themselves in the conscience of society. And therewith the ground had been cleared for that further advance represented by Insurance Legislation. Originated in Germany by Bismarck under conditions which will be examined in their place, it was taken over by the Liberal party under the leadership of Lloyd George, and in the period 1906–1911 led to the adoption of four notable types of insurance for working people. The afflictions which render the worker's lot particularly cruel are sickness, accident, invalidism through old age, and unemployment. The great British Insurance Code attempts to alleviate these four evils by benefits from public funds created in varying ways by contributions from three sources, the employers, the employed, and the state.

Undeniably socialist in character but put through by the Liberal party, the British Insurance Code measures the distance travelled by economic opinion since the emergence of *laissez-faire* over a **Labor organizes its own political party** hundred years before. But let us not deceive ourselves. The Liberal party, the party of the middle classes, had by the beginning of the twentieth century become the champion of socialist measures for the sole reason that it wished to keep its labor following from passing out of its camp. Long before 1900 certain radical workingmen had indicated a desire to abandon the old parties, which, although they had undoubtedly made concessions to the lower orders, were basically and ineradicably bourgeois, and to form a party pursuing an exclusive labor program. In the early nineties such a party was actually launched, but the organized workers in their vast majority fought shy of it as something unfamiliar and perilous. Before another decade the Trade Unions themselves at last reached the conclusion that their interests would be best promoted by a political party of their own, and accordingly, in 1900, their party, called the Labor party, saw the light. Presenting itself to the public with a moderate program, it has gradually adopted the full socialist demand of collective ownership of mines, railroads, and factories. On the whole the Labor party has since its inception steadily grown in parliamentary representation, although the ingrained British conservatism, noticeable even among workingmen, keeps a considerable proportion of their number loyal to the older parties. In any case since 1900 there have been three, instead of two, predominating parties fighting for control in Great Britain. Should the Labor party continue to add to its strength, it may happen in the not too distant future that all elements opposed to its program of complete socialization will combine, regardless of the old Liberal-Conservative differences. A single party upholding the existing individualist order would then confront a Labor party dedicated to the creation of a collectivist society.

One of the gravest issues confronting Great Britain since 1815 has been Ireland. All the grievances of Ireland can be summed up in a single phrase: it was a conquered country. In order to break its resistance the conquerors had gradually dispossessed the **The case of** Irish of their land, had imposed their own Anglican **Ireland** Church upon the island in spite of the fact that the natives staunchly adhered to Catholicism, had planted Anglo-Scotch colonists in the province of Ulster, had organized a purely Protestant local administration, and finally, in 1800, had destroyed the last remnant of Irish independence by merging the Irish parliament with the British parliament at Westminster. Rarely in history has one people forged more terrible chains for another people than the English forged for the Irish.

Not long after 1815 a movement began among the Irish which aimed at removing some of the disabilities resting upon them. Its leader, Daniel O'Connell, directed his efforts against the exceptional laws in force against Catholics and was largely instru- **Settlement** mental in producing the legislation of 1829 which won for **of the reli-** all Catholics throughout the British realm full civil rights. **gious and** He next agitated for a repeal of the Act of Union (1800) **land issues** in the hope of gaining for Ireland a modest measure of autonomy. The government responded by suppressing him and his movement by force. However, the Irish, now thoroughly aroused, continued their agitation by means of secret societies which did not scruple to carry on private warfare against the English landlords by maiming cattle, burning farms, and even by occasional murders. By the sixties the situation had become so intolerable that Gladstone at the head of a Liberal ministry resolved to ease the situation by removing some of the more conspicuous evils of which the Irish complained. In 1869 he passed an act which disestablished the Anglican Church in Ireland, known to the law as the Irish Church. The tithes which the Catholic peasants had been obliged to pay to maintain a hostile establishment thus disappeared; and although the Anglican Church was permitted to retain its buildings and a part of its estates, it was put henceforward on an equal footing with the Catholic Church. This resolute step toward righting Irish wrongs Gladstone immediately followed by another. In 1870 he passed the first Land Act which planned to protect the Irish tenants against the excessive powers of their landlords. These, as a result of the confiscations of the previous centuries, were not only, generally speaking, English gentry but, in addition, absentees who managed their estates through agents. Owing to the fact that the law had been made by the conquerors, the Irish peasants enjoyed no security on their farms and could be evicted from them at the pleasure of the owners. Another evil, over-population, made a bad situation worse by inducing the peasants to raise the rent by bidding recklessly against each other to the delight and advantage of the landlords. However, the terrible famine of 1845 followed by emigration on a large scale to America gradually reduced this particular affliction. What the Act of 1870 and a second Gladstonian measure of 1881 tried to do was to give the farmers a better tenure; but no sooner had the Irish gained this point than they made it plain that nothing short of complete repossession of the land would satisfy them. In 1891 the Conservative ministry of Lord Salisbury, weary of the interminable agitation of the lesser island, resolved to meet the Irish wishes and by means of the Land Purchase Act of that year enabled the peasants to buy their lands out of a fund put at their disposal by the government. Prospective purchasers had to agree to reimburse the government by means of small annual interest payments extending over a number of decades. The Land Purchase Act of 1891 together with supplementary legislation of a later date has effectively settled the vexed land question by abolishing the landlords and raising the Irish farmers to the level of active and self-respecting peasant-proprietors.

Meanwhile the movement for autonomy or home rule begun by O'Connell had never entirely died out. In the eighties it powerfully revived under the guidance of a clever politician, Parnell, who

resolved to employ his following of approximately 80 Irish members
to obstruct the business of the house of Commons until home rule
was given a fair hearing. When, as a result of the elections of 1885,
neither Conservatives nor Liberals commanded a majority **The Irish**
without Irish help, the Liberals entered into an agreement **demand**
with the Irish by virtue of which, in return for Parnell's **home rule**
support, Gladstone promised to back the Irish demand. However,
his Home Rule Bill was defeated in the Commons by the default
of a section of the Liberal party (1886). On returning to office
in 1895 Gladstone successfully pushed a second Home Rule Bill
through the Commons only to have it defeated in the Lords.
Thereupon for more than a decade, during which the Conservatives
governed the country, the home rule issue slumbered. Even after
the Liberals had again gained power (1906), they failed to take action
on home rule until a decline in the number of their supporters forced
them once more to seek the alliance of the Irish party. As a result
a third Home Rule Bill was introduced into the Commons in 1912
which passed that body and would in 1914 have gone into effect, had
it not been suspended by the outbreak of the World War.

At this juncture it becomes necessary to observe that from 1912
on the chief objection to Irish autonomy came not from the British
parliament but from the Anglo-Scotch colonists settled since the
seventeenth century in the province of Ulster. A power- **The Act of**
ful and active group of Protestant farmers and indus- **1920**
trialists centered about the thriving city of Belfast, they **creates two**
refused to be separated from the mother-country and **states:**
Northern
prepared to resist the application to themselves of home **Ireland and**
rule with force. This uncompromising attitude of the **the Irish**
Protestant North had the dire effect of bringing the **Free State**
irreconcilable elements of the Catholic South to the front. Organized under the Celtic name of *Sinn Fein*, meaning Ourselves
Alone, they prepared the ground for a complete separation from
Great Britain and the establishment of an Irish republic. On
Easter day, 1916, a small extremist group of Sinn Feiners actually
rose in rebellion, resolved to take advantage of the embarrassment of
the British lion caught in the net of the World War. With a force
hurriedly despatched to the Irish shores the London government
swiftly and bloodily suppressed the mad attempt. However, if the
Irish masses did not approve the armed rebellion, it soon appeared
that they were behind the independence program of Sinn Fein almost

to a man. On the termination of the World War the Irish problem
therefore presented an entirely new face: the suspended Home Rule
Act of 1914 was rejected by the Irish of the North because it conceded too much and by the Irish of the South because it did not concede enough. Not only was it impossible to apply the Act, but a
passionate unrest, accompanied by wild excesses of arson and murder,
seized upon the whole country. In an effort to compose the strife the
British parliament passed (1920) a new Government of Ireland Act
which, frankly acknowledging that Ireland was made up of two
peoples, created two states, North and South, each with its own parliament and executive. The Irish North, consisting of six counties of
northeastern Ulster, was hardly one-sixth as large as the Irish South
but it contained one-third as many people. Against the settlement of
1920, which the North accepted, the South at first raised a wild outcry;
but, a year later, a group of leading Sinn Feiners signed an agreement
with the British government at London which represented a compromise. While the demand for unqualified independence in the form
of an Irish republic was surrendered by the Irish negotiators, they
were offered and accepted the same measure of self-government as is
enjoyed by Canada and the other dominions of Great Britain; furthermore, in order to proclaim its relative sovereignty to the world the
southern section was to be known as the Irish Free State. Although
a minority of irreconcilable republicans refused to accept this compromise and even went the length of offering armed resistance, the
Irish Free State has apparently succeeded in winning the support of
the people. Its greatest remaining problem consists in evolving a
method of harmonious coöperation with its neighbor state to the north.
Only if these two groups and polities succeed in finding common
ground can the Irish problem be said to have expelled its last and most
deep-seated poison.

Far and away the greatest single interest of British life and politics
since 1815 has been the continued marvelous expansion of the British
Empire. While the eighteenth century had brought Great Britain
a secure ascendancy in Canada and India, it had more
than balanced this advantage by the loss of the prosperous colonies which became the United States of America. There followed the long conflict with Napoleon
which confirmed the British command of the seas; and
from this naval supremacy, taken in connection with the rapid multiplication of British trade under the stimulus of the Industrial Revo-

The
marvelous
expansion
of the Brit-
ish Empire

lution, sprang a new era of colonial expansion which completely
dwarfed the earlier one. Already the Vienna settlement of 1815 had
poured into Britain's lap a veritable cornucopia of strategic naval
stations, such as the islands of Malta, Ceylon, and Heligoland; best
of all, it had yielded the former African colony of the Dutch, the
Cape of Good Hope. The following generations witnessed a steady
enlargement of authority proceeding from a dozen separate centers.
In India the British direct rule was constantly extended and at the
same time more and more native states were by diplomacy or war
brought under indirect control by acknowledging British suzerainty.
In Canada the vast, half-frozen stretches of the west and north,
traversed by a few scattered tribes of Indians, were gradually sub-
dued and endowed with an effective administration. Using the Cape
of Good Hope as a starting-point, British colonials slowly pushed
northward in southern Africa until they were rewarded with the
prospect of another mighty conquest. Somewhat later, in the
eighties, a footing was won at the other end of Africa, in Egypt.
These two positions at the extreme north and south prompted the
desire to join them together by securing the heart of the continent,
the equatorial jungle. One of the finest, if not immediately the
most profitable, acquisitions was the island-continent of Australia.
The earlier colonial movement had neglected it, largely because of
its inaccessibility. With the development of steamships this difficulty
was largely overcome, and beginning with the generation after 1815,
Great Britain took up with constantly increasing energy the settlement of the vast and sparsely inhabited plains of this remote land.
To recapitulate: India, Canada, South Africa, Egypt, Equatorial
Africa, Australia with New Zealand constitute the proud roster of
British colonial enterprises developed since 1815. But scores of
scattered possessions, chiefly islands distributed over the face of all
the seas, would have to be enumerated if full justice were to be done
to Britain's amazing colonial fabric.

These almost countless territories assembled under the British
crown make up the present British Empire. On the eve of the World
War the Empire embraced nearly a quarter of the land surface of
the globe and slightly more than a quarter of the world's population.
Created primarily by an invincible navy, the immense structure
rested, and continues to rest, on this instrument of power. However, this primacy of the fleet does not mean that the army has
had no part in amassing the territories in question. It has played a

distinguished role, especially in Africa and Asia, where numerous, if backward, populations resisted British rule until persuaded of its advantages by the argument of the sword. And yet, fully admitting The Empire that armed power was and is a leading factor in the colo-created by nial system, we should not fail to see that the main urge commerce and sus- behind the expansion movement was undoubtedly com-tained by merce. Most appropriately therefore Great Britain is armed force symbolized not only as a helmeted goddess with a trident in one hand and a sword in the other but also as John Bull, the shrewd trader, standing on the deck of a ship or sitting on a wharf amidst crowded bales and boxes.

Though the London authorities failed to draw an immediate lesson from the revolt of the American colonists, they gradually gave increased consideration to the problems of colonial government Colonial and in the course of several generations have worked out govern- a system which has aroused a very general admiration. ment: (1) Broadly speaking the colonies fall under two heads: (1) the self-governing self-governing colonies; (2) Crown colonies. Self-govern-colonies ment was by careful degrees conceded to all those colonies predominantly settled by whites from the homeland as well as from the other states of Europe. Conspicuous in this group toward the middle of the nineteenth century were Canada, Australia, New Zealand, and Cape Colony (South Africa). On the basis of laws passed by the British parliament the management of local affairs was increasingly put into provincial hands until in the end the home government retained for itself little beside the control of foreign policy. But not only did these colonies become self-governing under a ministry responsible to an elected assembly, but presently contiguous settlements were given the right to federate. The decisive step in this direction was taken in 1867 by the formation of the Dominion of Canada composed of the four originally separate provinces of Quebec, Ontario, New Brunswick, and Nova Scotia. Later additions brought the vast areas of the west (British Columbia) and the north (Hudson Bay Territory) into the Canadian union. This agglomeration of self-governing units involved the elaboration of a federal Canadian constitution with a federal parliament and ministry. By the end of the century Australia had reached the point where it was prepared to follow the Canadian example. At that time six separate colonies — New South Wales, Victoria, Tasmania, South Australia, Queensland, West Australia — were enjoying a prosperous existence to which they resolved to give a greater security by federating under the name of the Commonwealth of Australia (1900).

Obstacles to federation, difficult to surmount, were encountered only in South Africa. They had their root in history. Cape Colony, acquired in 1815, had been originally settled by Dutch peasant-farmers, familiarly called Boers. As the establishment of British authority was unwelcome to them, considerable numbers sought new homes by trekking northward. There, in the haunts of savages and wild beasts, they founded the two republics of the Transvaal and the Orange River Free State. The accidental discovery of gold (1884) in the Transvaal disturbed the quiet existence of the simple farmers by drawing a flood of adventurous foreigners, chiefly British, into their territory. These newcomers, instinctively hostile to the ponderous, patriarchal government of the Boers, desired annexation to Cape Colony and created a state of friction which led ultimately to a war. In a fierce and prolonged struggle (1899–1902) the British government championed the cause of its nationals against the two republics. Although the Boers defended themselves valiantly, they were overwhelmed by the great forces mobilized by their powerful enemy and in the end the two farmer-republics were extinguished. However, in spite of its use of military means, Great Britain soon gave evidence of not having lost faith in the self-governing system which it had evolved. Before many years had passed the Transvaal and the Orange Free State were conceded a measure of home rule, and in 1909 all four contiguous colonies — the Cape, Natal, and the two ex-republics — were fused into a single state called the South African Union. Owing to the fact that a population of about 1,000,000 whites was confronted with 6,000,000 native blacks it was considered advisable to form a single strong government rather than a federation of four weak states. In this respect therefore the South African Union differs from Canada and Australia which are genuine federations of self-governing units.

On turning next to the Crown colonies, we observe that the Crown exercises authority in them through an appointed governor, but that a certain measure of self-government, varying in amount with each instance under examination, is not unusual. The distinguishing feature of the Crown colonies is that they are settled by natives (black, brown, or yellow) who are, judged by European standards, of a backward mentality. Exceptions to this criterion for Crown government are points like Gibraltar and Malta, which, though their population is preponderantly white, are ruled as Crown colonies because of their supreme strategical importance. At the beginning of the twentieth century India and Egypt were far and away the most important possessions of Great Britain with non-European populations. In each a system of control obtains which is technically Crown government but which is individual enough to call for a special word.

The government of Egypt presents so many anomalies as to be fairly *sui generis*. When the country of the Nile was occupied in 1882 by force of arms, the government of the local ruler, the khedive, **The** was not disturbed nor the fiction challenged that Egypt **government** was a province of the Ottoman Empire. However, the **of Egypt** government of the khedive was expected exactly to carry out the orders of the British resident at Cairo, whose power rested in last analysis on an occupying British force. In 1914, on Turkey's entering the World War on the side of Germany, Great Britain usurped the place of the Ottoman Empire and without particularly changing its methods of control proclaimed Egypt a protectorate. The long war worked a great change in the mental attitude of the Egyptians. They loyally coöperated with Great Britain while the conflict lasted, but, expecting to be rewarded with an improved status, in 1919 they almost unanimously demanded the recognition of their independent status. In the face of a torrential nationalist sentiment Great Britain offered concessions, and in 1922 went the length of declaring Egypt "an independent, sovereign state" and of conceding to its ruler the title king. However, since London reserved its rights in the Suez Canal zone as well as in the province of the upper Nile, known as the Sudan, and moreover, since the newly fledged Egyptian government insists on disputing these rights, the situation contains dangerously explosive elements. It remains to be seen what the recently conceded independence of Egypt will amount to in the end.

What is familiarly known as British India is really a vast tropical and semi-tropical continent, cut off from the rest of Asia by the Himalaya mountains and supporting a mass of 325,000,000 inhab-**The case** itants. They are of forty or fifty different races, speak **of India** over one hundred distinct tongues, and have as the leading element of union the Hindu religion which boasts about 200,000,000 followers. However, the existence of 70,000,000 vigorous Mohammedans must not be overlooked as an element of religious differentiation. After the expulsion of the French in the eighteenth century the area under British control was steadily enlarged. All this time the political control was shared between the merchants of the East India Company and a board appointed by the government. There can be no doubt that good work was done and that a greater measure of security was attained than the distracted realm had known for many a generation. However, there were frequent wars, chiefly on the border toward Afghanistan; and one extremely dangerous revolt occurred which must be recorded because it had important political consequences. In 1857 the native soldiers, called Sepoys, mutinied and raised a rebellion which was put down only by the greatest exertions on the part of the home government. Blaming the mutiny to the policy of divided control, the parliament took the important step of extinguishing the East India Company and vesting the sovereignty of India solely in the Crown, represented in England by a Secretary of State for India and in India itself by a Viceroy with an executive council (1858). Thus ended one of the most famous commercial companies of history. After some decades of experimentation with the new system the natives were given an inconsiderable voice in affairs by representation in a legislative council, made up preponderantly of British officials. Although the Indians, like the Egyptians, gave Great Britain loyal support during the World War, under the excitement of the struggle they developed fond hopes of a self-government which would ultimately expand into complete independence. To placate the popular clamor the British parliament passed (1919) a bill which conceded an increased measure of native participation both in the central and the provincial administrations. But the extremists, led by a saintly spirit, Gandhi by name, have rejected the British concessions, and by a policy of non-coöperation, which strictly eschews violence, have attempted so to disgust the British with their task as to persuade them voluntarily to abandon it. No one may say what will become of the issue. Undoubtedly the British still maintain an iron grip on the peninsula; but encountering passive resistance and sullen looks on every hand, they are by no means bedded on roses.

The British Empire is one of the most impressive features of the world of today. While its future seems assured, it also raises a wealth of interesting questions. So far as the self-governing, English-speaking colonies are concerned, their uninterrupted growth in numbers and power is as certain as anything can be on this uncertain earth of ours. As for the dark-skinned, subject peoples, on the other hand, such as the Indians and Egyptians, their case carries a The future much larger element of risk. Will they cut the British tie, of the Brit- and having cut it, will they, oriental groups without a ish Empire commanding national tradition, be able without external help to endow themselves with occidental institutions and an occidental mind? Any answer to this question would be wholly speculative. Again, conceding that the bond between the mother-country and the white dominions is still strong, may it not be slowly transformed into a matter of spirit and good will rather than of law and authority? Certainly the tendency throughout recent decades has been for the dominions to assert an increasing measure of political and moral independence. Nevertheless the threads the spirit spins are powerful, as the vigorous support given the homeland by the dominions during the World War amply demonstrates. Granting that spirit ties are tenuous indeed, it may yet be that they have that about them which makes them stronger and more enduring than ponderous political machinery.

Sovereigns of Great Britain Since the Eighteenth Century

George III, 1760–1820
George IV (son of George III), 1820–1830
William IV (younger brother of George IV), 1830–1837
Victoria (niece of William IV; *m*. Albert of Saxe-Coburg) 1837–1901
Edward VII (son of Victoria and Albert), 1901–1910
George V (son of Edward VII), 1910–

REFERENCES

C. J. H. HAYES, *Political and Social History*, II, pp. 28–37, 102–16, chs. 22, 29
C. D. HAZEN, *Europe Since 1815*, I, chs. 21–26
J. S. SCHAPIRO, *Modern and Contemporary Europe*, chs. 4, 5, 13, 15
E. FUETER, *World History*, chs. 6, 14, 18, 20, 21
C. M. ANDREWS, *Development of Modern Europe*, II, chs. 2, 8
A. L. CROSS, *History of England*, chs. 46–49, 54–57
G. B. ADAMS, *Constitutional History of England*, chs. 17–20
G. SLATER, *Making of Modern England*, chs. 15–23
Cambridge Modern History, IX, ch. 23, X, chs. 18–20, 22, XI, chs. 1, 11–13, 26, 27, XII, chs. 3, 4, 16, 17
G. P. GOOCH, *History of Our Time*, chs. 1, 6–8; *History of Modern Europe*
C. OMAN, *England in the Nineteenth Century*
G. M. TREVELYAN, *British History in the Nineteenth Century; Lord Grey of the Reform Bill; Life of John Bright*
J. H. ROSE, *Rise and Growth of Democracy in Great Britain; William Pitt and the National Revival*

J. A. R. Marriott, *England Since Waterloo*
W. L. Davidson, *Political Thought in England*
F. A. Ogg, *Economic Development of Europe*, chs. 3-8
H. de Gibbins, *English Social Reformers*
W. L. Blease, *Short History of English Liberalism; The Emancipation of English Women*
F. Jenks, *Short History of English Law*
B. L. Hutchins and A. Harrison, *History of Factory Legislation*
B. H. Holland, *The Fall of Protection*
J. Morley, *Life of Richard Cobden; Life of W. E. Gladstone*
G. Balfour, *The Educational System of Great Britain and Ireland*
L. Strachey, *Eminent Victorians; Life of Queen Victoria*
J. W. Morris, *Great Britain and Ireland*
E. R. Turner, *Ireland and England*
H. Plunkett, *Ireland in the New Century*
F. Hackett, *Ireland*
F. S. Marvin, *Century of Hope*, chs. 8, 12
A. F. Pollard, *The British Empire*
H. H. Fyffe, *The New Spirit in Egypt*
A. D. Innes, *England and the British Empire*

CHAPTER XXIX

ITALY, FRANCE, GERMANY, AND AUSTRIA-HUNGARY
FROM 1870 TO 1914

ITALY

As we have seen, in the period 1861–1870 the main interest of the new kingdom of Italy turned around the acquisition of Venice and Rome. None the less the problems of internal reconstruction **The new** claimed a large measure of attention, and after 1870, **kingdom of** with the government triumphantly established in the **Italy faces** ancient capital on the Tiber, they pushed more insistently **the prob-** than ever to the front. Owing to the pressure of a strong, **lems of** unitarian nationalism, the federal idea was rejected by **domestic** **reconstruc-** the royal government in favor of a centralized adminis- **tion** tration on the French pattern. New Italy was cast into a single, solid, and unbroken mold, but this administrative leveling and fusing of the historical provinces of Italy demanded as its corollary a general equalization in the social and economic fields. And this was far from easy because of a profound cleavage between the North and the South of the peninsula which dated back to the Middle Age. During the Renaissance the North had become the leading city area of the world; and although, beginning with the sixteenth century, it had greatly declined in relative importance, it was still a region of urban middle classes sufficiently alert to attempt to appropriate the advantages of the Industrial Revolution. In this effort, inaugurated toward the middle of the nineteenth century, the northern towns met, however, with only partial success owing to the fateful circumstance that Italy had few mineral resources and practically no iron or coal, the familiar bases of every effective industrialization. Italy was obliged to import these articles, thus making them unduly expensive. Fortunately a partial compensation for the country's fuel deficiencies was gradually secured through the development of electricity from the ample streams flowing from the Alps. The Italians refer to the upland snow which feeds these streams as their "white coal," and from its progressive appropriation and transformation into motive power they confidently expect an intensive future industrialization. Up to 1914

588

this was at best in its early stages and was moreover strictly limited to the North.

Although its industry was advancing, the North continued to depend for support largely on its agriculture. Its staples have been and still are wheat, wine, and olive oil which together provide the diet of the average Italian. The division of the land of the northern provinces into small holdings worked by a laborious peasantry created what may be described, on the whole, as a satisfactory social situation, although the absence of modern farming implements and methods revealed a backward economic system. But if the non-industrial, wholly agricultural, South was already out of harmony with the North by reason of the absence of a city culture, it was further differentiated from the more advanced section by virtue of its peculiar agrarian organization. For the southern land was held in great estates by the descendants of the old feudal barons and was cultivated by peasants working in great gangs as day-laborers. They constituted an agricultural proletariat, more wretched even than the urban proletariat produced by the industrialization of the North. There was also a difference in the products of the soil. The South, too, grew wheat, olive oil, and wine, but its warm climate enabled it to cultivate, besides, such citrous fruits as oranges and lemons.

The urban North confronts an agricultural South

These facts will serve to emphasize that there were really two Italies, the one removed from the other by the whole distance which separates the Medieval from the Modern Age. An active urban North leaning on a self-respecting responsible peasantry was confronted with a feudal South of great lords resting on oppressed laborers and boasting no more than a scattering of townsmen to leaven the dull agricultural mass. The problem before the government of Victor Emmanuel II was therefore grave; and with entire propriety legislation took the form of an effort to raise the backward South somewhat nearer the level of the more advanced North. Railroads and highways were built, brigandage, one of the rooted evils of the South, was suppressed, and the frightful illiteracy rather half-heartedly attacked by the opening of occasional public schools. The educational situation even in the North was none too good, and, owing to the pressure of other needs, was not systematically taken in hand till 1877 when the first step was taken toward making elemen-

Public works, education, and national defense produce heavy taxation and an annual deficit

tary education universal and compulsory. As schools cost money and Italy is poor, the new public school system only slowly spread into the remoter provinces with the result that, though illiteracy has steadily decreased, it still afflicts a considerable proportion of the population, especially in the South. If to the outlay occasioned by these and other productive public enterprises are added the unproductive expenditures incurred in connection with the national army and navy, with which the youthful kingdom, aspiring to play the role of a great power, believed it was unable to dispense, we can understand another phenomenon which presently arose to vex the country. This was the necessity of heavy taxation coupled, in spite of its severity, with the inability of the government to make the budget balance. However, toward the close of the nineteenth century the steadily growing prosperity of the country at last returned sufficient revenue to wipe out the deficit, and Italy entered the twentieth century under happier financial and economic auspices. They ruled undisturbed until the outbreak of the World War.

None the less one social-economic evil, emigration, continued to trouble the improved fortunes of the nation. While it was due primarily to the high birth-rate and the accompanying phenomenon of over-population, it flowed in part from the depressing conditions of the South, as is clearly proved by the fact that the emigrants hailed and continue to hail chiefly from that section. Many factors enter into the problem. The introduction of machinery, wherever it takes place, makes it possible to work the fields with fewer hands; the increased competition among laborers lowers wages and swells unemployment; finally, since the close of the nineteenth century American producers have flooded the north-European markets with citrous fruits and cut down the south-Italian exports. That emigration was the only possible escape from this critical situation is proved by the statistics showing that anywhere from a quarter to a half million people, chiefly south-Italians, have since the beginning of the twentieth century left the peninsula every year. They have gone to every country of the world but more particularly to South and North America (the Argentine and the United States). When foreign countries decide for reasons of their own to close the doors to the Italian influx — and signs pointing to a restrictive policy began to multiply long before 1914 — the problem of emigration will enter for Italy upon a new and directly dangerous phase. For with unemployment breeding misery and discontent and with all avenues of escape barred by restrictive legislation the country will be exposed to violent internal fermentation.

Another domestic issue, which has so far defied all solutions, is presented by the latent war between the state and the Church. The papacy, in its temporal aspect an Italian state, had opposed Italian unification with the result that its outlying territories were seized by force and that in 1870 Rome itself was taken and proclaimed the nation's capital. Resolved to carry through a transformation in accordance with modern secular demands, the young kingdom closed many monastic establishments and repeatedly confiscated the property of the Church. In exchange, it is true, it undertook to pay the salaries of the clergy. In view of his historic claims the pope could not but meet these measures, one and all, with implacable hostility. Following the capture of Rome, he appealed to Catholics the world over for help, and in order effectively to dramatize his situation he declared himself a "prisoner in the Vatican," closely beset by the Italian kingdom as by a besieging army. Largely to placate Catholic sentiment with solemn assurances of the pope's essential liberty of action, the Italian parliament, immediately after the occupation of Rome, adopted (1871) the Law of the Papal Guarantees, by which the government pledged itself to treat the pope as a sovereign on a par with the king of Italy, to permit him freely to send and receive ambassadors, and to concede to him all other rights associated with sovereignty. As a guarantee of his independent status his two great palaces with their gardens, the Vatican and the Lateran, were made extra-territorial, that is, the authority of the Italian government was declared not to extend over them. Pius IX promptly refused to recognize this law from fear that his acceptance of it would be construed as a relinquishment of all his other claims. His successors have without exception taken the same stand. Nevertheless the royal government which passed the law considers itself bound by it and hopes with a policy of patient waiting to bring the papacy to a more conciliatory frame of mind. Many people have professed to see a first evidence of papal yielding in the practical abolition under Pius X (1903-1914) of the so-called *non expedit*. This was a Bull issued by Pius IX forbidding faithful Catholics to vote or hold office under the royal government. However, even though this prohibition has been withdrawn, it may well be that the permission thus accorded to Catholics to accept public responsibilities was inspired by the papal desire to gain a

[margin note: Latent war between state and Church]

greater influence in domestic politics. Undeniably the state and the Church have since the beginning of the twentieth century come to a somewhat better understanding, but it would be a gross exaggeration to declare that their latent warfare has come to an end.

Like all states caught in the currents of modern life Italy has become increasingly democratic. For many years property and educational qualifications limited the vote to the well-to-do, but successive **Democracy,** extensions of the suffrage culminated at last in the reform **nationalism,** of 1912 which practically established universal manhood **and foreign** suffrage. Italian foreign policy has been inspired by the **policy** characteristic modern forces of democracy and nationalism with of course the Industrial Revolution as a contributory factor. Since after 1870 certain small areas of Austria-Hungary, more particularly the Trentino (the area around the city of Trent) and the Adriatic littoral around the city of Triest, although Italian in character, still remained outside the kingdom, they were hotly coveted by nationalist circles. In so far as these same circles exhibited the type of thinking imposed by capitalism and the industrial movement, they looked, rather than to Trent and Triest, to the Mediterranean sea as an appropriate field for Italian expansion. Since a policy directed toward further Austrian acquisitions implied war with Austria and since a Mediterranean advance might precipitate war with France, the government maintained a fluctuating attitude in foreign affairs until brought to a decision by an aggressive act of its Latin neighbor. In 1881 France seized Tunis, which brought her colonial territory close to Sicily. Thereupon Italy, which desired Tunis for itself, showed its resentment by entering into an alliance, celebrated as the Triple Alliance, with Germany and Austria-Hungary (1882). From now on Italy, fortified by the Triple Alliance, was free to proceed more boldly with its Mediterranean plans and embarked on an imperialist policy which did not prove an unbroken record of success. The government gained a foothold in Eritrea on the Red sea, but when it attempted to proceed inland and subjugate the independent state of Abyssinia, it met with a signal defeat (1896). Somewhat sobered, the country refused for a while to sanction further African adventures. Therefore it was not till 1911 that the government considered itself strong enough to appropriate Tripoli, for which it had felt a furtive passion for over two decades. As Tripoli belonged to the Ottoman Empire, a war had to be fought with the Turks (1911–1912) before the Tripolitan fruit could be harvested.

This war, enthusiastically supported by the population, indicated that the nationalist and imperialist sentiments were rapidly mounting to a flood. As the same phenomenon, observable at this time everywhere else in Europe, was setting the stage for the World War, Italy's participation in the struggle, in the hope of sharing in the spoils, might be looked on as assured.

FRANCE

It was the National Assembly which, as the ruling power of France, made peace with victorious Germany in 1871 and at the same time put down the savage insurrection of the capital, known as the Commune. It next took up the task of giving France a defini- Why the tive government. Perhaps because the elections to the monarchist Assembly had occurred during the distractions of the Assembly war, perhaps because the sentiment of the country was to establish not yet friendly to republicanism, about 500 out of the a monarchy 700 deputies elected were monarchists. Nothing therefore would have been easier than to abolish the republic, provisionally proclaimed on September 4, 1870, if only the monarchists could have agreed on a monarch. But here they encountered a difficulty. A large body of Orleanists desired to restore the grandson of Louis Philip, a smaller body of legitimists held out for the grandson of Charles X, and a handful of deputies were even found audacious enough to champion the heir of the discredited Napoleon III. Under the circumstances the monarchists so successfully frustrated themselves that their cause was lost. Only once, in 1873, did a ray of hope illumine their sky. By an agreement between Orleanists and legitimists the count of Chambord, the legitimist chief, was recognized as king on the understanding that he would acknowledge the Orleanist count of Paris as his successor. So far so good. But when the count of Chambord now insisted on the white banner of his Bourbon ancestors, the whole project collapsed because the Orleanists identified themselves with the revolutionary tricolor on the simple ground that French public opinion would accept no other flag.

Reluctantly therefore the Assembly took up the work of making the republic permanent. Thiers, the former Orleanist statesman, who served as the first president, indicated the gradual swing of opinion when he said. "The republic divides us least." However, when he came out somewhat too strongly for the republic, the monarchists revenged themselves by deposing him and electing Marshal MacMahon, a confessed monarchist, in his place (1873). Then by slow stages, yielding less to the behests of affection than of necessity, they passed the Constitutional Laws which established the republic (1873–1875). By these enactments the executive was vested in a president elected for a term of seven years by the two houses of the legislature meeting in common session. The two houses were called the Senate and chamber of Deputies respectively. While the senators were elected by local departmental bodies, the deputies directly represented the nation, which elected them on the basis of universal manhood suffrage. As the ministry must command a majority in the chamber of Deputies, this body has the power to make and unmake governments and must be accepted as the ruling element of the system. Its predominance so strikingly parallels that of the British house of Commons that the government of the French republic may be put in the same category as that of its neighbor across the channel. It may therefore be described as a parliamentary government with a purely decorative president charged, like the British king, with the exercise of merely representative functions.

The constitution of the Third Republic

When on the extinction of the National Assembly (1875) fresh elections were held, the republican parties carried the chamber of Deputies. The proof was thus given that the country was being converted to republican ideas. Of course the monarchists fought hard for their views, but their continued divisions lost them the favor of the voters, and in the elections of 1879 the upper house, too, was carried by their adversaries. Thereupon the monarchist President MacMahon resigned to make way for Grévy, a thorough-going republican. Thus, after a decade of uncertainty, France had become endowed with a constitution, a legislature, and an executive that were all republican. More and more firmly with each succeeding decade the republic became established in the good graces of the body of French citizens with the result that the monarchists gradually dwindled away to a negligible faction.

The nation converted to republicanism

In the light of its history since 1879 the republic may be described as democratic, nationalist, anti-clerical, and bourgeois. That means that the middle classes have consistently enjoyed the favor of the electors and have been able to impose the policies which accorded with their outlook and their interests. Of course they have encountered opposition not only from the monarchists and their close allies, the clericals, but in steadily increasing measure from the workingmen represented by the socialists. They have in consequence made occasional concessions both to the Right and to the Left, more particularly to the Left in the form of that *The administrative and military systems* Social Legislation with which every modern country has attempted to protect its industrial population against the extreme exploitation of the capitalists. Despite such favors to opponents, the history of the Third Republic remains, as stated, the record of a capable, energetic, and successful bourgeoisie. Its administrative system will bear out the contention. The centralization imposed on France by the first Napoleon and symbolized by the prefect who is appointed by and remains responsible to the national government, so exactly suited the unitarian sympathies of the bourgeoisie that no attempt was made to alter it. A slight concession to local opinion may be seen in the fact that with the prefect, head of the department, was associated a general council elected by manhood suffrage. However, as the central government reserved to itself the right to veto any act of the general council, the omnipotence of the ministry was hardly challenged. Among the earliest measures of the republic was the complete reorganization of the army, as was only natural after the military chaos precipitated by the German victory. It was natural, too, to imitate the system of the victors by adopting the principle of universal, compulsory military service. Enthusiastically nationalist in accordance with French middle class tradition, the republic has, since its establishment, spared no expenditures on either the army or navy and by tireless efforts has attempted to keep them on the same level of efficiency as the forces of the great rival state to the east.

More than by any other group of measures has the internal history of the Third Republic been colored by its open anti-clericalism. The reason why the Catholic Church drew the fire of the republicans is to be found in the circumstance that in the crucial *Anti-clericalism; the republic takes direction of primary education* decade of 1870 to 1880 the Church had hotly supported the cause of monarchy. No sooner did the republicans come into secure possession of the government than they showed their hand by launching a campaign for a public school system to be maintained by the state. This was a direct attack on the Church not only because the Church had always insisted that the education of the young was its own proper function, but also because in so far as there already existed a general primary school system in France it was under ecclesiastical direction. To be sure, the relatively large number of French illiterates proved that the system was very defective. Although this bad feature justified reform, it is undeniable that the republicans were moved to action chiefly by reason of their anti-monarchical bias. Beginning with 1881 they enacted a number of educational laws which gradually covered the country with public schools, taught by lay teachers and offering instruction free of charge. This state-directed system at once stimulated the Church to unwonted efforts with the result that the ecclesiastical schools, where teaching orders of brothers and sisters dispensed instruction, multiplied with great rapidity. Thus, France, which had always conspicuously lacked primary schools, suddenly had too many, that is, it had two rival systems competing with each other for the favor of the public! Not only did this competition frequently assume an exacerbated form, but the ecclesiastical schools were too often successful owing to the decisive moral influence exercised by the parish clergy over the minds of the peasants. At last the state resolved to end the conflict and set up an educational monopoly by closing the ecclesiastical schools. Instead however of striking a direct and open blow, it passed (1901) the Law of Associations which forbade a member of any unauthorized order (or association) to give instruction in a French school. As the ecclesiastical schools were staffed by orders (both brothers and sisters) which had never received formal authorization from the state, the teachers were automatically eliminated and most of the institutions obliged to close. In this manner the issue was decided in favor of the national system of free, lay schools.

Warming to the combat, the republicans now resolved to attack the Church in its last stronghold, the Concordat of 1801.[1] Not till Church and state had been completely divorced would they rest The divorce content, and since the Concordat of Napoleon's time made of Church the two institutions mutually dependent, there was and state enacted in 1905 the Law of Separation. By its terms the Concordat was abrogated; the state declined to continue to pay the salaries of clergymen; and the seizure of ecclesiastical property in 1789 was rounded off with a new confiscation. However, in order that public worship, with which the law professed not to interfere, might not be interrupted, the churches were to be made over to associations of Catholic laymen who assumed responsibility toward

[1] See p. 446.

the state. From this feature it is plain that the execution of the law depended on the willingness of the worshippers to form lay associations. But as such a directive activity on the part of the laity in Church affairs was contrary to canon law, and as, moreover, the pope clinched the matter by forbidding laymen to submit and by publicly condemning the law *in toto*, a complete deadlock resulted. It seemed more than likely at one time that the police would close the churches and that public worship would cease throughout the country. To avoid this grave offense of Catholic sentiment the parliament wisely gave way and passed (1907) a supplementary law permitting, as the canon law required, the clergy to take over the churches without the intervention of lay societies. That the last word has been spoken in this issue is very unlikely. However, as matters stand since 1905 Church and state in France are separated, the state no longer pays salaries to priests, and though public worship continues without interference, latent war exists between the ancient partners since the Church nurses a grievance and, speaking through the pope, has definitely refused to recognize the Law of Separation as binding.

The passionate and consistent anti-clericalism of the republican government has precipitated a number of crises which have threatened the very life of the state. The two most famous carry the respective labels of Boulanger and Dreyfus. Boulanger was a general who took advantage of the monarchical and clerical sentiments of the majority of the army officers to organize a violent opposition to the government. Though assuming dangerous proportions, at the moment for action the gallant general's courage failed him and, instead of organizing the expected *coup d'état*, he fled ignominiously to Belgium (1889). In sharp contrast to Boulanger, Dreyfus was not a conspirator but a victim. He was a captain in the army, a republican and a Jew, whom his Catholic and monarchical fellow-officers hated so fiercely that some of them went the length of forging documents, on the strength of which Dreyfus was degraded and sentenced to a long prison term as a traitor (1894). As a result of an agitation inaugurated by the novelist Zola, he was, after vigorous resistance on the part of the guilty army clique, at last fully cleared of the charges against him (1906). The interest in both the Boulanger and the Dreyfus case centers in the revelation that the army was honeycombed with monarchical and clerical sentiments. None the less the victory in both crises fell to the republic, which profited from them to no small

The Boulanger and Dreyfus incidents strengthen the republic

extent since the worst reactionaries were dismissed from the service
and special care was taken to train an officer body of sound republican
views.

A characteristic interest of the dominant French bourgeoisie was
to promote material prosperity in every possible way. Attentive to
the counsels of bankers and capitalists, the parliament strongly
The French supported public works such as highways, railroads, canals,
colonial and harbors, and, above all, threw itself enthusiastically
empire into colonial expansion. Colonialism, it is true, represented no new departure. As early as the eighteenth century France
had acquired a trans-oceanic empire, which, however, except for a
few insignificant fragments, she had been obliged to surrender to
Great Britain. In 1830, under the restored Bourbons, she made a
new effort at expansion by directing an expedition against Algeria
opposite her own southern shore. The governments of Louis Philip
and Napoleon III pursued the work thus begun by fighting and sub-
jugating the native tribes until a considerable area had been brought
under French domination. Napoleon III also developed French
authority in the Senegal river district of western Africa and in Indo-
China in southeastern Asia. Therefore on coming into power the
Third Republic found several promising colonial centers already in
existence; and, busily and tirelessly extending its claims, it had by
1914 succeeded in assembling an extra-European empire of such vast
extent that it was exceeded only by those of Great Britain and Russia. Its chief strength lay in northwestern Africa, almost the whole
of which had been brought under French rule; but the Indo-China
position was important and the possession of a long chain of islands,
in which chain Madagascar, off the coast of southeastern Africa, is
the largest link, added greatly to the solidarity and vigor of this empire ruled from Paris. Meanwhile the older colonial urge of the
European powers had, under pressure from the Industrial Revolution,
assumed the more aggressive form of imperialism. Imperialism, as
we shall presently see, came around 1890 to dominate the foreign
policy of every European power, producing the fiercest kind of competition among them. By its side and often merging with it the
older force of nationalism continued to manifest its strength. Nationalist assertiveness and imperialist expansion together ruled the
foreign offices of all the European powers and invariably furnish the
explanation of the attractions and repulsions manifested among them
during the generation before the outbreak of the World War. In

the case of France we find that in the early nineties she reached a
friendly hand toward Russia, and concluded a close alliance with
the empire of the tsar which in the twentieth century was expanded,
by the addition of Great Britain, into the famous Triple entente.
But therewith we have broached international relations, the systematic treatment of which is reserved to a special chapter.

GERMANY

The German Empire, forged in the fire of three wars fought between 1864 and 1871, rested on the constitution of 1867 together
with the modifications adopted on the occasion of the incorporation
in the Empire of the four South German states (1871).
The constitution, which, like the Empire, was the work The German
of Bismarck, aimed at combining three factors: (1) the constitution
ascendancy of Prussia, (2) the self-government of the a compro-
twenty-five component states, and (3) the national soli- mise between
darity of the German people. This last feature was to absolutism
be secured by means of a lower house (*Reichstag*) elected and liberalism
by universal manhood suffrage. While something like
a balance was obtained among the three above-mentioned historical
agencies, it is undoubtedly true that Bismarck reserved the decisive
political role in the new state to Prussia and its king, raised in respect
of the new federal structure, to the dignity of German Emperor
(*Deutscher Kaiser*). These circumstances make it difficult to classify
the new government. While it was constitutional, it was not parliamentary, at least not in the British or French sense since the ministry
was not responsible to the legislature. Because the emperor appointed the chancellor and the other ministers and because they
held office at his pleasure, he resembled an autocrat; but then,
on the other hand, his autocracy was seriously impaired by the
circumstance that taxes could not be voted nor laws passed without
the consent of the Reichstag. It is approximately correct to think
of the German system as a compromise between absolutism and
liberalism. That liberalism, dissatisfied with its half-triumph, did
not at once proceed to sweep the remnants of absolutism off the
boards as it did everywhere else in western Europe was probably due
to the immense prestige won by the Prussian monarchy through its
realization of the middle class dream of German unity.

The outstanding event in the history of the new Empire between

1871 and 1914 was its rapid and thorough-going industrialization. This meant an accelerated advance in the power and numbers of the middle classes. If the government had openly and systematically Unitarian antagonized them, they would in all likelihood, in spite legislation of their gratitude to Bismarck for his achievement of unity, have begun an agitation aiming at his overthrow and the revision of the constitution in their interest. But the chancellor more than met them half-way, as a review of Reichstag activity amply shows. Act after act was passed to the end of endowing the Empire with a body of efficient national legislation; and although these measures redounded to the advantage of the whole population, they were preëminently bourgeois in the sense that they constituted the very substance of the middle class program. A national coinage system was adopted (its unit the *mark*), a national bank (the *Reichsbank*), and a national (metric) system of weights and measures. The Prussian army organization with its feature of compulsory military service was extended to the South German states. One of the most sweeping reforms consisted in remodelling the whole edifice of justice. Not only were the courts endowed with a simplified and uniform procedure but special commissions were appointed to prepare new codes both of criminal and civil law which were debated and in due time passed by the Reichstag.

A noisy quarrel with the Catholic Church belonging to the seventies, also had, in large part at least, a bourgeois origin. To be sure, Bismarck made the quarrel his own on the ground that the Catholic The *Kultur*- Church enjoyed too great an authority in Prussia and *kampf* the other German states. Laws were passed (1872–1875) which aimed to bring the clergy more completely under state domination; but the clergy, enthusiastically supported by the Catholic laity, resisted so successfully that Bismarck was obliged to acknowledge himself beaten in this conflict usually referred to as the *Kulturkampf*. The obnoxious anti-Catholic legislation was gradually withdrawn, and after a decade the only advantage which remained to the state was obligatory civil marriage and the confirmation of the state's control of education. As for the Church it came out of the struggle with the heightened prestige resulting from the successful defense of its claims; and of this strengthened position the most striking evidence was the Center party formed among the Catholic voters for the support of their beloved mother, the Church.

From all that has been said it must be clear that the massive figure of the Iron Chancellor completely overshadowed every phase of German political life and that nothing happened in the whole vast field without his consent. During the seventies he coöperated with the party of the National Liberals, in whom middle class policy found its chief expression. But just before the close of the decade he adopted two policies which only a section of the National Liberals would accept. *Bismarck breaks with the National Liberal party* The first was an expression of his conversion from free trade to protection; the second signalized his alarm over the spread of socialism. It characterizes his contempt of established parliamentary procedure that he did not seek a preliminary understanding with his liberal supporters about his new plans but shaped them in the light of his personal view of the situation. Then he announced his program and challenged the National Liberals to rebel against him if they dared. As a group among them actually did dare, the party was split in two. None the less by combinations with other parties (the Conservatives, the Catholic Center, or both) Bismarck carried not only a protective tariff (1879) but also a series of measures dealing with socialism which are important enough to deserve a more detailed description.

While the Industrial Revolution had strengthened the middle classes, it had of course enormously swelled the numbers of wage-earners, who, yielding more and more to a very clever agitation conducted by Marx and his followers, were drawn into the Social-democratic party, organized for the conquest of political power. As soon as this party with its subversive *Bismarck's Social Legislation* aims succeeded in getting a solid block of representatives elected to the Reichstag, Bismarck took alarm and resolved to make an effort to turn the workingmen away from the Marxist camp. On the one hand, he had the Reichstag pass an anti-socialist law which tried by drastic punishments to suppress all socialist agitation whether of newspapers, books, or public meetings; and, on the other, he championed an elaborate labor code in protection of the workers and as a proof to them that they were not handed over for exploitation to the capitalists but that they were cherished and befriended by a patriarchal state. The anti-socialist law may be said to have been a complete failure in so far as the suppression of the movement was concerned. The government itself came to see the futility of meeting socialism with force, and in 1890, immediately on Bismarck's retirement from office, dropped the measure. The chancellor's ameliorative labor code is in another class. While a part of it dealt with the labor of women and children and provided more humane conditions in the factories, that is, followed a line already taken by the older industrial countries, another part, far more original, in fact representing one of the most important contributions ever made to Social Legislation, took up the issue of workingmen's insurance. Three types of insurance were inaugurated: (1) insurance against accident; (2) insurance against sickness; (3) insurance against invalidism and old age. As the workingmen were required to make contributory payments to the funds established in connection with types two and three, they were permitted to share the control of these funds with the employers. The responsibilities of management coupled with the coöperation imposed on employers and employees exercised a beneficent influence on the whole economic situation. In fact, according to almost universal opinion, the Bismarckian Insurance Legislation did much toward developing in Germany one of the most efficient bodies of workingmen to be found in the world. But though they gladly profited from the insurance enactments, which, carried in the period 1883–1889, constitute a genuine step toward socialism, they did not show the least inclination to give up their antagonism to the bourgeois state or to abandon the Social-democratic party.

In 1888 William I, the first ruler of reunited Germany, died at the advanced age of ninety-one years. As his son, Frederick III, who was already dwelling in the shadow of death at the time of his accession, reigned only three months, the scepter passed to Frederick's oldest son, William. William II (1888–1918) was an alert, ambitious, and autocratically-minded sovereign, who soon showed his restiveness under the tutelage of Bismarck and in 1890 dismissed him from office. By successively appointing more subservient and less authoritative men to the chancellorship, he reduced the importance of his ministers and became in his own person the director of German policy. His plan in essence was to promote material prosperity in every possible way by giving support to industry, commerce, and agriculture alike. This was far from easy since an antagonism often appears among these rival economic interests; but that Germany under William II advanced materially at an extraordinarily rapid rate can not be challenged in view of the great expansion registered in such matters as the merchant marine, the value of agricultural products, and foreign trade. A detailed analysis of the foreign trade would furnish interesting evidence of the amazing multiplication of machine-made goods. As a single statistical item illustrating German domestic growth we may note that the population increased between 1870 and 1914 from forty-one millions to close to seventy millions.

Translated into political terms, William II's economic program signified that he was resolved to lean upon the Conservatives, representing the Prussian landlords and the German farmers generally, and on the various groups of Liberals identified with the middle classes. By serving the interests of these groups he gained their attachment and loyalty and was enabled to push his imperialist schemes which centered on the maintenance of a large and effective army and navy. While the army had by William's time become an established feature of Prusso-German tradition, the navy was an innovation, largely due to the emperor's personal initiative. Not without difficulty he managed to persuade his followers in the Reichstag to embark on a naval program which in the course of the first decade of the twentieth century gave Germany the greatest fleet in Europe after Great Britain. Although its growing navy increased the apparent power of Germany, we should not fail to observe that it really weakened the German position since, by arousing the hostility of Great Britain, it pushed that country into the ranks of William's enemies. Of this more will be said in the chapter dealing with general European relations. In this purely domestic review it will suffice to point out the connection between William's naval policy and the political and social support on which he relied to carry it through. But caressing as he did the possessing classes, he offended the workingmen organized in the Social-democratic party. Hence it was give-and-take between them with the immediate advantage resting with the emperor, who from his loftier platform hurled the thunders of his wrath at their heads. However, after 1890, with the expiration of the anti-socialist law, it must be conceded he did nothing directly to obstruct their propagandist activity. By making it clear that the chasm between himself and the socialists was unbridgeable, he entered on a silent struggle with them in which he had the satisfaction of maintaining his ascendancy by reason of upper and middle class support. None the less the Social-democratic party continued steadily and ominously to grow. In the general elections of 1912 it came

The imperialist policy of William II in open conflict with socialism

dangerously near to polling as many votes as Conservatives and
Liberals combined and returned a membership which made it the
largest single party in the Reichstag. This separation of Germany
into a monarchical and a republican faction was probably inevitable,
but that William hastened it by his provocative attitude is incontrovertible.

A country which, like Germany after 1871, was politically powerful
and economically dominated by the Industrial Revolution, was
bound to embark on the colonial movement. The cautious Bismarck at first discouraged the merchants who looked
Colonial and imperial policy beyond the seas for territory, but when, in the eighties,
he saw an opportunity to go ahead without encountering
too much opposition from the older countries already in the field,
he assumed for Germany the protection of certain areas in Africa.
The policy thus inaugurated William II, throwing Bismarck's caution
to the winds, continued with enthusiasm until in 1914, at the end of
a quarter of a century, his country had amassed a considerable colonial empire. To be sure, owing to Germany's late appearance on
the scene, her extra-European possessions could not compare either
in extent or value with those of such older powers as Great Britain,
France, and Russia, but they were formidable enough to make her a
factor in the colonial race. The bulk of them lay in Africa (Togo,
Kamerun, German Southwest Africa, German East Africa) but her
Pacific territories, consisting chiefly of scattered island groups, like
the Marshall Islands and the Carolines, and her flourishing colony
at Kiao-chau in the Chinese province of Shan-tung were important
additional positions. In any case, taken in connection with her
powerful army and navy and her expanding commerce and industry,
her colonies sufficed to push Germany into the imperialist game. Although we shall study German imperialism in connection with all
the other imperialisms at a later time, it may be pointed out here
that it did not dominate German foreign policy till the reign of William II. Under Bismarck, whose nature was rooted in the realities
immediately surrounding him, foreign policy was determined almost
exclusively by the hereditary enmity with France. That the restless
and ambitious William II persuaded himself to disregard the enmity
of France and, pursuing imperialist designs, plunged into world
politics, represents the turn which became decisive for the German
destiny. By aligning Russia and Great Britain with France William
provoked a combination which drew an iron ring around his country.

AUSTRIA-HUNGARY

Between 1859 and 1866 the Austrian Empire suffered a series of defeats which drove it out of Italy and Germany and obliged it to effect a complete reorganization. Although the emperor, Francis Joseph I (1848-1916), became persuaded that the tradi- Austria tional absolutism would have to be given up, the ques- becomes tion as to what was to replace it proved exceedingly (1867) the dual empire difficult. There were those among his advisers who be- of Austria-lieved that the unity of the Empire should be maintained Hungary at all costs by the creation of a central parliament at Vienna, while others favored a decentralized and federal system which would break up Austria into its component provinces and nationalities. In the end neither of these proposals, neither centralization nor federalism, triumphed but a third program championed by the Hungarians. It is known as the Compromise (*Ausgleich*) of 1867 and is characterized as the dual system, since it divided the Hapsburg territories into two sections, Austria and Hungary. Under this arrangement Hungary embraced the eastern territories, that is, Hungary proper and her historical dependencies, Croatia, Slavonia, and Transylvania, while Austria included the western and northern provinces, seventeen in number. Each half of the monarchy was to have its own separate constitution, parliament, and administration. As the executive, called emperor in Austria and king in Hungary, was the same person, he would constitute the chief bond between the two sections. However, in order to assure harmonious counsels in diplomacy and war and leave to the united monarchy the status of a great power, certain additional interests like foreign affairs, army, and navy were recognized to be common to both areas. These common interests were presided over by common, that is, Austro-Hungarian ministers responsible to two *delegations* of sixty members each from the parliaments of Vienna and Budapest, the respective capitals of Austria and Hungary.

It thus appears that the combined state, no longer called Austria but Austria-Hungary, was based on a bargain between the two strongest national groups, the Germans and Magyars (Hungarians). Neither, it is true, could claim a majority of the population in its particular section, but each, by judiciously limiting the franchise, might aspire to maintain control in its half of the monarchy. Naturally the less favored groups, chiefly Slavs, protested against this system.   However, since it conceded them representation, though not in proportion to their numbers, they ended by accepting it and sending representatives to the parliaments at Vienna and The dual   Budapest charged with replacing as soon as possible the system   dual with a loose, federal system more calculated to give based on   each racial group the direction of its interests.   In each the ascen- dancy of the   parliament therefore, from the start, the nationality ques- Germans in   tion was constantly to the fore, the Germans and Magyars Austria and   trying by means of a restricted suffrage to maintain their of the Hun- garians in   ascendancy, while the opposition, consisting of Rumanians, Hungary   Italians, and, above all, of the numerous groups of Slavs, such as the Czechs, Poles, and Ruthenians in the north and the Serbs, Croats, and Slovenes in the south, tried, in order to get the full advantage of their numbers, to achieve universal suffrage and with this lever to put an end to the German and Hungarian ascendancy.[1]   That the Austro-Hungarian monarchy assumed on the basis of the Compromise of 1867 a form so complicated as to make classification impossible and even description difficult has generally been recognized.   However, the main point is as clear as day: the dual system represented an attempt to set up a constitutional government in which all the nationalities of the polyglot Hapsburg realm were to be conceded fundamental rights, but in which, chiefly by means of suffrage limitations, an ascendancy was to be secured in Austria to the Germans, in Hungary to the Magyars.   The wild struggle among the Hapsburg nationalities, inaugurated in 1848, continued therefore without abatement after the Compromise of 1867.   However, as it was conducted not with shot and shell but with harmless, though explosive words fired in the parliaments of Vienna and Budapest, the hope of an ultimate accommodation was never quite abandoned.   Let us now follow first the history of Austria and Hungary considered as separate entities, the second, the history of Austria-Hungary, under which title the Hapsburg monarchy continued to do business as a great power.

The Austrian parliament composed of two houses showed a laudable energy in modernizing the state.   Complete religious toleration was decreed; public schools were founded with compulsory attend-

[1] In 1910 Austria-Hungary had 51,300,000 inhabitants, distributed as follows among the leading nationalities; 12,000,000 Germans, 10,000,000 Magyars, 8,500,000 Czechs and Slovaks, 5,000,000 Poles, 5,000,000 Serbs and Croats, 4,000,000 Ruthenians, 3,200,000 Rumanians, 1,200,000 Slovenes, 750,000 Italians.

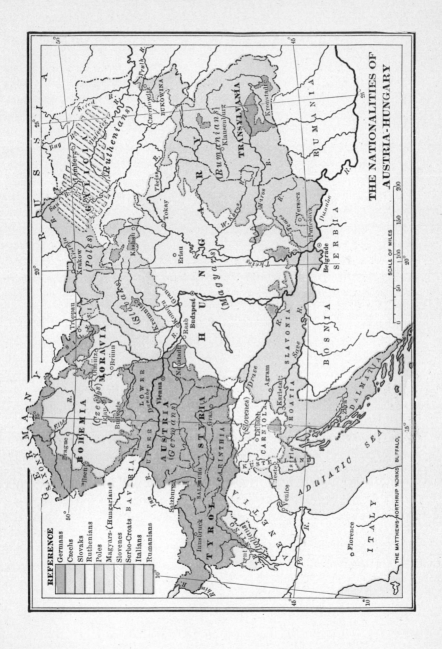

THE NATIONALITIES OF
AUSTRIA-HUNGARY

REFERENCE
Germans
Czechs
Slovaks
Ruthenians
Poles
Magyars (Hungarians)
Slovenes
Serbo-Croats
Italians
Rumanians

SCALE OF MILES
0   50   100   150   200

THE MATTHEWS-NORTHRUP WORKS, BUFFALO

ance; the judicial system was reformed and to a certain extent popularized by the introduction of trial by jury; and the army was
renovated by the adoption of the Prussian system of universal compulsory service. The citizens, encouraged by these evi- Moderniza-
dences of new life, developed an unexpected initiative tion of
and undertook to appropriate the advantages of the Austria
Industrial Revolution. The coal and iron resources, under the
chiefly of Bohemia and Moravia, served as the basis of tional
a development which gradually carried Austria into the system
ranks of the industrial states. Wealth grew rapidly, cities expanded,
workingmen tried to combat low wages and evil living conditions by
means of strikes and unions, in short, renovated Austria in the last
decades of the nineteenth century followed in the footsteps of Great
Britain, France, and Germany.

The Industrial Revolution was championed, in Austria as everywhere, by the middle classes and the Austrian middle classes were,
generally speaking, German. But what the Germans gained in wealth
and consideration as the leaders of business, the Slavs Political
gained in numbers by supplying the factory workers. and
The Industrial Revolution therefore intensified the nationalist
nationalist conflict, for the workers demanded the vote and democra-
every democratic advance proved to be a threat directed Austria and
against German ascendancy. However, so decisive was decline of
the economic expansion that there was no resisting the German
democratic movement. By successive stages the vote ascendancy
was extended to additional groups until in 1907 a law was adopted
establishing universal manhood suffrage. Already a generation
before 1907 the Germans had lost control of parliament, which with
its many parties along national lines exhibited a picture in miniature
of the ethnical situation in the state. After 1907 the national rivalries flared up more heatedly than ever, tremendously complicated
at times by the newer class rivalries connected with the problems
of capital and labor. Numerous were the observers who declared
that the Austrian state structure would not be able to stand the
strain much longer; but the contentious groups, perhaps because
they were dependent on one another economically, perhaps because
they felt a common loyalty to their aged ruler, Francis Joseph,
always drew back from the final, irrevocable step. Besides, the Poles,
Czechs, Slovenes, and other Slav peoples enjoyed the not inconsiderable satisfaction that the existing system permitted them

steadily to increase their rights in the schools, the courts, and the administration at the expense of the Germans. By 1914 there was as good as nothing left of the former political ascendancy of the Germans, though their social and economic predominance, unaffected by their political decline, enabled them to exercise a broad general influence which was the real cement holding the tottering structure of the state together. Austria's history between 1867 and 1914 proved that it is only with the greatest difficulty that a state composed of many diverse nationalities, each of which occupies a distinct area, will be able to resist the dissolving tendencies of the modern nationalist propaganda.

The internal history of Hungary after 1867 differs most conspicuously from that of Austria in that the Magyars successfully maintained their ascendancy in politics, justice, education, and administration. There were several reasons for this. First, the Magyars formed a solid central block surrounded by a rim of Slovaks, Ruthenians, Rumanians, and Serbo-Croats, incapable of uniting because they spoke different languages and were not in physical touch with one another. Second, the Magyars were traditionally a ruling group which owned the land, while the Slavs and Rumanians were, at least in overwhelming measure, backward and unorganized peasants. Third, the Industrial Revolution, which regularly carried in its wake a strengthened bourgeoisie and an aggressive proletariat, hardly penetrated Hungary. For all these reasons Hungary remained predominantly an agricultural state, essentially feudal and Magyar in spirit and organization. However, its wealth rapidly increased since the soil was extraordinarily fertile and the landlords, commanding capital and amenable to modern, scientific methods, doubled and trebled the value of the crops. Conscious of their power and resolved to maintain it at all costs, the Magyars had set up a franchise capable of such unscrupulous manipulation that the non-Magyar groups remained almost unrepresented in the parliament at Budapest. Of course they found leaders who agitated in their behalf, demanding if not universal manhood suffrage, at least a more equitable voting system. But as political democratization would unerringly have ended Magyar domination, the reform was violently resisted by the ruling group. When the World War broke out the actual political situation was still essentially what it had been since 1867. There was, however, this difference: the struggle for democracy and national rights had

The maintenance of Magyar ascendancy in Hungary

become so embittered that it did not seem credible that an unbending Magyar ascendancy could be maintained very much longer

A state like Austria-Hungary made up of many rival and contentious nationalities could not possibly play as decisive a role in Europe as the nationally compact powers all around it. Above all, as it lacked the impulse communicated by their homogeneous The interest nationalism to Great Britain, France, Germany, and Italy, of Austria-it could not venture upon an active, imperialist policy, Hungary directed to or it could venture on it only with certain paralyzing reser- the Balkan vations. For this reason the foreign policy of the dual peninsula monarchy, after the elimination of its influence from Italy and Germany, seems relatively tame and unenterprising. Southeastern Europe became almost exclusively its field of interest, and here it pursued as its main purpose the rather negative policy of hindering Russia from gaining such an influence over the small Balkan nationalities and the infirm Ottoman Empire as to expose the monarchy to attack on its Danubian front and to block its economic access to the Near East *via* the Ægean sea. In consequence of this fear of Russia the emperor-king became greatly agitated when, in 1877, Tsar Alexander II began a new war against the sultan which threatened to bring the whole Balkan peninsula under Muscovite domination. As Great Britain was equally alarmed by the prospect, Russia was forced to submit the Ottoman question to the powers at the Congress of Berlin. By the verdict of the assembled statesmen Austria-Hungary was entrusted with the administration of the two Ottoman provinces of Bosnia and Herzegovina (1878). From this moment the rivalry with Russia became the foremost, nay, almost the exclusive consideration of the Viennese foreign office. It led in the following year (1879) to a close alliance with Germany, which in 1882 was enlarged by the admission of Italy into the Triple alliance. As all this will be treated elsewhere, it will suffice if in this review, concerned entirely with domestic developments, we take note that the ultimate fate of the Austro-Hungarian monarchy as a whole hinged on the occupation of Bosnia, the rivalry with Russia, and the Triple alliance.

REFERENCES

J. S. Schapiro, *Modern and Contemporary Europe*, chs. 11, 12, 16, 17
E. Fueter, *World History*, ch. 26
C. M. Andrews, *Development of Modern Europe*, II, chs. 7, 9, 10–12
C. D. Hazen, *Europe Since 1815*, I, chs. 18–20

C. J. H. HAYES, *Political and Social History*, II, pp. 331–378, ch. 24
Cambridge Modern History, XI, ch. 25, XII, chs. 5–8
J. H. ROSE, *Development of European Nations*, I, chs. 4–6
G. P. GOOCH, *History of Our Time*, chs. 2–4, 6–10; *History of Modern Europe*
A. L. LOWELL, *Governments and Parties in Continental Europe*
F. A. OGG, *Governments of Europe; Economic Development of Modern Europe*
E. M. SAIT, *Government and Politics in France*
J. R. M. MACDONALD, *France*, III, ch. 40
J. C. BRACQ, *France under the Republic*
A. TILLEY, *Modern France*, pp. 170–184, 379–389
B. WENDELL, *The France of Today*
A. L. GUÉRARD, *French Civilization in the Nineteenth Century*
H. D. SEDGWICK, *Short History of Italy*, ch. 39
W. R. THAYER, *Italica*
F. M. UNDERWOOD, *United Italy*
B. KING AND J. OKEY, *Italy Today*
E. F. HENDERSON, *Short History of Germany*, II, chs. 11–13
C. G. ROBERTSON, *Bismarck*
W. H. DAWSON, *The German Empire; Evolution of Modern Germany; Municipal Life and Government in Germany*
H. LICHTENBERGER, *Germany and its Evolution*
F. K. KRUEGER, *Government and Politics of the German Empire*
R. H. FIFE, *The German Empire between Two Wars*
F. HOWE, *Socialized Germany*
H. W. STEED, *The Hapsburg Monarchy*
G. DRAGE, *Austria-Hungary*
A. R. COLQUHON, *The Whirlpool of Europe*
L. LEGER, *History of Austria*
R. W. SETON-WATSON, *Racial Problems in Hungary; The Southern Slav Question and the Hungarian Monarchy*

CHAPTER XXX

THE LESSER STATES OF EUROPE

The lesser states of Europe boast the same civilization as the greater states and their history in the nineteenth century has been shaped by the same general movements. That means that they have all, though in varying measure, been affected by the attempt to break away from the many bondages and re- *The lesser* strictions imposed by the Middle Age; that they have *states re-* *peat with* adopted the results of science and have felt the breath of *variations* the Industrial Revolution; that they have experienced *the experi-* the growth of power of the middle classes; and that they *ence of the* *great* have been swept by the political agitation connected with *powers* constitutionalism, democracy, and socialism. Our brief review can do no more than indicate the effect on the lesser states of the above general agencies in the period 1815–1914 and to note certain resulting variations due to the operation of special local conditions.

SPAIN

Having already dealt with the Spain of the Restoration Period, we have learned that the Bourbon monarch, Ferdinand VII, tried with the help of the Church and the nobility to reëstablish the abso- lute régime and that he met with opposition on the part *The* of certain liberal elements which had come into existence *struggle* during the struggle with Napoleon. Obliged (1820) to *between* *absolutism* concede a constitution, he was with the aid of the Holy *and* Alliance enabled to overthrow his opponents and reassert *liberalism* his power (1823). Perhaps the worst consequence for Spain of his uncompromising attitude was the estrangement of the South American colonies and their successful assertion of their independence.

Plainly the question which emerged in Ferdinand's day was whether Spain would hold fast to its eighteenth century organization or whether it would succeed in accommodating itself to the newer demands of constitutional government. But this question, political in nature, had social and economic implications, and the victory of

611

the constitutionalists would depend on the quiet but effective transformation of Spain by education, science, and industrialism. Now
it is a fact that this transformation was not carried through or
rather that it made headway at so snail-like a pace
The struggle continues indefinitely because of the lack of middle class strength that many decades passed before liberalism acquired
sufficient momentum to push absolutism off the boards.
The situation was further complicated by a disputed
succession. When the narrow-minded and bigoted Ferdinand VII died in 1833, he left the crown to his infant
daughter Isabella, thereby setting aside his brother
Carlos, who considered himself to be the lawful heir. Civil war
followed between Carlists and Christinists, so-called from the regent-
mother, Christina; and when this had been decided in favor of the
latter, the victors fell out among themselves. The fact that Isabella
became of age and reigned in her own name effected no improvement: the dreary civil struggle dragged on and on, without rhyme
or reason. Liberal promises were made and broken, constitutions
were published and annulled on no higher ground than a fancied
momentary advantage. At length the long-suffering public lost
patience with the dishonest game and Queen Isabella was obliged
to flee abroad before a general rising (1868).

A period of agitated experimentation followed. In reality the
power passed into the hands of successive dictators. During the
ascendancy of Generals Serrano and Prim the crown was offered to
Leopold of Hohenzollern-Sigmaringen, thereby producing
Establishment (1875-1876) of constitutional monarchy under Alfonso XII the famous Spanish incident which precipitated the
Franco-German war of 1870. On Leopold's refusal, an
Italian prince, Amadeo of Savoy was chosen king and
actually reigned two years before he gave up in disgust.
Thereupon a republic was staged which cut so ludicrous
a figure that the country at length declared itself ready
and eager to return to the Bourbons in the person of the banished
Isabella's youthful son. In 1875 he mounted the throne under
the title Alfonso XII and ruled for ten years on the basis of a
constitution which, at least so far as appearances went, established
parliamentary government. On Alfonso's death in 1885 the power
passed into the hands of Queen Maria Christina acting in behalf of
her son, Alfonso XIII, who did not reach the legal governing age
till 1902 when he assumed the reins in person.

Before the end of the nineteenth century therefore constitutionalism had definitely displaced absolutism. But the intimate changes in Spanish society and in the Spanish mind had not been such as to give the constitutional system its necessary underpinning. Spain remained obdurately outside the strong currents of modern life. Although the Inquisition had finally disappeared in the first half of the nineteenth century, the Catholic clergy continued to dominate thought and education; the bourgeoisie, owing to the backwardness of commerce and the absence of industry remained weak; and the masses, sunk in superstition and prone to indolence and beggary, failed utterly to impress themselves upon the situation. To the province of Catalonia with its busy capital, Barcelona, it is true, this description does not apply. The Catalans of the east coast had never been more than superficially assimilated to the Spaniards and a vigorous section among them had never ceased to ask for the home rule which they had enjoyed up to the time of Philip II. By the development of commerce and industry and the introduction of modern scientific and educational methods they tried to bring themselves into line with the rest of Europe and chafed impatiently under the backward government at Madrid. Catalonia is undoubtedly a modern anomaly in Spain; but perhaps because it is a small area, it did not succeed in the period under review in wresting autonomy from the central government. The heart of the Spanish phenomenon is mental immobility. Is it due to the unbroken rule of the Catholic Church? Or to the geographical isolation caused by the barrier of the Pyrenees? Or to the extreme poverty of a large part of the Spanish soil? Or to fundamental racial traits by reason of which the Spaniards are less enterprising and energetic than their European neighbors? A satisfactory analysis of the Spanish situation would have to reckon with all these factors.

Spain outside the main currents of modern thought and life

A decadent country in the midst of an expanding age was not likely to be able to maintain its colonies. We have already observed how the lusty South and Central American dependencies cast off the Spanish yoke in the first quarter of the nineteenth century. Cuba and the Philippines represented about all that was left of what had been once the greatest colonial empire in the world. Here, too, incurable mismanagement created chronic discontent and in the second half of the nineteenth century led to serious risings against Spanish corruption. It took

Decadent Spain loses its colonial empire

the mother-country ten years to suppress the Cuban rebellion of 1868. In 1894 Cuba rose again, and when a large Spanish army had almost reduced the island to a desert, the United States interfered, provoking the Spanish-American war of 1898. The quick and decisive triumph of the powerful young republic obliged Spain to sue for peace, by the terms of which Cuba was declared independent and Porto Rico and the Philippine Islands were ceded to the victors. All that remained to Spain after 1898 were the Canary Islands, the Rio de Oro region of West Africa, and a few isolated points like Ceuta on the Moroccan coast. When in 1904 Great Britain and France reached their famous Mediterranean agreement, which, among other matters, assigned the bulk of Morocco to France, Spain was placated with the promise of its eventual succession to the Moroccan area opposite its own shores. On the seizure of Morocco by France in 1911, Spain presented its promissory note and duly received an ample coastal segment. Mountainous, difficult of access, and without roads, it is inhabited by hardy, spirited tribes who, animated by the Moslem faith, are not minded to put up with Spanish rule. Whether Spain can bring them under subjection and maintain a modest imperialism among the vigorous grasping imperialisms of its neighbors remains to be seen.

PORTUGAL

The history of Portugal in the nineteenth century runs a course strikingly parallel to that of Spain. There is the same struggle between absolutism and constitutionalism, the same weakness of liberalism owing to the failure of the country to effect a thorough-going social-economic transformation, and when constitutional government is at last victorious, there is the same absence of that fresh national vigor which other happier countries drew from the well-spring of modern thought and enterprise.

Parallel movement of Portugal and Spain

We are aware that when Napoleon seized Portugal in 1807, King John VI and the royal family sought refuge in the great Portuguese dependency of Brazil, where they chose to remain even after Napoleon's rule had been overthrown. Great Britain, which had been drawn to Portugal by its struggle with Napoleon, continued its control after 1815 until the rising of 1820 brought the Liberals into power, who championed a constitutional régime. In order to save his throne John VI, on the urgent invitation of his subjects, returned to his native land, and with an intelligence and adaptability unusual in a legitimate sovereign, agreed to accept a limitation of his absolutism. However, as soon as the Brazilians discovered that John had abandoned them, they became disgruntled in their turn, declared themselves independent of the mother-country, and offered the throne to John's son, Pedro (1822). On John's demise in 1826, Pedro succeeded to Portugal, but as the Brazilians would have none of him on these terms, he was obliged to resign the Portuguese crown in favor of his infant daughter, Maria. In this peaceful way Brazil and Portugal were separated never to be joined again.

The peaceful separation of Portugal and Brazil

Although King John agreed to be a constitutional sovereign and his youthful successor, Maria, did the same, powerful reactionary elements within the country resisted this development and plunged the country into domestic disturbances similar to those which troubled neighboring Spain. Gradually, however, the situation consolidated, and under the reign of Maria's sons and successors (Pedro V, 1853–1861; Luiz I, 1861–1889) the country seemed to have settled down to an orderly evolution in a constitutional sense. The quiet turned out to be deceptive. Under Carlos I (1889–1908) administrative corruption, financial crises, and electoral frauds promoted by the party leaders in their private interest gained the upper hand and involved the country in renewed tumult. In 1908 King Carlos paid the cruel price of failure by meeting death at an assassin's hand. His youthful and inexperienced son, Manoel II, succeeded to a quaking throne and two years later was driven into exile by a republican rising. Since 1910 Portugal has enjoyed the doubtful blessing of a republic, doubtful because the people have experienced no essential change of heart or mind and are as little ready to turn the republic into an active, going concern as they were the constitutional monarchy. The corruption of officials and the brazen manipulation of elections continue exactly as before. Only one difference deserves to be noted. Republican Portugal, perhaps in imitation of republican France, has adopted a severely anti-clerical policy. In 1911 the religious orders were expelled and a law passed separating Church and state. To resist this movement the strong conservative elements are ready to go far, even to the length of revolution. The republic may live, but many years must pass before it can become secure, honest, and efficient.

The constitutional monarchy followed by a republic, 1910

Perhaps Portuguese patriots take comfort in the thought that the real and greater Portugal is their former colony of Brazil. Become an independent empire in 1822, it has steadily grown in wealth and power, gradually working back into its immense tropical hinterland. Emperor Pedro I was followed by his son, Pedro II, a prince with a modern mind who, when he discovered after a beneficent reign of over four decades that his subjects preferred a republic, resigned without a struggle. Since 1890 Brazil has been a prosperous federal republic. Portugal's other colonies, however, have remained under its ægis. In area they are not inconsiderable, comprising as they do the extensive African territories of Angola and Mozambique (Portuguese East Africa). Being undeveloped, they are rather a liability to the treasury than an asset, and may, especially if they should suddenly disclose any promising economic resources, be taken over, doubtless on moral grounds, by some strong power like Great Britain. Her near-by island possessions, the Azores and Madeira, are Portugal's surest as they were her earliest acquisitions. Populated with Portuguese, they are not governed as colonies but directly incorporated with the home country.

The independence of Brazil and the decline of Portuguese colonial power

SWITZERLAND

On dealing with the Swiss Confederation in the Period of the Reformation, we noted that it had grown steadily from small beginnings until it occupied an acknowledged position in the system of European states. In the Peace of Westphalia (1648) its independence of the Holy Roman Empire was made an article of international law. In spite of these promising beginnings the seventeenth and eighteenth century represent a period of stagnation through a convergence of extraordinary difficulties, which may be briefly enumerated. (1) The Confederation was a loose union purely for defense among thirteen sovereign cantons. (2) There existed a wide diversity of governing principles among the cantons; while some maintained a very democratic system, the majority were ruled by narrow oligarchies. (3) There were regions classified some as allied, others as subjected districts; in neither case did they enjoy equality with the thirteen constituent cantons. (4) The fierce religious animosities carried into Switzerland by the Reformation continued to smolder in spite of the settle-

Stagnation in the post-Reformation Period

ment of Kappel (1531). In the period after 1648 the Confederation fell into a complete state of coma and such feeble public life as there was unfolded itself within the limits of each canton.

When the storms of the French Revolution broke, this whole antiquated system went down in ruin. The French did not scruple to interfere in Switzerland and first, the Directory and later, Napoleon imposed a more compact organization on the country which lasted till the Corsican's downfall. Swept, owing to resentment against French tyranny, by an unreasoning reactionary sentiment, the Swiss returned in 1815 to the loose union of prerevolutionary days, while the old oligarchies once more successfully established their cantonal power. The allied and subjected lands, however, which during the French disturbances had won their independence, were happily left in possession of their new-won rights. Thus it was a group not of thirteen but of twenty-two free cantons which revamped the old constitution. The Congress of Vienna presented the renovated Confederation with a guarantee of perpetual neutrality, by which it was fortunately freed from the necessity of entering the perilous game of European politics.

Destruction (1798) and reconstitution (1815) of the loose federal system

A few years of reaction sufficed for the revolutionary sentiments to revive and produce a general ferment. The oligarchical cantonal governments were attacked by opposition parties representing popular rights. At the same time the liberals proceeded to assault the impotent federal government by demanding a more centralized system. Shortly after the July Revolution of 1830 the oligarchies, as though stunned by the new spirit which was abroad, began to give way with such surprising swiftness that before long the cantonal governments had been generally democratized. Aware that the turn of the feeble federal constitution had now come, the seven Catholic cantons formed a league of resistance against the innovators called the *Sonderbund*. As this was tantamount to secession, the other cantons declared war and in a brief campaign won the victory (1847). They crowned it by drawing up (1848) a new constitution, which established an effective union imbued with democratic principles and which with slight changes is still in operation.

The victory of democracy and union (1848)

By the constitution of 1848 the supremacy of the federal over the cantonal powers was raised beyond a doubt, but the cantons were not deprived of their local rights. In its dovetailing of federal and state powers Switzerland offers a strong resemblance to the political system of the United States. The national legislative power is vested in a *Federal Assembly* of two houses: the *Council of States*, much like

The consti- the United States Senate, consists of two delegates from
tution of each canton, while the *National Council*, comparable
1848 to the House of Representatives, is elected by the

people on the basis of universal manhood suffrage. The national executive is not a single person, but a committee of seven, called the *Federal Council* and elected by the Federal Assembly. Although one of the seven presides under the title of *President of the Council* his authority is hardly greater than that of his other six colleagues.

Since the fundamental reforms effected between 1830 and 1848 the Swiss have not ceased to bring the democracy to which they are dedicated to an ever fuller expression. In some of the smaller

The agricultural cantons there had survived from past ages
triumph of a kind of enlarged town meeting, called *Landesgemeinde*,
democracy which despatched its business directly by electing magis-

trates and voting laws. This system appealed also to the larger cantons, even though geographical necessity obliged them to legislate indirectly through elected representatives. The result of much reflection along democratic lines was the adoption of the *referendum* and *initiative*, first for cantonal legislation and later, for federal legislation as well, to the end of making the laws as far as possible the direct expression of the will of the body of the citizens. By the referendum laws passed by the legislature, whether cantonal or federal, are submitted for a final verdict to the vote of the people; by the initiative the right is conceded to a certain number of citizens to suggest a measure which, if the people favor it in a special election, must be converted into law by the legislators. It is probable that democracy has been more broadly applied and has achieved a more complete success in Switzerland than in any other country of the world.

Switzerland presents an anomaly in a nationalist age, since, although composed of three nationalities, it is not threatened with disruption. If to the German, French, and Italian groups we add

Switzerland the small body in the valleys of the Grisons who speak
a state of a dialect derived from Latin called Romansch, we may
four nation- even speak of four Swiss nationalities. That about 71
alities per cent. of the population speak German, 21 per cent.

French, and 6 per cent. Italian brings out the fact that the Confederation, which began among German peasants and townsmen, is still preponderantly German. If the language groups do not quarrel, it is because German, French, and Italian enjoy equal recognition as official languages and further, because each group, treating the others with respect, refrains from attempting to gain an unfair advantage at their expense.

The great political advance of Switzerland in the nineteenth century was prompted by the remarkable expansion of the economic and mental life of the whole Swiss community. The country has shared as fully as its numbers and resources permitted in the newest phase of western civilization. Its educational system from the obligatory public school at the bottom to the professional institutions at the top enjoys a merited renown. Illiteracy has practically ceased to exist. A people so alert and disciplined was sure to draw every possible advantage from the Industrial Revolution. There has therefore been a steady and notable increase of manufacturing in the towns. At the same time there has been an impressive advance in the dairy industry which represents the original occupation of the upland valleys. A Swiss specialty, the tourist industry, deserves mention since it rests upon the scenic beauties of the Alps and bears witness to an intelligence which neglects no opportunity to draw an honorable return from the resources of the country.

Switzerland in the mid-current of modern civilization

BELGIUM

Not born till the Revolution of 1830, Belgium is one of the youngest states of Europe. When the great powers found themselves unable to undo the Belgian revolt, they made the best they could of a bad business and not only accepted Belgian independence but tried, as in the case of Switzerland, to protect the new state against attack by guaranteeing its neutrality. The constitution adopted in 1831 by the liberated Belgian people is still in use. It established a hereditary monarchy together with a bi-cameral parliament, of which the upper house was chosen by rather involved methods, while the lower house was elected directly by the eligible voters. Owing to a relatively high property qualification the eligible voters were for many decades limited to a small body of citizens. Leopold, a German prince of the house of Saxe-Coburg, was elected king and proved an exceptionally intelligent sovereign (1831-1865).

The Belgian constitution

He was succeeded by his son, Leopold II (1865-1909), equally intelligent but shrewd and grasping. Leopold's successor was his nephew, Albert I (1909–).

On attaining independence Belgium embarked on a career which has brought it amazing prosperity. The country has taken full advantage of its fortunate geographical situation on the North sea and Intense   has tied up the great port, Antwerp, with its populous hinterland by one of the most elaborate net-works of canals activity   and railways in the world. It has made its rich coal-beds the basis of an industrial development which enables the country to compete with such great manufacturing nations as Great Britain and Germany. And it has witnessed, on the part of its numerous small landholders, the application of scientific methods to agriculture, whereby the wealth and comfort of the country people have been greatly increased. By 1910 little Belgium had reached a population of 7,400,000 and was the most densely settled area of Europe.

The limited suffrage put the development of Belgium after 1831 in the hands of the middle classes who divided their favor between a Catholic and a Liberal party. Having identical economic interests, Catholic   Liberals and Catholics differed chiefly as to the control of control; the education. At one time the Liberals were sufficiently suffrage and strong to eliminate clerical influence from the public education   schools; but in 1884 the Catholics gained the elections issues   and continued in power uninterruptedly to the end of the period under consideration (1914). Of course they restored religious instruction in the public school; but, what is more surprising, yielding to popular clamor, they cancelled the property qualification and established manhood suffrage (1893). However, they showed a lingering distrust of the common people by conceding one or two additional votes to citizens of wealth or education (plural voting). In 1899 a much discussed political device, proportional representation, was adopted in order to permit minorities to be heard in parliament. Though the Liberals had meanwhile almost completely disappeared, their place as an opposition party was taken by the Socialists, who made a point of defending the interests of the growing body of workingmen. In conformity with the views of their brethren throughout Europe, the Socialists have persistently attacked both plural voting and the clerical control of the schools. While they constitute a threat for the Catholic majority, they have not yet replaced it.

Belgium has an incipient nationality issue due to the fact that in a country which is about equally divided between French-speaking Walloons and a Flemish-speaking Teutonic people (Flemings), the French language enjoys an ascendancy, though by The nation- no means a monopoly, in the administration and in the ality issue; schools. A policy of concessions to the Flemings has been colonialism inaugurated which it may be hoped will preserve the domestic peace. In 1908 Belgium made a daring plunge into colonialism by taking over the huge African territory of the Congo after it had been developed by the personal enterprise of King Leopold II. It was in 1885 that Leopold obtained from a colonial conference held by the powers at Berlin recognition of himself as the sovereign in his own name of the Congo Free State. Devoting himself to its development like any other money-making capitalist, he soon succeeded in drawing truly princely revenues from its vast resources of ivory and rubber. When it was discovered that the abnormal profits were ground out of the black natives by a cruel system of forced labor, a cry of indignation was raised throughout Europe which obliged Leopold to introduce reforms and, finally, to transfer the colony to the Belgian state. With colonialism added to the other issues agitating the Belgian people it is plain that they feel the full breath of modern life.

HOLLAND

The kingdom of the Netherlands, established in 1815 by the Congress of Vienna, was dismembered in 1830 by the revolt of its Belgian provinces. Reduced to the area of the former Dutch Republic, it has continued to operate under the official The con- name adopted in 1815, but is in English-speaking coun- stitution tries generally referred to as Holland. The powers at of 1848 Vienna recognized William I of the historic house of Orange-Nassau as king of the Netherlands. A conservative typical of his age, he granted a constitution which left the power substantially in his own hands. Not even the Belgian disaster broke his stubborn, autocratic will, and it was not till the reign of his son, William II (1840-1849), that a new and more popular fundamental law was adopted. Doubtless the general ferment of 1848 was the moving cause of the royal liberality. By the constitution of that revolutionary year the power of the king was held in check by a parliament of two houses. The upper house was composed of members elected by the legislatures of the eleven provinces composing the kingdom, while the lower house was chosen directly by the voters, a limited body determined on the basis of property. By conceding important rights of self-government to the eleven constituent provinces, the Dutch system took on a balanced federal character like that of Switzerland and the United States. The narrow suffrage invited attack on the part of the Liberals, but such is the conservatism of Dutch society that, in spite of two extensions of the body of the voters (in 1887 and 1896), manhood suffrage has not been realized as in the surrounding countries. William II was succeeded in 1849 by William III, on whose demise in 1890, his daughter Wilhelmina mounted the throne. A strictly constitutional sovereign, she enjoys to the full the traditional devotion of her countrymen to the Orange family.

The inhabitants of the kingdom are a homogenous group of Germanic origin speaking the Dutch language. Perhaps the domestic question which has agitated them more than any other is the place **Education** of religion in the educational system. Their Calvinistic **and religion** faith has been such a factor in their history that large numbers of conservative Protestants feel an aversion for an education divorced from religious instruction. In this they are of one mind with the Catholics who constitute a not unimportant minority. However, in Holland as elsewhere, a Liberal party advocates strictly secular schools and in this position the Liberals are supported by a party of more recent origin, the Socialists. The solution of the educational problem arrived at among these rival groups was in the nature of a compromise. A public school system without religious instruction was created, at the side of which operate the private school systems of the Calvinists and Catholics, enjoying alike since 1889 the support of monies from the public purse. Attendance at either a public or a private school has been made compulsory.

The economic development of Holland has steadily continued along the lines determined by its glorious past. It was the full utilization by the people of its sea-board position that won for the **The** country its seventeenth century eminence. The startling **economic** decline since that epoch has, after all, been relative rather **situation:** than absolute, for, considering its small size and its **agriculture,** population of about 6,000,000, Holland still maintains a **commerce,** population of about 6,000,000, Holland still maintains a **colonies** very notable position in commerce and agriculture. Among its rich lowland meadows a dairy industry had developed which matches that of the Swiss upland, while a commerce, concentrated in the two sea-ports of Amsterdam and Rotterdam, throws a bridge from Holland to every country of the world. The still considerable remnant of Holland's colonial empire contributes in no small degree to the nation's prosperity. The Dutch possessions consist of Guiana (South America) and Java, Sumatra, Borneo, and other East Indian islands which supply the European market with spices, coffee, sugar, and other tropical and semi-tropical products. The commerce of the East Indies amounted in 1913 to about a half billion dollars. Owing to the absence of mineral resources Holland did not turn to manufacturing like its neighbor Belgium. That, in the light of all the facts, the country has made the best possible use of its natural advantages admits of no dispute.

Like Belgium, Holland occupies a dangerous position between France and Germany and directly opposite the English shore. Switzerland and Belgium, in spite of the neutrality guaranteed to them by the powers, have not failed to provide for their defense by the creation of considerable armies. Evidently they nurse a conviction that their independence rests in the last resort not on international promises but on their own prowess. We need therefore feel no surprise that the kingdom of the Netherlands, which enjoys no similar international guarantee, has been at particular pains to provide against attack. Beginning with 1898 the militia was reorganized with a provision for compulsory personal service. This reform has enabled the Dutch to mobilize at need a large and serviceable force. *The dangerous position of the Dutch in the midst of three great powers*

As the grand-duchy of Luxemburg, wedged between France, Belgium, and Germany, was in 1815 attached as a personal possession to William I, king of the Netherlands, a word concerning it may be inserted at this point. Although William ruled in Luxemburg as grand-duke, the territory was for geographic and military reasons incorporated in the German Bund. When the Bund disappeared as a result of the Austro-Prussian war of 1866, Luxemburg, left high and dry, was coveted by Napoleon III and might have been surrendered to him for a consideration by its then sovereign, King William III, if Prussia had not interfered. To adjust the uncertainties which enveloped the status of the grand-duchy, a conference of the powers, held (1867) in London, confirmed William as grand-duke, and renewing the declaration of the little *The grand-duchy of Luxemburg* territory's independence, put it under the collective guarantee of the powers. On William III's death in 1890 he was succeeded in Holland by his daughter Wilhelmina but in Luxemburg by his nearest male relative, Adolphus of Nassau. Since then Adolphus and his descendants after him have ruled this Lilliputian state as constitutional princes.

THE SCANDINAVIAN STATES

The three Scandinavian states, Denmark, Sweden, and Norway, have, in spite of their being inhabited by three peoples speaking three different languages, so much in common that it is proper to group them together. Danes, Swedes, and Norwegians represent branches of the same North-Germanic stock; they adhere alike to the Lutheran faith; they live by agriculture, commerce, and fishing, rather than by manufactures; they are intellectually alert and have provided themselves with advanced educational systems; and they have passed in recent years through a similar social and political evolution. They are not a numerous people, the population of Denmark being in 1910 about 2,775,000, that of Sweden 5,500,000, and that of Norway 2,400,000, but by their sturdiness and enterprise they have won an honorable position in the modern movement of civilization.

Danes, Swedes, and Norwegians three branches of a common tree

(a) DENMARK

To punish the king of Denmark for clinging to Napoleon, the victor powers transferred (1814) his dependency, Norway, to Sweden. In 1864 he lost Schleswig and Holstein, which two years later were incorporated in Prussia. By these reductions of the kingdom to a compact Danish group the ground was cleared for an accelerated domestic development. Up to the middle of the nineteenth century the Danish political situation was marked by stagnation and the king's absolutism was hardly challenged. But the revolutionary fervor which seized on Europe in 1848 weakened the royal position. Frederick VII issued a constitution (1849), which, revised in 1866, is still in force. Christian IX, who ruled from 1863 to 1906, tried to oppose the democratic trend and, against the wishes of the lower house, insisted on carrying through a policy of military preparedness. He appointed ministers at his pleasure, and when he could not get a majority for his budgets

Peasant prosperity and democratization

enacted them by royal decree. It was a serious situation, luckily solved without war by the irresistible advance of the small Danish farmers, who constitute the bulk of the nation. Steadily improving their condition by intensive dairy-farming coupled with an amazingly effective chain of coöperative societies, they gradually came to dominate so completely both the economic and political situations that the king in 1901 wisely ended the domestic conflict by installing a cabinet representing the majority party in the lower house. Since this popular victory the democratization has proceeded apace. It was championed by the Liberals and latterly even more ardently by a growing group of Socialists. Under Frederick VIII (1906–1912) and Christian X (1912–) the army was put on a strictly militia basis, while sweeping electoral reforms reduced the age limit of electors from 30 to 25 years and granted the suffrage to women. In conformity with the politico-social outlook of a prosperous community of socialized farmers, Denmark has shown so little taste for colonialism that, instead of reaching out for new colonies, it has disposed of most of those that it had. In 1903 Iceland was granted a measure of home rule which was subsequently expanded to independence; and in 1917 the three Danish West Indian islands, St. Thomas, St. Croix, and St. John were sold to the United States. True, Denmark still owns Greenland but its possession does not arouse any rosy dreams of colonial grandeur.

(b) SWEDEN

That Sweden had in the seventeenth century been a great power has in more ways than one subtly affected Swedish history down to our own time. It was the Russia of Peter the Great that had dragged Sweden from its eminence and absorbed most of the Swedish conquests along the east shore of the Baltic. A century later, in 1809, Tsar Alexander I crowned the work of Peter by capturing Finland from his Scandinavian neighbor. It was at this juncture that Sweden sought to strengthen its hand against Russia by electing one of Napoleon's marshals, Bernadotte, heir to its last and childless sovereign of the Vasa line, Charles XIII. Once in Sweden Bernadotte, instead of playing Napoleon's game, joined the allies and was rewarded for his help by the cession of Norway. Up to this time (1814) Norway had belonged to Denmark. Outraged by this treatment of them as a mere diplomatic pawn, the Norwegians rose in arms and forced

Loss of Finland (1809) and acquisition of Norway (1814)

Sweden to recognize their independence under their own separate constitution. Then they elected the king of Sweden as their own king, thus establishing the familiar form of connection between two separate states known as a personal union. In addition to the monarch the two kingdoms had no institution in common other than the diplomatic service. Even this restricted association led to friction which culminated in 1905 in a complete rupture. We shall treat of it in the following section.

In 1818 Marshal Bernadotte became king under the title Charles XIV and reigned till 1844. He and his descendants have identified themselves so thoroughly with Swedish interests that, though of French origin, the family could not be more popular if it

Political and economic transformation

were a native house. Sweden, in distinction from democratic Norway and Denmark, was in the days of Bernadotte an aristocratic society of great landholders set above a dependent peasantry. This upper order nursed dreams of Swedish greatness, favored military preparedness to resist further Russian encroachments, and set its face against the liberal movement. It was of one mind with Charles XIV in standing by the old system of government inherited from feudal times. However, the modern movement gradually strengthened the middle classes, and in 1866 under their influence the ancient diet was replaced by a modern parliament of two chambers. A fairly high property qualification restricted the body of electors and proved the conservative character of the reform. Not till 1909 were constitutional amendments carried celebrating the full triumph of democracy by the establishment of universal manhood suffrage. This political transformation must, as usual, be interpreted in the light of the contemporary social-economic movement. The Swedish natural resources, chiefly of iron and water-power, have served since 1850 as the basis of an industrial movement which has strengthened both the middle classes and the proletariat. While the land-holding aristocracy is still powerful, it can no longer stand up against a union of the newer orders represented in politics by the Liberal and Socialist parties. Many signs indicate that in the future the struggle for control will be between these two latter groups as the really decisive factors in present-day Sweden. Conservatism, resting on the power of great landlords, is apparently a lost cause.

(c) NORWAY

We have seen that it was due solely to the firm resolution shown by Norway in 1814–1815 that the country gained its independence under its own constitution and was joined to Sweden in a purely personal union. Even this loose association proved irksome for a number of reasons. Norway is a coast and mountain land of small farmérs, fishermen, sailors, merchants, and pastors, as democratic a society as can be found anywhere in Europe. Even the constitution of 1814, constructed in a period of general reaction, was for its time an unusually democratic document since it vested supreme authority in a parliament (*Storthing*) and gave the vote to all tax-payers. Now the energy of the Norwegians was in the nineteenth century poured chiefly into commerce. They developed the carrying trade to such a degree that by 1900 their merchant marine had reached a tonnage which ranked it above the merchant marines of even the great powers with the exception of Great Britain and Germany. That signified an increase of national self-esteem which made the domination of Sweden in the consular service, the business of which it is to look after shipping, decidedly irritating. The people raised a clamor for the Norwegian flag on Norwegian ships as well as for Norwegian consuls, and when the king, who was Oscar II, refused to yield, the Storthing at last dissolved the union (1905). The crisis ended by Oscar wisely accepting the situation. Norway, free of the last Swedish bonds, thereupon elected to its throne a Danish prince who took the title Haakon VII (1905–).

The union with Sweden and its dissolution

A society which, like that of Norway, was founded on the vigorous self respect of farmers and sailors, was sure to prove friendly to the democratic doctrines current in our age. From 1870 on they would have been incorporated in the Norwegian political system in short order, had not the conservative-minded Swedish king imposed a halt. Only slowly was his resistance overcome. In 1884 he was obliged to accept the parliamentary system, that is, he declared himself ready to concede the ministerial posts to representatives of the majority party in the Storthing. In 1898 the limited franchise was replaced by universal manhood suffrage. With the Swedish brakes removed (1905) the democratic chariot moved forward with accelerated pace. In 1907 women received the vote, first with certain limitations, finally (1913) on the same

Democratization

broad basis as men. Norway claims the honor of being the first sovereign state of Europe to permit women not only to vote in national elections but also to sit in parliament.

REFERENCES

C. D. HAZEN, *Europe Since 1815*, I, chs. 27–30

J. S. SCHAPIRO, *Modern and Contemporary History*, chs. 18–20

C. J. H. HAYES, *Political and Social History*, II, pp. 378–392, 435–446

C. SEIGNOBOS, *Europe Since 1814*, chs. 8, 9, 10, 18

Cambridge Modern History, X, chs. 7, 8, 9, XI, 8, 23, 24, XII, 9–11

F. A. OGG, *Governments of Europe*, chs. 33, 34

B. CLARKE, *Modern Spain*

C. E. CHAPMAN, *History of Spain*

M. A. S. HUME, *Modern Spain*

H. M. STEPHENS, *Portugal*, chs. 17, 18

H. A. L. FISHER, *Republican Tradition in Europe*

W. D. MCCRACKAN, *Rise of the Swiss Republic*

J. M. VINCENT, *Government in Switzerland*

W. OECHSLI, *History of Switzerland*

H. D. LLOYD, *A Sovereign People*

P. BLOK, *History of the People of the Netherlands*

R. C. K. ENSOR, *Belgium*

C. SMYTHE, *The Story of Belgium*

R. N. BAIN, *Scandinavia*, chs. 16, 17

K. GJERSET, *History of the Norwegian People*

G. LUNDBÖRG, *Sweden, its People and Industries*

F. NANSEN, *Norway and its Union with Sweden*

CHAPTER XXXI

RUSSIA AND THE OTTOMAN EMPIRE IN THE
NINETEENTH CENTURY

From the very beginning of this book interest has been focussed on western civilization and the position has been taken that it originated within the area of the medieval Latin Church. In the period of the Renaissance its slowly accumulated energy burst $_{\text{Russia}}$ through these narrow geographic bounds, crossed the seas, takes over and sought to bring America and Asia within the field the superof its activity. Though it gained at first no more than a features of foothold on these continents, it has ever since been en- western gaged in the attempt to bring them thoroughly and civilization entirely under its influence. In the vast eastern plain of Europe identical with Russia the expanding civilization of the west celebrated toward the end of the seventeenth century a victory of a somewhat different kind. Under Tsar Peter the Great it encountered that sincerest form of flattery, imitation; and although Peter was no magician and could not in a twinkle make over his people's settled Slav mind, he could perform a number of more superficial miracles such as the reorganization of the Russian army and administration after a western, more specifically, a German pattern. The effect was to give the vast Russian mass a slow but irresistible momentum, by virtue of which it soon pushed the weakening might of Sweden from the Baltic and, in the days after Peter, overran Poland and crowded the once irresistible Ottoman Empire from the northern shore of the Black sea.

When with exceptional frankness the Tsarina Catherine II indicated that the goal of Russian political endeavor would for her and her descendants be Constantinople and the straits, it became clear that the Ottoman Empire was doomed unless it found means of bringing the Russian offensive to a halt. Now the only effective way of doing that would have been for the Ottoman Empire to follow the Russian example and to carry through a reform of the army and administration, in other words, to adopt a frank policy of westerni-

629

zation.   But that was, at least without several generations of preparatory labors, wholly out of the question.   The Turks, who had built up the Ottoman Empire and on whom it continued to rest,

Reasons why the Ottoman Empire was unresponsive to western civilization
were entirely too hostile to Europe to befriend themselves easily with either its attitudes or institutions.   That they were Mongoloid Asiatics was perhaps in itself enough to dig a hopeless chasm between themselves and their Caucasian neighbors to the west; but as they were besides of the Moslem faith, they stubbornly locked and double-locked their minds against influences emanating from the
hated Christians.   In the days of their glory and as late as Solyman the Magnificent (d. 1566) the Turks had maintained a governing system which was in many respects superior to anything in contemporary Europe; but since the seventeenth century this system had fallen into open and undisguised decay.   The army, the once famous Janissaries, had become a wretched, undisciplined militia; the administration maintained by the provincial governors or pashas had degenerated into a sink of corruption; and the once war-like sultans had been replaced by feeble voluptuaries content to pass their lives in the enervating atmosphere of the imperial harem.

But if the Turks, though threatened with destruction, sealed their ears to the siren voices of the west, such was not the case with the Christian peoples of the Balkan peninsula who had been brought

The revival of the conquered Christian nationalities of the Balkan peninsula
under Ottoman subjection in the fifteenth century.   Before the end of the eighteenth century the Greeks and Serbs began to exhibit signs of restlessness giving evidence that they were stirred with a new hope.   At the same time intellectual leaders appeared among them, who, having traveled in the west, preached the necessity of spreading the knowledge of western ways by those characteristic instrumentalities, the school and the printing press.   The
effect was seen in the revolt (1804) of the Serbs of the Belgrad area which by 1817 had led to the enforced grant on the part of the sultan of a not inconsiderable autonomy.   When in 1821 the Greeks were in their turn encouraged to rise, they gained, as we have seen, not only autonomy but independence.   In this way a notable breach was made in the Ottoman house by action from within.   And what Serbs and Greeks had wrung from a decrepit master, could not Rumanians, Bulgars, and Albanians gain also?   Sooner or later the nationalist awakening, based on a new self-reliance as well as on the

absorption of the western outlook and methods, would reach all the Balkan groups, and the feeble sultan, the Sick Man of Europe as he was coming to be called, would be confronted with the more or less coördinated rebellion of his Christian subjects.

Advancing Russia, decadent Turkey, and the awakening Christian nationalities are three leading factors in the general nineteenth century situation of the Ottoman Empire; but there is a fourth. If the end of the Mohammedan state was at hand, it was not likely that the other European powers would leave the field to Russia as sole eventual heir. We are aware that Austria from the time of Prince Eugene had taken a keen interest in the Balkan peninsula; and the Mediterranean powers, France and Great Britain, did not fail to see the advantages beckoning in the Ottoman coastal areas. When somewhat past the middle of the nineteenth century Italy and Germany emerged into the light of day, they too turned a fascinated attention on the opportunities presented by the Near East. In this manner the decay of the Ottoman Empire became a general European concern, and the play of the imperialist appetites and enmities of the great powers must at all times be reckoned with as one of the directive forces in the movement of events.

The imperialist hunger of the great powers

If the initial Christian revolt, the revolt of the Serbs in 1804, had on the whole presented itself to view as a local, an Ottoman occurrence, that had not been the case with the Greek revolt of 1821. Its very significance lay in the fact that it produced an intervention of the powers and was followed by a war between the sultan and the tsar. Concluded by the Peace of Adrianople (1829), this conflict greatly strengthened the position of the Muscovite by conceding to him what amounted substantially to a protectorate over the principality of Serbia and the two principalities of Moldavia and Wallachia, the nucleus of modern Rumania. By an irresistible, patient procedure Russia was pushing into the Balkan peninsula. And at this promising juncture fate itself seemed to play into the Russian hands. The sultan's most powerful provincial agent was Mehemet Ali, pasha of Egypt. We have encountered him in the Greek war, wherein he took a part which might have proved decisive, had not the powers interfered and wrecked his fleet at Navarino. Mehemet's distinction was that he had provided himself with an army and a navy on the European model. He was in consequence

The sultan disastrously defeated on two occasions by the pasha of Egypt

more powerful than his over-lord, the sultan, and when he demanded a reward for his sacrifices to the common cause in the form of southern Syria, he could enforce his request with threats. From this situation there developed in 1831 a war between master and man, in which the pasha was successful, in fact so extraordinarily successful that Mehemet's army, commanded by his son Ibrahim, might have taken Constantinople itself if Tsar Nicholas had not interposed his veto (1833). In consequence of a protection asked for and received the sultan, Mahmud by name, was reduced to the status of a Russian ward and burned with thoughts of vengeance on his disobedient vassal of Egypt. In 1839 he renewed the war with Mehemet only to be again disastrously defeated. As in the very midst of the conflict Mahmud died, leaving the scepter to a youthful son, a general disintegration seized upon the Ottoman Empire which seemed to prognosticate its end.

If Tsar Nicholas could by his sole action in 1839 have "saved" the Ottoman Empire a second time, he would beyond a doubt have completed its reduction to a Russian province. But this time the other powers were on the alert and insisted on also having a hand in "saving" the Moslem state. The result was that, though only after a terrible crisis in which the specter of a general war loomed over Europe, the powers together undertook to regulate the affairs of the Near East. After a severe chastisement at the hands of European forces Mehemet was swept back into Egypt, which he received as his hereditary possession, though subject to the sultan as suzerain. So much but not a jot or tittle more would the powers concede to the pasha in return for his two victories over his master. This done, Mahmud's young son was enthroned on the Bosporus. The new ruler owed his existence and security to all the powers, not to Russia alone — that is the point to be noted. The tsar had acted with the other powers and in apparent agreement with them had restored the Ottoman Empire. And yet at bottom he saw the Ottoman problem in a radically different light from them. For it is clear as day that the Muscovite ruler interpreted the informal European protectorate as a preliminary step to a partition, while the other powers, and particularly Great Britain, because a partition would inevitably carry Russia to the key-position of Constantinople, opposed a partition and were resolved to use the protectorate to the end of "reforming" the Ottoman Empire in order that it might become strong enough to resist all further Russian encroachment.

Europe assumes an informal protectorate over the Ottoman Empire (1839)

Such are the elements that account for the Russo-British antagonism which ruled the Near East for the rest of the century. Great Britain was set on the policy of reform and because of its friendly interest in the government completely gained the ear of the sultan and of a small enlightened group of Ottoman officials. In fairness it must be admitted that some changes were effected, largely due to British pressure. Already Sultan Mahmud had in 1826 got rid of the worthless and ever mutinous Janissaries. On the foundations laid by him there was now built up a new Ottoman army equipped, disciplined, and organized in the manner of Europe. Undeniably this reformed army became the most important single factor in the prolongation of the life of the state. There was also a hesitant reshaping of the administration in the spirit of centralized control. On the other hand, as the terrible corruption persisted and as, in the main, the Turks fiercely opposed the spread of European ideas, the old evils proved ineradicable. The signs of discontent multiplied, if anything, and repeated risings furnished Tsar Nicholas with all the ammunition he needed to sustain his favorite thesis that Ottoman reform was a delusion and that the only logical course for the powers was to arrange for an early amicable division of the sultan's lands. Aware that, to carry this policy, he would have to gain the consent, first of all, of Great Britain, the tsar repeatedly approached the British cabinet with partition projects which London firmly rejected. The upshot was that, disappointed and enraged, he resolved to proceed alone. In 1853 his ambassador at Constantinople was ordered to present an ultimatum which called for the recognition of himself as the protector of all Greek Christians on Ottoman soil and which by implication signified the substitution of a Russian for the general European control of Turkey.

It was this ultimatum which led to the Crimean War (1854–1856) which we have already treated.[1] As Russia was defeated, the victors, Great Britain and France, in dictating the Peace of Paris, deprived the great Slav power of all the special advantages within the Ottoman Empire accumulated by previous wars and reduced it, in respect of that feeble state, to an exact level with all the other European states. Furthermore, in order to give the sultan the greatest possible security against a renewed future aggression, the two western powers

Great Britain backs and Russia opposes Ottoman reform

The Crimean War and Peace of Paris (1856)

[1] See p. 546.

went the length of forbidding Russia to maintain a navy on the Black sea. Finally, the informal general protectorate maintained since 1839 at Constantinople was abolished and the Ottoman Empire welcomed as a sovereign state into the comity of European nations.

Carefully examined the Treaty of Paris represented an attempt to secure the perpetuation of the Ottoman state by diplomatic devices. That it failed goes without saying. What was the use of stating

Folly and failure of the Treaty of Paris

that all was well in the sultan's realm when it was as plain as a pike-staff that decay persisted and that it was evidenced by the constant risings of oppressed populations? Presently one or the other power or several in combination interfered at some exposed point to put out a conflagration and restore tranquillity. They thus violated the sovereignty which they themselves had so sonorously proclaimed and indirectly endorsed the position of Russia that the Ottoman weakness was irremediable. Furthermore, Russia rapidly recovered from the Crimean disaster and evolved plans for undoing its effects. The war of 1870 between France and Germany was a golden opportunity. As soon as Europe was fully absorbed with that struggle, the tsar struck from his limbs the chief shackle imposed by the Treaty of Paris by issuing a declaration to the effect that he would no longer hold himself bound by the Black sea clause. To mark the complete resumption of his independence in the Black sea waters he undertook the construction of a navy and of a naval base. Fifteen years after the capture of Sebastopol Russia rebuilt that ruined port, thereby symbolically resuming the interrupted march on Constantinople.

The self-assertion which lay in this nullification of solemn treaty obligations was no isolated act of Russian policy. The Crimean defeat had convinced certain elements of the Russian people that some-

Alexander II takes up reform

thing was wrong with their state and that the time had come for a thorough reconstruction. It was now a hundred and fifty years since Peter the Great had initiated among his resisting and unwilling subjects a revolution from above. Among its by-products, hardly foreseen by the enterprising tsar, had been the creation of a small but active Russian middle class, which together with the more mobile elements of the land-holding nobility gradually formed an enlightened upper crust friendly to the program of reform and to western ideas in general. On the heel of the defeat of Russia in the Crimean war these people energetically came forward, declaring by book, pamphlet, and newspaper that the hour had struck to resume and intensify the eighteenth century reform movement. They insisted that the oppressed and submerged Russian people had at last made its appearance on the scene of history and in no uncertain terms prophesied a revolution from below if the work of Europeanization was not carried forward to a new stage. The young tsar, Alexander II (1855–1881), a humane and sensitive man, proved to be agreeably responsive to the pressure put upon him. Partly because the old institutions were manifestly antiquated, partly in order to conciliate hostile criticism, he inaugurated an important era of reform.

Three measures indicate that Alexander was willing to go far to bridge the wide gap between his country and western Europe. He introduced a new legal and judicial system inspired by western models; he endowed the constituent provinces of the Russian state with self-governing assemblies called *zems-* *tvos;* and he emancipated the serfs. This last measure _{The emancipation of the serfs} carried Alexander's reputation around the world because it elevated the legal and moral status of millions of peasants, who in the primitive, agricultural society constituting Russia made up the bulk of the population. Beginning with edicts liberating the peasant-serfs on the vast imperial estates, he ended with the decree of 1861 sweepingly applicable to the whole Russian territory. At the same time the attempt was made to convert the liberated agriculturists into peasant-proprietors. In return for a compensation paid out of state funds each landlord agreed to surrender a part of his property, which, assigned to his former subjects, was distributed among the households constituting a village group. As on this basis of apportionment the individual peasant-farm was so small as barely to suffice for subsistence, certain evils put in their appearance which rapidly assumed extraordinary proportions. For one thing there were presently far more peasants than the existing peasant land would support, and for another the surplus peasants constituted an impoverished agricultural proletariat animated by an unquenchable land-hunger. While some elements of this body were, it is true, gradually diverted toward the vast, unoccupied tracts of Siberia, others remained behind with rage and misery in their hearts and with a growing tendency to look for relief from their cramped conditions to the large and comfortable estates of the nobility. Decidedly emancipation, however laudable it may have been in raising the peasants to a human status, was far from solving all their economic problems.

Successfully launched on a policy of reform, Alexander was, before the first decade of his reign had passed, seized with doubts and fears that brought him to a halt. Perhaps the decisive factor in his **Alexander II reverts to reaction** change of front was the Polish revolution. In 1863 the Poles rose against him as they had risen thirty years before against his father, and although his armies quickly stamped out the rebellious embers, he became convinced he had himself nursed the serpent, revolution, by his support of modernizing measures. When, therefore, liberal sentiment raised its voice in behalf of an extension of the zemstvo idea to the whole realm in the form of a general Russian parliament, he abruptly broke with his former allies and, falling under the sway of reaction, enacted every conceivable measure conducive to the suppression of free opinion. The culminating act was the reintroduction of Nicholas I's infamous secret police system, known in the annals of Russian martyrdom as the Third Section.

With this dramatic change war was declared between Alexander and the Europeanizing intelligentsia which, like all thwarted groups, soon gave evidence of turning more and more to radical solutions. **The terrorists assassinate the tsar** While some liberals took up a sardonic and disillusioned rationalism, akin to eighteenth century enlightenment and called nihilism, others amused themselves with socialist and anarchist views, and still others, filled with a fanatic need for action, formed societies of terrorists pledged to the idea of wringing concessions from the government by deeds of violence. They murdered unpopular officials and in effect levied private war upon the tsar. Of course the threatened government met the attack by doubling its repression and, seizing its victims by the thousands, sent them marching in endless chain-gangs into the ice-bound wildernesses of Siberia. In March, 1881, Alexander II himself fell a victim to the ferocious struggle. A bomb thrown by a terrorist assassin ended his life.

Before Alexander perished he had been enabled to strike another and measurably successful blow against the old enemy of Russia, the sultan. It was in 1875 that the Balkan question once again **The Russo-Turkish War of 1877-1878** became pressing by the fresh rebellion of a subject people. The Christian Serbs of Herzegovina and Bosnia rose against their Ottoman masters, and by gaining the support of the two small Serb states of Serbia and Montenegro created a situation which alarmed and agitated all Europe.

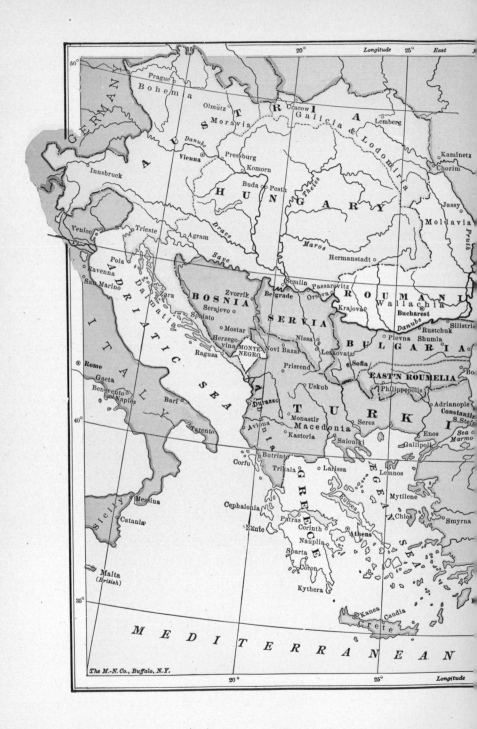

When the sultan was on the point of getting the better of his adversaries, the powers interfered to protect them against excessive punishment, but unable to persuade the Moslems to see reason, abandoned the field to the Russians, who, wanting nothing better than a chance to attack their ancient foe, issued a declaration of war (April, 1877). Pouring through the provinces of Moldavia and Wallachia, which since the Peace of Paris had been organized on a self-governing basis under the name of Rumania, they quickly drove the Ottoman forces before them toward the passes of the Balkan mountains. If it had not been for Osman Pasha, the war would have been for the Turks the story of a swift, ignominious collapse. Osman alone saved the honor of the Turkish army, for, gathering such forces as he could lay his hands on, he threw himself into the fortress of Plevna and there held the whole Russian army at bay for many months. However, when, in December, Plevna yielded, owing to starvation, and surrendered, the Russians encountered no further obstacle and poured in an irresistible stream across the Balkans into the Thracian plain. In January they camped on the shores of the sea of Marmora in view of the minarets of Constantinople. Reduced to utter helplessness, Sultan Abdul Hamid II was obliged humbly to sue for peace.

At this turn an enormous excitement seized upon the chancelleries of Europe, more particularly of Austria and Great Britain. They saw Russia in complete possession of its prey and in order to bring home to the tsar that they did not intend to let him devour it by himself in total oblivion of his neighbors, they made frantic gestures, Austria by mobilizing an army on the Rumanian border, Great Britain by despatching a fleet to the Dardanelles. It was a critical situation that became positively explosive when Russia in a treaty negotiated at San Stefano (a suburb of Constantinople) at last revealed the terms she was willing to concede to her beaten foe. The main feature of the treaty was the reduction of Turkey-in-Europe to such small dimensions that its Balkan role might be looked on as a closed book. Except for this Turkish remnant around Constantinople and except for the already liberated states of Greece, Serbia, Montenegro, and Rumania, the Balkan area was to be constituted as Bulgaria. This Big Bulgaria, manifestly under Russian tutelage, was the ominous novelty of the San Stefano pact; and as it seemed to Austria and Great Britain to secure to Russia the control of the peninsula, they protested clamorously against it. Insisting that the Treaty of San Stefano

Russian ascendancy secured by the Peace of San Stefano

must be submitted for revision to a congress of the powers, they would undoubtedly have gone the length of war, had not Russia given way. That the tsar yielded caused him and his people deep chagrin but was due to the fact that he was without a single friend in Europe on whom he could positively count for help.

In June, 1878, there took place the Congress of Berlin, which under the presidency of Prince Bismarck revised the Treaty of San Stefano according to the wishes of Austria and Great Britain. To **The Treaty** be sure, Russia was not deprived of all the fruits of victory. **of Berlin,** She received southern Bessarabia from Rumania, which **1878** carried her boundary to the mouth of the Danube. For this loss Rumania, her ally in the late war, was compensated by the Dobrudja taken from Bulgaria. Furthermore, the tsar was permitted to strengthen his position at the other end of the Black sea, in the Caucasus, by the acquisition of a part of the Armenian borderland. However, even for these relatively scanty territorial rewards Austria and Great Britain insisted on a full equivalent for themselves. Bosnia and Herzegovina, the Serb lands where the conflagration had started, were entrusted to Austria "to occupy and administer," while Great Britain secured the island of Cyprus on much the same terms. However, the outstanding measure of the Treaty of Berlin was that the tsar was obliged to forego his stranglehold on the Balkan peninsula secured by his plan of a Big Bulgaria. At the bidding of the Congress of Berlin Big Bulgaria was broken into three sections. Between the Danube and the Balkan mountains a self-governing *principality of Bulgaria* was set up with no obligation to the sultan save the payment of an annual tribute; south of the Balkans a province, to be called *Eastern Rumelia*, was conceded civil autonomy on the understanding that it was to be occupied by Turkish military forces; and finally, the important province of *Macedonia*, commanding the Vardar valley, was handed back to the sultan in order to enable him to continue to play an effective Balkan role. Though more hesitantly than at Paris twenty-two years before, the congress tried to blow the breath of life into the moribund Ottoman state.

None the less it should not be overlooked that the Treaty of Berlin represents a signal advance in statesmanship over the Paris arrangements in that for the first time the powers outlined a constructive plan for the Balkan peninsula. The Christian states, Serbia, Montenegro, and Rumania, which had, largely by their own heroic efforts, broken the Ottoman yoke in the course of the recent decades, were, albeit grudgingly, given increases of territory and acknowledged to be henceforth free and independent. In the case of the tiny mountain eyrie of Montenegro this international guarantee of liberty was hardly necessary, for the brave mountaineers had as early as the eighteenth century renounced every vestige of dependence on the sultan. As Greece, hailed as an independent kingdom since its war of liberation, also received a better boundary by the addition of the province of Thessaly, the congress proved that it was attempting to dispense its favors among the small Christian states with an even hand. If to these acts we add the creation of the Bulgarian principality, by virtue of which another awakened people, the Bulgars, were set upon the path of freedom, we are justified in saying that although the congress resuscitated the Ottoman Empire, it at the same time envisaged a not too distant future in which the Balkan peninsula would be taken over wholly by the liberated Balkan peoples. And that was not only for the immediate beneficiaries but also for the great European states a far happier prospect than the thought which had hitherto been the nightmare of all the foreign offices, to wit, that the Balkan peninsula was destined to fall like a ripe apple into the lap of Russia.

The independent Balkan states

In the period following the Congress of Berlin the young Balkan states justified the confidence placed in them. The princes of Rumania and Serbia took the title king in celebration of their full sovereign status; and both these countries and the kingdom of Greece as well took up with eagerness the work of spreading through their backward communities the science and education of the west as well as the railroads, banks, and industries which were the basis of the modern economic system. However, the most notable progress after 1878 was perhaps made by the Bulgars, who as the last people to rouse themselves from slumber had also the greatest distance to travel. The official status of their principality as defined at Berlin was still far from satisfactory. An assembly, elected to nominate a ruler, called to office Alexander of Battenberg, a nephew of Tsar Alexander II. But Russia, which had liberated Bulgaria, could not divest itself of the idea of control and kept the young prince in strict leading-strings. When Tsar Alexander III (1881–1894) succeeded his father, the situation became worse, for the new tsar was a gloomy despot who expected the Bulgars to show their eternal gratitude to him by obedience to his every wish. As a result

The progress of Bulgaria

the Bulgars swiftly developed a strong resentment against the tsar
and resolved to take affairs entirely into their own hands. In 1885
their government entered into a conspiracy with the political leaders
of Eastern Rumelia, on the strength of which Eastern Rumelia was
incorporated with the principality. As from the nationalist viewpoint Eastern Rumelia was Bulgar territory, the ultimate union of
the two sections of one whole was inevitable; but since it was contrary to the Treaty of Berlin it caused an immense disturbance of
opinion throughout Europe. The grieved tsar promptly withdrew
from his too independent ward such favor as he had still been inclined to dispense, while neighboring Serbia in a burst of jealousy
even went the length of declaring war on its young sister-state. This
Serb attack Bulgaria victoriously repulsed and a peace was quickly
patched up through Austrian intervention (1885). An ominous
novelty, however, had made its appearance in the Balkan world.
The youthful Christian organisms, having got rid of their Moslem
master, were making ready in their vigorous self-confidence to dispute the remaining Balkan ground with one another. In this connection let us observe that the most considerable province still in
possession of the sultan was Macedonia. Inhabited by representatives of all the Balkan nationalities, really the only extensive no-man's
land of the peninsula, it might well lure the ambition of every eager
neighbor government. If the time came, as it surely would, for
Macedonia to be wrested from the sultan's weakened grip, would not
a tremendous storm be loosed among the lusty Christian states all
alike eager for the booty?

Russia's disappointment over recalcitrant Bulgaria coming as a
climax to her disappointment over the Treaty of Berlin provoked
her government to adopt an extreme measure. It instigated or at

Russia turns to the Far East
least participated in a conspiracy to get rid of Alexander
of Battenberg, who had made himself offensive because
he had sided with the Bulgar people against his Muscovite
relative and benefactor. Alexander was dethroned by a *coup d'état;*
and although he might have had himself reinstated by his grateful
subjects, he chose exile in the hope of thereby placating the tsar.
However, as the incensed Bulgar parliament refused to accept the
Russian candidate and offered the vacant throne (1887) to the candidate of the extreme nationalists, Ferdinand of Saxe-Coburg, the situation was from the Russian angle not in the least improved. Deeply
angered, Alexander III turned his back, as it were, on Europe and

DISTRIBUTION
OF
BALKAN PEOPLES

Scale in miles
25   0   25   50   75   100

Slavs   Rumanians   Greeks

Turks ▨▨ Albanians ▨▨ Magyars ▨▨ Germans

fronted toward Asia. His son and successor, Nicholas II (1894–1917),
followed the same course and therewith plunged Russia into a strange
and startling adventure.

Of course Asia represented no new interest for Russia since the
penetration of the vast stretches of Siberia had begun as long ago as a
century before the accession of Peter the Great. The movement had
gone on steadily ever since. Owing to the extremely sparse Russia ex-
population, it had not encountered many obstacles; but tends her
also, on account of the failure to pursue a policy of system- Asiatic
atic colonization, it had not been particularly profitable. empire
Not till the second half of the nineteenth century did the extraordinary agricultural and mineral possibilities of the immense north-Asi-
atic plains begin to dawn upon the governing circles at St. Petersburg.
By that time the Russian claims extended clear across Siberia to the
sea of Okhotsk on the Pacific ocean. With the improved prospects
in this area it became desirable to extend control southward to warmer
waters, but the execution of this purpose necessarily meant a clash
with the empire of China. However, as this great state had centuries
ago turned away from war to dedicate itself exclusively to the pur-
suits of peace, it was not found difficult to wrest from it first, the
Amur district (1858), and two years later, seven hundred miles of
coast fronting the sea of Japan. At the southernmost end of this
coastal stretch the triumphant Russians founded a new commercial
capital, Vladivostok (1860). As at the same time military expeditions had begun to push south from Siberia into central Asia and as,
during the reigns of the second and third Alexander, they had gradually established Russian ascendancy throughout Turkestan, the
Asiatic expansion of Russia must be admitted to have prospered
extraordinarily in the age of these two tsars.

Now with Russia balked in Europe by the failure of her Bulgarian
plans, the Asiatic movement gained in the last decade of the nineteenth century a new interest and momentum which naturally took
the form of a southward expansion in search of warmer
waters. For Russia, greatest of land empires, fronted Russia
everywhere on seas frozen during many months of each outlet south
year — a situation involving a heavy handicap which the of Vladi-
powerful government was firmly resolved no longer to vostok
bear. The exception to the rule of frozen water-front was the Black
sea. But though the Black sea was happily immune against ice, its
free use was interdicted to Russia by the Ottoman control of the

straits.   Even the newly acquired Vladivostok had proved a disappointment since the severe winter season regularly suspended shipping.   In 1891 the Russian government began the construction of the great trans-Siberian railway, the eastern terminal of which would of necessity be at Vladivostok.   But could not a more suitable terminal be found farther to the south on water open all the year?   St. Petersburg had only begun to revolve this question when the Far East was shaken by a war between Japan and China.

In sharp distinction from China the empire of Japan had, ever since, under American pressure (1854), its gates swung wide to world trade, embarked on a policy of systematic Europeanization.

Rise of Japan and its defeat of China (1895) and of Russia (1904–1905)
We need not rehearse the stages of this process since this book has dealt with them again and again.   The amazing feature about the Japanese transformation was its rapidity and apparent thoroughness.   By 1890 a climax had been reached by the introduction of a parliament which exercised the usual legislative functions under the hereditary ruler, the mikado.   What chiefly prompted the Japanese to break so resolutely with their past was the clear-headed perception that unless they equipped themselves with the institutions and mental outlook of Europe they would inevitably be subjugated by the occident.   Being a cramped island-people, they interested themselves, as soon as they had reformed their government, in the Asiatic mainland as a possible area of expansion, and more particularly in near-by Korea.   Over this important peninsula they began in 1894 a war with China which they easily won because the larger empire, clinging tenaciously to its past, had hitherto refused to make the least gesture toward the assimilation of western efficiency.   In the peace (1895) dictated by Japan, this enterprising state acquired not only a veiled hold on Korea but also the direct possession of Port Arthur, a sort of potential Gibraltar of northern China.   Immediately Russia was up in arms, for Port Arthur was the very point she had secretly fixed on as the terminal of her trans-Siberian railroad and as the Pacific base for her fleet.   Persuading France and Germany to join her, she not only obliged Japan to relinquish Port Arthur but a few years later (1898) persuaded China to lease Port Arthur to herself. As at the same time, in connection with her extensive railway plans, she wrung from the Pekin government the military occupation of Manchuria, she now commanded a power in the Far East which was like a sword thrust at the very life of Japan.   Sharp notes were

exchanged and high feeling was engendered on both sides till the inevitable happened. In February, 1904, the desperate Japanese threw themselves on Russia and in the ensuing war beat her repeatedly on land and water. In August, 1905, with President Roosevelt acting as mediator, a peace was signed at Portsmouth (New Hampshire) by the terms of which Russia retired from Manchuria and transferred her lease of Port Arthur to Japan. As a result of the war Russia still remained a great Pacific and Asiatic power, but Japan had successfully protected its interests and made good its claim to be treated as an equal not only by Russia but by every other European state.

Worse for Tsar Nicholas II than his defeat at the hands of Japan was the domestic agitation launched against the government on account of its manifest mismanagement of the war. Since the terrorist activity which we have related and which culminated The in the murder of Tsar Alexander II the internal situation Russian of Russia had experienced a notable change. Beginning Revolution, with Alexander III and continuing under Nicholas II 1904-1905 the government had made a sustained effort to introduce the Industrial Revolution in order to bring the backward country somewhat nearer the western level in the matter of military efficiency and general economic productivity. Western capital was invited into Russia on favorable terms, vast railway constructions were carried out under governmental direction, and factories sprang up like mushrooms in such great centers as St. Petersburg, Moscow, Kiev, and Odessa. True, the transforming impulse came chiefly from above while the money was supplied from abroad; none the less the usual social and economic changes did not fail to put in an appearance. By 1900 Russia had acquired a strengthened middle class of bankers, business men, and engineers and a wholly novel group of factory workers. Furthermore, as might have been expected, the middle class aligned itself politically with western liberalism, while the workers, influenced by an effective propaganda, passed in a body into the socialist camp. In the face of this situation a desire for a modification of the traditional absolutism made itself felt which was much more effective in producing results than the system of sporadic murder practiced by the terrorists. In fact for the first time in Russian history the conditions had been created for a successful revolution of the people; and no sooner was the government engrossed by the war with Japan than it showed its face. To be sure the terrorists, whom the government police hunted like wild game but could not suppress, redoubled their activity and destroyed many a prominent official with pistol-shot or bomb, but in the main it was the new phenomenon of an organized pressure from liberals and socialists which brought the tsar to terms. When his first vague promises only increased the agitation, Nicholas II at last in October, 1905, took a decisive step. He issued a manifesto in which he guaranteed to his subjects the western liberties of conscience, speech, and association and at the same time called a *duma* into being, that is, a Russian parliament.

To this striking defeat of absolutism another factor contributed which must not be overlooked. The immense area of the Russian Empire covering eastern Europe and northern Asia was settled not The by one but by some scores of peoples who had all been Russian brought under the Russian scepter by military might. Empire a The Russians were indeed the central nucleus of the state, state of many na- but along the western border, in the Caucasus mountains, tionalities and thoughout Siberia other groups, great and small and representing every conceivable divergence of blood, speech, and customs, made their home, accommodating themselves as best they could to the fact of Russian domination. Closely scrutinized, Russia was not a consolidated national state but an agglomeration of discordant nationalities like Austria-Hungary. Along the western border alone there were more than half a dozen distinct peoples: Finns in Finland, Esths, Letts, and Germans in the Baltic provinces, and farther south, Lithuanians, Poles, and Ukrainians (Little Russians). In the nineteenth century these had all been sorely afflicted with the so-called "Russification" policy of the tsarist government. This was a systematic attempt to deprive them of their language, religion, and whatever other inheritance they cherished with a view to transforming them into obedient Orthodox Russians. As a result they nursed a deep though secret grudge against their master, and when the revolution of 1904–1905 broke out they joined the movement of revolt as far as they dared. Especially the Finns and Poles, among whom the memories of independence were a burning fire, exhibited ominous signs of unrest. These stirrings all along the border made a deep impression on the frightened government and undoubtedly constituted a considerable factor in the swift surrender signified by the October manifesto.

Great rejoicings were released among the victors by what looked to them like the fall of Russian absolutism. But the bonfires were premature. The first duma met in 1906 and, elected on a broad suffrage, was animated by the desire to complete the revolution. Meanwhile, as usual, the forces of reaction had set in. Nicholas II was able to rally the strong conservative forces about him consisting of officers, officials, landowners, and peasants, and in the course of the next few years he successfully broke the power of his adversaries. But though he disciplined the duma and reduced its authority, he did not abolish it. Failure of the revolution, 1906–1907 As a solely consultative body under an autocratic tsar it cut after 1907 rather a sorry figure; but undeniably its mere existence, apart from proving that the revolution had not been wholly in vain, not unreasonably inspired hope that it might yet serve as the nucleus of a gradual constitutional development.

The swift revival of the Russian autocracy enabled it to continue almost without interruption its expansionist policy; and, checked in the Far East, it now turned restlessly once more toward the Ottoman Empire. We shall trace in the following chapter how this shift of attention provided the opportunity for spinning the thread of the combination of powers known as the Triple entente. Both for the members of this group and The Turkish revolution, 1908 for those of the rival organization, the Triple alliance, the Ottoman Empire now became even more than before a center of passionate interest. The main reason was that never for a moment after the renewed lease of life conceded by the Congress of Berlin had the decay of this rotten edifice been brought to a halt. There had been a steady succession of risings and massacres — in Crete, in Macedonia, in Armenia — and the only cure conceivable to the reactionary sultan, Abdul Hamid II, had been bloody repression coupled with the maintenance of his unimpaired autocratic régime. But even this corrupt citadel of oriental immobility had at last been invaded by the forerunners of European civilization. Under their influence a Turkish intelligentsia, known familiarly as Young Turks, came into existence, who, in spite of Abdul Hamid's persecution, succeeded in spreading their doctrines far and wide, especially among the officers of the army. Suddenly in July, 1908, the world was surprised to hear that so irresistible a revolution had broken out in Constantinople that the sultan had yielded to it without demur. A parliament and constitution on the western pattern were the result and the Ottoman Empire seemed not only to have surrendered its traditions in order to trod the paths of Europe, but also to have brought to a conclusion the ancient disorders in its house! Of course these turned out before long to be exaggerated expectations. Neither Turkey nor any other state can pass over night from one world of thought and experience into another. However, it remained a fact that the Turks had indicated their desire to be assimilated in outlook and organization to their Christian neighbors, and as a mile-stone in the triumphant progress of occidental civilization the Ottoman revolution was and will always remain a notable event.

The Tsars of Russia (House of Romanov)	The Ottoman Sultans (House of Osman)
Alexander I (son of Paul I), 1801–1825	Mahmud II, 1808–1839
Nicholas I (brother of Alexander I), 1825–1855	Abdul Medjid I, 1839–1861
Alexander II (son of Nicholas I), 1855–1881	Abdul Aziz I, 1861–1876
Alexander III (son of Alexander II), 1881–1894	Murad V, 1876
Nicholas II (son of Alexander III), 1894–1917	Abdul Hamid II, 1876–1909
	Mohammed V, 1909–1918
	Mohammed VI, 1918–1923

REFERENCES

E. Fueter, *World History*, chs. 17, 22, 23
C. D. Hazen, *Europe Since 1815*, I, chs. 31, 32, II, chs. 34, 35
J. S. Schapiro, *Modern and Contemporary History*, chs. 21–23, 27
C. A. Fyffe, *Modern Europe*, III, chs. 3, 7
C. J. H. Hayes, *Political and Social History*, chs. 25, 26, 27
C. M. Andrews, *Development of Modern Europe*, II, chs. 8, 13
Cambridge Modern History, X, ch. 14, XI, chs. 9, 22, XII, chs. 12–14
E. R. Turner, *Europe 1789–1920*, ch. 7
J. H. Rose, *Development of Modern European Nations*, I, chs. 7–11, II, chs. 2, 9, 11
F. Schevill, *History of the Balkan Peninsula*, chs. 22–30
G. P. Gooch, *History of Modern Europe, 1878–1919*
R. W. Jeffery, *The New Europe*, chs. 13, 16
W. R. A. Morfill, *History of Russia*
R. Beazley and others, *Russia from the Varangians to the Bolsheviks*
A. Kornilov, *Modern Russian History*
D. M. Wallace, *Russia*
J. Mavor, *Economic History of Russia*, II, Bks. 4, 5, 7
F. A. Ogg, *Economic Development of Modern Europe*, ch. 15
P. Miliukov, *Russia and its Crisis*
B. Pares, *Russia and Reform*
J. R. Fisher, *Finland and the Tsars*
F. H. Skrine, *The Expansion of Russia*
K. P. Pobiedonostsev, *Reflections of a Russian Statesman*
K. Asakawa, *The Russo-Japanese Conflict*
W. Miller, *The Balkans; The Ottoman Empire*
Forbes and others, *The Balkans*
J. A. R. Marriott, *The Eastern Question*
S. P. H. Duggan, *The Eastern Question*
C. N. E. Eliot (Odysseus), *Turkey in Europe*

G. Young, *Nationalism and War in the Near East*
S. Lane-Poole, *Turkey*
H. M. Brailsford, *Macedonia: its Races and their Future*
H. W. Temperley, *History of Serbia*
E. Dicey, *The Peasant State*
L. Sergeant, *Greece in the Nineteenth Century*
C. A. Chekrezi, *Albania, Past and Present*

CHAPTER XXXII

THE NATIONALIST–IMPERIALIST PHASE OF FOREIGN POLICY (1871–1914) AND THE OUTBREAK OF THE WORLD WAR

Much space has been given in this book to foreign policy, the instruments of which are diplomacy and war. The justification for this procedure is that the relation of states to one another inevitably falls under the observation of every historian regardless of his definition of history. It may well be that the various categories of domestic happenings elicit a greater interest, but so long as states behave toward one another as free and independent organisms responsible to no one under God, they call for the closest scrutiny. And therewith we have touched on the most outstanding circumstance to keep in mind about the European states in the centuries covered by this history. Each is a struggling organism concerned with development, that is, it desires like everything that lives and grows to add to its strength and become as powerful as possible. However, as the lesser states, such as Switzerland and Denmark, are surrounded and held in check by larger ones, the principle in its pure and unadulterated form applies only to the group of states called the great powers. Of each one of them it may be said that the only restraint upon its ambition is the ambition of the others together with the circumstance that they have all developed a civilization based on productive labor and therefore inherently opposed to war as a destructive force. None the less war is still the last resort, the *ultima ratio* of the great powers since they have always acted on the principle that there is no limit to their jealously asserted sovereignty.

This being true, the form of government of a given state has, general opinion to the contrary notwithstanding, very little bearing on its foreign policy. Undoubtedly many people incline to think of the absolute monarchy as prone to war largely because it is absolute; but an oligarchy or a republic may just as readily appeal to arms because, so far as foreign affairs are concerned, it is no less absolute than the monarchy unlimited in all respects. European experience shows that monarchies, oligarchies, and republics alike have looked upon

The great states engaged in a struggle for power

Foreign policy independent of the form of government

648

themselves as free to pursue what they regard as their selfish interest subject only to the necessities of the situation. It is for this reason that if a state, giving up monarchy, radically reshapes its administrative, economic, or any other domestic inheritance, it rarely if ever changes its foreign policy. The case of France will serve as illustration. Between 1789 and 1914 France changed its government at least eight times, often as the result of what looked like a cataclysmic storm, but its foreign policy in that long period continued without essential deviation to follow the path marked out by Richelieu and Louis XIV.

But if the central principle governing the action of every great power in the foreign field has steadily remained the same throughout the Modern Age, its application has varied in response to the changing European situation and, above all, to the new and splendid opportunities connected with the radiation of occidental influence over the whole earth. Though the end of every foreign office has always been power, when this history opened power was contentedly sought within the narrow bounds of Europe itself. Then came the colonial movement with which certain favored trans-oceanic areas fell within the vision of the competitive states. As a result the seventeenth and eighteenth centuries rang with colonial wars. In the nineteenth century attention was for a time diverted from the colonial issues by the unification movement in Italy and Germany. This was based on the sentiment of nationalism which, gaining ground also in multinational states like Austria-Hungary, Russia, and the Ottoman Empire threatened to disrupt them and effect their reorganization on a strictly nationalist basis. Inevitably this critical movement within Europe drew the attention of the various foreign offices; but it did not interfere with their taking also all the other continents into consideration as soon as the new means of communication facilitated intercourse and the system of machine production increased beyond all expectation the prospect of profits to be derived from distant markets. It is possible therefore to speak of four or, more conveniently because of the contemporaneousness of the last two developments, of three phases of European foreign policy. During the first phase Europe, and more particularly western Europe, constituted the very limited field of vision of the rival statesmen; during the second phase the field of vision included together with the whole of Europe the new colonial areas in India and the Amer-

The three phases of European foreign policy

icas; and during the third phase not only Europe, agitated by the new force of nationalism, but also the whole earth with all its lands and seas fell within the scrutiny of the fiercely contentious foreign offices. This third phase extending from approximately 1871 to 1914 may be called the nationalist-imperialist phase and will be treated in this chapter.

Of the two main ingredients of foreign policy in the last and contemporary period, nationalism has been repeatedly dealt with. It manifested itself as the firm determination of those national groups **The nationalist factor in foreign policy** which through some accident of history had been broken into fragments or had been brought into subjection to some powerful neighbor to regain their unity and independence. But though after the achievement of Italian and German unity the chief field for nationalism was eastern and southeastern Europe, we should not fail to note that by a kind of mental sympathy it also reached such countries as France and England which had no immediate need for it since they had been unified many centuries before. Under these circumstances nationalism became a universal energy, and like a wine too freely quaffed mounted to the heads of all the European peoples. In every one of them may be encountered the phenomenon of the super-patriot. Joining with others of his kind, he constituted a band, small perhaps but noisy, which caused extraordinary mischief by exciting the corresponding bands of super-patriots in all the neighboring countries and thereby creating a very dangerous condition of general nervous tension.

Here lay a peril for the peace of Europe which was indefinitely multiplied by the second element of foreign policy, imperialism. This was, closely considered, nothing else than the colonialism of the **The imperialist factor in foreign policy** eighteenth century revived and intensified by the Industrial Revolution. Let us by rapid tabulation visualize the more important elements of the situation. The new means of communication — railroads, steamboats, telegraph — destroyed distances and brought all countries to the door of Europe. This is basic to the movement. Equally important is the enormously increased machine production for which Europe required non-European consumers. But the non-Europeans could pay for goods delivered to them only with native raw products such as wheat, fruits, minerals, rubber, etc. As inventions multiplied and articles serving our human convenience were put forth which surpassed even the dreams of visionaries it was disclosed that there was no country or climate which did not desire these comforts and devices and which did not possess something of its own capable of being exchanged therefor. For all these reasons a dense net of traffic was thrown around the earth from pole to pole. And as each national group of traders wished to be as secure as possible in a newly opened region, it persuaded the home government to step in and, raising the country's flag, to effect a political annexation. In this way a fierce and lawless scramble was inaugurated among the European powers for all those backward areas which had not been included in the colonial struggle of the eighteenth century. The movement may be compared to the famous gold-rush to California or the Klondike. At any rate in the course of a little more than a generation following the Franco-German War of 1870 much of Asia, most of Africa, and all of the Pacific archipelago had been appropriated by the jealous rivals. By the beginning of the twentieth century the backward areas which might be conceived as still available for seizure were reduced to Morocco at the northwestern corner of Africa, China and Persia in Asia, and the Ottoman Empire straddling Europe and Asia at the straits of the Bosporus and Dardanelles.

In measure as the prospective booty narrowed, the competition for it inevitably became more intense. Louder and louder rose the clamors of greedy traders and capitalists which the heated super-patriots did not fail to reënforce with their own peculiarly raucous cries. The great powers of Europe were six in number and they were all committed to the game. The three older and more successful states, Great Britain, France, and Russia, wished to round off the empires already amassed, while the more recent arrivals, Italy and Germany, were spurred to increased energy in order to make up for lost time. Even manifestly declining Austria-Hungary was not willing to forego its stake in the near-by Ottoman Empire. As the years rolled by it became quite clear that a peaceful partition of the prizes still subject to appropriation would prove very difficult. Only the most moderate and skillful diplomacy on the part of all the European capitals could possibly succeed in avoiding a catastrophe. The following account of diplomatic relations after 1871 unfolds the breathless tale of how the foreign offices succeeded for a while but failed in the long run to control the nationalist and imperialist forces astir in the world and steered their countries into the destructive maelstrom of 1914.

The Franco-German war of 1870-1871 created a new situation in Europe. The signal victory won by united Germany made the new empire the leading continental power and caused the other govern-

Germany dominates the diplomatic situation after 1871
ments to look forward with interest and anxiety to the policy which it would adopt. Bismarck, who, as the architect of German unity, enjoyed such authority that he exercised undisputed sway over German foreign affairs, was not long in disclosing his hand. In order that his country might consolidate the result of the three successful wars of 1864, 1866, and 1871, it needed, in his view, above all things a long peace. Since the only probable immediate disturber of the peace was France, which, as a defeated power wounded in its deepest feelings by the loss of Alsace-Lorraine, was patently animated with the hope of revenge, Bismarck applied all his skill to bring about the diplomatic isolation of his western neighbor. His thought was that France would prove dangerous only in case she succeeded in attaching to herself an ally.

Since Great Britain was in the early seventies prompted to keep aloof from continental affairs, the main factors in Bismarck's calculation were Russia and Austria-Hungary. Italy, as not immedi-

Bismarck creates the league of the Three Emperors
ately bordering on Germany, could be dismissed from the reckoning. Only in case France won the close friendship of either Russia or Austria-Hungary would she care to risk a war with her Rhenish neighbor. With these circumstances in mind Bismarck set to work to attach both Russia and Austria-Hungary to Germany and succeeded so well that in 1872 the rulers of the three empires entered into an alliance with one another.

However, an agreement yoking together Austria and Russia was a precarious affair and almost certain to go by the boards the moment the Turkish question was mooted between them. Both had for

Shipwreck of the league of the Three Emperors over the Ottoman question
generations entertained with regard to the Ottoman Empire ambitious and conflicting projects which, though often adjourned because of the pressure of other interests, had an uncomfortable habit of making a periodical reappearance. A grave crisis in Ottoman affairs in 1875 immediately aligned Russia and Austria-Hungary on opposite sides; and when, in 1877, Russia went to war with the Ottoman Empire the Hapsburg government looked on with disapproval, promptly converted to alarm, on Russia's winning

a brilliant victory and imposing on the sultan the peace of San Stefano. Since Great Britain took the Russian successes even more to heart than Austria, the two aggrieved governments by acting together were able to force the Tsar to a revision of his San Stefano treaty at a congress held at Berlin (1878). Russia, getting less than she considered her just due, was outraged, blamed her mid-European friends for her discomfiture, and grumblingly withdrew from further coöperation with them. The Bismarckian league of the Three Emperors was at an end.

Since the bitter competition over the Ottoman Empire produced a clear case of domestic incompatibility between Austria and Russia, Bismarck was obliged to be content with the association of either one or the other of his eastern neighbors and chose the Danubian monarchy. In the year 1879 he took the momentous step of concluding a defensive alliance with that state. Two years later occurred an incident destined to bring an important accession to the Austro-German partnership: France and Italy engaged in a diplomatic clash over the Mediterranean. France, already in possession of Algeria, desired to extend her African control and in 1881 seized Tunis, nominally an Ottoman province, though really an independent state. Having herself cast a covetous eye on Tunis, Italy resented the action of France but without avail. Here was European imperialism in action with a typical seizure of a backward area by one power followed by the jealous protest of another. The anti-French indignation of Italy mounted to such a point that the Italian government applied to Bismarck for admission to the German alliance with Austria, thus converting it (1882) into a Triple alliance.

[margin note: Creation of the Triple alliance of Germany, Austria, and Italy]

The Triple alliance of the three central European powers, though avowedly defensive in character, directed an unmistakable edge against Russia and France and operated to draw these two unattached states together. Radically dissimilar in political organization, the absolute monarchy of the tsar and the democratic French republic hesitated a long time before joining hands and fortunes. Finally, in 1890, driven by diplomatic necessity and disregarding every consideration but that of safety, they effected a preliminary arrangement which in the following year (1891) ripened into a formal alliance. Thus before the close of the century Europe fell into the two opposed camps of the Triple and Dual alliances, which maintained a delicate and perilous

[margin note: Creation of the Dual alliance of France and Russia]

balance of power with Great Britain swinging between them in the role of a wandering comet attached to neither system.

The British governments of the time, Conservative and Liberal alike, held the view that the two alliances dividing Europe had crystallized over purely continental matters which interested Great **Great** Britain remotely if at all, since she was a colonial power **Britain re-** almost exclusively pursuing objects lying beyond the **solves to** confines of Europe. In consequence Great Britain main- **join the** **Dual** tained what was proudly proclaimed as "a splendid **alliance** isolation." However, granting that the two alliances were immediately concerned with near-by matters, the five member powers involved had alike embarked on an imperialist policy and any given power, whenever it launched a forward movement in Africa or Asia, very naturally turned for support to its allies, since it was sure to meet with naught but ill-will and resistance from its rivals. Thus imperceptibly the two systems extended their influence so as to take in the whole world; and presently Great Britain found that her isolation was injurious, perhaps even dangerous, and that, in order to get backing for her particular projects, she would be doing well to join hands with either the Triple or the Dual alliance. After flirting for a while with the Triple alliance, with the coming of the twentieth century she veered about and definitely threw in her lot with France and Russia. This momentous step was chiefly due to the grave alarm excited in Great Britain by the economic development and naval policy of Germany.[1]

We have noted the remarkable industrial and commercial development of Germany following her unification. True, it was no isolated movement, since the economic expansion was general, a **Industrial-** world phenomenon, but the German development pro- **ized** ceeded apparently at a more rapid pace than that of its **Germany** neighbors, and in any case visibly provided Germany, a **becomes** **colonial and** hitherto divided and backward nation, with a very **imperialist** capable industrial organization, a vast merchant fleet, and commercial relations extending over all the earth. Though continuing, from an economic viewpoint, to remain inferior to Great Britain, she was undoubtedly pressing more and more closely on British heels. Moreover, following the common trend, she

---

[1] It may be noted that the earliest step of Great Britain signifying an abandonment of her "splendid isolation" was taken in 1902 by means of an alliance with Japan covering Asiatic interests.

adopted in the eighties a colonial policy, acquiring territory chiefly in Africa. As we have seen, colonialism, starting as an economic enterprise, usually develops into imperialism, concerned with territory and power, and in the nineties German policy became definitely imperialist.

The important change in foreign policy occurred simultaneously with a change of rulers; it may even be said to have been at least partly occasioned by that change. In 1888 a new sovereign, William II, came to the throne, shortly after his accession dismissed Bismarck from office (1890), and then with masterful self-sufficiency undertook to be his own chancellor and foreign minister. What Bismarck had cautiously refrained from doing, that is, from identifying himself *Imperialism championed by the new sovereign, William II* with an out-and-out imperialist course looking to territory beyond Europe, the ambitious William II took upon himself, and as the most appropriate step toward the realization of his hopes, planned the construction of a navy. Hitherto Germany had had no navy worth mentioning and the innovation was an open announcement that she was about to make a bid for sea-power.

Sea-power was sought and in varying degree possessed by every imperialist power of Europe but it was undoubtedly the special weapon of England. In fact, the British empire rested on the control of the seas, and the very first German navy bill authorizing expenditure on a large scale (1898) caused a shock which made itself felt from John o' Groats to Land's End. When the first bill was followed by others still further increasing construction, Great Britain unhesitatingly took up the challenge, strengthened her navy *The issue of sea-power ranges Great Britain against Germany* by enormous appropriations, and successfully maintained an easy preponderance over Germany. She had for generations held to the so-called two-power standard, which meant that the British navy was always to be a match for any two possible rivals combined, and alarmed by the action of the power across the North sea, she attached herself to the program of the two-power standard more ardently than ever. Nor was that all. As already said, early in the twentieth century, Great Britain made up her mind to give up the friendly neutrality which she had maintained for a decade between the two groups of powers and to throw her influence into the scales on the side of the Dual alliance and against Germany.

Though the story of Anglo-German rivalry is complicated with innumerable details which have no place here, it turns substantially, as indicated, around the question of German imperialism. Tact-lessly pushed by Emperor William II in and out of season and given in English eyes a formidable character by the feature of a powerful navy, German imperialism moved the British government to turn its face to France and Russia and as a measure preliminary to a better understanding with them, to attempt an accommodation of all out-standing differences. It must be remembered that the French and Russian imperialisms had been the most successful imperialisms in Europe after that of Great Britain, and that all through the nine-teenth century the friction among these three rivals had, as a result of the relentless pursuit of their respective interests, been constant. The Crimean War of 1854, to mention but a single instance, was a combination of France and Great Britain formed to hinder Russia from bringing the decaying Ottoman Empire completely under its control. Since then the diplomatic clashes among the three im-perialist leaders had been frequent, but as between France and Russia they had been brought to an effective end by the alliance of 1891. If Great Britain desired to get support against Germany from these two ancient rivals of hers, it was plain that she would have to give their ambitions larger play, and, fully aware of this condition of success, she opened negotiations first with France and then with Russia.

Great Britain draws near to France and Russia

In 1904 Great Britain and France came to an agreement by virtue of which France, in return for conceding Egypt to Great Britain, was given a free hand in Morocco. Of course the treaty did not use this crude language because certain decencies had to be observed, owing to the circumstance that Egypt belonged technically to the Ottoman Empire and that Morocco was an independent state under its own Mohammedan ruler. In fact Morocco was, as already noted, one of the few independent states still left in the world among those classifiable as "backward." The treaty established what became known as the Franco-British entente, a word signifying a diplomatic understanding of a less formal character than an uncompromising alliance. Three years later, in 1907, Great Britain composed her leading difference with Russia by a treaty touching Persia. By its terms Russia and Great Britain assumed control respectively of

Creation of the Triple entente. Agreement over Egypt, Morocco, and Persia

northern and southern Persia while the shah, hitherto an independent sovereign, was left in doubtful possession of the reduced middle section of his ancient kingdom. By these arrangements Great Britain, France, and Russia began an intimacy famous under the name of the Triple entente. Beginning with 1907, the alignment of the six great powers of Europe took the form of Triple entente versus Triple alliance with each group inclined to seize upon every incident that arose as an occasion for the display of temper and the assertion of prestige.

From the moment Great Britain joined with France and Russia, German imperialism labored under a heavy disadvantage. Closely examined, each and every imperialism, directed in accordance with the actual situation in the world to the control and seizure of primarily African and Asiatic territory, depended on sea-power, and with Great Britain flanked by France and Russia blocking the sea paths, German imperialism was threatened with paralysis. At this turn of affairs the German government was not slow to show its chagrin. It complained in acrimonious terms about being hampered and hemmed in by a policy of encirclement and did its best to hinder the Triple entente from disposing of Egypt, Morocco, and Persia without giving Germany a voice in the matter or paying it off with some sort of compensation. Over Morocco more particularly which, in spite of deceitful declarations to the contrary, was secretly assigned to France (and Spain), Germany provoked a crisis which repeatedly (1905, 1911) threatened war; but since the Triple entente maintained an unshaken front Germany had resentfully to give way. By 1911 France had effected possession of the larger part of Morocco, not however without having thrown Germany as a sop a relatively worthless piece of central African jungle.

The checkmating of German imperialism

Her conspicuous failure to participate adequately in the appropriation of Persia and Morocco made Germany cling all the more resolutely to the imperialist policy she had developed with regard to the one territory which was accessible to her by the land-route, that is, the Ottoman Empire. Here her great military power might make itself felt without the overwhelming naval power of the Triple entente being able to thunder a veto. With the new century and in exact measure as her other prospects, lying farther afield than the Ottoman Empire, began to grow dim, Germany concentrated her expansion policy more and more narrowly on the Near East.

Germany's attention concentrates on the Ottoman Empire

We have already seen that throughout the eighteenth and nineteenth centuries the Ottoman Empire, as a decaying power, had excited the territorial greed of the European states. At first its most immediate neighbors, Austria and Russia, obtained
Ottoman decay and European covetousness
a rather exclusive advantage from the decline of the Ottoman might; but in the nineteenth century Great Britain and France advanced claims in their turn which in the course of time netted France the provinces of Algeria and Tunis and Great Britain the fertile land of Egypt. When France, under the circumstances just recounted, acquired Morocco, the action, though not directed against the Ottoman Empire, since Morocco was an independent state, at least proved the energy of the French imperialist appetite. After this consummation the worthless desert of Tripoli lying between Egypt and Tunis stood out as the last stretch of north African shoreland outside of European control and as the last remnant of Turkey-in-Africa. Unwilling to see it gobbled up by Great Britain or France, as it was likely to be, Italy in 1911 suddenly seized and annexed it with no better excuse than Italy's civilizing "mission." Like every other European power, Italy was quick to discover a "mission" when it came to appropriating a backward area.

Meanwhile Turkey-in-Europe gave evidence of passing as certainly out of the sultan's hands as his African provinces. Austria and Russia, which in the eighteenth century had frequently fattened
The rise of the Balkan states
at Ottoman expense, would in the nineteenth century have continued the pleasant game, if it had not been for the revival of the sultan's subject nationalities, the Greeks, the Serbs, the Bulgars, and the Rumanians. We have traced the moving tale of how they rose, smote their tyrant-master, and after many tribulations won their independence. Before the end of the nineteenth century the respective states formed by the Greeks, Rumanians, Serbs, and Bulgars presented the picture of hopeful, if somewhat backward, commonwealths of an essentially west-European type.

Though in the light of these developments the Balkan situation was in slow process of clarification along nationalist lines, two particularly serious problems remained which the European powers at the Congress of Berlin (1878), instead of solving, on account of their incurable jealousies succeeded in involving in but worse confusion. One of these problems bears the name of Bosnia; the other

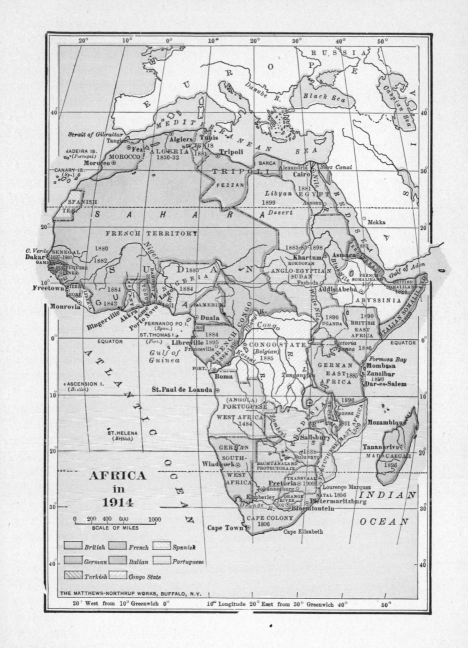

that of Macedonia. Bosnia together with the small province of Herzegovina, though inhabited by South Slavs (Serbs and Croats), was given to Austria, not in sovereignty, it is true, but for an indefinite occupation capable of being converted, sooner The or later, by the legerdemain, which was included in the problems of repertory of every European foreign office, into unqualified Bosnia and sovereignty. At the same time Macedonia, the great cen- Macedonia tral region of the Balkan peninsula where all its many races meet and mingle, was given back to the sultan. For the moment the two ill-considered actions, involving a flagrant disregard of the principle of nationality, provoked but little protest. In the long run, however, they were sure to cause difficulty: Bosnia, as between Austria and Serbia, which latter would lay claim to Bosnia on the ground of its being a land of Serbs; and Macedonia, as between the Ottoman Empire and the various Christian states of the peninsula, which would be stirred to liberate Macedonia from Turkish misrule and divide it among themselves.

Around the year 1900 the uninterrupted decay of the Ottoman Empire more than ever impressed observers with the conviction that its last days were at hand. And just as Great Britain, France, and Italy either had already taken or were about to take action The great to possess themselves of the north coast of Africa, so and the Austria-Hungary and Russia among the great powers, and small Greece, Rumania, Serbia, and Bulgaria among the small, powers stake out were on the alert to make, each for itself, the best possible Turkish bargain touching European Turkey in the event of the claims expected Ottoman demise. While the small powers directed their gaze at Macedonia and the contiguous territory of Thrace, Austria counted confidently on converting her provisional hold on Bosnia into permanent sovereignty and Russia turned a glazed and hypnotized eye on Constantinople and the adjoining straits. Ever since the days of the famous Catherine II Constantinople had been the dream of the tsars and each successor of Catherine affirmed his belief that when the collapse of the Ottoman Empire at last occurred the Russian imperial standard would be planted on the Constantinopolitan minarets.

Into this welter of projects excited by Ottoman decay, all of them, of course, in fluid state because of the uncertainties of the situation, Germany now plunged with a project of her own. Since every one was making sure of some part of the sultan's lands when the

day of division came, Germany undertook to stake out a claim in
Asia Minor, which she looked upon as reasonably accessible to a
land-power like herself.   Asia Minor, almost incredibly backward
The Ger-   because of Turk neglect and ignorance, had very luring
man stake: potentialities from a colonial viewpoint.   By means of
Asia Minor concessions from the Turkish government German
and the
Bagdad   capitalists, following the usual course, built up, be-
railway   ginning with the nineties, special economic interests in
the decayed peninsula.   Among other matters they constructed a
railroad which, penetrating into the interior of Asia Minor, joined it up
with Constantinople; and, finally, they acquired the famous charter
permitting the extension of the existing railway system through
and beyond Asia Minor to the city of Bagdad on the Tigris (1899–
1903).   Only then did the German projects become fully manifest.
If they worked out German interests would presently exercise control over the transportation system and therewith over the resources
of Asia Minor and would, without more ado, walk into complete
possession when the sultan's knell was at last sounded.

The prospect produced a tremendous commotion in the camp of
the Triple entente, particularly at London and Petrograd.   As
London saw the situation Germany, once at Bagdad, would only have
Growing   to run her railway line to the Persian Gulf to possess
concentra- at some future date a land-route from central Europe
tion of   to the orient considerably shorter than the water-route
imperialist
rivalries at via the Suez Canal controlled by Great Britain.   In the
Constanti- eyes of Petrograd, on the other hand, the evil of a trunk
nople   line under German management lay rather in its giving
Germany control of the Turk capital, thereby proving absolutely
fatal to the ancient hopes entertained by Russia touching Constantinople and the straits.   Protests, claims and counter-claims filled
the columns of the press and echoed through the halls of the European
parliaments.   Though the rival European imperialisms were clashing
at many points, they met at Constantinople, in connection with
the Bagdad railway project, with greater vehemence than anywhere
else, because the Bagdad project, if realized, would extend German
power in a manner disconcerting to every member of the entente.

In spite of the diplomatic defeats administered to Germany by
the entente in connection with Morocco and Persia, the German
government persisted in the Bagdad scheme, making steady headway
with the construction of the line in the years following 1903.

While the entente was resolute that the invaluable railway must not be monopolized by Germany, it could for the moment apply no convenient lever to the situation, especially as the sultan attached himself so closely to Germany that substantially he presented himself to view as Germany's ally. Then a faint possibility, hardly considered at first, dawned in Serbia. Through this little state ran the railroad which linked Berlin and Vienna with Constantinople and of which the projected Bagdad line was in effect nothing more than the Asiatic extension. Midway on the stretch between Vienna and the Golden Horn lay Belgrad, the capital of Serbia, and, what is more, the natural door into the Balkan house from central Europe. A hostile Belgrad might conceivably become an insuperable obstacle to the southeastward advance of Germany and her ally, Austria-Hungary. Now Serbia, as we have seen, had been made bitterly hostile to the Hapsburg monarchy because the Emperor Francis Joseph had occupied Bosnia, to which Serbia on nationalist grounds laid claim. Serbia, therefore, exercised a potential check on the Austro-German plans of eastern penetration and, properly encouraged by Russia and the other members of the entente, might prove a considerable nuisance. Under these circumstances little Serbia was lifted to an accidental and dizzy eminence, becoming a leading center of European intrigue where Triple alliance and Triple entente fought a bitter diplomatic battle over the absorbing issue of Balkan ascendancy.

German plans supported by Turkey but threatened by Serbia

Suddenly, in 1908, came a crisis which brought war knocking at the door of Europe. In order to put an end to all further debate as to her relations to Bosnia, Austria, in October of that year, issued a proclamation converting her occupation of Bosnia, conceded at the Congress of Berlin, into formal sovereignty. Serbia, backed by the entente, violently protested against this high-handed assumption of new rights, and on Germany's supporting Austria the strain became terrible. War hung on a thread and was only averted by the entente's gradually withdrawing its support from Serbia. The last entente power to yield was Russia, which finally in March, 1909, notified the Serb government not to expect any help in an eventual war with the Danubian monarchy. Serbia, isolated, was obliged to promise Austria to discontinue her nationalist agitation directed at Bosnia and other Serb areas under the Hapsburg crown. In this manner the first

The Austro-Serb crisis of 1908

Austro-Serb crisis, properly a general Balkan crisis involving all the varied Near East interests of the two rival European leagues, came to an end — a very provisional end — with a victory of the Triple alliance.

And now crisis followed on the heel of crisis in that simmering witch's kettle of the Balkans. Space forbids us do do more than to recall the Young Turk revolution (1908), which in 1909 led to the deposition of the red-handed Abdul Hamid II. Of deep interest, too, is the Albanian rising (1910), which proclaimed the awakening of the last of the submerged Balkan nationalities. Aiming to concentrate on the absolutely indispensable events, we shall follow the issue precipitated by the cruel situation of Macedonia until the Austro-Serb crisis of 1908, supposedly settled, rose like Banquo's ghost from the grave and this time applied the torch to Europe and to the world.

Steady succession of Balkan crises

The misery which with the coming of the new century overtook the Turkish province of Macedonia beggars description. Its many racial groups, Bulgars, Greeks, Serbs, and Albanians, moved by the spirit of militant nationalism, engaged in bloody internecine war, which the Ottoman overlords, owing to their habitual inefficiency, were unable to suppress. Little wonder that the small Balkan states bordering on Macedonia at last resolved, in their own interest, to bring the Macedonian chaos to an end. Forming an alliance, Bulgaria, Serbia, Greece, and Montenegro, impatient of further delay and alarmed lest Macedonia fall not to them but to the newly awakened Albanians, in October, 1912, declared war on the sultan. Taken by surprise and completely defeated on every front, the Turks were in May, 1913, obliged to sue for peace. The jubilant victors demanded the cession not only of the disputed Macedonia but also of the province of Thrace to within a few miles of Constantinople. Except for the capital and the all-important area of the straits, Turkey-in-Europe had come to an end.

The Balkan war of 1912

It might have been better for all concerned if the allied success had not been so great, for over the extensive Turkish spoils the intoxicated victors promptly came to blows. In the summer of 1913 a second Balkan war was fought in which Greece, Serbia, and Montenegro were pitted against their late ally, Bulgaria; and though powerful enough by themselves to finish the enemy, they were directly helped by Rumania and even received aid of an indirect nature from their recent enemy,

The second Balkan war of 1913

Turkey. Of course Bulgaria was swiftly overwhelmed, and when in August, 1913, peace was signed at Bucharest and the Ottoman booty distributed, the victors took what they pleased, leaving Bulgaria completely out of the reckoning. More particularly Macedonia, racially indeed a mixed area but preponderantly Bulgarian, was partitioned between Serbia and Greece. Closely examined, the two Balkan wars may be considered to have contributed to an improved Balkan order in so far as they had effected the elimination of the Mohammedan Turk from the lands in which he was essentially an alien and which for generations he had exploited and misgoverned; but unfortunately they left also a heritage of hate among the Christian powers because the victors, like victors from the dawn of time, could not refrain in their hour of triumph from punishing the vanquished in such a manner as to leave a gnawing resentment in his soul.

It was the curse of the Balkan situation that though disturbance followed disturbance nothing was ever settled. The Serb crisis of 1908, for instance — was it possible to speak of its settlement so long as the Serb nationalist aspirations turned longingly toward the neighboring province of Bosnia, and Belgrad, the capital, continued a focus of international intrigue? Big Austria and little Serbia continued to exchange bitter looks and words which gained, if anything, an added malignancy from Serbia's triumph in the Balkan wars of 1912 and 1913. Having in rapid succession defeated the Turks and the Bulgarians and having successfully doubled their territory, the Serbs were disinclined to hold to their promise of 1909 concerning nationalist agitation in Hapsburg lands. Secret agents, subventioned by Serb societies, traveled through Bosnia and southern Hungary preaching hatred of the imperial house. It was only too probable that the resulting tension would, sooner or later, lead to an act of violence. It befell on June 28, 1914, an ever memorable date, for on that June day a number of Bosnian youths murdered the heir to the Austrian throne, the archduke Francis Ferdinand, together with his wife, as they were driving through the streets of Sarajevo, the capital of Bosnia. Here was the Serb crisis back again and alarmed Europe, expecting the worst, straightway went taut with anxiety.

The renewed Austro-Serb crisis of 1914

This time Austria resolved on nothing less than the complete humiliation of Serbia. On July 23, 1914, the Viennese government presented a peremptory ultimatum at Belgrad intended to crush

The Austrian ultimatum to Serbia followed by war   Serb nationalist agitation once and for all. On Serbia's refusing to meet each and every Austrian demand without reservation or discussion, Austria, on July 25, broke off diplomatic relations with Serbia and three days later declared war on its little neighbor.

The Austrian program being to punish Serbia for a nationalist policy which made relations of good neighborhood impossible, it behooved the Austrian government to attempt to make this policy **Russia resolves to protect Serbia and partially mobilizes** acceptable to the world and particularly to the members of the Triple entente, which had constituted themselves as Serbia's official protectors. To promote this purpose Austria, though only after an unfortunate delay which added to the suspicions poisoning the situation, issued a promise to the effect that no territorial acquisitions from Serbia were contemplated. But Russia, which, as the leading Slav power, felt closest to Serbia and which moreover was not minded to surrender its prestige in the Balkans, refused to be placated by the Austrian territorial assurance. Russia took the position that she could not possibly remain indifferent in a war between Austria and Serbia, and as early as July 25 ordered a partial mobilization of her troops. With that bold act the Serb crisis entered upon a new phase, raising the question of a war among the powers. And immediately the interest shifted from Vienna and Belgrad to the other European chancelleries and particularly to Berlin and Petrograd.

Throughout the crisis precipitated by the murder of the archduke Germany gave her ally's policy a full and unwavering support because she argued that unless the Serb nationalist agitation was sup-**The question of general mobilization raised between Germany and Russia** pressed, Austria, her best support in Europe, would be presently undermined and fall to pieces. She therefore took upon herself the task of trying to persuade Russia to concede to Austria the satisfaction of a punitive expedition into Serbia in exchange for the Austrian pledge not to annex Serbian territory. Russia, alarmed about Serbia and her own probable loss of influence in the Balkans, refused to entertain the idea and, as already said, on July 25, took the decisive step of effecting a partial mobilization of her forces. From that moment Germany turned her attention to the new phenomenon. She notified Russia that if the mobilization continued, Austria, which had thus far mobilized only on the Serbian border, would have to arm to meet the Russian movement, and, further, that if the Russian mobilization became general, extending to the German border, Germany in her turn would have to issue a mobilization order, making war inevitable.

In this connection it should be remembered that under the prevailing European system of universal military service a general mobilization empties the fields and workshops, converts millions of men in the twinkling of an eye into soldiers, and sets the whole social and economic framework of a nation throbbing with war. All men in authority in Europe knew that a general mobilization was the certain signal for war and indeed the Franco-Russian military convention of 1892 expressly endorsed this view. The significance of the Russian action can not therefore be overlooked, for, disregarding the German warnings and counting on the certain support of France and the probable support of Great Britain, the tsar resolutely continued a progressive mobilization. It culminated in the early evening hours of July 30 in the fateful general order calling every eligible Russian to arms throughout the length and the breadth of the empire. On this action being reported at Berlin, the German Government despatched an ultimatum to Petrograd setting Russia a time limit of twelve hours to withdraw her measure. When Russia ignored the request, the German emperor, in the late afternoon of August 1, ordered general mobilization in his turn and at the same time declared war on Russia.

The Russian mobilization of July 30 followed by the German declaration of war of August 1

It is thus clear that the European war began over the clashing Austro-German and Russian imperialist designs in the Near East and particularly over the Austro-German resolve to remove the menace of little Serbia from the path of their imperialist advance. But war once begun, it was sure, owing to the treaty obligations as well as to the interests of the various powers, to rapidly extend its circle. On France, for instance, the effect of the Russian-German breach was instantaneous, for France was obliged by the terms of her alliance with Russia to respond to the Russian mobilization by ordering her own. The automatic response of France was so clearly understood by the German government that, after granting France a brief delay to avow her intentions, it declared war also against its western neighbor. The case of Great Britain was not quite so simple. Toward Russia the British government had only informal obligations, while, though the cabinet in power had bound

While France enters the war automatically Great Britain hesitates

itself in a very specific way toward France, it had kept the agreement secret and was nervously uncertain whether the parliament and public would permit it to live up to its self-assumed obligation.

From this embarrassing situation, which, to the grave alarm of Russia and France, kept Great Britain hanging fire, the British cabinet was extricated by an ill-considered and indefensible act of Germany, the violation of the neutrality of Belgium. In her desire to get at France without delay Germany, on August 2, requested at Brussels an unmolested passage for her army through Belgium; and when the demand was indignantly rejected, Germany, on August 4, committed an unprovoked act of war against Belgium by sending troops across the border. As soon as the violation of Belgian neutrality became known across the channel, it released a storm of furious resentment both as an act of lawless arrogance and as a direct attack on British security. In consequence the ministry, only privately pledged to come to the aid of France, was enabled to merge the French and Belgian issues before the parliament and public and amidst the passionate acclaim of the whole island to declare war on Germany (August 5).

The German breach of Belgian neutrality followed by the declaration of war of Great Britain

The feverish attention of the world now swung to Italy. As a member of the Triple alliance she was expected in some quarters to throw in her lot with Germany and Austria; but after brief consideration she declared that inasmuch as Austria had begun an offensive war against Serbia, the Italian government, only defensively bound to its allies, recognized no obligation of coming to their support. For the present Italy adopted a waiting attitude.[1] Not so Japan. The empire of the mikado had ever since 1902 been bound by treaty to coöperate with Great Britain in the Pacific ocean. It was therefore under no obligation to join in the European struggle. However, the opportunity afforded by the embarrassment of Germany to eject that power from the Shantung peninsula in China proved irresistible, and on August 17 the mikado served an ultimatum on the German emperor followed shortly after by a declaration of war.

While Italy proclaims her neutrality, Japan declares war on Germany

Thus the Balkan issue, with which the war began, was found to be so intimately tied up with a dozen other nationalist-imperialist issues,

---

[1] In 1902, in return for the promise of Tripoli, Italy gave assurances to France not to engage in war against her. Italy thus became an insecure member of the Triple alliance. "Henceforth Italy had one foot in either camp." (Gooch)

and the competing powers, sharply ranged in two groups, were found to be so deeply pledged to one another that the Serb-Austrian disturbance, affecting a comparatively small area in central Europe, became in the course of a few days a conflagration which *Every* spread until the whole of Europe, the dependent colonial *imperialist* areas of Africa and Asia, and all the highways of the sea *issue* were lighted with the fierce glare of war. Germany *thrown into the crucible* and Austria faced Russia, France, Great Britain, and *of the* Japan (not to mention Serbia and Belgium), while Italy, *World War* neutral for the moment, anxiously tried to make up her mind which way to jump. Never since the dawn of history had the world rocked with such an earthquake. The human rancors, piled mountain-high by the too ardent pursuit ever since the Industrial Revolution of wealth, colonies, and power, suddenly leaping to flame enveloped the globe with a ring of fire and raised the question whether the appalling spectacle unfolded before the eyes of men was not the end of civilization itself and the twilight of all the ancient gods.

REFERENCES

E. FUETER, *World History*, chs. 28–31, 33
G. P. GOOCH, *History of Our Time*, chs. 6–10; *History of Modern Europe, 1878–1919*
J. S. SCHAPIRO, *Modern and Contemporary History*, ch. 29
C. J. H. HAYES, *Political and Social History*, II, ch. 30
Cambridge Modern History, XII, chs. 1, 16, 17–20, 22
N. ANGELL, *The Great Illusion*
C. SEYMOUR, *The Diplomatic Background of the War*
A. C. COOLIDGE, *Origins of the Triple Alliance*
B. E. SCHMITT, *England and Germany*, 1740–1914; *The Triple Alliance and the Triple Entente* (in American Historical Review, April, 1924)
W. M. FULLERTON, *Problems of Power*
F. VON BERNHARDI, *Germany and the Next War*
H. A. GIBBONS, *The New Map of Europe* (1911–1914)
G. W. PROTHERO, *German Policy Before the War*
G. HANOTAUX, *Contemporary France*
A. TARDIEU, *France and the Alliances*
F. SCHEVILL, *History of the Balkan Peninsula*, chs. 31, 32
F. PRIBRAM, *The Secret Treaties of Austria-Hungary*, 1879–1914
E. DURHAM, *Twenty Years of Balkan Tangle*
EARL LOREBURN, *How the War Came*
M. JASTROW, *The War and the Bagdad Railway*
E. M. EARLE, *Turkey, the Great Powers, and the Bagdad Railway*
E. D. MOREL, *Ten Years of Secret Diplomacy*
M. MONTGELAS, *The Case for the Central Powers*
CROMER (EARL OF), *Modern Egypt*
H. H. JOHNSTON, *History of Colonization in Africa; The Opening-up of Africa*

R. K. Douglas, *Europe in the Far East*

K. K. Kawakami, *Japan in World Politics*

G. H. Perris, *Our Foreign Policy and Sir Edward Grey's Failure*

G. Murray, *The Foreign Policy of Sir Edward Grey*

J. H. Rose, *Origins of the War*

S. B. Fay, *New Light on the Origin of the War* (publ. in American Historical Review, 1920–1921)

H. E. Barnes, *Assessing the Blame for the World War* (Current History, May, 1924)

CHAPTER XXXIII

THE WAR AND THE PEACE (1914–1919)

It is hardly necessary to say that it will be impossible in a book of this scope to do more than call attention to a few leading facts and aspects of the World War. Important matters of great and legitimate concern will have to be resolutely excluded from considera- Limited tion. There will be no description either of the instru- purpose of ments which have revolutionized warfare on land and this chapter water, such as the giant gun, the scouting and bombing airplane, the trench-bomb, the tank, poison gas, and the submarine, or of the altered tactics and strategy imposed upon generals and admirals by the new tools of destruction. Attention will not be directed to the outstanding personalities of the various nations, the conspicuous and fast-shifting leaders in the field and council-chamber, nor to the heated domestic politics of each warring state, including such matters as its pro- and anti-war groups, the search for revenue to meet the vastly increased expenses, and the measures of economic reorganization for war production on a titanic scale. Our concern will be solely to set down a few salient features of the prolonged fighting, notably such as profoundly influenced the issue, and to define and interpret the peace which the victors dictated to the defeated central powers.

When Germany broke the neutrality of Belgium, in spite not only of the certainty of adding Great Britain to her enemies but also of the opprobrium which she knew beforehand would be visited upon her for her act, she disclosed the extreme importance she The purpose attached to the swift defeat of France. France once dis- of Germany posed of, Germany would turn upon Russia, which coun- in striking at France try, owing to its unwieldy bulk, the German general staff through supposed would get ready slowly and not prove imme- Belgium diately threatening. There followed the rapid march of August, 1914, through Belgium and northern France. It was bravely resisted by the small Belgian army and the forts along the Meuse, aided by the English and French troops hurrying up to stem the tide, but, conducted with superior numbers and equipment, it broke for a while through every obstacle. Not till the Germans were almost within sight of Paris, their military objective, were they stopped by a direct frontal attack combined with a flanking movement which threatened to envelop their right wing. The battle, lasting several days (September 5–10), is famous as the battle of the Marne. The Germans, beaten, had to retreat to the Aisne, where they entrenched. Having failed to reach Paris, they had failed to eliminate France from the situation. Therefore they had lost the campaign, and though by way of compensation they succeeded in occupying and holding almost the whole of Belgium and certain very valuable coal- and iron-producing regions of northern and eastern France, they would thenceforth be in serious danger the moment their enemies became strong enough to attack in their turn.

This theoretic peril of the Germans, due to their distance from their base and to the long line of communications which they were obliged to maintain, was in practice greatly reduced for them by their **The deadlock on the western front** resort to trench warfare, the so-called war of positions. Adopted by one side, it had perforce to be adopted also by the other. Both sides dug themselves in, forming an immense zigzagging battle-line stretching for six hundred miles all the way from the sea at Nieuport (Belgium) to the Alps on the German-Swiss border. During the next few years first one side and then another undertook an offensive with the purpose of breaking through, and though some of these attacks were conducted on a vast scale, as, for instance, when in the spring of 1916 the Germans tried to break through at Verdun or when in the summer of the same year the British and French conducted the campaign of the Somme, the battle-front, generally speaking, remained unchanged until March, 1918. For almost four years the situation on the western and decisive front was deadlocked.

Exactly as the German supreme command had miscalculated the Franco-British resistance in the west with the result that its attack was stopped at the Marne, so it indulged in a wrong assumption **The Russian invasion of Germany and Austria** as to the mobilization of Russia. The rush toward France was, as we have seen, predicated on the slow advance of the Russian army. The Russian army, however, conducted its mobilization not only rapidly but with enormous effectives and undertook, while the German army was sweeping on to Paris, to drive across the plains of the Vistula and the Oder to Vienna and Berlin. The German forces were driven from most of East Prussia and the Austrians from eastern Galicia before a German counter-attack at Tannenberg (August 26–September 1) turned the Russian advance into East Prussia to a disastrous rout. Hindenburg, the German commander, followed up his victory by crossing the Russian boundary and invading Poland and Lithuania.

The Austrians, however, in their sector had no such success as the Germans and continued to give way until the Russians threatened the forts of Cracow and extended an indirect menace to Vienna itself. Thus matters stood during the winter till May, The 1915, when the Austro-Germans combined in a vast Russian offensive which pushed back the Russians at every point defeats and ended in their complete defeat. Not only did the central powers now drive far into Russia but they succeeded in so severely crippling the Russian equipment by the destruction and capture of material that the great Slav empire began to show signs of approaching exhaustion. True, it manifested fine daring by engaging, in the summer of 1916, in a partially successful offensive against Austria conducted by General Brusiloff, but thereafter the army showed little fight, partly through discouragement and partly because of the civil break-up behind the battle-line which is the usual accompaniment of defeat.

The war had in the first instance led to a great outburst of patriotism and unified Russia as it unified, through the same patriotic sentiment, every other fighting country. But the old social and political divisions continued to stir uneasily under the The surface, and when the Russian defeats took place the Russian angered public laid the blame on the well-known incom- revolution petence and corruption of the tsarist régime. In March, of 1917 followed by 1917, an uprising took place in Petrograd which immedi- peace with ately gathered such momentum among both civilians Germany and soldiers that the tsar, deserted by his people, was obliged to abdicate. What next? The absolute system had crashed to the ground: would a moderate middle class or a radical socialist régime succeed it? The first result was a compromise, certain middle class groups coöperating with a moderate wing of the socialists and conducting a government pledged to the allies and resolved to keep Russia in the war against Germany. Through the summer of 1917 this government, becoming ever more radical, struggled on only to meet defeat in the end at the hands of the extreme socialists, known as the Bolsheviki.

In November these extremists set up their uncompromising revolutionary rule. From the point of view of the war, which alone concerns us here, the enormous significance of the triumph of Lenin and Trotsky, the Bolshevik leaders, was that they resolved to take Russia out of the struggle by making peace with Germany. This peace Germany, a victorious, militarist power, ruthlessly imposed on the beaten enemy at Brest-Litovsk in March, 1918. By virtue of this treaty Russia renounced title to her vast western borderland, including Finland, the Baltic provinces (Esthonia, Livonia, Courland), Lithuania, Poland, and Ukraine, all conquered by her since the days of Peter the Great and inhabited by a great variety of nationalities but in no case by Russians.

An obvious drawback of the method here adopted of treating each battle-front in turn is that it fails to bring out the intimate coherence of events in the east and west. The campaigns on these two fronts and on all fronts whatever should, especially if military *Interdependence of all the fighting fronts* enlightenment is sought, be studied as a unit. Fighting in the east constantly affected the situation in the west and vice versa, as will appear by glancing back once more, for the purpose of illustration, to 1914. The Franco-British forces won the decisive battle of the Marne, but their victory was largely due to the unexpected invasion by Russia of East Prussia and to the consequent diversion by Germany of troops, destined for the west front, to her eastern marches.

This intimate concatenation of occurrences in all quarters should be borne in mind as we turn next to trace the course of events on the Balkan front. The war, though beginning in the Balkans as a conflict between Austria and Serbia, assumed at once so *The Balkan front greatly affected by the entrance into the war of the Ottoman Empire* overshadowing an importance on the west and east fronts, where millions of men were under arms, that the Balkan front where Austria, because of having her hands full with Russia, made but a feeble effort, sank into relative insignificance. But not for long. Early in November, 1914, the central powers were greatly strengthened in their struggle by being joined by Turkey. Turkey's entrance into the war, due to the friendship existing between the Young Turks, the political masters of the Ottoman Empire, and Germany, profoundly affected the situation in the Balkans and for that matter in large areas of the Mediterranean sea and the whole Near East. Russia, in particular, was hard hit, for the Bosporus and Dardanelles were immediately closed to the ships of the entente, with the result that Russia was unable to receive the military supplies of which she stood in need. Her defeat in the campaign of 1915 was partly due to this circumstance, once more exhibiting the close interdependence of events on every fighting front. It was to break the intolerable barrier at the straits and establish the sorely needed contact with Russia that the western powers undertook their first Balkan campaign.

In February, 1915, a Franco-British squadron suddenly attacked the Dardanelles with the purpose of silencing the Turkish forts and forcing a passage to Constantinople. On losing in this hazardous enterprise several large battleships, the allies changed their plans and began to land troops, British for the most part, on the Gallipoli peninsula, with the object of taking the forts from the rear. All summer this campaign continued at ruinous cost, only to be acknowledged a failure and to be given up at the coming of winter. What gave the enterprise the finishing blow was a new and important development in Serbia. A recognized minor area of conflict, the little Slav kingdom was not seriously threatened by the Austrians till December, 1914, when an Austrian invasion was victoriously repulsed. Almost a year later, in October, 1915, Serbia was obliged to face a second and more ominous crisis. An Austro-German force under the German general, Mackensen, gathered on the Danube opposite Belgrad, while the Bulgars, elated by the prospect of revenge upon the Serbs for the loss of Macedonia in the second Balkan war of 1913, resolved to give up their neutrality and join the central powers. While the Austro-Germans pushed southward from the Danube, the Bulgarian army attacked Serbia from the east, that is, in the Vardar valley. The entrance of Bulgaria into the war was a commanding event, because it planted the central powers firmly in the heart of the Balkan peninsula; and when Serbia was now overrun, together with Montenegro and most of Macedonia and Albania, the longed-for, unimpeded connection between Berlin and Constantinople was at last made perfect.

Thus the year 1915 proved a very prosperous one for Germany, since it brought the realization of the dream of a Middle Europe under German direction extending from the North sea to the Dardanelles. The only offset for the Franco-British forces was the occupation of the Greek city of Saloniki at the head of the Ægean

The Gallipoli and Serbian campaigns of 1915

and the successful establishment there of a military base strong
enough to save southern Macedonia from the central allies, to
threaten Bulgaria with a future offensive, and to force Greece,
The Balkan   although only after the use of military power, into the
states   ranks of the allies. The definite accession of Greece to
obliged to   the entente came about in 1917 and not till after the
choose   remaining Balkan power, Rumania, had passed through
sides   a disastrous experience to be presently related. The
whole history of the war goes to show that the small powers of the
Balkans, so deeply involved in some of the main issues of the struggle, could not remain neutral. But to choose sides was a very
delicate matter because it was far from clear which side would prove
victorious. And yet life itself hung for them on picking the winner,
for these small governments were but helpless pawns in the game of
the great powers and were sure to be ruined if they crossed the path
of an irresistible moving force. For their part, the two opposed
European groups recognized the value of the accession to their
respective sides of a Balkan combatant and hotly bid against each
other for favor at all the Balkan capitals. Under the play of these
difficult counter-currents the Ottoman Empire and Bulgaria at a
relatively early period joined the central powers, while Rumania
somewhat hesitantly and Greece only under military duress ranged
themselves on the side of the entente allies.

It was in August, 1916, that Rumania threw in her lot with the
allies with the result that she was straightway invaded, crushingly
Defeat and   defeated, and almost entirely occupied by the central
conquest of powers. In the winter, 1916-1917, Germany was appar-
Rumania,   ently more securely entrenched in the Balkans than ever.
1916   The only cloud on the horizon was the allied front firmly
maintained at Saloniki.

A last European front remains to be listed, the southern or Alpine
front created when Italy, terminating the neutrality proclaimed by
her at the outbreak of the war, threw in her lot with the entente.
The   This decision was taken in May, 1915, and was imme-
Italian   diately followed by an attack in force on Austria along
front   the whole of the Italo-Austrian mountain border. Slow
Italian advances culminated in the capture of the city and fortress
of Gorizia in the summer of 1916. In the autumn of 1917, however, the gains made were lost and much else besides when the
Austrians, aided by German troops, broke through the Italian lines

at Caporetto, captured many men and much equipment, and were not brought to a halt till they reached the line of the Piave River, northeast of Venice. In the spring of 1918 Italy was a source of grave anxiety to the entente which, however, the events of the summer and autumn of that year scattered to the winds by revealing the recovered morale and resistance of the Italian troops.

At this point, though chiefly concerned with Europe, we must at least indicate the leading conflict-areas outside the little continent. The diminished Ottoman Empire of the twentieth century was largely Asiatic, embracing Asia Minor, Syria, Mesopo- The tamia, and Arabia. In all these provinces the vast strug- campaigns gle raged with the main feature of an attack by Russia in Asiatic and Great Britain upon the shaking Ottoman house. Turkey Russia made her forward thrust from the Caucasus into Asia Minor and conducted it, on the whole, victoriously until her collapse at home in 1917. Great Britain followed two separate and converging lines of penetration, the first leading from the Persian gulf into Mesopotamia, the second from the isthmus of Suez into Palestine and Syria. In spite of difficulties and setbacks these British offensives proceeded steadily, culminating in the year 1918 in a series of victories which resulted in the total collapse of the Ottoman state.

Inevitably, too, every German colony was at least a potential fighting area. But owing to the small German forces abroad and their inability to receive reinforcements on account of the British control of the seas, most of the colonies fell with little The war in resistance into the lap of the allies. Thus the German the German stronghold in China, Kiau-chau, was taken by the Jap- colonies anese after a few weeks' siege, and the scattered German forces in Southwest Africa and in German East Africa were gradually picked up, largely in guerrilla fighting, by the British or rather by the British colonial forces of South Africa.

Having enumerated, however briefly, the main fighting areas on land, we must now turn to take account of the sea. Perhaps, when all is said, the sea-front was the greatest of all the fighting fronts, or, to speak more accurately, the most decisive. The domi- The nating factor in the situation was Great Britain's control decisive of the world's seaways by means of her overwhelming influence of naval forces. Her fleet at once drove the German fleet sea power and merchant shipping from the ocean, gradually captured the merchantmen which failed to reach a safe port, and pursued and finally destroyed such German raiders as undertook to prey upon the enemy commerce. At the same time the British established a long-distance blockade of the German coasts in order to deprive Germany of needed supplies and, to make the measure thoroughly effective, began the regulation and control of neutral commerce, above all, of that of Holland and the Scandinavian countries adjacent to Germany, and of that of the United States, the greatest producer of raw products in the world. To break this British strangle-hold Germany had a gambler's chance in the mysterious and as yet untried weapon of the submarine. She declared in her turn the British coast in a state of blockade and attempted to make good her threat against vessels seeking British ports with a fleet of submarine vessels. But while the British blockade of Germany was wholly effective because no merchant vessel, neutral or otherwise, could pass into the North sea without being detected by the British guard-ships, the German blockade of the extensive British coasts was at best casual and would necessitate, to be even partially effective, the submarine's sinking its prize since it was out of the question to bring it safely some hundreds of miles to a German port. However, to sink a ship with its cargo had the very evil feature of imperiling the lives of passengers and crew since the submarine, hardly more than a toy, though a toy with a sting, was unable to take the victims on board and had no better alternative to offer them than the uncertain chance of getting to shore in life-boats.

Over this situation the United States was drawn into the struggle. When the war broke out the great American republic at once declared its neutrality and with this aloofness the citizen body was for The neutral a long time satisfied, although public sentiment from the rights of the first overwhelmingly favored the entente. Many factors United contributed to this state of mind, most conspicuously States the humanitarian indignation aroused by the outrage injured by Great done by Germany to Belgium in seizing and holding the Britain and little land in an iron military vise. But the war came close, Germany was woven into the texture of daily American experience chiefly through the interests of American commerce. It was plain that Great Britain was determined to make the United States sell goods exclusively to her and her allies, and it was just as plain that Germany was minded to have her share of American articles, failing which, she was resolved to interrupt the supply of Great Britain with her submarine weapon. Purposing with deadly intensity to

hurt each other, they instituted their respective blockades, besides
enforcing measures regulative of sea-borne trade which unquestionably signified a serious encroachment on the rights of neutrals and
therefore of the United States.

Protesting against the illegal ordinances of both combatants,
President Wilson began a lively exchange of diplomatic notes with
London and Berlin. From the first, however, the notes exchanged
with Germany had a special edge, absent in the case of The United
Great Britain, because Germany's breaches of the sea law, States
involving the use of the novel weapon, the submarine, enters the
war over the
imperiled American lives and thereby deeply stirred the submarine
sentiment of humanity, already aroused over the invasion issue
of Belgium. The diplomatic argument was still being conducted in
rather general terms when there occurred an event which sharply
defined the issue between the two countries. On May 7, 1915, a
German submarine torpedoed and sank without warning the British
liner *Lusitania*, pitilessly drowning over a thousand men, women,
and children, several hundred of them of American nationality. The
indignation in the United States was so intense that the American
government passed immediately from discussion to command and
insisted that the submarine conform to the laws of the sea and the
rules of humanity, in a word, that its unrestricted use cease forth-
with. The German government yielded, and though there were
occasional transgressions of the conditions laid down by the United
States, a precarious peace was maintained till January 31, 1917,
when the German government published a declaration notifying the
neutral world of its determination to resort without more ado to the
unrestricted use of its tool. Plainly the British octopus grip, continued for over two years, had begun to tell in the starvation and
reduced production of Germany. The German leaders themselves
admitted it and justified the ruthless employment of the submarine
on the ground of its being the sole means in their power of striking
back at Great Britain with her own program of hunger and commercial isolation. President Wilson promptly broke off diplomatic relations and on April 6, 1917, the Congress of the United States declared
war on Germany. The die was cast.

At this juncture it becomes necessary to analyze the motives and
program with which the United States entered the war two and a
half years after the struggle had begun. Owing to the small attention
paid in the United States to affairs in Europe, the bewilderment over

the sudden conflagration of 1914 was extreme and the neutrality proclaimed by President Wilson not only met the wishes of the American people but expressed the undeniable fact that the explosion

The motives resulted from the rivalry of Triple alliance and Triple
animating entente and was no concern of the Washington government.
the Ameri- But during the ensuing months and years that alert section
can public of the public which took pains to inform itself as to the
causes of the outbreak — a section which was undoubtedly a minority
but which, if it possesses resolution, always achieves leadership in
a democratic community — slowly came to the conclusion that the
war was due to a chain of rivalries and rancors reaching back for
generations and involving every sort of bitter contention over markets, raw products, colonies, military and naval establishments, in
sum, involving all the issues of imperialism. At the same time this
enlightened minority was plied by the propagandists of both sides in
the hope of winning its sympathy and support as a step preliminary
to drawing the United States into the struggle. And here the Franco-
British propaganda exhibited from the first a vast superiority over
that of Germany. Not only did it enjoy because of the British command of the sea, which brought with it the control of the cables, a
practical monopoly of information, but Franco-British opinion sensed,
as the German did not, that America could not be won except on the
basis of an idealist program which sweepingly condemned the existing order of things. Nor was it other than natural for the small but
compact liberal groups of France and Great Britain actually to feel
the horror they expressed for the monstrous developments of the
European system. Aligning themselves therefore with the liberal
intelligentsia of the United States, they poured the vials of a justified
wrath on the evils most immediately in view, such as militarism,
secret diplomacy, autocratic government, and hostile balanced alliances. What the world needed, they argued, was to get rid of these
hoary anachronisms in order to make room for a universal league
pledged to preserve peace and expressive of the brotherhood of the
human race, and as they were able to exhibit Germany on account of
her rape of Belgium and her narrow militarist code of conduct as
particularly identified with the evils which afflicted the world, they
persuaded themselves and in increasing measure the American masses
that the defeat of Germany was the necessary preliminary to the
dawn of a new era. If now to this expanding idealist conviction be
added the sense of injured dignity and violated interests aroused by

the submarine issue, the main influences will be realized which pushed the United States into the war.

In measure as American opinion about the war clarified it found a spokesman in the country's president, capable and ready to translate what stirred the general mind into eloquent and moving words. He signalized the entrance of the United States into the war with a ringing indictment of the autocratic and mili- President Wilson's tarist government of Germany, while voicing at the same idealist time his continued good-will toward the German people peace and pledging his country to the pursuit of unselfish ends. program From time to time, in further illustration of his position, he made additional declarations culminating, on January 8, 1918, in a peace program of Fourteen Points, which demanded, among other things, the abolition of secret diplomacy, the freedom of the seas, the reduction of armaments, the redrawing of the map of Europe along national lines, and the creation of a League of Nations as a guarantee of peace and good-will. President Wilson's ringing pronouncements appealed to European as well as to American idealism and unified liberal opinion the world over as it had not been unified before. Slowly a Wilsonian peace began to outline itself which not only was directed against Germany but which purposed to go to the bottom of things by bringing the greedy imperialism of the great powers and the ruinous nationalist rivalries of great and small alike under the control of the unified peoples of the world.

With refreshed spirits the allies resumed the war on the entrance into it of the United States. In 1917 the American participation hardly caused a ripple for the reason that America had first to get ready. Besides, the defection of Russia from the allied The ranks broke the iron ring around Germany and greatly decisive relaxed the pressure exercised upon her. The next cam- campaign of 1918. paign, however, the campaign of 1918, proved decisive. Germany's It began in March with a supreme effort by the German offensive command to break down French and British resistance followed by on the west front before American reënforcements in the offen- sive of the sufficient number were at hand. For three months the allies Germans battered the allied lines, achieving considerable success but failing in the main purpose of breaking through. In their hour of greatest need the allies unified their command more completely than ever before, put the French leader, Marshal Foch, in supreme control, and presently, in July, assumed the offensive in their turn. The next months brought the most ferocious fighting which the war, from first to last unexampled in ferocity, had witnessed. Irresistibly the French, British, and Americans drove forward, pushing the Germans back until it was clear that they could no longer maintain themselves in the invaded districts of Belgium and France.

The outlook for Germany was already somber when through occurrences on the other fronts it settled into the blackness of night. In the late summer the British began to apply their final pressure upon the Turks in Syria, resulting in the rout of the Turks and the utter breakdown of Turk resistance. Simultaneously the allies, moving north from Saloniki, broke through the Bulgarian lines (September, 1918) and obliged Bulgaria, unable to get sufficient support from Austria and Germany to steady its panicky forces, abjectly to sue for peace. Thus Turkey and Bulgaria were broken to bits and eliminated from the struggle. Inevitably the Austrian morale was badly shaken by these disasters in the immediate Austrian rear, and when, in October, the Italians undertook an offensive along the Piave, they easily crumpled the Austrian lines, captured division after division, and proceeded to strike for Vienna. Following defeat in the field, the whole Austro-Hungarian political fabric collapsed without delay: the house of Hapsburg was deposed, the various nationalities merged in the composite state declared their independence, and the war ended on this front with an armistice, signed November 4, that left the Italian army in complete control of the situation.

The allies victorious on the Syrian, Macedonian, and Italian fronts

These events, taken in connection with their own losing struggle on the west front, positively obliged the Germans to treat for peace. In those autumn weeks, while blow after blow was being delivered by the allies on every front, the shaken government of the kaiser slowly crumbled to destruction. The opposition groups of the Reichstag, seizing control, opened negotiations with President Wilson, but presently had to retire before a rising of the angered masses who drove the Reichstag, together with the imperial family, from power in order to set up a republic. A moderate group of socialists took over the government. Recognizing the hopelessness of stemming the revolutionary tide, Emperor William II left the army and fled to neutral Holland (November 10). Meanwhile President Wilson, acting as the spokesman of the allies, offered the German people his

The German government sues for peace

program of the Fourteen Points as the basis of a general peace. This having been accepted, on the day following William II's flight, on November 11, 1918, an armistice was signed which required the Germans to retire beyond the Rhine and effectually to disarm themselves. By an enormous coördinated effort the resistance of the enemy had been broken and the victory won. What would the peace bring?

The peace! Plainly it was as important as the war; in fact the war would have been fought in vain if the peace did not undertake honestly to grapple with the evils which afflicted the world before the war began and which were the real causes of the war. In consequence of the immensity of the victory the arrangements for peace would be exclusively in the hands of the victors, for of the four enemy states Austria-Hungary had disappeared from the map, the Ottoman Empire and Bulgaria were crushed and all but annihilated, and Germany, disarmed and passing through the throes of a revolution, *The peace congress certain to be wholly dominated by the five victorious powers* might plead the protection of the Fourteen Points, but was absolutely impotent to enforce consideration of her views. At the time when the long and terrible struggle came to an end, over a score of states, great and small, were joined together as allies or associates against Germany, and as soon as Paris had been agreed on as the place of meeting, representatives of the victorious states wended their way to the French capital to take part in the great congress which was to settle the disturbed affairs of the world. Of course the final decisions would be taken by the great powers, Great Britain, France, Italy, Japan, and the United States. They might listen to suggestions from the smaller states, but in accordance with immemorial usage they would always reserve the last word to themselves. When, in January, 1919, the peace conference was called to order, everything therefore depended on the temper and program of the five supreme representatives of the five victor powers, but also, we should not fail to note, on the temper of the respective publics which they served, since, no matter what an individual leader might think, he could not afford to put himself out of touch with his people. The people, however, of all the victor countries, persisting in the stern and exultant frame of mind produced by the war and its triumphant ending, were sure to make their influence felt in favor of a severe retribution to be visited on the vanquished.

It is difficult, if not impossible, to present the work of the peace

conference of Paris in an objective, historical light because we are
still too close to see its problems and decisions in their true perspective.
Suffice it to call attention to some of the more outstanding clashes
Conflict of   and conclusions and, to begin with, to the issue which
the old and   leaped to life the moment the congress opened its doors.
new diplo-   During the war an idealist program had sprung into being
macy, of
realism and   which, under the name of the Fourteen Points, had, as
idealism   already noted, generally won the adherence of the liberal
elements the world over. What is more, to this platform, formulated
by President Wilson, the governments themselves had become committed when, in connection with the armistice negotiations, they
offered it to Germany as a basis of discussion. Inevitably, however,
the victory, immense in its scope and won after a terrific, nerve-
racking struggle, reinvigorated the nationalist and imperialist designs
which had never ceased to prompt the diplomacy of Europe and
which were admittedly a leading factor in the war. These designs
had been discussed by the respective foreign offices in the course of
the struggle and had finally led to secret agreements among the
allies which enumerated in more or less definite terms the territories
and economic advantages each power might expect as its reward in
the event of victory. All the powers, with the single exception of
the United States, were involved in these elaborate transactions, and
it was a serious question how, if at all, the old-fashioned realist
diplomacy which they represented was to be brought into harmony
with the idealist program represented by President Wilson and his
Fourteen Points.

For the better understanding of the nature and the gravity of the
issue at Paris it is necessary to take a closer view of the secret treaties.
Signed, sometimes between two, sometimes between three and
The secret   more powers, these treaties were very numerous, although
treaties of   their exact number was not known and their contents,
the allies   nay, their very existence had been sedulously kept from
the general public. Gradually, however, in one way or another,
enough information leaked out to permit the curious to get a reasonably secure picture of the territorial distributions to which the victors
had become mutually committed. Thus the Ottoman Empire,
long a chief bone of European imperialist contention, was partitioned
among Great Britain, Russia, France, and Italy in such a manner
that each power received that portion to which it particularly aspired.
Further, the German colonial possessions of the Far East were

divided between Great Britain and Japan, Japan getting the lion's share as heir to Germany in China. Again, not only was France to recover Alsace-Lorraine, lost in 1871, but she was also given definite assurances involving the control, if not the possession, of the whole German territory on the left bank of the Rhine. And finally, Italy was promised, in addition to the coveted and genuinely Italian districts of the Trentino and Trieste, a portion of the Austro-German Tyrol and such Adriatic areas as Istria and northern Dalmatia, where the Italian element was numerically inferior to the Slovenes and Croats, two South Slav peoples, closely related to the Serbs.

When the sessions at Paris opened, the three great European victors were represented by their prime ministers, Lloyd George acting for Great Britain, Clemenceau for France, and Orlando for Italy. The directive influence exercised by the secret treaties From outside Europe they were joined by the Marquis Saionji representing the government of Japan and by President Wilson who, pursuing a course without precedent in his country's history, crossed the ocean to conduct the case of the United States in person. Russia, it should be observed, was not represented. Its Bolshevist government, committed to a vast revolutionary experiment aiming at nothing less than a new communist order of society, had broken off relations with the allies; or, it would be just as correct to say in view of the incompatibility manifested by both sides, the allies had broken off relations with the Bolshevists. Alarmed at the propaganda issuing from Moscow and Petrograd and appealing to the workers of the world to rise everywhere in revolution, the western nations had closed to Russia all the routes of trade and intercourse which they commanded and had gradually drifted into a relation with the Bolshevist government hardly distinguishable from war. Russia, therefore, was ignored when the distributions to be effected under the secret treaties were brought up for discussion. The other interested powers, however, that is, Great Britain, France, Italy, and Japan, resolved vigorously to insist on their bond, although in view of the power and prestige accumulated by the United States they were unable to exclude from consideration the program of the Fourteen Points.

Under these difficult circumstances President Wilson had not been long in Paris before he saw that he would be obliged to make concessions to the fierce egotism which dominated the counsels of his associates and which was consecrated by their secret treaties.

Undoubtedly these arrangements greatly disconcerted him; but since they represented the solemn mutual pledges of his fellow combatants, he considered it advisable, while trying to mitigate some of their worst provisions, to accept them and in exchange for this concession to insist on a League of Nations, pledged thenceforward to substitute the processes of peace and conciliation for the practices of a rapacious imperialism. The conflict among opposed opinions at Paris was sharp, but the President carried his plan. Without exaggeration it may be said that the League of Nations is the child of Wilson's loins.

President Wilson secures the acceptance of the League of Nations

In April, 1919, the Covenant of the League was completed and published to the world. Of course it was violently criticized by the conservatives of every country, who thought it went too far in the experiment of internationalism, no less than by the liberal opinion of the world, which contended that it did not go far enough. Its two chief features are an Assembly and a Council. The Assembly is a general body in which all the states, members of the League, are represented and in which each state is equal to every other by reason of its casting, regardless of size and might, a single vote. The Council, a smaller and far more important body, is composed of representatives of the five victor powers (the United States, Great Britain, France, Italy, and Japan) together with four representatives of four other members of the League chosen by the Assembly, that is, nine in all.[1] The Council is, among other matters, empowered to formulate plans for the reduction of armaments, to abate the evils which have arisen from the private manufacture of munitions, to act as a body of conciliators in case of a dispute which threatens war, and to formulate the terms under which a backward area is to be committed to the control and rule of a member-state acting as the agent or mandatory of the League. Since the chief purpose of the League is to settle contests among nations without recourse to war, the Covenant establishes as one of its most important creations a permanent court of international justice. Subject to a new decision of the Council, the seat of the League is established at Geneva in Switzerland. The court of international justice is located at The Hague.

The Covenant of the League

[1] Since the United States refused to join the League there are now (1925) only four permanent members of the Council. On the other hand the rotating members have been increased from four to six.

With the Covenant of the League of Nations accepted by all the delegates, the path was cleared for the treaty of peace with Germany. Besides five great powers, over a score of smaller states had either engaged in war against the Teuton empire or had broken Germany off diplomatic relations with it, and the harmonizing of signs the the often conflicting claims of this mass of victors was Treaty of Versailles, no easy matter. However, on May 7, 1919, the completed June 28, treaty was presented to a German delegation called for that 1919 purpose to Versailles. They were told peremptorily that no round-table discussion was to be allowed but that they might communicate in writing their objections to the terms submitted. This they accordingly did, passing at last from piece-meal criticism to an elaborate set of counter-proposals. On these having been answered and rejected the Germans were told to sign without delay on pain of a resumption of the war. To this curt ultimatum the government of Berlin yielded and on June 28, in a formal session held in the famous palace of Louis XIV, where the German Empire had been proclaimed in 1871, the document which registered its demise received the signature of vanquished and victors. By a no less remarkable coincidence the day marked the fifth anniversary of the historic pistol-shot which killed the Austrian archduke and which had ever since been going round the world in deafening echoes.

The Treaty of Versailles was a drastic document of 80,000 words which humbled Germany utterly. By means of its territorial provisions she was curtailed both east and west, losing Alsace-Lorraine to France and the bulk of the two provinces of Posen The terri- and West Prussia to the resuscitated state of Poland. In torial losses addition, certain districts in northern Schleswig and far of Germany more extensive ones along the eastern confines of Prussia, particularly upper Silesia with its invaluable coal-fields, were designated as plebiscite areas, where it was left to the population to decide by vote whether they wished to remain in the German communion. In another important German coal region, that of the Saar, a Prussian district adjoining Lorraine, the coal mines were given to France outright but politically the region was put under a commission responsible to the League of Nations with the understanding that the inhabitants would, after fifteen years, have the privilege of determining their ultimate fate by a popular vote. Finally, the German colonies in Africa, Asia, and the Pacific ocean were distributed among the victors, in some cases not as owners in full sovereignty but under

the mandatory system which reserved a right of supervision to the
League of Nations. Without doubt it was an intelligent proceeding
to give the League of Nations this power of review since only by
means of an active participation in the affairs of the world could thê
League prove its vitality and acquire a needed prestige. In pursuance
of this aim, particularly dear to President Wilson, chief sponsor of
the Covenant, the execution of the whole Treaty of Versailles was
put more or less in the hands of the League.

In the important matter of disarmament Germany agreed to surrender to the allies practically the whole of her war equipment — her
fleet, her submarines, her cannon, her machine guns, her munitions,
her military and naval aircraft. She further agreed to
maintain henceforward a navy so small as to be negligible
and to support an army which shall not exceed 100,000
men. Universal military service, with which her history
was peculiarly interwoven, was to be abolished and the
army was to be recruited solely by voluntary enlistment. In sum,
Germany was disarmed in the present and made powerless in the
future. But even more crushing were the reparations imposed on
Germany together with the economic consequences which they entailed. The beaten nation had in the armistice agreement accepted
full responsibility "for all damage done to the civilian population of
the allies and to their property by the aggression of Germany by land,
by sea, and from the air." Under this comprehensive, if somewhat
indefinite, obligation Germany was saddled with a vast burden of
payments. She agreed to replace, ton for ton, all shipping destroyed
by the submarine terror or from other causes; she pledged her resources to the rebuilding of the devastated areas of France and Belgium; she promised to assemble and hand over without delay large
quantities of live stock such as milch cows, heifers, stallions, mares,
and sheep, and annually, for years to come, to deliver many million
tons of coal. But the weightiest of all reparation items was the money
indemnity. Because the victors could not agree on the total amount
to be paid by Germany, they patched up a provisional arrangement
calling for the immediate payment of some billions of gold marks
but putting off the fixing of the definitive sum to May 1, 1921.
Finally a permanent committee, called the reparation commission,
was established to hold Germany to the exact fulfilment of the financial and economic terms imposed on her. In effect the reparation
commission undertook to manage Germany as a bankrupt estate in
the interest of the creditors.

The disarmament and reparation clauses

Resolved to get their full rights under the treaty, the allies did not overlook military coercion. They occupied with their armed forces the whole area west of the river Rhine together with the three important bridge-heads on the east bank at Mainz, Co- The blenz, and Cologne. The occupation was fixed for a term military of fifteen years and was to be at the expense of the Ger- coercion mans. Moreover, the treaty reserved to the victors the clauses right to seize additional German territory whenever Germany was adjudged to be in voluntary default in its obligations. Although there were many other articles in the treaty, each of which canceled some property or treaty right of Germany within or without her political boundaries, enough has been said to make clear that she was stricken from the list of the powers and, as far as lay with the victors, reduced to beggary and impotence.

With the Treaty of Versailles out of the way, President Wilson and the leading dignitaries went home, but their delegates remained behind at Paris to draw up the documents which, besides establishing peace with Austria, Hungary, Bulgaria, and Turkey, Additional should regulate the boundaries and impose certain ob- labors of ligations on the many new nations established on the ruins the peace of the ancient empires of the Hapsburgs and Romanovs. conference The labors of the peace conference continued therefore through 1919 and much of 1920.

The treaty with Austria, now a small German republic of about six million inhabitants, of whom two million lived in the single city of Vienna, was ready first and was duly signed at St. Germain in September, 1919. By its terms Austria obligated herself The treaty to meet a bill for reparations so greatly in excess of her with Austria assets that she, too, had to be taken over as a bankrupt concern by the same reparation commission appointed as receiver for Germany under the Treaty of Versailles. Although she had, as was natural enough in view of the triumph throughout the world of the nationalist principle, expressed a wish to join Germany, the conference, still filled with the fear of its late enemy and unwilling to see Germany strengthened by the addition of new territory, ruled otherwise. For the present at least Austria was to be a minor German republic dwelling in the shadow of its greater brother. Finally, after recognizing the sovereignty and independence, within the boundaries drawn by the conference, of the states formed wholly or in part from the Hapsburg wreck, to wit, Czecho-Slovakia, Jugo-Slavia, and Poland, Aus-

tria submitted to all cessions of territory required of her in favor of
these states as well as of Rumania and Italy, which, as active members of the victor group, had not failed to claim a share in the Hapsburg heritage.

Next came the treaty with Bulgaria, which, signed at Neuilly,
another Paris suburb, in November, 1919, imposed on the defeated
state a large but definite indemnity of something over two billion
gold francs and limited the Bulgarian army henceforth
to 20,000 men. In addition Bulgaria was obliged to
accede to various losses of territory, the most grievous
being the province of Thrace together with the Ægean
seaboard. Macedonia, to which Bulgaria could put forth,
on purely nationalist grounds, as good a claim or better than any of
her neighbors, had been lost for the first time in the war of 1913 and,
though regained in 1915, was in 1919 redivided between Greece and
Serbia. In the light of the Bulgar treaty the Balkan peninsula,
which had been a leading, though by no means the only storm
center of Europe throughout the nineteenth century, and which had
set the match to an inflammable continent in 1914, will doubtless
persist as a zone of danger. Its pacification is highly desirable, and
perhaps by means of a loose federation of all its states, if it were
feasible, the way might be cleared for a relaxation of the violent
tension and the triumph of a more placable spirit. But with Bulgaria nursing a grudge on national and economic grounds and with
no one of the Balkan states particularly well-disposed to any other,
the creation of a federative commonwealth is hardly to be expected,
at least not until much water has run down the Danube.

The treaty with Bulgaria and the Balkan outlook

The treaty with Hungary was greatly delayed, owing to the peculiarly violent domestic disturbances in that mid-Danubian land
which followed its defeat in war. No sooner had the Hapsburg
dynasty been deposed than, as in the case of Russia and
Germany, a republic was proclaimed. However, in
March, 1919, the communists or "Reds," who drew their
inspiration from the Russia of Lenin, overthrew the middle class, excluded them from power, and set up a purely proletarian régime.
Not till the month of August were the communists overthrown by
an invasion from Rumania, whereupon a strongly conservative
group of politicians succeeded in seizing the reins at Budapest. Thus,
in the year following the armistice, control fluctuated violently to
and fro. When in January, 1920, the allies laid the Treaty of Tria-

The treaty with Hungary

non before the Hungarian delegates summoned to this end to Paris, it was found to be modeled closely on the Treaties of Versailles and St. Germain. The amount of reparations to be paid was left unsettled; the army was reduced to 35,000 men; and very large slices of territory, preponderantly inhabited by Rumanians, Slovaks, and Serbs were handed over respectively to Rumania, Czecho-Slovakia, and Jugo-Slavia. By these decisions the new republic of Hungary was reduced in territory to one-third of the former kingdom and in population to about nine million inhabitants.

Owing to the disturbed condition of the disrupted Ottoman Empire and of the whole Near East, as well as because of differences of opinion among the victors, the treaty with Turkey, called the Treaty of Sèvres, was not ready till the summer of 1920. The treaty The chief stone of stumbling among the conferees proved with Turkey to be the age-old problem of Constantinople and the straits. By a secret treaty drawn up in 1915 France and Great Britain had promised this area to tsarist Russia, which therewith came into sight of a goal obstinately pursued for generations. By going Bolshevist, however, and deserting the allies, Russia was accounted to have forfeited the prize. After prolonged discussion Great Britain, France, and Italy, the powers alone concerned with drawing up the Treaty of Sèvres, agreed to declare the shores of the straits an international area to be governed by an international commission. Most of the remaining territory of the conquered empire was distributed among the victors, though often with important qualifications. Mesopotamia went to Great Britain and Syria to France but in either case the country given control agreed to regard itself as a trustee for the League of Nations. In southern Syria an interesting experiment was inaugurated with the ancient land of Palestine, for it was proclaimed a Jewish homeland under the protection of Great Britain, acting in this case also as a mandatory of the League. In Arabia was set up the independent Arab state of the Hedjaz under the rule of the sherif of Mecca. Although this ruler was awarded the sounding title king, it remained of course to be seen how far he could command the obedience of his subjects and give them protection against the wild tribesmen of the desert. So far as the Treaty of Sèvres went the only territory left to the sultan was Asia Minor and even this was to come to him in a sadly reduced form. Smyrna and its hinterland were assigned to Greece, while extensive spheres of interest were reserved to France, Italy, and Great Britain. Finally, the treaty declared for an independent Armenia in eastern Asia Minor with boundaries to be determined later. A strict execution of all these provisions would probably render nugatory the sultan's hold on even the single province nominally left in his hands. The backward Ottoman Empire had been, as we have seen, the chief apple of discord among the rival imperialist powers. By the Treaty of Sèvres the apple was claimed and divided among Great Britain, France, and Italy, with a not inconsiderable slice promised to the appetite of Greece in order to induce that state to serve as the victors' carving-knife.

REFERENCES

E. Fueter, *World History*, ch. 34

C. J. H. Hayes, *Political and Social History*, II, chs. 31, 32, 33; *Brief History of the Great War*

J. S. Schapiro, *Modern and Contemporary History*, ch. 20

E. R. Turner, *Europe Since 1870*, chs. 17, 18

C. D. Hazen, *Europe Since 1815*, II, chs. 26, 27

G. P. Gooch, *History of Modern Europe*, chs. 15-19

W. Lippmann, *The Stakes of Diplomacy*

J. T. W. Newbold, *How Europe Armed for War*

G. G. Coulton, *The Main Illusions of Pacifism*

H. A. L. Fisher, *The War, its Causes and its Issues*

C. Seymour, *The Diplomatic Background of the War*

J. B. Scott, *Diplomatic Documents Relating to the Outbreak of the War*

M. Montgelas, *The Case for the Central Powers*

F. Bausman, *Let France Explain*

A. J. Toynbee, *Nationality and the War*

E. B. Krehbiel, *Nationalism, War, and Society*

W. Weyl, *American World Politics*

A. F. Pollard, *Short History of the War*

F. H. Simonds, *The Great War*

W. E. Dodd, *Woodrow Wilson and his Work*

R. S. Baker, *Woodrow Wilson and World Settlement*

E. H. House and C. Seymour, *What Really Happened at Paris*

C. H. Haskins and R. H. Lord, *Some Problems of the Peace Conference*

E. J. Dillon, *Inside Story of the Peace Conference*

A. Tardieu, *The Truth about the Treaty (of Versailles)*

H. W. V. Temperley, *A History of the Peace Conference of Paris* (7 volumes)

A. P. Scott, *An Introduction to the Peace Treaties*

CHAPTER XXXIV

POST-WAR EUROPE

It was an amazingly altered appearance that Europe presented to view as a result of the war and the peace which concluded it. To leave to one side for the present the radical mental and moral changes among the many peoples whom we have in mind The new when we pronounce the word Europe and to concentrate map of on so relatively simple a matter as the new boundaries, Europe it is certain that neither the Treaty of Westphalia (1648) nor that of Utrecht (1713) nor the Final Act of the Congress of Vienna (1815) authorized even remotely such incisive alterations of the map as the treaties signed in the various suburbs of Paris. The whole vast middle of Europe took on a new shape. Let us first look at Germany. Besides losing Alsace-Lorraine to France, certain small sections (Eupen, Malmedy) to Belgium, a tiny Silesian district to Czecho-Slovakia; and most of Posen and West Prussia to Poland, the new government was obliged to hand over the Saar basin to the League of Nations, to resign the title to the district of Memel to the allies, to agree to the constituting of the city of Danzig as a Free State, and to acknowledge certain sections of Schleswig, East Prussia, and Upper Silesia as plebiscite areas, whose final allegiance should be determined by a popular vote.

Serious as was the immediate reduction of Germany, it would be worse if the plebiscites went against her. The Schleswig issue was the first to be settled, the first (northern) zone voting overwhelmingly for Denmark, the second as decisively for Settlement Germany. The two Prussian zones, called to choose of the between Germany and Poland, voted almost unanimously German for Germany. There remained Upper Silesia, a peculiarly boundaries and the contentious area because of its invaluable deposits of remaining coal, lead, and zinc. Although the vote was a German uncertain-victory, three-fifths of the population declaring for the ties old allegiance, so determined were the allies that these natural resources should not fall to Germany that Upper Silesia was divided between Germany and Poland in such a way that its natural

691

wealth fell preponderantly to Poland. It was not till the close of 1921 that the Silesian controversy was adjusted and the German boundary given a certain definiteness. Even so the Saar area will be alienated until a vote in 1935 shall determine the preference of the inhabitants, while the whole left bank of the Rhine, remaining in occupation by the armies of France, Belgium, and Great Britain, is, though administratively German, hardly an assured German territory so long as it is held by the forces of the victors. The Treaty of Versailles provided that, in case Germany fulfilled her obligations, the Cologne area should be evacuated in January, 1925, the Coblenz area in 1930, and the Mainz sector in 1935. In January, 1925, the allies refused to give up Cologne on the ground that Germany's disarmament was not complete according to the letter of the treaty. While this may be true, it is clear that the allies and more particularly France will never find it difficult to allege an infraction of the treaty if they consider it advantageous to exercise a continued threat against their defeated foe.

Even before the allies at Paris decreed the dissolution of the Austro-Hungarian Empire it had gone to pieces through the revolt of its component nationalities. Its place has therefore been taken

The succession states of the Hapsburg monarchy

by the so-called succession states — Austria, Czecho-Slovakia, Jugo-Slavia, Poland, and Hungary. Besides, Italy acquired certain sections of Austrian territory (Trentino, the southern Tyrol, Trieste, Gorizia, Istria, Zara), while Rumania received the Bukovina from Austria and Transylvania and the eastern section of the Hungarian plain from Hungary. The historical significance of the passing of the Hapsburg monarchy lies in the sweeping victory of the nationalist idea. In the main the distribution of the Hapsburg territories authorized at Paris accorded with the principle of nationality; but certain important modifications should be noted which we may explain as concessions to the hard facts of victory and its attendant passions. Also the circumstance that the various peoples were often so closely intermingled as to defy a clean mutual extrication must be in fairness taken into account in judging the new boundaries. Of the outstanding breaches of the nationality principle the most important instances deserve enumeration. Of the territories ceded to Italy the southern Tyrol, that is, the territory immediately south of the Brenner pass, is German and most of Istria is Slav; on the territories constituted as Czecho-Slovakia reside over 3,000,000

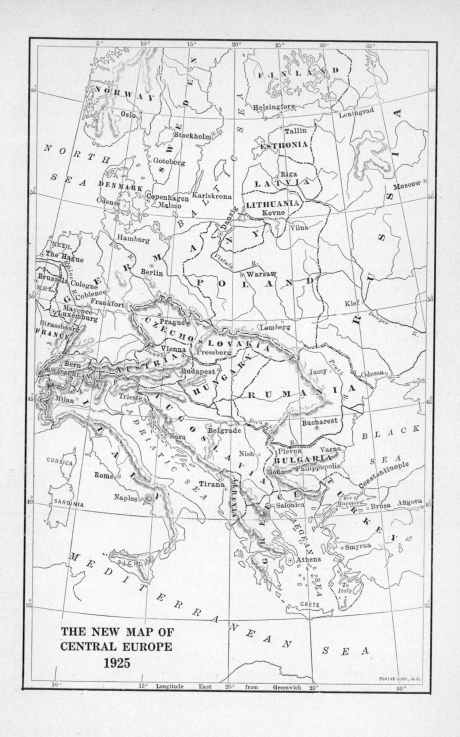

THE NEW MAP OF
CENTRAL EUROPE
1925

Germans and about three quarters of a million of Magyars, while Czecho-Slovakia's easternmost province, Carpathian Russia, is wholly inhabited by Little Russians (Ukrainians); of the former Austrian territory incorporated with the republic of Poland the eastern section of Galicia is populated not by Poles but by Ukrainians. Amidst the jubilations over what looked like the universal victory of nationalism the new Austrian Republic, the German core of the former empire, was with resolute inconsistency put under an antinationalist ban. On the morrow of the revolution an Austrian assembly voted the inclusion of Austria in the German family as represented by the German Republic; but the peace conference, moved by fear of a strengthened Germany, forbade this consummation. Only in case the Council of the League of Nations gives its unanimous consent can Austria in the future be merged in the German national state.

Passing from the former Austro-Hungarian Empire to southeastern Europe, we note that the principle of nationality, having worked its wonders there during the nineteenth century by rousing from their Rip Van Winkle sleep the Greeks, Serbs, Rumanians, Bulgars, and Albanians, found nothing left for it to do but to effect a possible readjustment of the boundaries. Perhaps Albania, which had not been constituted as a separate state till 1913 and which had proved so weak that it disappeared in the whirling maelstrom of the World War, may be looked on as a creation or at least a re-creation of the Paris conference. In any case the Paris conference undertook to draw for Albania, Serbia (in its enlarged form commonly called Jugo-Slavia), Rumania, Greece, and Bulgaria their new and authentic boundaries. While taking its cue in the main from considerations of nationality, the conference agreed to set the seal of its approval on the excessive demands of the victors, more particularly on those of Jugo-Slavia and Greece. In this way Macedonia, certainly more Bulgar than it is Serb or Greek, was divided between Belgrad and Athens. Again, another mixed area, Thrace, with probably as many Bulgars or Turks as it has Greeks was attributed to Greece.

The new boundaries of southeastern Europe

Nowhere in Europe did the principle of nationality triumph more completely than in Russia. The Russian core of the vast empire might obediently yield to Bolshevist rule, but along the western border as well as

The revolt of the various peoples subjected to the former Russian Empire

in the Caucasus the non-Russian peoples vigorously asserted their right of self-determination. True, the three Caucasus republics of Georgia, Armenia, and Azerbaijan were in 1921, only two years after they were founded, obliged to forego complete independence and to associate themselves with Soviet Russia. It may be doubted that they are today (1925) enjoying even a measurable remnant of independence.

But the states of the Russian western fringe, Poland, Lithuania, Latvia, Esthonia, and Finland were and are in a different case, partly because they possessed greater means of resistance than the tiny would-be republics of the Caucasus, partly because they were strengthened by the proximity of the western victors, who, as sworn enemies of the Soviet régime, are almost certain to give the new states aid in case they are attacked by Moscow. The republic of Poland, partitioned in the eighteenth century among its three neighbors of Russia, Austria, and Prussia, represents one of the remarkable resurrections of history. Resolved as the Paris conferees were to restore it along national lines, they found themselves confronted by the perhaps unsolvable problem of drawing correct racial frontiers in the vast east-European plain, where natural barriers do not exist and where peoples of different strains have been freely intermingling for centuries. However, favoring Poland against Germany, the victorious allies conceded to it the so-called Vistula or Danzig corridor which opened to Poland an immediate access to the Baltic sea; favoring Poland against Lithuania, they only protested feebly when Poland seized by military might the Vilna district attributed to Lithuania; favoring Poland against the Little Russian (Ukrainian) people, they permitted the new republic to take over eastern Galicia; and finally, favoring Poland against Russia, under pressure particularly from France they encouraged Poland to make war (1920) on the Bolsheviki. This struggle, concluded by a treaty between Poland and exhausted and defeated Russia, gave Poland an eastern frontier including a broad belt of non-Polish peoples, chiefly White and Little Russians. In sum, Poland is, though perhaps not in the same degree as Czecho-Slovakia, an inflated state containing numerous non-Polish nationalities.

The inflated state of Poland

Lithuania, which in the Vilna matter proved to be at the mercy of Poland, would seem from every angle to be a rather feeble creation. However, in 1923 it imitated the Polish action against Vilna by suddenly seizing the city and district of Memel, once the possession of Germany but held since 1919 by the allied powers. These, taken aback by the predatory act, finally agreed to abandon Memel to Lithuania. Latvia (the country of the Letts) and Esthonia (the country of the Esths) have, although small, exhibited considerable energy in setting their governments going. Even more vigor has been shown by Finland, long autonomous under the tsars of Russia and well prepared by history and the cool temper of its people to assume the responsibilities of self-government.

Lithuania, Latvia, Esthonia, Finland

It will summarize the extraordinarily novel political situation if we take note that in place of the three great empires of Germany, Austria-Hungary, and Russia we now have, on what was once their territory, an aggregate of seventeen states. Two of the seventeen, Russia and Germany, remain, in spite of the reductions suffered, sufficiently large and populous to aspire to play the part of great powers. The rest are patently small powers, though Poland and Czecho-Slovakia more particularly enjoy considerable resources and have already proved themselves by no means negligible factors in the post-war game of diplomacy. As eastern neighbors of Germany they enjoy the interested patronage of France, which by reorganizing their armed forces and by the loan of large sums for equipment has brought them definitely within her political orbit.

Seventeen states established on the territory of the former empires of Germany, Russia, and Austria-Hungary

In the light of the situation here set forth the most significant feature of the new map of Europe is the sweeping triumph of nationalism. We have followed the nationalist movement through the nineteenth century, beginning with the unification of Italy and Germany. Penetrating the Balkan peninsula, the new and revolutionary sentiment slowly dissolved the Ottoman Empire by calling back to life the submerged Christian peoples. Even on Europe's western fringe its clangorous tongue made itself heard by effecting the resurrection of Belgium, Norway, and Ireland. Its crowning achievement, however, was reserved to the World War, in the hot fires of which the great multi-national empires of Austria-Hungary and Russia were substantially melted down to their component elements. Without pretending to be able to give a certain answer, we yet may, nay, we must at this juncture raise the question of the

Does the nationalist organization of Europe make for security and peace?

outlook for the security and peace of Europe under the new system. And undoubtedly it is proper to begin the argument by recognizing that since nationalism had penetrated to the remotest corner of Europe and since it had received everywhere an almost ecstatic welcome as the modern way of salvation, it was a distinct gain that the fond hopes entertained of it had been realized and that Europe had with almost religious fervor during and after the World War affirmed its adherence to nationalism as the fundamental principle of its political organization. Might one not now reasonably expect some weakening of tension, some decline of the red-hot passions which had dangerously charged with electricity the whole public atmosphere of Europe? Perhaps; yet nothing of the sort has thus far taken place. Undeniably nationalism burns over Europe with a fiercer flame than ever. Is this because, as some pessimists would have it, it is by its nature a destructive force destined to rage until it has leveled European civilization with the ground? Or is the optimist view admissible that the nationalist passions continue to blaze because nationalism has after all not yet effected its final liberations nor realized its visioned, even-handed justice?

To whatever opinion we may incline let us pass the present situation in review and uncover the leading causes of the continued friction and exasperation. In the first place the new boundaries were drawn by a group of victors with the conscious purpose of doing the vanquished as much injury as possible. We have noted many instances of this biased procedure at Paris, the chief victim being the leading central European people. Many millions of Germans were by the express action of the conference excluded from the communion of their kin. But if many boundaries, drawn under the prompting of passion, may be expected to be some day rectified when a better feeling comes to prevail, how about the boundaries of those areas where different peoples have become inextricably intermingled through the accidents of history? The Serb-Bulgar, Bulgar-Greek, German-Czech, German-Polish, and Polish-Lithuanian contact areas are a few of the regions where the clean disentanglement which is the nationalist ideal is simply out of the question. Inevitably the group momentarily dominant will do its best to diminish and even to get rid of its rival or rivals. To prevent the worst oppression the Paris conferees imposed on all the national states of their creation, harboring within their borders

Reasons why the nationalist settlement is attended by continued unrest

considerable minorities of one or more peoples, the obligation to grant to these minorities a number of fundamental rights such as security of person, property, religion, and education. But is it not possible for governments, filled with ill-will, to achieve underhandedly what they agree not to do in the sight of the world? And since by the treaties signed at Paris the only legal protector of the minorities is the League of Nations and the League is far away and none too powerful, need offending governments fear retribution for tyrannizing over the groups in their midst whom they passionately desire to have disappear? And as for these minority groups, what is to hinder them, if their case becomes desperate, from entering into treasonable plots with their co-nationals across the boundary?

Here are real difficulties which will not yield to either sentimental generalities or frenzied exhortation and which have been made worse by the wanton creation of tariff and other impediments to free intercourse across the frequent territorial boundaries. It was *The folly of economic isolation* perhaps natural that the new states in the pride of their fresh statehood and in their injudicious animosity against their neighbors, always rivals and often hereditary enemies, should surround themselves with walls and barbed wire entanglements. But how can such a policy be brought into harmony with the modern system of world markets and world communications? In practically every instance each new state, practicing an exaggerated exclusiveness, has made a business not only of irritating its neighbors but incidentally also of injuring itself by — as the saying is — cutting off its nose to spite its face. Let us hope that the hermit policy characterizing the economic legislation of the new Europe will incontinently be abandoned, for unless it is, even the qualified prosperity of the pre-war period will never again be reached.

The outlook for Europe offered by these considerations would be dark to the point of blackness were it not for the League of Nations. Granting the imperfections of its origin and its manifest lack of present authority, we can not fail to see that it sketches *The League of Nations considered as a league of Europe* an European commonwealth which under favorable circumstances may become strong enough to bring the many conflicts agitating the ancient continent to some sort of settlement. Even today we may declare with assurance that were it not for the League of Nations, not only would the precarious peace maintained since 1919 be much more precarious but a great many border quarrels that have at least been temporarily patched up would have terminated in open war. From the angle of nationalistically organized post-war Europe, the League of Nations is not so much a world league as a league of the peoples of the troubled little continent, which is culturally as well as geographically a single unit. Indeed from this same angle the League is pan-Europe, the logical and unescapable supernational façade of the loosely constructed national house of many chambers.

The remainder of this chapter will be devoted to a discussion of the main issues around which the history of Europe has turned during the six years which have elapsed since the drawing up of the peace treaties. They are (a) the policy of the United States; (b) the rejection by the Turks of the Treaty of Sèvres and the resumption of the war in Asia Minor; (c) the policy and vicissitudes of Soviet Russia; (d) German reparations; (e) inter-allied debts; (f) the League of Nations.

The six leading issues which have agitated Europe since 1919

When by its entry into the war the United States of America decided the issue, it was universally assumed that the powerful western republic would thenceforth have a large part in the affairs of Europe. The vigorous leadership of liberal opinion throughout the world taken over by President Wilson fortified the impression; and when the president successfully imposed the League of Nations on the Paris conference, the expectation became general that his country would eagerly serve as the mainstay of the novel venture. But it befell otherwise. Within the senate of the United States, which body would under the constitution have to ratify the Treaty of Versailles, a partisan opposition developed to those sections of the treaty dealing with the League of Nations; and on the newspapers taking the matter up it quickly appeared that the country was unwilling to range itself behind its official chief. The profound American emotion over President Wilson's policy is not difficult to explain. It was felt that the League was primarily an European affair and that it was folly for the United States, which had been providentially spared the alarms and antagonisms of Europe, to identify itself with the older continent without necessity and in child-like ignorance of the merits of the innumerable European quarrels. More important still was the consideration of national sovereignty. It had become a fetish and even a ruling divinity in the course of recent centuries and no people showed the least willingness to give up its worship. If the European

(a) The United States rejects the League of Nations

nations had yielded so far from the extreme assertion of sovereignty as to consent to the creation of the League of Nations, they did so, in the first place, on the understanding that the League was to remain a feeble infant and, in the second place, because they were assured by their leaders that the new institution would infringe barely if at all upon their precious self-sufficiency. Undeniably the League was accepted reluctantly even in Europe and for the pressing reason that the alternative was almost certainly renewed war and ultimate chaos. But as these considerations did not weigh with the United States, its people at once sniffed the air suspiciously and ended by reacting violently against what they persuaded themselves was a plot to drag them into the European bog. In the presidential election of November, 1920, President Wilson's party was overwhelmingly defeated. As a result, so far as the western republic was concerned, the League of Nations issue quietly expired and with it the Treaty of Versailles of which it was an integral part. On March 4, 1921, President Wilson vanished, a man broken in health if not in spirit, from the public scene, and his Republican successor, President Harding, hastened to conclude a separate peace with Germany.

The League of Nations has since remained a dead issue in the United States and is not likely to be brought back into politics at an early date. For that it fills, as the American people instinctively felt, first and foremost an European want is undeniable. The League Into the embittered local contentions of Europe the United of Nations States is properly extremely loath to be drawn. But in analyzed from the so far as the League may succeed in serving, besides an American European, a world function it may well be that the United point of States will at some future time discover that a regularly view instituted session of the powers interested in world questions will prove a convenience for the American people, perhaps even a necessity. Without assuming the robe of the prophet it would seem to be possible to declare that the favorable development of the relations of the United States to the League will depend on the latter body's willingness and power to regulate outstanding imperialist interests and ambitions. For once more let us recall that the World War grew out of both nationalist and imperialist antagonisms and that the League of Nations has therefore naturally and inevitably a double set of functions. Certainly it is only on the side of its projected regulation of imperialist issues that it touches or may hope to touch any immediate concerns of the United States.

Even before the Treaty of Sèvres had been completed by the allies and as soon as it became apparent not only that the Ottoman Empire was to be thoroughly dispersed but that the Turks them-
(b) The Turks reject the Treaty of Sèvres
selves were to be brought under the permanent tutelage of the victors, an energetic leader who had distinguished himself in the war, Mustafa Kemal by name, organized his people in Asia Minor for resistance. Mustafa's movement had a distinctly nationalist cast. It will be remembered that as early as 1908 a section of the Turks showed that they had been Europeanized sufficiently to institute a revolution which had both a liberal and a nationalist character. It was this same Europeanizing group, the so-called Young Turks, who six years later plunged the Ottoman Empire into the World War on the side of Germany. While the defeat discredited the political leaders of the war period and obliged them to flee precipitately from Constantinople, it did not alter the attachment of the Turks to nationalism, especially as all the neighboring peoples of the Near East had been seized with the same consuming emotion. Certainly the Arabs of Arabia, Syria, and Mesopotamia made it quite clear that if they renounced Ottoman rule, it was not because they desired to bend their neck to the yoke of a victor power, no matter how beneficent that yoke purported to be. If the Arab leaders expressed the true opinion of their people, the Arabs intended to have an Arab state all of their own, preferably a pan-Arab state. This was also the idea of Mustafa Kemal and his Turks. Adopting nationalism with naïve literalness, they declared that they were willing to give up the non-Turkish provinces of their former empire of conquest, but that Asia Minor (Anatolia) together with Constantinople and eastern Thrace constituted a genuine nationalist Turkey and that for this Turkish nucleus the Turks would fight to the death. As early as 1920 it became clear that if the articles of the Treaty of Sèvres referring to the areas claimed as Turkish by Mustafa Kemal were to be executed, the allies would have to impose their will by armed force.

Unprepared for various reasons to levy war on the determined Mustafa, the allies commissioned Greece to act in their behalf. The result was a passionate Turco-Greek war which throughout 1921 and 1922 swayed to and fro between Smyrna, the Greek military base on the Asia Minor coast, and Angora, Mustafa's inland capital. At last the Greek forces were disastrously routed and Smyrna itself taken and burned (Oct., 1922). To save their self-respect the allies were obliged to intervene in behalf of their discomfited agent and, after protracted negotiations at Lausanne (Switzerland), in July, 1923, signed with the Anatolian Turks a new treaty. This, as emphatically registering a Turkish victory as the Treaty of Sèvres had registered a Turkish defeat, marks the accept- **The Turks impose the** ance of the main Turkish demands. While the Ottoman **Treaty of** Empire was happily not recalled from the shades, its resid- **Lausanne on the allies** uum, nationalist Turkey, was recognized within the boundaries demanded by the Kemalists. The chief loser by the Treaty of Lausanne was Greece, which had followed the lure of an overweening ambition and which now sat physically and spiritually broken amidst the wreckage of its hopes. The International Zone of the Straits, which represented the Sèvres solution of the ancient problem of the Dardanelles and Bosporus, was completely scrapped under the new arrangements. The most the victorious Turks would agree to was the demilitarization of the straits and that they were to be open in both peace and war to merchant vessels and warships of all nations. What this means, if it means anything at all, only the future can determine. The suspicion can not be avoided that the Turks have again clinched the control of the straits. Further, the idea of an independent Armenia was abandoned at Lausanne and the Armenians themselves, in so far as they reside on Turkish soil, were delivered to the mercy of the Turks. An interesting, novel provision fraught with countless personal tragedies was the wholesale transplantation of Greeks from Turkish to Greek soil and vice versa in the hope of effecting as clean as possible a disentanglement of these two hostile peoples. Finally, the extraterritoriality enjoyed for centuries by the European powers on Ottoman soil and familiar under the name of the Capitulations has been canceled. Freed of all reparation claims, Turkey has been accepted into the full comity of nations on the somewhat hazardous theory that it is an ordered, civilized state.

The new Turkey, due largely to the bold initiative of a single man, has declared itself a republic under a constitution which vests both the legislative and executive power in a National Assembly elected for two years. The sultanate and califate have both been **The new** abolished. The ancient house of Osman has been driven **Turkey** into exile. The only possible interpretation of these startling measures is that under Mustafa Kemal's leadership Turkey is resolved to make a complete break with its past and to establish a state which shall be as close a realization as possible of what presents itself to the imagination of the Near East as western progress. That this will be a difficult program to carry through goes without saying. In view of the character and mental outlook of the Turks and with due regard to the difficulties of their situation in the midst of so many old and new enemies it may prove beyond their strength.

It was in November, 1917, that the Bolsheviks, whose program was an extreme radical socialism, more properly defined as communism, seized the power in Russia. Their program, so flattering to the workers and peasants, ranged these oppressed classes in (c) The Bolshevik triumph in Russia sufficient numbers behind the Bolshevik leaders to put them in secure possession of the country. None the less, undoubtedly encouraged in some instances by Great Britain and France, groups of monarchical and bourgeois opponents, usually lumped together under the designation of Whites, undertook to overthrow the Bolsheviks, commonly called Reds. We need not go into these attempts, which continued for three years after the Bolshevik triumph, further than to note that they all failed. Because the Whites, by accepting foreign support, aroused nationalist resentment, because the masses continued to rally enthusiastically behind their revolutionary leaders, and finally, because the Bolsheviks boasted in Lenin an impressive political leader and in Trotzky a capable and magnetic military organizer the Reds trampled in the dust all armed opposition and with a sort of elemental fury set about the realization of their politico-economic program.

The outstanding feature of that program was to destroy the capitalist system and to effect a complete economic equality among men not by persuasion and by gradual measures, but by a single sweeping The communist system act based on the exercise of an irresistible force. The land of the nobles and well-to-do was seized and distributed among the peasants; the factories, banks, mines, and other private businesses of every kind were appropriated with a view to operating them as public concerns for the benefit of the common people. Resistance on the part of the individual owners was punished by imprisonment and in numerous cases by death. The attempted realization of the communist theory breathed force at every turn, force without stint or limit. The transformation effected by these measures and the failure and success of the whole communist program can not yet be discussed with anything resembling assurance. Judgment on the Bolshevik experiment must wisely remain in suspense.

However, there is one thing which the student of European history will always do well never to lose from mind in weighing the phenomenon called the Russian revolution: it is that that revolution did not take place in an old and typical European state but among a people which had only recently been brought under the influence of the west and which in organization and mentality was utterly different from the peoples of the Atlantic seaboard. It is therefore quite possible that what happened in Russia in the way either of the destruction of the older economic order or of the creation of a new society of equals may not be particularly relevant for Europe. In spite of the prophetic gestures of Lenin and Trotzky as well as of the nucleus of followers they command in every country of the world, the Russian revolution, even if ultimately successful, may prove to be suited only to Russia, to be in effect a social reorganization of purely Russian import.

Let the reader entertain no doubt however that the above does not represent the view of the promoters of the Red revolution in Russia and elsewhere. Holding the Marxian view of history, they declared and for some decades before 1917 had been declaring that the capitalist system was approaching an inevitable transformation to be marked by the seizure on the part of the workers of the means of production. As under the strict theory the transformation was to be inaugurated in the most highly industrialized centers, such as England and Belgium, it was something of a disappointment that industrially backward Russia should have rung in the new era. But the Russian leaders themselves lost no sleep over this historical vagary. Frankly recognizing that an isolated Russian communism was foredoomed to failure, they rejoiced in the possession of political power which they could utilize to bring about a communist revolution in other countries. They consequently called into being the Third International, representative of international communism, with a permanent organization at Moscow; and providing this huge propaganda organization with a blank check on the Russian treasury, they bade it go ahead and produce at the earliest possible date a world-wide communist upheaval.

The aim of the Russian revolution is world revolution

It is in this propagandist form that the western governments encountered Russia after 1917 and it is not surprising that they should have interpreted the Russian activity as latent war. They went therefore the length not only of giving support to the various

civil risings in Russia associated with the Whites but also of more
or less ruthlessly suppressing all the sympathetic radical manifestations in their own midst.   Finally, they sternly broke off diplomatic

Russia and and economic relations with the Soviet régime and sur-
the western rounded their all but avowed enemies with a sanitary
govern-   cordon as though they considered them to be in the grip of
ments lay
the founda- a contagious disease.   This last group of measures
tions of a amounted to a policy of complete non-intercourse.   But
frail peace such a policy was difficult to keep up in our modern world
of mutually interdependent parts.   Wonderful economic opportunities beckoned within the vast Russian dominion; and if these attracted the foreign exploiters by the prospect of gain, they signified to the
Russians themselves industrial goods of which they stood in clear need
and which they could never hope to produce by themselves because
of their lack of capital and technical skill.   Hesitatingly negotiations
were initiated between the bitter opponents, between Moscow and
the various capitals of Europe.   Of course the western statesmen put
at the head of their demands the cessation of all propaganda aiming
at the overthrow of the existent politico-economic system of their
respective countries.   In the end the Russians always granted the
request, moved by the hope of generating that moral confidence
among their neighbors without which capital would not embark on
the perilous journey to Muscovy.   It may well be — and the charge
has been repeatedly voiced — that the Bolshevik promise to desist
from agitation is given with the tongue in the cheek, for, as we have
seen, the issue for Russia is and must be: world revolution or failure.
None the less the Bolsheviks have in many instances pledged their
word to desist from propaganda in response to the pressing need of
their country for goods and conveniences destroyed by the war and
incapable of being replaced by Russian effort.   They have a deep
distrust of one another, the semi-oriental Russians and the wholly
occidental English, French, Italians, and Germans; but slowly,
driven by the unescapable necessities of economic exchange, they
have drawn together and between 1922 and 1924 have signed treaties
patching up a precarious *modus vivendi*.   As late as 1925 the United
States of America voiced a firm refusal to follow the European lead.
For reasons satisfactory to itself the Washington government prefers
to play a lone hand.   Whether the timorous resumption of diplomatic
relations between communist Russia and capitalist Europe will bring
in its wake a profitable economic exchange it is yet too early to say.

Quite likely it will not, unless the experimental communist system is gradually abandoned in favor of a return to the older capitalist method of production. It is doubtless the hope of such a consumma- tion as this which inspires the governments of London, Paris, Rome, and Berlin. The game of Moscow, on the other hand, seems to be to hold out resolutely for communism and yet to offer opportunities calculated to draw private capital and engineering skill of foreign origin to Russia. Arrangements based on such contradictory consid- erations would hardly appear to offer a fair assurance of success. Besides, there remains the troublesome matter of propaganda. Is it not an irritating ambiguity that, although the Russian government agrees to discontinue its own radical agitation, it permits its *alter ego*, the Third International, to function exactly as before?

It was pointed out in our discussion of the Treaty of Versailles that, as the reparations to be assessed on Germany could not be at once agreed on, the matter was put in the hands of a reparation commission with the understanding that the total sum (d) German was to be fixed on the basis of its recommendations reparations on May 1, 1921. When this day came, the sum to be paid by Ger- many was set at 136,000,000,000 gold marks with annual payments beginning at once amounting to 3,000,000,000 gold marks. Since under other articles of the treaty considerable payments had already been made by Germany and since, owing to the revolutionary crisis holding Germany in its grip, the country was at a sorry pass politi- cally and totally without credit, the Germans protested their inability to pay this huge sum until a military threat from the allies forced them, exactly as in June, 1919, to sign on the dotted line. However, this renewed violence settled nothing. In spite of frenzied effort to meet the required payments divided between remittances in specie and deliveries in kind the German government fell behind and was obliged to ask for a moratorium. Again and again the allied governments met in conference to consider the request. Of the two leading creditors Great Britain was inclined to concede delay as well as a reduction of the total debt; but France was stern and on January 11, 1923, under the guidance of its prime minister, Poincaré, took the momentous step of occupying with military might the rich industrial basin of the Ruhr.

The French thesis was that Germany was well able to pay the sums she was assessed and that she was merely a recalcitrant debtor who needed to be brought to terms at the point of the bayonet.

The French therefore set up an economic control in the Ruhr, the object of which was to divert the profits of this great coal and iron area into their national treasury. So far as lay in them in their dis-

The occupation of the Ruhr and the collapse of the German currency
armed state the Germans opposed the French plans by a policy of passive resistance throughout both the Ruhr and the Rhineland. A grave tension manifested itself everywhere in Europe. However, before the autumn arrived the French had won, at least technically, for the German government was obliged to bring the passive resistance to an end and humbly to accept the French occupation. It was the total collapse of the German currency that had precipitated the German surrender. Like all other European countries Germany had, during the war, abandoned the gold basis and taken to paper currency. With the country's defeat and the issuance of ever new masses of greenbacks, their value steadily dropped. When, in May, 1921, the reparations bill was presented, the decline was accelerated. For henceforth when a cash payment fell due, the government, having no cash to transfer, printed and sold paper marks for what they would bring in London or Amsterdam. Presently they brought less and less and by the end of the Ruhr fight nothing at all. The German currrency had been wiped out. It was useless for even domestic transactions and Germany was threatened with complete economic chaos.

It was not till 1924 that a first ray of common sense burst upon these insane perturbations. In April, 1924, a non-political committee of economic experts was permitted to take up the problem of

The Dawes plan of 1924
Germany's future payments in connection with Germany's economic rehabilitation and worked out a series of recommendations known from the American chairman of the committee as the Dawes report. The scheme called for an elaborate series of payments by Germany after a foreign loan had been floated and put at the disposal of Germany for the restoration of its currency and economic life in general. There was also to be a short respite from the full burden of reparations in order to enable Germany to recover its breath. In August the interested governments, including Germany, accepted the program and France formally promised to retire from the Ruhr in the course of the ensuing year. With a degree of general good-will not experienced in Europe since 1914 the conference, held at London, came to an end. As we peer into the future we can not tell whether the Dawes plan will work, whether

its schedule of annual payments is or is not excessive. But we can say that if the creditor nations will listen to economic reasoning rather than to political rancor and that if, instead of threatening Germany with military execution, they will invite her to join them in friendly, round-table discussions, the vexatious reparations problem, the supreme nightmare of Europe since 1919, may be found to be at last approaching a settlement.

Glooming in the European background like a cloud capable at any moment of discharging a storm has been the question of the inter-allied debts. These were contracted during the war by the extension of credits to one another on the part of the gov- (e) The ernments of the victor group. Of course the strongest inter-allied and richest governments were most profuse in extending debts credits, the United States of America in particular literally showering its associates in the war with gold. As no interest payments were forthcoming even after the war had ceased, the total debt of Great Britain to the United States amounted in 1924 to four and one half billion dollars, that of France to four billion dollars, and that of Italy to about two billion dollars. In addition there were smaller but still tidy sums owing to Washington from Russia, Belgium, Poland and the smaller states of Europe. These facts make it clear that in respect of these inter-allied obligations the United States was wholly a creditor nation. Great Britain and France, on the other hand, were creditor and debtor at the same time. Having borrowed from the United States, Great Britain had turned over as much and more than she had borrowed to France, Italy, Russia, and others, while France for her part had given smaller but still extensive credits chiefly to her continental neighbors. On the basis of a general, all-around settlement the United States might claim a total of eleven billion dollars and Great Britain a total of perhaps half that sum. All the other countries would show appalling deficits, those of France and Italy amounting in each instance to approximately five billion dollars.

These facts and figures can leave no reasonable doubt in any one's mind that the two creditor nations, the United States and Great Britain, have the issue of the inter-allied debts securely in their hands. Immediately after the war there was much loose talk of a general forgiving of debts. It received a sharp rebuff when the United States firmly insisted on being reimbursed. In January, 1923, the British treasury took the lead in opening negotiations for a settlement and signed an agreement at Washington for the extinction of its debt by installment payments spread over a long period of time. However, no major country has thus far (1925) followed the British example. Declaring that their budget will not support a heavy annual interest charge, they have evaded the pressure the Washington government has brought to bear upon them. But ever since the British government has undertaken to repay the United States, it not unnaturally has become increasingly insistent about being squared by its own numerous debtors. The resulting situation is delicate in the extreme. Having come to terms with each other, the United States and Great Britain are natural financial partners and are sure henceforth to make more or less of a common cause against the body of continental debtors. So far they have been content with the veiled allusions with which polite creditors remind their victims of their obligations. From such courteous warnings to the more brutal methods of political pressure it is only a step. If the governments of London and Washington should at some future day make up their minds that France, Italy, and their many petty continental satellites are spending money for armament which they might better apply to the settlement of their debts, what is to hinder them from saying so, though perhaps at first only in the circumlocutory language of diplomacy? In this way the issue of the inter-allied debts may quite possibly become tied up with the vaster issue of disarmament and peace. That it is and has from the first been linked also with German reparations goes without saying, since such ability as France may develop to settle with Great Britain and America will depend entirely on the regular flow of reparation payments from across the Rhine. In sum, the inter-allied debts constitute a world problem of today and tomorrow; and not the least interesting feature about the complicated issue is that it confers an extraordinary degree of control on the two outstanding money powers, the United States and Great Britain.

The issue in the hands of the United States and Great Britain

That between 1919 and 1925 the League of Nations has been much in the public eye results both from its being a novel institution and from the strong and conflicting feelings which it has aroused. While a handful of champions have exalted it to the sky and certain uncompromising enemies have loaded it with curses, numerous intermediate opinions have been voiced, ranging all the way from lukewarm approval to kindly, ironical rejection. As is alone suited

to the candor of historical study we must see the League as
objectively as possible, viewing it less in the light of fleeting opinion,
favorable or unfavorable, than under the aspect of its purposes, that
is, of the principles which underlie it. In this connection (f) The
let us recall that its chief sponsor, President Wilson, League of
thought of it as an association of all the states of the world, Nations
great and little, for the maintenance of peace. Here is a preliminary
criterion for measuring its present usefulness. But it is general and
rather vague. We may refine upon it by recalling the conditions
of European peace, and more particularly that in recent generations
peace has been chiefly threatened from two sources, nationalism and
imperialism. It therefore follows that we can improve upon our
first criterion by giving it a more specific character something in
this fashion: can the League placate the nationalist, can it placate
the imperialist rivalries of Europe?

Any fair-minded attempt to answer this sweeping question must
begin by recognizing that the League is incomplete, that it is a torso.
Owing to the circumstances of its origin already recounted it came to
life as a league of victors; and even as a league of victors The insti-
it was destined to remain imperfect because of the prompt tutional
defection of the United States of America. Well-wishers weakness of
have not failed to point out that it must change its the League
original character and achieve the universality at which it aims by
absorbing Germany and Russia. But that is by no means easy, as
Germany and Russia have been systematically taught to see in the
League an institution organized against themselves. Nor may the
Genevan association, if it craves effectiveness, give up the hope of
receiving the United States within the fold, although an early and
complete realization of such a purpose is apparently out of the
question. In short, considered purely in the light of a world institution the League is rather frail and without much likelihood of
becoming stronger in the immediate future.

By setting forth these flaws in its mechanism we have already given
a reasonably definite answer to the central question of the control by
the League of European peace. The organization looks back upon
five years of existence. It has by no means been inactive Its manifold
in that time. It has exercised a surveillance over the man- activities
dated areas; it has kept an eye on Danzig and the Saar basin; it
has decided some important disputes involving boundaries and the
rights of minorities; it has superintended the economic rehabilitation

of Austria and Hungary; it has set up an International Labor Organization at Geneva; and it has created, also at Geneva, a permanent secretariat charged with preparing the work and executing the decisions of the Council and Assembly. Instinctively feeling that it can justify itself only by finding something to do, it has made itself useful in the hope of becoming ultimately indispensable. Especially in the matter of toning down somewhat the hot passions which blaze across the European frontiers it has enjoyed a slight measure of success. After all the League is first of all an European organization; it is or must aspire to be pan-Europe.

However, when it comes to the great world issues included in the concept of imperialism the record of the League is approximately zero. Imperialist issues affect the great powers and the great powers have not yet acquired the habit of carrying their problems and disputes to the bar of the League. This was well illustrated by the Washington Conference of 1921–1922. When President Harding arrived at the conclusion that a new race of armaments was creating a situation akin to that which had precipitated the war of 1914, he summoned the great powers to the American capital to consider ways and means of alleviating the situation. Nor was the session futile, although it was found impossible to adopt a sweeping program of armament limitation. The agreement finally made applied solely to naval armament and among the various factors of naval strength only to so-called capital ships. Such modern weapons as submarines and airplanes were expressly excluded from limitation. With regard to capital, that is, battle-ships it was agreed that Great Britain, the United States, and Japan, the three leading naval powers, were authorized to maintain battle-fleets in the proportion of 5–5–3, and that for a period of ten years they should abandon further battle-ship construction. Moreover, by a four-power pact concluded among the United States, Great Britain, Japan, and France, these states substantially guaranteed the *status quo* in the Far East by promising to respect each other's insular possessions in the Pacific ocean. That these were useful arrangements lessening the tension among the naval powers and giving a valuable assurance of continued peace in a circumscribed oceanic area is undeniable. But they were made at Washington among the naval powers treating directly among themselves in scornful disregard of the pretensions of the League of Nations.

The Washington Conference, 1921–1922

With the caution imposed by a very fluid situation we may say that the great powers are not minded to accept the control of the League in matters touching their vital interests. Jealously defending their traditional sovereignty, which they desire to preserve intact, they refuse to regard the League as a super-state to which they owe allegiance; and indeed there is nothing in its present constitution to warrant such a claim. The most that can be said for the Genevan body at this time is that it provides new means of coöperation among states and that by a score of not always minor instances it has already facilitated the regulation of the world's business. What makes most vigorously for its perpetuation is that the post-war world is more of a unit than ever before and that some sort of world organization, far from being the vacuous dream of sentimentalists, corresponds to the unescapable realities of modern commerce, finance, communication, thought, and science. Prophecy is not the function of the historian. The League of Nations may dwindle and disappear or it may grow until it effects a modification of the existing notions of sovereignty and acquires a position at the side of and even over the existing states. Let Time supply the answer. All that the historian may point out with some measure of assurance is that great social forces have been astir during recent generations to bring the ends of the earth together on the basis of a common human effort. Throughout this book treating of Europe since the Middle Ages there runs like a red thread a single theme: the unfolding of occidental civilization. Undeniably our story of the successive phases of that civilization has been marked by the almost uninterrupted conflict among larger and smaller social groups. It is therefore not impossible that struggle is a necessary condition of the incessant movement which we vaguely call progress and hail as the essence of our age. In sharp opposition to this view the supporters of the League of Nations hold, either consciously or unconsciously, that our civilization has arrived at a new phase, a phase of unity, and that at least in the hideous and lawless form of organized warfare conflict not only can but must be overcome if we would realize the highest possibilities of our human situation.

Will the League survive or perish?

REFERENCES

C. D. Hazen, *Europe Since 1815*, II, chs. 38–54
C. J. H. Hayes, *Political and Social History*, II, chs. 34, 35
E. R. Turner, *Europe Since 1870*, chs. 18, 19

I. Bowman, *The New World*

J. F. Bass, *The Peace Tangle*

W. A. Phillips, *The New Poland*

L. Voinovich, *Dalmatia and the Jugoslav Movement*

C. A. Beard, *Cross-Currents in Europe Today*

A. J. Toynbee, *The Western Question in Turkey and Greece*

E. M. Earle, *Turkey, the Powers, and the Bagdad Railway; The Trek of Near East Minorities* (Asia, January, 1925)

E. G. Mears, *Modern Turkey*

G. F. Abbott, *Greece and the Allies (1914–1922)*

A. F. Kerensky, *The Prelude to Bolshevism*

N. Lenin and L. Trotzky, *The Proletarian Revolution in Russia*

J. Spargo, *Bolshevism, the Enemy of Political and Industrial Democracy*

P. K. Miliukov, *Russia Today and Tomorrow*

J. M. Keynes, *The Economic Consequences of the Peace*

H. G. Moulton and C. E. McGuire, *Germany's Capacity to Pay*

R. H. Lutz, *The German Revolution of 1918–1919*

G. Young, *The New Germany*

S. P. Duggan (*editor*), *The League of Nations*

A. Sweetser, *What the League of Nations Has Done*

I. Fisher, *League or War?*

R. L. Buell, *The Washington Conference*

Current History, 1919–1925

INDEX

A

Aachen, Peace of (1668), 320; Peace of (1748), 356–357, 375, 377
Abdul Hamid II (sultan), 645; deposed, 662
Absolutism, its function, 384; and constitutionalism, 384–385
Act of Settlement (1701), 369, 371
Act of Supremacy (1534), 167–168, 179, 180
Act of Uniformity, 173, 179, 180, 305
Act of Union (1800), 382, 577
Adrianople, Treaty of (1829), 479
Albanians, rising of (1910), 662; constitute a state, 693
Albigensians, 22
Alcabala (Spanish tax), 148; in the Netherlands, 200–201
Alexander (of Bulgaria), 639–640
Alexander Farnese, duke of Parma, in the Netherlands, 203–208
Alexander I (of Russia), 451; at Tilsit, 452; resists French invasion (1812), 458–459; at Congress of Vienna, 462, 468; and Holy Alliance, 470–471, 478; as king of Poland, 487
Alexander II (of Russia), succeeds to throne, 546; reforms of, 634–635; murder of, 636; fights sultan (1877), 636–638
Alexander III (of Russia), and Bulgaria, 639–640
Alexander VI (pope), 69–70
Alfonso XII (of Spain), establishes constitutional monarchy, 612
Alfonso XIII (of Spain), 612
Algeria, taken by France, 598, 658
Alsace, conquered by France, 254, 322; ceded to Germany, 563; regained by France, 685
Alva, duke of, sent to Netherlands, 198; recalled, 201
Amerigo Vespucci, 53
Amiens, Peace of (1802), 444
Amsterdam, 211, 270, 274
Anarchism, 524–525
Anglican Church, founded by Elizabeth, 179–180; reëstablished by Restoration, 305–306; and Methodism, 387

Anne, of Austria (regent), 314
Anne, of England, reign of, 370–371
Anthony (of Navarre), 220, 221, 222
Aragon, joined with Castile, 75; Mediterranean expansion of, 77–78
Armada (Spanish), 153, 187–188
Army Reform Bill (Prussian), 555–556
Arts, Seven Liberal, 31
Arts, the Fine, of the Renaissance, 37–43; decline in Italy, 259; state of in Germany, 259; in Spain, 260; in Netherlands, 260
Asiento, 374
Assignats, 419, 441
Astronomy, Renaissance advance of, 45–46; from Kepler to Galileo, 265–266
Augsburg, diet of (1530), 112; confession of, 112; Peace of (1555), 117–119, 236
August I (of Poland), defeated by Charles XII of Sweden, 335–336; restored, 338
Ausgleich (Compromise) of 1867, 605, 606
Austerlitz, battle of (1805), 449
Australia, acquired by Great Britain, 581; transformed into self-governing federation, 582–583
Austria, early history of, 351–352; acquired by house of Hapsburg, 352; gradual formation of Austrian Empire, 352–353; struggle with Ottoman Empire, 353; attempts centralization, 354; and the Pragmatic Sanction, 354; failure of Joseph II to unify, 362–363; at war with France, 422–423, 436, 438–439; joins second coalition, 442; defeated, 444; defeated at Austerlitz (1805), 449; at Wagram, 457; at Leipzig, 461; in revolution (1848), 497, 501–502, 504–506; driven from Italy, 548–549, 552–553; in Danish War, 557; driven from Germany, 558–559; transformed into Austria-Hungary, 605; domestic history of between 1867 and World War, 606–608; a republic (1918), 687; under treaty of St. Germain, 687; forbidden to join Germany, 693